A Dictionary of Soldier Talk

A Dictionary of Soldier Talk

Colonel John R. Elting, USA Ret.
Sergeant Major Dan Cragg, USA Ret.
Sergeant First Class Ernest L. Deal, USA Ret.

THE SCRIBNER PRESS

Charles Scribner's Sons ★ New York

Library of Congress Cataloging in Publication Data

Elting, John Robert.
A dictionary of soldier talk.

Bibliography: p.
Includes index.
1. Military art and science—Dictionaries.
2. Soldiers—Language (New words, slang, etc.) I. Cragg, Dan. II. Deal, Ernest L. III. Title.
U24.E38 1984 355.1'03'21 82-42642
ISBN 0-684-17862-1

This book published simultaneously in the United States of America and in Canada—Copyright under the Berne Convention.

1 3 5 7 9 11 13 15 17 19 F/C 20 18 16 14 12 10 8 6 4 2

Printed in the United States of America.

☆☆☆☆ Contents

☆☆☆☆ Acknowledgments

Most of this book came from our own experience and reading. The rest was given us by interested and helpful friends of all ages, services, and places, and chance-met strangers who produced new words or helped to sharpen old ones.

To the following, who took the time to review large portions of the manuscript and make comments and suggestions toward its improvement, we render a very special acknowledgment for their scholarship and physical endurance: Lieutenant Colonel Karl Sakas, USA; Major Vernon D. Moss, USA; Dr. Jonathan Lighter of the English Department, the University of Tennessee; Captain Fitzhugh McMaster, USN-Ret.; Captain Howard S. Browne, MC, USN-Ret.; Colonel "Red" Reeder, USA-Ret.; Captain George S. Grove, USN-Ret.; and Colonel Samuel A. Owens, USAFR-Ret.

We also thank Ann M. Elting, who "packed up her placket to follow the drum" in 1935 and now has typed much of this manuscript, besides checking our senior officer's punctuation and spelling—even though, she maintains, her typewriter blushed at some of the items that passed through it. And our fellow old soldier, Everett Bleiler, has been a good and helpful comrade as well as our editor.

The bibliography contains a list of printed sources consulted during the preparation of this book. We recommend all of them to readers who are interested in further study of military topics.

☆☆☆☆ Introduction

"Then a soldier," wrote William Shakespeare, "full of strange oaths. . . ."

The Armed Forces of the United States, like every other serious trade, have their own professional languages that are more or less incomprehensible to those outside. We have seen a Navy officer instruct an Army sergeant to "put a chart of Formosa on that bulkhead"—and the sergeant, with a somewhat glazed look about his eyes, depart in search of an interpreter. Eventually a Marine officer advised him that "chart" was Navy talk for "map" and that "bulkhead" meant "wall."

We have heard another Army sergeant encourage his platoon across a battered hillside with "Hiyaku! Right goddam ima! Move!" (Shakespeare, who may have trailed the "puissant pike" in the Low Countries as a youthful corporal, certainly would have approved.) And we have known a legal camp follower, Turkish-born and French-educated, to instruct her friend at a busy Tokyo street intersection, "Turn sukoshi gauche."

American fighting men have appropriated words and phrases all across the world from ally and enemy alike. They may employ deliberate mispronunciations and occasional elaborations—such as *beetle crusher* for *infantryman*—but their speech remains terse, plain, and handy. Service talk—whether by soldier, sailor, marine, or airman—makes increasing use of abbreviations and acronyms; a technical discussion between two veterans may sound more like an exchange of encoded messages than ordinary conversation. Its vocabulary lacks a sentimental touch; its nicknames seldom are kindly ones, and the few exceptions are hard-earned indeed. Its rare sympathy is offered wryly, and its general philosophy seems best expressed by the Old Army adage, "Never call a spade a spade when you can call it a goddam shovel." A modern sociologist would dismiss service talk as racist, sexist, chauvinist, and scatological. But it is the natural speech of men who exist for the basic purposes of life and endure proudly where sociologists do not venture.

It is also a traditional, conservative style of speech. Old terms, especially in the Navy, remain current; their meanings may change through the centuries, but seldom drastically. They express an ancient professional courtesy and comradeship, still echoing the thought of some forgotten captain of Queen Elizabeth I: "Let the soldier then go proudly, for he is not as other men." And their not-infrequent self-mockery is a mood that only the competent and self-respecting can admit.

Every foreign war has seasoned American service talk with strange new words, often somewhat twisted by American pronunciation and American humor. Our Senior Officer still employs French phrases he learned—eagerly—from World War I veterans who taught him the gunner's art on the old iron-tired, horse-drawn French 75mm field gun. Today, SAC officers stationed at English bases salt their daily conversation with words like *hooch* and *moose*, even though they may never have been east of Suez or west of San Francisco.

Men and women entering the service bring in expressions from every corner of the United States—and, indeed, from half the world. Leaving the service or going on leave, they carry service talk back into the civilian world outside. It can be exceedingly difficult, and sometimes impossible, to establish whether the origin of many common terms was the barracks or Main Street.

Within the Armed Forces the exact meaning of words may vary from service to service and even from unit to unit, especially when they are names invented for a new weapon, piece of equipment, or technique. Battalions and regiments may have their own private vocabulary, although the rapid turnover in the Armed Forces today makes this less common than it was in the long-service, self-sufficient outfits of the Old Army.

We offer this study of the Armed Forces' language with full acknowledgment that it is incomplete. Together we have served the United States of America for some eighty-five years as artilleryman, tanker, infantryman, marine, paratrooper, medic, and signalman—not to mention a variety of staff assignments and service schools—and have mastered our trade from the trigger squeeze and hippology to thermonuclear weapons. All three of us are students of military history. Yet there are many things we have neither done nor seen, and there are places and wars we never knew. Our joint military service began only in 1928 and ended in 1980. Unintentionally, we have slighted the Coast Guard and not done too well by the Air Force. The private languages of black servicemen require a special study, and our treatment of the female portion of the Armed Forces may be dated. In fact, we are certain that a complete coverage of this subject would require the proverbial "five-foot bookshelf."

Research of the World War I–Old Army period was hampered by the tricky memories of its veterans. One we consulted had been much more impressed by the peculiar French agricultural customs than by his share of combat. Another, a retired banker and former state senator, took much more delight in recalling the details of how he stole a watermelon after his return home in 1919.

We have done our best, yet we doubt that our definitions and derivations will be accepted by all of the millions of our fellow American servicemen. We shall be happy to learn from them, knowing, as Dr. Samuel Johnson, grandfather of all lexicographers, first explained, that "dictionaries are like watches; the worst is better than none, and the best cannot be expected to go quite true."

Finally, we are honor-bound to warn readers that this is real "Army talk"—with a good supplement of its Navy and Marine Corps equivalents. It is frequently bawdy, often profane, sometimes foul. This book is nothing to leave around where curious pre-teens or proper maiden aunts might explore it. One of our contributors—a thoroughly adjusted former Marine officer—has suggested that it probably will be banned in Paris. Our senior officer's dutiful wife, who gallantly typed the gentler historical entries, reports that her typewriter is still blushing.

This is in salutation to the Armed Forces of the United States—their hard beginnings, their mighty yesterdays, and their unknown tomorrows—to the men and women who served, are serving, and will serve in the unchancy years to come, to those who went to the wars with us, and to those who did not return.

John R. Elting
Dan Cragg
Ernest L. Deal

Note: All terms in the main body of this book are Army talk unless otherwise identified.

Abbreviations ☆☆☆☆ and Chronology

ABBREVIATIONS

AAV	*Aces and Aerial Victories* (U.S. Department of the Air Force)
AH	*All Hands* (U.S. Department of the Navy)
AID	*Army Information Digest* (now *Soldiers*)
ANJ	*Army and Navy Journal*
AR	*The Army Reporter* (U.S. Department of the Army)
AS	*American Speech*
AT	*Army Times*
BN	*Bugle Notes*
CD	*The Century Dictionary*
Cordiner	"The Cordiner Report" (U.S. Department of Defense, *Report of the Defense Advisory Committee*)
DAE	*Dictionary of American English* (William A. Craigie et al.)
CSA	Confederate States of America
JAF	*Journal of American Folklore*
Linebacker	*Linebacker II* (U.S. Department of the Air Force)
OED	*The Oxford English Dictionary* (Sir James Murray et al.)
s.	slang, unofficial, or unauthorized expression, as opposed to formal, official language

SM	*Soldiers* (U.S. Department of the Army)
TB	*The Tale of Two Bridges* (U.S. Department of the Air Force)
TM	*The Times Magazine*
USA	United States of America

GENERAL CHRONOLOGY

Ancient	Pre-1689
Colonial	1689–1775
Revolutionary	1775–83
Considerable Antiquity	It's old, but we can't determine *how* old. Assume early 19th century at least.
War of 1812	1812–15
Mexican War	1846–48
Civil War	1861–65
Indian Wars	1866–90
Spanish-American War	1898
Philippine Insurrection	1898–1901
Old, Old Army	1900–17
World War I	1917–18
Old Army	1919–41
World War II	1941–45
Occupation of Germany	1945–Present
Occupation of Japan	1945– c. 1957
Post–World War II	1945–68
Korea	1950–53
Vietnam	1965–73
Modern	1973–Present

NAVAL CHRONOLOGY

Old Sailing Navy	Pre-1689–1861
Old Steam Navy	1861–c. 1900

A Dictionary of Soldier Talk

AA (World War II to Modern; all Services) Antiaircraft Artillery.

AAA-O (World War II) Anything, Anywhere, Anytime, Bar Nothing. The badge of the 39th Infantry Regiment, worn on the front of helmets and painted on everything it owned.

AAFES (1948 on) Army and Air Force Exchange System. The successor to the Army Post Exchange system; now includes the Air Force, which had been established as a separate service in 1948.

A & R (World War II to Modern) Athletics and Recreation. An officer on every post takes care of such matters. Assignment to the duty is usually "in addition to" for some unfortunate line officer.

AB See *area bird.*

abort, to abort, an (World War II to Modern; also Air Force) To fail to carry out a mission, or to cancel a mission after it has begun, for reasons other than enemy action, such as engine trouble, icing, or cowardice. A plane that is turned back for such reasons was called *an abort.* In modern usage, a missile is called an abort if its flight is terminated before destination.

ACAV (Modern) Armored Cavalry Assault Vehicles. During the Vietnam War these were tanks or armored personnel carriers (M132 or M113) armed with M10-8 flamethrowers and coaxially mounted machine guns. Also called *big boys, Dragon Lady, Zippo.*

accompanied tour (Modern) A tour of duty, especially overseas, in which the soldier is authorized to take along dependents. The opposite is *unaccompanied tour.*

accordion effect (At least as old as World War II) Columns of troops or vehicles moving across broken terrain or along hilly roads tend to bunch up or open out —like the sections of an accordion—as they meet, respectively, difficult or easy going. This slows the march and makes it hard to control. The same thing can happen in dismounted drill if the leading unit takes too long a step. This results in the last soldiers in the column alternately running and half-stepping.

accountable Answerable, especially for classified documents, property, or funds. Although colloquially held to be equivalent to *responsibility, accountability*, strictly speaking, means that you are required to explain the whereabouts or disposition of something. *Responsibility* means that if something is missing, you pay for it. Payment may be in cash or a bent career, depending on what the missing item is.

ace (World War I to Modern) *s.* A fighter pilot with a record of at least five enemy planes shot down. The term is unofficial and rather vague.

ack ack (World War I) *s.* Antiaircraft artillery or, especially, its fire. The term originated from the British code for AA.

ack emma (World War I; Aviation Section) *s.* An aircraft mechanic, from the phonetic alphabet for *AM*. Undoubtedly a borrowing from the Royal Flying Corps, which had a language all its own. Another RFC term, possibly used by Americans, was *Comic Cuts*, meaning the Corps Communiqué, which gave the official version of aerial activity over the British sector of the Western Front.

across the river (Early 20th century; extent of use and status as a service expression uncertain) Dead. It is likely that this expression was inspired by Stonewall Jackson's last remark, "Let us cross over the river." This is probably reinforced by our general cultural concept that death is like a river (*over the river, the river Styx, across the Jordan*, etc). As James S. Albert wrote in *Panama Patchword*:

Close the door—across the river
He has gone
With an abscess in his liver
He has gone.
Many years of rainy seasons
And malaria's countless treasons
Are among the many reasons
Why he's gone.

acting Temporarily performing the duties of an absent superior, as when a captain acts as a battalion commander, or a private as a squad leader. In both cases, he has the full authority and responsibility, plus the chance to prove his abilities for higher rank, but his pay remains the same. See also *jack*.

acting jack See *jack*.

action officer (Comparatively Modern) The officer responsible for a particular project, staff study, test, or similar task. The word *action* alone is often used in this sense: "Who has the action on that?"

active (Modern; all Services) Full-time duty on military service, regardless of the length of the service involved: "I had two years active." The term is also used adjectivally, as in *active service* and *active Army* (as opposed to the Reserve or National Guard).

adjutant general See *AG*.

Adjutant General's Corps AGC (Colonial to Modern) Established as the Adjutant General's Department in 1813; given its present name in 1950. The US Army has had an adjutant general (AG) since 16 June 1775. Originally the adjutant general and his assistants were the Army's principal staff officers and might see a good deal of combat. Today, they are purely administrative; their responsibilities include personnel records and statistics, publications, postal service, and bands.

adjutant's call A bugle call announcing that the adjutant is about to form the troops for a ceremony. The traditional words to the call are "Colonel wants you, colonel wants you, colonel wants you." Also called *adjutant's walk*.

administrative absence (Modern) A period of absence not chargeable as leave or temporary duty, granted so that soldiers can participate in semiofficial activities considered of some benefit to the Army. At one time this was a much abused privilege, especially in connection with "religious retreats," in which soldiers were invited to travel to some secluded spot for religious instruction and contemplation. Often, soldiers whose religious motivation was minimal would apply for administrative absence simply to get away from military routine for a few days. There is the sad story of the marine named Clancy, who put in for administrative leave for Passover and the Jewish New Year. When the Christmas holidays came around, he found himself detailed to CQ.

admiral (Modern) 1. (All Services) *s.* An ironic term for a sailor. 2. (Air Force) *s.* The senior enlisted intelligence technician on board aircraft that are flying electronic warfare missions.

advance (Modern; all Services) A payment disbursed against a soldier's next regular paycheck before he or she departs for a new assignment, in order to defray traveling expenses. Repayment may be staggered over several pay periods.

advanced (Post–World War II) *s.* Short for *Advanced Individual Training.* The period of training that followed basic combat training and was intended to give the soldier special skills related to his MOS: "I took my advanced at Fort Dix." It was also called *second eight,* since it usually lasted eight weeks. It is now called *Initial Skill Training* (*IST*) and lasts from three to forty weeks, depending on the individual's MOS. See also *basic.*

advance leave (Modern) Leave granted before the soldier has earned it, on the reasonable expectation that the soldier will be able to repay it during the remainder of his active period of service.

advance party (Considerable Antiquity to Modern) A detail sent to a new site of operations in advance of the main body of troops, to prepare for the arrival of the unit.

AEF (World War I and later) American Expeditionary Force. The US forces in Europe during World War I and shortly thereafter. They were mostly Army, but did include a brigade of Marines and some small Navy units. One impolite doughboy translation of *AEF* was *After England Failed.* More typical were *American Expeditionary Farce* and *Ass-End First.*

affirm (Modern; all Services) *s.* Short for *affirmative*; radio-telephone language for *Yes, that's right,* etc., as in "That's affirm!" The term has crept into ordinary military conversation, and our sergeant major reports that it is not uncommon to hear otherwise eloquent speakers who hold down staff jobs at the Pentagon engaged in conversations like the following: First Army Major: "Shall we play some handball at lunchtime, George?" Second Army Major: "That's affirm!"

A-5 container (Modern) A container used for aerial delivery of equipment. It is dropped by a rayon parachute, the color of which indicates the contents of the container—ammunition, rations, etc.

AFQT See *Armed Forces Qualification Test.*

A-frame (Modern; also Air Force) A light wooden back frame shaped like a capital letter *A*, used by the Koreans to carry heavy loads. This contrivance is still widely used in Korea and so has been taken as symbolic of Korea by many military clubs. It is not at all uncommon to hear veterans speak of the good times they had eating and drinking in, for example, the A-Frame Club at Yongson Compound in Seoul.

AG Adjutant General. Specifically, the adjutant general (or adjutant) of a particular headquarters, organization, or installation. He handles the paperwork. *Adjutant general* is a staff position and not a specific grade. All major headquarters, organizations, and installations have an adjutant general; in organizations smaller than a division, he is termed *adjutant.* An adjutant general's office (AGO) makes an excellent repository for any peculiar responsibility that needs to be picked up and cherished. We remember the adjutant general of the Military District of Washington's task of riding herd on officers awaiting separation from the Army for due cause. Most Monday mornings he had at least one hung-over specimen on his carpet, vowing utter remorse and repentance—which, unfortunately, would evaporate in a day or two.

AG AGC See *Adjutant General's Corps.*

AGCT (World War II and later) Army General Classification Test; either the test itself or the score obtained by a soldier. This was the Army's aptitude test or IQ test. During the years of the draft it was extremely important because one's scores on this test often determined what military job one would get. The average of the total field taking the test was projected at 100, and scores above and below this were distributed on a Gaussian curve. Thus, regardless of the edition of the test used, if the soldier answered the average number correctly for that edition, his score would be 100. Scores were divided into five categories: Grade I, 130 and up; Grade II, 110 to 129; Grade III, 90 to 109; Grade IV, 60 to 89; and Grade V, below 60. If a soldier believed that his score was not representative, he was permitted to take the test a second time. For admission to OCS during World War II, a soldier had to have an AGCT of at least 110, although waivers were available.

Aggressor, the (Modern) A mythical enemy army, complete with its own uniforms, tables of organization, weapons, and the like. It was "organized" in 1946 to represent the enemy during tactical exercises and maneuvers, in an effort to make them more realistic.

Agnew (Civil War; USA) Apparently the first uniform item worn by nurses (in this case belonging to the Sanitary Commission) serving with the Army. It was a plain Army-issue shirt, worn with the tails out, sleeves rolled up, and collar open, over a plain skirt without hoops. The name came from a Dr. Agnew who lent one of his shirts to a nurse during the 1862 Peninsular Campaign and thus set the style.

aiguillette An ornamental braid or cord worn about the shoulder when performing duty as a presidential aide, an attaché, an assistant attaché, or an aide to a general officer. There are two types, service and dress. The aiguillette is sometimes worn on the right shoulder and sometimes on the left, depending on the duty assignment. It differs from a shoulder cord in being more ornate and in terminating in a three-inch metal tip or ferrule. Also called *fire hose.*

aiming stakes (World War II; North Africa) *s.* A term used by company officers for their insignia of grade—bars. By order of Gen. George Patton, these insignia were painted in white or yellow on the front of the helmet. They were markers (it was feared) for enemy snipers. Officially, aiming stakes were poles used by the artillery in laying guns for indirect fire.

airborne (Modern) 1. As *the Airborne*, paratroopers, who are borne into battle on the air, by parachute. 2. *s.* A qualified parachutist: "He's airborne." 3. *s.* A gung-ho response to a question or order, meaning *Can do!*: "Our company was pinned down . . . and we had to . . . leave our dead. I said to our men, 'We have to go back there and get them.' They answered 'airborne!' " (*Washington Star*, 29 August 1979).

airborne boogie (Modern) *s.* The Jody chants used by some paratroop units. See *Jody*.

Airborne Club (Modern) *s.* An imaginary organization; a facetious reference to officers who have taken parachutist training. So many officers, as a ticket-punching exercise, seek parachute training that lack of a qualification tends to make an officer feel he has been left out of the "club."

airborne copulation (Modern) *s.* A euphemism for *I don't give a flying fuck*.

airborne shuffle (Modern) *s.* A sort of jogging pace, something like the half step in drill, performed on the balls of one's feet. It may have originated with the paratroopers (whence the *airborne* qualifier). It is used to maintain a relatively easy gait during long runs.

airborne wings (Modern) *s.* The parachutist's badge, conferred after the requisite course in airborne training. See also *ice cream cone with wings*.

airdough (World War II) *s.* Supposedly a name airborne troops applied to themselves. We have never heard it, but it has appeared in print.

Air Medal (1942 to Modern) A medal awarded in recognition of single acts of merit; sustained operational activities against an enemy; or heroic acts while participating in flight. It is awarded to US and foreign military and civilian personnel in both peace and war. It is unique among medals in that subsequent awards are indicated by bronze arabic numerals.

airphibious (Modern) *s.* Involving ground troops transported in helicopters. Paralleling *amphibious*: "There had been no large air-phibious attacks" (Tregaskis).

Alamo Scouts (World War II) A small force of specially trained scouts organized by the US Sixth Army in the Southwest Pacific in 1943. Their specialty was reconnoitering islands held by the Japanese. Their title apparently derived from the fact that the Sixth Army had been activated at Fort Sam Houston, Texas.

albatross (World War II, possibly earlier) *s.* Chicken, as served in the mess hall. One would expect this term to be naval in origin.

Alcoholics Anonymous (Post–World War II) The 82d Airborne Division. Expanded from the letters *AA* (*All American*) on its shoulder patch. The 82d is also known as *Almost Airborne, Eighty Deuce*, and *Eighty Niggers and Two White Men*, the last from an alleged racial imbalance in its ranks since the integration of black soldiers into formerly all-white organizations in 1948.

alibi (At least as early as World War II, to Modern) A weapon or ammunition malfunction that authorizes a shooter on the firing range to take his or her shot (or shots) over again. Alibis were entered on an *alibi list* by the officer in charge.

Almost Airborne (Modern) Nickname for the 82d Airborne Division, not recommended for use where veterans of the division congregate. It is based on the letters *AA* that form a prominent feature of the divisional shoulder patch. This nickname is usually applied by members of other airborne units.

amah (Old, Old Army to Modern) A nurse or nursemaid for children. The word came into use in the military when America took over the "White Man's burden" in the Philippines. Ultimately of Portuguese origin, *amah* is used all over the Indian subcontinent and the Far East.

ambulance 1. (Early 19th century) A dressing station or field hospital. Derived from French *hôpital ambulant* 'mobile hospital'. This was French usage, and not common in the American service. 2. (Early 19th century to Modern) A vehicle specifically designed for the transportation of wounded or sick soldiers. From French *voiture d'ambulance* 'hospital vehicle'. Such vehicles seem to have been first used in the US Army during the Mexican War. 3. (Civil War, Indian Wars) The "Rucker pattern" ambulance. Introduced during the Civil War, it was a comfortable, four-wheeled spring wagon. A good many general officers acquired them for personal headquarters wagons. After the war many officers purchased such wagons for use in transporting their families and possessions from one post to another, especially in the West. Whatever their use, these wagons were still called *ambulances*. Similar wagons were also occasionally called *ambulances* in civilian life.

Ambush Academy (Modern) *s.* Any of the various courses on jungle warfare or unconventional warfare, especially those operated in Vietnam for newly arrived infantrymen.

America (Pre–Civil War) The frontier soldier's name for the civilized portion of the United States. A fairly equivalent modern term would be *Land of the Big PX*.

American Luftwaffe (World War II) *s.* The US 9th Tactical Air Force, a constant hazard to US and Allied ground troops because of its tendency to attack anything seen moving down below, regardless of recognition signals.

American *Turtle* (Revolutionary) America's first submarine, a clever one-man, hand-powered contraption invented by David Bushnell. It just missed being successful. Also called the *Famous Water Machine from Connecticut*.

AMF (Modern) *s.* Adios (or Aloha) Mother-Fucker. An emphatic way of saying good-bye or breaking off a relationship. Lighter defines it as "the finish."

amigo (Philippine Insurrection) *s.* A Filipino, especially one whose friendship was dubious. Insurrectionists, and just plain bandits, customarily insisted, "Me amigo," even when caught red-handed.

ammo *s.* A handy abbreviation of *ammunition*.

ammo humper (Modern) *s.* Specifically, an ammunition storage specialist; loosely, any artilleryman.

amnesty box (Modern) A receptacle installed at an overseas military air terminal in which personnel leaving the command may deposit—no questions asked—contraband like weapons, ammunition, drugs, drug paraphernalia, etc.

Anacdutra (Modern) Annual Active Duty for Training. Such Pentagonese acronyms save the AG time and space, and keep the rest of the Army dependent on him to interpret them.

anchor clanker (Modern; all Services) *s.* A sailor.

anti-dim (World War I to Modern) A chemical that is supposed to keep the eyepieces of a gas mask from fogging over. A little tin containing a rag impregnated with it is issued with every mask.

Anything to preserve the Union (Civil War; USA) A catchphrase, the Yankee soldier's version of *C'est la guerre* of World War I and *That's the way the cookie crumbles* of recent years. In other words, "We know we're in the Army now; we didn't expect eggs in our beer; and we'll do our best to sweat it out." This wins wars.

ANZAC (World War I) Australian and New Zealand Army Corps. A British acronym picked up by American troops. Sometimes applied to Australians and New Zealanders in general, as *Anzac.*

Angry Nine (World War II and later) *s.* The powerful ANGR-9 radio. It took up the entire backseat section of a jeep. Keeping its batteries charged was rough on the motor of the jeep, but it had a splendid "reach."

ankle boots (1830s through Civil War) High shoes, something like present-day jodhpur boots. They were laced in the front, with a single lacing, and were worn under the trousers. They were standard issue for all mounted men during the cited period, and most regular cavalrymen in the Civil War wore them. In 1872 they were officially replaced by boots.

Anzio Express (World War II) *s.* A German 280mm railroad gun used to bombard the Anglo-American beachhead at Anzio, Italy, in 1944. Its rounds sounded "like a freight train coming to a stop sideways."

AO (Modern) 1. Area of Operations. 2. Action Officer.

AP Armor Piercing (ammunition). Sometimes applied to the vocal endowments of service wives.

APC (World War II to Modern) Armor Piercing, Capped (projectile). The cap was a sort of windshield fitted over the head of the projectile to streamline it and provide faster, more accurate flight. 2. Armored Personnel Carrier. 3. The Army version of aspirin, a general cure-all containing aspirin, phenacetin, and caffeine. Army medics were accused of using "Give him an APC and mark him Duty" as their standard sick-call prescription. Wartime GI movie audiences were likely to chorus that sentence when some hero of the silver screen was dying gloriously after having made the world safe for democracy. The APC pill was also known in civilian life, but there it had many competitors.

ape (Modern; Air Force) *s.* An air policeman, from the initials *A* and *P.*

APO (World War I to Modern) Army Post Office. These were first used in World War I. The five-digit code used today became effective at the same time as the zip code for civilian addresses, on 1 January 1966. Prefixes in use today are 09, New York; 96, San Francisco; 98, Seattle. The Air Force uses the Army system, but the Navy and Marine Corps use FPO (Fleet Post Office).

apple sauce enema (Modern) *s.* To give a chewing out (the enema) to a subordinate, but to do it so tactfully and gently that he goes away feeling better for the experience.

AR See *Army Regulations.*

ARA (Modern) 1. Aerial Rocket Artillery. Helicopter gunships, widely used during the Vietnam War:

Let me tell you of a Cong named Charlie
On that tragic and fateful day

He put two rounds in his pocket
And went out to zap the ARA.

2. Aerial Reconnaissance Aircraft.

Archie (World War I; early World War II) *s.* Antiaircraft artillery, especially that of the enemy. Used by the Royal Flying Corps around 1915 and picked up by US troops in 1917–18. During 1939–40, the term was replaced by *flak*. The origin of *Archie* is not known. One theory is that it is derived from the refrain "Archibald, certainly not" of a popular song of 1913 and a little later. On the other hand, Partridge (1970) records, from about 1910, before the song was written, *Archibald* as "the airbump over the corner of the Brooklands aerodrome."

ardent, the (Civil War) *s.* Intoxicating liquor. A variant of the polite term *ardent spirits*. From civilian use.

area 1. (Antiquity uncertain, to Modern) A clearly and specifically defined space. The company (or larger unit) area includes all the buildings and grounds assigned to the unit, as is the case with headquarters area and hospital area. An individual area is the space allotted to one man in the barracks or quarters, and includes a specific number of square feet, within which are placed his bed, foot and/or wall locker. This concept of area, which is not to be found in the dictionaries consulted, seems to be only American and military. 2. (Since at least 1900; West Point) As *the area*, the Academy's barracks courtyard, where cadets walk punishment tours.

area bird AB (West Point) *s.* Since at least 1910, a cadet who has been forced to walk punishment tours in *the area* (the barracks courtyard). Also called *tourist*.

area sergeant (West Point) *s.* The cadet in charge of the punishment tour detail.

arigato (Occupation of Japan and later) The Japanese word for *thank you*, a useful word that indicated that you weren't an absolute, big-nosed, hairy barbarian. Like *dozo* and *benjo*, often carried over into civilian life by veterans. (A trick played on a newcomer to Japan was to tell him what a delicious drink arigato was, in the hope that he would go and make an ass of himself demanding it in Japanese bars.)

Armed Civil Service (Modern) *s.* The US Armed Forces of today, as seen by various disgruntled veterans, who are quite positive that things have gone generally to hell.

Armed Forces Gestapo (Korea) *s.* The MPs, the SP, and the Air Police, especially those watching over R & R activities in Japan.

Armed Forces Qualification Test AFQT (Modern) A mental aptitude test administered to prospective soldiers by recruiters. It classifies testees into five groups. Category 5 (the lowest 9 percent) is not accepted, and category 4 (the tenth to thirtieth lowest percentile) is taken only in limited numbers. This test is not to be confused with AGCT, the Army General Classification Test.

armored cow See *canned cow*.

armored Diesel (World War II) *s.* A tipple of whiskey, sugar, and lemon juice to taste, mixed with shaved ice. Reportedly popular with the better-equipped echelons of the US 3d Army.

armored Frigidaire (World War II) *s.* A tank, from the trade name of a commercial refrigerator. Sitting in a tank for hours during the winter of 1944–45 could leave you feeling like a barely animated ice cube.

armpit sauce (Vietnam; all Services) *s.* A powerful Vietnamese sauce, known to the

Vietnamese as *nuoc nam*. It is the essence of fermented raw fish, slowly percolated through various strange materials. One veteran correspondent compared it to "a garbage truck running over a skunk in front of a whaling factory in a pulp mill town."

army (Ancient to Modern) 1. The land military forces of a nation. 2. The largest tactical and administrative unit of ground forces. It consists of two or more corps and supporting troops, and is usually commanded by a general officer. 3. Capitalized, the US Army.

Army banjo (World War I, and possibly earlier, to World War II) *s.* An entrenching tool (shovel). Also called an *Irish banjo*.

"Army Blue" (1846 to Modern; West Point) One of the most famous Army songs, sung by cadets since at least as early as 1846. There are at least two versions of the lyrics, both of which express anticipation of donning the blue (the color of the old service uniform) and mild regrets at leaving the Academy. The music is now generally familiar as adapted in the 1950s by Elvis Presley as "Love Me Tender."

Army brats (Antiquity uncertain to Modern) *s.* The legal offspring of Army personnel; traditionally precocious, ubiquitous, underfoot, and insubordinate. *See* also *brown-spit babies, Class F dependents, hanger bats, house apes, rug rats.*

Army Crimes See *Army Times*.

Army dining facility (Modern) A very fancy name for the good old mess hall.

Army Green (Modern) The general-duty uniform authorized for year-round wear by officers, warrant officers, and enlisted men and women. It is basically a dark blue-green, although the shades (44, 244, 344, 444) may vary. Army Green was adopted as the official uniform on 1 October 1957, and by 1960 had replaced all others.

Army is all right, The (Modern) A catchphrase meaning that the Army definitely is *not* all right. Usually rendered as *The Army is al-l-l-l-l right!*

Army Mine Planter Service A specialized little navy belonging to the US Army. It formed part of the now defunct Coast Artillery Corps. Its mission was to plant, maintain, and take up coast defense minefields.

Army name (Ancient to approximately World War I) An alias under which a man enlisted in the Army. For many different reasons, men might enlist in the Regular Army under assumed names. (There was no way of checking identity in those days—no Social Security numbers, no fingerprint systems—and, after all, no one really cared.) Some men forgot their new names under stress and thereby loused up the monthly company muster. Wise topkicks therefore made it a point just beforehand to tell everyone, "Remember your Army names."

Army Register, The A multivolume set that lists all Active Army officers (Regular and Reserve commissions) and all retired officers. It gives biographical and service information. Also called the *Stud Book*.

Army Regulations A group of serial publications, distributed throughout the Army according to unit needs, describing missions, responsibilities, policies, and administrative procedures. They are numbered according to subject matter. Colloquially they are called *ARs* and *Regs*.

Army Slimes See *Army Times.*

"Army Song, The" (Modern) The shortened name of the official Army song, "The Army Goes Rolling Along." The lyrics are by Dr. Harold Arbert, and the music is that of the venerable "Caisson Song" (also known as "The Field Artillery March" and "Over Hill, Over Dale"). Old Army artillerymen don't approve.

Army strawberries *s.* Prunes.

Army Times A weekly newspaper, founded in 1940, that contains information, commentary, and articles of interest to soldiers of all ranks. Although it is not an official information organ of the Department of the Army, the *Army Times* is often the first to provide soldiers with news of official policy. It is published in Washington and is distributed through the PX system. Nicknames are *Army Crimes* and *Army Slimes.*

arriero (Mexican War and later) Mexican civilian muleteer, hired to handle the Army's pack trains. Arrieros were cheerful, expert workers, although understandably nervous when Mexican irregular cavalry hung closely about the rear of the column. Just as the American cowboy learned his trade from the Mexican vaquero, so did the American packer from the arriero.

ARTEP (Modern) Army Training and Evaluation Program, a system for testing the combat readiness of an organization.

Article 15 (Modern) Article 15 of the *Uniform Code of Military Justice* provides commanders with the authority and procedures to impose disciplinary punishments upon military personnel for minor offenses without the intervention of a court-martial. For this reason, Article 15 authority is usually referred to as "nonjudicial punishment," because punishments imposed under this article of the *Code*, unlike court-martial sentences, are not considered federal convictions for criminal offenses. Article 15 is intended to provide a swift, efficient, and relatively easy method for punishing minor offenses, maintaining discipline, and deterring future offenses by encouraging positive behavior patterns. Punishments that may be imposed, although less severe than those of a court-martial, range from oral reprimand to reduction in grade, fines, restrictions, extra duty, or a combination of all of these. Article 15 may not be imposed if the accused demands trial by court-martial. Article 15 is not a legal proceeding, and beyond those restraints imposed upon a commander by the *Manual for Courts-Martial*, his or her authority is virtually unrestrained by legal process. Rules of evidence and provision of defense counsel at an Article 15 hearing do not necessarily apply. Nevertheless, the accused does have some protection against arbitrary or capricious use of authority under this article, which includes the right to consult with counsel and to appeal.

Articles of War (Revolutionary to Modern) The legal code and procedures of the US Army and (later) Air Force. First enacted by the Continental Congress in September 1776 and revised in 1806, they remained in effect until replaced by the *Uniform Code of Military Justice* in 1950. The *Articles of War* were periodically read to the troops, at least a two-hour session and thoroughly boring.

artificer (Colonial to 20th century) A skilled workman. During the 18th and 19th centuries artificers included both soldiers and hired civilians. There were two general types of soldier artificers: artillery artificers, who prepared ammunition, fuzes and military pyrotechnics, and built and repaired gun carriages; and regimental and company artificers, who were responsible for maintaining the equipment, vehicles, and quarters of their organizations. Typical artificers were farriers, armorers, blacksmiths, carpenters, wheelwrights, and harness makers. During the early 20th century the increasing complexity of equipment of even an infantry regiment made it impossible for an artificer to possess all the necessary skills. After World War I, old-style artificers were gradually replaced by technicians such as motor mechanics and radio repairmen.

artillery bull (Modern) *s.* Complete failure to hit the target on the rifle range.

artillery ears (Modern) 1. *s.* Loss of hearing caused by prolonged exposure to artillery fire or comparable loud noise. 2. *s.* Unwillingness to hear certain unwanted things.

Artillery punch (Ancient to Modern) A refined form of brave-maker, acceptable in the most polite society. Originally, it was a mixture of whatever liquors a group of Royal Artillery officers might have handy. American gunners developed it into a judicious blending of "good green tea," Catawba wine, St. Croix rum, choice brandy, real rye whiskey, select gin, brown sugar, preserved cherries, and orange and lemon juice—served over ice, with equal amounts of the best champagne. Regrettably, such careful preparation is too much for some alleged artillerymen of Dr. Spock's Army. Even the Officers' Open Mess at the Artillery School at Fort Sill substituted a muddle of Tom Collins, ginger ale, straight alcohol, and red food coloring, thereby casting grave doubts on their ability to lay a gun straight. We hear this degenerate trend has recently been checked.

artillery raid (Vietnam) A highly effective American technique of jungle warfare in which Chinook helicopters would lift an entire battery of field artillery deep into enemy territory. There the battery would fire at preselected targets detected by air reconnaissance and intelligence agents. Before the enemy could react, the Chinooks would return to shift the battery to another position. One battery achieved a total of thirty-six different fire positions in twenty-four hours.

ARTY LO (Modern) Artillery Liaison Officer. Such officers are assigned to infantry/armor units at brigade or division level to coordinate artillery support for troops in combat.

ASAP /'ay-sap/ (Modern; all Services) *s.* As Soon As Possible. This expression is so overworked that it has become a joke in a profession where everything is required yesterday. "We need dust-off ASAP" (Groom).

ash and trash (Modern) 1. *s.* Headquarters and housekeeping units, or any miscellaneous collection of men used to perform menial tasks. Often used adjectivally, it is the equivalent of British 'odds and sods'. 2. *s.* Garbage detail.

ash can (World War I) *s.* A large-caliber German artillery shell. See also *GI can, marmite, Jack Johnson.*

Ashcan City (Modern) *s.* From ASCOM City (an acronym of Army Service Command), a processing center for Army personnel, located at Inchon, the port of Seoul, South Korea.

Asian two-step (Modern) *s.* A krait native to the jungles of Vietnam. According to soldier lore, this snake's poison is so virulent that its victim has time to take only two steps before dying.

Asiatic (Generally Spanish-American War to Modern; also Marines, Navy) *s.* Someone who acts abnormally. Originally it meant a service type who had gone bamboo from too much service in the Far East, but later was applied to anyone appearing slightly deranged. Probably originally a naval term, but Boatner lists it among words then current in the Army. "It was not inconceivable that the Company Commander himself had gone Asiatic" (Groom).

ass 1. (At least as early as World War II, to Modern) *s.* Oneself, in certain expressions: "My ass is dragging." "Get your ass in gear." "Drag your ass out of here." 2. (Post–World War II) *s.* Short version of *red ass.*

assault fire (About 1920 to 1942) Fire delivered by attacking infantry and armor to make the enemy keep his head down. By 1942 the term *marching fire* had taken its place.

assholes and elbows See *elbows and assholes.*

ass in gear, to get [one's] (Modern; all Services) *s.* To get moving, to get to work. "He tells you to get your ass in gear . . . you move out" (Bunting). See *move out smartly.*

ass is grass, your (Modern; all Services) *s.* You've had it. Infinite wrath is about to descend on you. A military adaptation of Isaiah 40:6, "All flesh is grass." The authority who is going to cause the trouble is often referred to as the *lawn mower*, thus extending the phrase. "You'll think your ass was grass and the airborne was the lawn mower" (Doulis).

Associators (Colonial to Revolutionary) A sort of Pennsylvania volunteer militia, first formed in 1754 to meet raids up the Delaware by French privateers. Since the Quaker-dominated provincial assembly refused to take any measures to defend the colony, Benjamin Franklin inspired the organization of an "Association" of individual citizens who organized, equipped, and armed themselves. The Associators reappeared in 1775 and gave good service during the Trenton-Princeton campaign. In early 1776, they were redesignated the *Philadelphia Brigade.*

Assumption is the mother of all fuck-ups (Modern) *s.* A catchphrase often ruefully stated by commanders and supervisors after having made an unfortunate assumption.

ass up, to get [one's] (At least as early as Civil War, to Modern) *s.* To act big and authoritative, pull rank, and be generally and unpleasantly officious. "A damned Irishman always gets his ass up in about two days after he is promoted."

ASTP (World War II) Army Specialized Training Program. A program, started in late 1942, that detailed some of the more intelligent or educated soldiers to study at various colleges and universities. Officially, the program was based on military needs—language specialists, premedical training, engineering—but a sub rosa explanation for its establishment was that it would keep American colleges from withering on the vine. The instruction was sometimes "forced-draft." As one ex-member has stated, if you dropped your pencil, you missed a month of advanced math. Unfortunately, the men so detailed were mostly excellent NCO material, badly needed in combat units. In February 1944 the growing shortage of replacements for combat units forced its reduction and eventual abolition in early 1945.

As you were! (Of great antiquity) A necessary command that cancels the previous command, permitting a quick correction. For example, a drill sergeant means to say, "Right—face!" but he is distracted by a passing blonde and begins, "Left—" instead. Catching himself, he bellows, "As you were! Right—face!" *As you were!* is equally handy if men who are being drilled misunderstand a command or bungle its execution. An officer in a staff conference may use the phrase to retrieve a slip of the tongue or to get the discussion back to its original subject. Another use occurs when an officer passes a group of enlisted men. Rather than have them come to attention and salute, he might say, "As you were!"

AT (World War II to Modern) 1. Antitank. An AT gun is a flat-trajectory, high-velocity weapon designed to punch holes in tank armor. 2. A training plane for aviation cadets.

At ease! A command the meaning of which has changed in detail from time to time, although its general intention has remained much the same. 1. (Before World War I and during World War II) A command given to troops in formation, releasing them from the stiff position of attention. It was permissible to stand in a relaxed manner as long as one foot was kept in place. Silence was maintained. 2. (World War I until just before World War II; after World War II to Modern) A command like British *Stand at ease!* During the earlier period the left foot was advanced a prescribed distance; the rifle was held in the right hand, tilted forward, butt resting on the ground near the right foot, and the left forearm was placed horizontally in the small of the back, waist high. This position looks smart and is slightly more comfortable than standing at attention. (During World War II this position was called *Parade rest.*) The present interpretation of *At ease!* is similar. The right foot is kept in place, silence is maintained, but small body movement is permitted, which was not the case in the earlier period. 3. (World War II to Modern) A command equivalent to *Quiet!* with no indication of position. Since the command includes the notion of silence, *At ease!* is often used in squadrooms, mess halls, barracks, and at indoor gatherings to command silence, in order to get attention for an order or announcement. Our senior author remembers its being used at an officers' club. Our marine has often heard it used (since at least as early as 1958) in the rhyming line *At ease, disease! There's a fungus among us.* 4. (World War II to Modern) A command specifically canceling a previous order of attention. When an officer enters an area where enlisted men are present, the first soldier to notice him would give the command *Attention!* The officer generally responds with *At ease, men!*, which means that the men are to remain silent, in relaxed position, but not in formation. A stronger release is *As you were!*, which permits enlisted men to carry on with what they had been doing before the officer entered. This formality also applies to officers, as when a superior enters a meeting, briefing, or some official gathering. *Attention* is called, those present rise, and the superior says *At ease!* 5. (World War II to Modern, perhaps earlier) Colloquially and unofficially, Calm down, cool off, shut up: "At ease, Mac, at ease!"

At ease, disease! There's a fungus among us (Modern) *s.* A catchphrase meaning "Shut up; you don't know what you're talking about." Usually said jokingly. The components *disease* and *fungus among us* do not seem to have any special meaning except to make rhymes.

ATS (World War II; British) Auxiliary Territorial Service, the British equivalent of the American WAC. Although not so smartly uniformed, they were handy, hearty women whose comradely ways produced the unofficial explanations of their title *Any Time, Soldier* and *Army Tail Service.*

auger in (World War II; Air Force) *s.* To crash-land, to crash an airplane. See *buy the farm.*

Aunt Jemima (World War II) *s.* The T1E3 "mine exploder," a modified Sherman M4 tank. It pushed two roller units, each consisting of five steel disks 96 inches in diameter and 2.75 inches thick, which were supposed to detonate any mines in a 33.75-inch-wide path in front of each of the tank's tracks. The disks were powered by roller chains from the tank's front sprockets. The whole attachment weighed approximately 29 tons, or almost as much as the tank itself (36.5 tons). Aunt Jemima never moved faster than a slow waddle, was very difficult to steer, and bogged down whenever there was a heavy dew.

AUS Army of the United States. It consists of the Regular Army, the Army National Guard of the United States, the Army Reserve, and all other persons taken into the service by appointment, enlistment, or conscription. The present concept is that these elements together constitute "one Army," but Regulars still refer to themselves as USA—United States Army.

AUTOVON (Modern; all Services) Automatic Voice Network. A telephone-microwave relay-satellite network that enables persons with access to the system to direct-dial any military telephone number in the continental United States. Access to military telephone networks in overseas areas is also possible using this system, through local military switchboard operators.

avalanche (Civil War) *s.* A soldier's typical misnaming of *ambulance.*

aviation English (World War II, possibly later; also Navy) A strange patois spoken only by zoomies; largely unintelligible to anyone else.

awkward squad (Ancient into World War II) A group of slow-learning recruits who were trained separately. In the average company, troop, or battery, those recruits who were slow to learn, for whatever reason, received separate instruction by a capable NCO. He was always tough, and frequently an intuitive psychologist. (The term *awkward squad* was beginning to be regarded with disfavor in World War II, and such men were sometimes called the *special group.*) Today, with all training schedules decreed by higher headquarters, such separate training is almost impossible, especially since training must now be nontraumatic.

AWL (Old Army) Absent With Leave. An enlisted man on furlough or an officer on leave. We can recall the term from our early days of service, but it never attained the popularity of its opposite, *AWOL.*

AWOL awol */pronounced either as initials or as* 'ay-wall/ (Perhaps Civil War, to Modern) Absent Without Leave. The major difference between this offense and desertion is that the AWOL serviceman presumably intends to return. After thirty days of absence, a soldier is considered a deserter. *Absent Without Leave* is a very old official designation, found in both the American and British services at least as far back as the early 19th century. Some sources claim that the acronym *AWOL* came into common use during the Civil War, but we have been unable to verify this. The Old Army frequently used the expression *A W O Loose*, and more recent interpretations of the initials are *After Women Or Liquor and A Wolf On the Loose*. In World War I the short form *to go absent* was also used.

He licked a coffee cooler
Because he said he'd tell.
He's ten days absent without leave.
O'Reilly's gone to hell.

According to Army legend, the highest-ranking soldier ever to go AWOL was General of the Armies John J. Pershing. Late in his lonely last years at Walter Reed Army Hospital, the eighty-odd-year-old "Black Jack" became literally fed up with hospital grub and went out unannounced for a night in Washington, D.C. Frantic searchers finally found him in an exclusive restaurant, luxuriating over the last of a gourmet dinner consisting of everything the hospital dieticians had banned—and were told to wait until he finished his coffee and cognac. 2. In everyday speech an *AWOL* is an individual absent without leave: "The 24th hasn't had an AWOL in six months."

AWOL bag /'ay-wall/ (World War II and later) *s.* A small grip or handbag, originally of canvas, with a zipper top. It is just large enough to carry toilet articles, pajamas, a change of underwear, and a bottle—about what a soldier would take if he were going AWOL. The term has been extended; it is often applied to almost any kind of small handbag. During World War II a superior leather bag was sometimes available in the PXs. These were occasionally referred to simply as *pigskin AWOLs*.

AW 103 (Early 19th century to 1957) The Article of War that caused a soldier to make up time lost through his own fault. If, for example, he caught VD, he lost all time and pay while hospitalized. Then, when he was released from the hospital, he was jailed for catching VD, and lost time and pay for that, too. This situation, plus the fact that penicillin was unknown in those days, caused the soldier to take certain precautions in his amours. AW 103 did not, as some alarmists predicted, cause sex to vanish among military personnel. Eventually, AW 103 came to be considered a form of cruel and unusual punishment. See *bad time*.

baby shit (At least as early as World War II, to Modern) *s.* Mustard.

b-ache (West Point) *s.* Bellyache. Complaint.

b-ache, to (West Point) *s.* To bellyache, to complain.

backbone of the Army (Ancient to Modern) The NCO corps. This concept is so widely accepted today on faith alone that no responsible officer would dream of contradicting it. Noncoms have been known to grow misty-eyed when contemplating its deeper meanings. One wonders if the expression was not coined in antiquity by some artful sergeant and has not been faithfully perpetuated by his successors ever since. Grose (1783) advised sergeants to "make people believe, that serjeants are the only useful and intelligent men in the corps." Kipling probably did much to immortalize the expression when he wrote, "The backbone of the Army is the noncommissioned man!" ("The 'Eathen," 1896). The 1915 graduating class at West Point had a somewhat different idea of what the backbone was:

> If you talk to a veteran Doughboy,
> He'll say in a whisper to you,
> "My boy, the backbone of the Army
> Is wearing the white and the blue."
>
> ANJ 52:41

White and blue were the colors of the Infantry.

backchannel (Modern) 1. General officers' personal message traffic sent by electrical means. Backchannel messages, because of their extreme sensitivity, are not handled by ordinary signal communications centers but by special security detachments. Backchannels give their users a means of expressing themselves frankly and off the record. "Once there, my schedule . . . would be arranged through backchannel communications" (Marshall, 1979). 2. Any out-of-channel or unofficial communication, maneuver, or procedure. See *frontchannel, jump channels.*

back trouble (World War II) *s.* A euphemism for pregnancy among WACs: "McCarthy kissed everyone in the motor pool good-bye." "How'd she get out?" "Back trouble!"

bacon can A component of the 1910 mess equipment: a flat, rectangular metal box with a tight lid, designed to hold two days' rations of bacon or salt pork. To reduce wear on the soldier's pack, in 1916 a new model with rounded corners was introduced.

Badlands, the (1950–55; also Marines) *s.* Korea. At that time reputed to be the only place on earth where one could stand neck-deep in mud in a midwinter downpour and have dust blowing into one's eyes. It was rough, folks. What's more, our air mattress sprang a leak.

bad time (At least as early as Old Army, to Modern, although the definition has changed) Time that has been lost from a soldier's enlistment because of his own misconduct and that must be made up. At present, bad time consists of time that has been lost through being AWOL or under confinement. Before leaving the service, a soldier must make up such time or forfeit an equal number of days' pay. In the past, time lost in the hospital for injury or sickness (such as VD) resulting from misconduct was also counted as bad time and had to be made up. See *VD.*

bag-drag (Air Force) *s.* A fail-safe measure: for every cell of three bomber aircraft on a sortie, one additional airplane is provided. If anything goes wrong with one of the primary bombers, its crew can transfer to the spare plane and the mission can go ahead as scheduled.

bail out, to (World War II, probably older) *s.* 1. Originally an Air Force term for making an emergency parachute jump from a disabled plane. Later adopted by ground troops. "The krauts hit our lead tank with a panzerfaust, but the crew managed to bail out." 2. A euphemism for avoiding work or for goofing off.

Balbo (1933 into early World War II; Air Corps) *s.* A large formation of aircraft. The term is based on the name of an Italian airman, Gen. Italo Balbo, who led a mass flight of planes from Italy to the United States and back in 1933. It was effective propaganda for Fascist Italy, and the starveling US Army Air Corps was duly envious.

baldy (World War II) *s.* A GI haircut, so called from the way it made you look—naked from the eyebrows up.

ball-bearing WAC (World War II and later) *s.* A male soldier performing what had come to be regarded as women's work: typing in higher headquarters, clerking in a field PX, working in a post headquarters message center, running a mimeograph machine, and such. Also called a *titless WAC.*

ball cartridge A small-arms cartridge consisting of a case, a projectile, and a propelling charge. See *live ammunition.*

ball game (Modern) *s.* Any military operation, whether practice maneuvers or actual war.

balli-balli /'bah-lee-'bah-lee/ (Korea and after) *s.* Quickly. From Korean *balli* 'quickly', also transliterated *palli.* Literally, *quickly quickly*, from the common American misapprehension that everything must be repeated at least twice before Orientals will understand it.

balls up (World War II) *s.* Total, pointless confusion. An old British expression comparable to American *everything is balled up.*

Baltimore Whore (World War II; Air Force) *s.* The B-26 medium bomber, so called from its place of manufacture and its tricky characteristics. See *Flying Prostitute.*

bamboo (Philippine Insurrection into 20th century) *s.* Used in expressions like *gone bamboo* or *bamboo juicer*, it originally meant a soldier who had served too long in the Philippine Islands. It originated during 1899–1905 and came back into use in the 1950s to describe characters—especially DACs—who were getting a bit too sodden from prolonged exposure to the underside of Japanese culture. The real Old Army bamboo type could easily be identified by his habit of carefully shaking out his shoes and socks before putting them on. This was not a symptom of incipient psychosis; it merely meant that he had learned that scorpion stings were painful.

bamboo telegraph (Philippine Insurrection and later) The system whereby some tribes in the Philippines could transmit news through almost uninhabited country with uncanny speed. Generally, the system worked through runners who used little-known back trails, drum signals, voice signals, and even kites.

ba-me-ba bameba (Vietnam) A beer brewed in Saigon by the French-owned Brasseries et Glacières de l'Indochine (BGI) brewery; so called for its trademark, "33," in Vietnamese *ba mưòi ba.* This beer became very popular with Americans. Taken in the French way (with ice), a strong, cold glass of "33" drunk in the shade of a sidewalk cafe along Saigon's Tu Do Street, was a very nice way to fight a war. Most Americans believed that the brewers used formaldehyde to hasten the aging process. At first taste, one might think so, but after some exposure, ba-me-ba could grow on you. Also pronounced *bomb-ne-bomb* and *bamidy-bam.*

ba-me-lam (Vietnam) *s.* A man with a voracious sexual appetite, a sexual athlete. The term comes from Vietnamese *ba-mưòi-lăm* 'thirty-five', which is Vietnamese slang for a roué or oversexed man. The expression is said to have originated from a once-popular lottery in which the prize for drawing number 35 was a goat. "*Bam Melam,* . . . the pilots told us proudly, indicates the sexual power of a goat" (Tregaskis).

banana clip (Modern; all Services) *s.* A clip designed to hold thirty rounds of ammunition; so called because it is slightly curved. This type of clip was very popular in Vietnam, where personnel armed with the M1 (semiautomatic) and M2 (automatic) .30-caliber carbine often taped two of these clips together in order to double the magazine capacity of their weapons. Since one clip was upside down, this practice was called *tape and turn.*

band-aid (Modern) *s.* A medical corpsman.

bandit (Modern) *s.* Enemy aircraft.

bandsman (Revolutionary to Modern; all Services) A member of an organized band and, in theory at least, a skilled musician. During the Revolution and the War of 1812, a few regiments had bands, usually made up of soldiers detailed from the ranks. Until 1832, bandsmen were outfitted at regimental expense; officers might contribute one day's pay a month for the support of the band. After this date, each regiment was allowed ten musicians. Colonels frequently put them into fancy uniform for parades and reviews. Bandsmen, unlike the field music, were semi-noncombatants. In action, they usually served as stretcher-bearers. Some Civil War generals, like Philip Sheridan, had the habit of ordering their bands to "play the troops into action." The Army now has fewer bands, but they are mostly very good.

bang-bang (Modern; all Services) 1. *s.* Any firearm, but generally the infantryman's rifle or individual weapon. 2. *s.* The act of copulation, in Pidgin English. This term is widely used in the Far East.

Bang-clap (Modern; all Services) *s.* Bangkok, Thailand, a very popular R & R spot for Americans in Southeast Asia during the Vietnam War. *Clap*, of course, refers to gonorrhea.

Banhof queen (Modern; also Air Force) *s.* A streetwalker. From the years of the Occupation of Germany and later, when prostitutes regularly advertised their goods in and around the railroad stations. From German *Bahnhof* 'railroad station'.

BAR The Browning Automatic Rifle. A .30-caliber gas-operated air-cooled automatic rifle that could fire around 350 rounds per minute. A fine weapon, if a little heavy and awkward to handle.

bare-ass (Modern) *s.* A play on *barracks*: "Let's go back to the bare-ass and change into civvies."

bare base kits (Modern; Air Force) Made-up cargoes containing portable shelters, power generators, field kitchens, fuel storage containers, and similar supplies. These kits can be flown in anywhere in the world where a runway, parking space for aircraft, and potable water are available, and can be set up quickly to establish a functioning forward air base.

barracks bag B-bag (World War II to Modern) A large, sturdy cloth bag with drawstrings that served as the soldier's trunk, closet, hope chest, and whatnot. It was often tied to the head or the foot of the soldier's bunk. It is not to be confused with a duffle bag. The barracks bag crops up in several Service expressions, notably "Blow it out your barracks bag!" Said in chorus, this was a World War II catchphrase, meaning approximately "Shut up!" Said on an individual basis, it could be less polite, a not-so-veiled way of telling a person to go have a bowel movement.

barracks breeze *s.* Gossip, rumor, idle chatter. The Army equivalent of Navy *scuttlebutt* and Air Force *prop wash.*

barracks rat (Modern) *s.* Anyone who lives in the barracks.

Barracks 13 (Old Army) *s.* The guardhouse, imprisonment. One of many terms: *the Mill, Company Q, the bull pen, the stockade, Cross-bar Hotel*, etc.

barrel drill (Civil War; USA) *s.* A punishment for minor offenses. The culprit had to stand on a barrel for a specified length of time. In one case, the offender also stood "with a stick of wood on his shoulder from Reveille to Retreat for 2 days." In other cases, soldiers guilty of theft had to stand on a barrel while wearing a placard labeled "Thief" and holding the stolen articles.

barrel overcoat (Late 18th century through the Civil War) *s.* A punishment used in the field for minor military offenses. The offender had to don a barrel with a hole cut in the top for his head and two holes for his arms. Sometimes he had to stand on the head of another barrel while wearing this "overcoat."

bars The insignia of rank of captains and lieutenants. *To get one's bars* means to become an officer, to become a second lieutenant.

baseball cap (Modern) *s.* The utility or fatigue cap, so called because of its resemblance to a baseball player's cap. See *flattop Army.*

base pay base (All Services) A fixed amount of monthly pay, established by law, not including various allowances, extra pay, or special-duty pay. Base pay does include increases for length of service (longevity). "What's your base?"

basic (At least World War II to Modern) *s.* Short for *basic training, basic combat training*, the initial infantry-type training every enlisted soldier receives. The objective of this training is developing a disciplined, motivated, arms-qualified, and physically conditioned soldier drilled in the fundamentals of the infantry. "I took my basic at Fort Dix." Currently called *initial entry training.*

bateaux men /bat-'toe men/ (Colonial to Revolutionary) Men who handled the bateaux—flat-bottomed riverboats, typically 28–32 feet long, with flaring sides. They were used for transporting troops and supplies on the rivers and lakes of northern America. Originally, the bateaux men were civilians, but in 1756 the terrible-tempered Lt. Col. John Bradstreet organized 2,000 of them on a military footing and made them into as tough an outfit as Rogers' Rangers.

bat-horse /*originally* bah-horse *or* baw-horse/ (Colonial to Revolutionary) A packhorse for carrying an officer's baggage in the field. The term is derived from French *bat* 'pack', 'packsaddle'.

bathtub (World War I into World War II) *s.* A motorcycle sidecar. Also called a *buddy seat.*

bat-man /*originally* bah-man *or* baw-man/ (Colonial to Revolutionary) A soldier detailed to lead and care for a bat-horse. At present, batman, the personal orderly of a British officer.

battalion (Ancient to Modern) A unit composed of a headquarters and two or more companies or batteries. It may be part of a regiment and be charged only with tactical functions, or it may be a separate unit and charged with both administrative and tactical missions. It is usually commanded by a lieutenant colonel.

battery (Colonial to Modern) Originally an indefinite number of guns, sometimes of different calibers, emplaced together in the same position. By 1846, however, the light companies of the artillery were commonly termed *field batteries.* During the Civil War, *battery* replaced *company* as the official designation of the basic artillery unit. The older meaning continued in use with the Coast Artillery.

battery acid (Old Army to Modern) *s.* Coffee. Not infrequently an accurate description. Cooks start the coffee before they begin to prepare the breakfast so that they can have an eye-opener. Then the coffee sits and bubbles, and gets vicious by the time they have breakfast ready. We solved the problem by getting our company cooks their own coffee pot.

battle sight (Old Army into World War II) The U-shaped open sight on the Springfield '03s and certain other military rifles. When you were engaging the enemy at 300 yards or less, you seldom had time to put up your sight leaf and make fine adjustments for range and windage. The '03 would put your shots where you pointed it at that range.

Bay of Pigs, the (Modern) *s.* From about 1961 to the present, a derogatory term for the WAC quarters. The references are to the aborted invasion of Cuba at the Bay of Pigs (April 1961), *pig* as an ugly woman, and *bay* as a living area for troops. The term is fast becoming obsolete among today's generation of young soldiers living in coed barracks.

bayonet (Colonial to Modern) A knife (of various lengths and designs at different times) that can be fixed to the muzzle of a rifle and is a standard item of issue to infantrymen. For many years the bayonet has served as a very useful weapon, but with the introduction of rapid-fire weapons, it has gradually fallen into disuse in battle.

bazooka (World War II) *s.* A recoilless shoulder-fired antitank rocket launcher. Its name comes from the musical contraption invented by radio comedian Bob Burns in the 1930s. The weapon and its name are now obsolete, but older people and those not familiar with military weapons still use the term.

B-bag b-bag See *barracks bag.*

BC Battery Commander. The artillery used this term instead of *CO, Old Man,* or *captain.*

beam (World War II and possibly earlier; Air Force) A radio signal, transmitted along a narrow course to guide aviators through fog or darkness. They could be *on* or *off the beam*—expressions that were soon applied to situations other than aerial navigation. If aviators followed the course of a railway, they were *flying the iron beam*; if following the course of a river, *flying the wet beam.*

beanette (West Point) *s.* A new name for a woman plebe.

beanhead (West Point) *s.* A plebe.

beanie (World War II) *s.* A small knit cap of OD yarn, designed to be worn in cold weather under the steel helmet. Some soldiers liked to wear them without helmets, but only until General George S. Patton, Jr., saw them. The term probably comes from civilian slang of the 1930s, where a somewhat similar felt cap was called a *beanie.* The ultimate reference is to *bean,* the human head.

beast (At least as early as 1890; West Point) *s.* A cadet plebe (freshman). Dr. Lighter (letter to Cragg, 19 July 1980) traces the term to an 1871 source.

beast barracks (Post–Civil War to Modern; West Point) *s.* Specifically, the barracks area at the US Military Academy where the new plebes were kept while undergoing initial processing, indoctrination, training, and incidental hazing. Generally, the whole process was titled the *beast barracks.* As part of the present regime of sweetness and light, the name has been abolished and the process (much diluted) redesignated *Cadet Basic Training.*

beast detail (West Point) *s.* The duty assigned to cadet upperclassmen (members of the first class) to supervise the month-long intensive basic military training administered to plebes. The detail is under the overall supervision of the officers of the Tactical Department. Today, any use of the term is unofficial and probably naughty.

beat (Ancient to Old Army) A particular drum signal, such as assembly or reveille.

beat for recruits, to (Ancient to early 19th century) To try to enlist men. Recruiting parties normally included drummers and fifers to attract potential recruits. The expression may also reflect the hunting concept of sending out beaters to flush game.

beating orders (Ancient to early 19th century) Written orders given to an officer authorizing him to "raise men, by beat of drum."

beat off, to (Ancient to Modern) To repulse an attack.

beat up, to (Ancient into 19th century) To launch a surprise attack that breaks up the enemy's outpost system. Washington's attack on Trenton in 1776 was an excellent example of beating up an enemy's winter quarters. From the old English hunting term for striking bushes to flush game.

beat up the girl friend, to (World War II; Air Force) *s.* To do some stunt flying over your girl friend's house. If the neighbors objected, you might be grounded.

beautification detail (At least as old as World War II, to Modern) A troop detail on Army posts that cuts grass, rakes leaves, and performs general police of the communal areas; sometimes called *post beautification detail.* Also similar work done on lower levels, down to the company area. Beautification projects may include lining up stones and painting them with aluminum paint and whitewashing the trunks of trees to a height of eight feet.

bed check (At least Old Army to Modern) A paternal custom, now fast becoming obsolete, in which a kindly NCO tiptoed through the barracks after Lights Out, making certain that all were safely tucked into their bunks, instead of injuring their health by shooting craps in the latrine or sneaking out for a night in town.

Bed-Check Charlie (World War II, Korea) *s.* An enemy reconnaissance plane that regularly flew over around bed-check time. North Koreans used old-fashioned string, wood, and canvas aircraft that could not be picked up by radar and that flew too low and too slowly to be intercepted by the swift American jets.

Bedlam Old Bedlam (At least as early as mid-19th century, occasionally heard post–World War II) *s.* The bachelor officers' quarters on a frontier military post. It was usually cavernous, sketchily furnished, and very noisy. Sometimes it included the kitchen and dining room of an officers' mess. In one veteran's estimation it was "correctly named."

bedpan commando (World War II on) *s.* A derogatory term for a medical corpsman, especially a corpsman assigned to duty in a medical ward in a fixed hospital installation.

beehive (Modern) *s.* 1. A 105mm artillery shell loaded with antipersonnel flechettes. 2. Certain now obsolete government housing.

beenie weenie (Modern) *s.* The beans and frankfurters in the C-ration meal pack, named after the commercial brand of beans and frankfurters found in most supermarkets.

beetle crusher *s.* An infantryman.

behind the butt plate (Modern, especially among paratroopers) *s.* On the firing line in combat. The butt plate is a protective metal strip covering the butt end of a rifle's stock.

being on his knees (World War II; Air Force) *s.* In an advanced state of intoxication. One source describes it as the stage beyond "standing on his cap badge."

bellhop (Probably late 19th century; still in use) *s.* A member of the Armed Forces (particularly a soldier or marine) in Dress Blues. Often the confusion was the result of a perfectly honest mistake. Prior to the 1950s the average civilian so seldom saw Armed Forces personnel in full dress that one could easily confuse them with bellhops or doormen. (We remember an ROTC cadet at a Monterey hop in 1931 who innocently handed his cap and his date's coat to a first lieutenant, Regular Army, in Dress Blues.) Recently the term seems to have been used maliciously by civilians in the Washington, D.C., area. One marine was heard retorting, "The last belle I hopped was your wife!"

belly punchers (World War I) *s.* Medical personnel at a dressing station (modern term, *air station*). The nickname arose from the practice of injecting antitetanus shots into the stomach walls of wounded soldiers who were brought in. (Men wounded in the stomach reportedly were not given this injection.) The needle was "large enough to be used by a veterinarian inoculating an elephant" (Eaton).

belly-robber (World War I) *s.* A mess sergeant.

below the zone See *secondary zone.*

bend the throttle, to (World War II) *s.* To speed up the motor, to travel at the highest possible speed. A reckless driver might be called a *throttle-bender.*

Be nice! (Vietnam and later) *s.* An expression used while feigning shock or disgust. Vietnamese bargirls and prostitutes, accustomed to the rough and straightforward advances of the American fighting men, cautioned them to be nice, while otherwise leading them on. A facetious interjection. See *Sorry about that.*

benjo banjo (Occupation of Japan to Modern; all Services) *s.* A toilet. From Japanese *benjo* 'toilet'. Widely used today in Korea as a loan word.

bennie (Modern; all Services) *s.* Short for *benefits,* of which (the recruiters assure us) there are multitudes to be found in the service. Ordinarily used by servicewise personnel in a deprecating manner.

Benning School for Boys (Modern) *s.* The Infantry Officer Candidate School, Fort Benning, Georgia. Also called *Calley Hall.*

benny bennie (World War II) *s.* A foul-up in a military formation or in drill, caused by an inexperienced or inattentive soldier.

"Benny Havens" "Benny Havens, Oh!" (About 1840 on) Perhaps the oldest song of the US Army, "Benny Havens" commemorates a historical person and his tavern, which stood at various locations in and around West Point from 1825 to its destruction by fire in 1934. Although Havens and his wife were banned from setting foot within the Academy grounds (because of selling hard liquor to the cadets), his tavern was a favorite eating and drinking place of the cadets and Academy staff. The authorship of the song, which is sung to the tune of "The Wearing of the Green," is disputed. The two attributed composers are a Lt. Lucius O'Brien, who visited West Point in 1838, and Dr. John Thomas Metcalf, a cadet of the Class of 1838. Metcalf is generally considered to have the stronger claim.

Bent Whore (Vietnam; also Air Force) *s.* A play on the name of the city Bien Hoa, South Vietnam.

benzine board B-board (1869 to Modern) *s.* A board of officers appointed to determine whether an officer who has received unfavorable efficiency reports should be retained in the service or returned to civilian life. The term apparently was first used in 1869, when Congress cut the number of infantry regiments from forty-five to twenty-five, forcing the relief of 750 officers with one year's pay. Benzine being an early cleaner's solvent, this board—which was to clean out the officers' corps—became the *benzine board.* Unfortunately, many of its victims were capable officers.

berm 1. (Antiquity uncertain to Modern) A mound, wall, or ridge of earth built around a firing range to deflect or to stop bullets. In the European field fortifications of the 18th century, a berm was the small strip of level ground between a moat (or fosse) and a fortress wall. 2. (Post–World War II to Modern) The earthen dikes in a rice paddy, which resemble rifle-range berms. "Rice-paddy dikes, which everyone called berms" (Heinemann).

between retreat and reveille *s.* A catch-phrase meaning that if there is not time to do something in duty hours it can be done after normal duty hours. Our sergeant major remembers first hearing this phrase in 1959 when his first sergeant told him: "Pfc Cragg, you can always finish those reports between retreat and reveille!"

B4 bag (Modern; all Services) Bag, assembly, Flyer's Clothing, Type B-4. A general borrowing from the US Air Force. It is a handy piece of canvas luggage that is nearly waterproof. It has heavy-duty zippers, capacious side pockets, and an interior almost roomy enough to hold all a soldier's initial-issue clothing.

BG (Antiquity uncertain) Brigadier General. "He made BG." This is the lowest grade of general officer. One cynic noted that BGs come in handy because their proximity can expedite necessary action without materially contributing to it.

Bible *s. Army Regulations.* Up until 1920 they were contained in a single 6-by-9-inch blue-bound book. Today, they are a 5-foot bookshelf of loose-leaf binders, but the old name lingers on in wistful memory.

bic, to /bik/ (Modern; all Services) *s.* To understand, to comprehend, in Pidgin English. From Vietnamese *biet* 'to understand'. "I no bic you, GI!"

big boys (Modern) *s.* Tanks. See *ACAV.*

Big Eight, the (Occupation of Japan, Korea, and later) *s.* The most important American military prison, in Japan, located near Yokohama.

big five, to give the (World War I) *s.* To render a really snappy salute.

big-load drivers (Modern; Air Force) *s.* Pilots of B-52 Stratofortresses. "The big-load drivers" (Broughton).

Big Man (World War II; black soldiers) *s.* A senior officer; the CO.

Big Pond, the *s.* The Atlantic Ocean or the Pacific Ocean. For many years the term *the Big Pond* was used for the Atlantic, but during World War II it was sometimes also applied to the Pacific (Sanders and Blackwell). During the Vietnam War, the term again became popular, but at that time exclusively for the Pacific. Most of the 2.5 million men who served in Vietnam had to cross the Pacific at least twice. The fact that vast numbers of men crossed the Pacific by air tended to reduce its size in their minds to that of little more than a pond.

Big PX, the (Post–World War II, mostly Far East) *s.* The United States. See *Land of the Big PX.*

Big Red One, the The 1st Infantry Division, so called because of its insignia, a red numeral 1 on an OD shield and because of its splendid combat record.

Big Rice (Occupation of Japan) *s.* A Japanese nickname for the United States, occasionally used (in translation) by Americans. It is based on a Japanese pun. The character *bei,* which forms the first part of the Japanese word for the United States, can also be read as *rice.*

billet (World War I to Modern) The place where a soldier sleeps when "quartered on the inhabitants." It may be a room in a private house, a hayloft, or a large public building. The term comes from the *billet* (French for 'ticket') that a soldier received, with the address of his temporary quarters. *Billet* was a common European term, with some use in the English service, by the 17th century, but Americans had little knowledge of it until the AEF went overseas in 1917.

big thing, a (Civil War; USA) Something on the order of the mountain that labored and gave birth to a mouse; a big project that trips over its own feet. *Big thing* was sometimes howled in chorus, to the everlasting confusion of the recipient. Gen. George McClellan was a big-thing specialist.

bingo (Air Force) *s.* Minimum fuel level on an aircraft; also a signal given by the first pilot in a formation who had dropped down to minimum fuel level. "Flight had reached Bingo fuel level and had to retreat for home" (AAV, p. 110).

bint (World War II into the 1950s) A woman. If young, good; if pretty, wonderful. A British Army term, from Arabic *bint* 'girl', 'woman'. Picked up by Americans serving in the Near East and the CBI.

bird (World War I to Modern) *s.* Any type of aircraft, fixed-wing or rotary-wing. The term is probably as old as the art of heavier-than-air flight itself. Lighter cites an August 1918 source documenting its use during World War I.

birdbath (Modern) *s.* A concrete area in a motor pool or tank park used for washing vehicles. It resembles a birdbath.

bird colonel (Antiquity uncertain, but probably old, to Modern) *s.* A "full" colonel. So called because his insignia of grade is a silver eagle.

bird corporal (Modern) *s.* A specialist fourth class (pay grade E-4), the specialist parallel to a corporal. So called because the golden spread eagle is the basic insignia for specialists.

bird dog (Modern) *s.* The L-19 light-observation, fixed-wing aircraft used by forward air controllers to spot for artillery and tactical airstrikes. The term replaced the somewhat older *butterfly*, current in 1962. "The keen eyes of the pilot of a 'Bird Dog' aircraft" (Marshall, 1968).

bird-dog, to 1. (World War II and later) *s.* To supervise, or to keep an eye generally on someone or some activity, possibly surreptitiously. 2. (Vietnam and later; probably originally Air Force) *s.* To work hard at something, with the hope and intent of hacking it.

birdland (Modern) *s.* Quarters for senior officers on a post; so called from the fact that they are generally occupied by officers in the grade of colonel (*full colonel, bird colonel*) on up (Brosig).

bird time (Modern) *s.* The time that a helicopter has been aloft. "I've got about two hours bird time."

bird watching (Vietnam; all Services) *s.* Girl watching. From the early days of the Vietnam War, when many Americans stationed in or visiting Saigon spent at least some of their time in the sidewalk cafes, sipping iced ba-me-ba, and admiring the exotic beauty of the Vietnamese women passing by. The sensation of bird watching was heightened by the flowing, varicolored silk dress (*áo dài* 'long dress'), which is the traditional garb worn by Vietnamese ladies.

biscuit bitches See *donut dollies.*

biscuit gun (Early World War II; Air Corps) *s.* An imaginary weapon, said to be used to shoot food up to student pilots who could not muster the skill or courage to land their planes.

bitch (Well established by World War II) *s.* As a noun, a complaint. As a verb, to complain, usually loudly, persistently, and fervently. Why such activity is called *bitching* is not known, but a good guess is that it comes from *bitch* meaning a quarrelsome, querulous, complaining woman—or complaining like an old woman. Another theory is that the term comes from the frequent references to *bitches* and *sons of bitches* included in the complaint. A *bitch session* is a group of soldiers bitching in chorus or comparing bitches. This latter often develops into a liars' contest. Bitching is a favorite Army recreation; it requires no special equipment and often can be carried on simultaneously with one's normal duties. Our senior officer's sainted uncle, who began as a private in the Indian Wars and finished as an Old Army sergeant, advised him when he became a lowly shavetail, "Never worry about men complaining; the time to worry is when they stop."

bitch box (World War II to Modern; all Services) *s.* A loudspeaker system, especially in training camps and repple depples. Strange, irritating sounds come reverberating out of it hour after hour. Frequently the thing is out of adjustment or the clown reading the announcements has not mastered basic English. When you have given up trying to translate the noise and have stopped listening, something is broadcast that you really should have heard.

bite the bullet, to (18th century on) *s.* To steel oneself to undergo extreme pain, hardship, or embarrassment. The expression, no longer often encountered, was Army slang during the late 18th and 19th centuries, at which time it meant to undergo an amputation or other painful operation. Since painkillers of any sort (even raw, new whiskey) were often lacking, surgeons would give a wounded soldier a soft, lead musket ball to bite down on while they worked. According to report, such balls with tooth indentations have been found at Continental Army battle sites.

bitter (Post–World War II to Modern; also Air Force) *s.* A deliberate mispronunciation of the German *bitte*—meaning 'please'—frequently used by Americans.

bivouac (Apparently early 19th century, to Modern) Originally, a camp (or to camp) in the open without tents. The soldiers would sleep on the ground around their campfires—if wood were available and rain and wind did not put the fires out. With the introduction of the shelter half during the Civil War, *to bivouac* gradually came to mean to camp with such tents, as contrasted to billets. Today, again, tents are less used in combat situations, and troops bivouac around their vehicles, using sleeping bags and/or improvised shelters.

BJ (At least as early as 1900; West Point) *s.* Bold before June, meaning an impertinent cadet. Such a person puts on airs, presuming an authority and status conferred only after graduation in June.

blackberry picker (Civil War; USA) *s.* A professional straggler, a coffee boiler. Blackberry pickers might deliberately lag behind their unit (under the pretext of hurriedly picking fruit) in order to be captured by the enemy and thus be safe from the hardships of the war. Southern prisons sometimes taught them there were worse places than combat.

blackbird *s.* A soldier who is assigned to an Army school before class actually begins. Possibly from the fact that such personnel hang around like blackbirds, waiting for things to begin. See *snowbird.*

black book (Ancient to Modern) *s.* A book, actual or imaginary, that is supposed to contain the names of persons designated for censure or punishment. The term can also be used as a verb, meaning to enter in a black book. During the Indian Wars some contrary-minded officers of the 10th Cavalry Regiment complained that their colonel had threatened to *black book* them, thereby harming their chances for promotion. Nowadays, with the general degeneration of our language, soldiers are more apt to use the expression *shit list*. The origin of the term *black book* may be military, arising from the memorandum books carried by officers and sergeants to note down matters of daily routine, which would naturally include the names of soldiers guilty of various offenses. On the other hand, black books and white books are very old, and the first recorded examples of *black book* come from the days of Henry VIII and Queen Elizabeth I, where the use is not military.

black box (Korea and later) *s.* A black metal or plastic cover over some particularly secret or complicated piece of equipment, preventing the organization's own maintenance specialists from trying to fix the equipment when it malfunctions. Or, the equipment itself. Black-box repair work must be done by a highly paid civilian black-box specialist, who works for the firm that manufactured the faulty item—if he is sober, if he is not too busy with his own affairs, and if you can find him. The situation is fine for morale: your best maintenance people all want out so that they can get black-box specialist jobs themselves.

black death (World War I) *s.* Coffee at the officers' mess. A Royal Flying Corps definition that seeped into American lingo.

Black Hole (Early 19th century; West Point) A covered pit, approximately eight feet square, used by Capt. William Partridge, Superintendent of the US Military Academy (1815–17) to give cadets guilty of fighting, insubordination, or attempting to burn down their barracks a quiet place for a half-hour's contemplation of their sinful ways. It was probably named after the infamous 1756 Black Hole of Calcutta.

Black Jack Gen. John J. Pershing of the AEF. He had earned this nickname—the source of which is disputed—well before World War I, but some bruised subordinates declared that it thoroughly expressed his style of command.

Blacklist Forty (1945) The code name for Korea used during its occupation in 1945. Once a soldier got a whiff of its rice paddies, he became convinced that he had been blacklisted. In recent years the Korean government has banned the use of human feces as fertilizer.

blade time (Modern) The time a helicopter is actually in flight. See *bird time.*

blanco (At least World War I to World War II) A commercial product used to color web equipment so that it all looked the same, whether new or old. Despite the suggestion of whiteness in the term, blanco came in several shades, ranging up to a dirty light-greenish tan. According to Partridge (1970), from a British trade name of about 1895.

Blanket Division (Modern) *s.* The 1st Air Cavalry Division, because of the size of its shoulder patch, the largest one authorized for any Army unit.

blanket drill (At least as early as World War I to Modern) *s.* Sleep. One usually *does* or *performs* blanket drill.

Blanket party (World War II and earlier) A lynch mob within the unit, a term probably borrowed from the Imperial Prussian Army and the Old, Old British Army, when it was limited to extremely unpopular NCOs. In the US, a *blanket party* was generally used on barracks' thieves, snitches, and other low vermin. The idea was to inflict severe physical punishment without any participants being identified. A blanket was thrown over the head of the "guest of honor" and held there by two or three brawny individuals while the contents of the blanket was beaten to a pulp. The practice reduced barracks' theft and white ratting to a minimum.

bless, to (Modern) *s.* To approve officially, particularly of a staff paper.

blighty (World War I to World War II) 1. *s.* Home. Borrowed from British forces in the Near and Middle East. Derived from Hindustani *bilayati* 'foreign', 'European', ultimately from Arabic *wilayati* 'province'. In World War II, *Old Blighty* specifically meant England. An American soldier might say, "I've got a week's leave in Old Blighty." 2. *s.* By an extension of meaning (also British), a wound that necessitates sending one home: "I got my blighty at Wipers."

blind (World War I and perhaps earlier, to at least World War II) *s.* A fine, especially a fine imposed by a court-martial, usually two-thirds of a culprit's pay for three months (see *three and two-thirds*). Also, other pay deductions, such as for lost or damaged government property. The term was probably borrowed from poker, where a blind is the stake put up by the elder hand, before the deal.

blind shell (Civil War, probably earlier) A shell used for target practice.

blister 1. (World War II) *s.* A sexually attractive female. 2. (World War II and later) *s.* A glass or transparent plastic bulge or dome on the fuselage of an airplane, forming a gun turret or cockpit cover.

blisterfoot (World War II) *s.* An infantryman. See *mud crusher, gravel agitator, beetle crusher*.

blister rep (West Point) *s.* The cadet who is assigned to the duty of administering first aid to other cadets' blistered feet.

blister squad (West Point) *s.* Cadets temporarily excused from marching or standing in ranks because of their blistered feet (Mardis).

blitz (World War II) The German word *Blitz* 'lightning', used in various combinations, especially *blitzkrieg.* The British and some Americans applied the term *the blitz* to heavy aerial bombardments, especially the German raids over England in 1941.

blitz, to 1. (Before World War II to Modern) *s.* To polish metal (see *Blitz Cloth*). 2. (World War II to Modern) *s.* To pulverize something, destroy something.

Blitz Cloth (Before World War II to Modern) The trade name for a chemically impregnated cloth used to give a quick shine to brass belt buckles, collar insignia, buttons, etc. *Blitz* is the name of the company that manufactures these cloths. Our sergeant major reports that Blitz Cloths work well on his wife's brassware, but that soldiers much prefer French's Brasso.

blitzkrieg (World War II) 1. *s.* German for *lightning war*, a term that describes

German strategy and tactics during the campaigns of 1939–41. 2. *s.* A fast line of talk designed to get the admiration and cooperation of a pretty girl, or a loan, or a pass before the other party can think up a good reason for saying "No." A snow job.

blivit blivet (World War II to present; all Services) 1. *s.* Originally a trick word used to elicit a question, to which a specific nonsensical reply would be given. "If he doesn't cut it out, I'm going to hit him with a blivit." "What's a blivit?" "Ten pounds of shit in a five pound bag." In this sense, almost always used with *hit* or a similar word 2. *s.* A petty nuisance. 3. *s.* A sarcastic way of referring to correspondence from some higher authority, usually a directive of some sort: "A blivit from the front office."

blockbuster (World War II) *s.* Unofficial term for a high-explosive aerial bomb weighing from 4 to 8 tons.

blood *s.* Ketchup.

bloodhounds in the boudoir *s.* WAC slang for inspections.

blood stripe (Modern) *s.* A promotion at the expense of another. When an NCO is demoted for misconduct, the promoting authority may decide to confer the unfortunate soldier's stripes upon a more deserving member of the unit. The metaphor is from the battlefield and promotion to fill vacancies caused by death or disability.

Bloody Back (Revolutionary) *s.* A jeering reference to a British soldier, possibly referring to his red coat, but more likely to have been based on the use of flogging as a common form of military punishment. See *lobster*.

Bloody Bucket (World War II) *s.* The US 28th Infantry Division, which had a very rough time in the Normandy bocage, Hürtgen Forest, and the Ardennes. Originally a Pennsylvania National Guard organization; its division insignia was a red keystone, which—with the organization's perverse fortunes and heavy casualties—inspired this nickname.

Blooey Blooie (World War I) *s.* Blois, France, the Officers' Reclassification Center, where incompetent officers were stored. Officers sent there were said to be *blooeyed*. Probably also the origin of *blooey*, civilian slang of the 1920s, meaning *all messed up*.

blooker blooper (Modern; also Marines) *s.* The M79 grenade launcher. "You'll be runnin' around handin' out fuckin' tangerines to people steda shooting ya blooker, I bet!" (Groom). Also called *chunker, '79, thump gun*.

blooker balls blooper balls (Modern; also Marines) *s.* Ammunition for the M79 grenade launcher.

blouse 1. (Civil War; USA) An unlined blue-flannel coat, worn for fatigue duty and field service. 2. (1920s to Modern) The dress uniform coat. In civilian life it would be called a coat or a jacket.

blouse, to 1. (Antiquity unknown to Modern) To tuck one's trousers into the tops of one's boots, leaving a neat overhang. One blouses trousers, not boots, but the expression *bloused boots* is common. The term comes from civilian dressmaking. 2. (Modern) *s.* To give or receive a black eye.

blow away, to (Modern) *s.* To kill. Perhaps assimilated black argot. "Blew away everybody but Ivy, the driver" Heinemann).

Blow it out your barracks bag! See *barracks bag*.

blow smoke, to (Approximately Vietnam to Modern; also Air Force, possibly Navy) *s.* To obfuscate, to do a snow job on, to bamboozle, to flank. Often phrased, "He thinks he's blowing smoke up my ass."

blow Zs, to (Modern) *s.* To sleep, to snore. Probably from comic strip rendering of snoring. "Maybe he'd just stay in his tent and blow *Z*s for a few days" (Smith). Also as *to cut Zs.*

blue (Modern; all Services) The color of water features on maps; hence, a river or stream. "We set up this side of the blue."

Bluebelly Blue Belly (Civil War; CSA) *s.* A US soldier. From Southern lips *Blue-bellied Yankee* was a major insult.

Blue Book (West Point) *s.* The book of cadet regulations. Now obsolete. Also called the *Commandant's Bible.*

Blueboy (Modern) *s.* The US Air Force. Any airman. "I called Blueboy" (Tregaskis).

Blue Dart (West Point) *s.* A special report rendered on one cadet by another. As these reports do not have to be signed, they often amount to a stab in the back. They are printed on blue paper. " 'Blue Dart' . . . the light blue forms with which one cadet could pillory another" (Truscott).

Blue Hen's Chickens (Revolutionary) *s.* The Delaware regiment of the Continental Line, famous for its valor and discipline. Capt. Jonathan Caldwell, commanding a company raised in Kent County, was a well-known cockfighter who took two of his best gamecocks along to the wars. These were from the brood of a certain blue hen, famous for the fighting qualities of her offspring. The nickname was applied first to Caldwell's company, then to the whole regiment.

blue pill blue mass (19th century, especially Civil War) A cathartic much favored by Army medical officers. It consisted of metallic mercury mixed with chalk.

blue plumb blue plum (Revolutionary) A musket ball. The term is of British origin and may refer to lead as plumb.

Blues, the (World War II) The Infantry, from the blue color traditionally ascribed to friendly forces in map problems and exercises (Garber and Bond). Perhaps influenced by the fact that the Infantry color was sky blue.

Blues Dress Blues A type of uniform. In Gen. Winfield Scott's opinion, blue was the "national color" and thus the proper color for American Army uniforms. During the Colonial Wars, a good many Americans wore blue; and blue was the standard uniform color, with some exceptions, until 1898, when a khaki field uniform was adopted for tropical service. In 1902 this was followed by an OD wool service uniform, blue uniforms being used only for full-dress ceremonies. Blues were abandoned when we entered World War I. Since then Dress Blues have had an off-again, on-again existence. At present, officers wear them on appropriate occasions, but only in certain special units (notably the 3d Infantry Regiment, the Old Guard) does the whole outfit have them.

Blue Star Rangers Blue Star Commandos (World War II) *s.* Troops in the ETO communications zone and/or rear-echelon types in general, who were never shot at but were apt to give themselves airs. The Services of Supply insignia featured a large blue star.

blue-suiter (Modern; Air Force) *s.* An airman. "The first blue-suiter he met . . . was Chief Master Sergeant of the Air

Force James M. McCoy" (*Airman*, May 1980).

blue ticket *s.* A discharge, neither honorable nor dishonorable, given to a soldier separated from the service under Section 8 for inaptitude. It was originally printed on blue paper, and the term stuck even after the color of the paper had been changed.

blue time (Modern) *s.* Productive time, or the actual time that a Regular Army adviser spends with a Reserve or National Guard unit. This does not include travel time, but does include any time actually spent with the unit, whether in drinking coffee, advising, or swapping stories.

boarder (West Point) *s.* A cadet who is resigning or being dismissed from the Academy. Boarders are relegated to the Boarder's Ward, a barracks reserved for such unfortunates, where they stay until they can be processed out of the Corps of Cadets. The origin of the term may be that such persons are no longer considered cadets but merely boarders at the Academy. Possibly related to *board out*, because cadets are dismissed only after the action of a board. "They were no longer cadets. They were boarders" (Truscott).

board out, to boarded out, to be (Modern) To be eliminated from the service by the action of a board of officers convened to determine one's suitability for retention on active duty. Usually such boards consider undesirable personal traits or performance below par. Boards are also convened to determine medical disability ratings.

bobtailed discharge bobtail (Old, Old Army) *s.* A discharge from the service under less than honorable conditions. Not a dishonorable discharge, but the next thing to it. The term came from the practice of clipping off the final section of the discharge form, which covered the dischargee's character. In World War II called a *discharge without honor*.

boche Boche (World War I primarily, perhaps a little use in World War II) A German. Probably the most common French slang term for a German, taken over to a small extent by journalists and members of the AEF. The native American terms *Heinie, Kraut*, and *Fritz* seem to have been much more common. The origin of the term is obscure. According to Dauzat, it probably comes ultimately from *tête de boche*, via the 19th-century forms *allemoche* and *alboche* (combining *allemand* 'German' and *caboche* 'hobnail', 'pig head').

body count (Vietnam; mostly Army) A count of the enemy dead left on the field after an engagement. In the hit-and-run fighting of guerrilla warfare, this was the best possible indication of how badly the enemy had been hurt before he faded back into the bushes. Unfortunately, the term was not felicitous. It jarred civilians back home, exacerbating antiwar sentiment.

body shop (Modern) *s.* A mortuary or a hospital ward for prosthetic surgery. The term undoubtedly comes from the automotive repair industry.

body snatcher (World War II) 1. *s.* A stretcher-bearer, whose job is to pick up the wounded and carry them back to the aid station. 2. *s.* A streetwalker, particularly an aggressive one.

bogey bogie (Air Force) *s.* An unidentified or suspicious aircraft, or a blip on a radar screen. Bogies are not necessarily bandits (enemy aircraft).

Bohemian Brigade Bohemians (Civil War; USA) A collective name war correspondents gave themselves as they followed Union armies in the field. What the soldiers, and especially the generals, called them was something else. The term *Bohemian* probably had several connotations at the time: a wandering Gypsy-like occupation, as opposed to work at a desk; roughing it, in the manner of Paris Bohemians; and the Bohemian centers of journalism in New York, like Pfaff's Tavern. " 'The Bohemian Brigade' was the name the little corps of army correspondents and artists that soon assembled at Jefferson City had received. . . . We adopted the true Bohemian code of doing the best we could for our comfort and of laughing away the multifarious annoyances" (Browne).

boilermakers (Old Army into World War II) *s.* An Army band. In premodern times, when boilers were hammered together out of copper and brass, a boilermaker's shop was generally considered the ultimate in discordant noisiness.

bolo, to 1. (Old Army until at least through World War II) *s.* To fail the rifle marksmanship qualification tests. A soldier who so disgraced his unit might be called a *bolo.* Army folklore had it that in some units his rifle would be taken away from him and replaced with a real bolo (the heavy working-fighting knife of the Filipino farmer), as better suited to his abilities. Such a soldier might be placed in a bolo squad for special training. 2. (World War II) *s.* To have a zero score on the rifle range or to miss the target completely.

bomb, to bomb out, to (Beginning in World War II or somewhat later, probably originally Air Force) *s.* To wash out, to make a mess of things, to fail. This is one bit of military slang that has become thoroughly civilian in recent years.

bombardier 1. (Colonial into early 19th century) An artillery NCO who prepared ammunition and fuzes. Bombardiers were especially responsible for loading and firing howitzers and mortars. (Since these fired explosive shell, they had to be handled with especial care and skill.) There were several bombardiers in each artillery company. 2. (World War I and later) The member of a bomber crew who operates the bombsight and bomb-release mechanism.

bombed (Antiquity uncertain, probably World War II on) *s.* Drunk or otherwise incapable of coherent speech, thought, and action. Possibly the term is derived from the dazed condition of individuals after prolonged, heavy bombardment.

bombproof (Civil War) 1. A general term for a dugout or underground shelter. 2. *s.* By extension, a coward, whether a soldier who avoided combat or a civilian who evaded military service.

bomb up, to (World War II; Air Force and Navy) To put a plane's bomb load aboard it in preparation for an air raid.

bone, to (Perhaps about 1850 on; West Point, with some diffusion into the Regular Army) *s.* To work hard at, to study diligently. It has been used in many combinations: *to bone check*, to work hard at saving money; *to bone dis*, to observe strict discipline; *to bone file*, to strive for class standing; *to bone make*, to work hard for promotion; *to bone a reverse*, to be regarded with disfavor; *to bone tenths*, to work for high grades; *to bone parade and drill*, to work hard at parade and drill. *To bone* is sometimes taken as a peculiarly military word, but there are many civilian uses from an earlier date, and we still speak of *boning up* on something.

boobies (Modern) *s.* Booby traps.

boodle (From about 1900; West Point) *s.* Extra goodies, such as cookies, candy, and ice cream. The boodler's was the place in the cadet area where such things could be purchased legally. Plebes are permitted to buy boodle, but not to keep it in their rooms. The term itself was originally a slang word for illicit gains or loot.

boodle fight (West Point) *s.* A gathering where boodle is served. Now obsolete.

book *s.* The existing regulations, text, and doctrine on any subject. It is used in several common expressions. *To go by the book* is to follow regulations exactly. If you gum things up, you may not be court-martialed, but somehow you may be overlooked when promotions and decorations are awarded. *To throw the book away* is to invent your own solution to a problem. The phrase has a fine, free ring, but it usually indicates that the person saying it has not bothered to read the book in the first place. *To throw the book at someone* is to inflict the maximum punishment.

boom-boom (Modern) *s.* Sexual intercourse. A term widely used throughout Asia and the Pacific. It is usually accompanied by gently (or not so gently) punching one's fist into the palm of the other hand, while lasciviously winking and leering. Perhaps a military counterpart to civilian *bang-bang* and *to bang a woman. Boom-boom, bang-bang*, and *to bang* are not present in these senses in Partridge or Wentworth and Flexner, although all have been in common use since at least World War II. "One sat in Slagel's lap and said, 'You boom-boom, GI?' " (Smith).

boomerang (World War II) *s.* An abort, so called because, like the true boomerang, it has returned to its place of origin. From the British.

boondocks boonies (Philippine Insurrection on) *s.* Somewhere out in the backwoods, the sticks. From Tagalog *bundok* 'mountain'.

boondockers (World War II to Korea) *s.* Field boots.

boonie hat See *Gabby Hayes hat.*

boonie rat (Modern) *s.* An infantryman or combat soldier, so called because he spends so much time in the boonies. "When the hard-core Boonie Rat returns home from a tour in Vietnam . . ." (Pratt and Blair). See *field rat.*

bootee (19th century) The equivalent of a modern high-cut shoe. The term was changed to *shoe* in 1875.

boots and saddles (Ancient into World War II) A Cavalry trumpet call, adopted 1841, indicating that troops are to fall in mounted, armed, and equipped for service. The term is a corruption of French *boute-selle* 'saddle up'.

bootstrapper (Modern) *s.* One who participates in the Degree Completion Course (known as Operation Bootstrap), a program that enables Army personnel to complete academic degrees by attending college full-time while still on active duty. Once open to enlisted personnel, this program is now authorized only for officers.

BOQ (Old Army to Modern) Bachelor Officers' Quarters, where the unmarried officers of a post or unit live. Traditionally, it had all the home comforts of Mammoth Cave during a hard winter. Existence there could turn a young officer's thoughts toward matrimony. (Occasionally there were dark mutterings that a post or unit commander with a clutch of homely daughters might deliberately let the place run down.) We recall a Navy officer on detached service with the Army who looked at his two rooms in the BOQ and refused to believe that he was not the victim of a major hoax. See *Bedlam*.

bottlecap colonel (Modern) *s.* A lieutenant colonel, so called perhaps from the resemblance between the silver oak leaf insignia and a bottlecap or the tinfoil on the inside of a bottlecap. Derogatory, since a bottlecap is a throwaway thing.

boudoir (Of some antiquity) *s.* A soldier's sarcastic name for his place to sleep—tent, hut, dugout, or foot of a tree. Frequently mispronounced, and not common of late.

bounce a quarter, to (Modern) During inspection, to test a soldier's bed-making technique by tossing a quarter onto the blanket. If the quarter bounces (and the higher the better), the bed is tightly made and the bed-maker has paid commendable attention to the principles of good military living. Our sergeant major reports that in the days when a quarter was really worth something, he spent much time dreaming of inventing a bed that would not give the quarters back.

bounced (World War I to Modern; Air Force) *s.* To get hit by a surprise attack from above.

Bouncing Betty (World War II) *s.* A fiendishly clever German antipersonnel mine (the S-mine), which, when tripped, popped up out of the ground and exploded at approximately waist level. It is possible that there may be a very vague folk memory of the terms *bouncing bet, bouncing betty*, or *bouncing betsy* for a common weed.

bounty jumper 1. (Civil War; USA) A volunteer who enlisted for a bonus and then deserted. Because of the difficulty in getting recruits for the Army, by 1862 the federal and state governments had begun to offer cash bounties up to $1,000 to volunteers. Predictably, bounty jumpers—usually professional criminals, sometimes operating in gangs—would enlist, draw their bounties, desert, and then enlist again. One bounty jumper confessed to having repeated the process thirty-two times. By some rank miscarriage of justice, he was sentenced to four years in prison instead of hanging. As soldiers, bounty jumpers were cowardly and worthless. 2. (Indian Wars) *s.* In the plural, two small rolls of cloth at the bottom of the back seams of the Cavalry shell jacket that were intended to support the saber belt with its load of cartridge pouches, saber, and revolver. Soldiers considered them troublesome and often removed them.

bowlegged *P* (Modern) *s.* The letter *P* in parentheses after one's rank to indicate that one has been selected for promotion: *MSG (P), Maj. (P)*, etc. Officers sometimes flaunt this designation and claim the privileges of their rank-to-be, before actual promotion. (They can flaunt too hard or in the wrong place and learn that "the Army giveth and the Army taketh away.") It is considered highly ridiculous for an enlisted soldier to try to pull rank with his bowlegged *P*.

bowlegs (Old, Old Army to World War II) *s.* A cavalryman.

bowser (Modern) *s.* A Canadian Army term taken into the vocabulary of the New York Army National Guard, more or less in self-defense, after joint maneuvers. The Canadians probably picked it up from the

British, for Partridge records it from the RAF in the 1930s. A bowser, the Canadians explain, is a long, hollow, cylindrical object with wheels under it and a motor in front, used for transporting gasoline—in other words, a tanker. Other terms from the Canadian are *PUFO* and *sharp point*.

box ambulance (Modern) *s.* The AM725 series military ambulance, which is square and boxlike. Also called the *crackerbox ambulance*.

Boxcar Flying Boxcar (Post–World War II; also Air Force) *s.* The Fairchild C-82 transport aircraft.

box kicker (Modern) *s.* A logistician or supply specialist, so called from the notion (perhaps justified) that supplies are inventoried merely by kicking boxes to see if they contain anything.

box respirator (World War I) The standard gas mask developed during World War I. The filter was in a metal box or canister carried in a bag suspended on the soldier's chest. It was connected to the face piece of the mask by a rubber hose.

Box 3 Box 13 Formerly the mailing address for prisoners in the stockade. It was less embarrassing for them and their families for mail to go to a cover address. According to Kendall and Viney, once very common in the Army. See also *drawers, Special Processing Company*. Post records,

Oh, send my mail to Box Three,
It's the last of me you'll see;
Just send my mail to Box Three
Till I'm free.

Boy Scouts (Modern) What is the difference between the Boy Scouts and the Army? Part of a thoroughly scurrilous riddle game played in the barracks. The response to it is, "The Boy Scouts have adult leadership." Our sergeant major reports that he first blanched at this hateful aspersion in 1958.

brace bracing (Originally West Point, but the practice and the term have been adopted elsewhere) The exaggerated position of attention assumed by cadets, with the chest thrust forward like a pouter pigeon's, and the chin tight enough to create at least three wrinkles. The command is *Brace!* or *Grab a brace!* In the equivalent commands *Hit the wall!* or *Grab a wall!* during personal inspections by upperclassmen, the cadet receiving the command assumes a brace with his back against the wall of the room.

bracket (World War I to Modern) The standard method of adjusting artillery or mortar fire on a target, by splitting the difference between overs and shorts until your fire lands right on target and you can go into fire for effect. The width of the desired bracket depends on the nature of the target. Troops on the move require a wider bracket than a dug-in defensive position:

For you'll wear a wooden jacket
After Heinie gets your bracket,
And you'll never see your sweetheart anymore!

The term naturally passed into the artilleryman's everyday language: "The topkick sure got a bracket on Private Slick."

Bragg's Bodyguard General Bragg's Bodyguard (Civil War; CSA) *s.* Lice.

brag rags (Modern) *s.* Service stripes (see *hash marks*). Wentworth and Flexner define the term as meaning campaign ribbons.

brain box (World War II; Air Force) *s.* Any device, especially an electronic one, used to control a mechanism.

brain bucket (World War II; Air Force) *s.* A crash helmet.

branches of the service The present branches of the service are as follows: Adjutant General's Corps (AG, AGC). Air Defense Artillery (AD, ADA). Armor (AR, ARM); established as Cavalry in 1776 and redesignated as Armor in 1950. Branch Immaterial (BI). Chaplain's Corps (CH). Chemical Corps (CM, CMC, CMLC). Corps of Engineers (CE). Field Artillery (FA). Finance Corps (FI, FC). General Staff (GS). Infantry (IN, INF). Inspector General (IG). Judge Advocate General Corps (JA, JAC, JAGC). Medical Service (MS), including Army Medical Specialist Corps (AMSC), Army Nurse Corps (ANC), Medical Service Corps (MSC), Veterinary Corps (VC). Military Intelligence (MI). Military Police Corps (MP, MPC). Ordnance Corps (OC). Quartermaster Corps (QM, QMC). Signal Corps (SC). Transportation Corps (TC). The Women's Army Corps (WAC) has been discontinued as such.

brass (Considerable antiquity to Modern) 1. Peacetime insignia and buttons made of brass. The time and energy spent in keeping them bright kept many a soldier out of mischief. In many Old Army units this brass included the eyelets and snaps on the cartridge belt and leggings. 2. Empty cartridge cases. What you always have to police up after a long, hot day on the range. 3. *s.* High-ranking officers, especially staff officers. In this sense, *brass* and *brass hat* seem to have come into the Army during World War I from the British, whose staff officers wore nicely decorated caps and had been nicknamed *brass hats* by the resentful Tommies.

brassard (Antiquity uncertain, but civilian British use in 1870, to Modern) An armband worn on the left upper sleeve to identify personnel who are performing special duty, usually of a temporary nature.

brassed off (World War II) *s.* Angry, disheartened. Approximately the same as *browned off*. It has been suggested that the term is a euphemism for the more scatological *pissed off*, but Partridge (1970) records *to brass off* (to grumble) at an earlier date. This suggests that the term may originally have been connected with *brass* (insolence).

brass hat *s.* An officer. See *brass* 3.

brave-maker (Old, Old Army, probably of civilian origin) *s.* Any alcoholic stimulant that makes you feel capable of singlehandedly licking the whole Sioux nation —or even your first sergeant.

Brave Rifles The 3d Cavalry Regiment, originally raised as the Regiment of Mounted Riflemen, redesignated as cavalry in 1861. Gen. Winfield Scott gave them their title in Mexico in 1847.

bravo (Modern) *s.* An infantryman, from the letter suffix to the infantryman's military occupational specialty number—11B. In the phonetic alphabet *b* is rendered as *bravo*. See *infantry* for other synonyms.

break (At least World War II to Modern) *s.* A short rest period, a cessation of activity. Common in such expressions as *take a break, a ten-minute break.*

break, to 1. (Colonial to at least Old Army) *s.* To reduce in grade or rank; the equivalent of modern *bust*. To discharge, usually under dishonorable circumstances; to cashier. "Broken from the service." The expression *a broken old soldier* commonly meant one disabled by wounds and hardship, but this seems to have been more a civilian usage. 2. (World War II to Modern; Air Force) *s.* To cause an aircraft to make an emergency turn to avoid being tracked by an enemy fighter pilot. "Hey Lead, break right, break right, they are firing at you" (TB).

break arrest, to To leave one's quarters or barracks after having been placed there under arrest.

break quarters, to (Modern) To leave one's quarters or barracks deliberately after having been confined there by a doctor's orders, as a result of sickness.

Break rank, march! (Civil War) Equivalent to the modern *Fall out!*

break ranks, to (Possibly Colonial to Modern) To break formation or to fall out. No longer used as a command, except in a negative sense: "Who the hell told you you could break ranks?"

brevet (Colonial to early 20th century) A type of promotion that raised an officer to a higher grade in the Army as a whole than that which he held in his regular unit. Brevet rank might be employed, for example, to give an infantry lieutenant extra authority when he was detailed as an assistant adjutant general, or in recognition of ten years of honorable service in one grade; or as a reward for valor; or to give a Regular Army officer sufficient rank to deal with militia officers or allies. Congress periodically changed the rules concerning the award of brevets, the wearing of the insignia or uniform of brevet rank, and the use of brevet rank in official correspondence. The result was constant and impressive confusion in both the Army and Congress, and many bitter quarrels among officers as to who really ranked whom. The only certain fact was that a brevet promotion brought no increase in pay unless the officer was given duty commensurate with his brevet grade. The confusion became especially painful after the Civil War. Veteran officers who had won several brevets and had served as division and corps commanders suddenly reverted to their permanent grades—in one case, from major general to captain! The practice died out, in effect, in the 1890s. The last brevet promotion, that of Maj. Gen. Tasker H. Bliss to lieutenant general in May 1918, was to give him rank equal to French and British representatives on the Supreme War Council in Paris. See *Mexican rank.*

brevet second lieutenant (Early 19th century) In many years the US Military Academy graduated more cadets than there were vacancies for second lieutenants in the Army. The unlucky surplus graduates were rated as brevet second lieutenants, attached to regiments, and put to work until there were vacancies for them. Sometimes this took as long as two years. A few enlisted men were also awarded this grade for valor during the Mexican and Civil wars.

Bridgman's Bull Battery (Philippine Insurrection) Light Battery G, 6th US Artillery, 1898–1900. It landed in the Philippines without its horses and, finding the native Filipino variety too small to haul its 3.2-inch field guns, utilized over a hundred Brahma bulls. These were trained to obey bugle calls and gave good service. Photographs indicate that native drivers were used.

brigade (Colonial to Modern; also Marines) In its usual sense, two or more regiments (now, battalions) grouped together as a major component of a division. However, from colonial times through the War of 1812, various confusing foreign usages have appeared in American campaigns. In the British Army a brigade of engineers might consist of only two or three officers attached to the headquarters of an army; a brigade of artillery was a company of artillery fully equipped with cannon (five guns and one howitzer) and vehicles, or the rough equivalent of a modern battery. In the French service the army bakers were organized in brigades of four men—a brigadier (master baker) and three helpers.

brigade, to (Colonial to Modern; also Marines) To form several separate regiments or battalions into a brigade. These are then said to be *brigaded* with one another.

brigade major (Colonial to Revolutionary) In the British and American armies, the principal staff officer of a brigade. He received and distributed the brigade commander's orders and kept the brigade records and duty rosters.

brigadier (Colonial through 1815) 1. In the British Army, an officer, usually a lieutenant colonel, acting temporarily as the commanding officer of a brigade. George Washington served as a brigadier in 1758 during the last campaign against Fort Duquesne. American historians frequently confuse the term with *brigadier general*, a grade that the British did not have during the American Revolution. 2. In the French Army, a corporal of mounted troops or the chief of a small detachment of bakers. "Brigadier Gerard," the hero of A. Conan Doyle's stories about a Napoleonic soldier (in *The Adventures of Gerard*), was a typical British misconception of French military grades. Gerard would have been a general of brigade.

brigadier general (Revolutionary to Modern) A general officer ranking below a major general and above a colonel. His insignia is a single silver star. A brigadier general usually commands a brigade. Nicknames for the rank are *gigadier breneral* and *gigadier brindle.* Abbreviated *BG, Brig. Gen.*

bright crowd (World War II) *s.* A British insult, meaning exactly the opposite. Learned from a Royal Marine Commando officer, who was describing an unfortunate "colonial" unit.

bring a brick with [one], to (Civil War; USA) *s.* To return to camp under the influence of Jersey Lightning or other varieties of the ardent.

bring smoke, to (Modern) *s.* To bring retribution on, to punish, to discipline, to attack. Probably derived from the procedure of marking enemy positions with smoke to make them visible to pilots conducting airstrikes. "Let's bring smoke on those fuckin' gooks!" (Smith). See *smoke bringer*.

broken-backed war (Modern) A brutally blunt description of the type of war probable after the first major strike and counterstrike of an all-out nuclear war. Communications will be shattered; each surviving military unit will have to regroup the best it can, while hitting out with what it can muster at whatever foes it can reach. The overly housebroken commander who insists on waiting for orders, rather than acting on his own initiative, will not last long.

broken-feather chief (Post–World War II) *s.* Usually a field-grade officer—a battalion commander or senior staff officer—who has major responsibilities, but little independent authority, in the modern Army's highly centralized command system. One of them, feeling immoderately supervised, created an Army ditty found on many bulletin boards, especially in higher headquarters:

I'm not allowed to run the train,
Or see how fast t'will go.
I ain't allowed to let off steam
Or make the whistle blow.
I cannot exercise control
Or even ring the bell.
But let the damn thing jump the track—
And see who catches hell!

broken-wing award (Modern) *s.* Unofficial recognition given to any Army aviator who successfully lands or crash-lands a disabled aircraft.

brolly (World War II; Air Force) *s.* A parachute. The term is derived from the Royal Air Force, and ultimately from lower-class British slang for an umbrella.

Bronze Star Medal (1944 to Modern) An award for heroism or meritorious achievement, service, or acts performed in connection with military operations against a hostile armed force. It may be awarded to US or foreign personnel, military or civilian. It ranks below the Soldier's Medal and above the Meritorious Service Medal. A bronze V device is worn to indicate awards for valor.

brought up to the bullring, to be (Civil War; USA) *s.* To be brought up for military punishment, particularly execution.

brown bar (Modern) *s.* A second lieutenant, because of the color (gold) of his insignia of grade.

brown bomber (Modern; all Services) *s.* A large, brown laxative pill with a quick and devastating effect. The term is probably connected with *the Brown Bomber,* the nickname of the boxer Joe Louis.

brown boy (West Point) *s.* Formerly the tan cotton quilt issued to West Point cadets. Now called a *green girl.* "Brown Boy, the tan cotton quilt every cadet slept with" (Truscott).

brown nose (World War II and later) *s.* A person shamelessly eager to curry favor with his superiors. Such a person can also be called a *brownie,* and the same idea can be conveyed by stroking one's nose and looking significantly at the person in question.

brown-nose, to (World War II and later) *s.* To curry favor with superiors shamelessly.

Brown-shoe Air Force (Post–World War II) *s.* The one-time US Army Air Corps/Forces—an organization suffering intensely from the frustration of still being part of the Army, but occasionally useful. (When the Air Force became an independent branch of the US Armed Forces in September 1947, it quickly adopted a new uniform that included black shoes.)

Brown-shoe Army (Modern) *s.* The post–World War II/Korea Army of OD uniforms and brown leather shoes and equipment, before black shoes and boots became standard. Actually, the old brown shoes and boots were known officially as "boot [or shoe] russet." Department of the Army Circular 670-22 (21 January 1958) authorized dyeing brown combat boots black and gave specific instructions on how to do it. (It was hard work. You employed lots of warm water, GI soap applied with a GI brush, elbow grease, and black dye.) To be called *brown-shoe* is to be recognized as hard, tough, and dedicated, if old-fashioned.

brown-spit babies (Old, Old Army) *s.* The legal offspring of enlisted soldiers, tough as a mule's nose and weaned on sutler's chewing tobacco.

Brown-water Navy (Vietnam; all Services) *s.* US Navy forces engaged in operations along the waterways of South Vietnam, as part of the Army–Navy Mobile Riverine Force. It was a tricky and dangerous, but highly effective, business that has never received due credit.

brunette (Indian Wars) *s.* A black soldier. One respected squadron of the 9th Cavalry was Henry's Brunettes, named after their scar-faced commander, Maj. Guy V. Henry.

Bryan howitzers (World War I) *s.* Imitation cannon, made of wood and stove pipe, used in training artillerymen because of the lack of real guns. Secretary of State William Jennings Bryan, a confirmed pacifist, was blamed for delaying American preparedness.

bubble (Modern) 1. *s.* The OH-6, OH-13, and OH-23 helicopters, so called because of the configuration of the transparent plastic that covers and protects the pilot. 2. *s.* Inflatable shelters used to house the elements of the Medical Unit Self-Contained Transportation (MUST) hospitals. Deflated and folded, bubbles are 6 by 15 feet, but inflated they form structures providing 20 by 60 feet of working space.

bubble dancer (1920s into the 1940s) *s.* A KP assigned the job of washing dishes. Other designations were *pearl diver* and *China Clipper*. See also *pot walloper*.

buck (19th century to Modern) *s.* The lowest level of certain grades, used in such combinations as *buck private* (a private, as opposed to a private first class) and *buck sergeant* (the lowest grade of sergeant). Webster's *Third* refers to a *buck general* (presumably a brigadier general), but we have not heard the expression. The origin of the term *buck* in this sense is not known, but it may derive from such expressions as an *Indian buck*, which originally meant an adult male Indian, but shifted to mean a tribesman, as opposed to a chief. From the Old, Old Army into World War II, *buck* or *Johnny Buck* could mean a buck private.

buck, to (19th century to Modern) *s.* To fight against, to oppose a trend or operation, as in bucking the system.

buck and ball (Colonial into Civil War) A peculiarly American form of ammunition developed during the first Indian Wars. It contained one musket ball and several buckshot. It was excellent for dealing with the agile Indian as he slipped from tree to tree. If you did not hit him square, you had a good chance of nicking him. Buck and ball later became a standard load for the infantry musket cartridge. The British, who were on the receiving end of it in 1812–15, considered it a minor atrocity. Buck and ball was used until the old smoothbore musket was replaced by the more accurate rifled musket —in some regiments, not until mid-1863.

Buckeye (Civil War) *s.* A soldier from Ohio. The nickname seems to have been well established by 1830.

buck for, to (Perhaps 19th century to Modern) *s.* To work hard to achieve a desired end; sometimes the term implies temporary zeal and ostentation to impress one's superiors. An ambitious private can buck for private first class. He can also unintentionally buck to get an undesired result: "What the hell's the matter with you standing inspection drunk! Are you bucking for the guardhouse?" Connected with this use of *buck*, although without the unfavorable aspects, is the custom (at least as old as Old Army, into World War II) of *bucking for orderly*. The smartest soldier in a guard detail would be selected as the commanding officer's orderly for the next twenty-four hours. It was an easy detail, with a full night's sleep, and was usually followed by a twenty-four-hour pass. There was much competition among companies, and the best man from each company on the guard detail would be carefully prepared and coached. In mounted outfits, he might be lifted into his saddle, to avoid stains and wrinkles. All these usages of *buck* are probably connected with the early 19th-century civilian usage of *buck* as a very well dressed person, sometimes a playboy, and mid-19th-century use of *buck up* for *spruce up*.

bucking and gagging (Revolutionary through Civil War) A rough form of military punishment used in the field, especially for drunkenness and insubordination. The offender was seated on the ground, his knees tight up against his chest. A stout stick was run under his knees, his arms placed under the stick, and his hands then tied in front of his shins. To keep him from annoying his more virtuous comrades with complaints, a tent peg or bayonet was inserted crosswise in his mouth and tied in place behind his ears.

buck sergeant (Old Army to Modern) *s.* The lowest grade of sergeant, with three stripes on his sleeve. A basic element in the backbone of the Army. The older term *line sergeant* seems to have gone out of use.

buck slip buck sheet (At least as early as World War II, to Modern) An office form, usually locally procured, used to pass a problem along to someone else for action, opinion, or advice. Some staff types develop an amazing degree of artistry in the employment of buck slips, keeping their own desks clear and their hottest problems in circulation until someone else solves them or the crises pass. Here, *buck* is obviously derived from *passing the buck*, a general expression ultimately derived from poker or a related game.

Buddha belly (Modern; all Services) *s.* An obese person, particularly one with a beer gut. Widely used in the Pidgin English of Buddhist Asiatic countries.

Buddha head (World War II; among Nisei troops) *s.* An American soldier of Oriental, particularly Japanese, ancestry.

Buddhist priest (Modern; all Services) A mild interjection, a play on *Judas priest!*, which in turn is a play on *Jesus Christ!* Widely used in Vietnam to express mild surprise/dissatisfaction; equivalent to *Oh, son of a gun!*

buddy system 1. (Modern) A system whereby friends could enlist in the Army and be guaranteed training and perhaps even initial stationing together. 2. (At least World War II) A system requiring two or more persons to remain near each other for mutual protection and assistance.

BUFE buffie (Vietnam) *s.* Big Ugly Fucking Elephants. Ceramic elephants produced in vast quantities in Thailand and South Vietnam for sale as souvenirs to US personnel. They were available on the local open market or at the Army and Air Force Regional Exchanges. They were just small enough to be mailed home through the service post office systems. While buffies were often very colorful and attractive, enlisted men sometimes came to hate them, since so much time had to be spent packing them and shipping them home for various senior officers.

BUFF BUF (Modern; Air Force) *s.* Big Ugly Fat Fellow (Fucker), Big Ugly Fella. Nicknames for the B-52 Stratofortress bomber. Apparently the acronym was originally coined by Strategic Air Command pilots and used affectionately by them. But fighter pilots used the term disparagingly. "BUF stands for *big ugly fellows* in polite conversation, but is suitably amplified in true fighter conversation" (Broughton). Broughton also cites the Strategic Air Command directive that the acronym was *not* to be used by ground personnel or flight crews.

buffalo soldiers (Indian Wars) *s.* Black soldiers, especially the 9th and 10th Cavalry Regiments. The term was supposedly of Indian origin, based on the resemblance of the troopers' hair to buffalo fur.

Buff Sticks Buff Strap *s.* The 3d Infantry Regiment, which has a distinctive insignia on the left shoulder: a half-inch-wide strap of black leather through which is woven a quarter-inch strip of buff leather. The insignia supposedly dates back to the Legion of the United States in the 1790s.

bug bugs (World War II; Air Force) 1. *s.* Usually in plural form, defects in a plane, vehicle, weapon, organization, or procedure. 2. *s.* An oak-leaf cluster added to a decoration to indicate that it had been won a second time. 3. *s.* The key in radio or wire telegraphy.

bug juice 1. (Old Army; Marines) *s.* Bad hard liquor, usually whiskey, which resembled a grasshopper's digestive juices in color and quality.

O'Reilly's gone to hell,
Since down the pole he fell;
He drank up all the bug juice
The whiskey-man would sell.

2. (World War II; Air Force) *s.* Propeller deicing fluid. 3. (Modern) *s.* Insect repellant. 4. (Vietnam to Modern) *s.* Kool-Aid. From the Vietnam War, when Kool-Aid was served to the troops in vast quantities because it was easy to make and made water more palatable. Whether the troops adopted the term because the drink tasted like insect repellant or because it attracted insects is not known. "Kool-Aid, known as 'bug-juice' because it invariably attracted gnats and other insects, which died immediately upon touching it and then floated around on top" (Groom).

bugle, to (West Point) *s.* To avoid recitation in the classroom by contriving to remain standing at the blackboard until the end of the class, which was formerly announced by a bugle. From around 1900, but now obsolete.

bugle oil (Old Army and later) *s.* An imaginary substance that rookies might be sent to obtain from the supply sergeant, along with a tent wrench and six yards of skirmish line.

bug out, to bug, to (Korea) To run away, to retreat without orders, to play the coward.

"Bugout Boogie" (Korea) A popular song by Hank Snow. By other units attributed to the US 2d Infantry Division, commemorating its rout at Kunuri in November 1950. Officially proscribed, but still sung, it has the catchy refrain "We're buggin' out, We're movin' on!" but its theme is sad. Also known as "Moving On."

bull 1. (From about 1910 to 1940) *s.* Bull Durham tobacco. The little bag it came in fitted your shirt pocket neatly and the package was within the enlisted man's purchasing power. (Golden Grain and Duke's Mixture were just as popular, but somehow they are not remembered.) To watch an old-timer roll a Bull Durham cigarette with one hand, in a high wind, was truly to gaze upon a work of art. *Bull* could also mean tobacco in general. See *tailormades*. 2. The bull's-eye of a target.

bull colonel *s.* A colonel, as opposed to a lieutenant colonel.

bullet launcher (Modern) *s.* The individual infantryman's rifle or any other individual firearm, including handguns.

bullet squirter (Indian Wars) *s.* A Gatling gun.

bull pen (Revolutionary to Modern) *s.* The guardhouse or stockade.

bull ring (Early 19th century into World War II) *s.* An enclosed area—actually a small outdoor riding hall—where horses and riders were exercised and trained. Also, by extension, in World War I, the forward areas where divisions received their final training before going into the line. In World War II the term was applied to separate training areas for new recruits and draftees before they were assigned to their units.

Bull (Bull's) Run, Third Battle of (World War II; Army and possibly Navy, but only in whispers after the third drink) The northern end of the naval battle of Leyte Gulf (1944), when Adm. "Bull" Halsey insisted on chasing a Japanese decoy force and almost wrecked the US invasion of the Philippines. Fortunately, the senior Japanese admiral present was equally stupid.

bully soup (Civil War; USA) *s.* A hot soup much served in Army hospitals. It was made from corn meal, mashed hardtack, ginger, and wine cooked together, with some water added. Eliza Harris, a Sanitary Commission worker, is credited with having invented it in a desperate effort to produce from available supplies something that could be fed to seriously wounded soldiers. Another version of the recipe, credited to Clara Barton, added brown sugar and whiskey. Its official name was *panda*, sometimes *ginger panda*.

bumf (World War II to Modern; all Services) *s.* Unnecessary paperwork. Used mostly by officers and not as often as it deserves to be. From the British *bumfodder*, a slang term for toilet paper.

Bumfuck, Egypt (Modern) *s.* Synonymous with Timbuktu, except that *Bumfuck* is a much more expressive name for an incredibly remote (here imaginary) place, the ultimate in hardship tours. A similar station in World War II was *West Fungoolistan, fungoo* being one of the variants of *fuck you*.

bummer (Civil War, specifically among the troops under the command of Gen. W. T. Sherman in 1864–65) *s.* Irregular foragers who, taking advantage of Sherman's limp discipline, left their units and lived off the countryside along his army's line of march.

bunch quitter (Old, Old Army to 1940s) An independent-minded horse who is always looking for opportunities to go over the hill. It cannot be trusted to graze peacefully with the other horses of its unit. Even when hobbled, it can disappear while the herder is lighting a cigarette.

bunk (Old Army) A soldier's bed, whatever form it might take. A man's bunk was his home and his castle; no one sat on it without his permission and his seniors touched it only in line of duty, as during inspections.

bunk boy (Pre–World War II) *s.* A Filipino hired as a dog robber by an American enlisted man. For literally pennies he would shine shoes, make beds, take care of the laundry, police up the area, and—if the NCOs and officers were lenient—even take over KP details. In China, the Forgotten Fifteenth had a similar system.

bunk fatigue *s.* Sleep. One *took some bunk fatigue, did some bunk fatigue*, or *performed some bunk fatigue.* Also (World War I) *bunk police* (Nason, 1928).

bunk flying (World War II; Air Force) *s.* Off-duty discussions of flying techniques or experiences by men in their sleeping quarters. Sometimes a man was much better at that than at the real thing. Hence, a *bunk flyer* was a fly-boy long on talk, but short on delivery. See *prop wash.*

bunkie (Old, Old Army) *s.* A close comrade and friend. Well into the late 19th century soldiers slept two to a bunk.

bureau (Civil War; USA) *s.* A knapsack (pack). "Each man had a large, well-filled knapsack, of the kind new recruits usually carried on coming first to the front, and which the older soldiers spoke of humorously as bureaus" (Buell). Veterans tended to discard such bureaus, carrying what few items they needed in their knapsacks and horseshoe or horse-collar blanket rolls.

burn, to (Modern; all Services) 1. *s.* To kill. Assimilated black argot, perhaps, but the term has been used by the underworld since at least the 1920s. 2. *s.* To make a copy of a document. This term originated when Thermafax-type reproduction equipment became standard in government offices. These machines used heat during the copying process, and even though modern reproduction machines use different processes, the word *burn* is still used. Our sergeant major likes to tell the story (perhaps apocryphal) of the young soldier who was told to burn a lengthy and important document and took his sergeant's instructions literally.

burn bag (Modern; all Services) A paper bag specially designated and often specially marked (bright red stripes, etc.) to hold classified waste destined for pulping and burning.

Burn before reading! (World War II to Modern) A catchphrase, as in "Shoot bearer; burn before reading," parodying official security classifications like *secret* and *top secret.* It may also be used semi-seriously, to indicate that a subject or assignment really is highly classified, without being needlessly specific as to its nature. There are many variants and similar expressions, the most drastic we remember being *Commit suicide before reading!*

burner (Air Force) Short for *afterburner*, an auxiliary burner attached to the tail pipe of a jet for injecting fuel into the hot exhaust gases and burning it to provide extra thrust. "I went 'burner' and held minimum 'burner' throughout initial engagement" (AAV, 40).

burp (Modern) *s.* The Army infantryman's name for a US Marine.

burp gun (World War II) *s.* The German Schmeisser 9mm MP38 submachine gun. One British officer described it as having a "peculiar emetic sound," but its bite was worse than its burp.

burrhead (Modern) *s.* A recruit, from the short haircut traditionally given to newly enlisted soldiers. Perhaps connected with *burrhead*, a derogatory term for a black male, since the Army haircut resembled the short haircuts once popular among blacks.

bus (World War I, World War II; Air Force) *s.* An airplane.

buscar, to (Probably older than Mexican Punitive Expedition to World War I) *s.* To steal, to make a moonlight requisition. While in Castilian Spanish *busca* means a search, in Mexican Spanish it can mean a theft (particularly of government or public property), a shady deal, or getting a little something on the side.

bust (Old Army to Modern) *s.* A reduction in grade. Like *break*, which applies, however, more to officers. "Corporal Halfbright got a bust back to private." The age of the term *bust* is unclear. Wentworth and Flexner speak of it as in common use after World War I. Partridge (1970) mentions it as a late-19th-century British term. Mencken (1948) considers this meaning of the word to go at least as far back as the Civil War, but no early quotations survive.

bust, to (Old Army to Modern) *s.* To reduce in grade. "They busted Corporal Halfbright to private." A soldier can be busted to only one grade, that of private. If it is wanted, for example, to reduce a sergeant to the rank of corporal, he must first be busted to private and then appointed corporal.

butcher *s.* A form of genial insult, applied to the company barber and sometimes to medics. In the pre–World War II Army the chief surgeon of a hospital might be called *Butch*. The post carpenter was a *wood butcher*.

butcher charts (Modern) *s.* Instructional charts prepared on large sheets of flimsy white paper, usually mounted on a stand with the long axis vertical. The paper resembles that used by butchers to wrap meat. Butcher charts are generally used for informal desk-side briefings.

butcher's bill (Civil War; USA) *s.* A casualty list. *To present the butcher's bill* was to read off a list of casualties or to hold a roll call immediately after combat. This phrase may have been used before the Civil War. After that, it passed into common use, especially among journalists.

butt 1. (Post–Civil War through Old Army; now obsolete) *s.* That portion of an enlistment still to be observed. A conversation: "I've got a year and a butt to do." "How much butt?" "Eleven months and twenty-nine days." Dr. Lighter has traced this meaning to an 1888 source referring to the Civil War. From an old English term for anything left over; now obsolete or technical in civilian life, but it has survived longer in the military. 2. (At least as early as 1910; West Point) *s.* Something left over. "There are 161 and a butt days until Christmas leave" (i.e., 162 days). 3. Ancient to Modern; all Services) The handle end of certain weapons, or the end toward the user: a rifle butt, a revolver butt, a spear butt, etc. 4. *s.* A cigarette, even an unsmoked one.

butt can (At least as early as World War II, to Modern) *s.* A tin can, usually an empty food container, placed as a receptacle for cigarette butts or ends. It is usually partially filled with sand or water.

butterbar (Modern; also Marines) *s.* A second lieutenant, whose bar insignia of grade is gold. From the commercial candy, Butterbar. The connotation is of something soft and sweet, from the tradition that most second lieutenants are sweetly innocent of their military duties.

butterfly 1. (Colonial to early 19th century) *s.* A light fieldpiece, usually a one- to three-pounder, mounted on the standard type of carriage and towed behind a limber. This is in contrast to the galloper or grasshopper models, which had no limbers. 2. (Vietnam) *s.* A light-observation, fixed-wing spotter airplane. See *bird dog*.

butterfly, to (Korea to Vietnam; all Services) *s.* To bestow sexual favors indiscriminately, as a butterfly flits from flower to flower. A favorite expression among Korean and Vietnamese bargirls was "You butterfly me, GI!" a harsh and usually justified accusation of infidelity.

butterfly bomb (World War II) *s.* A German aerial antipersonnel bomb. Its casing opened to form two "wings" as it fell, slowing its descent so that it would explode in the air.

butternut (Civil War; USA) *s.* A Confederate soldier, especially during the last years of the war. As the South ran out of imported cloth and dyestuffs, it replaced its regulation gray uniform with clothing dyed various shades of brown with butternut or walnut shells, or with copperas solution.

button board (Old Army into World War II) A now forgotten contraption consisting of two pivoted arms, cut away on the inner edges, designed to fit around the row of brass buttons on the front of a soldier's blouse and thus protect the fabric while the buttons were being polished. Usually it was made of brass, but some early examples were made of wood.

button chopper (At least Old Army to Modern) *s.* A laundry.

button up, to (World War II to Modern) Used by armored troops to indicate that all hatches were closed, specifically, that of the tank commander, who usually rode with his head protruding for better visibility. Buttoning up was essential under heavy artillery, mortar, or sniper fire.

butts (All Services) Always used in the plural. In the strictest sense, an embankment built across the far end of a rifle range to stop the bullets and protect the sand rats. In common usage, the whole target end of the range, including the pits. Men assigned to work the targets may be called the *butts detail*.

buy, to (Modern; all Services) *s.* To agree with, to approve of, to concur, to accept an action from a staff office.

buy a farm, to (Approximately World War II; Air Force) *s.* To crash, with or without fatal results. It was felt that the owner of the property where the crash took place usually demanded as much as the whole property was worth as compensation for alleged damages, regardless of the actual amount of harm done.

buy the farm, to (Date of origin uncertain; all Services) *s.* Usually used in the past tense. To be killed, to die. "Well, Murphy bought the farm."

buy it, to (Modern; all Services) *s.* To be killed.

buy out, to (Old Army) *s.* Officially known as "purchase of discharge," a policy whereby a soldier could, after one year of service, buy his way out of the Army for a stipulated sum. The amount decreased with the total years of service, up to eleven. The amount varied also according to the geographical department to which the soldier was assigned. It cost more for a soldier stationed overseas, because part of the purchase price went to defray transportation expenses. The maximum price was $170 for a soldier with one year's service stationed in the Philippine Islands, to $30 for a soldier with eleven years' service stationed in the United States. This practice was in effect in the Army from 16 June 1890 (pursuant to an act of Congress approved that date) to 7 April 1952. It was suspended during World War II.

buzz (Modern) *s.* A type of haircut in which the hair is closely cropped. Once required of all new recruits. See also *burrhead, skinhead, GI* haircut.

buzzard (Mid-19th century on) *s.* A discharge from the service and/or the Army Discharge certificate issued on that occasion. The name refers to the national eagle insignia at the top of the discharge. The term was in common use by 1850 and may survive today.

buzzards (Antiquity uncertain) *s.* A "full" colonel's silver eagle insignia of grade.

Buzzicot (Old Army; also Marines) An early field range, a collapsible sheet-iron affair that would burn anything combustible. It would also work in a heavy rain and generally was a lot better than cooking over open campfires, as the Army had done from colonial times through the Spanish-American War.

Bypass, haul ass, and send for the Infantry! (World War II) The infantryman's version of the armored divisions' standard tactic of bypassing stubborn centers of resistance, leaving them to be mopped up by the infantry divisions following.

by the numbers 1. (Ancient to Modern) A deliberate type of drill in which each movement is executed in accordance with a series of numbered steps. For example, "By the numbers! Right shoulder—arms! One! Two! Three! Four!" This system trains recruits to perform actions accurately, smoothly, and in unison, not only for the aesthetic effect but also to keep some careless clown from poking the muzzle of his piece into the next man's eye. 2. (World War II) *s.* To do things in a rigorously disciplined way, with no room for individuality. Drill sergeant: "By the time I get through with you rookies, you'll shit by the numbers!" 3. (World War II) *s.* As in *fucked up by the numbers,* really fucked up.

☆☆☆☆C☆☆☆☆

CA, to (Modern) *s.* To be transported via helicopter on a combat assault mission. "Brigade sent them some slicks and they were CA'd in" (Glasser).

cab (World War II; Air Force) *s.* The cockpit of an airplane, by analogy with the cab of a truck or locomotive.

Cab rank (World War I; Royal Flying Corps) A term for flight line. Occasionally used in archaic manuscripts written by US Army Air Service veterans who had been on detached service with the RFC.

cabron (Mexican Border Service) In Castilian Spanish, it means a billy goat or a cuckold. In the Mexican Spanish that Americans picked up, it is a stronger, more potent insult, implying that the person so addressed is not a sufficient man and that his wife must seek consolation elsewhere.

caca dow (Modern) *s.* A Vietnamese slang expression, the precise meaning of which our sergeant major has never been able to discover. Some think it might represent *cạc cai đao* 'kill the duck', and others, 'knock your block off'. The general meaning of the expression, always delivered facetiously, is a threat of violence to someone. 'I caca dow you, GI!" was an expression commonly heard in Saigon bars, usually accompanied by the universal sign for murder, a forefinger across the speaker's throat. Slang expressions meaning to kill various sorts of animals, but applied figuratively to humans, occur in many languages. The Vietnamese *gà chềt* ('The chicken is dead') and German *die Katze ist verreckt* ('The cat is dead') are only two to which American soldiers have been exposed over the years, and in English there are always *a dead duck* and *a gone goose*. The variant form *cec ce dao* is still pronounced *caca dow*.

cadence (Antiquity uncertain, to Modern) 1. The uniform rhythm in which a drill movement is executed. 2. The number of steps per minute that a soldier marches or a movement is executed. Synonymous in this sense with time. 3. A command to the soldiers to count "one, two, three, four" in unison with their marching step, as in *Count cadence, count!* Used primarily with recruits.

cadet (Ancient to Modern) A young man or woman attending the US Military

Academy at West Point, New York, usually for the purpose of obtaining a commission in the Army. Cadets rank just below warrant officers and just above enlisted personnel in pay grade E-9. They are addressed as *Miss* or *Mister*. Cadets undergo a four-year period of instruction, from fourth class (equivalent to freshmen) to first class (equivalent to seniors). Their life is rich in service customs and lore, much of which is focused upon members of the fourth class, who are most commonly known as *plebes*. The Corps of Cadets is organized as a brigade, with ranks identified by a system of chevrons that has been in effect since 1817. Persons attending the US Air Force Academy at Colorado Springs and senior ROTC advanced courses are also called *cadets*, but men and women attending the US Naval Academy at Annapolis are called *midshipmen*.

cadre (World War I to Modern) A detachment of officers and enlisted men assigned to organize and train a new organization, of which they form the nucleus. Also, the permanent staff in training installations, as in basic. From French *cadre* 'framework', 'skeleton'.

cagg keg (Revolutionary) *s.* An informal oath to refrain from drinking (or at least from getting drunk) for a certain period. It was usually observed rigorously. Used by British enlisted men, it was apparently carried into the American service by deserters.

caisson (Early 19th century to World War War II) A vehicle for transporting artillery ammunition in the field. A company of artillery normally had one caisson for each gun. During the 18th century, the British and Americans commonly termed such a vehicle an *ammunition cart*. After the Revolutionary War, Americans adopted the cumbersome French four-wheeled caisson, but this gave way to a more mobile two-wheeled type during the modernization of the artillery before the Mexican War. When the artillery was motorized during the early 1940s, the caissons vanished with the horses that had pulled them, except for a special model of caisson used in armored field artillery units. At West Point, in 1951, we had to explain to cadets just what caissons were.

"Caisson Song, The" (Old, Old Army to Modern) The Field Artillery's own march, which was composed in the Philippine Islands around 1907 or 1908 by Lt. Edmund L. Gruber. It was not published commercially until 1918, when John Philip Sousa, who apparently wrote the piano music and the orchestral score, brought it out as the "U.S. Field Artillery March." It is a fine rousing tune, perfect for mounted units. Unfortunately, in a moment of inexplicable mental poverty, the Army appropriated the music for its own official song, which is notable chiefly for the kindergarten quality of its words. "The Caisson Song" is also known as "Over Hill, Over Dale" and "The Field Artillery Song."

Calamity Jane (World War I to Vietnam) Originally, the gun that fired the last artillery round of World War I. The name was later applied to a 155mm howitzer that was part of the defenses at Pearl Harbor. This gun was used to fire the first and last 155mm rounds of the Korean War, went to Vietnam in 1966 as part of the 2d Battalion, 11th Artillery, 101st Airborne Division, and fired the battalion's one-millionth round there (ANJ, 13 September 1971).

calibogus (Colonial) A potent early American drink—spruce beer spiked with rum—which protected both the soldier's health and his morale. The term is spelled in various ways.

Calley Hall (Modern; Army) *s.* The Infantry Officer Candidate School, Fort Benning, Georgia. First Lt. William Calley, convicted of participating in the massacre at My Lai, Republic of Vietnam, in March 1968, was a graduate of Infantry OCS at Fort Benning. Also known as *the Benning School for Boys.*

calls (Civil War to Modern) Bugle calls used as signals. At the time of the Civil War, bugles gradually replaced drums, and a large number of bugle calls were developed both to control troops in combat and to regulate the daily life of a military post. During World War I the use of bugle calls in combat became impractical. Since then, their use in peacetime also has declined. (On some occasions, live buglers have been replaced by a recording, which is usually poorly done and scratchy.) Certain calls—especially *retreat, to the colors, reveille*, and *taps*—remain well known. More respectful of its traditions, the Navy still uses the boatswain's pipe for its shipboard calls.

Calvary (Antiquity uncertain, but surviving at least into World War II) *s.* The arm in which many old-time cavalrymen served. It does seem easier to say than *Cavalry.*

Cambo (Modern) *s.* Short for *Cambodia.*

camel gun (Late 19th century) *s.* A short-barreled Gatling gun, Model 1874, designed to be light enough to keep up with the cavalry.

camion (World War I) Originally a horse-drawn dray, but during World War I a truck.

camp (Ancient to Modern) A temporary station. See *post.*

campaign hat (Early 20th century to Modern) A hat with a wide brim and a high crown, made of fur-felt material, OD in color, and with a Montant peak. It is officially known as *hat, service*, to distinguish it from *cap, service.* It was used around the turn of the century, discontinued, and then reissued in 1964 for use by Army drill sergeants. Also called *cowboy hat, Smokey the Bear hat.*

camp canard (Civil War; USA) Something uncomplimentary, widely believed, but untrue. For example, the many stories told in the Army of the Potomac in 1862, claiming to prove that Gen. Irvin McDowell (a devoted, if sometimes obtuse officer) was a traitor.

camp colors (Colonial to early Civil War) Little flags, approximately 18 inches square, used to mark the campsite of a regiment. Normally they were the color of the regiment's facings and were marked with its name and/or number.

camp follower (Ancient to Modern) Anyone who would "pack up her placket [petticoat] and follow the drum"; the nonmilitary part of an army. Originally the term meant the wives, legal or temporary, of the enlisted men and their offspring, as well as the gaggle of sutlers, bootleggers, prostitutes, gamblers, entertainers, and related harpies that followed an army and preyed on it and the countryside. "The rogues and whores that went with the baggage." Today, practically all the wives and children are legal; they follow the soldiers' outfit from station to station in peacetime only. In war, we have the Red Cross, the YMCA, TV and newspaper representatives, and sundry such.

can (Modern) *s.* The latrine. See *crapper, necessaries, Old Soldiers' Home.*

Canaan Happy Land of Canaan (Civil War; USA) The Promised Land, or at least the hereafter. "The Happy Land of Canaan" was a popular hymn at the beginning of the Civil War. Union soldiers used it as a marching song, with inevitable alterations to its lyrics. The Yankee artillerymen had their own version, which stressed "sending Rebels to the Happy Land of Canaan!"

C & E Clothing and Equipment.

can do can-do attitude (Modern) *s.* The attitude that no mission or responsibility is so great that it cannot be attempted. When given a mission that seems impossible, the soldier is expected to approach it with a can-do attitude.

Can-Do Boys The US 15th Infantry Regiment, from its motto, "Can Do." This unit, also known as the *Forgotten Fifteenth,* was long stationed in China, and its motto is in Pidgin English.

Can do, Madame Nhu No can do, Madame Nhu (Vietnam) Rhyming catchphrases from the early stages of the Vietnam War meaning that something is, or is not, possible. Madame Nhu, the wife of Ngo Dinh Nhu (brother of Ngo Dinh Diem, President of South Vietnam), was a flamboyant and powerful figure in the Saigon government before Diem's overthrow in November 1963. She was a female activist, and her efforts to impose high moral standards on Saigon bargirls were openly derided by most Americans and many Vietnamese. See also *Dragon Lady, never hachi, Never happen, said the cap'n.*

canned cow (Old, Old Army to Modern) *s.* Canned condensed milk. It had a robust flavor all its own, sufficient to blunt the edge of Army coffee. It also made an excellent substitute for glue. After about 1940, this term was generally replaced by *armored cow.*

cannon cocker (World War II to Modern) *s.* An artilleryman. Also called *ammo humper, jo humper.*

cannoneer's hop *s.* The old "standing gun drill," during which members of a gun crew rotate through their various duties. Hard work, but practical.

cannon fever (Civil War; USA) *s.* A violent, numbing aversion to the sounds and sights of combat; it could be cured only by transfer to a safe rear-area assignment. Chaplains reputedly were especially susceptible to it. Similar to the *gangplank fever* of World War II.

canopy 1. The cloth surface of a parachute. Also called a *shroud.* 2. (Vietnam) Overhead foliage, especially that found in thick jungle.

cans (World War II) *s.* A radio operator's headphones.

canteen 1. As in civilian life, a durable, sturdy flask. Although it is intended to hold water, it has been known to contain other liquids. 2. (Colonial to Revolutionary) A small chest made of wood or leather, in which an officer's eating utensils, liquor, and food were stored. In Grose's *Advice,* an officer's servant is reminded that "When he is on guard, you may invite company to his marquis, and it is hard if you cannot get a key that will open his canteens." 3. (Colonial to early 20th century, but with some change of meaning) At first, a sutler's establishment that sold food and drink to officers and men. Such canteens evolved into establishments operated by Army posts, and eventually became the modern PX. 4. (World War I, World War II, and later) Snack bars operated by social-service organizations where servicemen and women could get coffee, doughnuts, sandwiches, or their equivalents. Since World War II, such bars have been operated by the USO.

canteen checks (Old, Old Army to World War II) Small books of detachable coupons, good for purchases at the PX. They were issued to enlisted men on credit on jawbone paydays several times a month and were paid for on monthly payday. See *company collection sheet.*

canteen commandos (World War II; British-American) *s.* Rear-area troops given to posing as rough, tough fighting men. Apparently identical with Bill Mauldin's *garritroopers* and the *rear-guard rangers.*

cantina (Mexican War on; probably still used) A saloon.

capon colonel (World War II) *s.* A noncombatant colonel, usually commissioned directly from civilian life for some specialized service, such as the Venus fixers. A play on *chicken colonel.*

captain (Ancient to Modern) A company-grade officer ranking below a major and above a first lieutenant. His insignia of rank is two silver bars. Captains usually command companies, batteries, troops, and units of similar size. Abbreviations are *Cpt.* and *Capt.*

captain lieutenant (Colonial and Revolutionary) 1. A grade found in the British and American services; an officer with the job and authority of a captain but with only the pay of a lieutenant. The grade was commonly held by those officers actually commanding the field officers' companies. The said field officers drew the captains' pay in addition to their own. 2. In the British Army, and presumably the colonial forces, too, meat between veal and beef; that of a very old calf.

Carabaos (Philippine Insurrection and later) A fraternal organization of officers who served during the Philippine Insurrection; properly, *the Military Order of the Carabao.* The carabao, of course, is the water buffalo of the Philippines and other places in the Orient, a powerful, slow, ungainly animal, with a distinct dislike for the scent of a white man. More than one husky American has been rescued from an angry carabao by a bare-tailed Filipino child, not much higher than his knee, who quickly slapped and screeched the beast into submission. On one occasion, an infantry regiment was routed when it stirred up a carabao herd after dark.

career manglement (Modern) *s.* A wordplay on *career management,* which personnel officers proudly believe they can effect.

career reservist (World War II into at least the 1960s) A Reserve officer on extended active duty who liked the Army and would serve as long as permitted. We can personally testify that they were a hardworking lot. They had to be.

care package (Modern; all Services) *s.* A package of goodies such as candy or canned goods received from home or friends. The name is taken from the CARE organization.

carpenters (Colonial to Revolutionary) In the American, British, and French services, men capable of felling trees and performing rough construction and repair work on bridges, roads, fortifications, and the like. Usually each regiment detailed one soldier per company for such service. For North American campaigns, whole companies might be recruited, or large numbers of civilians hired. During the late 18th century, Americans and British tended to term such troops *pioneers*, while the French called them *sapeurs*.

carpet, on the (Old Army to Modern; probably still in use) *s.* A summons to the commanding officer's inner sanctum for a one-sided discussion of your alleged sins of omission, commission, and just mission. Or similar takedown by a superior. While the expression may be of civilian origin (Partridge [1970] records it from the early 19th-century treatment of British servants), it fitted military circumstances well, for in the old days the commanding officer's sanctum was usually the only room with a carpet on the floor.

carrier pigeon (World War II) *s.* A messenger. They were also, as in World War I, called *runners*.

case case shot (Civil War) A bafflingly inexact term that may mean either canister or shrapnel, depending on who used the term. The correct meaning would seem to be an early form of shrapnel—spherical case shot for smoothbore guns, case shot for rifled guns.

cashier, to casheer, to (Colonial to Revolutionary) To discharge an officer dishonorably from the service. In 1777, Gen. Philip Schuyler remarked that some of his Continental officers "have so little sense of honor that cashiering seems no punishment" to them. It was occasionally applied in a similar sense to the discharge of an enlisted man.

cat's eyes (World War II to Modern) *s.* Tiny, semicrescent-shaped dim blue lights placed above the regular head and taillights of a vehicle, used in night driving. If you could see them, you were awfully close; if you suddenly lost sight of them, you were in trouble.

cat's whisker (World War II and later; probably all Services) *s.* The long, thin fine-tuning indicator in radios and similar equipment.

cattle country *s.* Troop compartments aboard troop ships, so called because they were overcrowded.

cavalryman (Old Army) *s.* An officer who was apt to shift rapidly from boundless enthusiasm to complete inertia, such shifts reputedly being a tendency among horse soldiers. We remember from our first shavetail days hearing senior infantry and artillery officers saying things like "Jones won't do. He's too much of a cavalryman. He'll get everybody all stirred up, and then quit cold." Such expressions naturally made actual cavalrymen furious enough to chew horseshoes and spit nails, but there was not much they could do about it.

CBI (World War II) The China-Burma-India theater of operations. Probably the most confused military effort in the history of mankind, as well as the most miserable place possible to fight a war.

CC pill (World War I and somewhat later) The Medical Corps's cure-all when there were no visible open wounds or broken bones. *CC* supposedly stood for *compound cathartics*. A CC pill at least kept you so busy that you tended to forget your real troubles, and it *was* somewhat better than the calomel pill it replaced. It, in turn, gave way to the APC pill in World War II.

CD (Modern) Certificate of Destruction. The form on which classified documents are listed as having been destroyed.

CD, to To destroy classified documents.

C-day (Modern; all Services) Conversion Day. The date selected (with great secrecy) on which a series of Military Payment Certificates is to be changed.

Cees Cs (Modern; all Services) Combat rations. First developed in 1940. They consisted of six cans of food, two for each meal. The meals contained three meat units, three carbohydrate units, and powdered drink units. "At lunch they'd sit alone together . . . while the greenhorns gobbled their Cs" (Smith). Also *C-rats, C-rations, Charlie's rats.*

Cement City *s.* A cemetery.

century man (West Point) *s.* A cadet who has walked a hundred or more punishment tours in the area. See *area bird, area sergeant.*

C'est la guerre (World War I) A borrowing from the French, mistranslated to mean 'In case you don't know it, there's a war on'. US civilians, especially sales clerks and their ilk, used the American version freely during World War II. Rough equivalents are *That's the way the ball bounces* and *That's the way the cookie crumbles.* See *Semper fi* in the Appendix.

CG Commanding General.

chairborne (World War II to Modern) *s.* A takeoff on *airborne* applied to staff, office, and administrative personnel, especially those in the ZI. Even when a GI admitted the need for their existence, he never considered them better than a necessary evil. (The British used the term *Whitehall Warriors* for the same groups.) Also, by extension, an armchair strategist. See *ball-bearing WAC, flatpeters, RAMF, Remington Raiders, REMF, titless WAC.*

chairborne commandos (World War II to Modern) *s.* Generally, office personnel: clerk typists, file clerks, etc.

chamber a round (Modern; also Marines) To work the slide of an automatic or semiautomatic weapon to feed a bullet from the clip into the firing chamber. To prepare a weapon for immediate fire; hence, to mean business.

Chancre Jack (World War II and later) *s.* Chiang Kai-shek, the Chinese Nationalist generalissimo. Although in civilian life the word *chancre,* meaning an ulcer from venereal disease, is technical and perhaps not generally known, it was very familiar to troops from Mickey Mouse films, and the allusion would have been obvious.

chancre mechanic (Also Navy) An enlisted man of the Medical Corps assigned to dispensary duty; also *pecker checker* or *penis machinist.* These are peacetime (or at least rear-area) names. In combat the GI generally speaks of the medics serving with him in more respectful terms.

change of base (Civil War) *s.* A retreat. Gen. George B. McClellan explained his withdrawal from in front of Richmond in 1862 as merely a "change of base," according to plan. Soldiers in both armies thought this humorous. "If a dog were seen running ahead of another dog as if wishing to get away, a shout would go up, 'Look at him changing his base!' "

change [one's] base, to (Civil War) *s.* To retreat.

channels go through channels, to The normal routing, up and down, of military correspondence and communications. A letter from a corps commander to a company commander, for example, will pass through the headquarters of the division, brigade, and battalion commanders. The reply, if any, returns by the same route. This practice ensures that all concerned parties are kept fully informed and have an opportunity to express their opinions.

In essence, it expresses the Army's philosophy of efficiency—perhaps not the least effort, but the most foolproof, a concept that is sometimes criticized, but has its justification. Jumping channels seldom saves much time and usually ends with someone's not getting the essential word. Consequently, it is resented by those jumped. An officer who makes a practice of jumping channels rapidly loses the confidence of his subordinates. Similarly, an enlisted man who has a request—perhaps for a pass or furlough—does not approach his company commander directly but goes through channels via the orderly room. For the exceptional instance, see *Inspector General.*

Chaos Boys (Occupation of Germany) Agents of the US Treasury Department or like-minded members of the US Army Military Government in Germany in the first years of the military occupation of that nation. Inspired by Secretary of the Treasury Henry Morgenthau's determination to visit Old Testament vengeance upon Germany, they were distinctly unhelpful.

char cha (World War II) Anglo-Indian for the beverage tea. Reputedly used more by Tommies than by their officers. Adopted occasionally by American troops. Since *cha* is almost a Pan-Asiatic word, American soldiers in Japan took over the Japanese equivalent, *o-cha.*

character guidance (Modern) A once mandatory training program administered by Army chaplains to the troops on a monthly basis. The program was established in August 1948 and affirmed under an executive order of 27 October 1948 to be "the policy of the Government to encourage and promote religious, moral and recreational welfare and character in the Armed Forces." These generally nonsectarian morality lectures were received by the troops with universal cynicism. During the years of the draft, many soldiers who attended these sessions were better grounded in ethics and philosophy than the chaplains who conducted them. Our sergeant major remembers some chaplains becoming outraged when confronted by uninterested, inattentive, and uncooperative audiences. Post records,

Oh, what a monstrous hypocrisy
To say we keep the world safe for
democracy
When all we do is sit
And listen to this shit
From a member of the theocracy.

chargee chargie cha-gee (Korea and later; all Services, but principally Army) *s.* Korean pidgin for the penis. See *hotchee, suckahachi.*

Charlie Charley Mister Charles Sir Charles (Vietnam) *s.* A Vietcong or North Vietnamese soldier—actually largely the same person, especially after the abortive Tet offensive of 1968, in which the North Vietnamese command managed to get most of its Vietcong veterans killed off wholesale. They were stout fighters, but not as vicious as their American admirers. The name *Charlie* is the designation of the letter *c* in the phonetic alphabet. See also *Bed Check Charley.*

charlie bird (Modern) *s.* The helicopter used by a tactical commander to oversee (command and control) his troops during combat operations. *Charlie* is the phonetic alphabet equivalent for the letter *c.* This helicopter is also called *charlie charlie.*

Charlie's rats See *Cees.*

charm school (Modern) *s.* Any kind of professional or orientation course or school, especially one conducted for officers.

chase a prisoner, to (At least as early as World War I to Modern) *s.* To guard a garrison prisoner, particularly one who is on a work detail. *Chasing* is the standard term for this even though it does not involve pursuit. Wentworth and Flexner seem to consider it prison slang. Partridge (1970) defines *to chase* as "to stand over and keep urging (someone) to do and get on with a piece of work," from about 1920.

Cheap Charley Cheap Charlie (Modern, since Vietnam; all Services) *s.* A miserly person, especially one who will not buy something or who tips in a very niggardly fashion. Widely used by Vietnamese bargirls. The expression may not have originated in Vietnam, but it had widespread currency there. Naturally it had other meanings. As early as 1962, the Chong Nam restaurant on Hai Ba Trung Street, Saigon, was being called Cheap Charlie's because its prices were so reasonable. But the excellent Chinese cuisine of Cheap Charlie's was a far cry from the bargirl's patois, as in "You numbah fuckin' ten Cheap Charlie, GI!"

check into the net, to (Modern) To check in, to see what is happening. To check out of the net is to leave.

cheese eater (Late 1940s) *s.* A character who plays any sort of a low trick. For example, if your buddy finds the pint hidden in your laundry bag and drinks it all, allegedly to keep you from getting into trouble over it, when you mention his name, you say that *he ate a pound of cheese*. In other words, he is a rat.

cheese knife (At least as old as the Civil War; all Services) *s.* A sword or saber. In the Marines it is specifically the sword worn by staff NCOs during formal ceremonies.

cherivallies (Revolutionary to War of 1812) A type of waist-high overall, often reinforced with leather, worn over expensive britches and boots to protect them from dust and wet. There were many styles. The fancier ones buttoned up the outside of the legs and were very showy. Used principally by staff officers and cavalrymen, although infantry officers and artillerymen might wear them in the field. Derivation probably is from *charivara*, a westernized version of the Hungarian 'esquavar', a type of leg covering worn by 18th-century hussars.

cherry (Modern) *s.* A new man in a unit, a replacement. From the slang term for the hymen or virginity.

cherry juice (Modern) *s.* Hydraulic fluid. "Tankers call hydraulic fluid 'cherry juice,' because it is red" (Reed, *Army Times*, 21 May 1979).

chevron (Early 19th century to Modern) 1. A V-shaped stripe, which since 1902 has been worn point upward. Synonymous with *stripe*. 2. An insignia of rank formed of such stripes, perhaps combined with other elements—arcs (rockers), lozenges (diamonds), eagles, letters *T*, horizontal bars, etc. Such an insignia of rank is presently worn on the upper arm. While at one time in the early 19th century company officers wore chevrons, for the past 150 years chevrons have been worn (in the active Army) only by enlisted men. Chevrons are also worn by cadets at the US Military Academy, but these do not follow the same system as those in the active Army.

chewer (Mid-19th century to Modern) *s.* A tobacco chewer. Now comparatively scarce, tobacco chewers used to be rather common in the cavalry, where smoking on night patrol in Indian country or striking a match while astride a spooky remount could be hazardous to your health. There are stories, probably true, of the ability of skilled chewers to use tobacco juice as an emergency weapon against rattlesnakes and such.

chewing-gum salute (1944–45) *s.* A peculiar style of saluting that had a fleeting popularity in back areas of the ETO. It has been described as giving the impression that the saluter was attempting to remove a wad of chewing gum from his right eyebrow.

chew out, to (World War II to Modern; all Services) *s.* To rebuke, to berate, to reprimand, to tear off a strip, give a bawling out and otherwise make your displeasure emphatically evident. Only from a superior in rank to an inferior.

chichi chi-chi chee-chee (Modern; all Services, but principally Army) *s.* A woman's breasts. From Japanese *chichi* 'breasts'. A very common word in Korean Pidgin English.

chicken 1. (At least late 19th century to Modern) *s.* Various shades of meaning centering around a new soldier: a new recruit, a new person in an outfit, a particularly young and scrawny recruit, etc. At a somewhat earlier period, particularly in naval slang, a boy or youth used as a catamite. 2. (At least World War I to Modern) *s.* Cowardly. An insulting catchphrase in World War II was "What's the color of chicken? Yellow, yellow, yellow." 3. (World War II to Modern) *s.* Apparently an abbreviation of *chicken shit.* Overly fussy, petty, demanding, spit-and-polish. "I want out of this chicken outfit."

chicken colonel *s.* A "full" colonel. See *eagle colonel.*

chicken coop with a roof (Modern) *s.* A specialist fifth class. The insignia of this rank is a spread eagle surmounted by an arc (the roof).

chicken corporal (Modern) *s.* A specialist fourth class, because of the spread eagle device of his rank. A specialist fourth class is in the same pay grade (E-4) as a corporal.

chicken food chicken feed (World War II and later; USA, British) *s.* A high-level intelligence term for rumors and faked intelligence passed out in neutral countries to mislead Axis intelligence agents or others. Usually it was tailored to confirm similar stories leaked "in confidence" by the Allied diplomatic staffs to the press and leading citizens of the neutral country. The term probably came from the American slang expression *chicken feed,* meaning *small change* or a *trivial amount of money.* But it would have taken a dumb cluck, indeed, to believe much of it.

chicken guts (Old, Old Army to Modern) *s.* The loopings of gold braid on the sleeves of officers' Full Dress and Mess Dress uniforms.

chicken house (Modern) *s.* The WAC quarters on an Army post. The term is becoming obsolete since the abolition of the WAC and the institution of coed barracks.

chickenplate (Modern; Air Force, with some Army use) *s.* The flak jacket.

chickens *s.* A colonel's eagle insignia.

chicken shit *s.* Cheap, demeaning, disagreeable in petty ways. Synonymous with *chicken* 3. Our senior officer recalls it as being in use in 1928; it became more than common during World War II, and has so continued. Also *owl shit*.

Chicom (Korea; all Services) *s.* The Chinese Communists, especially the "volunteers" serving against us in Korea. The term was used as much in headquarters as by the troops in the lines. Also *Old Joe Chink*.

chief (Modern) *s.* An informal mode of address or reference to a warrant officer of the upper three grades (CW2, CW3, CW4). Also, in the Navy, for chief petty officers.

chief of smoke (Modern) *s.* The NCO (chief of section) who is responsible for the laying and firing of a gun.

chief of staff 1. (Ancient to Modern; at present, all Services) The principal officer of a military staff. He coordinates and supervises the work of the various staff sections and may serve as an adviser to the commanding officer. 2. (Modern) *s.* Colloquially, an officer's wife. "Let me check with my chief of staff and see if she has anything planned for tomorrow night." Many officers, including our senior officer, use it habitually.

chiefs and Indians (Antiquity uncertain; very old in general use, but probably first systematized during World War II) *s.* Chiefs are people with enough authority to give orders and have even their dumber ideas given serious consideration. Indians do the work, whether they are enlisted men policing up the post, or lieutenant colonels and majors trying to put a chief's ideas into practical form. "Too many chiefs and not enough Indians" is a common complaint, especially on high-level staffs. *Heap big chief*, of course, means a real VIP and is very old usage. A *broken-feather chief* is either a downgraded big chief or an officer occupying an uncomfortable intermediate position with limited authority and extensive responsibilities to a whole tribe of irritable chiefs.

chiêu hôí /chew-hoy/ (Vietnam) *s.* To give up, to surrender. From the Chiêu Hôí program of the Vietnam War, which was intended to encourage Vietcong and North Vietnamese soldiers to surrender and join the forces of the government of South Vietnam. The term means *open arms*.

China Boy Companies (Vietnam) *s.* The Special Forces' "Mike Force," possibly called *China Boy* because these units were composed largely of ethnic Chinese recruited from among the Nungs of South Vietnam. "The China Boy Companies, as they are called" (Marshall, 1969).

China khaki A cloth used by US Marines stationed in China in the 1920s and 1930. It was used for trousers and neckties ("field scarves") of the summer cotton uniform, but not for shirts, since shirts were of lighter weight poplin. Custom-tailored to the individual and paid for by him, it was a light coffee and cream color. In spite of its total lack of uniformity with khaki, it was permissible to wear it in ranks on posts in the US. A modern I.G. would throw a fit to see a summer turnout at NOB, Norfolk, right after the transport *Autores* had dumped a group of mixed pickles from Panama, Puerto Rico, Hawaii, Olongapoo, and China wearing four different colors of leather equipment and two colors of "khaki."

Chin-chin, Ho Chi Minh (Vietnam) *s.* A very popular toast among Vietnamese bar-girls. The idea was that dear old "Uncle Ho" deserved a drink because he was not going to get anything else from the Americans and their South Vietnamese allies. This, of course, was during the optimistic years of the Vietnam War, when even the people running the US government still believed that America would never abandon a faithful ally. The expression *chin-chin* has long been a popular toast in British naval circles and club society, dating back at least as far as the middle 19th century (Hotten, 1873). It is recorded even earlier in English-language sources as a Chinese greeting. *Chin-chin* is probably Mandarin *ching-ching* (an invitation to do something), which in the Chinese of Shanghai would be rendered as *chin-chin*. The most reasonable suggestion for its adoption is that it was picked up by naval and trading circles either in Shanghai or Singapore. Ware describes it as common in Singapore in 1890 or so. The expression seems to have been used throughout the Far East, and it was popular in Saigon long before the US Army landed in force.

Chinese fire drill (All Services) 1. *s.* Any showy but pointless exercise or operation involving noise, activity, and showmanship. The term comes from the elaborate semiacrobatic displays put on by Chinese fire companies, leaving spectators dazzled but extinguishing no fires. Sometimes useful in snowing unfriendly visitors, military or civilian, Chinese fire drills are usually merely the product of a commanding officer with more imagination than intelligence and a useless wearying of everyone else involved. 2. *s.* Specifically, in OCS, an exercise that stresses "organizing time." The candidates fall out in front of their barracks and are then ordered to run inside, change into different uniforms, and fall in again, in two minutes.

Chinese landing (World War II; Air Force) *s.* Coming in on Won Wing Low.

Chinese rot (1920s and 1930s) *s.* A virulent fungus infection common in the Far East.

ching pao juice (World War II) *s.* *Mao tai*, a powerful, fiery South Chinese liquor distilled from rice. Probably from Cantonese *chung pao* 'heavy artillery', although some veterans claim it means 'air raid'. An overload of *mao tai* could be just as devastating as either.

chino khaki (20th century) Light gold-colored khaki fabric. By World War II, it had become the standard shade, replacing the light greens and browns of early years. Why it did is unclear, for one dirty look would smudge it.

chit (All Services) A voucher for money owed at the mess or elsewhere for food and liquor; sometimes loosely used for any sort of voucher or receipt, or even a note. From a Hindustani word (*ciṭṭha*) adopted by the British and later picked up by Americans, probably during World War I.

choggie chogie chuggie (Korea and later) *s.* To run, to walk, or to move. "Choggie down the street." From Korean *chøgi* (also transcribed as *jogi, chugi*), an adverb of place meaning 'over there', away from the speaker. In reduplicated form, *choggie-choggie* 'hurry up'.

choi oi (Vietnam and after) An exclamation, from the common Vietnamese interjection *chối ối* 'good heavens'!

chop 1. (Modern) Food. "Three-star war food, the same chop they sold at Abercrombie & Fitch" (Herr). Since at least the middle of the 19th century *chop* has been the word for food and eating in the lingua franca of the West Coast of Africa. It is not clear whether the modern use is connected with this. 2. (Probably Modern) Concurrence obtained when staffing a paper. Probably ultimately from Hindustani *chhap*, an identification seal, through British English, where *chop* has several related meanings. Concurrences are usually obtained by initial or signature of various staff officers to whom papers have been submitted for approval.

chop-chop (Spanish-American War through World War II; all Services) *s.* Pidgin English for *hurry up*, from Cantonese *kap kap*. Once commonly used by American soldiers in the Far East, but since World War II, Korean or Japanese terms seem to have crowded it out.

chop-chop, to (Vietnam and later) *s.* 1 To eat. The origin of the term is unknown. Various explanations have been offered: imitation of the noise of chop sticks in a bowl; an assumption that the *chop* of chop sticks meant food; a borrowing from British soldiers once stationed in West Africa, plus reduplication. "Let's chop-chop." 2. To perform fellatio. "You chop-chop, suck my cock" (Smith).

chopper (Modern) A helicopter.

chow (Antiquity uncertain, but around 1900 for civilian use, to Modern) Food. Probably from Chinese *chao* or *jao* 'to cook', 'to fry', brought to California by Chinese emigrants, many of whom became cooks or restaurateurs in the "days of '49." Although the term is recognized by civilians, it is much more important in the Army, where it is a standard word. It is found in various combinations: *chow hall* (mess hall); *chow line* (line waiting outside the mess hall for food); *chow time* (eating time); *to chow up* (to eat, to eat a lot); *to chow down* (to eat), etc.

chow hound (Antiquity uncertain, but at least as early as Old Army, to Modern) *s.* A soldier with an oversized appetite. He is always the first man in the mess line and the first man back wanting seconds. He is usually mildly resented and may be the subject of continual ribbing, but he also may be a first-class soldier.

chrome-dome (World War II and later) *s.* A bald-headed man.

chunker (Modern; also Marines) *s.* The M79 grenade launcher. Also called *blooker, '79, thump gun*. "Lynch and Henderson, get your chunkers firing!" (Smith).

chute patrol (Army) A semiofficial patrol provided by parachute outfits to make life easier for the MPs. The idea is to grab your own drunks before the MPs do. Sometimes this ends up with everyone in jail.

CIB (World War II to Modern) Combat Infantryman Badge. A badge awarded to soldiers who perform duty while assigned or attached to an infantry unit when the unit was engaged in active ground combat. It is not awarded to general officers or to personnel of headquarters companies of units larger than brigade. Only one award of the badge is authorized for each war in which an individual is eligible, and subsequent awards are indicated by stars. The badge was first approved for wear in 1943. "Our CIBs shining blue and silver" (Heinemann). "The great prize of honor: the Combat Infantryman's [*sic*] Badge" (Groom).

CID /*pronounced as initials or as* sid/ (World War I to Modern) The Criminal Investigation Command. A rather curious example of an institution that has never existed as such. "The Army has no Criminal Investigation Division and never has had one," said Maj. Gen. William H. Maglin, Provost Marshal General (AID 10:3, 1955). This is true, but when criminal investigation was under the jurisdiction of the Army Provost Marshal's Office, there were criminal investigation *detachments* throughout the Army; this may account for the letter *D*, although the very famous CID of New Scotland Yard may also have contributed to the legend. During World War I the AEF had a Division of Criminal Investigation (DCI) in France, and Lighter (letter to Cragg, 19 July 1980) has traced the initials CID to a 1919 source. In World War II the Provost Marshal General had a staff division for criminal investigation, but it exercised no control over active investigation. Today, the US Army Criminal Investigation Command (USACIDC) retains the "silent" useless letter *D*, perhaps out of respect for the past or perhaps to distinguish itself from the Counter Intelligence Corps (CIC).

cigarette roll (World War II to Modern) A peculiar parachute malfunction in which an odd twist in the canopy rolls it up progressively, until suddenly you are no longer in the shade. Although nearly everyone claims to have had one, it is a fact that in fourteen years of parachute duty one of our authors never beheld one and avows it is a total myth. This assertion is always good to start a fight in a bar frequented by parachutists.

cinch, to (World War II and perhaps earlier) *s.* To finish up something selfishly, to take the last portion of food out of a serving dish at your table in the mess hall. The term may have come from the card game cinch, one of the forerunners of bridge, where cinching meant cutting off another player's chances of making points. At some posts (like Fort Custer, Michigan) the definition was a little different. There, the second-last man to take food from the serving bowl would be considered as having cinched the food and would have to refill the dish. This definition prevented arguments with sneaky soldiers who would leave a very small quantity of food in the dish, then claim that they had not cinched it.

circular file (World War II to Modern) *s.* A wastebasket, often the most useful article in an office. See *File 13*.

circus 1. (World War I) A name given to several German air units, the most famous being the one commanded by Baron von Richthofen (and later by one Hermann Göring). The term was probably applied because of the gaudy colors of the planes and because of the fact that the organization (like a conventional American circus) had its own train, enabling it to shift its base personnel rapidly from one sector of the battlefront to another. Flying, in those days, was also still something of a novelty and associated with circuses. 2. (World War II; Air Force) A powerful air force sent out to draw enemy fighters into action. It consisted largely of fighters but included some bombers to stir up enemy fighters.

cit cits 1. (West Point and probably elsewhere) *s.* Around 1900, a term for a civilian. 2. (West Point, Army) *s.* By 1900, in the plural, as *cits*, civilian clothing. Probably older than *civvies*, this term was very popular in the Army before World War II. However, it has vanished, leaving very few traces.

citizen-soldier (Modern) 1. *s.* A National Guardsman or an Army Reservist, "a citizen in uniform." 2. *s.* A draftee. Used derogatorily.

civil serpent (Modern) *s.* A play on *civil servant*.

civvies civies (20th century; all Services) 1. *s.* Civilian clothing. Recorded in Great Britain from the 1890s and probably picked up by soldiers of the AEF in World War I. Mencken notes that the term was in use in World War I, but was an enlisted man's word, officers preferring *cits.* The first printed reference occurs in an anonymous satirical poem, "A Ballad of Danny Deever (With Apologies to RK)," published in the 24 June 1920 issue of the *Army and Navy Journal*:

> Their rank, rispect an' spirit they
> are takin' it away;
> O! They're gettin' into "civies" for
> to earn a decent pay.
> An' the officers are a-quittin' in
> the Army.

The word is placed in quotes and its meaning is explained in a footnote, indicating that it was not then in wide use in the Army. It should be noted that during World Wars I and II, American military personnel were not permitted to wear civilian clothing, whether on or off post. 2. *s.* Civilians in general. Partridge (1970) notes that this meaning was in use in the British Army as early as 1895. See also *cit.*

civvy street (Modern) *s.* Retirement into civilian life. "With two teenage kids, it's tough on civvy street."

clackers (Spanish-American War, especially Philippine sector) *s.* Centavos, the Spanish equivalent of pennies.

clank, to clank up, to (World War II; Air Force) *s.* To become nervous, to freeze up.

clap checker (Probably 20th century) *s.* A medical specialist. See also *pecker checker, pricksmith, bedpan commando, pill pusher.*

claps (Modern) *s.* A play on *clasps,* invoking comparison with venereal disease. The bronze bars denoting successive awards of the Army Good Conduct Medal or battle and service credit on certain campaign medals and ribbons. "He was awarded the Good Conduct Medal with three claps" is a wry comment on a soldier's service.

Class F dependents (World War II on) Dependents acquired without benefit or blessing of clergy.

Class VI supplies (World War II) *s.* Alcoholic beverages, preferably hard, whether locally procured or (rarely and niggardly) issued. The term is nonregulation and is based on the fact that there were only five official classes of supplies at that time.

clean sleeve 1. (Modern) *s.* A buck private, who has no chevrons. 2. (West Point) *s.* A member of the first class (a senior) who has either remained a private in the Corps of Cadets throughout his four years or been busted back to private.

clean up on, to (Modern) *s.* To get the better of someone or something, to kill, to destroy.

clear, to (Considerable Antiquity) To get yourself officially relieved from responsibility. On a PCS, you *clear your quarters,* a matter of policing them up until the responsible authorities agree that they are as spotless as when you moved in (some military families hire professional cleaners to do the job for them); then you *clear the post* by turning in post property, paying bills, picking up any records you should take with you—in short, *clearing away* all outstanding obligations. In the modern Army, clearing is accomplished by getting the appropriate signatures in the appropriate spaces provided on DD Form 137, Installation Clearance Certificate. The completed form is presented during out-processing as evidence that you have "cleared" all the proper facilities and activities.

clerks and jerks (Modern) *s.* Administrative and support personnel. See *overhead, chairborne.*

click (Post–World War II to Modern) *s.* A kilometer. "At least you could buy you some pussy over here [Vietnam] without going sixty clicks for it" (Smith). Used before the Vietnam War, particularly in Germany during the 1950s.

Close stations! March order! (20th century) The command for an artillery unit on the range or in action to get ready to move out. Sometimes used to get a fatigue detail out of the shade and back to work or to signal that it was time to stop talking and go.

clothing allowance (Modern) Money paid to enlisted personnel to help defray the cost and upkeep of clothing. The exact amount varies, but it is never very much.

clown (Ancient to Modern) A term of disapproval. It has been used by angry noncoms in its original sense of an ill-bred, stupid, loutish boor since at least the days of William Shakespeare. The British applied the term to American soldiers at the beginning of the Revolution. A *clown of misery* is something like a clown, but much, much worse.

club, to (Colonial into 20th century; also British) *s.* To throw a formation into confusion by an incorrect command or by the incorrect execution of a command. Common in the days of intricate close-order drill, it has now been replaced by a variety of more earthy expressions.

cluster fuck (Modern) *s.* Synonymous with *gang shag* or *gang fuck* of civilian slang. Possibly an adaptation of *cluster bomb unit,* a type of aerial ordnance developed during the Vietnam War.

Clutching Hand (World War I) *s.* The de Havilland 5 training aircraft, clumsy but safe. Borrowed from the Royal Flying Corps by American flying cadets in Great Britain.

clutter (World War II) Unwanted images that appear on a radarscope, obscuring observations. They may be caused by anything from passing birds to obscure atmospheric phenomena. Up in foggy Alaskan waters, during World War II, the US Navy fought a major engagement with some of the latter sort of clutter in its famous "Battle of the Blips."

CO 1. Commanding Officer, from shavetail to colonel. 2. Conscientious Objector.

Coast, the (Old Army into World War II) *s.* The Coast Artillery. See *Cosmoline Gang.*

cobb cobbing (Colonial to early 19th century) A punishment, normally for minor military offenses, consisting of blows with a light stick or scabbard across the offender's bare posterior. In the British service, where the practice originated, the traditional number of blows was twelve. It was often administered by the soldiers themselves to comrades who had broken barracks rules for cleanliness or decency, or had hung back in a fight.

cocksucker bread (World War II to Modern) French bread, so-called from a widely held notion about Frenchmen. Similarly, *cocksucker toast* is French toast.

Code of Conduct (1955 to Modern) A code developed after the Korean War for the purpose of rendering more clearly to the serviceman what he should, and should not, do if captured by the enemy. It consists of six articles written in the first person, its main topics being surrender; the duty to try to escape; refusal to accept favors from the enemy or to give parole; refusal to aid the enemy or to make disloyal statements; refusal to give information beyond name, rank, serial number, and birth date.

coffeeboiler coffee-boiler (Civil War; USA) *s.* Generally, a straggler of the professional type; he never missed a payday or a meal but would drop out just before a hard march or an engagement and spend his time safely and comfortably brewing coffee with his fellow scoundrels. Specifically, a straggler who deliberately set out to be captured by the enemy so that he could spend the war safely in a prison camp. "The terms *coffee-boiler* and *blackberry picker* were considered the worst terms of opprobrium we had in prison. They were applied to that class of stragglers and skulkers who were only too ready to give themselves up to the enemy [saying they had just] stopped to boil a cup of coffee . . . when they were gobbled up" (McElroy). Some of them learned a thing or two in Confederate prison camps. The weak discipline of most of the US volunteer regiments and the lack of effective military police made such evasions comparatively easy. Most coffeeboilers undoubtedly later acquired pensions for their heroic services, cut a wide swath in their hometown GAR affairs, and ran for political office as worthy veterans.

coffee call (Modern) Coffee break, the term being based on the system of bugle calls that once regulated Army life.

coffee cooler (Old Army) *s.* A loafer who has a soft job that allows him to consume his coffee leisurely while you are out in the hot sun or icy wind gulping yours down scalding hot or icy cold. The term was generally applied to all administrative personnel, from the company clerk to the post quartermaster. On occasion, as during the Philippine Insurrection, the term was extended to whole regiments on rear-area garrison duty. A coffee cooler is not to be confused with the Civil War coffeeboiler, who was something a lot more degraded.

coffin corner (World War II) *s.* In a large bomber formation, the position on the extreme rear and outer flank. The bomber there is the most vulnerable to fighter attack, while by the time it comes along, enemy flak has had plenty of time to adjust its fire.

Cogle (Mexican War) A mythical malefactor among the Kentucky volunteers. He was blamed for all thefts and other offenses against military discipline. See *Locks.*

cold 1. (Modern) Not receiving enemy fire, as in *a cold LZ,* a landing zone not under enemy fire. Obviously related to the general term *cold war.* 2. (Since at least as early as 1920; West Point) *s.* Absolutely perfect, as in "cold max."

cold-beverage corporal (West Point) The plebe responsible for serving the cold beverages at each table in the mess. See *dessert cutter, gunner, hot-beverage corporal.*

cold burning (Ancient to early 19th century) A punishment for minor offenses, often administered by soldiers to a comrade guilty of some infraction of mess or barrack conduct. The offender had a cup of cold water poured slowly down the sleeve of his upraised arm, the executioner pulling at his clothing so that it ran down the length of his body. This practice was already well established when John Smith used it at Jamestown in 1608 as a cure for profanity. A modern variant is throwing the offender under a cold shower.

cold turkey (Antiquity uncertain; all Services) *s.* An easy job or mission.

cold turkey, to talk (Antiquity uncertain; all Services) *s.* To speak bluntly, without mincing words.

colonel (Ancient to Modern) A field-grade officer ranking below a brigadier general and above a lieutenant colonel. The colonel's insignia is a silver spread eagle, and a colonel usually commands a regiment or a brigade. Most of the nicknames for the rank are based on distinguishing a colonel from a lieutenant colonel: *bird colonel, bull colonel, chicken colonel, full bird colonel, full bull colonel, full bull, full colonel.* Abbreviated *Col.*

colors (Colonial to Modern) Flags of an infantry or other dismounted organization. Flags of a mounted or motorized organization are called *standards.*

Columbiad 1. (Early 19th century; also Navy) Apparently the first American-designed type of cannon. It was developed by Capt. George Bomford, who in 1805 was the eighth graduate of the US Military Academy. Used both for seacoast defense and aboard ships, it was a short, lightly built, large-bore weapon usually employed as a shell gun. It was not a successful design, and relatively few pieces were built. 2. (Mid-19th century) A powerful 8- or 10-inch coast-defense gun introduced by Bomford (by then head of the Army Ordnance Department) during the early 1840s. It continued in use through the Civil War.

Column of ducks (Modern) Soldiers in column, two abreast.

Com (Since at least as early as 1900; West Point) The commandant of cadets at the US Military Academy.

Combat Arms Branches of the service whose mission it is to engage in actual fighting: at present, Infantry, Field Artillery, Air Defense Artillery, Armor, and Corps of Engineers (which also serves as a combat support arm).

combat-happy, to go (to turn, to be, to get) (World War II to Modern; all Services) *s.* To be mentally disturbed through overexposure to the strain and pressure of being in a combat area too long. "[Combat-happy] could mean anything from turning chicken to killing forty prisoners" (Smith). Also called *battle-happy. Happy* is a common enough suffix meaning either breakdown or overenthusiasm for something: *cunt-happy, slaphappy, trigger-happy*, etc.

Combat Infantryman Badge See *CIB.*

Combat Medical Badge (World War II on) A badge awarded to members of the Army Medical Department in the grade of colonel or below. Wartime service criteria for awarding the badge are otherwise the same as for the CIB.

Combat Support Arm Branches of the service providing operational assistance to the Combat Arms: at present, Corps of Engineers (which also serves as a combat arm), Signal Corps, Military Police Corps, and Military Intelligence Corps.

combatticals (Modern) *s.* Jocular name for the fatigue or utility uniform.

come-along (World War I and later) A slip collar and leash improvised from barbed wire, used to make a balky prisoner follow his captors. The term itself is probably taken from the civilian police come-along, a form of handcuff.

Come and get it! (Antiquity unknown) The mess sergeant's traditional yell to indicate that chow is ready to be served.

comfort halt (Considerable Antiquity) The polite name for a halt longer than usual, allowed periodically so that men can relieve the pressure on bladders and bowels. The slang term is *pee halt*. During stateside maneuvers and practice marches, such a halt seems to attract curious civilian spectators, even in the most thinly populated areas.

comical warfare (Modern) *s.* A wordplay on chemical warfare.

command decision, to make a (Modern) To be decisive; to make a decision, even an inconsequential one, regardless of whether one is actually in command of anything. Generally used facetiously. "One of my more striking command decisions" (Marshall, 1979).

command of execution (Considerable Antiquity) As in "Forward! March!" *March* is the command of execution and is supposed to ring loud, clear, and sharp. In the old days, mounted or horse- or mule-drawn units employed the longer "Forward! Ho-o-o-o!" to give the animals a moment to gather themselves and go. Naturally, some cavalry and artillery officers and NCOs might unconsciously use it for dismounted drill. When, as was common in World Wars I and II, veteran cavalrymen found themselves transferred to the infantry, there would be interesting developments. Let a "H-o-o-o-o!" echo across the parade ground and every field-grade beetle crusher within earshot developed instant lycanthropy.

command sergeant major CSM (Modern) With the exception of the office of Sergeant Major of the Army, the highest-ranking noncommissioned grade in the Army, pay grade E-9. The insignia of the grade is three stripes above three arcs enclosing a wreath, within which is a single five-pointed star. The grade was first established in 1968. The CSM serves as the senior enlisted adviser to a commander at battalion level and higher, and is first and foremost a troop leader. He outranks the sergeant major, who is also in pay grade E-9, and is addressed as *sergeant major*. The nickname *top* is occasionally used.

COMMFU (Modern) *s.* Complete[ly] Monumental Military Fuck-Up.

commissary 1. (Colonial to Revolutionary) An administrative official, almost always a civilian, serving with an army. The Commissary General of Stores and Provisions and his deputy and assistant commissaries were responsible for the supply of food. Other commissaries oversaw an army's financial records and muster rolls, or care of its horses or prisoners of war. These were safe jobs and very profitable. 2. (1812–1912) A military officer of the Subsistence Department, headed by the Commissary General of Subsistence, which supplied rations to the Army. Rations were issued from commissary warehouses or stores, which in turn became known as commissaries. The department also sold rationed items to officers and to married soldiers who were allowed to eat with their families. 3. By extension, the modern system of post commissaries.

commo (Modern) *s.* Short for *communications*. Our sergeant major remembers being earnestly counseled by a senior communications NCO not to use this informal term. Communications personnel apparently detest it because it is used by the uninitiated to describe commo personnel's esoteric calling in a slightly disrespectful manner.

commodore (Modern, as a military term, but otherwise Ancient) 1. A naval grade of flag officer next below a rear admiral. Until 1982 this grade was not used in peacetime, but in war it might be applied to the commanding officer of a convoy or to the senior captain when two or more warships are cruising together. 2. *s.* An officer who forgets to button or zip the fly of his trousers. Possibly based on the opinion that an officer old enough to be a commodore is apt to be somewhat senile. The term has been picked up by Army and Air Force officers serving in joint headquarters and by their wives. We know one Army wife who checks out her absentminded husband with the question "Are you Army—or Navy?" before he leaves the house.

company (Ancient to Modern) Along with its administrative equivalents, the battery and the troop, the basic unit of the Army. It is usually formed of two or more platoons and a headquarters and, in the combat arms, is usually one of the components of a battalion. In service units and units with special missions, there are many exceptions to this ideal organizational pattern. It is normally commanded by a captain, assisted by other officers, a first sergeant, and other noncommissioned officers.

company bean boiler (Civil War; USA) *s.* The company cook. Beans were an important part of Yankee rations, and a man who knew how to cook them properly was a useful citizen.

company clerk (Ancient to Modern) The assistant to the first sergeant in a company. He sees that the day-to-day paperwork is done, often assists the company commander and the other officers with their forms and reports, acts as general receptionist to keep the other enlisted men from bugging the officers and the first sergeant, and very often amounts to acting first sergeant when the topkick is on furlough, temporarily "incapacitated," or lazy. Although he is usually only a specialist, he enjoys prestige and influence beyond his rank, for he is both at the center of power and in close contact with the rank and file. On the debit side, he often has a superiority complex because he fancies himself the only literate man in the company. He also poses as company oracle, what with inside information he has picked up. The straight-duty men often regard him as a perishable form of life that will melt if exposed to outside weather. Yet, despite all this, a good company clerk is a priceless asset, with a thankless job. His nicknames are *company clown, company jerk, company monkey, company punk, company queer, company stooge.*

company collection sheet (Old Army) A device for making the soldier pay for things he bought jawbone with money he did not have, such as haircuts from the company barber, canteen checks, alterations from the post tailor, occasionally a contribution for the company day room. On payday, a collection sheet showing each soldier's outstanding indebtedness lay on the pay table. Once the soldier had his pay in hand, he promptly settled his accounts. Usually there was not much left over for riotous living.

company fund (Early 19th century to Modern) A fund to be spent by the company commander for the benefit of the enlisted men of the company. Typical expenditures were for fruit and such extra delicacies for the mess, athletic equipment, and reading material. The character and sources of the fund changed considerably over the years. Originally, the money came from the company's share of the tax levied on the sutler and from savings made by establishing a post bakery for bread. A bakery would permit a considerable saving in the flour ration. Expenditures from the fund were controlled by a company council, consisting of all officers present for duty. Such funds were rigorously inspected at least annually.

company headquarters (World War II and later) The orderly room. An example of what happens to service speech when you get the Army all cluttered up with a lot of well-meaning civilians.

company officers company-grade officers (Ancient to Modern) Captains and lieutenants.

company punishment (Ancient to Modern) Minor punishment awarded by a company commander. In its 20th-century form it is limited to a short period of restriction to a given area and/or extra duty, usually of a menial sort. The soldier must be willing to accept it rather than risk court-martial. Company punishment is appropriate for first offenses or for the well-meaning but chronic minor offender. Now called Article 15.

Company Q 1. (Mexican War to 20th century, possibly to Modern) *s.* The guardhouse, imprisonment. Artillerymen called it *Battery Q*. The *Q* may have some relation to quod, an old slang term for prison. 2. (Civil War) *s.* The sick list of hospital rats. 3. (Civil War; CSA) A holding organization of Confederate cavalrymen who had lost their horses and were unable to replace them. (In the Confederate service, cavalrymen supplied their own mounts.) One of J. E. B. Stuart's staff wrote that "hundreds of such dismounted men were collected in a useless crowd, which was dubbed 'Company Q.' " 4. (Civil War; USA) A company made up of officers who had been reduced to the ranks for cowardice in action and were being given an opportunity to redeem themselves by serving as privates. There were at least two such organizations in the Union armies. Most of the men in them fought well and many finally regained their commissions. 5. (20th century, perhaps earlier) A provisional company, formed from odds, ends, sods, and strays in combat.

company street In garrison this may be an actual paved street in front of the barracks, and in the field it may be merely a cleared area in front of the tents or hooches. It is the area where the company falls in for drill, inspection, and other formations.

compliments (Old Army) As the adjutant said to the colonel, "Sir, the general's compliments, and your regiment may advance." Free translation: "Move out!" See *respects*.

compound (Korea and later) A walled enclosure containing living quarters, offices, and/or storehouses. In Korea and Vietnam such installations were often garrisoned and fortified. From Malay *kampong* 'a cluster of buildings'. The term was occasionally used by old China hands before World War II, but did not come into general use until the Vietnam War.

Com Z (Modern) Communications Zone. "The part of a theater of operations just behind the combat zone, and in which communications, supply, and other activities for the support of field forces are established." Combat men visualize it as a sort of Mohammedan paradise.

con (West Point) *s.* Confinement to quarters for breaches of discipline. The form *cons* was earlier, but was dropped around 1900.

conchie conchy conshie (World War I and later) *s.* A conscientious objector. By claiming this status, one was not automatically deferred from the draft, but was subject to performing noncombat duties or alternate service. Also the more modern *CO.*

Concrete Battleship (Old Army to World War II) *s.* Fort Drum, built 1909–19 on tiny El Fraile Island at the entrance to Manila Bay. The entire island was built up into a massive structure of reinforced concrete, mounting four 14-inch guns in two turrets, four 6-inch guns, and a fire-control mast, so that its outline resembled that of a battleship. It was the only American stronghold to resist Japanese air and artillery bombardments in 1941–42. Its guns were still in action up to the final US surrender on 6 May 1942. Garrison duty "aboard" it in peacetime, however, was not popular.

condiment can (Old, Old Army, World War I) A small rectangular can, divided into two compartments by a partition. It had a screw cap at each end. One half of the can held sugar, the other, ground coffee. One screw cap contained a small compartment for salt. It was a part of the soldier's individual mess equipment developed around 1910. See *bacon can, meat can, mess kit.*

condom 1. (18th century) The oilskin cases for the colors of a regiment. From British use. 2. (Modern) *s.* A plastic bag for aerial delivery of water; designed to be dropped from a low altitude without a parachute. Sometimes it survives this treatment. When it does, you wish it had not, because your platoon leader will not let you drink the water. He makes you shave with it. But if you do drink it, you regret it because the plastic gives the water the flavor of paint. Undoubtedly invented by a Russian agent. Like definition 1, the term is derived from the contraceptive.

conductor (Colonial to early 19th century) 1. A civilian assistant to a commissary, responsible for the movement of supplies. Those with the artillery were in charge of the ammunition wagons. 2. A person charged with recruiting Indian war parties and accompanying them into the field.

confidence course (World War II and later) A nicer name for the obstacle course, intended to make you think positively about it and thus eager to face it. As a matter of fact, successfully living through the course did give you confidence in your ability to do unreasonable things.

Cong, the (Vietnam) *s.* A term used indiscriminately by American soldiers for members of the National Liberation Front, or Vietcong, as a whole, including the National Liberation Army, the Territorials, the Main Force, and paramilitary elements. The plural could be either *the Cong* or *the Congs.*

consecrated milk (Civil War; USA) *s.* Concentrated milk, an early form of condensed milk issued as a ration supplement in the Union armies.

conservatory (World War II; Air Force) *s.* A glass-enclosed machine-gun turret, usually power-driven. It resembled a small greenhouse.

contact, to make (to get) (Modern) Either to fire upon, or to be fired upon by, the enemy. "The word 'contact' is little more than an ambiguity" (Marshall, 1969). "One of the companies from third brigade got contact" (Smith).

Continentals (Revolutionary) The regular American army, raised by the states for the national service. No other American army has endured so much for so long, accomplished so much with so little, or been so callously neglected by its fellow citizens.

contraband (Civil War; USA) 1. Trade in goods prohibited by federal law, or the goods themselves. All Confederate imports or exports were thus considered contraband and subject to seizure by the Union forces. 2. An escaped slave. A Virginia slave owner demanded that Maj. Gen. Benjamin Butler, then commanding at Fort Monroe, Virginia, return to him three blacks who had fled behind Union lines. Butler (later to be known as Beast Butler in New Orleans and to have his portrait painted on the inside bottom of Southern ladies' chamber pots) was a poor general, but an astute criminal lawyer. He solved the legal problem by declaring the slaves to be contraband. The designation caught the fancy of Union soldiers and sailors.

cook-house rumors (Old, Old Army, World War I) *s.* The same as latrine rumors, the mess being another place where soldiers could gossip together and exchange misinformation. The Navy had *galley yarns.*

Cookie Division (Modern) *s.* The 9th US Infantry Division, from the octofoil design of its shoulder sleeve insignia.

cookie pusher (20th century) *s.* A mildly contemptuous term sometimes applied to gentlemen of the State Department, which is generally regarded with considerable justified suspicion by members of the Armed Forces. Probably of civilian origin, with reference to a tea party. A State Department veteran tells us that the term was used in the State Department itself, to mean a useless or spineless member of that organization.

cook's police (World War I and possibly earlier) The equivalent of *KP.*

cootie cooty (World War I) A louse, particularly the body louse. The term is probably borrowed from the British, since it comes from Malay *kuti.* Occasionally used later than World War I.

copacetic copasetic /ko-pah-'see-tik, kop-pah-'set-tik/ (1930s into World War II; possibly still used) *s.* Completely satisfactory, under control, all right. "Everything copacetic around here?" Apparently civilian slang brought into the service by recruits and Reservists. Its origin is not known. Suggestions have been made that it is of black origin, of Yiddish origin, or a humorously pretentious corruption of *antiseptic.*

copain (World War I) *s.* The French word for *buddy,* adopted to a certain extent by the AEF.

cops and robbers (Post–World War II) *s.* Practice maneuvers, particularly by the National Guard or Reservists.

corned Willie (World War I) *s.* Canned corned beef. Also sometimes called *corned Bill.*

corner pocket (1930s and 1940s) *s.* Another term for the guardhouse. From pool.

cornet (Colonial through War of 1812) The lowest grade of commissioned officer in the cavalry; equivalent to an infantry ensign. The title is still retained in the Philadelphia City Troop of the Pennsylvania National Guard, in memory of excellent service in the Revolutionary War.

corporal (Ancient to Modern) A junior noncommissioned officer serving in pay grade E-4. He ranks below a sergeant and above a private first class and, within the pay grade, outranks a specialist fourth class. His insignia of rank is two stripes. Until very recently a corporal commanded a squad, but today corporals are usually assistant squad leaders. The grade of corporal may be low, but a soldier never forgets the initial experience of having made corporal. It is his first real step up. From *Stars and Stripes* (22 February 1918):

Oh, the General with his epaulettes,
a leadin' a parade,
The Colonel and the Adjutant a
sportin' of their braid,
The Major and the Skipper
[captain]—none of 'em look
so fine
As a newly minted corp'ral, comin'
down the line!

The abbreviations for corporal are *Cpl.* and *Corp*. Nicknames are *corp, corpuscle, double PFC, two-striper.*

corps 1. A special branch or department of the Army, with a specialized function —like the Medical Corps. 2. A tactical unit on a command level below an army, composed of two or more divisions and auxiliary troops. It is usually commanded by a lieutenant general.

corpsman (World War II on; usually Navy, Marines) *s.* A member of the Medical Corps, particularly an aidman or medic. Used only for enlisted personnel, not for officers and/or doctors. Also called *band-aid, bedpan commando, clap checker, pecker checker, pill pusher, pricksmith,* etc.

corpuscle (World War II to Modern) *s.* A jocular term for a corporal. In pronunciation it often shaded over into *corpsuckle*, etc.

cosmoline (20th century) Technically, a trade name for petrolatum, but used as an ordinary word. A stiff, heavy, greasy jelly, like a thicker vaseline, used to protect weapons against rust. Removing it was an experience in frustration. After you got it off the weapon, you had to get it off yourself.

Cosmoline Gang Cosmoline Slingers Cosmoline Artillery (World War I and Old Army) *s.* The former Coast Artillery, which had to keep its guns coated with cosmoline to protect them from the weather. In World War I slang a *cosmoline antiaircraft outfit* would be a Coast Artillery unit serving as antiaircraft artillery.

costume worker (Post–World War I; AEF) *s.* An operative of the DCI who went about in disguise as a civilian Frenchman or other national.

Cotton Balers The 7th Infantry Regiment, in commemoration of its service at the Battle of New Orleans in 1814. The legend that the Americans fought behind breastworks of cotton bales is, unfortunately, completely false. A few bales were used to line the flanks of the gun emplacements, but had to be removed because of their tendency to catch fire.

count off, to To call out one's numerical position in a line of troops, starting with *one*. The command is *Count off!*

county fair 1. (Modern) *s.* A method for instructing or examining large groups of soldiers in several subjects by having them attend a series of continuous lectures, demonstrations, and/or examinations. 2. (Pre–World War II) Groups of displays of weapons, equipment, or service life through which visitors pass. One put on by the Special Forces at Fort Bragg featured such things as smokeless cooking of rattlesnake meat (with free samples), wall scaling, and unarmed combat. This is excellent for a dramatic briefing and snow job for visiting brass or for impressing the general public on Army Day and other holidays.

court-martial A court consisting of military personnel appointed to try members of the Armed Forces who are charged with offenses against military law. Courts-martial are temporary tribunals that may be convened whenever and wherever required—for example, aboard a transport or during combat. In time of war their jurisdiction includes civilians serving with the armed forces, enemy spies and prisoners of war, and civilians in occupied areas. There are three levels of courts-martial, in ascending order:

Summary court-martial. Normally termed "summary court," it consists of one officer, selected for education, experience, and judicial temperament. This resembles a civil trial by a justice of the peace or federal magistrate. Jurisdiction is limited to enlisted personnel.

Special court-martial. Consists of three or more members, who are equivalent to a civilian jury, and a trial counsel (prosecutor) and a defense counsel. In cases that may result in a BCD (bad conduct discharge), a military judge is assigned as presiding officer. (Under combat conditions or other circumstances of military exigency, a special court may impose a BCD when a military judge is not available but only if the accused is guaranteed the right of competent military counsel and a complete written transcript of the trial is maintained.) If the accused is an enlisted person, he or she may request that at least one-third of the members of the court also be enlisted. (In that case, they must always be higher in grade than the accused.) The accused also can request trial by the military judge alone. A special court has authority to try both enlisted personnel and officers.

General court-martial. Consists of five members, plus a trial counsel, defense counsel, and military judge. Both counsels must be qualified lawyers. They may try any person subject to military law and persons charged with violations of the laws of war. Punishments may be the maximum authorized, including death.

In all court-martial proceedings, findings of guilty are subject to exhaustive review, including in some cases the all-civilian Court of Military Appeals. Sentences involving general officers or the death penalty cannot be executed without the President's approval. Normal American judicial standards are observed—the presumption of innocence, protection against self-incrimination, the right to call and cross-examine witnesses, and proof of guilt beyond a reasonable doubt.

See also *Article 15* and *company punishment.*

coushay avec /ˈcoo-shay a-ˈvek/ (1917 to Modern; also Marines) *s.* To have sexual intercourse with. Short form of *Voulez-vous coucher avec moi?* 'Do you want to go to bed with me?' The German equivalent was *schlafen mit. Coushay avec* was sometime used as a nickname for someone whose aspirations were always urgent and entirely horizontal.

co van (Vietnam) An American adviser to the South Vietnamese Armed Forces. From Vietnamese *cố vấn mỹ* 'American adviser'.

cover 1. Concealment and protection from the enemy. 'You, Jones, take cover behind that tree there." 2. A hat, a protective device.

cover, to 1. To watch out for the safety of another, to protect. "And you, Donovan, cover him." 2. To align men in ranks, from front to rear.

COW cow 1. (Old Army) *s.* Commanding Officer's Wife. Usually she ran the other wives of her husband's post or unit with an iron hand, no less effective for being concealed in a lace glove. The better ones were a combination of fairy godmother, Dutch aunt, military Emily Post, Red Cross, and Army Relief. The worst were interfering old biddies who also ran their husband and as much of the Army as he theoretically controlled, and were one of the worst curses of the service. 2. (West Point) *s.* Lower-cased, a cadet in the third year (second classman). Also an Annapolis third-year midshipman, and an Air Force third-year cadet. See *sow.* 3. (West Point) Lower-cased, a milk pitcher in the cadet mess.

cowboy 1. (Revolutionary) A Tory (Loyalist) irregular, especially in the lower Hudson Valley. Like their usual opponents, the allegedly pro-American *skinners*, they were little more than bandits. 2. (World War II and later; also Air Force) *s.* A reckless driver or pilot who delights in scaring his passengers half to death.

cowboy hat (Modern) *s.* The campaign hat worn by Army drill sergeants. It is the same Montana-peak model introduced in 1910–11.

CP Command Post. The headquarters and operations center from which a commander conducts tactical operations.

CPX Command Post Exercise. A simulated combat situation or war game that is worked out by commanders and their staffs, usually "in addition to other duties," without involving any troop units. It is economical; tests communications, plans, and staff functioning; and gives the officers and NCOs practice in going without sleep.

CQ Charge of Quarters. A noncommissioned officer who is on duty at headquarters after normal duty hours and is the representative of the commanding officer and whatever noncommissioned officer is ordinarily in charge. This may be in a company orderly room or in the headquarters of a larger unit. Among the CQ's duties may be maintaining order, conducting bed check on a company level, putting lights out, taking messages, supervising orderlies or runners, and serving as a link between higher headquarters and unit, and troops and commander. The position is usually filled by rotation among the noncoms.

crab (West Point) *s.* A midshipman at the US Naval Academy.

crackerbox crackerbox ambulance (World War II) *s.* The AM725 series ambulance, so called for its shape.

crackshack (Modern) *s.* The WAC quarters on a post. Now becoming obsolete, what with coed barracks. *Crack* equals *vulva.*

crack troops (Modern) *s.* Female soldiers. Often *America's crack troops.*

crapper (Modern) *s.* The latrine.

crate (World War I to Modern) *s.* An airplane of any type. Occasionally *hot crate* for a fast, high-performance aircraft.

C-rats C-rations See *Cees.*

crawl, to (World War II to Modern) *s.* To reprimand, to chew out. Reportedly originated at West Point, and not very common outside.

creamed foreskins (World War II on) *s.* Creamed chipped beef on toast. Sometimes considered the same as *shit on a shingle*, but the latter was usually ground beef.

creature, the (19th century) *s.* Hard liquor, generally whiskey. Usually phrased as *the friendly creature* or *good creature.* Probably from Irish slang, where it is often spelled *cratur*.

creeping crud (World War II on) *s.* A vague term for intestinal disorders or sometimes for some indefinable malaise, suggestive of malingering. "Look! You don't ride my sick book with your goddamned creeping crud, unless you want a couple of spells of KP!"

creeping Jesus 1. *s.* A slow-moving, ineffectual person of limited mentality. Parallel to civilian *creeping Moses*, which was usually applied to a lethargic black. 2. (World War II) *s.* A chaplain's enlisted assistant.

crib 1. (Old, Old Army to 1940s) The hay rack in a stall in an Army stable. 2. (Old, Old Army to Modern) *s.* A house of prostitution. Usually small, one-woman units, built in a rowhouse arrangement along a street in a red-light district.

cribber (Old, Old Army to 1940s) A horse that chews on the crib and other wooden parts of its stall. Cribbing is a serious vice. The horse often swallows splinters or gets them in its mouth, besides damaging the stall.

Crime of 1901 The Army reorganization of 1901, in the opinion of Regular officers. A generally praiseworthy piece of legislation, it brought approximately twelve hundred new officers into the Army. Some were promoted from the ranks; a few were graduates of the better tin schools; some were transferred from the Volunteers. A good number of the officers translated from the Volunteers came in as captains and field-grade officers, thus badly scrambling prospects of promotion for the Regulars.

Crossbar Hotel Cross Bar Hotel (20th century) *s.* The guardhouse, imprisonment.

cross-country methods (World War II) *s.* Getting supplies by informal methods rather than through established channels. Perhaps a friend in the supply dump will turn his back while you load up. See *drawing over the left, moonlight requisition.*

Crot (West Point) *s.* A plebe. Perhaps a shortening of the older *Ducrot*, reinforced by *crotch.*

crotch cobra (Modern) *s.* The penis. In an essentially male environment, as the Armed Forces remain, machismo is highly rated. Women are viewed as weak and deficient in warrior qualities, and the penis is often thought of as an aggressive organ. Other similar terms are *drawers dragon, one-eyed zipper snake, pants python, trouser worm*, etc.

crotch crickets *s.* Lice, specifically Phthirus pubis, the crab louse.

crow (World War II) *s.* Mess-hall chicken. Also called *albatross.*

Crowbar Hotel Crow Bar Hotel (20th century) *s.* The guardhouse, imprisonment.

crow tracks (World War II) *s.* The chevrons of a noncommissioned officer.

crud s. Although this word does not appear in military language until relatively late, it is otherwise old. In Shakespeare's *Henry IV, Part Two* (act IV, scene iii), the fat knight (and captain of infantry)

Sir John Falstaff speaks of "crudy vapors." The word ultimately comes from Middle English *crudde*, 'curd'. The adjectival form of the modern word is *cruddy*. 1. (World War II) A moderately polite synonym for shit. "That's a lot of crud!" 2. A disliked person. "Do you know what that crud just did?" 3. (World War II) A sickness. Originally a skin affliction, but extended to bowel complaints or anything uncomfortable. See *creeping crud*.

cruit croot *s.* Short for *recruit*.

crunch cap (Modern; Army) *s.* Another name for the boonie hat (see *Gabby Hayes*) issued to troops in Vietnam. So called because it could be crunched up and stuffed into a pocket or pack.

CSM See *command sergeant major*.

C3 (World War II) The combat beverage of the 3d Armored Field Artillery Battalion. Equal parts of cointreau, champagne, and cognac. Fire for effect!

cue ball (World War II; all Services) *s.* A man who has just had a close haircut. Also, sometimes, a naturally bald man.

culture shock (Vietnam) The effect on newly arrived Americans of the Vietnamese way of doing things. The most aggravating thing about the Vietnamese way was that it always took longer than we wished. Very frequently heard.

cunt cap (Apparently some small use in World War I; extensive use in World War II and later) *s.* The present garrison cap, so called because of a fancied resemblance to the vulva. This is one of those terms that are heard almost every day and come to sound perfectly natural. But soldiers often forget themselves in mixed company. Our sergeant major tells the story of a friend, home on leave after his basic, who shocked his mother (a refined and decorous lady) by asking her, "Mother, have you seen my cunt cap?"

Cuntsville (Modern) 1. *s.* A term for the United States during the Vietnam War. Probably mirrors soldiers' expectations on arriving back in the United States after their tour in Vietnam. 2. *s.* A wordplay on *Huntsville*, Alabama.

cush (Civil War; CSA) A favorite campaign dish made by frying the fat from bacon and then adding small pieces of beef to the fat and sautéing them. Later, crumbled corn bread or hardtack, or a paste made from corn meal or flour would be added. The mixture was then cooked until the liquid boiled away or was absorbed. Also called *slosh*. The word *cush* is an African word of slave origin and is probably related to *couscous*, a North African dish.

Custer ring (Modern) A tight, easily defended perimeter, usually assumed in desperate situations. Based on the popular myth that Custer and his cavalrymen formed such a ring to make their "last stand" at the Battle of the Little Big Horn. "The company would form a Custer ring at the center of the clearing" (Marshall, 1969).

Customs of the Service According to Moss, this is the "common law of the Army." These are the unwritten "rules" of conduct that every soldier learns and to which he is expected to adhere. They are not prescribed by regulation or established law, and in this respect they differ from the rules of conduct called military courtesy. Examples are that a junior in rank walks to the left of his superior and that a soldier in uniform does not carry an umbrella.

cut a choggie, to (Korea and later; also Marines) *s.* To run, to retreat, to move away fast. Pidgin Korean used by American troops. From Korean *kada* 'to go' and *chøgi* 'over there' (see *choggie*). Partridge (1970) speculates that *cut* may be reinforced from the expression *cut and run*, but this expression is literary rather than colloquial.

cut and paste, to (Modern) *s.* To edit, as of a staff paper. Such papers are sometimes literally cut apart with a scissors and reassembled with paste or tape, with sections in a different order from the original.

cut orders, to (World War II to present) To publish orders. In the days before multilith offset and fast-copying machine processes, orders were mimeographed and the letters were literally cut into the surface of the stencil. "My orders were cut for June 10, 1944" (Marshall, 1979).

cutter cap (Generally World War II) *s.* The overseas cap.

cut [one's] teeth on a bugle, to (Old Army) *s.* To be born into an Army family. See *Army brat, brown-spit baby.*

cut Zs, to (Post–World War II) *s.* To sleep. Probably from the comic strip use of a string of Zs to indicate that a character is snoring.

CYA (Relatively Modern) *s.* Cover Your Ass, a military aphorism meaning that you should always consider your professional health. If the company commander whom you are replacing assures you that all company property is complete and paperwork is up to date, then begs you to "please sign here" and assume all accountability and responsibility so that he can depart at once to reach the bedside of his dying mother—ignore his lamentations and insist on a joint inventory. If you are told to do something odd, insist on having your orders in writing. If a soon-to-be-transferred couple suddenly starts slathering you with hospitality, do not feel obligated to buy their out-of-tune piano.

cyclo (Vietnam; all Services) *s.* The *cyclo-pousse* and its motorized version (*cyclo-may* to the Viets) are both common forms of transportation in Vietnam. The *cyclo-pousse,* or pedicab, provided the customer with a very comfortable seat protected by an awning, which could be extended for protection from the rain and the sun. (This was about the only protection you had when riding in one of these things.) Hiring a cyclo for a tour of downtown Saigon was a pleasant and leisurely way to spend an afternoon. The motorized version, however, was noisy, dirty, expensive, very dangerous, and wildly exciting. In both models the passenger sat in front of the driver (pedaler), but whereas the pedicab traveled at a slow speed and was extremely maneuverable, the cyclo-may traveled very fast. As a result the passenger sometimes found himself whizzing toward a collision with no more protection than a flimsy footrest jutting out in front of the passenger seat.

cyclo boy and cyclo girl (Vietnam; all Services) *s.* A pimp and his prostitute. Quite often the cyclo boys made extra money pimping among their customers for prostitutes or for the owner of a bordello.

D Dee (At least as early as the 1920s; West Point) *s.* Deficient, or below average in academics. "Dee . . . meaning Deficient, flunking" (Truscott).

DA Department of the Army.

DAC (World War II to Modern) Department of the Army Civilian employee. A sort of hazard introduced to keep the Army from becoming too military. In the Old Army, civilian employees consisted of a few skilled craftsmen at each post and a few typists in Washington. Nowadays, they come in thousands and in every degree of importance. They have become indispensable, largely because it is impossible to figure out your civilian "assistants' " filing systems during an ordinary tour of duty. Since they are protected by both the Civil Service and their government employees' union, they are almost impossible to correct or discipline. In keeping with Finigal's Law, their tribe increases as the number of combat soldiers decreases. The Air Force and Navy have the same problem.

daddy bus (Modern; West Point) *s.* A small Army brat's name—now adopted by adults—for the bus that picks daddy up in the morning and brings him home from work in the evening.

daily (West Point) *s.* Daily inspection.

daisy chain (World War II and later) *s.* Two parabundles attached to each other. The parachute of the upper (second) bundle is jerked open by the static line attaching it to the aircraft from which it is dropped. The parachute of the lower (first) bundle is opened by the line connecting it to the upper bundle.

daisy-cutter (World War II) 1. (Army) *s.* A shell coming in just above ground level. 2. (Air Force) *s.* An antipersonnel fragmentation bomb, fuzed to burst on impact with the ground or heavy vegetation.

Dandy Jack (Old, Old Army) *s.* An officer who was very spiffy and particular about his uniform and horse equipment.

dawn patrol dawn patrolling (World War I to at least World War II; mostly Air Corps) 1. A patrol of fighter aircraft, sent out over the lines in the very early morning. 2. *s.* By normal transition, getting up before reveille. This was not uncommon with older soldiers whose bladders (grown less elastic with age) would get them out of bed early. Once up, the more dedicated or obnoxious of them might decide to stroll around and see what sins of commission or omission they could detect. Garbage racks seemed to be their favorite target.

day of grace Until recently, the day following the last day of leave indicated on the soldier's DA Form 31 "Request for Leave or Absence" or, at an earlier date, his furlough papers. If the soldier was due to return on the fifth, he had until the midnight of the sixth to return to his unit. He was not considered AWOL on the sixth, and the extra time was not charged to him as leave. No longer practiced, since a more liberal policy of granting extensions and better transportation have made the custom unnecessary.

day room A room or small building (sometimes even a whole barracks) set aside for the recreation of troops assigned to a particular unit. It is furnished and may contain a pool table, writing desks, drink- and food-dispensing machines, TV sets, magazines, etc. It provides a relaxed atmosphere in which troops can enjoy their leisure time in the unit area, but it may be haunted by sergeants suddenly in need of a detail.

day-room orderly See *DRO*.

DB (Old Army to Modern) Disciplinary Barracks. Institutions designed to teach the insubordinate and irresponsible how to behave, and also not to come back for a second session. Of course, since their rigors have been softened in later years, some GFUs would rather be in a DB, with no exposure to inclement weather or enemy action, than with their outfits.

DB (Modern) Daily Bulletin. A sheet covering official details, such as Officer of the Day, special events, and other items of interest. Your wife always expects you to bring it home with you.

D-bar ration (World War II) An emergency combat ration issued to all men for use when no other supply of food was possible. It was a four-ounce chocolate bar enriched with sugar, oat flour, vanillin, and vitamins. See *Hitler's secret weapon*.

DCI (Post–World War I) Department of Criminal Investigation. Established by the AEF in France to combat black-marketing and organized crime among American soldiers and deserters.

DD 1. Department of Defense. 2. Dishonorable Discharge. "He got five years in Leavenworth and a DD." 3. A much less frequently used version of *dee dee*, which see. 4. See *Donald Duck*.

D-day (World War I to Modern) The cover name for the actual date on which a major military operation is to begin. (See *H-hour*.) The plans for such an operation are prepared well in advance, but the day and hour on which it starts are not announced, for obvious security reasons, until the last possible minute. Therefore, plans and preliminary orders state that the operation will begin at H-hour on D-day and that certain actions will be taken on D-day plus or minus a certain number of days. The term may be remembered better than the actual date; thus, the World War II landing in Normandy is frequently recalled as *D-day* rather than as 6 June 1944.

D-day dodger (World War II and thereafter) *s.* Anyone who was not present at the Allied landing in Normandy, 6 June 1944. The epithet was invented by the comparative handful who were there. Americans and Britons who had been across North Africa and Sicily and up the boot of Italy, including the Salerno and Anzio landings, naturally retorted, "Which D-day do you mean?" They even had an ironic song, "They Call Us the D-day Dodgers."

deadbeat (Mexican War to Modern) *s.* A worthless soldier, always dirty and usually trying to play sick. The term has carried on into present military and civilian speech with much the same meaning, plus the specific implication of financial irresponsibility.

deadhead (At least as early as World War II, to Modern; all Services) *s.* Probably from a civilian term in trucking and shipping. 1. The return flight of a transport aircraft without payload. 2. A ride on an aircraft making such a flight.

deadhead, to *s.* To fly on a deadhead. "I'm going to try to deadhead back to the States."

deadline (Especially Civil War) A line around the perimeter of a military prison, inside its fence, which prisoners were forbidden to cross. As at Andersonville, a prisoner who put even a hand or foot across it would be immediately shot by the guards. Its purpose was to prevent prisoners from suddenly rushing the prison enclosure in attempts to escape.

deadline, to (World War II to Modern) *s.* To take a motor vehicle (or sometimes a radio set or similar piece of complex equipment) out of service for needed repairs. In keeping with peacetime Army ways, such items are *deadlined*—lined up neatly—until the grease monkeys can get them fixed.

dead soldier (Probably quite old) *s.* An empty liquor bottle.

Dear John (World War II to Modern) 1. *s.* A letter from *the* girl at home, telling you that she has met an essential civilian with a fat paycheck. It did not happen in the Old Army. *They* didn't know anyone back home or, if they did, probably had joined the Army to escape them. The company mail usually could be carried in the company clerk's shirt pocket. 2. *s.* Reserve officers on active duty also called the official letter terminating their services a *Dear John.*

Death Factory (World War II) *s.* Hürtgen Forest, Germany. A bloody, freezing battlefield during November-December 1944.

dee dee di di DD (Vietnam and later; all Services) *s.* Short for *dee dee mau,* from Vietnamese *đi mau* 'to go quickly'. " 'Di di' means 'get outa here' and 'di di Mao' means 'get the fuck out of here' " (Haldeman). Also a dishonorable discharge.

deep kimchi, to be in (Korea and later; also Air Force) *s.* To be in serious trouble, synonymous with *to be in deep shit.* Widely used in Korea by Americans stationed there, Korean service veterans, and the general Army population, which has picked up the expression by diffusion. The expression is reinforced by the almost universal American dislike for kimchi. See *kimchi.*

deep shit, to be in (World War II and on) *s.* To be in serious trouble. "Boys, as you can see, we're in deep shit up to our necks" (Marshall, 1969). Similarly, *deep shit up to our ears, deep shit up to our knees,* etc.

dekko (World War I, revived in World War II, and still lingers) *s.* *To take a dekko* is Indian Army British for *to look around* (from Hindustani *dekhna* 'to look'; imperative form, *dekho*). One of those handy words picked up to give the impression that the speaker is an old hand who knows his way around England and its former empire "east of Suez." Do not believe him. Be dubious of even an Englishman given to studiously casual employment of such words.

deliberate disobedience (Ancient through World War II) Doing something after you have been told not to do just that. In the unenlightened days of old, this was certain to get you severe punishment, perhaps capital.

deliver ordnance, to (Modern) To bomb and/or shell.

delousing (World War II) *s.* Clearing an area of enemy mines and booby traps, a detail that could be as risky as driving the enemy out of it in the first place.

DEML (World War II) Detached Enlisted Men's List. An organization of men not assigned to other units, usually doing administrative work in post headquarters and similar jobs.

deploy, to 1. (Ancient to Modern; also Navy, Marines) To spread troops or ships out of column into line or battle formation. For example, a Civil War brigade advancing down a road would deploy its regiments into line of battle on coming into contact with a considerable enemy force. Each regimental commander would order one or more of his companies to deploy as skirmishers—a loose, open formation—to feel out the enemy position. The term is still proper, but no longer so much a matter of infantry close-order drill. 2. (Modern; all Services) Of a parachute, to open up fully in midair.

DEROS /'deer-rose/ (Modern) *s.* Date Eligible for Return from Overseas. "The Vietnamese soldier has no DEROS" (Mulligan).

DEROS blues syndrome (Modern) *s.* A psychological disorder from which some personnel suffered during the Vietnam War. The syndrome consisted of depression stemming from long-term tension and stress, as a result of suppressed uncertainties and anxieties. It was characterized by a desire to "escape." See *DEROS*.

desecrated vegetables (Civil War; USA) *s.* Desiccated vegetables, a mixture of carrots, beets, onions, string beans, cabbage, and other garden truck that had been shredded, scalded, dehydrated, and compressed into sheets and bales. This was intended to be used in stews and soups when fresh vegetables were not available, but it gave the effect of a kettle of dried leaves, and soldiers did not like it. Also called *bailed hay*.

desert stove (World War II; North Africa) *s.* A small hole dug in the ground and half-filled with water topped with gasoline; used for heating C-rations. It could also remove your eyebrows and forelock if you added too much gasoline. Another version was an empty No. 10 can partly filled with sand so that the gasoline would burn more slowly.

desk-drawer letter (Modern) *s.* An official letter of reprimand intended to fulfill a commander or supervisor's obligation to punish a soldier for some misdeed, but not intended to become a part of his official file—thereby saving the soldier from permanent stigma. A letter of this kind is intended to be kept in a desk drawer for a time and then destroyed, if the soldier behaves.

desk-top leave (Modern) *s.* Leave charged against a soldier's account, but not taken because he comes to work anyway. This may be out of "devotion" to duty or because of a summons back to attend to some problem. Literally, leave taken at one's desk. See *flagpole leave, pocket leave.*

dessert cutter (West Point) The plebe at each table responsible for seeing that all desserts that require cutting are sliced into the appropriate number of pieces. The dessert cutter sits opposite the gunner. See *cold-beverage corporal, hot-beverage corporal.*

detach, to (Ancient to Modern; all Services) To send off or detail military units, ships, or individuals from their normal assignment for a special mission or duty. A serviceman who is detached from his unit in this fashion is called *on detached service (DS).*

detached volunteers (Civil War; USA) A method of replacement used during the Civil War. Because of an ineffective replacement system, batteries in the field (especially the Regular batteries) were seriously understrength and could not replace their casualties. Generals therefore resorted to the time-honored practice of detaching infantrymen from their regiments for temporary service as artillerymen. This practice was never very successful, infantry colonels too often detailing the men they best could spare, but for lack of anything better it continued until the end of the war.

detachment (Ancient to Modern; all Services) A number of troops, ships, or aircraft detached for a special duty or mission. In the Army, a detachment may be made up of individuals or of small units from several larger organizations. The term is often loosely used, however, and it can mean any small unit operating at some distance from its main body.

detail (At least 17th century) A job, the assignment of men to it, the actual list of names (read by the first sergeant and/or posted on the bulletin board) of men assigned, and the men themselves. Men are *detailed* to the garbage *detail,* which means both the work to be done and the group of men doing it. Officers get *detailed,* too—usually "in addition to" their ordinary duties. Army life is full of *details*—guard, KP, and especially fatigue. That fact is recorded in one verse of an Old Army song: "All the tail we get is detail." The term comes, via the British, from the French verb *detailler* 'to cut up' in the sense of dividing duties. An interesting early American use is to be found in George Washington's Order of 14 March 1780: "The fatigue party for finishing the new orderly room is to be furnished by detail from the line of the army."

det cord (Modern) *s.* Short for *detonation cord,* used with explosives. " 'Det cord, detonation cord.' Looked just like plastic clothesline" (Haldeman).

deuce-and-a-half (World War II and later) *s.* The 2½-ton truck. In its six-by-six type, it was big, heavy, mechanically complex, but rugged, roomy, and able to move cross-country over an amazing variety of terrain. As lend-lease in World War II, it gave the Russian 1944–45 offensives their decisive mobility—quite possibly another outstanding example of our national shortsightedness.

device for incinerating seven brothers (World War II) A Russian nickname for the US M3 (General Lee) medium tank. (A token of Russian appreciation for our lend-lease.) It was a big target, and its gasoline engine made it far more likely to catch fire than were the diesel-powered Russian tanks.

Devil's Article (Old Army) *s.* Article 99 of the *Articles of War* in force at that time. It punished "disorders and neglects . . . to prejudice of . . . order and military discipline." It was a legal catchall designed to take care of the cagey offender who could not be pinned down by the more specific articles and an excellent way of dealing with the useless and genuinely undesirable. For that reason, it was considered a crime by progressive legal eagles.

Dextrose Joe (World War II) The Chindit's (British deep-penetration forces operating in Burma) nickname for Lt. Gen. Joseph Stilwell, known to Americans as Vinegar Joe. Undoubtedly an example of the nearly impenetrable British sense of humor.

dhobi dhobi-wallah (World War II) *s.* A laundryman. A borrowing from Anglo-Indian talk.

DI (Immediately after World War I; AEF) A member of the DCI; also, a drill instructor.

diamond (Vietnam) *s.* The one good, gallant, or lucky idea, deed, or happenstance amid the universal crud and squalor. A catchphrase goes, "It shines like a diamond in a goat's ass."

diamond, to get the (Antiquity uncertain, to Modern) *s.* To be appointed first sergeant. The diamond (or lozenge) has been the insignia of the company first sergeant since 1847.

Diarrhoea Rangers Diarrhoea Blues (Mexican War) *s.* Troops suffering from aggravated cases of Montezuma's revenge or other debilitating sicknesses who were left behind as part of the garrisons of Veracruz and (especially) Puebla during Gen. Winfield Scott's advance on Mexico City.

dice (World War II; Air Force) *s.* A fast, low-level fight over an important area, usually for photoreconnaissance. Probably from British RAF slang, where *dicey* meant *chancy, dangerous,* and where a dangerous mission could be called a *dicer.*

diddly shit (Modern) *s.* Worthlessness. "One of the few men . . . worthy of that most uncommon of military distinctions: a diddly shit" (Suddick).

diddly squat (Modern) *s.* Worthlessness. Absolutely nothing. "You don't know diddly squat."

ding, to (Modern) *s.* To shoot, to wound, to kill. "Dingin' gooks with my forty-five" (Heinemann). Although the term is fairly recent among military personnel, there is a comparable archaic or dialectic word *to ding*, meaning *to knock down*: "Which pauncht his horse and dinged him to the ground" (Thomas Kyd, *The Spanish Tragedie* [1592]).

dingdong (Modern) *s.* A stupid person.

dining facility manager (Modern) A neologism for the older and better-known mess sergeant. Army image-makers, ignorant of the etymology of the word *mess*, coined this phrase to "clean up" the image of the ancient respectable mess sergeant.

dining in (Intermittent) A formal gathering of officers or NCOs of a unit to share a meal in comfortable surroundings and foster bonds of friendship, loyalty, and esprit, by paying tribute to a unit's current or past achievements. This sort of ceremonial occasion was popular in the Army up to the time of World War II, but it died out in the postwar years and is only beginning to come back into fashion. In the British Commonwealth armies, however, dining in is a respectable and long-established military custom.

dining-room orderly *See DRO.*

dink (Modern; all Services) *s.* A derogatory term for a Vietnamese. The earliest known ethnic application of *dink* seems to have been in Australia, in the 1920s, where it meant a Chinese. It has been explained as rhyming slang for *Chink* or as a portmanteau word for *damned Chink*. It is not known whether the term died out in Australia, but it appeared in Vietnam during the Vietnam War. Several explanations have been offered for this later manifestation: (1) From *dinky*, American colloquial for something small, trivial, and cheap—a description that, in the minds of many soldiers, aptly suited the peoples of Southeast Asia. Americans in Vietnam often did consider the natives small and backward, except when they were armed, when they suddenly became brilliant strategists and determined fighters. (2) From *rinky-dink* for cheap, tawdry junk. "Suits 'em just perfect, rinky-dink. 'Cept that was too long, so we cut it down some and that's why we call 'em dinks" (Herr). (3) Short for Vietnamese *điên cài đầu* 'crazy head', which was very quickly picked up as pidgin *dinky dow* by American troops. Our sergeant major first heard it in shortened form as *dink*, in 1962, as a nickname for his unit's Vietnamese day-room orderly. The orderly's favorite expression was "You dien cai dau, GI!" Later this became a frequently heard expression, used by the Viets toward us and among ourselves. (4) From a Vietnamese word or phrase meaning a "hairy man from the jungle," first applied by the Vietnamese to us and then applied by us back to them. "It turned out that the enemy started calling us 'dinks' first . . . at least, that was the story" (Downs). (5) From a derogatory term of sexual origin. Read points out that *dink* is a reduction of *do-dinkus* for the penis. This meaning could subliminally reinforce the derogatory connotation of the word, especially among American males, where to call someone "a little prick" is to poke fun at his sexual adequacy. According to our standards, the average Vietnamese is not a very macho figure. Our sergeant major has never heard the term applied to anyone but a Vietnamese; this suggests that no matter what its origin, dink is very strongly linked to *dinky dow*.

dinky dow (Vietnam and later) *s.* Crazy, insane. See *dink*.

dip (Vietnam and later) *s.* Short for *dipshit*, another derogatory ethnicism for the Vietnamese. See also *dink, gook*.

direct exchange A wartime system of free clothing issue. When an organization comes out of the line, soldiers can exchange their torn, dirty clothing for new.

direct order An order given by an officer in person.

Dirty Gertie from Bizerte (World War II) The first of the Army's antiheroines, encountered during the North African Campaign. She

Hid a mousetrap 'neath her skirty,
Baited it with fleur-de-flirty,
Made her boy friends' fingers hurty.

Things did not improve when the troops moved on into Italy. There they met *Filthy Annie from Tripani* or some such place.

dirty officer (Modern) *s.* A play on *duty officer*. See *sheriff*.

Dirty Shirts (War of 1812) *s.* American frontier militia or volunteers, who usually were "uniformed" in hunting shirts. Specifically, those who came down from Kentucky and Tennessee to help Andrew Jackson defend New Orleans in late 1814. The name—undoubtedly accurate, if derogatory—probably was of British origin, but was proudly adopted by the Americans.

discharge stick (World War II to Modern) *s.* A crutch. If you are disabled enough to need a crutch, you will probably be discharged.

disciplinary barracks Military correctional facilities today have the mission of rehabilitating their inmates, either for return to duty or to civilian life. Minor offenders are confined in the SPC (Special Processing Company) or the stockade (euphemistically called the "personnel control facility" in today's Army) of the post where they are stationed or of the organization to which they are assigned. Prisoners convicted of serious offenses by a general court-martial are incarcerated in a US disciplinary barracks, the oldest and best-known of which is at Fort Leavenworth, Kansas. (The term *military prison* has not been used since 1915.) Another well-known facility is the Naval Retraining Command at Portsmouth, New Hampshire. In times of war, these are supplemented by various types of disciplinary training centers, detention centers, and rehabilitation centers designed to retrain military offenders sufficiently to fit them for combat duty. Also called *Big 8, Box 3, Box 13, Crossbar Hotel, Crowbar Hotel, Drawers, L.B.J., Screenhouse, Wire City,* etc.

dishpan helmet (World War I, World War II) *s.* The wide-brimmed shallow helmet worn in World War I and the early days of World War II. Also called *pie pan helmet.*

Disneyland East (Modern) 1. *s.* The Military Assistance Command Headquarters complex, formerly at Tan Son Nhut Air Base, Saigon, from which Gen. William C. Westmoreland and Gen. Creighton W. Abrams directed operations in Southeast Asia from 1967 on. 2. *s.* The Pentagon Building, in Washington, D.C. 3. *s.* Any one of a number of sprawling business enterprises existing in the vicinity of American base camps in South Vietnam. It was originally applied to the complex of bars and bordellos that sprang up around An Khe, the base camp of the 1st Air Cavalry Division, and was sometimes called *Sin City* or *An Khe Plaza.* Initially, at any rate, the sky troopers could purchase a short time for from $2.50 to $5.

Distinguished Flying Cross DFC (1926 on) An award established in 1926, which may be conferred in both peace and war to military personnel who perform acts of heroism in the face of great danger. It ranks just below the Legion of Merit and just above the Soldier's Medal. Enlisted personnel awarded this decoration who retire after twenty years or more of service may be awarded a 10 percent increase in their base pay.

Distinguished Service Cross DSC (1918 on) The second highest Army decoration for valor, bestowed in recognition of extraordinary heroism in connection with military operations in time of war. Enlisted personnel awarded this decoration who retire after twenty years or more of service may be awarded a 10 percent increase in their base pay.

Distinguished Service Medal DSM (1918 on) Awarded to any person who, while serving in any capacity with the Army, distinguishes himself by outstandingly meritorious service. It ranks just above the Silver Star.

ditch (Civil War; CSA) *s.* The Confederate soldier's usual term for *trench.*

Ditch Big Ditch *s.* The Panama Canal, constructed and made safe from yellow fever by US engineer and medical officers under Col. George Goethals and Col. William C. Gorgas.

ditch, to (World War I to Modern; Air Force and Navy) *s.* To bring a land-based plane down on a body of water. The British also term it a "hard landing."

ditty bag (All Services) A small cloth bag with drawstrings, generally used for holding toilet articles and small items of various sorts. Originally a naval term, but now known to all services. (The etymology of the word has been disputed, with suggestions for its source running from native Australian languages through Hindustani and dialect English.) Specifically, the ditty bags containing razor blades, toothpaste, soap, paperback books, and similar objects distributed free by the Red Cross to soldiers in Vietnam. "They distributed 1232 ditty bags" (Bunting).

division An administrative and tactical unit that is smaller than a corps but is self-contained and equipped to conduct prolonged combat operations. It usually consists of two or more brigades and is commanded by a major general.

dobe-wall, to (19th century through World War I) *s.* To stand someone up against an adobe wall and shoot him. An expression from the Southwest frontier. Apparently no longer used.

dobie itch (Philippine Insurrection through the 1930s) *s.* A skin irritation caused by mites. (There are variant spellings.) The victim scratches and a secondary infection may follow. American medics were not prepared for such unpleasant effects from our new tropical empire. The term probably covered several different afflictions. Some marines remember it as a ringworm type of fungus and believe it was spread by infected laundry, whence the association with the Anglo-Indian *dhobie*. Whatever it was, it certainly made a lot of Americans wish they were back home. Oddly enough, we cannot recall any trouble with it in the 1946–47 Philippine Scouts.

Dr. Spock's Army Dr. Spock's generation Spock's Army (Modern; probably other Services) *s.* Rightly or wrongly, or with partial justice, veteran officers and NCOs blamed the child-rearing theories of Dr. Benjamin Spock for the mental attitude of the recruits and draftees of the late 1950s and 1960s. It was difficult to convince these soldiers that frustration, hardship, and danger could be the common lot of mankind or that their "constitutional rights" did not include doing just what they wanted to do exactly when they wanted to do it. Probably Spock's performance as an anti-Vietnam War activist reinforced the veteran officers' low opinion of Spock the pediatrician.

dodo (Probably dating from World War I; Air Force) *s.* Any nonflying Air Force personnel, whether a pilot trainee who has not yet flown solo, a qualified pilot who has decided that it is safer to fly a swivel chair, or an airman who wants to fly but has been drafted into a desk job.

DOG (Early 20th century to Modern) *s.* Disgruntled Old Grad. A graduate, age immaterial, of the US Military Academy who is positive that the place is going to the dogs and does not want any more newfangled changes. Every so often, we suspect, he is right.

dog-and-pony show (Modern; all Services) 1. *s.* A briefing conducted with slides and viewgraphs or simply a briefing, whether or not visual aids are employed. 2. *s.* Any formal, elaborate occasion.

"Doesn't mean that they can't recognize Christmas, but no dog-and-pony show" (Groom).

dog biscuit (World War I; probably still around) Hardtack.

dogface (Pre–World War II to Modern) *s.* An infantryman. Probably from the unshaven, hangdog appearance of the combat infantryman's face when he is suffering from the physical and mental exhaustion of combat. The term is exclusively an Americanism. It gained wide popularity in World War II, although it was in use in the Army at least as early as 1935 ("Service Humor," ANJ 72:10, 9 November 1935). In this citation, it is used as a familiar term, without emphasis, indicating that it was common enough in the services that its meaning was understood. There is a diminutive, *doggie*, which Heinl lists as a Marine Corps word for an Army infantryman.

dogfight (World War I to Modern; all Services) *s.* An engagement between airplanes; it originally referred to only two planes, but later, to large numbers.

doghouse (Indian Wars to the 1930s) *s.* A pup tent.

dog robber (Civil War to Modern; also Marines) *s.* An expression of disapproval, obviously of American origin. Apparently it was first a Civil War term for a cook (particularly one for a small, informal mess) or for a camp follower who helped with cooking and other chores. During the late 1860s the term was applied to the cooks and orderlies assigned to an officers' mess. As a major perquisite they were permitted to devour all leftovers, supposedly leaving nothing for a hungry dog. Thus, *dog robber* easily became the enlisted man's name for an officer's personal orderly or striker. Today, with only general officers having "enlisted aides," *dog robber* is degenerating into a name for a scrounger or sycophant, enlisted or officer. In the old Marine Corps, officers at least used both *dog robber* and *striker*. The term *dog robber* was also applied to the company clerk. See also *bunk boy*.

Dog Soldiers (Indian Wars) One of the military societies found among the Plains Indian tribes. Such societies acted—usually in turn—as camp police and controlled the great buffalo hunts and the migrations. They were particularly important among the Cheyennes, where they formed a separate village of the tribe's finest warriors. Always hostile to the whites, they were finally surprised and broken at Summit Springs, Colo., in 1869.

dog tags (1906 to Modern) *s.* At present, two noncorrosive metal identity tags worn around the neck, indicating the wearer's name, blood type, Social Security number, and religious preference, if any. Dog tags, which were first prescribed in 1906, have changed considerably over the years. The earliest tags, which were issued free to enlisted men and at cost to officers, were round and about the size and thickness of a half dollar. They indicated the soldier's name, rank, and organization. Serial numbers were later added, while rank and organization were dropped. For a time during World War II the dog tag indicated next of kin, but this practice was discontinued when the Germans began to release false casualty data to the relatives of captured soldiers. In case of death, one tag was left on the body, the other attached to the grave marker, hence the World War II prayer "May my dog tags never be separated." During World War I, according to Fraser and Gibbons, American troops referred to their dog tags as *mermaid's visiting cards*, an allusion to possible attack and sinking by German submarines while troops were en route to Europe. The term *dog tag* is related to the metal license tab worn by a dog. The official term is *identification tag*.

dog tent (Civil War) *s.* An early name for the pup tent or shelter half, supposedly applied because, when pitched, it "would only comfortably accommodate a dog and a small one at that."

do it or have it done, I will (Modern) *s.* A catchphrase meaning that the speaker is positive he can do the job. "Sergeant, will you please have this typed for me?" "Sir, I'll do it or have it done!"

don (Spanish-American War) *s.* A Spaniard. Probably used more in the newspapers than by the troops.

Donald Duck DD (World War II and later) *s.* A facetious expansion of the initials *DD*, which stand for *duplex drive*, a feature of Sherman tanks modified for amphibious operations. A tank would be fitted with a flotation collar to give it added buoyancy and with two propellers to drive it through the water at approximately five miles an hour. Once the tank was ashore, the collar was lowered and the propellers were disconnected and swung up out of the way. These Donald Ducks rendered valuable service during the Normandy landings in June 1944.

donkey dick 1. (Since World War II, but probably earlier in origin, when donkeys were more commonly seen) *s.* Sliced salami, bologna, or other cold cuts. Probably so called from the resemblance of a whole sausage to the animal's penis. Such cold cuts were once staples at Sunday suppers. The quality of the meat was often inferior—salty, tasteless—and this may have encouraged some soldiers to speculate on its origin. See *horse parts*. 2. (Modern) *s.* The cable or cables connecting a tactical vehicle (jeep, truck) to its trailer.

donkey shern (Modern; also Air Force) *s.* A play on German *danke schön* 'thank you'.

Donovan's Dragoons (World War II) A name given by Army staff officers to Col. William "Wild Bill" Donovan's Office of Strategic Services, better known as the *OSS*. Operating very much on its own hook, the OSS had its nose, two left feet, and eleven greasy thumbs in everyone else's business and contributed vastly to the general confusion. Sometimes, not entirely by accident, it even confused the enemy.

Don't call me sir! (Modern) A rejoinder when one enlisted soldier inadvertently or facetiously addresses another as "sir," the salutation reserved for officers. The implication is that officers do not work for their pay. "Don't call me sir! Ah work for a livin' " (Doulis).

Don't rock the sampan! (Vietnam; all Services) *s.* An updated version of the ancient *Don't rock the boat!* Another, somewhat older, version is *Don't make waves!*

Don't shit the troops! (Modern) *s.* A catchphrase, probably of British origin, equivalent to *Don't lie to me* or *Don't kid me*. Partridge (1970) notes that this expression has been in use in Great Britain since about 1920.

donut dollies doughnut dollies (Vietnam; all Services) *s.* American Red Cross volunteers who operated Clubmobiles in the Vietnam War theater during 1965–72. More than 600 college-age women served in this program, providing American soldiers with coffee, confections, and sympathy. They deserve unstinted praise for their courage and self-sacrifice. It was commonly believed among enlisted men that these women extended special sexual favors to the officers. Also called *biscuit bitches*.

Doodle From the song "Yankee Doodle." 1. (War of 1812) *s.* A British nickname for American soldiers. 2. (Civil War; CSA) *s.* A Confederate nickname for US troops, as in

Hark! The Doodles have broken loose,
Roaring 'round like the very deuce!

doodlebug (World War II) 1. *s.* A German "self-propelled mine." A small, remote-controlled, full-tracked vehicle carrying a large explosive charge, it was used against the Anglo-American positions at Anzio. Overexcited people called them *robot tanks*, but they were not tanks and they certainly were not robots. 2. *s.* American tanks or reconnaissance vehicles; applied variously early in the war. The term seemingly met an early death through neglect.

doodlesack dudelsack (Colonial to Revolutionary) Bagpipes. From Dutch *doedelzak* or German *Dudelsack*.

dope off, to (Modern) *s.* To fuck off. Soldiers tend to say *fuck off*, but *dope off* may be used if the circumstances or company present requires gentler speech.

double-digit midget See *two-digit fidget*.

double Pfc (Old Army to pre-Modern) *s.* A corporal has two stripes. From 1920 to 1965 a Pfc had a single stripe. Since 1965 the chevron of a Pfc is a stripe and an arc.

double-slotted kitchen mechanics (Modern; all Services) *s.* Women, since the female body has two "slots." A disparaging reference to the stereotyped role of the woman as housewife, not much good for anything else.

doughboy (Mexican War to Modern, especially World War I and a little later) 1. *s.* An infantryman. This is the nickname par excellence. The earliest known citation is from 1859, with reference to the Mexican War: "No man of any spirit and ambition would join the 'doughboys' and go afoot when he can ride a fine horse and wear spurs like a gentleman" (Chamberlain). The origin of the term is not known, although there are many theories. First, the term is related to *doughboy*, a dumplinglike item made of flour or corn meal, sometimes baked in the ashes of a camp fire. This is related to the infantryman because it was a favorite dish of his; because it resembled the spherical buttons worn by soldiers; and because, when baked in ashes, it resembled the mud-encrusted feet of the infantryman. Second, *doughboy* has been related to *adobe* (commonly pronounced *'dobe*), either because soldiers in the Southwest spent much time in making adobe bricks or because they lived relatively comfortably in adobe buildings. Another theory relates *doughboy* to the doughlike appearances of the pipe clay used as a whitener on the soldiers' belts. In damp weather this clay would become sticky and doughy. Fourth, when the infantryman slogged through mud, his feet would become encased in doughy masses. This last theory fits in with other nicknames of the infantryman. 2. *s.* Any American soldier, but particularly (and then often capitalized) a member of the AEF in World War I and shortly thereafter. During this period certain journalists, notably those of *Stars and Stripes*, tried to force the use of *doughboy* as a general term for an

American soldier, paralleling *Tommy* for the British and *poilu* for the French. The campaign was not successful, although one may still refer to any soldier of the AEF as a *Doughboy*.

doughboy captain (World War I) *s.* A captain of the AEF who was not wearing his insignia of rank or officers' accoutrements. It was common enough in combat for officers to conceal their rank in order to escape snipers.

doughfoot (Probably World War I and later) *s.* Another term for the infantryman, probably because of the mud that often encrusts his feet.

dovetails (Modern) *s.* WAC (or women) second lieutenants.

DOW (20th century) Died Of Wounds.

downhill (Roughly World War II) *s.* Refers to the last part of an enlistment, when you are really over the hump and have only a short butt left. The opposite is *uphill.*

down range 1. In rifle-range terminology, in the direction of the targets. 2. Colloquially, in the line of fire, verbal or otherwise.

dozo (Occupation of Japan and later; all Services) The Japanese word for *please*; not infrequently used as a reply to a threat. Its use continued on into civilian life.

DR (Modern) Delinquency Report. A report submitted by the MPs concerning infractions of regulations or military laws: traffic violations, uniform violations, minor misdeeds. "I see you do this again and I'll issue you a 'Delinquency Report,' a ticket" (Heinemann).

Drachen (World World I) *s.* A German observation balloon, from its German designation, *Drache* 'dragon'.

draft Selection of men for compulsory military service. Until the Civil War, the United States relied upon militia, volunteers, and small Regular Army forces. In April 1862 the Confederacy instituted the first draft; this was followed by the Union in March 1863. Neither system worked well. In World War I it was again necessary to resort to a draft, and in May 1917, the Selective Service Act was passed. In 1940, before the United States entered World War II, the draft was reinstituted. Actual drafting came to an end in 1973, and the law was allowed to lapse in 1975. At present (1983) certain classes of men are being registered, but conscription is not talking place.

draft bait (World War II) *s.* Anyone liable to be conscripted in the near future.

draft dodger (World War I to Modern) *s.* A person who seeks to evade the draft. The technique may vary from trying to talk your way out of it to hiding in your mother's attic for thirty years.

drag 1. (Modern) *s.* The rear security element of a convoy. 2. (Since about 1939; West Point) *s.* A date. See *drag, to* 1.

drag, to 1. (At least as early as 1900; West Point) *s.* To escort, to accompany, to bring, to carry. The earliest meaning is to escort a young woman to a hop or other social event. *Drag* has come to refer to the woman herself; thus, one's drag is one's date. 2. (1920s) *s.* To apply water, shoe polish, or the like to the head of a deserving cadet, such as a recently appointed cadet officer.

Dragon Lady (Vietnam; all Services) 1. *s.* A female Vietcong terrorist who assassinated several persons in the streets of Saigon and Cholon in 1967. The name was applied to her by the Vietnamese press. 2. *s.* Madame Ngo Dinh Nhu, the sister-in-law of President Ngo Dinh Diem of South Vietnam (assassinated in November 1963). A person of considerable influence in the Vietnamese government, she received much publicity in the American press for her various moral crusades. The nickname came from the very popular comic strip "Terry and the Pirates," in which the Dragon Lady (whom Madame Nhu resembled physically) was a ruthless, bloodthirsty female pirate who roamed the China Seas. See also *ACAV, Can do, Madame Nhu.*

dragon ship (Vietnam; all Services) *s.* A transport plane, originally the C-47, but later, a larger aircraft, converted into a gunship by arming it with Vulcan guns (electric-powered Gatling guns). It was employed against enemy ground forces, its tremendous firepower enabling it to shred jungle positions. Also called *Puff, the Magic Dragon.*

dragoon (17th century to Civil War) Originally, as in European armies, an infantryman mounted on a light nag for greater mobility. Dragoons fought on foot and were considered a separate arm, whence the old saying "Horse, foot, artillery, and dragoons," meaning everyone. The word *dragoon* is derived from *dragon*, the name of a short musket or carbine that such troops originally carried. By the middle of the 18th century, the dragoon had evolved into conventional cavalry, with little or no capability of dismounted action. The two "dragoon" regiments added to the US Army in 1833 and 1836 were dragoons in name only. Although capable of dismounted action in an emergency, they relied primarily on their sabers and on shock action. In 1861, these two regiments were redesignated the 1st and 2d Cavalry Regiments.

drawers (Modern) *s.* Mailing addresses for prisoners in the US Disciplinary Barracks, Fort Leavenworth, Kansas, as in *Drawer A45.*

drawing over the left (Civil War; USA) *s.* Stealing. Other terms were *gobbling* and *raiding. Draw* is used in the sense of *drawing rations or supplies.*

dream sheet (Modern) *s.* Either DA Form 483 (Officer Assignment Preference Statement) or DA Form 2635 (Enlisted Preference Statement). These forms are filled out periodically (especially just before returning from an overseas tour) to aid personnel managers to match an individual's preference for an assignment to positions available for his grade and specialty. The options include geographical areas as well as type of duty. Since anyone seldom gets what he or she wants, these are widely referred to as *dream sheets.* According to a popular theory, the career-manglement boys throw these forms at the ceiling. Those that stick are considered; the rest go into File 13.

dress, to (Colonial to Modern) To form a straight line in rank (left to right). The commands are *Dress right!* or *Dress left!* at which the soldier turns his head and eyes and straightens the line, each man in relation to the man on his right or left. Space between soldiers is determined by placing the left hand on the hip, elbow out, and adjusting so that each soldier barely touches his neighbor. This can later be adjusted visually. A soldier who is not on line will be told, "Dress, up, there!"

Dress Blues and tennis shoes, to wear (Modern) *s.* A catchphrase meaning to be dressed up, to be in faultless attire. "I'll be there wearing my Dress Blues and tennis shoes."

dressing station field dressing station (Early 19th century through World War I) A medical station immediately behind troops engaged in combat, where the wounded had their wounds dressed by medical personnel. First-aid treatment, especially in World War I, came first.

dress parade A ceremony in which soldiers in dress uniforms take formation under arms.

dress uniform The uniform authorized for wear at social, ceremonial, and official occasions. Dress uniforms are the Army Blue, White, White Mess, Blue Mess, and Evening Mess uniforms. The Army Green uniform may be worn only by enlisted personnel when specifically authorized by a commander. Sometimes called *full-dress uniform.*

drill (Modern) *s.* Short for *drill sergeant.* "A posse of male drills was waiting as the trainees stepped cautiously from the bus" (Rogan).

drill sergeant A noncom selected to train recruits in the basic skills of soldiering. He is authorized to wear the campaign hat and the Drill Sergeant Identification Badge. The position of drill sergeant still exists, but the term itself has been discontinued.

Drive it into the hanger! (World War II; Air Force) *s.* Shut up! and/or Change the subject! Like the civilian *Put it into a paper bag!*

driver (Modern) *s.* An aircraft pilot. "I want to tell you about the Thud drivers" (Broughton).

DRO (Old Army to Modern) 1. Dining-Room Orderly. The detail of looking after the mess hall. A cushy job for a KP; his duties, depending on the custom of the outfit, may include keeping the room clean, filling salt and pepper shakers, setting places, refilling empty serving dishes, bringing bread, and filling juice pitchers. He is usually picked from among the first men to arrive at the mess hall for KP in the morning, but if the mess sergeant or the first cook (an irascible and narrow-minded breed of man) is feeling capricious, the DRO may just as easily be selected from the last to report for duty. Occasionally, for one reason or another, the DRO may be an unofficial semipermanent detail. The term *dining-room orderly* is unusual in being the only situation in which EM use the term *dining room* in preference to *mess hall.* 2. Day-Room Orderly. The enlisted man detailed to keep the company or unit day room neat and orderly.

drop 1. (Modern) *s.* A curtailment of an overseas tour, perhaps because of a reduction in the length of the tour or of the size of the forces deployed. "I got a thirty day drop." 2. (World War II to Modern) The delivery of troops, supplies, and/or equipment by parachute in one action. "We'll get a supply drop after dark."

Drop your cocks and grab your socks! (At least World War II, to Modern) *s.* Get out of bed! A favorite chant of first sergeants, barracks sergeants, or charge-of-quarters personnel.

drop your laundry, to (World War II and later) *s.* To prepare for sex.

drumming-out An ancient ceremony—probably based on the medieval degradation of an unworthy knight—associated with a dishonorable discharge for such serious offenses as theft, desertion, or cowardice. (In the Old Army a barracks thief was lucky to survive the judgment of his peers long enough to be drummed out.) After a culprit was thoroughly flogged, his head was shaved, his buttons and insignia cut away, and a placard stating his offense hung around his neck. In extreme cases, he might be branded, for example with a *D* for *deserter*. This done, he was marched under guard to the post boundary, while the field music played "The Rogue's March" and the other troops turned their backs on him.

Tarred and feathered and sent to hell,
Because he wouldn't soldier well.

After 1861, flogging and branding were forbidden, although there may have been isolated incidents during the Indian Wars. Drumming out lasted until at least the end of the 19th century.

drum out, to To expel from the service.

dry run (Late World War I to Modern) 1. On beginning rifle target practice, a session in which the targets were exposed for the regulation time while the shooters went through the motions of firing "with nothing in the barrel." 2. *s.* By extension, any sort of rehearsal or practice period. As CCB, 8th Armored Division, went up the gangplank somewhere in New York harbor in late 1944, a plaintive voice sounded out of the night, "This dry run is getting too damn wet!" 3. (World War II at least) *s.* Coitus reservatus.

DS Detached Service Duty away from one's own organization. "I'm on DS as an umpire with the Carolina maneuvers."

duck (Probably World War I to Modern) *s.* A small portable urinal, in shape something like a duck decoy, used in hospitals, hospital trains, and similar situations. The term is also in civilian use.

duck (World War I, World War II, and later) *s.* Various amphibian vehicles, such as any amphibious plane or any amphibious tank. Especially, in World War II and later, the DUKW, a 2½-ton amphibian truck, used in landing operations and river crossings.

duck (Old Army) *s.* Probably short for *deduct*. A small sum deducted from a soldier's pay for some form of jawbone purchase. Usually there were several such ducks against his name on the company collection sheet. As one soldier said of his pay, "De ducks done got it."

duck bills (World War II) *s.* Extended metal track grousers added to the tracks of US tanks to increase their width and so improve flotation in marshy ground and deep mud. Until duck bills were added, our tanks often bogged down in terrain through which the heavier, but better-designed, German tanks moved easily.

duckboards (World War I to Modern; also Marines) *s.* An openwork wooden walkway to keep one's feet out of the wet or the mud. When you see duckboards in a trench, you know that you either are in a training area or are going to change sectors soon. If you see them in a camp, you know that you either are in the division CP area or are going to leave soon. Sometimes used indoors in shower rooms or sink areas.

ducks in line, to get [one's] (Modern) *s.* To straighten out one's affairs or thinking. "It takes me that long to get my ducks in line or work out my own data plane" (Marshall, 1979).

Duckworth Chant (World War II to Modern) *s.* Another name for *Sound off!* Supposedly originated by Pvt. Willie Lee Duckworth during World War II.

dud (World War I to Modern) *s.* A shell or bomb that fails to explode, hence a person or enterprise that is not satisfactory. This word has a curious history. Ultimately it comes from Middle English *dudde* 'rag' or 'piece of clothing'. In one line of descent, the original meaning has been retained in *duds*, a colloquial term for clothing. In another line, a *dud* came to be a weak, raglike person. The wheel then went full circle. The British use of *dud* for a useless person became transferred to a useless shell during World War I. We picked up this meaning from the British and then reapplied it to persons.

dud out, to (Modern) *s.* To miscarry, to fail, to fail to explode. "Every grenade dudded out" (Marshall, 1971).

duffle (Modern; originally Naval, where it is considerably older) One's personal possessions such as might go in a duffle bag.

duffle bag A fairly long cylindrical cloth bag in which clothing and personal possessions are stored or carried. Duffle comes originally from the town of Duffel, near Antwerp, and was applied to a coarse woolen cloth.

duffle-bag drag (Modern) *s.* A permanent change of station or duty assignment. A soldier, after traveling great distances with all his uniforms and personal belongings crammed into his duffle bag, which is slung precariously over his shoulder, is sorely tempted to let it fall so that he can drag it along after him.

Duflicket Du John Dumflicket Doowillie (West Point) *s.* Various ways of speaking to, or about, a cadet whose name is not known; usually spoken to a plebe (freshman).

dugout (World War I and later) 1. An underground shelter, normally constructed as part of a trench system. Some, especially those constructed by the Germans in World War I, were elaborate and even comfortable. Originally slang, the name may have originated in the American West where it was a not-uncommon type of first-generation prairie dwelling. 2. *s.* A soldier, usually an officer, who has been *dug out* of retirement and ordered to active duty. See *retread, metalman.*

Dugout Doug (World War II) Gen. Douglas MacArthur. This was an odd nickname for a soldier of repeatedly proved courage, but it apparently was given to him by his troops on the Bataan Peninsula in 1942 because he remained on the offshore fortress island of Corregidor.

dumb bomb (Vietnam to Modern; Air Force) *s.* An old-fashioned bomb that is simply dropped toward its target, not guided to it. The opposite of *smart bomb.*

Dumbo (World War II; Air Force) *s.* A Martin Mariner PBM or Catalina PBY seaplane used in search-and-rescue operations, especially in the Pacific. The name was inspired by Walt Disney's flying elephant. Super Dumbos were converted B-17 or B-29 bombers used for longer range, more dangerous patrols.

dummy stick (Modern) 1. *s.* An Oriental carrying device. A long pole balanced on the shoulder; on each end of the pole is suspended something, perhaps a basket with produce for sale in the market. "Steaming pots of rice and boiled shrimp balanced at opposite ends of a dummy stick" (Mulligan). 2. *s.* A swagger stick carried by officers and NCOs.

dump (World War I to Modern) The common name for a place where supplies, especially ammunition and rations, are stacked by supply units for distribution to the combat units. The term probably comes from the usual practice of piling supplies under cover just off the road. Given bad weather, the place frequently does look like a dump.

Dunked Caterpillar (World War II; Air Force) A member of the Goldfish Club who came down into salt water on his parachute instead of riding his plane down.

duplex drive See *Donald Duck*.

duration, the (World War II; all Services) *s.* As long as the war is going on, until the war is ended. The Selective Service Act of 1941 specified that draftees would remain in the Armed Forces for the duration of the war. "Don't count on getting out soon. We're in for the duration and that's a long ways off." *The duration and six* meant the duration of the war and six months after that.

dust, to (Modern; all Services) *s.* To kill. Perhaps from black argot; perhaps from agricultural use, to dust crops to kill insects.

dustbin (World War II; Air Force) *s.* A gun turret on the underside of an aircraft. Sometimes expressed as a *dustbin gun. Dustbin* is the British term for *garbage can*.

dustcover (Modern; all Services) An Army blanket, folded and placed over the head of the bed, covering the pillow and sheet. It is tucked in under the head and sides of the bed. Also called *pillow blanket*.

dust-dust (World War I and World War II) *s.* According to Wentworth and Flexner, a newly promoted NCO, so called because he perpetually dusts off his new stripes. We have not heard this usage. Actually, as our editor recalls, it was more a business of admiring comrades pretending to dust off the gleaming new stripes (or imaginary ones, if the NCO had not had time to sew them on), rather than using the words *dust, dust*. However, it is quite possible that such words were spoken on occasion.

dust-off (Modern; all Services) 1. *s.* A medical evacuation helicopter. 2. *s.* The process of being evacuated by such a helicopter. Probably called this from the clouds of dust that helicopters raise in the downdraft from their rotor blades.

duty, the (Modern) *s.* Extra duty assigned to officers and NCOs, per a duty roster, requiring their attention during off-duty hours. Usually said as "I have the duty."

duty officer An officer assigned by roster to staff duty officer, officer of the day, or any other type of on-call or standby duty during off-duty hours. Also called *dirty officer, sheriff*.

duty roster (Modern) A form (DA Form 6) used by first sergeants and others to assign extra duties in the most equitable manner. It indicates the number of days since a soldier has last performed a duty, so that the soldier with the longest time can be selected.

dynamite gun (Late 19th century) A pneumatic cannon that threw a projectile filled with dynamite. The United States used a few of them for a short time during the Spanish-American War, both as field guns and as the main armament of the gunboat U.S.S. *Vesuvius*, although they were already obsolete. They were inaccurate, short-ranged, and tricky. Neither gallant gunner nor jolly tar wept when they were recalled.

DZ (World War II and later) Drop Zone, the area where parachute troops, weapons, and supplies are literally dropped from transport aircraft.

☆☆☆☆*e*☆☆☆☆

eagle eagles *s.* The spread-eagle insignia of a colonel, dating from the 1830s. *To get your eagles* is to be promoted to colonel, a long, rough process in which many are culled and relatively few are chosen. *To bear the eagle* is to be a colonel. See also *buzzards, chickens.*

eagle colonel s. A colonel, as distinguished from a mere lieutenant colonel. The latter —for convenience or flattery or both—is usually addressed or referred to orally as "colonel." In such a case it is sometimes necessary to ask, "Is he an eagle colonel or a light colonel?" Also called *bird colonel, buzzard colonel, chicken colonel, full colonel, bull colonel*, and *full bull.*

eagle day (World War II) *s.* Payday.

eagle flights (Vietnam) Detachments of helicopter-borne infantry orbiting in readiness to come down on enemy units located by air or ground reconnaissance.

eagle shits, the (Antiquity uncertain, but widely used in World War II, and still heard) *s.* Payday. The eagle is the federal government, and the comparison between excrement and military pay is intentional. Found in such variants as *when the eagle shits, the day the eagle shits, the eagle screams*, etc.

E & E (Modern) Escape and Evasion. Either formal training in ways to avoid capture and/or to escape from the enemy, or actual performance in combat. "They were looking for possible . . . E & E (escape and evasion) routes" (Marshall, 1968).

ear-banger (1930s) *s.* Another version of *hand-shaker.*

Easy 8 (World War II through Korea) *s.* The M4A3E8 Sherman medium tank. Equipped with wide tracks, a high-velocity 76mm gun, and an improved suspension system, it was a far more effective fighting vehicle than the original Sherman.

economy, on the (Modern; all Services) *s.* Using local native resources in a foreign country. *To live on the economy* is to live away from the local US installation in a foreign country. The term is also used to describe goods and services purchased from foreign agents and businessmen.

ED (Modern) Excused from Duty. On duty rosters first sergeants use the abbreviation *ED* to indicate that a soldier is excused from duty. "The General got me ED'd from all company duties."

edible and nonedible garbage (Old Army to Modern) Signs placed on GI cans outside mess hall segregating garbage into two categories: edible, or those leavings later sold to livestock owners for feed; and nonedible, or garbage fit only for dumping or destruction. Soldiers, in their quaintly humorous way, have always maintained that their next mess-hall meal is prepared from the contents of these cans.

egg 1. (World War I) *s.* A soldier newly arrived in France for duty with the AEF. 2. (World War II) *s.* An aerial bomb.

egg, to lay an (World War II) *s.* To drop a bomb—with luck, somewhere near the enemy.

egg in your beer *s.* Unnecessary, probably also undeserved, luxury. A chronic bitcher eventually will be asked, "Whaddyu want, an egg in your beer?"

egress, to (Modern; Air Force) Aviation English. To leave enemy airspace or a target area in enemy airspace. "The flight egressed with no other encounters" (AAV).

eight (Modern) *s.* Short for pay grade E-8, or master sergeant. "I should make eight on the next list." The term is not used in this manner for first sergeant.

eight ball (World War II to Modern) *s.* The sort of inept, useless fumbler that no one wants in his outfit, because he never totes his end of the load, but generates or attracts misfortune. This is the sort of man who clumsily trips a booby trap that kills better men, but is not scratched himself. The term is undoubtedly of civilian origin, based on the significance of the eight ball in pool.

eight ball, to be behind the To be in a difficult position with no escape handy, to be in trouble.

Eighty Niggers and Two White Men (Modern) *s.* The 82d Airborne Division, from the numerals *82* and a fancied racial imbalance in the ranks of the outfit.

Eisenhower jacket See *Ike jacket.*

elbows and assholes **assholes and elbows** (World War II and later) *s.* Policing an area. The term probably originated with the catchphrase *All I want to see is elbows and assholes*, as said by a noncom supervising a police detail. This is the position of the members of the detail, seen from the rear. In Korea there was a similar phrase, *shoe soles, elbows, and assholes,* but we have not pinned down its exact meaning.

elephant (West Point) 1. *s.* Around 1920, "a large ball of hash served in the mess hall" (*Howitzer*, 1920). 2. (Around 1939 and later) *s.* A cadet who cannot dance or is taking dancing lessons. Now obsolete. 3. See *see the elephant.*

elephant gun (World War I) *s.* The first German attempt at a specialized antitank gun. It resembled a much-enlarged bolt-action infantry rifle, and although it was clumsy to handle, it could make a colander out of most Allied tanks.

elephant walk (Modern) *s.* The ground movement of a B-52 aircraft. Also called *parade of elephants.*

eleven bang-bang **eleven bush** (Modern) *s.* An infantryman. The MOS code for an infantryman is 11B.

el tee (Modern) *s.* A lieutenant, from the letters *L* and *T*.

EM (All Services) Enlisted Man (or Men).

embalmed beef (Spanish-American War) 1. *s.* A descriptive term invented by Maj. Gen. Nelson A. Miles during postwar hearings on the conduct of the war. Once an aggressive and able soldier, Miles was suffering from professional frustration and presidential ambitions. At odds with President William McKinley's administration, he testified—although he refused to do so under oath—that the refrigerated beef furnished to troops in Cuba during the final stages of the war had actually been embalmed (that is, treated with preservatives that were harmful to the health of the soldiers). Subsequent investigation showed that Miles had no real evidence to back up his charges, but the newspapers gave them great publicity. 2 *s.* Canned boiled beef, which some genius in the Commissary Department decided to issue to the Cuban expedition as travel and field rations in place of the traditional corned beef. It was tasteless and tough, and began to spoil as soon as the cans were opened. It probably inflicted more casualties than the Spanish Army and Navy combined.

emergency ration (Old Army to Modern) A light, nonperishable ration designed to be carried by the soldier for use when the usual ration issue and preparation become impossible. As developed during the last of the Indian Wars, it consisted of powdered dried beef mixed with parched cooked wheat and a little sweetened chocolate. Much the same combination was used in World War I. In World War II it was replaced by the D-bar Ration and some specialized types of ration like the Parachute Emergency Ration and the Lifeboat Ration. See *Hitler's secret weapon*.

enfants perdus A borrowing from the French, literally 'lost children', frequently mistranslated as 'forlorn hope' (which was the same thing). The term, meaning volunteers for any especially hazardous duty, apparently dates back to the wars of the 16th century. During the Civil War, the New York Volunteers included a battalion of Enfants Perdus, which proved to be a lot of lost little men, indeed, and perfectly useless. "Most of them are foreigners, the roughscuff of New York City" (Wainwright).

Enfield American Enfield (World War I and later) The US Magazine Rifle, caliber .30, Model 1917. An American copy of the British service rifle, adopted when it proved impossible to rush the manufacture of enough Springfields to arm the entire expanding Army. It was heavier and longer than the Springfield and was not nearly so well designed. American soldiers did not like it. It had some use as a training arm in World War II.

engineer (At least as early as 1920; West Point) *s.* A cadet academically in the top of his class. Traditionally, the top classmen have chosen commissions in the engineers.

enguneer (Modern) *s.* A play on *engineer*, as in the catchphrase "Yestiddy I couldn't even spell 'enguneer' and today I are one."

enlisted aide (Post–World War II) The modern equivalent of a *striker* or *dog robber*. Only general officers have enlisted aides, who are noncommissioned officers. Their training in being useful around the house would have made the tobacco-eating character who polished our boots and groomed our horse when we were a shavetail (for which we paid him $10 a month out of our slender income) utter ungenteel comments. The institution of enlisted aide has definite usefulness, but it comes under periodic assault as undemocratic and a burden on the taxpayer.

enlisted men enlisted personnel Privates, privates first class, specialists, noncommissioned officers.

enlisted swine (Modern) *s.* Enlisted personnel. Used jokingly (of course!) among enlisted personnel and sometimes by officers, too (when they are in a good mood). See *junior enlisted swine, officer swine.*

E-nothing (Modern) *s.* An imaginary pay grade. Usually as in *Private E-nothing,* an extremely low-ranking enlisted soldier, below E-1. A sardonic play on the pay grades.

ensign (Colonial to early 19th century) The lowest grade of commissioned officer in the infantry, junior to a second lieutenant. American infantry companies had an ensign until some time after 1815. The grade is fairly old in European armies. Armies of the 16th century included one ensign (sometimes termed an *ancient*) in each infantry company. He had the duty of carrying its ensign (flag). Although company flags were abolished by the early 18th century, the grade of ensign was retained in the British Army until 1871.

entrenching tool (At least as early as Civil War to Modern) The official name for a small shovel carried on the full pack. Some models could be taken apart for easy carrying. It is used for digging trenches or foxholes. Also called *E-tool, Army banjo, Irish banjo.*

epaulette epaulet (Colonial to 1870s) A now obsolete form of shoulder ornament that either was an insignia of rank or bore an insignia of rank. It consisted of a strap that ended in a fringed pad. At one time, both noncommissioned officers and officers wore epaulettes, but their use was discontinued for noncommissioned officers in 1851 and for officers (except general officers) in 1872.

E pay grades (Modern) Pay grades for enlisted men are E-1, the lower grade of private; E-2, the higher grade of private; E-3, private first class; E-4, corporal and specialist four; E-5, sergeant and specialist five; E-6, staff sergeant and specialist six; E-7; platoon sergeant and sergeant first class (and formerly specialist seven); E-8, first sergeant and master sergeant; E-9, Sergeant Major of the Army, command sergeant major, and sergeant major. E-10, which is sometimes mentioned jokingly, is an imaginary grade, sometimes used for any high-ranking noncommissioned officer. See also *E-nothing.*

ER (All Services) Efficiency Report or Evaluation Report. Written reports on a standardized form commenting on the conduct, capabilities, and fitness for promotion of Army personnel. They are filled out at least once annually and under special circumstances, such as transfer or change of immediate superior. There are two separate forms, one for commissioned and warrant officers, and one for senior noncoms (SEER, or Senior Enlisted Evaluation Report). Each form goes through three hands: A rater (the immediate superior), an indorser, and a reviewer. The forms are theoretically important in promotions and assignments. While officer ratings have been in existence since at least the early 19th century, enlisted ERs date only from 1948. Such ratings, of course, have a subjective element, and the ER forms have become increasingly complex in an effort to reduce the possibility of even unconscious personal prejudice. But, especially in the officer's version, ratings now suffer from inflation, mostly because some raters give their subordinates unjustifiably high grades. Therefore, if others are not to suffer by comparison, they too have to be carried in a higher grade than they really deserve. It is a wry service jest that the best way to cut an officer's throat officially is to give him a strictly honest rating. To us, the best ERs were those given by the brigade commander of the 27th Infantry Regiment in August 1813. They include such gems as "Merely good, nothing promising," "More fit to carry the hod than the epaulette," and "Unfit for anything under heaven. God only knows how the poor thing got an appointment."

esprit de corps (Mostly World War I) The morale of a unit. A battalion with esprit de corps is gung ho and one for all and all for one.

essen, what's for (Post–World War II to Modern; also Air Force) *s.* What is there to eat? From German *essen* 'to eat'.

E-10 (Modern) *s.* An imaginary pay grade, generally used facetiously or deprecatingly, of any senior NCO grade but particularly those of sergeant major and command sergeant major. (The highest enlisted pay grade is E-9.)

ETO (World War II) European Theater of Operations.

E-tool (Also Marines) *s.* An entrenching tool (shovel). "Digging a cat hole with your E-tool" (Webb).

EUSTIS (Modern) *s.* Even Uncle Sam Thinks It Sucks, with reference to Fort Eustis, Virginia.

exec (Late 19th century to Modern) *s.* The executive officer of an organization or ship. He is the second in command and normally the man most active in supervising daily activities. Also *XO.*

executing a flank movement (Civil War; CSA) *s.* Turning one's underwear inside out to baffle the lice inhabiting the seams.

executioner (Colonial to at least the 1930s) *s.* A steady private, handy with his fists, who enforced the agreed-on rules of barracks and mess conduct among his peers. Ordinarily, he began by offering fatherly advice. If this was not heeded, the necessary lesson followed. It was a thoroughly democratic process, for the executioner acted only with the approval of his fellows. Officers and NCOs frequently knew nothing of the process; if they did, they studiously ignored it. See *cold burning.*

exercise (Colonial into early 19th century; all Services) Drill, especially in the handling of a soldier or sailor's weapons. The term was used at least as early as the time of Queen Elizabeth I, as in Sir Francis Walsingham's instructions for the training of shot or in a 1619 drill book dedicated to "jonghe and olde exercised Souldiours." Naval officers employed the term in the same sense, exercising their crews "at the great guns" or other necessary skills. The terms *drill, training,* or *school of the soldier* gradually replaced it.

Expert Infantryman Badge (1943 on) A badge awarded to any individual with an infantry MOS who has satisfactorily completed proficiency tests while assigned to an infantry brigade, regiment, or smaller unit.

express (Colonial to Mexican War) A dispatch rider.

extend, to (Modern; all Services) *s.* To stay longer voluntarily than the required time on an overseas tour or an enlistment. "I tried to extend, but they wouldn't let me do it" (Tregaskis).

extracted /'ex-tracted/ (World War II) *s.* Drunk on extract. In the early days of World War II the flavoring extracts still had an alcoholic base, and cooks and mess sergeants notoriously used them for no-cost jags. This, of course, was a time-honored practice, as old as the issue of such extracts. The development of non-alcoholic flavoring extracts made a lot of veteran mess sergeants *very* unhappy.

eyewash (Old Army to Modern) *s.* Extra prettying up and primping to make something—from a whole post to one jeep with driver—look more appealing to visiting dignitaries, military or civilian. A good IG ordinarily will give it the X-ray eye and wonder what training was neglected to find the time for the eyewash. But we still have generals who judge the efficiency of a unit by how recently the rocks lining the sidewalk in front of headquarters have been whitewashed.

Eytie (World War II) *s.* An Italian—a typical soldier mispronunciation. This form probably came from the British, who in North Africa in 1940 had a mocking little song:

> Oh, Sidi Barrani!
> Oh, Mersa Matruh!
> The Eyties will get there,
> And then what shall we do.

American soldiers usually referred to Italians as *wops*, less often as *spaghetti stranglers*, or *guineas*. In the song above, Mersa Matruh is often spelled Marsa Matruh in atlases. See *Itey*.

face The direction to which soldiers are commanded to turn. The commands are *Right face!, Left face!,* and *About face!* These commands are given only when troops are stationary.

fag (World War I, and perhaps later) *s.* A cigarette.

> While you've a lucifer to light your
> fag,
> Smile, boys, that's the style.

failure to repair (Modern) The official term for nonappearance at a formation or duty. A lesser offense than AWOL, failure to repair occurs when a soldier, usually through simple negligence, fails to show up. Generally, the intent is to delay doing something for personal reasons, such as recovering from hangover.

fair wear and tear FWT (20th century) Worn out by normal use or service. Applied to equipment. The expression goes back at least to the first decade of this century, when it was used in *General Orders #185* (4 September 1907). It describes property "worn out by fair wear and tear in the service which has no salable value." Determining the fairness of the wear is often impossible, and over the years soldiers responsible for items of government property have breathed thankful sighs of relief when no questions were asked as articles were turned in for replacement.

Fall in! Fall out! (Ancient) Military commands. *Fall in!* means that a unit should form up, that each soldier should take his proper place in formation. *Fall out!* means to break ranks, to leave formation. Individuals, too, may be ordered to fall out, as for example, to pick up items of equipment. Other similar terms (*to fall in with*, meaning to encounter; *to fall upon*, meaning to attack suddenly) no longer have definite military status. It is still proper usage, however, to say that someone *fell into an ambush*.

falling bricks (Old, Old Army) *s.* An exact descriptive phrase used for the effects of ranking out.

family member (Modern; also Air Force). The new official term for a dependent or legal camp follower, a cosmetic change made in recognition of the fact that the wives of our much-married, all-volunteer Armed Forces very much want more attention to their family comfort and convenience. The term also illustrates the fad that first appeared during the Carter administration of desexing the language: *sibling* for *brother* or *sister, workhour* for *manhour*, and ingenious sentence constructions to remove "sexist" pronouns like *he* and *she*.

farrier (Colonial into 20th century) A noncommissioned officer in each mounted troop, company, or battery responsible for the care of its horses. Originally, he seems to have acted as a rule-of-thumb veterinarian, as was the custom in the British cavalry, while the troop blacksmith took care of the horseshoeing. (The US Army, for some reason, did not establish a Veterinary Corps until 1916.) By the time of the Mexican War, the troop farrier also did the horseshoeing. By 1860 there were two farriers in each troop, supervised by a chief farrier in regimental headquarters.

fart sack (At least as early as World War II to Modern; all Services) *s.* A bedroll, sleeping bag, bunk, or other sleeping equipment. *To hit the fart sack* or *to climb into the fart sack* was to go to bed (for sleeping purposes).

Fast-Footed Virginians Flat-Footed Virginians (Civil War; USA) *s.* A most unkind damyankee takeoff on the semi-sacred initials *FFV, First Families of Virginia.*

Fat Boy Program (Modern) *s.* A periodic program in which the Army decides to browbeat overweight soldiers into losing pounds. While corpulent soldiers can be a disgusting sight, sloppy commanders let them get that way and thereby create victims for the excesses of the Fat Boy Program. The most recent ukase threatened to bar overweight soldiers from reenlisting if they could not lose certain amounts of weight by specified times.

fatcatting (World War II to Modern) *s.* Enjoying special treatment. We recall an Army medic in late 1945 who prescribed himself into the Fort Knox hospital on a diet of steak dinners and a shot of bourbon every hour. One source of information would also include as *fatcatters* those characters who are making an all-out effort to obtain such benefits.

fatigue (Ancient to Modern) Labor performed by military personnel, as opposed to training. Typical examples of *fatigue* would be policing the living areas, improving the training facilities, shifting supplies and equipment, or general cleanup work around the camp. A group of men detailed for such duty is a *fatigue detail*. In the 19th century such a detail could be called just a *fatigue*, but this usage seems to have disappeared. The term *fatigue* is also used ironically to mean the opposite of work: *bunk fatigue* (sleep) or *cunt fatigue* (sexual intercourse).

fatigues (20th century) The uniform worn while on fatigue duty, usually simple coats, trousers, and denim caps. Since World War II, fatigues have been commonly used in training, or even as hot weather uniforms in combat.

fattygews (Modern) *s.* A play on *fatigues.*

Faydleburg *s.* Fayetteville, North Carolina, just outside Fort Bragg.

FBI (World War II; mostly Army) *s.* Americans in the PGC (Persian Gulf Command) considered themselves the "new FBI—Forgotten Bastards in Iran."

FD (From about 1939 to present; West Point) Full Dress uniform.

FDC (World War II to Modern) Fire Direction Center. Each artillery battalion has an FDC to coordinate the fire of its three batteries; division artillery headquarters has one to tie the battalion FDCs together; and so on up the chain of command. All sorts of other outfits—chemical mortar battalions, tank battalions—and additional artillery battalions can tie in with this system at various levels. It works beautifully; ask the Germans, Japanese, North Koreans, Chinese, and North Vietnamese.

feather merchant (World War II; all Services) 1. *s.* A mental lightweight, promoted beyond his capabilities before anyone discovered what they were not. Frequently the implication was that he could talk a good war, but could not or would not fight one. 2. *s.* A civilian in essential industry or for other reasons not in the Armed Forces. Sometimes equivalent to *slacker*; at other times, without opprobrium.

FEC FECOM Far East Command.

fed up (World War I to Modern) *s.* Of British origin. It means that you have enough of something and are more than ready to quit and go home. Never mind who wins this war.

feeking stick feaking stick (Considerable Antiquity to Modern; servicemen from the southeastern states) A pole, at the end of which was a cloth pad or rag that had been dipped in turpentine. Drovers or drivers used it to stimulate tired cattle, oxen, or horses on a steep hill, at a difficult ford, or in a sudden emergency. Gently applying the pad to the animal's anus in such a crisis produced a spectacular burst of energy. Definitely not recommended for mules. Hence, a stimulus. "If Colonel Dumsquat doesn't get a move on, I'll have to get out my feeking stick."

few good men, a (Modern) From the Marine Corps recruiting poster announcing that the Corps is *Looking for a Few Good Men.* Soldiers are fond of using the expression derogatorily, saying that the Marines need more than a *few* good men.

FIAP /fee-'yap/ (Modern; all Services) *s.* Fuck It And Press, meaning "Don't worry; press on with the business at hand."

Fiddler's (Fiddlers') Green (Ancient; periods of American use uncertain) An odd corner of the Hereafter, located "half-way down the road to Hell." It was supposedly designed for those souls unfit for either Hell or Heaven. The idea may have come from the theological concept of Limbo, but the description of Fiddler's Green sounds more like a Mohammedan paradise: a "pleasant camping place" with adjacent houses of refreshment. One toplofty cavalry version held that "only shades of mounted men may halt at Fiddler's Green":

So when both man and horse go
  down
Beneath the sabers keen . . .
Or when the hostiles crave your
  scalp
Just empty your canteen—
And put your pistol to your head,
And go to Fiddler's Green.

The concept seems to have been popular among 17th- and 18th-century sailors, soldiers, and masterless men, who knew that they would not qualify for Heaven, but trusted that a merciful God would agree to their credo that "To live hard, to die hard, and to go to Hell afterward would be hard indeed."

field Originally, *in the field* meant *on campaign* or *on patrol*, well away from the home post or barracks. The term *field* has since taken on a less stark meaning. Troops on an overnight practice hike are *in the field*. The number of terms based on *field* is very great, and only a few of the more important are given below.

field belt (Between World War I and World War II) A leather harness for officers, worn in the field. (It took the place of the Sam Browne belt, which was worn on post.) It consisted of a heavy leather waist belt, with a suspender belt over each shoulder. It supported your pistol holster, a pouch for two extra pistol clips, a first-aid pouch, a canteen and cover, and a binoculars case. All of these cases had to be saddle-soaped and polished to an absolutely matching shade, which was designated by the regimental commander. But once you and your striker had achieved the de rigueur nuance of, say, cordovan red-brown, you would probably be transferred to an outfit that demanded a soft golden tone.

field cap See *overseas cap*.

field clerk (Old Army) A potent warrant-grade expert in paperwork, regulations, and red tape, who might descend from higher headquarters to check out your sins of omission and commission in these departments.

field day (Ancient) A day devoted to a display of military drill and equipment, to impress local citizens and taxpayers. It might often be a feature of militia or volunteer training. In the Marine Corps, a general clean-up.

field first (Modern) *s.* A noncommissioned officer, usually in the grade of platoon sergeant or sergeant first class, who oversees the daily training of troops in a basic training unit. He is not an actual first sergeant and does not wear the chevrons of that grade or draw comparable pay. It is to be observed that *field* here does not mean *field of combat* as it often does elsewhere.

Field-Grade Good Conduct Medal (Post–World War II to Modern) *s.* The Army Commendation Medal, so called because before the Vietnam War many soldiers believed that only field-grade officers received it. See *Green Weenie, Officer's Good Conduct Medal*.

field jacket (Mostly Army) An item of uniform, cut much like a civilian windbreaker, introduced in 1941 to give the soldier more practical clothing for field service. Made of heavy cotton fabric, it was water and wind repellant, but distinctly lacking in warmth. The original waist-length model was replaced in 1943 by a longer, four-pocket style, which was later furnished with a separate pile liner, a hood, and matching trousers. These became generally available to combat units by the time the war ended.

field music 1. Depending on the historical period, the drums; fifes and drums; bugles and drums; or bugles of a regiment; or the players thereof. (For cavalry, field music was always its trumpets.) The term probably is based on the fact that these musicians always went into the field with the troops, whereas regimental bands might be left behind or the bandsmen might be used as stretcher-bearers. 2. The music played by such soldiers.

field officers field-grade officers Majors, lieutenant colonels, and colonels. The term comes from the British service of the 18th century, in which a field officer was an officer of sufficient seniority and experience to command a regiment in the field.

field rat (Antiquity uncertain, to Modern) An infantryman or combat soldier. Fraser and Gibbons attribute it to "a Prussian Guard contemptuous term for ordinary linesmen" in World War I, implying that it is a loan from German, translated literally into English by the British troops. One might also infer that the term was then picked up by the members of the American Expeditionary Force and came into our present vocabulary in this rather circuitous passage. Unfortunately, none of this can be proved. None of the lexicons of German Army slang consulted by us or our correspondents contains a German equivalent of *field rat*. Most significantly, the term is not included in Max Fritz's *Schwäbische Soldatensprache im Weltkrieg* (Stuttgart, 1938). (In Swabian dialect the term would be *Feldratz*; in Standard German, *Feldratte*.) Neither does it appear in other modern lexicons. The closest equivalent seems to have been the *Frontsau* 'front pig' of World War I, meaning an infantryman, recorded in Fritz, although the possibility exists that *Feldratte* or *Feldratz* might have been used but not recorded. As in English the combination of words describing a dirty, bedraggled, and downtrodden infantryman would have been natural and instantly understandable to any German speaker. One thing is certain: the common experiences of German and Allied troops on the Western Front during World War I led to certain commonality of language. (Our thanks to Dr. Reinhold Aman of Waukesha, Wisconsin, and Mrs. Elly Brosig, of Stuttgart, FRG.)

field rations (Old Army to World War II) A ration designed for use in time of war or national emergency when the garrison ration was not used. It was issued in kind, and no ration savings were allowed. Field Ration A was to be issued in the continental United States, and overseas when possible; it included fresh fruits, vegetables, and meats. Field Ration B was for overseas use and consisted of nonperishable canned or dehydrated foods.

field soldier *s.* A soldier who prefers active service with a combat arms unit, in contrast to staff or administrative assignments.

field strip, to (At least as early as World War II to Modern; all Services) 1. Officially, to break a weapon down into its basic components, usually so that it can be cleaned. 2. *s.* To reduce cigarette or cigar butts to shreds so that they can be disposed of outdoors without leaving a noticeable residue. The technique, for a cigarette, was to peel off the paper and roll it into a ball, while scattering the tobacco. "Any man not field-stripping cigarettes deals with me personally" (Smith).

fifinella (World War II; Air Force) 1. *s.* A female gremlin. 2. *s.* A trainee with the Women's Airforce Service Pilots. See *WASP*.

FIFO (Comparatively Modern) First In, First Out. This has a variety of applications. The most recent we have seen was a motto to encourage quartermaster warehouse DACs to keep fresh fruits and vegetables from sitting in dark corners.

fifteen and two (Modern) *s.* A common punishment under Article 15 of the *Uniform Code of Military Justice*: fifteen days' restriction to specified limits, plus two hours of extra duty per day.

fifth wheel, the (Civil War; USA) 1. The spare wheel, carried on the rear of artillery caissons. Since it was used for spread-eagling military offenders, it also became 2. *s.* The soldier's term for spread-eagling.

fifty-mission bennie (1930s to World War II; Air Force) *s.* Properly, the Air Force crush cap. An authorized service cap for aviators, manufactured with a soft leather visor and without stiffening so that radio headphones could be worn comfortably over it. It could even be rolled up and stuffed into a pocket. The term *bennie* was undoubtedly a variant of *beanie*, a felt skull cap popular with boys in the 1920s and early 1930s.

FIGMO (Modern; all Services) *s.* Fuck it, I Got My Orders, meaning "I have my reassignment or separation papers, and I don't care anymore." Algeo traces this expression to the Korean War and notes *figmo attitude*, comparable to *short-timer's attitude.* When pressed to explain the acronym, some soldiers will render *fuck it* as *forget it*. See also *short-timer's attitude, stack arms, stack pencils.*

file (Colonial to Modern) 1. Various uses and meanings based on the common factor that a file is a column of men standing one behind the other, as in *single file* and *Indian file.* From this come a number of drill orders, such as *Cover in file!* (the rear-rank man shifts his position to stand directly behind the front-rank man of his file) and *Follow in file!* (move off in single file). In a formation, just as the ranks correspond to the lines of width, the files correspond to the lines of length or depth. See *rank and file*. 2. *s.* As derived from definition 1, a soldier, a person, a man. "So I heard the noise and looked up and there was this drunken file wandering up the company street."

file Until 1940 a method of regulating promotion of company-grade and field-grade officers—second lieutenant to colonel. Officers were promoted according to seniority, their relative positions being spoken of as *files.* Thus, "Smith has two files on me" means that Smith is two places ahead on the promotion list. An officer who was reduced in rank for misconduct was said *to have lost* (whatever number of) *files.* An older officer who would soon retire was a *good old file*, but an officer who was unusually young for his grade could be a *bad file* for older officers junior in grade, who might have to retire before he did.

file boner fileboner (Early 20th century; West Point) *s.* A cadet who exerts himself to obtain class or academic standing. Now obsolete. See *bone.*

file-closer (At least early 19th century, to Modern) 1. A soldier in the rear of a formation whose duty it was to supervise the men in ranks. 2. (Modern) *s.* An unnecessary or superfluous person. A straphanger. "An unheard-of array of VIP file-closers" (Marshall, 1968). 3. (West Point) *s.* The second-ranking cadet in a section. 4. (West Point) *s.* An academically undistinguished cadet.

File 13 *s.* The waste basket. Also called the *circular file.*

Filipino ration (Old Army to post–World War II) The peacetime ration of the Philippine Scouts. It differed from the usual ration by including considerable amounts of fish and unpolished rice. The Scouts also delighted in all manner of freshly baked breadstuffs. One of the hardest chores in the Scouts' short existence after World War II was reestablishing some semblance of the original Filipino ration. Our overstuffed G-4, who ate at a special division headquarters mess, fed us for weeks—meagerly—on canned Vienna sausage, canned peas, and unadorned wheat flour, and considered us downright unsoldierly and ungrateful when we asked for some yeast and a little fish now and then. We hope he got ulcers.

find, to (Since at least as early as 1910; West Point) *s.* To discharge for reason of academic failure. "Mike was found in Frog."

fined down (Indian Wars) *s.* Traveling light, with only the absolutely essential items of equipment. "There are few sights more inspiring to a military observer than a compact, well-disciplined column of cavalry, 'fined down' to a minimum of impedimenta, moving rapidly, silently, and with malice aforethought along the trail of an enemy" (Bourke).

finger-four (Air Force) *s.* A formation of aircraft in which planes occupy positions suggested by the four fingertips of the hand, when the hand is held upright. Also called *fingertip.*

fire (Modern) *s.* A match or cigarette lighter. A soldier wanting a light for his cigarette will ask a friend, "You have any fire?"

fire base **fire support base** **FSB** (Modern) A semipermanent tactical base established in a forward combat area, from which maneuver elements receive artillery and logistical support while engaged against an enemy. This tactic was widely employed during the Vietnam War. FSBs also provided a relatively safe area where troops could refit and rest. "A fire base. That's where they keep the big guns, artillery" (Haldeman).

fire cake (Colonial to Revolutionary) A bread substitute consisting of flour and water mixed together and cooked in the ashes or on a griddle, hot rock, or board. One German officer described them in 1777 as an "unhealthy floury paste." Also called *ash cakes, flour cakes.*

Firefly (Vietnam) Night combat missions flown by helicopters. The ships flew in three tiers: a command and control ship at approximately one thousand feet; a lightship, equipped with a cluster of seven powerful searchlights, at approximately five hundred feet; and a gunship on the deck (very close to the ground). This system provided rapidly movable, continuous pinpoint illumination of enemy ground activity, plus the firepower to knock it out. During the Korean War, flare-ship missions were also designated by the code name *Firefly*, and were also called *Lightning Bug* and *Old Lamplighter of the Korean Hills.*

fire for effect, to (World War I to Modern) What you do when you have a suitable bracket on your target and are ready to take it apart. "Fire for effect! Battalion, three rounds. Fire!" (The phraseology has varied somewhat over the years, but it conveys the same meaning.) By logical transfer, if someone says that the Old Man is *firing for effect* this morning, you need not be a genius to deduce that life is going to be somewhat hairy for everyone in his outfit.

fire hose (Modern) *s.* The aiguillette, the shoulder cord, or the fourragère. The cords and braids resemble hoses, and the brass ferrule of the aiguillette looks very much like the nozzle of a fire hose.

fire in the hole (World War II; attributed to the Engineers) *s.* VD. A play on the traditional warning given when a demolition charge has been ignited. In this case, it means that a woman in question has venereal disease.

fireworker (Colonial to early 19th century) A soldier, usually an artillery officer, skilled in the preparation of ammunition and military pyrotechnics. See *laboratory.*

firing line The point from which riflemen take aim and fire at their targets. Figuratively speaking, *to be on the firing line* is to be in the thick of things, to be afforded an opportunity to speak out, to be expected to produce results. This is a military expression that has gained wide civilian popularity. Millions of Americans are familiar with it from military rifle ranges, where they have heard, "Ready on the right! Ready on the left! Ready on the firing line!"

firing order (At least World War II to Modern) A group of riflemen in a prescribed course of familiarization or qualification in arms; all go through each stage of the course together.

firing party (Ancient to Modern) The detail that fires the three volleys at a military funeral. It is not to be confused with *firing squad*, which is employed in military executions.

first (Probably of some antiquity, to Modern) *s.* Short for *first sergeant*, the chief noncommissioned officer in a company.

First at Vicksburg The 13th US Infantry Regiment, for its valorous conduct there in 1863.

first-call men (Civil War; USA) Men who responded in May 1861 to the call for volunteers for three years' service. They came because of patriotism and love of adventure, and were the backbone of the US armies.

first captain (West Point) The commander of the brigade of cadets. His rank is identified by six chevrons over a star.

first class (West Point and other Service academies) The senior class, facing graduation and a reduction in status to mere second-lieutenancy. The informal term *firsties* is sometimes used by people of no breeding. What the plebes call them varies, but seldom implies adoration.

first cook Generally, the mess sergeant's deputy; senior man among the cooks.

firsties (West Point) See *first class*.

first john *s.* A first lieutenant. See *second john*.

first lieutenant The second-lowest rank of commissioned officer, pay grade 0-2, ranking above a second lieutenant and below a captain. His insignia is a silver bar. Nicknames are *first John, looey, loot*. See *lieutenant*. Abbreviated *1 Lt., 1st Lieut*.

first light Technically, the beginning of morning twilight. The sun is still below the horizon, but its light has just become barely perceptible. (The Arabs had a rule of thumb that first light occurred when you could make out isolated white hairs in the coat of a nearby black horse—or something of the sort.) You can begin to see where you are going, and it is a good time to stand to.

first sergeant (Revolutionary to Modern) A rank and a position that have varied over the years, but essentially the senior sergeant in a company, battery, or troop. In defining *first sergeant*, it is necessary to distinguish between the rank of first sergeant and the position of first sergeant, which have not always gone together in the history of the Army. 1. (Rank) At present, a first sergeant is a senior noncommissioned officer in pay grade E-8, who is assigned to the duties of a first sergeant. (He is selected by a local commander from a pool of master sergeants and assumes the title and insignia of a first sergeant only as long as he performs these duties. If he should be assigned to other duties, he reverts to master sergeant.) He ranks above a platoon sergeant (E-7) and master sergeant and below a sergeant major (E-9). His insignia is three stripes above and three arcs below, enclosing a diamond (lozenge). The modern rank of first sergeant was created in the reorganization of 1920, in which first sergeant (second grade) was created. His insignia then was three stripes above, two arcs below, and a lozenge enclosed. In 1942 the rank of first sergeant was upgraded to first grade, along with master sergeant, and the present insignia was adopted. The present rank of first sergeant dates from 1958. 2. (Position) The position of first sergeant has been recognized in the Army since at least 1779, when it was described by Baron von Steuben in his *Regulations*. Until very recently, most of the administration of a company was handled by the first sergeant and the company clerk. The choice of first sergeant has always been highly important, for a wrong choice can ruin a commander's career and can cause damage both to the noncommissioned officer concerned and the unit. A good first sergeant must have strength of personality, the ability to remain cool under hazardous or trying conditions, common sense, and objectivity. He must be a walking encyclopedia of Army regulations, customs, and traditions; a painstaking and careful administrator; and a practical psychologist skilled enough to manage two hundred or so men and women who represent the extremes of American society and every shade of social, educational, and ethnic background. The man who holds the position of first sergeant is not, however, always a first sergeant by rank. He may well be an acting first sergeant of lower rank. In such a case, although he wears the insignia of a lower grade, he is still referred to as first sergeant. Nicknames for first sergeant are many: *first, first hog, first man, first pig, first shirt, first skirt, first sleeve, first soldier, top, topkick, topper, tops, top sergeant, top soldier*, etc. Abbreviated *1 SG, 1st Sgt.*

First Team, the The US 1st Cavalry Division; a self-inflicted title.

first three grades first three graders top three graders The senior NCOs. At present, in ascending order, pay grade E-7 (sergeant first class and platoon sergeant), pay grade E-8 (master sergeant and first sergeant), pay grade E-9 (sergeant major and command sergeant major). In World War II, staff sergeant and technician third grade, technical sergeant, first sergeant and master sergeant.

first up (Modern) The Army aviator's equivalent of *point man*; the first or lead helicopter in a mission, the first aircraft to fly out on a mission.

fishnet (At least World War II to Modern) *s.* A net made of knotted cord, used to hold camouflage materials in place.

FIST (Modern) Fire Support Team.

five (Modern) *s.* Short for *pay grade E-5* or the rank of *sergeant* or *specialist five*.

Five Brothers (1930s) A packaged black burley tobacco favored by the more daring prewar marines and soldiers for chewing and pipes. It was claimed that any man who could smoke Five Brothers in a corncob pipe was tough enough to take a canoe around Cape Horn. Upon hearing this story, some ambitious recruits, "seeking the bubble reputation," tried it and came down with severe nicotine poisoning. The stuff was too cheap to appeal to the highly paid aristocrats of the US Navy. See *Bull, hardroll, tailormade*.

five-by-five (World War II and later) *I hear you five-by-five* is a radio operator's way of saying that the transmission he is receiving is "loud and clear." The expression is based on a scale showing the strength and clarity of radio reception. Also, a general expression of approval.

5 percent promotion (Modern) About 5 percent of officers selected for promotion are from below-the-zone (i.e., in the secondary zone). These officers are junior in rank to those who would normally be selected. Persons picked in 5 percent promotions must be outstanding in all ways. Also *below-the-zone, nickel promotion.* See *primary zone, secondary zone, pass-over.*

five-quarter ton (Modern) Paradoxical nomenclature. The 1¼-ton M37 series cargo truck, which replaced the ¾-ton truck.

five-striper (West Point) *s.* Cadet brigade officers, regimental executive officers, and battalion commanders, whose insignia of rank is five chevrons.

fixed wing (Modern) *s.* An aircraft kept aloft by propeller and stationary wings, as opposed to rotary wings.

flagging action (Modern) When a soldier is awaiting the outcome of disciplinary action, such as a court-martial, his personnel records are flagged so that he will not be selected for promotion, special assignment, etc. He can be reassigned while in this status only at the convenience of the government. He cannot volunteer or initiate any other action that would be favorable to himself.

flag officers General officers. They are authorized to display flags with the color of their branch and the appropriate number of stars.

flagpole, don't screw up around the (Modern) *s.* Don't let your foibles and peccadillos be known around the post where you are stationed—wise advice. In this and similar expressions, the flagpole is the symbolic center of Army life. See *ten miles beyond the flagpole.*

flagpole leave (Modern) 1. *s.* A leave spent at work, for whatever reason, but usually voluntarily. 2. *s.* A leave on which one does not go elsewhere; hence, to stay near the flagpole or the post. See *desktop leave, pocket leave.*

flagpole transportation (Old Army) *s.* No transportation at all when reenlisting. When a soldier was discharged at the end of his first enlistment, he was entitled to the cost of transportation to his home. At the end of subsequent enlistments, he received cost of transportation to the place where he had re-upped. If that place was the post at which he was currently serving, he got flagpole transportation—enough to take him to the post flagpole, absolutely nothing at all.

flak (World War II) 1. *s.* Antiaircraft fire. 2. *s.* By extension, objections, criticisms, and obstacles. "We're getting a lot of flak from division headquarters over the new training schedule." An acronym from German *Flugabwehrkanone* 'antiaircraft gun'.

flak alley (World War II; Air Force) *s.* An enemy area guarded by heavy antiaircraft defenses. See *Happy Valley.*

flak birds (Air Force) *s.* Flak-suppressing aircraft. "The 'flak birds' had two 750-pound bombs for good measure" (TB, p. 31).

flak jacket (Air Force) *s.* Body armor worn by air crews as protection against hostile fire.

Flaming Four (World War I) *s.* Aviators' name for the DH-4 biplane, built in the United States from a British model and equipped with the American-designed Liberty engine. It was moderately useful for observation and daytime bombing, but caught fire readily, whether from enemy action or by accident.

They've got no Sops,
They've got not SPADS.
They've got no Flaming Fours,
And little frosted juleps
Are served in all the stores.

Also called *Flaming Coffin, Flying Coffin.*

flaming horse turd flaming onion *s.* The insignia of the Ordnance Corps (properly a flaming grenade). See also *flaming pisspot.*

Flaming onion (World War I) An incendiary device in strings of four used by the Germans against aircraft.

flaming pisspot 1. *s.* The insignia of the Ordnance Corps (properly a flaming grenade). 2. *s.* The shoulder patch worn by personnel assigned to the US Army John F. Kennedy Center for Special Warfare (USAJFKCENSPWAR), Fort Bragg, North Carolina.

flank (Ancient to Modern) The right or left of a body of troops or the terrain immediately to the right or left. The term appears in many combinations.

flank, to outflank, to 1. (Ancient to Modern) To flank or outflank an enemy is to pass around his flank or turn his flank. 2. (Civil War; USA) *s.* A special use. To cut into a formation or sneak into a mess line before one's turn. 3. (Civil War; USA) *s.* To outsmart, evade, or successfully deceive someone, usually an officer, who had forbidden foraging, bringing liquor into camp, or fraternizing with the enemy while on outpost duty. A soldier who performed such behavior might be called a *flanker.*

flank companies (Revolutionary to about 1830) Two companies of picked soldiers in each infantry regiment, so called because they formed on its right and left flanks. By European standards, the right flank company was grenadiers; the left flank, light infantry. The existence of the light companies in America was an off-and-on matter. During the Revolution, a few regiments had grenadier companies, but eventually all regiments came to have light infantry companies. (These light infantry companies usually served detached in provisional light infantry regiments like those with which Mad Anthony Wayne took Stony Point, N.Y., in 1779). From 1820 to 1830 every Regular regiment had a company of grenadiers and one of either light infantry or riflemen. The topic requires much more research.

flanker 1. (Civil War; USA) *s.* A soldier who tried to break or sneak into a queue of soldiers. The term was particularly used among POWs. 2. (About 1920; West Point) *s.* A tall cadet.

flap (Perhaps World War I, but especially from World War II on) *s.* Hysterical excitement, a bugout, a stampede, an episode of utter confusion, unreasonable to-do, noisy unfair criticism, etc. Probably originally from the image of an excited hen. Dates of origin not known, but in use in British naval circles at the end of the 19th century. Picked up and rejuvenated during the North African campaigns against Rommel.

flare ship (Modern; all Services) An Air Force cargo-type aircraft modified to provide battlefield illumination, usually by dropping aerial flares. See *Firefly* and *Lightning Bug.* Used as synonym of *Puff, the Magic Dragon,* although, strictly speaking, flare ships provided only light and little firepower.

Flash Gordon (World War II) *s.* An early soldiers' nickname for Gen. George Patton, based on his unique taste in uniforms, and probably his dash and ubiquitousness during training and maneuvers.

flash-hider removed (Modern) *s.* Circumcised.

flash power (World War II to Modern; Air Force) *s.* The war-emergency power of an aircraft engine.

flat hat (Modern; also Navy, Marines) *s.* The flat-crowned service cap.

flatpeter flat peter (Modern) *s.* A person so stupid and clumsy that he is "always stepping on his dick." But most often used by combat soldiers as a derogatory description of rear-echelon personnel.

flattop flat top (World War II to Modern) *s.* An aircraft carrier. A *baby flattop* was an escort carrier, the smallest type within this category of warships.

flat-top Army (Modern) *s.* The US Army from the Korean War to 1963. The term refers to the blocked fatigue caps with stiff crowns and flat tops—like a kepi—that were very popular in units from the 1950s through the early 1960s. These caps were not issued, but many commanders required their men to purchase them from the PX because they looked more military than the shapeless, long-visored regulation caps that were hold-overs from World War II. The flat-top cap tended to lose its shape and stiffness after a washing or two, and the wire frame that reinforced the crown bent easily. As a result, soldiers who wanted to look sharp were forced to replace flat-top caps frequently. The present-day baseball cap was adopted in 1963, and by March 1965 the flat-top cap had been phased out.

fling wing (Modern) *s.* A helicopter, probably with reference to the action of its rotor blades.

Flip (Mostly Navy) *s.* A Filipino. Considered offensive.

flopper stopper (Old Army) *s.* A brassiere.

flub the dub, to (World War II) *s.* To foul up, blunder, and generally make a mess of your assignment, possibly more from innate stupidity than willful misbehavior. Perhaps from the old term *flubdub*, meaning pretentious nonsense or show, although civilian slang of the 1930s took the phrase to mean male masturbation.

flugelman flugleman See *fugleman.*

fluid four (Modern; Air Force) A fighter aircraft formation in which some of the aircraft are spread out horizontally and vertically in order to provide lookout and cover to other planes in the formation.

flute (Old Army) *s.* A sodomite; one who practices fellatio.

fly, to *s.* To work out, to be effective. Negatively, "It won't fly."

fly-boy fly boy *s.* An aviator.

fly by, to An air unit's version of *to march past in review.*

flying artillery (1800 into Civil War) The horse artillery, in which each soldier had his own horse. (In some early cases, soldiers without individual mounts rode in light wagons.) It could move rapidly enough to keep up with cavalry and was famous for its hell-for-leather ways. The term, apparently, was seldom employed by artillerymen themselves during the Civil War and thereafter went out of style. The word *flying*, in many of these older terms, does not mean volation, but simply highly mobile.

flying ashcans (World War II) *s.* Projectiles from heavy Japanese mortars.

Flying Assholes (World War II) The 11th Airborne Division, so called from the red disk, edged with white, in the center of its shoulder patch.

Flying Banana (Modern) *s.* The now obsolete H-21 helicopter, in which the tail section was angled away from the main compartment. The H-21 was kept aloft by six rotor blades, three aft and three forward. Riding in one was like being inside a washing machine. These machines were used extensively in the early years of the Vietnam War. "But right now we are stuck with flying bananas in Vietnam" (Tregaskis).

Flying Boxcar (World War II to Modern; Air Force) *s.* The C-82 cargo plane and the later C-119.

Flying Brickyard, the (Modern; National Aeronautics and Space Administration, Armed Forces) *s.* The US space shuttle, so called because of its outer coating of more than 32,000 ceramic tiles. These tiles are intended to serve as insulation against the heat generated by atmospheric friction as the craft leaves and reenters the earth's atmosphere. Thanks to our myopic politicians, it is our first space venture in almost six years. Meanwhile, the Russians have been at it hot, heavy, and successfully.

flying camp (Revolutionary) A strong force organized as mobile reserve to reinforce threatened points. Washington employed one at the beginning of his campaign of 1776.

Flying Coffin See *Flaming Four, Flying Prostitute.*

flying devil (World War I) *s.* A trench mortar shell with "wings" or fins to stabilize its flight. Reportedly used by both Germans and French. Apparently fired from a spigot mortar.

flying fuck at a rolling doughnut, Go take a (At least World War II, to Modern) *s.* Synonymous with other such expressions of defiance as *Go fuck yourself, Go piss up a rope*, etc.

Flying Milk Bottle (World War II; Air Force) *s.* The US P-47 Thunderbolt fighter, so called because of its shape.

flying pig (World War I) *s.* A German "aerial torpedo" launched from a heavy trench mortar. The name may have come from the noise that it made, like a pig's squeal.

Flying Prostitute (World War II; Air Force) *s.* The US B-26 light-medium bomber, so called because its comparatively small wing surface seemed to provide "no visible means of support." It also had bitchy peculiarities in its takeoffs and landings, which could shake up the most stouthearted pilot. Some pilots flying B-26s from English bases had local jewelers saw off the tips of their wing badges to match the stubby wings of their planes. Naturally, higher authority did not approve. Also called the *Baltimore Whore.*

flying saucer cap (Modern) *s.* The service cap, which with its circular design is somewhat suggestive of a flying saucer. See *flat hat.*

flying 25 (Modern) *s.* The first $25 paid to recruits shortly after their processing at the recruit depot. The money does not last very long.

FNG (Vietnam and later) *s.* Fucking New Guy. A replacement, a new man in an organization. "And sometimes, if you're a FNG, a fucken new guy" (Heinemann).

FO (World War I to Modern; also Marines) Forward Observer. An artillery lieutenant with a small detail and a radio who moves with the infantry or tanks to locate targets and adjust fire on them. During World War II, Korea, and Vietnam, Air Force officers sometimes operated in the same fashion and were called *forward air observers*. It was a splendid opportunity to show courage, initiative, and any suicidal tendencies in your make-up.

foal, to (Old Army; Cavalry and Field Artillery) *s.* To give birth. "My wife's foaling."

fogy fogey fogie (All Services) A word whose origin and history would probably be very interesting, if precisely known. The earliest form, which is civilian and from the middle 18th century, is *fogram*, meaning a superannuated person, an old fuddyduddy. 1. (Late 18th and early 19th centuries; British and American) An old or invalid soldier; hence, a garrison soldier. 2. (19th century, with some survivals; USA) Longevity pay, increase of pay for length of service. "I get another fogy next month, but my wife's already spending it." Also called *fogey pay, fogy pay*. Both *fogy* and *fogy pay* (with variants) are now becoming obsolete.

fooball (World War II; Air Force) *s.* A generic term for various types of German incendiary antiaircraft missiles, whether launched from the ground or from Luftwaffe fighter planes.

food service attendant (Modern) A simpering neologism for *KP*.

foo gas fu gas fougasse (Late 19th century to Modern) At present, a small mine utilizing explosives and napalm or gasoline that is buried at a strategic point along a fire base perimeter and detonated when the enemy threatens to break through the defenses. Sometimes the foo gas takes the form of a 55-gallon drum, filled with explosives and napalm, triggered with blasting caps hooked to hand generators. It may be covered with a little pile of broken rock to add to the enemy's woe. The term is a phonetic rendering of French *fougasse* 'small land mine'.

footlocker trunk locker A small trunk, olive-drab in color, issued to each soldier and stenciled with his name, number, unit, and sometimes his unit insignia. As the name suggests, it stands at the foot of the soldier's bunk in barracks. It is used for clothing and personal articles. Such lockers have been standard equipment since the last quarter of the 19th century, although earlier examples are smaller than the modern form.

footslogger *s.* An infantryman. Dr. Lighter cites an August 1918 use of the term.

forced issue (Considerable Antiquity to Modern) What you get when the quartermaster wants to be rid of some stuff cluttering up his warehouses. You requisition fresh beef, and he ships you surplus goldfish, left over from World War I and not aging gracefully. We got some veteran hardtack once instead of fresh bread!

force-out (Modern) An officer or enlisted soldier eliminated from the service by a reduction in force (RIF) or by the Army's Qualitative Management Program, which attempts to eliminate underachievers.

foreign duty pay Pay to which enlisted personnel are entitled while stationed in certain overseas areas classified as hardship tour areas.

Forgotten Fifteenth (Old Army) The US 15th Infantry Regiment, so called because it was stationed in Tientsin, China, from 1912 to 1938. A show-horse outfit, with Chinese boys for KP and fatigue. Sometimes called the *Can-Do Boys*, from its regimental motto, *Can Do*.

forlorn hope (Colonial to at least the Mexican War) A party of soldiers from different regiments who volunteer to lead the attempt to storm a fortification. They have a "forlorn hope" of surviving the fight, but if they do, they get first crack at the loot. Actually, this is a slight mistranslation of Dutch *verloren hoop* 'the lost group', 'the lost bunch'.

formation (Colonial to Modern) 1. An arrangement of elements of a unit in a prescribed manner. See *file, line, rank*. 2. Any formal gathering of troops, such as for reveille, retreat, etc. "Fuck formation. I'm tired of it" (Smith).

Form 20 (World War II and later) DA Form 20, Enlisted Qualification Record, now replaced by DA Forms 2 and 2.1. While it varied over the years, essentially it contained the basic personal data on a soldier, including a record of his assignments, promotions and reductions, test scores, education, decorations and awards, personal and family data, etc. It was kept in the soldier's 201 File (Personnel File), and when the DA levied a requirement for, say, a redheaded sergeant who spoke Urdu, Form 20s were screened until one or more candidates were identified. Low and probably malicious Army tradition had it that if there was more than one candidate, the personnel officer made his final decision by the same scientific process employed with *dream sheets*.

fort (Ancient to Modern) A permanent post or installation, as opposed to a camp, which is a temporary installation. Many of the forts occupied by US Army units have been given uncomplimentary nicknames: *Fort Dicks* or *Fort Pricks* (Fort Dix, New Jersey), *Fort Lost-in-the-Woods* (Fort Leonard Wood, Missouri), *Fort Mother-Fucker* (Fort Rucker, Alabama), *Fort Puke* (Fort Polk, Louisiana), *Fort Swill* (Fort Sill, Oklahoma), *Fort Useless* (Fort Eustis, Virginia), *Fort Uterus, Vagina* (Fort Eustis, Virginia), *Fort Turd* (Fort Ord, California). Less uncomplimentary was *Fort Custard* (Fort Custer, Michigan).

Fort Fumble (Modern) *s.* The Pentagon, in recognition of what seems to be its inmates' principal contributions to the national defense.

fort up, to (Colonial to 19th century) To take refuge in a frontier fort from large-scale Indian raids. Generally applied to civilians, sometimes used by soldiers and plainsmen, who, when under attack by superior numbers of Indians, might fort up in a handy gulch or buffalo wallow—or even behind their dead horses.

forty and eight (World War I) The standard French railway boxcar, a rather runty affair by US standards, capable of holding (and so labeled) *Hommes 40, chevaux 8*—forty men or eight horses. They were still around in World War II, but we did not depend on them so much, since we were a mechanized army. According to veterans of the AEF, we were lucky: their experience was that *chevaux* had always used them first.

forty dead men (Civil War; USA) *s.* A Yankee infantryman's optimistic term for the forty rounds of ammunition he carried in his cartridge box.

40-yenner (Occupation of Japan) The smallest, cheapest type of Japanese taxicab, so called from its basic fare of 40 yen, then equivalent to a little more than a dime. Its capacity was one average American, plus possibly a small *slanteye* companion. A 70-yenner seated two Americans comfortably, and a 100-yenner, four. Despite what newcomers were told, the drivers were not all ex-kamikaze pilots. No kamikaze was ever half so reckless.

4-F (World War II and later) A Selective Service classification meaning physically, morally, or psychologically unfit to serve in the Armed Forces. Also, a person so classified. This classification carried a definite stigma through the 1940s and 1950s, although some 4-Fs were willing and even eager to serve. During the Vietnam War the classification was a coveted distinction.

4F 4Fs (World War II) *s.* A reference to a catchphrase describing the technique of lechery: *Find 'em, fool 'em, fuck 'em, forget 'em.* Or, *Find 'em, feel 'em, fuck 'em, forget 'em.* A practitioner of this art might, as a gambit, refer to himself as a *4-F*, and then, if asked about it, explain. Probably an expansion of the civilian *three Fs* (omitting *fool 'em*), to parallel the draft category.

foundling (West Point) *s.* A cadet who is dismissed from the Academy. See *find*.

found on post Abandoned but serviceable government property found on an installation and put to use by a unit after a thorough search has failed to reveal its proper ownership. Sometimes the search is not so thorough.

four-by (Modern; all Services) *s.* 1. Short for *four-by-four*, a vehicle in which four wheels are driving wheels. Dual wheels are considered to be a single wheel for this classification. Usually written as *4 x 4*. 2. Short for *four-by-two*, or a vehicle in which two wheels are driving wheels. Usually written *4 x 2*. See *six-by*.

four-point-deuce *s.* The 4.2-inch mortar.

fourragère (World War I to Modern) A shoulder cord, similar to the aiguillette, awarded to units that have distinguished themselves in battle. The US Army does not award fourragères, but units may receive them from foreign governments. A soldier who served when the fourragère was awarded may continue to wear it no matter where he serves afterward, but a soldier who enters the unit after the award has been made is authorized to wear the fourragère only as long as he is with the unit.

four-star *s.* A full general.

fourteen and two (Modern) *s.* A common punishment under Article 15 of the *Uniform Code of Military Justice*. It consists of restriction to specified limits (usually the offender's barracks during off-duty hours) for fourteen consecutive days and concurrently two hours of extra duty for fourteen consecutive days. This punishment usually does not include suspension from duty, although such suspension, under the provisions of Article 15, is possible. Field-grade commanders may impose longer periods of restriction and extra duty: restriction up to sixty days, extra duty up to forty-five days.

fourth point of contact, Get your head out of [your] (Modern) *s.* Get your head out of your ass, in Army airborne talk. Other points of contact are the balls of the feet, the heels, the thighs, and the chest.

foxhole (World War I to Modern) A hastily dug pit large enough to give shelter to one or two men. Foxholes were usually dug by soldiers halted in contact with the enemy, but might be found around rear-area installations as cover during air raids. There is the story of a nurse who took shelter in a foxhole on such an occasion, found it already occupied, and emerged calling it a wolf hole. Before 1917 the foxhole was officially termed *skirmisher's* *trench*, and during World War II the term *slit trench* tended to replace *foxhole*. Also called *fighting hole* and *hasty pit*.

foxhole inspection (World War II and later) *s.* Medical examination of the vagina for VD. See also *manhole inspection*.

frag (Modern; all Services) *s.* Various uses derived from the words *fragment, fragmentary, fragmentation*. 1. A fragment of a shell. 2. Short for *fragmentary order*. An abbreviated operations order concerning an air flight or mission, issued on a daily basis, eliminating the need to repeat the information in the basic order. Also the flight arising from such an order. 3. Short for *fragmentation grenade*.

frag, to (Particularly in Vietnam) *s.* To use a fragmentation grenade. Originally to assassinate, murder, or try to murder someone with an explosive device, especially a hand grenade. The meaning has been extended to assassination by various other means, including firearms or even leading the victim into an ambush. Apart from random assassinations by deranged persons, the basic motive is vendetta: personal enmity, racial ill feeling, rebellion against authority, feeling of being imperiled by rash superiors, and similar situations. Actually, there were incidents in all such wars, although there were fewer correspondents in the past to report them. In the Mexican War a sergeant placed a shell under Capt. Braxton Bragg's bedroll one night and lit the fuse. The explosion wrecked the bedroll and tent, but Bragg emerged unhurt and more irascible than ever, as the sergeant soon learned.

frag breaker (Modern; Air Force) *s.* A bomb mission planner who translates fragmentary orders into an "understandable schedule for the wing" (Broughton).

fragging (Modern) *s.* Murder or attempted murder, as in *frag, to* 2. While the term is new, the practice is neither new nor confined to the American Army.

fraternization (Post–World War II) Any nonofficial association between US troops and the conquered Germans. Sparked by the meddling US Secretary of the Treasury Henry Morgenthau, official policy forbade personal relations of any sort between Americans and Germans. Gen. Dwight Eisenhower, who considered himself a 20th-century crusader, enforced the policy, or rather, tried to. It was the first time in history that any commander had had the unmitigated gall to tell his victorious troops that the conquered wine, women, and song were off limits. It was also pathetically stupid. There is no way to keep American soldiers from fraternizing with pretty girls or making friends with small children. In Japan, MacArthur avoided any such nonsense, remembering the advice of his soldier father never to give an order he knew would be disobeyed.

fraternize, to (Post–World War II on) 1. To associate with the people of a conquered and occupied land. Generally, this was not forbidden, but see *fraternization*. 2. *s.* To have sexual intercourse with, or to take as a mistress, a woman of the conquered people. In such cases, one did not *fraternize with*, one simply *fraternized*: "I'm going to find me a fräulein and fraternize her all night long."

freak (Modern; all Services) *s.* Short for radio *frequency*. "A strange voice came in on the command freak" (Marshall, 1969).

Freddy FADAC /Freddy 'fay-dack/ (Modern) *s.* Field Artillery Directional Automatic Computer. This is a computer that coordinates such data as powder charge, time of travel, deflection, and elevation for firing.

freedom bird (Modern; all Services) *s.* The aircraft (usually a Military Air Transport Service contract flight) that took soldiers (and others) home after they had completed their tours in Vietnam. "But you ain't got it made until you get on that freedom bird at Bien Hoa" (Bunting).

free mail Mail from a soldier in a combat zone, sent without postal charges. To take advantage of the franking privilege, the soldier writes the word *Free* in the upper right-hand corner of the envelope. Formerly called *soldier's mail.* In World War II it was available to all members of the Armed Forces, regardless of station.

French itch (World War I) *s.* A skin infection caused by a small parasitic mite, which for centuries had been the curse of armies operating in Europe. The term, however, was loosely used and might be applied to a wide variety of skin irritations.

French landing (Air Force) *s.* A landing in which a plane rolls along the ground on its two main wheels with its tail in the air, parallel to the runway, for some distance before coming to a stop.

French 75 (World War I to early World War II) 1. The French 75mm field gun, Model 1897, adopted by the US Army as its light artillery weapon. It was replaced by the 105mm howitzer. Although handicapped by its relatively light caliber, its flat trajectory, and its most peculiar sighting system (logical only to a Frenchman), it was a handy, sturdy, sweet-shooting gun. 2. A potent alcoholic beverage, inspired by the above and almost as deadly. According to our bartender's guide, it consists of an ounce of gin, the juice of one-quarter of a lemon, and half a teaspoon of powdered sugar, in a highball glass filled up with champagne. We remember it, however, as basically cognac and champagne. Probably the rigors of war made the other items unavailable.

fresh fish (Civil War) *s.* A term used by Union prisoners of war for newly arrived prisoners.

fresh meat (Modern; also Marines) *s.* A replacement or replacements. "Called me fresh-meat and told me to find some other outfit to get myself killed with" (Herr).

fried egg (West Point) *s.* The insignia on a cadet's dress hat.

friendly friendlies (World War I to Modern; all Services) One's own troops, gunfire, bombs, aircraft, etc. This definition results in such paradoxical terms as *friendly fire*, as in the Vietnam War, meaning that we have accidentally bombed or shelled our own troops. The term also applies to troops, either our own forces or the forces of allied nations. "Those are friendlies in that village, over there."

Fritz (World War I to World War II) *s.* A German, or things German.

frock, to (19th century to Modern) "To grant permission . . . to assume the style, title, uniform, and authority of the next highest grade [before actual promotion]" (Heinl). The term is based principally on naval practice. When a ship lost an officer, the vacancy was filled with a midshipman who had passed the examination for lieutenancy. He was appointed acting lieutenant, was addressed as *lieutenant*, and had the authority of a lieutenant. He no longer wore the short coat of a midshipman, but assumed the frock coat of an officer. In the Army only general officers are frocked (and then but rarely) when selected for promotion and assigned before the effective date of actual promotion to a duty position calling for a higher rank. For instance, a brigadier general selected for promotion to major general and assigned to a major general's position in a new command may, upon approval by the Deputy Chief of Staff for Personnel, Headquarters, Department of the Army, assume the two-star insignia, authority, title, and privileges (but not the pay) of a major general. There is, of course, an obvious parallel with frocking as the investiture of a person with a priestly office. The OED does not adduce any instances of the term before 1828. In the Navy, enlisted personnel are quite often frocked; Army enlisted personnel never are.

Frog 1. (Revolutionary to Modern) *s.* A Frenchman. Usually, in wartime, *those damned Frogs*. Also *frog eater* and *froggie*. 2. (West Point) *s.* The French language.

frogsticker (Uncertain antiquity; still heard in World War II) *s.* A bayonet. Not much used, to our knowledge. *Pigsticker* was more common.

from A word missing in much official Army language: "You will exit this post . . ."; "You will depart this command . . ."; "The aircraft egressed airspace above. . . ."

front and center 1. A portion of the ceremony of dress parade or guard mount in which the adjutant commands, "Front and center—march!" and the appropriate officers and NCOs come forward to receive the day's orders. 2. Similarly, a command used at special formations to call one or more soldiers forward to receive a decoration, promotion, or commendation. 3. At drill, to call men aside for special instructions. 4. *s.* In everyday Army life, *Smith, front and center!* means *Come here, Smith!* and may be used at any time.

frontchannel (Modern) An electrically transmitted message sent through normal communications facilities. See *backchannel, jump channels*.

front leaning rest position (Modern) *s.* A jocular description of the starting position assumed in push-ups. Arms, back, and legs are straight, and the weight is supported by the hands and the tips of the toes. As soldiers are sometimes punished by being made to perform push-ups, the threat to put someone in the front leaning rest position is common and meaningful. It is sometimes shortened to *leaning rest*, as in

If I die in the old drop zone
Box me up and ship me home.
Bury me in the leaning rest
And tell all the girls I did my best.

Here the expression also has a sexual significance. See also *Give me ten!* and *jack up*.

Frozen Chosin Frozen Chosen (Modern; all Services) A descriptive term applied by soldiers and marines to the Chosin (Korea) Reservoir area during the retreat in the disastrous winter of 1950–51; also, to Korea in general. *Chosen* is the Japanese parallel form to *Chosun*, the ancient name for Korea. Both *Chosen* and *Chosun* mean (Land of) Morning Calm.

fruit salad (Late World War II) *s.* A gaudy display of the ribbons of decorations and service medals. The term probably originated among envious rear-area types, but may have been created as self-derogatory irony by veterans who have a full fruit salad. Also used by the RAF in World War II.

FTA (Modern) *s.* Fuck The Army. In the 1960s and 1970s, *FTA* could be seen scrawled almost everywhere in Army installations, even on pieces of individual equipment and clothing. Our sergeant major reports an ingenious stratagem employed by certain young soldiers caught displaying the ugly letters. To avoid just and swift retribution, they claimed that the initials stood for *Fun, Travel, and Adventure.*

FUBAR /'foo-bar/ (World War II to Modern; all Services) *s.* Fucked Up Beyond All Recognition.

FUBB (World War II to Modern; all Services) *s.* Fucked Up Beyond Belief.

FUBIS /'foo-biss/ (Modern; all Services) *s.* Fuck You, Buddy, I'm Shipping Out. Wentworth and Flexner state that this originated in the 1960s. It is not heard much anymore.

Fuck 'em all (At least World War II to Modern) 1. *s.* Part of a catchphrase indicating resigned disgust, disdain, etc. There are various versions of the full statement: *Fuck 'em all but six and save them for pallbearers; Fuck 'em all but six, four to be pallbearers and two to count cadence*; etc. "Fuck 'em all but eight. Leave six for pallbearers and two to beat the drums" (Durden). 2. *s.* A substitute chorus for that popular British song "Bless 'Em All." According to Partridge (1970), *Fuck 'em all* was the original, later cleaned up.

Fuck 'em and feed 'em beans (At least as early as World War II) *s.* A catchphrase indicating the fate of a GI. Actually, beans were not that prominent a part of the Army diet.

Fuck 'em if they can't take a joke (Vietnam and later) *s.* A catchphrase often used when some dreadful military tragedy is revealed. During the Vietnam War it was most frequently used when friendly positions were accidentally bombed or shelled by our own troops. See *prosign.*

fucking A you're fucking A (At least World War II, to Modern) *s.* That's right! You're right! "Fuckin' A. We'll get a place in Berkeley and join the VFW" (Smith). *A* here probably stands for first class (as in A1), absolutely perfect, but we have found no etymology.

fucking up like a T/5 going to an NCO meeting fucking up like a spec five going to an NCO meeting (World War II and later in first version; 1955 on in second version) *s.* Being wrong and out of place. The first phrase was based on the fact that the technician grades of 1942–48, although officially defined as noncommissioned officers, were sometimes regarded as ambiguous. They were often considered out of place in any discussion of training, leadership, and morale. In the more modern version, a spec 5, although accorded most of the privileges of an NCO, is not primarily an enlisted leader. See *hard-stripe.*

fuck-off (Antiquity uncertain but common from World War II to Modern; all Services) *s.* A useless, idle, unreliable, lazy bum. Occasionally a *fuck-off* can be a deliberate troublemaker, but such a soldier is more properly a *fuck-up.*

fuck off, to To loaf, to shirk, to ignore one's duties, to hamper the work of others, to be an unmitigated nuisance.

fuck the duck, to (Antiquity uncertain but common from World War II to Modern; all Services) *s.* To goof off, to loaf, to sleep. In civilian slang *to fuck the duck* sometimes meant to masturbate, but this meaning does not seem to appear in the service. This expression is not the same as the World War II catchphrase Go *fuck a duck*, which was usually not offensive, and meant roughly 'Go away and don't bother me."

fuck-up (Antiquity uncertain but common from World War II to Modern; all Services) *s.* One of the basic, most common Army expressions, this has entered into a seemingly endless variety of compounds and acronyms, indicating confusion, spoiling, improper or inadequate performance, stupidity, irresponsibility, disaster, and just the nature of things. 1. Things that are fucked up. "What a colossal fuck-up! Don't you know that you don't put KP on a morning report?" 2. A bad soldier. He ranges from being an irresponsible bum and unfortunate soldier who messes up everything he touches to a deliberate, provocative troublemaker and shirker. He differs from an *old soldier* in doing what the old soldier might only think of doing and in getting caught at it. Readers may remember what happened to fuck-ups in James Jones's *From Here to Eternity*.

fuck up, to *s.* To screw up. "Everything is all fucked up! We'll never get it straightened out." "Will you stop fucking up the morning report and do it the way HQ wants it?"

fudge factor (Modern) *s.* A built-in allowance for error, as in a statistical report. From *to fudge*, meaning to cheat, lie, hedge.

fugleman fugelman (18th and 19th centuries) An intelligent soldier, expert at drill and the manual of arms, who is posted in front of a raw unit to give the members an example of correct execution of a drillmaster's commands. "Lieutenant Buford, who was detached to drill the Arkansas Cavalry, had me detailed for his orderly and I acted as 'Fugleman' for that regiment in the Carbine and Saber exercise" (Chamberlain). The derivation of the term is from German *Flügelmann* 'man on the wing', and the English forms *flugelman* and *flugleman* are sometimes met.

FUJIGMO /foo-'jig-mo/ (Modern; all Services) *s.* Fuck You, Jack, I Got My Orders. A statement of indifference and mild defiance. *Orders* in this sense means shipping orders. The soldier will be leaving soon and does not care.

full bird (Modern) *s.* A colonel, because of his eagle insignia. A lieutenant colonel, however, is not called a half bird.

full bull (Antiquity uncertain, to Modern) *s.* A colonel.

full-dress uniform This term is obsolete, although uninformed persons often confuse it with dress uniform.

full field full field layout full field inspection (Modern) Generally, an out-of-doors inspection in which the soldiers display all their field equipment, including weapons. The display is arranged in a prescribed manner and usually takes place before pitched tents.

full track (World War II to Modern) A vehicle (such as a tank or tractor) that moves on caterpillar tracks only. See *half-track*.

FUMTU (Post–World War II; all Services) *s.* Fucked Up More Than Usual. A second-generation offspring of *SNAFU*.

funk hole (World War I, still occasionally encountered) *s.* A foxhole, shelter trench, dugout—anything you can duck into for shelter against the wrath of your superiors. Earliest quoted use is from the British Army of around 1900.

Funky Fourth Funky Fo' (Modern) *s.* The US 4th Infantry Division. Also known as the *Poison Ivy Division* from the four ivy leaves on its shoulder patch.

funny money (Modern; all Services) *s.* Military payment certificates. "They resurrected the 'funny money,' the scrip currency used in Korea and post-war Germany" (Mulligan).

funny papers (Modern) *s.* Maps.

furlough (Revolutionary to Modern) 1. An extended period of authorized absence granted to an enlisted man. 2. The document issued to him to make his leave a matter of record, although the term *furlough papers* (even though it is a single sheet of paper) is more common. In the 19th century the verb *to furlough*, to let a soldier go on furlough, was used, but it is now obsolete. For some reason, in the American Army, a similar permission to an officer is called *leave*.

furniture (Civil War; USA) *s.* Eating and cooking equipment issued by the Army: "A spoon, fork, knife, and cup for each man and two cooking pans for a mess of eight."

☆☆☆☆ g ☆☆☆☆

GA (Modern) General of the Army.

Gabby Hayes Gabby Hayes hat (Modern) *s.* A field hat popular with the troops during the Vietnam War. A narrow-brimmed, low-crowned bush hat issued to soldiers in the combat zone, it was probably named after the floppy, crumpled, worn-out hat that was a prop for the Western character actor Gabby Hayes.

gadget 1. (West Point) *s.* A cadet. 2. (Army, Air Force) *s.* An Air Force Academy cadet. 3. *s.* According to Wentworth and Flexner, in World War II, a young woman.

gaggle (Air Force) *s.* A number of aircraft operating in close proximity to each other, but not necessarily in any semblance of formation. From the traditional group-designation for geese.

galloper 1. (Revolutionary into early 19th century) *s.* Also called *galloper gun*, it was a light cannon, usually a one- to three-pounder, mounted on a carriage with shafts like those of a buggy so that it could be towed by one horse or two horses hitched in tandem, without the use of a limber. It was a handy rig that could move rapidly over rough ground. It was often used for those guns directly attached to the infantry. See *grasshopper, butterfly*. 2. (Colonial to World War I) A mounted messenger. In older British usage, the term might mean an aide-de-camp.

galloping dandruff *s.* Crab lice.

galvanized Yank galvanized Reb (Civil War) *s.* A turncoat. This odd term does not seem to refer to galvanized iron, as is sometimes thought, but refers to the electrical experiments of the 18th-century Italian scientist Luigi Galvani, in which he brought a semblance of life to detached muscles. (This was popularly identified with bringing the dead back to life, as in Poe's story "Some Words with a Mummy" and Mary Shelley's *Frankenstein.*) Thus, a *galvanized* soldier was a soldier who had been brought back to life and activity, from a prison camp, but on the side of his captors. There were galvanized Confederate soldiers who signed up with the Union Army and were sent to the West to fight Indians, and there were galvanized Union soldiers (mostly bounty jumpers) who joined the Confederate Army to escape the prison camps. There is some confusion about the terms, for while most soldiers understood *galvanized Yank* to mean a Yankee who joined the Rebels, some modern historians claim it meant a Rebel galvanized back to life as a Yank. *Galvanized* was also used as a noun to mean a *turncoat*: "The boys resolved to use these [blacks] to wreak the camp displeasure on the Galvanized. [They would] approach one of the leaders among them [and ask] 'Is you a Galvanized?'" (McElroy, 1899).

Gammon bomb (World War II) An antitank hand grenade, designed for close-in defense by newly landed paratroops against enemy armor. Reportedly named after its inventor, a Sergeant Gammon of the Royal Engineers, it consisted of an explosive charge in a tarred canvas bag, with a tricky detonating device that supposedly went off on impact against anything hard. Although used with occasional success in Sicily and Normandy, it was not popular. Many paratroopers seem to have considered carrying one around a bigger hazard than the chance of a German tank attack.

gangplank policy (Modern) *s.* A policy that permits a soldier to extend his overseas tour at any time before his actual DEROS—virtually up to the moment he is scheduled to depart the theater or just before he "walks up the gangplank" to go home. "Some . . . are able to extend at any time under . . . the 'gangplank' policy" (*Pentagram News*, 3 April 1980). This policy also prevailed in Vietnam.

gangplank retirement (Modern) 1. *s.* A retirement that is forced, in advance of one's own plans, or retirement against one's will. In this sense, equivalent to walking the plank. 2. *s.* Less frequently, retiring suddenly, in a huff.

Garand (World War II) The US Garand .30-caliber M1 semiautomatic rifle, named after John C. Garand, its designer. It was adopted by the Army in 1940 as a replacement for the Springfield '03. While it was far less accurate than the Springfield, especially for ranges over 400 yards, it was an effective weapon. In a tight spot, a good shot could squeeze off the eight rounds in its clip in twenty seconds, and it took less time to train a soldier to use it than was needed for the Springfield. (Its front sight did occasionally work loose during sustained firing and might even drop off.) See also *M1 thumb*.

garbage can rattler (Modern) *s.* A somewhat cynical appraisal of the duties of a command sergeant major, who is sometimes seen as spending much of his time attending to the details of post police.

Garden Service (World War I) A temporary branch of the Quartermaster Corps set up within the AEF in France to provide fresh garden foods for the troops. It acted in cooperation with the local French authorities.

garrison (Ancient to Modern) 1. A permanent military post. 2. The troops stationed at such a post. 3. Used adjectivally, describing certain articles that are issued to, or permitted to, soldiers in garrison, but not to combat troops. See *garrison belt, garrison buttons*, etc. 4. (Age uncertain) Used adjectivally, to describe someone who is ignorant of how the "real Army" works, is a fuddyduddy, or is a martinet. A *garrison soldier* is one who observes all the rules and regulations, always salutes officers, starches his uniforms, and shines his shoes when no one else does. "I didn't know any different. I was still garrison" (Heinemann).

garrison, to To assign troops to a post.

garrison belt (Early 20th century to post–World War II) A broad, brown leather waist belt with an open brass buckle. It was introduced in 1902 and was worn with dress uniforms in garrison and on pass. Before World War I it was even worn with the Full Dress Blue uniform and black shoes, a combination not allowed thereafter. A soldier wearing a garrison belt was not considered under arms unless he had a side arm attached to it for drill or guard mount. In off-post brawls it made a first-class weapon, whether swung buckle-end first or looped around the fist as a knuckle-duster. (The Marines' white leather dress belt with its big, solid brass plate was even better.) The garrison belt vanished with the adoption of the Ike jacket.

garrison buttons (At least Old Army into World War II) Brass blouse buttons that could be purchased at the PX. They differed from issue buttons in having a smooth surface (instead of striated), being more convex, and in taking a superior shine. Some organizations permitted them; others did not.

garrison cap 1. (Not long before, and during, World War II) A flap-topped hat with a leather or composition visor. There were both OD and suntan types. It was almost the same as the modern service cap. 2. (Since World War II) A visorless soft cap that can be folded and is authorized for wear with the Army Green, tan, khaki, and Hospital Duty uniforms. This cap was originally called the *overseas cap*, because during World War I it was authorized only for overseas wear. During the 1920s the Army Air Corps adopted it, since it is convenient to wear in the restricted space of aircraft, and for similar reasons, motorized troops began to wear it in the 1930s. It was adopted throughout the Army soon after this. In the 1940s and 1950s, the tip edge of the curtain of the cap was trimmed with braid piping, which indicated by its color the branch of the service to which the soldier belonged; such piping is no longer used. At present officers wear a gold braid; warrant officers, silver; and enlisted personnel, a braid that matches the shade of the cap. This cap is also called the *cunt cap* (perhaps its most common name), the *go-to-hell cap*, and the *tit cap*. In the Marine Corps it is known as the *fore-and-aft cap* and the *piss-cutter cap*.

garrison flag The largest (20 by 38 feet) national (American) flag, used on military installations. Is it flown only on national holidays and special occasions.

garrison hat (Air Force) The Air Force service hat with bill.

garrison prisoner A soldier found guilty (by a court-martial) of a military offense who served out his sentence at the post (garrison) where his unit was stationed. His sentence could be commuted by the garrison commander.

garrison rations (Pre-1940) Not rations, but a monetary allowance made to units in peacetime, based on the current cost of the thirty-nine items included in the official rations. This allowance was computed monthly in two values, one for posts with government-owned bakeries, the other for posts without such bakeries. Each unit (company-sized at that time) could plan its own menu and serve whatever meals it thought proper as long as it kept within the value of the ration. Money not spent (*ration savings*) was paid to the unit, and was used for the purchase of extra or special foods. Companies, batteries, or troops with good mess officers, mess sergeants, and cooks could live high on the hog, while the outfit next door consumed beans. All this could be wonderful for unit morale, but it seemed easier to abolish the whole system than to get rid of the commissioned and noncommissioned incompetents who could not meet its requirements.

garrison school (World War I) *s.* A beating, in the form of a fistfight, delivered for disciplinary reasons. Usually such educational sessions were held out behind the stables by an NCO or the company executioner.

garrison shoes (Post–World War I to Modern) Good quality shoes, now oxford style, for wear on dress occasions. (The Army had them, as *post shoes*, from 1885 to 1887, but stopped issuing them because they were too comfortable. Soldiers used them for fatigue and field duty and wore them out too quickly.)

garritroopers (World War II) *s.* An element among service and headquarters personnel given to phony displays of military experience and personal toughness. They were "too far forward to wear ties and too far back to get shot" (Mauldin).

"Garry Owen" The famous song of the 7th Cavalry. It was introduced in the post–Civil War period when that newly organized regiment was filled with Irish immigrant soldiers.

Let Bacchus' sons be not dismayed
But join with me each jovial blade;
Come booze and sing and lend your aid,
To help me with the chorus:
  Instead of Spa we'll drink down ale,
  And pay the reckoning on the nail:
  No man for debt shall go to jail
  From Garry Owen in glory.

gas attack (Modern) *s.* Breaking wind.

gas barrage (World War I) *s.* Unnecessary and unwanted talk and bragging. Hot air.

gas curtain (World War I and later) A canvas or blanket at the entrance to a shelter, intended to keep gas out.

gas house gas tent A structure used in gas-mask training. Chemical warfare instructors were often termed the *Gas House Gang.*

gas house (Post–World War II) *s.* A beer hall, saloon, or other place of alcoholic refreshment. The GI version of German *Gasthaus* 'inn'.

gate, to (Air Force) *s.* To fly at maximum possible speed or power.

gate ghetto (Modern; also Marines) *s.* The collection of clipjoints, bars, amusement parlors, and other kinds of dives that cluster around the main gate to military installations. "Kin village . . . was nothing but a gate ghetto" (Webb). See also *Strip, Ville.*

Gatling gun A multibarreled, hand-cranked early type of machine gun, invented by an American, Dr. Richard J. Gatling, in 1862. In spite of a tendency to jam, it was used all around the world as an effective prop to the "White Man's burden." A two-gun section (manned by infantrymen) played a key part at San Juan Hill in 1898. The Russians, naturally, called it the Goroloff gun, after the Russian officer who supervised the production of their imitation of it. A modern, electric-powered version—the Vulcan gun—was introduced after World War II as an aircraft weapon.

gauntlet gantelope gantlet An ancient military punishment used up to the early 19th century. The culprit was made to walk slowly between two ranks of his comrades, each of whom was required to strike him once with a stick, gun sling, or switch. During the 1930s it was a favorite ceremony at the end of a National Guard encampment, those enlisted men who had completed their first period of active duty being put through the gauntlet as a rite de passage acknowledging their full comradeship. The favorite weapon employed on them was the holster of the .45-caliber automatic pistol, held by its tip. The flap really stung! The term has nothing to do with gauntlets as gloves, but is derived from Swedish *gatlopp* 'running the lane'.

gear 1. (At least 19th century) Military equipment or accoutrements in general. 2. (World War II and later; Signal Corps) Radio equipment.

geechie (World War II) *s.* A native girl on any of the Pacific islands occupied by US forces. We have been told that after a few weeks Americans began to realize that the geechies *were* beautiful. The origin of the term is uncertain; perhaps from the Southern term *geechie*, a black woman, or a variant of the omnipresent *chichi*.

gen, the /jen/ (World War II; Air Force) *s.* Information, the straight dope, poop. We have a suspicion that it was an informal shortening of *genuine*. Another source suggests that it is another borrowing from the RAF—the abbreviation for *general*, as in "general information for all ranks." "What's the gen on the outfit being transferred to the Far East?" Usually it turned out to be another number one rumor.

general (Ancient to Modern) 1. A generic term applied to all general officers: brigadier general, major general, lieutenant general, general, general of the Army. 2. At present, a four-star general officer ranking beneath general of the Army and above lieutenant general. A general usually commands an army, an army group, a theater, or higher command structures. The chief of staff of the Army is a general, and no higher appointment is made in the Army of today. Until World War II the rank of general was rarely filled. In the 19th century, only Grant, Sherman, and Sheridan were generals; and during and immediately after World War I, only two men held the rank, Pershing and Tasker H. Bliss (brevet rank). During and after World War II, however, appointments have been made to the rank of general. Abbreviated *Gen., G.*

General, the (Ancient to Old Army) A field-music signal, later replaced by first call. It was an alert, indicating that the whole force was to prepare to move out. The *Regulations* of 1779 provided that "the General is to beat only when the whole is to march, and is the signal to strike the tents and prepare for the march." An Old Army touch, dating back at least to the Civil War, was to have all the tents struck together so that they came down simultaneously with the last notes of the General. The cavalry used *Boots and Saddles* as an equivalent.

General Balzoff (World War II) *s.* One of a series of Allied generals whose exploits the GIs used to discuss in catchphrases, often before WACs who pretended they did not understand. "Hey, are the Russians rolling them up! It's that new general, Balzoff." "Never heard of him." "You never heard of Gen. Katya Balzoff?" Gen. Katya Balzoff had brother officers Terya and Ripya. Or, sometimes his full name was Katyabalzoff. Some of the more timid GIs used to worry if the Spaniards came into the war, because of their great general, Don Juan Tumeni. It was generally conceded, though, that the greatest military genius of all was the Chinese Nationalist general, Fah Kyu.

general officer An overall title for brigadier generals, major generals, lieutenant generals, generals, generals of the Army. Their insignia is the silver star: one for a brigadier general, two for a major general, three for a lieutenant general, four for a general, and five (in a circular pattern) for a General of the Army.

General of the Armies 1. This rank was created for George Washington by Congress on 3 March 1799. But President John Adams did not make the appointment, and when Washington died, about nine months after the creation of the rank, he was still a lieutenant general. In 1976, for the Bicentennial, Congress reinstated the rank of General of the Armies posthumously for Washington, and his appointment became effective on 4 July 1976. This grade of Washington's was clearly intended to rank higher than any other appointment of general officers made in the US Army, including the five-star generals of World War II. 2. In 1919, Congress created the rank and title of General of the Armies of the United States for John Pershing, who retained them until his death in 1948. The rank had only four stars.

General of the Army 1. On 26 July 1866, Congress created for General Grant the rank of General of the Army; this was considered to be a revival of Washington's unfulfilled appointment, despite the slightly different title. Grant thus became the first four-star general. Sherman and Sheridan were also later created Generals of the Army, but the title was allowed to lapse with Sherman's death in 1888. During this period the titles *general, General of the Army*, and *General of the Army of the United States* seem to have been considered synonymous. 2. During War II it was recognized that a rank higher than general was needed to put American officers on a par with their European counterparts, and the rank of General of the Army, a five-star general, was created. There have been only five five-star generals: George C. Marshall, Douglas MacArthur, Dwight D. Eisenhower, Henry H. Arnold, and Omar N. Bradley. Abbreviated *GA, Gen. of Army.*

general order An official order applying to an entire command. Such orders are usually numbered serially by the issuing headquarters through the calendar year.

General Orders General Orders of a Sentinel Formerly, a set of twelve standard orders given to all Army sentinels. Beginning with "To take charge of this post and all government property in view," they were designed to cover all likely problems a sentinel might encounter and had to be memorized verbatim. One of the delights of guard duty in a driving midnight rain was having the Officer of the Day appear and demand to know what the fourth—or any other—general order was. This practice reportedly has been abolished recently, apparently because it placed too severe a mental strain on our modern VOLAR personnel. After the outbreak of World War II, General Order Number 9, which pledged you not to allow anyone "to commit a nuisance on or near your post" was revoked. Presumably the Regular Army suspected either that its draftees were not properly housebroken (in which case there would be unnecessary stateside casualties and paperwork) or that no non-Regular knew what nuisance meant. In

1967 the General Orders were abridged to three.

general prisoner A soldier found guilty of a serious crime resulting in long imprisonment and dishonorable discharge. He was usually transferred to a disciplinary barracks or federal penitentiary.

general's car (Common in World War II, but probably older) *s.* A wheelbarrow. The term came from certain sergeants' odd ideas of humor. When they wanted someone to push a wheelbarrow, they would ask for a volunteer *to drive the general's car.*

general staff A group of officers in the headquarters of Army divisions, similar units, and larger units. The general staff assists its commanding officer in planning, coordinating, and supervising operations. The general staff is usually as follows: G-1, personnel; G-2, intelligence; G-3, operations and plans; G-4, logistics; G-5, civilian affairs or military government. Particular sections may be added or eliminated by the commanding officer. On some general staffs, for example, a G-6, communications, is added, while elsewhere the G-1 may be eliminated and its functions divided up among the other staff officers. Joint staffs and special staffs are similarly organized.

General Staff Identification Badge Established in 1920, a badge awarded to any officer (or noncommissioned officer if he has served in an action officer position) who has served a year or more on the Army General Staff. Upon issuance of a certificate, the badge may be worn as a permanent part of the uniform. Also called the *liver patch* or *liver pad.*

geographical bachelor (Modern) *s.* A married soldier who does not take his family with him on a permanent change-of-station assignment. The term is not used for married soldiers serving on unaccompanied status in overseas areas.

German Terms for a German (or the Germans) include *Boche, Dutch, Dutchman, Fritz, Fritzie, Hammerhead, Heinie, Hermann, Hun, Jerry, Katzenjammer, Kraut, Lugerhead, Rad, Squarehead.*

German ace (World War I) *s.* An aviation cadet with five or more flying accidents. See *ace.*

Geronimo (World War II and later) A shout uttered by members of the original 501st Parachute Battalion at Fort Benning, Georgia, in 1940, when jumping from an airplane. There is a hazy legend that a motion picture about Geronimo, the famous Apache chieftain, was being shown at the post motion picture theater at the time. *Geronimo* became the motto of the 501st Parachute Infantry Regiment, which was formed from the battalion, and was given considerable publicity. Its use, however, was by no means universal. Some paratroopers were reported to use *umbriago*, Jimmy Durante's catchword. One company of the 505th Regiment later affected the commonplace, if emphatic, "Fuckkit!"

[get, to] *Expressions using this verb are placed under the major word of the phrase.*

G-5 (World War II to Modern) The staff section (or the officer in charge of it) responsible for the military government of occupied territories. Unfortunately, too many of its members may be blissfully ignorant of the native languages, customs, and geography, and helplessly dependent on their assigned DACs.

G-4 (World War I to Modern) The staff section (or the officer in charge of it) responsible for supply and logistics. When

G-4 does work, it is probably the most essential staff section. However, like the Old Army supply companies, it is still a natural home for slow horses and fat men. Below division level, this is termed *S-4*.

GFU (World War II to Modern) *s.* General Fuck-Up. An exceptionally bad fuck-up. Applied only to persons, not to situations.

ghost (Civil War; USA) *s.* A white horse, probably because of its visibility after dark. Dangerous in combat, white horses were useful on night marches. "My guide properly rode a white horse which I could distinguish at twenty paces" (Wainwright).

ghost, to (1950s on) *s.* To sneak off from duty or to find a legitimate-sounding excuse for evading it. *Ghosting* was hiding out when the topkick was forming a fatigue detail. See *goldbrick*.

ghost turds (West Point) *s.* Small rolls of dust that collect under beds and other furniture in the barracks, driving the occupants frantic as they try to clean them up just before an inspection. "Sweep up the ghost turds collected under the beds" (Truscott).

ghost walks, the (Old Army to at least World War II) *s.* It is payday. Also *the walking of the ghost*. Victorian theater slang in origin, possibly with ultimate reference to Hamlet's father. See also *the eagle shits*.

GI /*Pronounced as initials*/ A very important word in the Army. A term of complex origin, indicating various aspects of military life as opposed to civilian. 1. (Pre–World War II to Modern) An enlisted person in the US Army. This was pretty much the standard term among both soldiers and civilians in World War II. While the term was usually considered inoffensive by enlisted men, it seems to have been regarded with some disfavor in higher circles. Gen. Douglas MacArthur apparently did not like it. When his surgeon, Colonel Roger O. Egeberg, casually referred to the troops under MacArthur's command as GIs, MacArthur is reported to have said, "Don't ever do that in my presence. . . . GI means 'general issue.' Call them soldiers" (Manchester). In other services, too, the term was frowned upon. "Never speak of an enlisted Marine as a 'GI' " (Heinl). Nevertheless, the term was generally accepted, along with its relative, *GI Joe*. In the Vietnam War, *GI* seems to have been the standard way the bargirls and their like addressed soldiers. 2. Adjectivally, indicating things issued by the Army, like *GI brushes, GI shoes*, etc. Here *GI* stands for *general issue* or *government* issue, and to discourage theft, the initials *GI* were sometimes painted or stenciled on articles not designed for personal use. The term *GI* also came to mean a particular style of object, as issued by the Army. The GI brush, for example, carried over into civilian life, and even today veterans may refer to a flatbacked stiff scrubbing brush as a GI brush. 3. Adjectivally, indicating things that are characteristic of military life, sometimes in contrast to civilian. A *GI party* is not a party; *GI blues* are unhappiness in the service; *GI haircuts* are crew cuts, etc. 4. Adjectivally, meaning the official way. Oddly enough, this can mean either well done or poorly done. Meaning correctly done, "Come on, men, let's do it GI!" or ". . . the GI way!" 5. Adjectivally, describing a rigid person who is a stickler for the rules and somewhat lacking in compassion for others. "Don't fuck with the top. He's a

GI son of a bitch and you'll be pulling KP before you know it." This is both a common and an important use. 6. As an adjective, it may stand for *galvanized iron*. The *GI can*, a basic of Army life, is simply a galvanized iron can.

In the complex, obscure history of *GI*, the original element seems to have been *GI* as *galvanized iron*, as stated by Colby and Lighter. The earliest quotation that has been found (A. E. Whitehead, "Handling a Wagon Train," *Cavalry Journal*, vol. 17, p. 64) uses *GI* as if it were a term familiar to his readers: "The following is the equipment of wagon trains sent from the post to the Ft. Riley maneuvers in 1906: Bucket, G. I. on strap near axle under body." *GI* for *galvanized iron* and *GI* for *government issue* or *general issue* apparently coalesced and became confused before World War I, with possibly still another component, *garrison issue*, a term once used to describe certain accessories to the uniform. Nason (1928), who wrote stories of World War I and is authentic as to language, refers to "G. I. cans, the initials signifying Government Issue." Precisely when *GI* became a term for a soldier is not known. Lighter refers to a cartoon of December 1918 that is captioned "A G. I. Christmas," but here the initials probably meant *general issue* or *government issue*—simply military. But by 1939 *GI* meaning a soldier had become part of West Point vocabulary (*Bugle Notes*, 1939). This can be interpreted as evidence for an earlier use in the Army in general.

GI, to To clean up. "We've got to GI the barracks before we can take off."

GIB (Modern; Air Force) *s.* Guy In Back. The backseat crew member in a fighter aircraft. "I and my GIB engaged a number of MIG 21's" (AAV, p. 109).

GI bath (Modern) *s.* A punishment meted out to soldiers by their fellows. It is reserved for persons whose standards of personal hygiene are below average, and it is accomplished by throwing the offender into a shower and then scrubbing him down with GI brushes and GI soap. Although the term is known, our sergeant major says that he has never witnessed a GI bath nor known anyone who would admit that he has.

GI brush (At least World War II to Modern) A large, wood-backed scrubbing brush with stiff bristles, used for heavy-duty cleaning. Our sergeant major, who claims to have spent many years whiling away the blissful hours at GI parties and on KP, is still trying to discover the name of the person who invented this ingenious and useful device.

GI can (At least World War I to Modern) 1. A galvanized iron can used principally as a garbage can, but sometimes diverted to such prosaic uses as a container for peeled potatoes in the mess hall, cans of beer at parties, washing mess kits in the field, etc. 2. (World War I) *s.* A heavy artillery shell, so called from the fancied resemblance to a GI can. 3. (World War II) *s.* A WAC of loose morals. You can put anything into a GI can.

gig /gig/ A variety of uses cluster around this word, which seems to have come from gambling and lottery parlance of the middle and late 19th century, where a *gig* meant a sufficient number of points to win something. The primary military meaning of *gig* is a minor bad mark or demerit, usually associated with failure at inspection. A certain number of gigs automatically causes suspension of privileges (passes, free time) or application of company punishment (KP, extra details, restriction, etc.). The more important meanings of *gig* are (1) an offense that can result in a gig; (2) enough marks to cause a loss of privilege ("Pfc. Murphy. Gigged for this weekend."); (3) to record or mark down a gig. Many special terms are associated with *gig*. *A gig flap* is an unbuttoned pocket, especially one that is discovered during an inspection. Inspecting officers have been known to cut or tear the offending flap off. A *gig line* is the straight line that results when the shirt front, the edge of the belt buckle, and the trousers fly are in perfect alignment. Old soldiers automatically adjust the gig line before stepping into public in uniform. A *gig list* is a list of possible offenses at inspection; it does not have to be written down.

gigadier breneral jigadier brindle (At least Civil War to Modern) *s.* A wordplay on *brigadier general.*

GI gin (Modern) *s.* A cough medicine compounded by Army pharmacists. The principal ingredient is ethyl alcohol, for which reason it is sometimes called *ETH* or *ethyl turpin hydrate.* The mixture sometimes includes codeine. It not only cures the cough, but if you drink it by the gulp instead of by the spoonful as prescribed, you will feel no pain whatever. Then you wake up four hours later to find that you are hungry and that it is 0200 hours.

GI gunboats (World War II) *s.* The heavy Army service shoes. Even when they fit, they looked too big.

GI Jesus (World War II and later) *s.* A chaplain.

Gimlets The US 21st Infantry Regiment.

gink (Modern) *s.* A derogatory word for the Vietnamese. Perhaps a combination of *gook* and *dink*, reinforced by civilian slang *gink*, meaning a stupid person or just a person.

GI party (Pre–World War II to Modern) *s.* A general cleanup, customarily held on Friday nights, so that everything would be sparkling clean for the traditional Saturday morning inspection. This practice, however, in the words of a veteran sergeant major, is now "unfashionable." The biggest and most exacting of these parties was the one to get ready for the IG's annual inspection. As one soldier put it in Post:

GI for the IG 'cause that's the thing
to do.
GI for the IG 'till you're black and
blue.
Oh, GI for the IG so when the Man
comes through
He'll see that you've GI'd for the
IG and won't gig you.

GIs GI shits *s.* Diarrhea. From *gastrointestinal*, but undoubtedly influenced and reinforced by *GI* meaning military. Probably taken over from civilian hospital use. "I've got the GIs." The term has been in use since at least as early as 1943 (*Yank*, 3 September 1943). During the Vietnam War the venerable GIs took on several modernizations: *Ho Chi Minh's curse* (probably influenced by *Montezuma's revenge* for a Mexico tourist's diarrhea), the *Saigon quickstep*, the *Viet shits*, etc. It was said of these disorders that "your youth drops purgatively out your asshole during your first week in Vietnam" (Suddick). Well, perhaps not the first week.

Give me ten! (Modern) *s.* A command to perform ten push-ups as punishment for real or imagined infractions of the rules. There may be a sardonic connection with the civilian slang expression *Give me five*, meaning "Shake hands with me." Note, also, that *Take ten!* is something very different. See *front leaning rest position* and *jack up*.

Give the tops of your shoes a party (Modern) *s.* Short for *Give the tops of your shoes a party and invite your trousers down.* The correct length for Army dress trousers is just sufficient to cover the tops of the shoes, with the crease just breaking over the laces.

gizmo gismo (World War II on) *s.* Any thingamajig or whatchamacallit. Probably of naval origin.

glider badge (World War II) A badge presented to a soldier who had satisfactorily completed glider training or who had participated in at least one combat glider landing in enemy-held territory. No longer awarded.

glider patch (Modern) The official Airborne insignia: a white parachute and glider on a blue disk with a red border; worn on the garrison cap.

glider riders (World War II) *s.* A paratrooper's term for those elements of an airborne division that landed (usually as the second wave of an airborne operation) in gliders. Until the middle 1940s they were treated like country cousins—neither jump pay nor jump boots, but lots of risks. Consequently, there was considerable friction between them and the lordly paratroopers. Also reportedly called *flack hacks*, although we never heard the term.

gloom period (West Point; Modern) *s.* The period immediately after return from Christmas leave, on through Easter.

gnome (West Point; World War II and later) *s.* A short cadet or a member of the second battalion. Also known as *duckbutt, runt.* Now replaced by *munchkin.*

goal knocker (Old, Old Army into World War I) *s.* A derogatory term, generally applied among enlisted men. Unfortunately, we have not been able to find a veteran who could give a detailed definition. What we got suggested someone of dubiously human parentage and no apparent virtues. Perhaps connected with the civilian expression *to knock someone for a goal* (to beat someone up badly).

goat 1. (Old Army, but still lingers) *s.* The junior officer in a regiment or separate battalion. He is well advised to remain a bachelor, because he will collect all sorts of interesting and time-consuming extra jobs. Probably related to the general use of someone's being *the goat* or *scapegoat.* 2. (West Point) *s.* The bottom man in a graduating class. Traditionally, each of his classmates used to give him a dollar. With the large classes of the 1960s and 1970s, graduating last could be profitable. Unfortunately, this practice was halted with the graduation of 1978. Perhaps related to the first definition of *goat*, but Partridge (1970) quotes *goat*, from the turn of the century, as meaning a stupid person.

gobble, to gobble up, to (Civil War and somewhat later) *s.* A variety of meanings centering around capture: to steal, to appropriate, to capture, to wipe out. "Forrest gobbled our outposts last night."

go boresight, to (Air Force) *s.* To fire weapons visually.

God (1950s–1960s) *s.* Gen. Curtis LeMay, commander of the Strategic Air Force.

go-go go-go bird (Vietnam) *s.* A CH-47 Chinook helicopter modified for close air support, with an armament of two 20mm Vulcan guns, .50-caliber heavy machine guns, and 40mm grenade launchers—plus anything else that could be hung on it. They were devastatingly effective, but they were big, slow targets and burned up ammunition at a rate that made resupply difficult. They were replaced by dragon ships and Hueycobra choppers. Also called the *Hook* and the *Shithook*.

go heat, to (Air Force) *s.* To fire a heat-seeking missile.

going downtown (Vietnam; Air Force) *s.* Flying a mission against Hanoi. A popular expression among pilots.

going to the sticks (Civil War; CSA) *s.* Going to the dogs, coming apart, becoming a monkey show, going to hell. Possibly a censored version of what a Southern gentleman really did say (Freeman, vol. 1).

goldbrick 1. (Early 20th century to World War II) *s.* A soldier on a special assignment that did not require him to participate in the usual training and fatigue details. Possibly the term was inspired by envy, with the implication that such men were just imitation soldiers and not the real article, but it did not indicate that they were not reasonably hard-working. 2. (World War I) *s.* A member of the Military Police. 3. (World War I, very common in World War II, to Modern; all Services) *s.* A soldier who tries to get out of doing work and shirks when he is put to work. A lazy bum. As one song had it, "In ducking jobs, he works like hell." The term is thus now thoroughly derogatory. A *goldbrick detail* is a particularly easy, effortless job that is sometimes just an excuse for goofing off.

goldbrick, to To avoid work, to loaf on the job.

golden flow (Modern) *s.* A urinalysis, to which soldiers are subjected before their departure from overseas commands. The purpose of the test is to detect the presence of harmful drugs in the urine.

Golden Goats (World War II) The US 13th Airborne Division. Its insignia was a "winged unicorn in gold on a blue shield."

Golden Turdhooks (World War II) The US 17th Airborne Division. Its insignia was a clutching golden claw on a black circular patch.

goldfish Army goldfish cold goldfish (World War I and later) *s.* Canned salmon. Apparently not a high-priced delicacy, as it is today, but a low-priced food, somewhat resented by the soldiers:

> I've et so much goldfish,
> I've growed me a tail.
> If I eat any more,
> I'll have fins like a whale!

Goldfish Club (World War II; Air Force) An unofficial group of airmen who had been shot down into, or forced to ditch into, salt water. Their emblem was a cloth patch showing a winged fish, done in silver embroidery, gliding over the waves. A second such occurrence entitled the airman to a goldfish cluster, a small embroidered goldfish. RAF airmen usually wore their emblems under a coat lapel or pocket flap, but most Americans displayed theirs openly. See *Dunked Caterpillar*.

gold-star man (West Point) *s.* A cadet whose academic average is 90 or more. Also called a *star man*.

golf suit (Modern) *s.* A set of fatigues with jacket and pants of different shades of green.

gomen nasai (Occupation of Japan and later; all Services) Japanese for *Excuse me.* Round-eyes used it even with one another.

gomer (Modern) 1. *s.* A dull, stupid person. 2. *s.* A trainee. 3. (Air Force) *s.* A first-year cadet at the US Air Force Academy. The origin of the word is uncertain, although it may be related to the Scottish *gomeral* 'fool', 'simpleton'. In hospital jargon, it means "an unkempt, unsavory, chronic problem patient" (George and Dundes). In the hospital sense, the word has been in use since at least 1964 and perhaps since 1950. Its present popularity may stem from the television program "Gomer Pyle, USMC." See also *Private Slipinshits* and *snuffy.*

G-1 (World War I to Modern) The staff section in divisions and larger organizations responsible for all personnel matters and administration. Also the officer in charge of that section. Both are emphatically noncombatant. Below division level they are termed *S-1.*

gong (World War II, Vietnam) *s.* A derisive term for a military decoration. Used in the British Army since the late 19th century, and periodically borrowed by Americans.

Good Conduct Medal A medal awarded to enlisted men for exemplary behavior, efficiency, and fidelity in active military service—officially. Actually, the award is virtually automatic and the decoration is considered a rather pointless joke by most servicemen. Recommendation originates with the individual's commander. The usual qualifying period of service is three years of continuous active service on or after 26 August 1940, but there are exceptions to this limitation. Successive awards are identified by a system of clasps and loops.

good posts *s.* There are only two good posts in the Army—the one you just left and the one you want to transfer to. This bit of service philosophy has been around for more years than our senior officer can remember.

good training (Modern) *s.* Anything unpleasant, presumably because unpleasant things harden the soldier for war. "The MPs just gave me a ticket for speeding on post!" "Well, that's good training."

goof burner (Old Army into World War II) *s.* Anyone who smoked marijuana; from *goof,* the slang term for marijuana. The Army had such characters, mostly from the Southwest, in the 1920s and 1930s. They were considered practitioners of a low and antisocial vice, suitable only for greasers.

goo-goo gu-gu gugu 1. (Philippine Insurrection and scattered use later) *s.* A Filipino. This seems to have been a local term, developed during the Philippine Insurrection and seldom used outside the Philippine Islands. During 1946–47 we heard it used only by a few old-timers. The origin of the term is unknown, although it has been suggested that it is related to civilian slang *googoo eyes,* meaning staring eyes. It is more probable that it is a contemptuous mouthing of nonsense syllables to imitate native speech. 2. (World War II; mostly Navy, but some Army) *s.* A native of the Pacific islands, particularly a Polynesian.

gook *s.* A derogatory term for ethnic groups in various parts of the world. 1. (American intervention in Nicaragua in 1912; Marines) A Nicaraguan and later, by extension, any Spanish-speaking native of Central America and the Caribbean. In the larger sense, *gook* was still being used up until as late as 1948. The origin of the term is not known, but it is a reasonable supposition that it grew out of *goo-goo*. 2. (World War II and a little later) Military usage for a variety of natives among whom American and Anzac troops served in the Pacific and the Far East. 3. (Korea and later) Localized and accepted as a basic term for a Korean or (less frequently) a Chinese. It has been suggested that this use was reinforced by the Korean word *guk* 'country', as in *Hanguk-saram* 'a Korean man'. 4. (Vietnam and later) Localized and accepted as a basic term for a Vietnamese. 5. (Modern, also largely civilian) Any nonindustrialized, brown-skinned people with whom we happen to be on bad terms.

goon (World War II to Modern) *s.* Any large, disreputable, and messy person, especially one with little intellect and a tendency toward meanness. From the comic strip "Popeye," where the goon was a subhuman monstrosity of great fighting prowess.

gooney bird (World War II and later; all Services) *s.* The C-47 transport plane—adaptable, rugged, and ubiquitous. See *dragon ship*.

goon gun (World War II) *s.* The US 4.2-inch chemical mortar, an accurate and powerful weapon.

goonie *s.* A service adaptation of *goon*. A small variety of that creature, more of a mess than a menace.

goon platoon **goon squad** (World War II to Modern) *s.* A platoon (or other unit) filled with awkward, misfit, or malcontent soldiers who are put in one place to better control them and keep them out of everyone else's way. "Captain Thurlo had made Brill's outfit sort of a 'goon platoon,' filling it with misfits and malcontents who did not perform well elsewhere" (Groom).

goose egg *s.* Complete failure to hit the target on the rifle range. A zero score. Also called *artillery bull, bolo, Maggie's drawers, washout*.

Gorgeous Georgie (World War II) Gen. George S. Patton, Jr.

go through [someone] like shit through a tin horn, to (World War II) *s.* To rout someone, to beat someone easily and disastrously. "And then Rommel turned around and went through them like shit through a tin horn."

go-to-hell cap (Before World War II) *s.* A Regular Army term for the overseas cap.

Grab-a-whore (Since about 1950) *s.* A play on Grafenwöhr, West Germany, the site of the 7th Army Training Center. Also called *Graf*.

Grab 'em by the balls (Vietnam; all Services) *s.* Short for "Grab 'em by the balls and 'their hearts and minds will follow.' " It is based on the slogan of the civic-action–revolutionary development groups who were preoccupied with getting the Vietnamese to love us by winning "their hearts and minds." The combat soldier's solution was more direct, if not as effective.

grade (At least early 19th century to Modern) The position of a soldier in the command structure according to officially defined steps. These range from private (E-1) to General of the Army (O-10—not currently filled) and include enlisted personnel, warrant officers, and commissioned officers. Common uses are *first* *three graders, company-grade officers, field-grade officers. Grade* is frequently confused with rank or seniority.

grandma (Early World War II) *s.* The compound-low gear of a motor vehicle. Safe enough for a grandma to use.

grapevine sling (Old Army to World War II; also Marines) *s.* The sling adjustment used for firing offhand; also called a *hasty sling*. The superlative marksmanship training of the Springfield '03 period included carefully tested instruction in the use of the sling to steady your aim.

grappa (World War II) From the Italian *grappa* 'brandy'. A sort of brandy distilled from the skins, seeds, and stalks of grapes after they have been pressed for wine. It might also be anything else an Italian entrepreneur could get into a bottle. The only certainty was that it would not do you any good.

grass cutting See *hedgehopping*.

grasshopper 1. (Colonial to Revolutionary) *s.* A light fieldpiece, usually a one- to three-pounder, with a carriage designed for use with mobile columns in rough country. This term was often interchangeable with *galloper*. Both terms were nicknames and applied loosely. Possibly the most characteristic type of grasshopper (light aircraft) was designed so that it could be carried stretcher-fashion by its crew. 2. (World War II and later) A light, fixed-wing aircraft for artillery air observers, couriers, liaison officers, and similar purposes. The name originally applied only to the L-4 and L-14 Piper models but came into general use for all aircraft of this type. Popular belief was that it derived from their ability to pop in and out of small fields. See also *butterfly, bird dog, puddle jumper*.

grass money (Post–Civil War) Rental fees paid by civilian cattlemen for the right to graze their cattle on Indian reservations. The Army frequently had the responsibility of seeing that it was paid and turning it over to the Indians.

G-ration (1947–49) The so-called *assault ration*, a small packet of concentrated food designed to sustain a soldier during the first twenty or thirty hours of an attack, when resupply might be difficult.

gravel agitator gravel crusher gravel pounder (Probably Old Army, still lingers) *s.* An infantryman. Like the parallel *beetle crusher*, probably coined by mounted troops who looked down upon the trudging doughboys. Such terms also illustrate the tendency of soldiers to use complex terms in place of simple ones.

grayback 1. (Civil War and later) *s.* A louse. Also *army grayback*. 2. (Civil War; USA) *s.* A Confederate soldier, so called for his gray uniform. Also *gray back*.

gray-hog (West Point) *s.* Truscott defines this person as a "super-straight" cadet.

grease (World War II and perhaps a little earlier) *s.* Butter.

grease, to (Probably post–World War II) *s.* To kill. "His father, who got greased in Korea" (Herr).

grease board (Modern) *s.* A chart board covered with plastic or acetate on which is shown the personnel strength and disposition of a unit. It is kept current by using grease pencil or China marker pencil, whence the name.

grease gun (World War II and later; all Services) *s.* A submachine gun, especially the US M3 and M3A1 .45-caliber submachine gun, which really resembled an automotive grease gun, but functioned far more effectively than the much-touted Tommy gun.

grease monkey (Around World War II to Modern) *s.* A civilian term for a motor mechanic, picked up by the Army.

greasepot (Generally World War II; largely Navy but heard occasionally in the Army) *s.* A cook.

greaser (Early 19th century to Modern) *s.* A Mexican. The term may have been used as early as the 1830s, but it came into common use with the Mexican War. It was apparently a frontier version of *greasy*, perhaps inspired by the worn leather working dress of Mexican cattlemen.

grease trap (Antiquity uncertain, but certainly in use in World War II; all Services) A sump near a mess hall where grease and food particles are collected from the dishwater before it drains into the sewer. Cleaning it was the exclusive and onerous task of the KP; one of the most unpleasant and most dreaded details of an unpleasant and dreaded detail. From Post:

> Up jumped the KP and leaped into
> the grease trap.
> "You'll never take me alive,"
> said he.
> And his ghost may be heard as you
> pass by that grease trap,
> Singing, "You'll come a peeling
> potatoes with me."

green, in the greened up (Air Force) *s.* Ready to go, ready to fire. "All flights 'greened up,' a term meaning that all switches were set so that appropriate munitions were ready" (TB, p. 17). "With all systems 'in the green' (e.g., indicating normal)" (Linebacker II).

green backs (Modern) The volumes of the excellent official history *United States Army in World War II*, so named from the color of their bindings; published by the Office of the Chief of Military History, Washington, D.C., US Government Printing Office.

green banana, to get the (Post–World War II) To be shafted.

Green Berets (1950s to Modern) The Army's Special Forces, organized for counterinsurgency operations, unconventional warfare, and psychological warfare. The nickname comes from their special headgear, created in an attempt to link them with Rogers's Rangers of the French and Indian Wars. (Someone had stated that Rogers's woodsrunners wore green Scots bonnets.) In sad fact, Rogers issued his men cocked hats. The Scots bonnets that the Rangers (as well both English and American provincial infantrymen) sometimes wore on patrol were purchased from sutlers and undoubtedly were the conventional blue. Other quaint "ancestral" touches included a phonied-up version of Rogers's ranging rules, inscribed on imitation birch bark. The Special Forces deserved better, and Rogers is probably rotating in his grave. Also called the *Green Beanies*.

green girl (West Point) *s.* The comforter issued to cadets. Formerly called *brown boy*.

Green Hornet (Early World War II) *s.* Gen. George S. Patton, Jr., so-called from his self-designed green tanker's uniform, with gold helmet, worn during maneuvers. The original Green Hornet was a comic book and radio character of the day.

Green Machine (Modern; also Marines) *s.* The military bureaucracy. The Marines have used this expression since at least as early as 1969 (Lighter, letter to Cragg, 19 July 1980).

greens (Modern) The Army green uniform. Also, the Marine green uniform.

green tape (Modern) A waterproof, highly adhesive green tape widely used and much sought after in Vietnam. It was employed for almost every purpose, from taping dog tags together so that they would not make noise to fastening extra clips of ammunition together. Its virtual indestructibility added to its versatility.

Green Weenie (Modern) *s.* The Army Commendation Medal. Between the Korean War and the beginning of American combat involvement in the Vietnam War (1965), the Army Commendation Medal was about the only decoration for meritorious service or achievement that most enlisted men and junior officers could hope to win. It was awarded sparingly during those years, and those who received it treasured it because it was earned and deserved. The cynical nickname probably arose among soldiers who did not get a medal, to show their disdain toward those who did. Later, when the decoration was passed out indiscriminately, the term *weenie* began to make sense. In the term, *green* is from the basic color of the service and suspension ribbons, while *weenie*, a frankfurter sausage, may have a phallic significance. See *Field-Grade Good Conduct Medal.*

greeting, to get [one's] (World War II and later) *s.* To get a notice that you have been drafted under the Selective Service Act to serve your country. From the opening phrase of the notice.

gremlins (World War II; mostly Army Air Force and civilian journalists) *s.* Mythical invisible elflike creatures supposedly responsible for all sorts of things that can happen to a plane. If your hydraulics do not work, your gyro compass points south, or there are mysterious holes in your wings, the gremlins must have done it. Gremlins increased noticeably around bases with poorly trained or badly disciplined air and ground crews and hastily developed aircraft. The original myth became quite elaborate, with many varieties of gremlins, all duly illustrated in *Life* magazine. Gravel agitators and cannon cockers rather suspected a fly-boy publicity stunt.

grenadier grenadiers (Ancient to early 19th century) During the 18th and 19th centuries, picked soldiers (usually selected from the tallest men in a regiment). Originally, they were armed with hand grenades. When improved muskets made it suicidal to use grenades in open battle, the grenadiers became the elite company of each regiment, enjoying extra pay, fancier uniforms, and freedom from most fatigue details, but getting the most dangerous missions. Contrary to popular belief, some Continental regiments had grenadier companies during the American Revolution. Also, from approximately 1825 to 1835 each American infantry regiment had a grenadier company as one of its two flank companies.

greyhounds to march and stayers in a fight (Civil War; USA) *s.* An apparently common characterization of good infantrymen or a good infantry regiment.

gross (West Point) An adjective describing a cadet who seems to lack the essential characteristics of an officer and gentleman.

ground apes (World War II and later) *s.* Derogatory term for blacks.

grounded (World War I to Modern) *s.* An aviation term referring to a pilot who is unable to fly because his plane was damaged or who is not permitted to fly because he is being punished for some misconduct—like buzzing the general's wife's afternoon tea. The latter sense has passed into general usage. Army brats are *grounded* when their parents will not let them use the car. Soldiers are *grounded* when they are restricted to camp. The term is also applied to air units that cannot operate because of bad weather or shortage of fuel.

ground guide (Modern) A soldier who walks in front of a vehicle (usually a track) to guide it safely over rough or built-up terrain. "The ground guides stood in front of the tracks" (Heinemann).

ground loop (Possibly World War I; still occasionally heard) *s.* A bad plane landing, involving a circular skid. Sometimes applied to describe the mental effect of shock or surprise.

groundpounder 1. (Modern) *s.* An infantryman. 2. (Vietnam; Air Force) *s.* A nonflying Air Force officer.

ground scout (Old Army) Scouts out well ahead of a unit moving across country; they are to detect and report terrain obstacles such as ravines or marshy ground.

group 1. (World War II) A temporary tactical formation of several battalions, plus a group headquarters company; roughly equivalent to a brigade. It served to control independent tank, tank destroyer, or artillery battalions. 2. (Air Force) An operational and administrative unit, normally consisting of two or more squadrons, which forms part of a wing.

grubcrabber (World War I) *s.* A soldier who is always complaining about his food.

gruesome twosome (World War II) *s.* WAAC and WAC term for their issue service shoes.

grunt 1. (Pre–World War II) *s.* An Army Signal Corps assistant. 2. (Vietnam to Modern) *s.* An infantryman, "because that's the noise you make when you shit." Originally a term used by the Marines.

G-3 (World War I to Modern) The general staff section (or the officer in charge of it) responsible for plans and operations. The most noisy and pushing section of the average staff, it usually operates in an atmosphere of innocent confusion. Below division level, it is termed *S-3*.

GT score (World War II to Modern) General Technical score, or the Army equivalent of an IQ score; it is derived from averaging the Verbal English and Arithmetic Reasoning scores on the AGCT.

G-2 (World War I to Modern) 1. The general staff section (or the officer in charge of it) responsible for intelligence and counterintelligence. During peacetime, as from 1919 to 1941, it is considered a handy place to drop goofballs, goof-offs, and well-connected nitwits. Pearl Harbor was a typical result. G-2 is usually bullied by G-3. Below division level, it is termed *S-2*. 2. Colloquially, the latest supposed facts on whatever is going on. "What's the G-2 on Colonel Bullbleat's transfer?"

guard ammunition 1. A special type of ammunition for the Springfield '03 rifle, used only for peacetime guard duty. It has a reduced charge, enough to kill a man at short range but not enough to endanger people in the next county, as '03 service ammunition would do. 2. Special ammunition for the military shotgun (riot gun), which was often used for guard duty. The shells had brass casings, which stood up to the frequent loadings and unloadings that would have quickly worn out standard paper cartridges.

guardhouse (Early 18th century to Modern) Often a dual-purpose building. 1. The quarters and office space for the post guard and the OD. 2. A place of confinement for garrison prisoners. Terms for the guardhouse and imprisonment are multitudinous and include *Barracks 13, Box 3, Box 13, bull pen, Company Q, Crossbar Hotel, Crowbar Hotel, drawers, Hotel Dee Barb Wire, Irish theater, mill, screenhouse, stockade, Wire City.*

guardhouse lawyer (Old Army to Modern) *s.* A soldier who sets himself up as an authority on Army regulations and is free with his advice on how to get around them. The term comes from the fact that his imperfect knowledge leads to frequent periods of residence in the post guardhouse—where he continues to dispense advice.

guard mount (Ancient to Modern) A formation at which the guards are mustered, told off, and sent to their posts.

guard room (Colonial to late 19th century) A room or rooms at the entrance of a fortified place or large barracks area for the shelter of the guards.

guard tent (Old Army) A pyramidal tent used as a guard room when troops were under canvas during summer training or field service.

guard the flagpole, to (Old Army) *s.* To be restricted to the post or camp as punishment for minor offenses.

guide (Antiquity uncertain, but British usage in late 19th century) The soldier responsible for maintaining the prescribed direction and rate of march in military formations.

guidon (Ancient to Modern) 1. A unit flag or pennant, wide at the lance end, narrower and forked (swallow-tailed) at the other end. Used in mounted units to indicate direction and place of formation. Also, loosely, other small flags. 2. The soldier who carries a guidon. Also called a *guidon bearer*.

gum blanket (Civil War) A rubber blanket issued to Union troops—and eagerly acquired by Confederates at every opportunity. *Gum* in this usage meant rubber.

gumshoe (Early World War II) *s.* A passing name for the Military Police. Also occasionally applied to G-2 personnel. From civilian slang for a detective. The *gum* meant is rubber, for soft treading, and the civilian term is 19th century.

gun 1. In its loosest use, any sort of firearm from which missiles are shot by the detonation of an explosive propelling charge. 2. A piece of artillery, a cannon, characteristics unspecified: "At Wagram (1809) Napoleon massed 188,800 men and 488 guns." 3. Specifically, a cannon with a relatively long tube (barrel), flat trajectory, and high muzzle velocity, used in tanks and antiaircraft units as well as field artillery. A howitzer has a shorter barrel and a high trajectory, the latter being useful for hitting enemy troops behind a ridgeline or in deep trenches, but less accurate and less effective against armor. Mortars have very short tubes, in proportion to their base, and a very high trajectory. The lighter types are smoothbore and are considered infantry weapons rather than guns; however, heavier types are rifled (see *goon gun*) and may be employed as a form of artillery. Modern developments in ordnance and ammunition have blurred many of the original distinctions between guns proper and howitzers.

gun bird See *gunship.*

gun bunny (Modern) An artilleryman. *Bunny* is derogatory.

gunge /gunj/ (Vietnam) *s.* A mythical tropical disease, generally described as a venereal infection that made a man rot "from his genitals outward." This legend produced one excellent motto: "Do not get the gunge. When the Army wants you to have it, it will be issued to you." Also called *crotch rot.*

gung ho (World War II to Modern; all Services) *s.* Describing individuals or organizations, in a state of active and zealous military enthusiasm. Originally taken in a positive sense, but in more recent years suggestive of naiveté. The expression is Chinese in origin, although its exact meaning and the date of its first use by American military forces are in dispute. According to the strongest theory, *gung ho* is a contraction of *gung-yeh hodzo* 'industrial cooperation', the name of an official group sometimes called the Chinese Industrial Cooperative Society Association. The contraction would mean *work together* in a very positive sense. According to this explanation, the term was picked up in China, during the years 1937–38, by Lt. Col. Evans Fordyce Carlson, USMCR, when he was an observer to the Red Chinese 8th Route Army. He then introduced the term into American English when he was commander of the 2d Marine Ranger Battalion.

gunmen (Early 19th century to Mexican War) A name given to, or adopted by, some Southern volunteer and militia units. Originally, at least, most of them appear to have been mounted riflemen.

gunner 1. (Army) The artilleryman who actually lays (aims) the piece. The rest of the gun crew are properly called *cannoneers.* In popular usage, however, *gunner* is applied to all artillerymen. 2. (West Point) *s.* The plebe responsible for sending serving dishes to the kitchen for refilling. There is one gunner at each table. He sits opposite the dessert cutter.

gunner's chant gunner's doxology (Ancient to early 20th century) *s.* A chant used by artillery NCOs while firing salutes; a technique for keeping the intervals between rounds uniform in those harsh days before everyone had a reasonably accurate watch. (There are also references to the Navy's using it.) We can barely recall it and so offer the beginning with considerable trepidation:

> If I had good sense, I wouldn't be here.
> Number One—Fire!
> I'd like to slip off for a pail of beer.
> Number Two—Fire!

gunner's creed (Old Army into World War II) *s.* The priorities taught to every new artillery shavetail and grimly observed in every self-respecting field artillery unit: "First the horses, then the guns, then the enlisted men—and then you can sit down." Also called the *Artilleryman's creed.*

gunner's punch (World War II to Modern) A drink developed in the 3d Armored Field Artillery Battalion, consisting of a quart of triple-strength tea, the juice of 12 lemons, sugar to taste, half a pint of curaçao, half a pint of brandy, and a quart of Jamaica rum. This mixture should be cooled for several hours and then mixed with equal volumes each of burgundy wine and carbonated water (courtesy of Maj. Gen. George Ruhlen, USA-Ret.). See also *Artillery punch.*

gunner's tap (World War I to Korea) *s.* A method of traversing the water-cooled Browning .30-caliber machine gun, which was faster and handier than using the traversing wheel. You loosened the traversing clamp very slightly so that the barrel could be traversed (turned horizontally) by tapping the butt with the heel of your hand. The knack of doing this was seldom acquired overnight, since a perfect tap was supposed to shift the barrel (and line of fire) just 3 mils.

gunnie gunny (Modern) *s.* An aviator who pilots a gunship.

gunship gunbird guns (Vietnam and later; all Services) *s.* A UH-1 helicopter armed with miniguns, rockets, 40mm grenade launchers, or any combination of these weapons. Also called *ARA, hogs, slicks.*

guntruck (Vietnam) A 5-ton cargo truck armed with .50-caliber or M60 machine guns and other weapons. Its chassis was armored to protect its crew. Used in convoy security.

gyrene garine girene jirene /ji-'reen *to rhyme with Irene*/ (Approximately World War II and later in the Army, but at least as early as 1894 in the Naval Academy) *s.* A Marine. While various folk etymologies have been proposed—portmanteau words from *gyre* and *marine, GI* and *marine*—Dr. Lighter (letter to Cragg, 17 September 1979) has offered what seems to be the definitive etymology. Lighter suggests that *gyrene* is derived from Latin *gyrinus* (or Greek γυρίνος), 'tadpole', with reference to the amphibious nature of the marine's mission. (In modern zoology, however, *Gyrinus* is a genus of aquatic beetles.) It has also been suggested that the term may embody a reference to *pollywog*, a naval slang term for a person who has not yet "crossed" [the equator], hence, a landlubber. The assumption is that an unknown naval midshipman stumbled upon the word *gyrinus* and recognized its descriptive and assonant qualities. (Our senior officer, however, remains unimpressed by this erudition, suspecting that *gyrene* simply reflects the usual soldier-sailor tendency to twist words, as in *fattigews for fatigues.*) There are many other spelling variants.

hack, to hack it, to (World War II, if not earlier, to Modern; probably all Services) *s.* To handle a problem or situation successfully. "We really hacked that new training schedule!" "They're sending Blow back to a quartermaster job. He couldn't hack it as a platoon leader." This gradually shades over into *to cope with* something or *to tolerate* something. "I just can't hack it back in the world" (Herr).

hacked (Civil War; CSA) *s.* Used up, worn out, weary of the war, and about ready to quit.

hacking stripes (Air Force) *s.* Service stripes, no longer issued. To earn them, one had to be able to hack the military life.

hairy (World War II to Modern) *s.* Difficult, embarrassing, dangerous. "That's a hairy question!"

halberd halbert (Colonial to Revolutionary) A pole weapon with a spearhead, an axlike cutting blade, and a beak opposite to the blade. It was the traditional weapon of the sergeant, although seldom carried in the field in North America. In the British service (and, to some extent, in American colonial units) *to get a halberd* was to make sergeant. *To go to the halberd* meant to be flogged; men thus punished were tied to a tripod formed of three halberds. A sergeant commissioned as an officer might be said *to carry the halberd in his face* or be termed *an old halberd.*

half-mast (At least Mexican War to Modern) Half-staff. *Half-mast* is a naval term, and the correct military expression is *half-staff.* But a lot of soldiers use *half-mast* anyway. It used to be a favorite trick of promotion boards for someone to ask a candidate to explain when the flag is flown at half-mast. The correct answer is "Never," because the Army does not use masts.

half-staff, to be at (Antiquity uncertain) *s.* To have one's fly partly open.

half step In drill, a 15-inch step, performed at ordinary marching time, 120 steps to a minute. The command is *Half step—march!*

half-step, to *s.* To move slowly in order to avoid doing something. "Me and Sergeant Wallace gettin' things set up so we can half-step all the time" (Smith).

half-track (World War II to Modern) A motor vehicle, usually lightly armored, with ordinary front wheels and short caterpillar tracks instead of rear wheels. Half-tracks were much used as personnel carriers for armored infantry, as combat ambulances, and as command vehicles. After World War II they were gradually replaced by full-track vehicles.

hammerhead (Old Army) 1. *s.* A horse with definite ideas of its own about where it wants to go. It usually hammers against the rider's grip on the reins. Kipling's "a raw rough dun was he, with the mouth of a bell and the heart of Hell and the head of a gallows-tree" is a fair description. 2. *s.* By extension, a stupid, obstinate individual.

hand-carry, to (Modern) To carry by hand. Usually applied to paperwork. When an action officer wants fast action on his project, he probably will hand-carry the pertinent papers from office to office, rather than entrust them to the message center delivery.

handcuffed volunteers 1. (Civil War; USA) *s.* A low type of replacement furnished to the United States armies in 1864; in large part bounty jumpers and substitutes. They had to be brought up to their regiments under armed guard. Once there, they frequently deserted, sometimes to the enemy. 2. (World War I) *s.* A figurative term for a draftee. Also *handcuff volunteer.*

H & I (Modern) Harassment and Interdicting. Artillery fire intended to disturb enemy troops or to disrupt their activities and movement in areas where their presence is suspected. It is random, usually unobserved, and fired at a slow and irregular rate.

handie-talkie (World War II and later; also Marines) *s.* A small radio set that could be held in one hand. The walkie-talkie was larger and was carried as a backpack, but the terms *handie-talkie* and *walkie-talkie* were used rather loosely.

hand pops (Modern) *s.* Pyrotechnics fired by hand.

handshaker (Old Army, but still used) *s.* A soldier who attempts to ingratiate himself with his superiors by effusive displays of friendliness. Not as revolting as a brown nose, but still uncomfortable to have around. Marines may call him an *ear banger,* although they also use *handshaker.*

handspike (Colonial to Civil War) A 6-foot bar, used in shifting gun carriages or for lifting the breech of a gun so that the elevating screw or quoins might be more easily adjusted. It was usually made of hickory wood and shod with iron. When boarders came over your rail or enemy infantry got into your gun position, handspikes were excellent skull crackers.

hang a lead bracelet around [someone's] neck, to (World War I) *s.* To have someone imprisoned in the guardhouse.

hanger bats (Modern; Air Force) *s.* Dependent children.

hanger pilot (World War II; Air Force) *s.* A bunk flyer, a man who talks a good job at flying, but is not much use up there in the "wild blue yonder."

hanger queen (World War I to Modern; Air Force) *s.* A plane that never gets out of the hanger simply because it is used as a source of spare parts for the other planes in the unit.

Hanoi Hanna (Vietnam) *s.* The nickname for the woman broadcaster who conducted regular English-language propaganda broadcasts aimed at US servicemen. She was never taken seriously. "That same night Hanoi Hanna came on the radio" (Broughton).

Hanoi Hilton (Vietnam) 1. *s.* Any prisoner-of-war camp. The nickname was used generically by US ground forces in South Vietnam, after Hoa Lo prison in Hanoi. 2. *s.* Any large Vietcong or North Vietnamese tunnel complex.

happy (World War II and later) *s.* An ironic term, used in compounds, to indicate an abnormal state of mind. Examples: *island happy*—you have been stationed too long on a small island and are socializing with frigate birds; *rice happy*—a soldier captive in a Japanese prison camp hoarded his rice ration for several days in order to have one good meal (usually an indication that he was about to give up and die); and *shell-happy*—shell-shocked.

Happy Valley 1. (World War I, World War II, Korea, Vietnam) *s.* A term recurrently applied to a particularly bloody, hard-fought battlefield. In World War I, the valley of the Somme; the name seems to have originated with the British Expeditionary Force. 2. (World War II; Air Force) *s.* The Ruhr area, so called because of the unusual opportunities it offered of being tickled by German flak and fighters while flying over it.

happy-to-glad (Modern) *s.* Refers to minor, nonsubstantive corrections to a staff paper. Probably from the penchant of some military editors for making very minor alterations, such as changing *happy* to *glad*, etc. "I got it approved with only a few happy-to-glad changes."

hard-charger (Relatively Modern) *s.* Aggressive, persistent, gung ho. Applied to units or an individual. In the latter case, it can mean someone who has a lot of push and an abrasive personality, even when it is not needed.

hard-core (Post–World War II to Modern; probably all Services) Dedicated, if on your side; indoctrinated, if on the other side. A soldier who swallowed a ramrod while young and has no tolerance for those weaknesses of the human flesh that contravene military regulations. He can be an uncomfortable daily associate, but he is there when he is needed.

hard-hat (Vietnam; also Marines) *s.* A Vietcong or main-force soldier of the National Liberation Force Army. Pike attributes the term to the fact that these soldiers wore metal or fiberboard helmets resembling the pie-pan helmets of World War I and early World War II.

hardhead (Old Army) *s.* A mule, specifically one in a jackass battery. A hardhead is also a kind of fish, and during World War II there was a submarine named the *Hardhead.* Its skipper—the wandering son of a respectable field artilleryman—took it into action with a pair of nickel-plated mule shoes mounted on its conning tower, and in the control room, alongside a photo of Jane Russell, a photo of a pack mule.

hardroll hardrolled (Mostly Marine Corps, occasionally Army) *s.* A factory-made cigarette, so called because it was likely to be firmer than a hand-rolled cigarette. The term was unknown in the pre-1940 Navy, since—in contravention to all fair play and decency—Congress had decreed that a seaman second class would have $42 a month as against the $21 of an Army or Marine private. Hence, only the poverty-stricken soldiers or marines rolled their own. (Needless to say, such soldiers and marines did not mention congressmen in polite company.) But by the time a soldier or marine had made sergeant and could afford hardrolls, he had learned how to impress recruits by rolling his own with one hand in a high wind, and he was not about to adopt sissified habits. During the 1940s, with the influx of draftees and with higher pay, many privates and Pfcs smoked hardrolls on payday. Bull Durham or Five Brothers was used the rest of the month, until we went overseas and hardrolls became a part of the ration—well, supposedly and sometimes. Also called a *tailormade.*

hardship tour 1. Any disagreeable duty anywhere. 2. An overseas tour where married personnel are not permitted to take their families and the amenities of civilization are few for everyone.

hard stand (20th century) An area paved or otherwise solidly surfaced in order to keep vehicles or supplies from sinking into the mud.

hard-stripe 1. (Modern) *s.* The stripes of a noncommissioned officer, as opposed to those of a specialist (see *soft-stripe*). Thus, a noncommissioned officer is referred to as a *hard-striper.* 2. (Modern; Air Force) *s.* The chevrons worn by personnel in the grade of E-6 (technical sergeant) and up.

hardtack (Early 19th century to 1930s; also Navy) A hard biscuit or cracker made of unleavened, unsalted flour, thoroughly baked so that it will keep for a long time. It used to be the standard bread ration for troops in the field and was thus generally known among commanders and quartermasters as *hard bread.* The usual sort of hardtack was approximately 3 inches square, and almost half an inch thick. It was palatable enough when not insect-infested or moldy. Similar fare in the Navy was called *ship's biscuit, sea biscuit,* or simply *biscuit.* The word *hardtack* originated as a combination of *hard* and *tack,* an old term for food. During the Civil War, Union soldiers had a variety of nicknames for hardtack: *teeth dullers, sheet-iron crackers, worm-castles,* and *Lincoln pies.* See *soft-tack.*

hard tail (Old Army to World War II) *s.* A mule.

Harness and hitch! (Old Army through World War I, to the disappearance of horse-drawn artillery and vehicles) A command to harness teams and hitch them up. Generally, *get ready to move out.* Usually preceded by *Roll packs!*

hash marks (Early 20th century to Modern; also Navy and Marines) *s.* Service stripes, one for each enlistment (hitch), worn on the lower left sleeve of a soldier's uniform. The institution of service stripes is very old, going back in the US Army to an order of 7 August 1782, issued by George Washington from his headquarters at Newburgh, New York. The origin of the term is not known, and various sources for it have been suggested: *hatch marks,* referring to the parallel lines of a series of service stripes; *hitch marks; hash marks,* referring to years of eating Army hash. It is always possible that some wit adapted *hatch marks* or *hitch marks* to *hash marks.* Over the years, the term has come to be applied to all the cloth insignia worn on an enlisted man's sleeves.

hate (World War I to World War II) *s.* An enemy bombardment. A British expression picked up by Americans. In World War I, the usual German artillery concentrations on roads behind the British front, to catch supply trains and reinforcements moving up under cover of dusk, was the *evening hate.*

hat up, to hat up and head out, to (Modern) *s.* To leave. The expression *to hat it up* is current black slang and may reinforce Army usage. But no soldier is ever supposed to go anywhere (with certain obvious exceptions) in uniform without his hat, so that the wearing of the hat becomes second nature to him. "Let's hat up, hey. Let's get . . . outa here" (Heinemann).

haul ass, to (1930s to Modern) *s.* To move rapidly, to depart hurriedly. "We sure hauled ass out of there fast." The expression *Haul your ass!* did not mean quite the same thing. It was equivalent to *Get moving. Stop your stalling.*

hava-no (Korea to Modern) *s.* Korean Pidgin English for *don't have, don't have any*, etc.

Have a go, Joe (World War II) *s.* A London prostitute's salute to a prospective customer. Picked up by the latter, it came to mean *Give it a try, Try your luck, See what you can do.* Some cynics used it to describe Anglo-American strategy in Europe between the Normandy breakout and the Battle of the Bulge.

Havelock (Civil War; USA) Named after Gen. Henry Havelock, a British general during the Indian Mutiny. 1. A "grey, round hat with a wide black visor," used to some extent by the US Sharpshooters in early 1862, but soon discarded because its "rebellious hue" often drew fire from other Union soldiers. 2. More commonly, a cap cover, usually white, with a long flap at the back to protect the neck from rain and sun, like the headgear that the Foreign Legion wears in motion pictures. Very popular in 1861–62; thereafter used for towels or cleaning rags.

hazing Mistreatment of plebes by upperclassmen at the US military academies. It apparently became systematized and serious at the end of the Civil War, but was almost impossible to stop because of an informal conspiracy of silence among the cadets, including the plebes. It had certain practical purposes: plebes learned to control their tempers and keep their wits under extreme pressure, and conceited or unruly cadets were disciplined. These worthy goals, however, too often became an excuse for violent and sometimes harmful horseplay. A more recent form required plebes to memorize great amounts of nonsense, to the detriment of their studies. At present, hazing appears to have been suppressed.

HE High Explosive. Applied as in *HE shell* or *HE bomb.*

head-and-head (Modern) *s.* Short and informal for *headquarters and headquarters company.*

head bucket (Early World War II) *s.* A short-lived term for the World War II helmet.

head count Keeping an accurate account of the soldiers eating in a mess hall, a detail usually performed by an NCO or specialist. The head count is also used to ensure that specified personnel (officers and enlisted personnel authorized to mess separately) pay the stipulated rates for the meals if they try mess-hall food for a change.

headquarter, to (Modern) To establish in a headquarters facility. "During its tour . . . the 135th has been headquartered in Blackhorse" (AR, 7:31 2 August 1971). Another example of the disreputable modern trend to make verbs out of nouns.

headquarters comedian (Modern) *s.* The headquarters commandant, who is the staff officer responsible for supply, repairs, motor vehicles, and other support services in nontactical units. As almost no one is ever satisfied with the services he provides, he is universally derided and condemned.

headquarters in the saddle (Civil War; USA) An unfortunate phrase (one of several) attributed to Maj. Gen. John Pope on assuming command of the make-shift Army of Virginia in 1862. Pope's subsequent defeat at Second Bull Run produced remarks to the effect that he had his headquarters where his hind-quarters should have been. Thus, *head-quarters in the saddle* became an Army joke on the level of McClellan's *change of base*. It rather obscured the fact that Pope was a stout fighter, if overconfident.

headshed (Modern) *s.* A headquarters.

headspace (Probably Old, Old Army to Modern; also Marines) 1. The clear-ance between the face of the bolt of a rifle or machine gun and the base of the cartridge. If there is too much headspace, the weapon will not fire. 2. *s.* By transfer from the above, the platoon sad sack, with the implication that he has too much of it. 3. *Checking the head space* is an essential and periodic armorer's rite. Long-service infantrymen and marines use the expression to describe any sort of routine investigation.

health-care consumer (Modern) Anyone who needs medical attention; formerly called a *patient*. The Old Army fre-quently called a spade a goddam shovel; the New Army tends to refer to it as a long-handled agricultural instrument with an iron blade designed to be pressed into the ground with the foot, used for digging. Other neologisms are *Army din-ing facility* and *dining facility manager*—respectively, mess hall and mess sergeant.

heart (Modern) *s.* Short for the *Purple Heart Medal*. "I got a heart in Vietnam."

Heavies **Heavy Infantry** (Civil War; USA) *s.* Regiments of "heavy artillery," oversized outfits raised to garrison the fortifications around Washington, D.C. It was a comfortable assignment—until U. S. Grant brought them down to the Army of the Potomac in early 1864 as combat infantry.

hedgehopping (World War I to Modern) 1. *s.* Flying very close to the ground, so that you practically have to go up a bit to hop over a tall hedge or tree line. It is a method of attack favored by planes out to strafe the enemy ground forces. More recent terms are *grass cutting* and the more official *contour flying*. See *dice*. 2. *s.* A short aerial flight, probably be-cause such flights are made at lower alti-tudes.

heifer barn *s.* A WAAC or WAC bar-racks, WAAC or WAC detachment.

Heinie (World War I) *s.* German sol-dier. Short for *Heinrich*.

hell buggy (World War II) *s.* A tank. One of the many resounding names thought up early in the war (usually by reporters) that never caught on with soldiers.

Hell Cats (At least 1910; West Point) *s.* The cadets' name for the field music of the West Point band—drums, bugles, piccolos. One of their duties is to wake the cadets in the morning, a task they used to perform with gusto. A former member confided that in winter the Hell Cats turned out at 0530 with overcoats over their pajamas and field boots. They played the cadets awake and then went back to bed. If they did not mind missing breakfast, they could stay in the sack until 0930 roll call. "One of the Hellcats blew taps" (Truscott). At present, except for summer camp, they no longer sound reveille.

hellfire stew (Civil War; USA) *s.* A stew made of anything available.

hell hole (Modern; all Services) *s.* A repair area on the underside of a helicopter.

Hell-on-the-Hudson (Antiquity uncertain) *s.* The US Military Academy, West Point, New York. Formerly a proud, disciplined, semimonastic institution that made a high percentage of its graduates into first-class combat officers and gentlemen. Now coeducational, but at least a recent attempt to reduce military instruction has been thwarted.

Hell on Wheels (World War II) *s.* The 2d Armored Division.

Hell's Half-acre (World War II) *s.* The hospital area of the cramped Anzio beachhead. It caught most of the German shorts and overs.

Hell with the Lights Out **Hell with the Fires Burned Out** (Civil War; USA) *s.* The Dakota Badlands, so christened by Gen. Alfred Sully when he drove the Sioux through them in 1864.

helmet The regulation protective headgear with a liner and chinstrap. Also called *head bucket, iron hat, kettle, pot, steel pot.*

henhouse **hen pen** (Modern) *s.* The WAC quarters. Now becoming obsolete what with coed barracks.

herd bound (Old, Old Army to 1940s) Describing a horse that does not want to leave the others belonging to its unit. If kicked, spurred, quirted, and cursed into doing so, it will take advantage of the first opportunity to get the bit in its teeth and bolt back. Not an animal to be given to a scout or courier.

Herky-bird (Modern) *s.* The C-130 Hercules transport plane. "Banked his 'Herky-bird' sharply to the right" (TB).

Herman (Modern) *s.* A faintly derogatory name for any German civilian.

hero medal (Modern) *s.* Any decoration, whether for actual heroism or for meritorious service, but generally applied only to the latter.

hero snatcher (World War II) *s.* The American "translation" of the nickname *Heldenklaue* 'Hero-claw', which German soldiers gave to Gen. Walther von Unruh. It was his mission to comb through rear-echelon units for men who could be transferred to combat units on the Eastern Front. American troops in the ETO badly needed similar support, but efforts to provide it were usually defeated by Lt. Gen. John S. H. "Courthouse" Lee, the Services of Supply commander.

Hershey bar 1. (World War II and later) *s.* A woman—prostitute or amateur—whose horizontal favors could be had very cheaply, for barter of such items as candy or cigarettes. 2. (World War II to Modern) *s.* The overseas service bar, a gold stripe worn on the lower right sleeve of the uniform. It denotes service in an overseas combat theater. The term *Hershey bar* was a double double entendre, since it suggested that such bars were as significant as a nickel candy bar and echoed the name of Maj. Gen. Lewis B. Hershey, Selective Service director.

H-hour The hour set for an attack. In preliminary planning, the time is expressed as *H-hour, D-day*, in order to preserve secrecy. The actual hour and day are disclosed to personnel "having need to know" only at the last practicable moment.

Hide and Hope (World War II) *s.* The second, very unofficial motto of the US Tank Destroyer units, meaning that it was much safer and more effective to ambush German armor than to tackle it head on. See *Seek, Strike, Destroy.*

high ball (World War II) *s.* A salute, especially one delivered with flair and vigor. *To give someone the high ball.*

high crawl, to do the (Modern) *s.* To extricate oneself quickly but cautiously from an embarrassing or potentially hazardous social situation. In official terminology, the high crawl is a technique used when good concealment is available, enemy observation is limited, and speed is necessary. See *low crawl.*

high private (Civil War; USA) *s.* A veteran private of extensive experience and definite opinions, frequently given to loud and disrespectful utterances.

hike (At least 1900 to Modern; also Marines) A foot march. This is still an essential military art—the one certain way of getting across the worst terrain—but the average American recruit, motorized from his birth, needs considerable practice and hardening. We can remember during World War II that a movement of trucks might be called a *motor hike.*

hike, to To march on foot.

hill, to go over the See *over the hill.*

hindquarters company (Modern) *s.* A play on *headquarters company.*

hip-pocket promotion (Modern) *s.* Retiring from active service in a grade not held while on active service. For example, John Sullivan, who holds a Reserve commission as captain, has served as an officer in the Active Army for ten or more years. In a reduction in force, he is reduced to enlisted status. While serving as an enlisted man, he is promoted to major in the Reserve. Shortly afterward, he retires with twenty years of active service. His highest active-duty grade was captain, but he would retire as a major. He has "carried" his Reserve promotion in his hip pocket until he could retire and claim it. The Army is attempting to secure legislation that will abolish hip-pocket promotions.

HISASS /hiz-'ass/ (Vietnam) *s.* Play on *HSAS* (Headquarters Support Activity Saigon), the Navy command that furnished logistical support to the Military Assistance Command, Vietnam. In April 1966 the Army assumed this function.

hish and hash (Civil War; USA) *s.* A field soldier's improvised one-dish meal, consisting of anything available. In one case "pork, tomatoes, potatoes, crackers [hardtack] and mushrooms all stewed together and seasoned with a little salt and pepper." The same dish might be termed *hellfire stew* or *hellfired stew.*

hit, to be hit, to get 1. (Modern; all Services) *s.* To make contact with the enemy; to be attacked. In general, *getting hit* means that enemy attacked first and has the initiative. 2. (At least as early as World War II, to Modern) *s.* To be wounded or killed.

hitch (20th century and perhaps older) *s.* A legally specified term of service in the Army; an enlistment or reenlistment. *He is on his first hitch* means that someone is still in his first period of enlistment. The origin of the term is not known. Some authorities have derived it from the concept of hitching up a horse to a wagon. Others have related it to marriage, from the common slang expression *getting hitched.* (This, in turn, goes back to hitching horses together to form a harmonious team.) The DAE also records a mid-19th-century use of *hitch* as a time period or occasion: "We shall clear up three load this hitch"; "She'll mind her stops, next hitch, I reckon."

hitching-post fort (Indian Wars to early 20th century) *s.* A small post garrisoned by one or two understrength companies, originally built as a patrol and supply base during the pacification of the West. Since such posts were a major source of income to the communities that grew up around them, there often was strong political pressure to keep them open, even though the interests of the Army would have been better served in closing them. To pacify Congress, the Army kept many of them open for years—slightly shabby, quiet little places scattered about in odd corners of the Western states.

hit for the weeds, to (Air Force) s. To maneuver an airplane close to the ground in an attempt to elude pursuing aircraft or missiles. "Knowing that the Sams had his range [he had to] roll over and hit for the weeds" (Broughton).

Hit it! (World War II to Modern) *s.* Our marine recalls: "Very wide use, but most common was in Parachute School at Fort Benning. Means *get down and knock out pushups* as a penalty for something. Was accompanied by finger pointing at ground." It is also used to urge more speed and effort. Possibly of paratrooper origin.

Hitler's secret weapon (World War II) *s.* The issue chocolate bar, whether the small version in the K-ration packet or the larger D-bar emergency combat ration. It was enriched, fortified, harder than armor plate, almost insoluble, and generally frustrating. We have heard it claimed—but never seen it demonstrated—that this bar made the best hand-thrown antitank weapon available. Our marine did see a sergeant of A Company, 377th Infantry saved by a D-bar he was carrying in his shirt pocket. It stopped a fragment of an exploding 105mm shell.

Hit the deck! (World War II on, but much earlier in the Navy) *s.* Usually, as a command, *Get out of bed!* See Appendix.

Hit the dirt! (World War II and later) *s.* Take cover, duck, get down. Often uttered at the sound of an incoming shell.

hit the sack, to (Very common from World War II on; all Services) *s.* To go to bed, whether in comfortable quarters or a muddy slit trench. Possibly ultimately of naval origin, since a *sack* is naval slang for a hammock. The comparable civilian expression, *hit the hay*, goes back at least to World War I.

hit the silk, to (World War I and later) *s.* To make a parachute jump, especially from a disabled plane. A parachute at that time was made of silk.

hive (At least as early as 1900; West Point) *s.* One who learns quickly; a cadet who studies hard and even seems to enjoy it. The adjectival form is *hivey*, meaning bright and clever.

hive, to 1. (Pre–Civil War; West Point) *s.* To purloin or secure through irregular channels. Thus, the pans and sugar the cadets used to make taffy over the gaslights in their quarters were hived from the mess hall. Actual theft, however, was considered a major crime. Much the same concept prevailed throughout the Army in World War II, where such borrowing would be called *midnight requisitioning.* 2. (At least as early as 1900; West Point) *s.* To understand, to study, to comprehend. Possibly related to meaning 1 of *hive*, since both refer to acquisition, articles or knowledge.

hiyaku /'high-yack-koo *or, properly,* 'hah-yah-koo/ (Occupation of Japan and later) *s.* Hurry up! Move! Taken over by American soldiers from Japanese *hayaku* 'quickly'.

hog See *gunship.*

hog ranch (Old, Old Army into early 20th century) *s.* An establishment purveying corrosive liquids and diseased horizontal companionship. Usually there was at least one located just outside the boundaries of every western post. All told, they probably inflicted more casualties on the US Army than all the tribes west of the Mississippi.

hold baggage (Modern; all Services) Personal belongings, including those of your legal camp followers, that you cannot carry along with you during a move overseas. Within established weight allowances, these follow you at government expense. *Hold* in this case means the hold of a ship. Reportedly this term sometimes is used loosely for goods shipped by truck within the country.

holey joe (Modern) *s.* A shotgun envelope, incorporating a wordplay on *Holy Joe* (a chaplain). An interoffice envelope with many large perforations so that it can be seen if the envelope is empty.

Hollywood jump (Modern) *s.* A parachute jump without combat gear. It is usually performed from a helicopter, never in a massed tactical formation. " 'Hollywood' jumps, not weighted down with necessary baggage, not ungainly, utilitarian exercise" (Doulis).

Holy Ghoster (Revolutionary) *s.* A Nova Scotian volunteer for the American forces. There were quite a few of them, but for some reason they were not welcomed.

Holy Ghosts (World War II) *s.* Among German prisoners of war in the United States, Nazi goon squads that tried to keep anti-Hitler Germans properly cowed. The term is a translation of *der Heilige Geist* 'the Holy Ghost', referring to their sudden nocturnal visitations. On occasion they went as far as murder. Considerable effort was required to eradicate them.

Holy Joe (Also Navy, Marines) *s.* A chaplain. Possibly the oldest of the present service nicknames for that office, dating back at least to the beginning of the 20th century. See *padre.*

hombre (Old Army) *s.* A man, from Spanish *hombre.* One of the Spanish words adopted by Americans along the Mexican border. It is usually used with at least one qualifying adjective, such as *good* or *damned mean.* For a wonder, the original Spanish pronunciation is retained.

home plate (Air Force) *s.* An aircraft's base of origin. From baseball.

homesteader (Modern) *s.* A soldier who by design or chance stays in one assignment for a long period of time, perhaps five years or more. Generally applied to those who stay in the United States for long periods between overseas tours, but recently it has also been applied to those who choose to remain in overseas areas beyond their normal tours.

homing pigeon (World War II) *s.* Another term for the *ruptured duck*; more descriptive, but not as popular. When you got the homing pigeon, you took off like a homing pigeon.

honcho honsho (Post–World War II to Modern) *s.* The boss, the one in charge.

From the Japanese, although it is not clear which of several possible origins is valid: *hanchō* 'squad leader', *honshō* 'the main office', *honsho* 'the main place', and other forms. "See Sergeant Darby. He's the main honcho down at the motor pool." Also used extensively by civilians.

Hong Kong (Vietnam on; all Services) *s.* Vietnamese pidgin English for anything cheap, imitative, or false. During the war the local markets were filled with cheap goods manufactured in Hong Kong. Many Vietnamese women affected brassieres filled more with sponge rubber than parts of themselves and *Hong Kong* came to be a term for a padded brassiere: "She's wearing Hong Kongs." It was a favorite pastime in Vietnamese bistros to accuse the hostesses of wearing Hong Kongs. A Navy commander known to our sergeant major claims to have experienced the ultimate put-down in this amusing game. He casually squeezed a young barmaid's ample bosom and asked her facetiously, "You Hong Kong?" The quick-thinking young woman, far from being affronted, placed her hand on his member, squeezed hard, and replied "*You* Hong Kong?"

honors Distinctions, usually in the form of battle or campaign streamers for the standard or colors of the unit; they are granted for outstanding conduct. For most of the history of the Army, honors were granted in a hit-or-miss fashion. Prior to, and during, the Civil War, some regiments simply had the names of their engagements painted or embroidered on their flags. Honors include awards by foreign governments during World Wars I and II (usually in the form of a fourragère) and the US Distinguished Unit Citation and Meritorious Unit Award. After World War II considerable emphasis was placed on unit honors as aids to morale. Unfortunately, the Pentagon inmates involved in the program appear to have been thoroughly civilian-minded. To them, unit honors were on the order of trading stamps or bubble-gum bonus cards. The height of their achievement was directing two divisions to exchange designations and honors.

hooch (Occupation of Japan to Modern) 1. *s.* A native shack of woven bamboo, grass, or similar materials, anywhere in the Far East. Soldiers' corruption of the Japanese *uchi* 'a house', with possible connections to the English word *hutch.* 2. *s.* A quonset hut used as a barrack. 3. *s.* Any kind of temporary billet for troops other than a tent. 4. *s.* Any kind of a house or place to sleep.

Hook (Vietnam to Modern) *s.* The CH-47 Chinook helicopter. Perhaps short for *Shithook* or just a contraction of *Chinook.*

hooker (At least Civil War to Modern; all Services) *s.* A prostitute, particularly a low-grade one. Military tradition, as persistent as it is tenuous, insists that the term originated around Washington, D.C., in 1862–63, among prostitutes who serviced the troops commanded by Maj. Gen. Joseph Hooker. ("Fighting Joe" did not exactly shun the more sensual pleasures himself, as a general rule.) But the DAE records *hooker* in 1859, as a sailor's term, and connects it with the whores at the Hook in New York. In all probability, though, the term is based on the older thieves' cant *hooker* for pickpockets, cheats, and aggressively dishonest merchants.

hooks 1. (Old, Old Army, still occasionally used figuratively) *s.* Spurs. *To put your hooks* into a horse was to spur him vigorously. The old-fashioned Army spurs with the sharp, dime-sized rowels were *really* hooks. Naturally, an officer or NCO was often described as *putting the hooks* to a sluggish or recalcitrant unit or individual. 2. (Old Army into World War II) *s.* An NCO's chevrons.

hop (Modern; West Point) *s.* A dance. An example of Army conservatism in language. Although *hop* was a standard word for a dance in the early 19th century, both in Great Britain and America, the word has almost disappeared (except jocularly) in civilian circles. It remains standard at West Point.

hop, to (Modern) *s.* To obtain a seat on a military aircraft, generally for semiofficial business. The hopper has a definite destination and some good reason for traveling, and is subject to payment of a nominal fee for transportation.

horde (Korea; also Marines) *s.* One or more North Joes or Chicoms. Although the Communists did employ massed infantry assaults at what they considered decisive points, most of their attacks were small-scale affairs, shrewdly directed at the flank or rear of a UN position. It is an ancient axiom, followed by all armies, that it is safer to tell higher headquarters that you were outnumbered than that you were outsmarted. Also called a *human sea.*

horizontal refreshment (Civil War and probably earlier, to Modern) *s.* Sexual intercourse on a catch-as-catch-can basis.

horn (Modern) *s.* The microphone on a field radio set. Any telephone instrument. A loudspeaker. "Get on the horn and tell Service Company to send up the water truck." "It just came over the horn."

horsefly (World War II; also Air Force) *s.* A light liaison-type aircraft (see *grasshopper*). A *horsefly mission* is the use of such an aircraft to guide friendly fighter bombers to an enemy ground target.

horse holder 1. (Early 19th century to World War II, and may still linger) When cavalry dismounted to fight on foot, one man in each four held the horses some distance to the rear and under whatever cover was available. Consequently, *horse holder* came to mean someone who was on your side but did not take an active part or risk getting his nose bloodied. This implication was not entirely fair. The horse holder had to be man enough to hang on to four frightened horses and also reliable enough to stick it out whatever happened. 2. (Modern) *s.* A disrespectful description of certain field-grade officer assistants to Pentagon chair-borne general officers. "Lt. Col. Jones is General Smith's horse holder" means that Jones tags along, runs errands, and caters to the general's every whim.

horse parts (1930s through at least World War II; also Navy, Marines) *s.* A somewhat bowdlerized term for cold cuts. During World War II, Army expressions became blunter: *horse cock* or *cold horse cock.* See also *donkey dick.*

horseshoe roll A traditional type of infantryman's pack, used in America at least as early as the French and Indian Wars. The soldier rolled up his blanket lengthwise and slung it over his shoulder. The two ends were then tied together with a thong or strap behind the right hip, giving the rig the general shape of a horseshoe. Extra articles of clothing and such could be rolled up inside the blanket. Sometimes the blanket was rolled inside a shelter half or "rubber" or oilcloth ground sheet.

hose down, to (Modern; all Services) *s.* To kill, particularly with automatic weapons. "A lot of them are going to get killed, hosed down no questions asked" (Bunting).

hospital rat (Civil War; CSA) *s.* A malingerer; someone who habitually rode the sick book.

hostiles (Indian Wars) Members of Indian tribes engaged in active hostilities against the whites and/or friendly Indians. The term continued into the Philippine pacification, where it was applied to insurrectos or plain bandits.

hot (Modern) 1. *s.* Receiving enemy fire. " 'Hot LZ' means the pilot won't land for fear of getting shot up" (Haldeman). 2. *s.* Firing on the enemy. "The 'guns' came in 'hot,' meaning with their rockets and machine guns firing" (Mulligan).

hot-beverage corporal (West Point) The fourth classman (plebe) responsible for serving the hot beverages at each table in the mess hall.

hotchee (Occupation of Japan and later) *s.* The penis. Commonly used in Korean pidgin English. The origin of the term is obscure. It may represent Japanese *hachi* 'eight', a figure often quoted in such circumstances. Or it may be a back formation from *shakuhachi*, the traditional flute, the name of which was corrupted by American soldiers to *suckahachi*, meaning fellatio. The *hachi* part could then have been taken to mean penis. See *suckahachi*.

Hotel Dee Barb Wire (World War I) *s.* Soldiers' humorous term for the stockade.

hotel out of your alpha, Get your (Modern) *s.* A catchphrase, meaning *Get your head out of your ass* or *Get to work; Stop goofing off*. *Hotel* and *Alpha* are the phonetic alphabet letters for *h* and *a*.

hotrep (Modern) *s.* Hot report. An in-depth reading of an aerial reconnaissance photograph.

hot rock (Approximately World War II, but still heard occasionally) *s.* An expert, hardworking individual, especially a hot pilot. Or a vain and aggressive person who thinks he is a hot rock.

hots (Modern) *s.* Hot meals prepared in a field kitchen or mess hall; also called A-rations, as distinct from C-ration meals. See *field rations*.

hot sheets (Vietnam and later) *s.* Sheets of steel (usually pierced steel plate) laid out as sidewalks, roadways, runways, etc. They would be heated to a high degree by the tropical sun. " 'Hot sheet' . . . sheets of steel soaking up the Vietnam sun and pushing it back through the soles of your boots" (Haldeman).

hot skinny *s.* Information.

house apes *s.* Dependent children, usually under twelve years of age.

housecats (Modern) *s.* Combat service support personnel. "Housecats—the vehicle mechanics and radio mechanics and cooks and clerks" (Heinemann).

household troops (Early World War II) *s.* Personnel of the Service Command responsible for "housekeeping" functions at posts, camps, and stations. The name had only a short existence and was seldom used without qualifying adjectives. The idea, however, was good, as it gave the troop units more time for training. Also, it utilized limited-service personnel, such as one post MP at Camp Cooke, California. His false teeth popped out every time he challenged. On a dark and stormy night, this could induce instant sobriety in any late-returning GI, however inebriated. In European usage, of course, the term *household troops* has the entirely different and much older meaning of elite troops guarding a sovereign and his palaces.

housewife (Ancient to Modern; also Marines) *s.* A small sewing kit for emergency repairs to clothing. Many soldiers carried their own, but in the 1930s at least every squad was issued one, which was carried by the corporal. Also *soldier's wife.*

How! (Old, Old Army into the 1950s) Sometimes *Here's how!* The traditional Army toast, which supposedly originated during the Seminole War of 1841 as an adaptation of the Indian salutation *How!* We have not heard it used in years.

Howard Johnsons (Vietnam) *s.* The little pushcarts that Vietnamese food vendors operated in the streets of Saigon and other South Vietnamese cities. From them the peddlers sold everything from hot soup to cigarettes. The term is from the American chain of highway restaurants. Our sergeant major notes that it was very popular among the Americans in Saigon as early as March 1962.

How are they all? (Modern; West Point) *s.* A stock question asked plebes by upperclassmen. The necessary stock answer is "They are all fickle but one, sir." Presumably "they" are females of the species and the one exception is the cadet's own sweetheart. See *plebe knowledge.*

how box (Indian Wars) The companion of most field-grade and higher officers when on campaign. It was carefully packed away in their headquarters wagons or ambulances when on the march and usually was the first item unloaded when the command made camp. A typical how box was approximately 18 inches square and 15 deep, and made of polished hardwood. Its interior was divided into compartments, each of which held a bottle of whiskey or its spiritous equivalent. Once the men and horses were cared for and guards had been posted, the owner of the how box might assemble his subordinate officers for a relaxing drink or two. The name obviously came from the traditional toast of the Indian-fighting Army—*How!*

How is the cow? (Modern; West Point) *s.* A stock question that upperclassmen ask plebes. The stock answer, which must be rendered precisely, is "Sir, she walks, she talks, she's full of chalk; the lacteal fluid extracted from the female of the bovine species is highly prolific to the nth degree." See *plebe knowledge.*

hows (Generally World War II) *s.* Howitzers. "The 121st Field Artillery Battalion is being reequipped with 8-inch hows."

HQ Headquarters.

hubi hubi (Post–World War II) *s.* Korean pidgin for *hurry.*

Hudson hip disease (West Point) *s.* An occupational hazard described as a bilateral growth of adipose tissue that often afflicts beanettes after a week or two of eating Army chow.

Huey (Vietnam) The UG-1 helicopter. See *gunship, slick.*

huffduff (World War II) *s.* Slang pronunciation of *HF/DF* (high frequency direction finding), a British device for locating the source of high-frequency radio broadcasts. It was much used during the Battle of the Atlantic to direct hunter-killer groups.

hump See *over the hump, promotion hump.*

hump, to 1. (World War II, perhaps later) *s.* To speed up, to work faster. "Come on, hump it, soldier, hump it!"

"We're going to have to hump it to reach Kaiserslautern tonight!" 2. (Modern) *s.* To cope with something, as "I can't hump it. The cook sits there drinking coffee with O'Neill, and I have to do all the work." 3. *s.* To do heavy work, to proceed with difficulty, to footslog. "For ten days the platoon humped the short range of mountains south of the river from Bong Son" (Smith). "Humping the boonies . . . you put a monster pack on your back, a gun in one hand . . . and you go out in the woods . . . lookin' for trouble" (Haldeman).

hump, to be over the (At least World War II) *s.* To have the worst part of anything behind you, usually an enlistment. "Yeah, I'm over the hump now. Only fifteen more months to go."

Hun (World War I) 1. *s.* Term of opprobrium for the Germans. In a typical blowhard speech, when sending troops off to help crush the Boxer Rebellion in China (1900), the Kaiser urged his men to make themselves as dreaded as Attila's Huns. In 1914, British propaganda resurrected that phrase and went all out to make the Germans appear even meaner. The term was not used much by American soldiers, but was a favorite of journalists. 2. *s.* What instructors in British flying schools called the typical US flying cadet they had to train.

Hungry Hill (Old Army) *s.* The area of a military post where married enlisted men had their quarters. Also *Soap Suds Row.*

hurry up and wait (20th century, but probably earlier versions) If you are on time, no one else is—one of the basic principles of civilized warfare. Also, if there is a general review at 1100, the participating battalions will have been checked minutely by their COs at 1000; the companies making up those battalions by their COs at 0900; the platoons in those companies at 0800; and the squads in those platoons at least as early as 0630. With all that accomplished and with everyone afraid to sit down for fear of wrinkling his trousers, some large stray dog will join the review and gambol merrily through the ranks of the band, completely hogging the attention of the observers.

husband (West Point) *s.* The ranking cadet of roommates at West Point.

hut hup hep The drill sergeant's way of saying *one.* "HUT two three four!"

hydrostatic lock (Modern) An imaginary article, like the skyhook, the left-handed monkey wrench, and the stove jack, which ingenuous personnel are sent to fetch.

hymn (Modern) *s.* Referred to as *hymn,* but actually *him. Him* is the first word of a mindless four-word soldier ditty that goes: *Him, him, FUCK HIM!* The hymn is performed to express resentment against and disrespect and dislike for a despised officer or noncommissioned officer, who is never identified by name. It is usually begun by two or three soldiers, who sonorously chant, "Him, him," with the troops all joining in on the "chorus," shouting "FUCK HIM!" as loudly as they can. Tregaskis mentions this as a favorite hymn among Americans stationed in the Mekong Delta in 1962. Our sergeant major witnessed it at Fort Bragg, North Carolina, in 1964. The noncom in charge of the troops was not particularly well liked. He knew perfectly well what the performance meant, but since he was unable to pinpoint any one soldier, he wisely chose to ignore the matter.

☆☆☆☆*i*☆☆☆☆

IAF 1. (World War I) Independent Air Force, a branch of the RAF formed in 1918 for strategic bombing missions. Its Handley-Page bombers could lift a ton of bombs, fly approximately 90 miles per hour, and reach the German Rhineland from bases in west central France. With favorable weather and lots of luck, its bombardiers could hit a good-sized city—a feat that the Bomber Command of the RAF and elements of the US Strategic Air Force had some difficulty in repeating through World War II. Some Americans served with IAF, integrated into British squadrons. It also mightily inflamed the imagination of Billy Mitchell.

I & I Inventory and Inspection Report. Government property rendered unserviceable "through fair wear and tear in the Military Service" was listed on this form by the officer responsible for the property and submitted to an inspecting officer. The inspector could order the property destroyed, turned in for salvage, or broken up to utilize its component parts. Before 1941 (and under the benign neglect of Secretary of Defense Louis Johnson between World War II and the Korean War), getting the inspector's OK frequently resembled extracting an impacted wisdom tooth. This original two-officer process was undoubtedly lacking in technological expertise, and it allegedly has therefore been replaced by the integrated efforts of a special Pentagon board, three senior DAC's, one GS-14 from the General Accounting Office, another from the Bureau of the Budget, and one computer. Naturally, the old I & I process gave rise to the verb *to I & I*, which was applied to people, plans, doctrine, or anything else that the Army looked over and decided to get rid of. (Come to think of it, we have not heard the term for years.) 2. (World War II) *s.* Insolence and Insubordination. 3. (Korea; also Marines) *s.* Intercourse and Intoxication. A blunt description of how R & R actually worked out once the heavy fighting was over and the men who went to Japan on leave were still full of vim and vigor.

IAW (Modern) In Accordance With.

IC (Civil War; USA) Invalid Corps. The Corps was established in April 1863 to utilize soldiers who were unfit for combat duty. Those who could still handle weapons were used for rear-area guard duty; those too disabled for such duty served as hospital cooks and nurses. The IC was a useful organization, but its members were often taunted as being "condemned Yanks" (see *I/C*) and in March 1864 its name was changed to *Veteran Reserve Corps*.

I/C (Pre–Civil War to Modern) Inspected and Condemned. *I/C* was placed on public animals, equipment, vehicles, and other Army property found unfit for further Army use. Usually such property was offered for sale to the general public, but such items were often adjudged adequate for issue to ROTC units, Philippine Scouts, and other underprivileged outfits. In 1946 the Philippine Scouts were issued I/C'd trucks, while new trucks stood on hard stands all around Manila until the tropical sun rotted their canvas and rubber or some hard-working Tagalog borrowed them. (The Philippine Command never bothered to explain why this situation existed. Since they were the people MacArthur decided not to take to Japan with him, they were probably too busy drowning their sorrows.) In the 24th Field Artillery Battalion of the Philippine Scouts, however, we managed. Two or three I/C'd trucks could be reassembled to make one serviceable truck. For the rest, we relieved some thieves of their booty and did not trouble Manila about it.

ice cream cone with wings (Modern) *s.* The parachutist badge, so called because of its resemblance to a cone (the fully deployed parachute), with wings flanking the parachute on the badge.

ich /*usually* ish/ (Post–World War II) *s.* The personal pronoun *I*, from German *ich*. Frequently used for emphasis: "And who gets stuck with that chicken detail? Old ich, as usual."

ichiban (Post–World War II) *s.* The best, Number One, from Japanese *ichiban* 'number one'. See *number ten* for a discussion of the Oriental rating system.

ID ID card (World War II to Modern) Identification card carried by service personnel and their dependents.

idewa iddiwa /'ee-dee-wa/ (Mostly 1950s on, although earlier use during the US occupation of Korea in 1945–49) *s.* Come here! The derivation of the expression is obscure. Most sources regard it as of Korean origin, but no comparable Korean form has been found. In all probability, it is pidgin Japanese, a corruption of *o-ide nasai* 'come here', in which *nasai* has been dropped and the nominative particle *wa* has (incorrectly) been added in its place.

idiot blocks (Modern) *s.* Blank lines typed on the bottom of a staff paper indicating options. They permit a decision maker to indicate his desires by using a check mark. For example: Approved ———. See me ———. Brief no. ———.

idiot board (Korea) *s.* A pack board for carrying supplies in areas fit only for men or mules—and the Army no longer has any mules. The Korean A-frame was far more efficient, but it was not designed for delivery by air. In contrast to *idiot stick*, the idea behind *idiot board* has an element of good sense. Where there is shooting to be done, no squad, platoon, or company commander is going to detail his best and brightest to run up and down the ridge lines carrying resupplies of ammo, food, and water.

idiot stick (World War II to Modern) *s.* Primarily a rifle, sometimes a shovel. The implications are that a smart soldier avoids the hazards and fatigues associated with either and that only those soldiers not intelligent, educated, or shifty enough to get a soft job end up toting a rifle in the combat infantry. The sad fact is that the modern combat infantryman needs more character than a bishop, more guts than a professional hockey player, and more brains than a US senator. Marines never call a rifle an *idiot stick*. It is part of their religion that carrying a rifle is a real man's job.

I don't get paid enough to think (Unknown antiquity to Modern) *s.* A cynical rejoinder to any question beginning with "Do you think. . . ."

IDR (Revolutionary to 1930s) *Infantry Drill Regulations*, one of the Army's principal theological works, based on original scripture by Friedrich Baron von Steuben, written at Valley Forge in early 1778. It finally was superseded by *FM 21-100* in 1939.

IET See *initial entry training*.

IFC (Modern) *s.* Idiots, Fools, and Clowns. A play on *IFC* for Integrated Fire Control.

If the Army wanted you to have a wife, it would have issued you one (Modern) *s.* A stock phrase, in the present version implying that soldiers have no business being married and that those who do have wives should keep their marital problems strictly personal. There are many variants to the expression, adapted to such other "unnecessary" things as education, intelligence, one's own opinions, etc.

IG. Inspector General.

IG inspection An annual inspection of a unit to determine how well it performs all aspects of its mission. The inspection is intended to help a unit maintain its readiness, not to destroy its commander's career by showing him up. But careers have been ruined by it.

ignorant stripe (Modern) *s.* A service stripe (hash mark). So called, probably, from the idea widely held among young and inexperienced soldiers that anyone who would stay in the Army long enough to qualify for a service stripe (three years) has simply *got* to be stupid.

IHTFP (Modern) *s.* I Hate This Fucking Place. The term gained wide popularity during the Vietnam War, when it was most often seen scrawled or carefully hand-lettered on helmet camouflage covers or cardboard placards.

Ike jacket (World War II) *s.* A snug, waist-length uniform jacket similar to the shell jacket worn by US Civil War cavalrymen and horse artillerymen. It was a comfortable and practical piece of clothing, but unfortunately not becoming on plump, chairborne, rear-echelon types. Also, it required less material than a full-length uniform coat, much to the distress of congressmen from states producing woolen cloth. Which of these two groups of selfless patriots had the greater share in abolishing the Ike jacket in the early 1950s is impossible to determine. In the States, sometimes called the *Eisenhower jacket*.

illegitimis non carborundum illegitimati non carborundum (World War II and later) s. Mock Latin for "Don't let the bastards wear you down." The expression is of British origin, and Partridge (1970) attributes it to Stanley Casson, although the attribution is only a guess. The first of the two forms above is the more "correct."

illum (Modern; also Marines) *s.* Short for *illumination*, meaning flares.

ima . . /ée-mah/ (Occupation of Japan and later) *s.* Now. From Japanese *ima* 'now'. Used by American noncoms for gentle chidings like "Right goddam ima!"

immediately, if not sooner (Modern) *s.* A catchphrase meaning *right away.*

immunes (Spanish-American War) Ten regiments—six of whites and four of blacks—of US Volunteer Infantry recruited in the southern states from men who were immune to tropical diseases. Unfortunately, many of them were not.

impact area That portion of a firing range where the projectiles strike. If you are an infantryman in combat, you probably think that you live in one large impact area—which is not far from the truth.

implement, to (Probably World War II on) A favorite headquarters word, meaning "No matter how impracticable or impossible this directive may be, you will somehow make it work—and don't bother us about associated details."

inclosure A supporting document sent along with a letter. The inclosures are always listed at the bottom of the letter so that the recipient can tell immediately which one the sender forgot to forward. Often abbreviated *incl.*

incoming (Modern; also Marines) Descriptive of enemy fire. The opposite of *outgoing* fire.

increments (World War I to Modern) Portions of the propelling charge of a mortar or artillery projectile. Depending on the range and/or elevation at which these weapons are fired, some increments from each round may be discarded. When this happens, they are promptly grabbed up by passing infantrymen, who use them for starting fires with wet wood. Since the increments burn at approximately 2000° F. without smoke, they are excellent for this purpose. However, it is not advisable to use increments in a stove. When so confined, they revert to their original explosive nature.

Indian country (Modern; also Marines) *s.* Unsecured enemy territory, usually outside the perimeter of a position; the area where patrolling and fighting are conducted. Undoubtedly suggested by Westerns.

Indian Heads The 2d Infantry Division, so called from its insignia; an Indian head in profile on a white star superimposed on a black shield.

indigenous personnel (Modern) The natives. Native employees at an overseas installation and, by extension, all foreigners. The expression has been common in the Army since the 1950s, but the preferred terminology is *local national personnel.* This sounds more pleasant than *indigenous,* which is sometimes misunderstood.

indorsement Military letters are not usually answered by means of a separate letter. Instead, the answer is added to the end of the original letter, in the form of a "1st indorsement." A letter going through channels from a lower to a higher headquarters picks up indorsements (consecutively numbered) at each echelon of the chain of command through which it travels. This system keeps all the known facts concerning the problem in question together for everyone's edification and for the senior commander's decision. There is also the pleasant Army procedure of "reply by indorsement hereon," by which a commanding officer invites you to explain in writing your—or your unit's—shortcomings and transgressions. The classic indorsement in such a case—which we fortunately never had the opportunity to use—is "Communication noted. No comment."

indorser (Modern) In the efficiency-report system, the individual next higher in rank than the rater. The indorser makes appropriate comments on the efficiency report forms for officers and enlisted men. On OERs, now called the *immediate rater*.

infantry infantryman (Ancient to Modern; also Marines) A soldier who fights on foot. The infantry, often called the *Queen of Battle*, has not always been the senior or preferred service in the armies of the world. Horse cavalry has often enjoyed more prestige. The infantryman's lot has always been fraught with dirt and hardship, sometimes followed by a very mean death. But there is scarcely a veteran of the infantry who is not intensely proud of his service as a foot soldier. The origin of the word *infantry* is somewhat unclear. It came into Renaissance English from Italian *infanteria*, via French intermediary forms. The Italian word is obviously connected with Latin *infans* 'child', which presumably shifted in meaning to refer to a youth, young person, armed servant, etc. Modern nicknames for the infantryman are legion and include *beetle crusher, blisterfoot, blue, boonie rat, bravo, dogface, doggie, doughboy, doughfoot, eleven bang-bang, eleven bravo, eleven bush, field rat, footslogger, gravel agitator, gravel crusher, gravel pounder, gravel pusher, groundpounder, grunt, leg, mudcrusher, mud thumper, pebblepusher, peon, rifle, straightleg, stump jumper*, etc.

infiltration course (At least World War I to Modern) A course designed to expose soldiers in basic training to combat conditions. Soldiers are required to crawl through the course while live ammunition is fired inches above their heads and explosives are detonated around them.

ingress, to (Modern; primarily Air Force) To enter enemy airspace or a target area.

initial entry training IET (Modern) Formerly called *basic combat training*. This can be ONESUT (One-Station Unit Training), in which the recruit takes initial and advanced training at the same post, or TWOSUT (Two-Station Unit Training), in which the recruit takes advanced training at a different post.

initial issue (Modern) 1. Clothing issued free to the inductee or recruit when he is processed from civilian life into the Army. When items of initial issue wear out, are lost, or are stolen, the soldier must replace them at cost. During the soldier's first six months of service, items that do not fit properly may be exchanged free for items that do. 2. Equipment not previously approved, but now issued; equipment supplied to newly activated units.

in on at (1920s to 1940s) Peculiarities of service talk. One serves *in* Hawaii, Panama, the Philippines, and China, but *on* Guam and *at* stateside posts.

in place (Ancient to Modern; also Marines) A drill command, meaning retain the present marching attitude when given the command to halt. For example, if you are marching at the oblique and are commanded to halt in place, you will halt at the oblique rather than facing to your original front, as you would normally do. Also—as in "In place, double time, march!"—to go through the motions of double time without changing place. Naturally, the phrase has been adapted to unofficial meanings, such as *orgasm in place*.

insert, to (Vietnam and later; also Air Force) To land troops in the enemy's rear areas by helicopter or parachute.

insignia insigne Traditionally, *insigne* is the singular form (and is still occasionally met), and *insignia*, the plural. But in usage, *insignia* is both singular and plural. A new plural form, *insignias*, is sometimes heard.

insignia of branch Insignia representing the branch of service to which a soldier belongs. A general officer or a warrant officer does not wear an insignia of branch. An enlisted man wears an insignia mounted on a gold metal disk; it is inserted in the left side of the shirt collar, on the tab, or on the left lapel of the blouse. An officer wears his insignia similarly, but his are without disks.

Inspector General (Revolutionary to Modern) Often referred to as *IG*. The Inspector General and Inspector General's Department, now a branch of the service, is the resident conscience of the Army. Operating outside the normal chain of command, the IG is charged with monitoring the Army's efficiency, economy, discipline, and ability to perform its mission. The IG conducts frequent inspections at all levels and handles complaints or requests for assistance from all ranks. Actually, handling complaints is a very small aspect of the work of the modern IG, and contrary to the common belief that the IG is all powerful, he can assist the soldier only as far as Army regulations permit. Any soldier can see any IG at any time, but an unwritten rule of demonstrated validity is that the soldier should not go to the IG until the chain of command has had a chance to operate. As often as not, the IG, to settle the soldier's complaint, merely refers him to the proper element in the chain of command that he should have consulted in the first place. It is also an unwritten rule that a soldier should not be punished for bypassing the chain of command by going directly to the IG.

instant artillerymen (Indian Wars) *s.* Cavalrymen and/or infantrymen detailed for service as artillerymen, usually with very sketchy training, if any. See *wagon soldier.*

instant NCO (Vietnam) *s.* An NCO who received his stripes immediately after completing a prescribed course of instructions in a particular MOS. Sometimes referred to as *Shake 'n Bake, Ready Whip, Nestle's Quick*, after the popular quick-food products. "An Instant NCO . . . with sergeant's stripes earned in three months of stateside schooling" (O'Brien).

instrument sergeant (Approximately 1900 to Modern) The NCO in an artillery battery or battalion who has charge of the BC scopes, aiming circles, range finders, and similar fire-control instruments. He helps with fire control and survey work.

interior guard Guards posted within the limits of a post, camp, or station.

in the Army (Modern) A soldier who is *in the Army* (as opposed to *of the Army*) is there to get it over with and return to civilian life with as many veteran's benefits as possible. See *lifer, of the Army.*

Intoxication and Intercourse See *I & I.*

iodine (Old, Old Army into World War II) A potent liquid antiseptic, comprising most of the exterior treatment practiced by Old Army medics. Standard sick-call treatment was to "paint him with iodine and mark him 'Duty.' " It really worked. It stung you enough to make you forget your original injury. For internal purposes a CC (or, later, APC) pill took its place. During the Philippine Insurrection the Medical Corps motto allegedly was "Give him a CC [or an APC] pill and paint him with iodine."

iodine spillers (War War I) *s.* Medical Corps personnel.

I remain in observation (Old, Old Army to Old Army) The customary closing of a report from a patrol that has detected some enemy activity, indicating that it would continue to observe it. Naturally, the phrase lent itself to other applications, especially where the activities of the fair sex were concerned.

Irish banjo See *Army banjo.*

Irish Brigade (Civil War; USA) A famous shock unit of the Army of the Potomac. It originally consisted of the 63d, 69th, and 88th New York Volunteer Infantry regiments. At various times the 28th and 29th Massachusetts and 116th Pennsylvania served with it, as did elements of the 7th New York Heavy Artillery. Each of its regiments carried a special green flag in addition to its regulation colors. A good many of the officers and men regarded the Civil War as practice for the liberation of Ireland and were later involved in the somewhat comic opera Fenian raids into Canada.

Irish musket (Revolutionary) *s.* A club.

Irish pennant (20th century; originally Marines and/or Navy) Something loose or flapping, like tag ends of a strap, loose threads on a garment or, commonly, around the edges of chevrons. Also called *rip cords.* Airmen call them *ropes.*

Irish promotion (Old, Old Army and later) *s.* A demotion.

Irish theater (Old, Old Army) *s.* The guardhouse.

Irish turkey (Antiquity uncertain, but probably early 20th century through World War II) *s.* Hash.

Iron Brigade Iron Brigade of the West (Civil War; USA) The only all-western brigade with the Army of the Potomac. Under the efficient leadership of Brig. Gen. John Gibbon, who gave it Regular Army drill, discipline, and dress, it immediately won distinction, particularly at Gettysburg. After this, possibly because of poorer leadership and replacements, its service was unremarkable. The brigade was originally known as the *Black Hat Brigade* (from the Regular Army dress hats that Gibbon issued). The nickname *Iron Brigade* was apparently coined by a reporter, not by the soldiers. The organization originally consisted of the 19th Indiana and the 2d, 6th, and 7th Wisconsin regiments of volunteer infantry. The 24th Michigan was added in October 1862.

iron mouth (Old Army) *s.* An intractable horse, prone to running away with its rider. Some iron mouths were tricky types, able to tongue their bits in between their rear teeth; others simply had mouths tougher than curb bits. If an iron mouth bolted with you during retreat parade, you could get a term in the mill. The horse got no punishment; it was not its fault that you could not ride it.

irritated orifice (World War II and later) The insignia of the 37th Infantry Division, a red circle centered on a slightly larger white one.

I shall return! (World War II to Modern) A catchphrase, usually delivered with a flourish, meaning that the speaker will be right back. A somewhat cynical response is "Don't take as long as MacArthur did." The statement originally became world-famous when General MacArthur used it in a speech at Adelaide Station, Australia, on 20 March 1942, but it seems to have been created by Carlos P. Romulo (Manchester).

Islands, the (Old Army) *s.* The Philippine Islands, known in the proud, old days by that short title. In these effete times, however, it probably means the Hawaiian Islands.

issue (Ancient to Modern) An adjective or noun indicating items that are issued, such as *issue clothing.* In this sense, *issue* often has a slighting meaning, since some soldiers prefer to buy what they consider smarter-looking or better-quality items from the PX or even from civilian merchants.

issue, to (Ancient to Modern) To give out clothing, equipment, or supplies to members of the Armed Forces according to appropriate regulations.

It all counts for twenty It all counts for thirty (Modern) *s.* A catchphrase meaning that the present problem or difficulty is trivial when compared with the totality of a service career or that one just has to put up with it. *Twenty* and *thirty* refer to years of service before retirement with half or three-fourths of your active-duty base pay.

Itey Itie Eytie (World War II) *s.* A derogatory term for an Italian. Borrowed from the British. More common American terms were *wop, dago, guinea.* See *Eytie.*

Ivan (Modern) *s.* A Soviet soldier.

jab, to get a (World War I) *s.* To get an inoculation or injection.

jack (Old Army) *s.* A corporal; almost always used in combination. A *limber jack* was the corporal in charge of an artillery gun section's limbers and caisson; a *lance jack*, a lance corporal; and an *acting jack*, an acting corporal.

jackass battery (About 1840 to World War II) *s.* A battery of mountain or jackass guns. "The shackass battery, by Gott—get out mit der way or we blow your hets off!" (Rear guard at Second Bull Run; Catton).

jackass gun (About 1840 to World War II) *s.* A light howitzer designed so that it could be easily taken apart and its component parts carried by several pack mules. Where terrain permitted, it was often towed by a single mule.

Jack Johnson (World War I) *s.* The shell or shell burst of a German 5.9-inch (150mm) howitzer. British origin. Named after the fabulous black heavyweight champion Jack Johnson. Partridge (1970) states that the shell emitted a heavy cloud of black smoke; Johnson's nickname was *the Big Smoke.*

Jackson (World War II) *s.* A form of address among enlisted men when names were not known and rank was not a question. While the term *soldier* might have been officially sanctioned in such cases, some GIs resented being called *soldier*. The term carried memories of a talking down by officers. *George, Jack*, and *Mac* were similarly used. "Hey, Jackson! Will you move that goddam jeep! You're blocking the snow path!"

jack up, to (Antiquity uncertain) *s.* To scold, to chew out. Wentworth and Flexner record the expression as from the 1890s and archaic by 1960, but do not cite an example or source. Partridge (1970) cites *jag* and *jag up* as British military slang from around World War I, meaning *to punish*, but this may not be the same term.

jarhead (General) *s.* Probably parallel to, or derived from, *jughead*, with a wide range of meanings similar to *jughead*. At present, the primary meaning is a US Marine. Morris and Morris cite *jarhead* as Old Army slang for a mule. Wentworth and Flexner define *jarhead* as variously a mule, a black male, or a marine. Dr.

Lighter (letter to Cragg, 22 October 1970) cites from *Leatherneck* (1933), where Army soldiers are called *jarheads*. Col. Albert Moe (letter to Cragg, 22 October 1979) writes that he first heard the word in 1942, used by marines as synonymous with *jughead*. On the other hand, an ex-Marine master sergeant with six years' experience around the time of the Korean War informs us that in his time a *jarhead* was a sailor, so called because the little white caps sat on their heads like jar lids.

jawbone (At least Old, Old Army to Modern) *s.* *Jawbone* has had a variety of meanings describing related situations that were promissory rather than actual, tentative rather than official, oral rather than written. A *jawbone* sergeant was an acting sergeant, *jawbone* in that he was a sergeant only on the captain's say-so and had not yet been confirmed in grade by official orders. (Those were the days when a company, battery, or troop commander was considered capable of picking his own NCOs from his own unit.) Credit was also *jawbone*, when a soldier could wheedle a local merchant into extending credit until next payday. In the old days of low pay, Post Exchange coupon books might be issued on *jawbone paydays*, once or twice a month, to be paid for on the company collection sheet at the end of the month. A *jawbone wedding* was an oral agreement to live together without benefit of clergy, like the modern shack job (or the even more modern upper-class "relationship"). In some countries, as long as the happy couple conducted themselves according to local standards of lower-class decorum, such an arrangement was respectable enough. As for the antiquity of the term, it was used in civilian life in the Old West, in San Francisco in 1862 (Hotten), but survived longer in the Army than outside.

Jayhawker (Civil War; USA, CSA) *s.* A soldier from Kansas. The nickname may have been applied originally to frontier freebooters during the fighting between proslavery and antislavery factions in Kansas before the Civil War. It was used at first for members of both parties, but later specifically for the antislavery group. The term may be a made-up word for an imaginary predatory bird that combined the most undesirable traits of a hawk and a blue jay. The undisciplined behavior of most Kansas volunteers made the term thoroughly appropriate. Occasionally used for lawless irregulars of either side.

J.C. maneuver (Air Force) *s.* A porpoise—a vertical, uncontrolled oscillating dive. "He entered a porpoise . . . better known as a J.C. maneuver. The best way to get out of it is to let go of everything and say, 'OK, J.C., you've got it' " (Broughton). *J.C.* here stands for *Jesus Christ*.

J.C. penny (Modern) *s.* The US dollar. The term is used by American servicemen stationed in Europe. The initials *J.C.* here stand for President *James Carter*.

jeep (World War II to Modern) *s.* Officially, "Truck, ¼ ton, 4 × 4." Probably the most practical and most versatile military vehicle ever manufactured. The M38 model of World War II was developed by Willys and manufactured mostly by Willys and Ford. Later versions were adopted in 1951 and 1959. The word *jeep* probably derives from the letters *G.P.* (for *general purpose*), which were stenciled on it, but this term may have been reinforced by the jeep, an imaginary humanoid creature that appeared in E. C.

Segar's comic strip "Popeye the Sailor." H.L. Mencken (1948), however, considered the comic strip the primary source for the term. During World War II the word *jeep* was transferred to other objects. A *jeep* could also be a new recruit or the Link Trainer used by the Army Air Forces. A *jeep carrier* was a naval escort carrier. The barracks inhabited by new recruits was known as *Jeepville*, as was Detroit (where jeeps were manufactured). The driver of a jeep was called a *jeep-nurse*.

Jefferson boots (1830s to 1870s) High-cut, laced shoes "rising 2 inches above the ankle joint and not higher," issued to all arms. Also called *bootees* and, later, *brogans*. In 1875, footgear of this sort finally was officially termed *shoes*.

Jerry (Mostly World War I, some use in World War II) *s.* A German. British usage borrowed by Americans. In British slang, a *jerry* is a chamberpot, which the German helmets resembled.

Jerry can Jerrycan Jerrican (World War II and later) *s.* A well-constructed narrow, rectangular, 5-gallon can with a built-in handle, used for anything liquid, but principally gasoline. It was originally a German product, whence its name.

Jesus boy (Modern) *s.* An overly religious, goody-goody soldier who frowns on barracks horseplay; a sissy; a square. "A soldier who sits on his bunk reading religious tracts is apt to be labeled a 'Jesus boy' " (AT, 4 June 1979).

Jewish chicken (Probably 20th century) Ham, bacon, or pork in any form. With such food the only meat available, a soldier of the Jewish faith, too hungry to observe his religion's dietary rules, is apt to compromise by requesting "Please pass the chicken."

Jewish infantry (World War II) *s.* The Army Finance Corps, from an allegedly high percentage of Jewish-Americans in that most noncombative branch of the service. Also sometimes applied to the Quartermaster Corps.

Jewish navy (World War II) *s.* The Coast Guard. We haven't the faintest idea what inspired this.

jink, to jank, to *s.* To maneuver an aircraft so as to avoid being hit by enemy fire. "The art of weaving, bobbing, twisting, and turning to avoid enemy gunfire" (Broughton).

jive bummer (Late 1940s) *s.* A character in the EM Club, usually far gone in drink and broke, who tries to mooch nickels for the juke box. It is best to give him a quarter and send him to the machine. Otherwise, he will hang around getting friendly until you sponsor his alcoholic weakness.

Jock (World War I, World War II) *s.* A Scots Highlander. Borrowed from the British, the term is the Scots for *Jack*.

jockstrapper *s.* An Army professional athlete, usually found in units commanded by a perpetual sophomore (a perpetual yearling, if he is a West Pointer) who thinks that the Army is meant for fun and games only. He insists on getting the most professional baseball, football, boxing, or whatever team possible. It may win games, but no one else gets to play and there is not much fun in the business. Since the jockstrapper is so important to his CO's ego, he is usually on special duty and thus exempt from KP, guard duty, and other onerous chores. He eats at a training table and is otherwise pampered. His company commander and first sergeant hate his guts, but they are nice to him because he is more important to a sophomoric colonel than they are. (Colonels have been known to promote jockstrappers without even consulting their company commanders if the jockstrappers have won an important game or wager for them.) In the barracks the jockstrapper ranks somewhere between a crab louse and spirochete, since someone else always has to pull his details for him. The worst outbreak of these pests was during World War II, when camps, schools, and other installations screened out professional athletes of all types in order to build up mighty teams. It even ended up with an "Army Football Team" of great publicity, which—so a nice old colonel who had once played second-string football or something at West Point assured us—would help the morale of combat soldiers. When we suggested that it would help morale even more to put his pets into the infantry, he was hurt. The only comparable outrage we can remember inflicting was on another nice old colonel at Fort Douglas in 1938, when we innocently suggested that the post golf course, which he had spent years cherishing through Utah's ornery weather, would make a good emergency pasture for mules.

Jody Jodie (World War II to Modern) *s.* A mythical civilian male who avoids military service and is renowned for his sexual achievements. His lust for the girl friends, sisters, wives, and mothers of servicemen is the universal theme of the Jody cadence songs sung and chanted by soldiers while drilling and marching:

You had a good home when you *left*.
(You're *right*!)
Jodie was there when you *left*.
(You're *right*!)
I don't know but it's been said
Jody's had your wife in bed.
I don't know if this is true
But Jody's had your sister too.

Two-mouth Mary, known for sin.
One mouth's for Jody and the other's
for gin

Joe Blow (World War II) The "John Doe" of military speech, a generic name for the enlisted man, especially a private. It replaced the older *Johnny Buck* or *Buck*. Not to be confused with dreadful examples like *Joe Dope*.

Joe Brown's pets (Civil War; CSA) *s.* The Georgia militia. Governor Brown kept them safe at home as long as possible.

Joe Dope (World War II) *s.* An imaginary soldier of absolute imbecility and irresponsibility, but much zeal. He was the central character of a set of clever posters designed to cause soldiers to take better care of their weapons and vehicles. From that, it was easy and natural to transfer his name to his living counterparts.

john (Antiquity uncertain, but probably at least 19th century) 1. *s.* A recruit. Sometimes as *Dumbjohn*. In the 19th-century British Army, *Johnny Raw* was used. 2. *s.* A new man in an organization, not necessarily a recruit. Common World War I usage. 3. *s.* A lieutenant, as in *first john, second john*.

john company (Indian Wars to at least World War I) *s.* A temporary organization set up to train a regiment's new recruits, or johns. (In those days recruits got little or no basic training before joining their organizations.) This term may have been partially inspired by the fact that regiments had no J company on their regular establishment (see *milk battalion*). The American *john company* is not to be confused with the 19th-century British *John Company*, which was a nickname for the East India Company or its private army.

John L's *s.* Government-issue long underwear, especially the woolen winter type. The bottom portion looked like the boxing tights worn by John L. Sullivan. John L's were certainly warm, but they took forever to dry out after washing—a problem in midwinter in the field. Also called *long Johns.*

Johnny Blowboy (World War II) *s.* A play on *Johnny Doughboy,* an infantryman or just a GI in general. He was also the subject of an obscene version of the sentimental song "Johnny Doughboy Found a Rose in Ireland."

Johnny Raw (West Point) *s.* A plebe.

Johnny Reb Johnny Johnnie (Civil War; USA) *s.* The commonest colloquial name for a Confederate soldier. Its origin seems to have been the Union soldier's habit of hailing his opponent, during the periods of fraternization common between outposts of the two armies, as *Johnny* or *Reb*, names the Confederates accepted in a matter-of-fact way. The term apparently was not considered offensive. See also *butternut, grayback.*

John Wayne (Vietnam and later) *s.* Various uses suggested by the macho, heroic war roles played by the movie actor John Wayne. As a noun, a macho hero type. As a verb, to act heroically: "Why you can even John Wayne it and pull [the grenade pin] with your . . . eyetooth" (Heinemann). "Have you ever thought about how many ways 'John Wayne' can be used? . . . linguistically speaking it's almost as versatile a word as 'fuck' " (Suddick). Among the Marines the P-38 can opener was sometimes called a *John Wayne.*

jo humper (Modern) *s.* Another name for an ammo humper, an ammunition storage specialist, or, loosely, any artilleryman. The component *jo* is from *projo*, short for *projectile.*

joker 1. (World War II) *s.* A wise guy, with many of the qualities of a guardhouse lawyer. Usually unreliable and an irritant to the industrious and serious-minded. This term slips in and out of the talk of all armies. Napoleon's hussars used it. 2. (Modern; Air Force) *s.* A preselected fuel level warning that bingo is approaching and that contact should henceforth be avoided.

Jolly (Vietnam and later) *s.* The HH-53 air rescue helicopter widely used during the Vietnam War. Short for *Jolly Green Giant*, after a brand of canned food.

Jonah (Civil War; USA) *s.* The awkward clod who never could do anything right and had no intention of learning how. His ineptitude and sullenness made him dangerous to everyone but the enemy. In later years he would be called variously *rear-rank Rudy*, a *blank file*, an *eight-ball,* or a *skull.*

josan (Occupation of Japan and later) *s.* A girl friend, a mistress. A corruption of Japanese *ojōsan*, which means a respectable young woman, a daughter. Not infrequently, we fear, the young woman also was corrupted. Widely used in Korea today.

Judge Duffy (Old Army to World War I) *s.* A summary court-martial. We are still trying to identify Duffy.

judy (World War I through World War II) *s.* A female of the human species, characteristics unspecified. Probably of British origin (Partridge, 1970).

Jug (World War II; Air Force) *s.* The Republic P-47 Thunderbolt fighter plane, also known as the *Flying Milk Bottle*. The word *Jug* was a shortening of *Juggernaut,* a name reportedly given to the P-47 because it was so big and so hard to handle on the ground.

jug fuck, to have a (Modern) *s.* To get drunk.

jughead (Old Army) *s.* A mule. Since mules were used for pack artillery, the term *jughead battery* might be used in place of the older *jackass battery*. A *jughead company* would be a machine-gun company that had mule-drawn carts. By extension, *jughead* came to be applied to stupid or obstinate horses or to unsatisfactory horses in general. From there, it was a minor shift to apply it to people of like disposition.

jump boots (World War II to Modern) Elegant boots issued to paratroopers and (during World War II) regularly affected by rear-area staff officers and NCOs.

jump channels, to (At least World War II to Modern) *s.* To go out of the established chain of command or channels of communication. See *backchannel, frontchannel*.

jumper *s.* A paratrooper.

jumping through his ass (1930s to 1940s) *s.* In a feverish panic of uncoordinated activity.

jumpmaster (World War II to Modern) The NCO in charge of a planeload of paratroopers. He sees that they are properly rigged, hooked up, and out of the plane in proper order.

jump-off (World War I) *s.* A loose term for the time and/or place an attack is to begin, although the place is properly called the *line of departure*. "Jump-off's at midnight."

jump [one's] bracket, to (World War I to Modern) 1. Technically, in artillery firing, to call for fire outside one's bracket instead of splitting the bracket obtained on an enemy target. This, of course, results in a complete miss and is an artillery faux pas comparable to cutting your salad with a steak knife at a formal banquet. 2. Colloquially, as *Don't jump your bracket,* an expression warning an angry or excited artilleryman that he is about to do something foolish. See also *bracket*.

jump pay (Modern) *s.* An utterly paltry sum paid to soldiers for jumping out of perfectly good airplanes. Rumor has it that paratroopers do this not for the money but because they like it.

jump sack (World War II) *s.* A parachute.

jump status, to have (Modern) 1. *s.* To be parachute qualified, assigned to an airborne unit. 2. *s.* To be drawing special or jump pay.

jump week (Modern) *s.* The third and final week of airborne training; the week during which airborne candidates qualify for their airborne wings.

jungle boots (Vietnam to Modern) Special boots designed for the wet, tropical climate of Southeast Asia. Now a standard item of issue.

jungle fatigues (Vietnam) Loose-fitting, lightweight fatigues that were standard issue for all service personnel in Vietnam. Also called *hot weather uniform* and *tropical combat uniform*.

jungle juice (World War II) *s.* In the Pacific theater, any available alcoholic drink, especially if improvised or locally produced.

junior enlisted swine (Modern) *s.* Army enlisted personnel ranking below the grade of sergeant first class. See *officer swine, senior enlisted swine.*

junior NCOs (At least World War II to Modern) At present, noncommissioned officers in the grades corporal, sergeant, and staff sergeant. In World War II, T/5, corporal, T/4, sergeant.

junk 1. (Revolutionary) A hastily cooked meal. ". . . a junk of fresh beef and that without salt . . ." 2. (Early 19th century into Indian Wars) *s.* Salted (corned) meat, a frequent item of issue at isolated frontier posts. See *salt junk.*

junk on the bunk (Modern) *s.* An inspection of one's equipment, displayed on the bunk in a prescribed manner. See *showdown inspection.*

kamikaze cabs (Occupation of Japan to Modern) *s.* Recklessly driven taxicabs. The expression was widely used in Vietnam and is still current in Korea, where the cabbies drive their machines as if they want to die. The term originated in Tokyo in the late 1940s and early 1950s. The driving habits of Japanese cabbies inspired the story that they were all survivors of the kamikaze corps. See *40-yenner*.

kangaroo (Early World War II) *s.* The sergeant of the guard. Apparently a short-lived term.

KATUSA (Korea to Modern) Korean Augmentation To the United States Army. Originally, in 1950, as a desperation measure, thousands of Korean civilians, ignorant of military life and the English language, were hastily drafted into under-strength American units. Many of them were refugees, half-starved and sick. Generally, they could be used only for work details. This term has since been used for the assignment of Republic of Korea (ROK) soldiers to selected American units to serve as fillers and to receive American military training.

Katzenjammers (World War I) *s.* The Germans; a term sometimes used by the AEF to denote the gallant foe from the east side of the Rhine. From the American comic strips "The Captain and the Kids" and "The Katzenjammer Kids."

KAWOL /'kay-wall/ (Modern) Knowledgeable Absent Without Leave. An AWOL with knowledge of classified information that might be useful to enemies of the United States.

keg, to See *cagg*.

keg hat (Civil War; USA) *s.* New Hampshire soldiers' name for the regulation black felt hat worn for full dress. See *war hat* for details.

khaki (Spanish-American War to Modern; also Marines) Khaki was originally a color term (from Urdu *khākī* 'dust-colored', 'dusty') adopted by British troops in India for their field uniforms from 1846 on. In American military usage, *khaki* has come to mean primarily a cotton fabric used for summer uniforms. It has gone through a variety of shades, both official and unofficial. The pre–World War II variety was a brownish or OD color that tended to fade after repeated washings until it was a "burnt-almond ice cream" shade. (Soldiers sometimes aged new khaki uniforms artificially with strong soap and a stiff brush to get rid of their shiny look.) Some commands, like the Panama Canal Zone, insisted on a greenish shade and even dyed the official issue to obtain the desired color. The more golden-colored "Hong Kong" or "Chino" khaki came in around the beginning of World War II; there was also a lighter, "silver" khaki. None of these shades was very practical, either for field service or garrison. They were conspicuous against any background and even a dirty thought would stain them. See *suntans.*

khaki-colored kids (Modern) *s.* The offspring of a racially mixed union (white-black, white-Oriental, black-Oriental). The skin color is often similar to that of the khaki uniform.

khaki teat, to suck the (Modern) *s.* To be in the US Army. Professional soldiers often refer facetiously to the Army as their teat, since Uncle Sam takes care of their basic needs. Leaving the Army is sometimes referred to as being *weaned from the khaki teat.*

khaki-wacky (World War II) *s.* Crazy about soldiers, sailors, and marines—a characteristic of Victory Girls.

KIA Killed In Action. The final word.

KIA Travel Bureau (Modern) *s.* Graves registration, in which the bodies of soldiers killed in action are prepared for return to the United States. "Bagged and tagged and shipped back home through what they call the KIA Travel Bureau" (Herr).

kick kick-out (Old Army to World War II, possibly later; also Marines) *s.* A dishonorable discharge, particularly when given in connection with a sentence to confinement at hard labor. Thus, a deserter might get "three years and a kick."

Kickapoo joy juice (World War II, perhaps later) *s.* Brandy of a sort, a GI version of grappa; it was usually produced by running any available wine through an improvised still. (Any aggregation of good-old-red-blooded, beady-eyed American boys has the know-how and skills to develop a small distillery, given free time and a few salvaged parts.) Kickapoo joy juice was rough, but far safer than the native Italian product, which was made from God knew what. The term comes from Al Capp's comic strip "Li'l Abner," where Kickapoo joy juice is a loathsome brew cooked (not distilled) by Lonesome Polecat and Hairless Joe.

kick ass and take names, to kiss ass and take names, to (At least World War II to Modern) *s.* A catchphrase, sometimes used jocularly, to describe the duties of an NCO or one's own leadership ability.

kid 1. (World War II; also Air Force) *s.* The copilot of an airplane. He is usually junior in grade to the pilot and so presumably younger. 2. Occasionally used as an "oblique reference" or third person designation for oneself. Sometimes as *this kid.* "Supply told me they didn't have any more rifle patches. But you can't fool this kid."

kill, to This is the soldier's basic mission, so often underplayed by recruiters and Pentagon public relations people. That soldiers have adopted and invented so many euphemisms and circumlocutions for this brutal activity may be the result more of a superstitious belief (albeit unconscious) that it is unlucky to talk openly about death than of any sense of guilt about being its instrument. See *blow away, burn, buy it, buy the farm, ding,* *dust, hose down, lightup, massage, use up, waste, zap.*

killemquick (Philippine Insurrection) *s.* Strong drink, possibly inspired by the effects of vino and tuba. Sometimes low-quality whiskey. In civilian slang of the period, also *killmequick*.

killer MOS (Korea to Modern) *s.* A combat MOS—rifleman, tank crewman, gunner, and the like.

Kilroy (World War II) The invisible point man of the American forces in North Africa and Europe. He always left "Kilroy was here" written in the damnedest places, some of them decidedly hot and unhealthy.

kimchi (Korea to Modern) 1. A Korean version of sauerkraut: Chinese cabbage, chili peppers, garlic, and sometimes other ingredients salted and fermented in their own juice. It is usually not cooked and is a staple at Korean meals. Like sauerkraut, it emits a foul odor while working, but the kimchi made during the winter is milder and its aroma less offensive to American nostrils than that made during the warmer months. American soldiers, on the whole, do not like kimchi, but oddly enough kimchi is now one of the most popular food articles in Chinese food stores that cater to white Americans. 2. *s.* Anything Korean, such as *kimchi cab, kimchi house,* and *kimchi fart*. 3. Anything of inferior workmanship or quality. See also *deep kimchi.*

King of Beasts (West Point) The first class (senior) cadet who is in charge of plebes during beast barracks, a period of basic military training conducted for each freshman class. This title continues in popular use, even though *beast barracks* is now a forbidden term. See *beast, beast barracks, beast detail.*

KISS (Modern) Keep It Simple, Stupid. Used by instructors of tactics and strategy in our service schools. Complex plans seldom work in war, as generals as different as Philip Sheridan and Paul von Hindenburg proclaimed. One Englishman had a somewhat differing opinion: "Simplicity by all means, but not the simplicity of an ape with a paintbrush." See *school solution.*

Kit Carson Scouts (Vietnam; all Services) Former Vietcong guerrillas who had "rallied" to the South Vietnamese government. After a period of indoctrination, they were assigned to American units, usually two or three to a company. Their knowledge of Vietcong tactics, trail markings, and booby-trap techniques made them very useful, for the Vietcong and North Vietnamese were surprisingly inflexible in such matters and seldom changed their methods. Kit Carson Scouts served with the Marines, the Army, district advisory teams, and the Brown Water Navy. The program was discontinued in 1971–72 when the US "crawled out of Vietnam standing up."

kitchen man (Modern) A KP assigned to assist the cooks in food preparation in the kitchen of the mess hall. This detail is preferable to pots and pans, tray man, or even outside man, but not so cushy as DRO.

kite (World War I, World War II, probably later scattered usage) *s.* An airplane.

kiwi /'kee-wee/ 1. (World War I and later) *s.* A nonflying Air Corps officer. From the hen-sized flightless bird found only in New Zealand. As Wentworth and Flexner nicely put it, "an officer who cannot, does not, or does not like to fly." The term *kiwi* is borrowed from the British, presumably suggested by some Anzac birdman. 2. (World War II; Air Force) *s.* A student pilot who had not yet qualified for his wings. He was supposed to wear his goggles under his chin while on the ground and to keep his heavy fleece-lined flying jacket zipped all the way up to his throat.

Kiwi (At least Old Army to Modern) The brand name of an excellent shoe polish, very popular with the Regulars. In World War I the British had the expression *Kiwi king*, meaning an officer who was meticulous about the appearance of leather (Partridge, 1970).

knapsack drill (Early 19th century to post–Civil War) *s.* A form of punishment for minor military offenses such as smuggling liquor into a barracks. The guilty soldier had to walk a certain distance or length of time with his knapsack filled with heavy objects—rocks, cannon balls, or sand. If no knapsack was available, as in some veteran units (see *bureau*), a heavy log or a bag of sand was substituted.

knee-level wind (Relatively Modern) *s.* A breeze that stirred up a lot of trembling knees, as when some route-step outfit has just learned that its new CO is a highly carnivorous smoke-bringer.

K-9 Corps (World War II and later) Dogs trained for Army service; established in March 1942. Of the 10,526 dogs accepted and trained in World War II, most went overseas and 2,290 were killed in action. The name is obviously a play on *canine*.

knobhead (Old, Old Army to World War I) *s.* A mule or a human of comparable disposition.

Knock it off! (Antiquity uncertain to Modern; all Services) *s.* Cease and desist from whatever you're doing, right now. Depending on the speaker, it may be anything from a plea to a direct order.

knot 1. (Modern; all Services) Originally a nautical unit of speed, 1 nautical mile per hour. Since a nautical mile is approximately 1.115 statute miles, a ship cruising at 30 knots is traveling about 33.5 miles per hour by a landlubber's reckoning. Today, the knot is also used as the unit of Navy, Army, and Air Force aircraft speeds. 2. (Modern) The loop representing a successive award of the Good Conduct Medal. See *claps*.

knothead (West Point) *s.* The junior permanent professor of a two-professor academic department of the US Military Academy. The senior is Professor and Head of the Department; the junior is Professor and *not head*.

knuckle knife (World War I to Modern; also Marines) *s.* The Model 1917 trench knife or Mark I trench knife, which had its hilt garnished with a set of spiked brass knuckles. It was not so good as a sharpened entrenching tool for chopping off North Joe's head, but it looks dangerous and thus has become a hard-to-get accessory for the dogface who wants to send home a photograph with a real combatty look.

KOW (Old, Old Army) *s.* A discreet form of COW (Commanding Officer's Wife). Used on those occasions when the literal abbreviation would be indiscreet, not to say unwise. See *COW*.

KP kitchen police (Antiquity uncertain, but very common pre–World War I to Modern) Soldiers detailed to assist the cooks in preparing and serving food, and in policing the kitchen and mess hall; also the work itself. This feature of military life has largely disappeared. As we remember it, the detail was hard work, but you sometimes ate better and more frequently, and could do part of your work sitting down. Its worst feature was a 14-hour day. One *pulls KP*.

KP pusher (Antiquity uncertain, but at least World War II to Modern) *s.* A soldier (usually a noncommissioned officer) in charge of the KP detail. In World War II it was sometimes felt that the cooks should confine themselves to preparing gustatorial delights and that they and the mess sergeant (who spent his day drinking coffee with the other senior NCOs) should not have to enforce discipline on the KPs. In such cases a KP pusher might be used. He did not need any knowledge of dietetics, just an alert eye and a forceful disposition, so that his charges did not goof off. An Old Army cook did not need a KP pusher. He picked his teeth with his cleaver and could part an erring KP's hair with it at twenty paces. However, the modern large consolidated messes have a lot of KPs, requiring someone's undivided attention.

Krag (Old Army) Properly *Krag-Jorgensen*. The service rifle from 1892 to 1903; replaced by the Springfield '03. A Swedish version of the Mauser action, it was the first standardized repeating rifle issued to the entire Army. Accurate and sturdy, although somewhat unhandy because of its protruding horizontal magazine, it was the Regular soldier's weapon during our brief imperial attempt to "civilize 'em with a Krag." Some Krags were used during World War I for drill and training. Legend has it that a battalion of engineers arrived in France in 1918 armed with Krags for appearance sake, but without ammunition. Their mission was rear-area heavy construction. Shoved into the lines when a German offensive cracked the British front, they had to wait for their allies to get hit so that they could take over their rifles.

K-ration (World War II) A combat ration originally developed for paratroopers. It was prepared in three forms—breakfast, dinner, and supper—and was packaged in waxed cardboard containers that burned very well. In addition to food, each package held cigarettes, chewing gum, water purification tablets, salt tablets, matches, and toilet paper. Except for the lemon-juice powder in the dinner ration—acid enough to melt holes in the side of a tank—the food was quite palatable for short periods in warm weather. In winter, K-rations could be a form of torture. Dumps of K-rations had to be guarded carefully, especially in Italy. Stray soldiers and civilians alike were inclined to rip the cartons open to get the cigarettes.

Kraut (World War I and some use in World War II, but probably more a civilian term) *s.* A German. Like *liberty cabbage*, an example of the inexplicable fixation that World War I propagandists had on sauerkraut.

kriegies (World War II) *s.* The term American prisoners of war in Germany gave themselves. Short for German *Kriegsgefangenen* 'prisoners of war'.

K-Town (Modern) Kaiserslautern, West Germany.

Kum City (Korea) *s.* Kumamoto, Japan. A fine place to blow all your pay while on R & R without being particularly singled out for attention by the Armed Forces Gestapo.

KYPIYP (Old Army, possibly to Modern) *s.* Keep Your Pecker In Your Pants. A blunt piece of advice given young soldiers before the Army had horror movies to scare them into the path of righteousness. We first heard it from a gray-haired PMST at the ROTC summer camp at the Presidio of Monterey in 1931. A cadet had acquired a galloping case of gonorrhea from an amiable lady in the adjoining town. The PMST assembled us for a little friendly advice. "Gentlemen," he rapped. "Some of you will put your family jewel into places I wouldn't even put the tip of my riding crop! KYPIYP!"

laboratory (Colonial into 19th century) A building where ammunition and military pyrotechnics were made up. (In the field a large tent might be used.) Even minor frontier forts had a hut or special room for this purpose. Working with black-powder ammunition was extremely dangerous. Nothing made of iron or steel could be used, for fear of striking a spark, and all soldiers working in the laboratory had to wear shoes made without nails.

ladders *s.* A captain's insignia. Also occasionally called *railroad tracks*.

Lafayette Escadrille (World War I) A small aviation unit of American volunteers formed by France in early 1916. Its CO and key officers were French, and its mascots were two lion cubs. It was a competent enough unit and was the pride and joy of war correspondents. (The larger number of Americans serving with the RAF somehow got little attention.) In 1917 it became the US 103d Areo Squadron, with additional American personnel. The insignia of both units was the profile of an Indian wearing an eight-feathered war bonnet with a swastika on its headband.

lager /'lah-ger/ (World War II; possibly still used) A position organized for all-around defense by a mobile force that has halted for the night, or a similar short period. Much used in Vietnam for night defensive positions. From the Afrikaans *laager* 'camp', a defensive position adopted by the Boers, and later the British, during their native wars in South Africa. When attacked, they formed their wagons in a circle and fought from behind them, as Americans did in the Old West. Americans picked up the term in North Africa, where British armored units customarily formed lagers (or lagered) when halting after dark.

lake fever (Colonial to War of 1812) A fever that caused much sickness and a good many deaths among troops serving in the Lake Champlain and Great Lakes areas. It was probably typhoid fever caused by contamination of lake water by sewage from camps and naval bases.

lamp post (Civil War) *s.* A heavy artillery projectile, usually from a naval gun. Other names were *camp kettle* and *boot leg*.

lance corporal lance sergeant (At least 1830s to post–World War I) An old term for an acting corporal or sergeant. While the exact nature of the rank differed from time to time, lance corporals and lance sergeants were, in general, temporary noncommissioned officers who had the authority, privileges, and responsibilities, but not the pay, allowances, or permanency, of their acting grades. The rank itself was abolished in 1920, although the term undoubtedly continued to be recognized. The origin of the term is obscure. It is often referred back to Italian Renaissance *lanciaspezzeta* 'broken lance', meaning a dismounted cavalryman reduced to serving as an infantry NCO, although this interpretation has been questioned as not existing in Italian sources. In any case, the term passed into other nations. In the army of Queen Elizabeth I a corporal's assistant was sometimes termed a *lance-presado*.

landing zone (Vietnam to Modern) A cleared area for landing helicopters. Also called *LZ or LIMA ZULU*, from the phonetic alphabet. "He wanted a rifle company to be inserted at the landing zone (called LZ LIMA ZULU)" (Tregaskis).

landlines (Modern) Telephone communications using cable rather than radio microwave relay.

Land of the Big PX, the (Occupation of Japan to Modern) *s.* The United States.

Land of the Round Doorknob (Modern; also Air Force) *s.* The United States, so called because doorknobs in this country are usually round, while in Europe, especially Germany (where this expression originated), the doorknobs are usually shaped like handles.

Land of the Twenty-four-hour Generator, the (Vietnam and later; all Services) *s.* The United States, so called because in Vietnam power failures were frequent. In most US installations power was provided by generators that would often break down for long periods of time, and Vietnamese commercial power sources were extremely unreliable.

langrage langridge /'lang-grij/ (Revolutionary into early 19th century; also Navy) An improvised substitute for canister, made up of small pieces of any available metal. Very messy at short range. Commonly used in naval warfare as an antipersonnel weapon.

lash-up lashup (Modern; also Marines) 1. *s.* The manner in which an organization or program works with other similar activities. 2. *s.* Any inefficiently organized unit, activity, or program. The term has been borrowed from the Marines, where it is a potent term of disapproval, applicable to almost anything. See the Appendix.

last post (World War I on) In the British service, the bugle call signaling the time to retire. It is the equivalent of American taps, and like taps, it is sounded at military funerals. During World War I probably, the term came into occasional American use in its funeral aspect. Thus, in publications related to military matters, *last post* may be used in the sense of *in memoriam*.

latrine (Antiquity uncertain, possibly pre–World War I) The soldier's toilet, whether it is modern plumbing in a barracks or a slit trench in the field. The term is of French origin, but was used in the British army in the 1870s. Earlier American terms for toilet facilities were *necessaries* and *sinks.* The latrine is a favorite retreat for goldbricks ducking work and something of a social center. Also called the *Old Soldier's Home.*

latrine orderly (At least World War I to Modern; also Air Force) A soldier detailed to keep the latrine clean and sanitary, or the work itself. It is not a choice assignment, but at least it keeps you inside out of the hot sun or bad weather. We have known soldiers, mostly of limited intelligence, who liked the detail and kept their latrines as spotless as a model kitchen.

latrine orderly in the WAC barracks (World War II and still occasionally heard) *s.* According to male chauvinist lore, the lowest, dirtiest job in the Army. "You couldn't even make latrine orderly in the WAC barracks" was a real insult—between male soldiers, of course. It meant that you were completely dumb and useless.

latrine rumor latrine-o-gram latrinogram *s.* Any wild story, because soldiers using the latrine frequently swap the latest gossip and rumors, which are seldom accurate. See *number one.*

laudable pus (Colonial to post–Civil War; Medical Corps) A standard early medical term for a type of suppuration that was considered healthy or a sign of healing. Before the discovery of antiseptics and antibiotics, few wounds healed at "first intention," most becoming infected in one manner or another. Laudable pus was a particular type of thick, whitish, creamy pus that offered a favorable prognosis.

laundry 1. (World War I) *s.* Air-ground recognition panels—pieces of cloth, usually white, that were spread out in various arrangements as signals to friendly aircraft. Sometimes the "friendly" aviators chose to regard laundry as a target or a clumsy attempt at deception. 2. (Early World War II; Army Air Corps) *s.* A review board that passed on the qualifications of air cadets and might wash out those not progressing satisfactorily.

lavandera (Old Army to World War II) In the Philippines, a washerwoman. In the Scouts, she often was a soldier's wife, as in the Old, Old Army days of Soapsuds Row.

lay, to (Ancient to Modern) To aim a gun.

lay pipe, to (Civil War) *s.* To intrigue, to play politics. Gen. Marsena Patrick, Provost Marshal of the Army of the Potomac, described a visiting politician as "laying pipe" for his son's promotion. Also recorded as a civilian expression in 1835.

LBJ (Vietnam) 1. *s.* Long Binh Jail for US Army prisoners. It is possible that there is a play on the initials of President Lyndon B. Johnson. 2. *s.* Long Binh Junction, a processing center complex and the headquarters for the US Army in Vietnam (USARV).

lead (Also Air Force) The lead aircraft, or its pilot, in a group of aircraft flying in formation.

leaders lead team (Early 19th century to World War II) The front (leading) team of horses of a field gun or caisson. They were lighter and more nimble than the other two teams, able to change direction at the gallop when a battery went into action across country. See *swing team, wheelers.*

leadersleep (West Point) *s.* The required course in leadership. The term expresses the inspiration the cadets derive from the course.

leaping over the sword jumping over the sword (Colonial to early 19th century) An informal but normally binding military wedding ceremony. The couple to be married joined hands. A sword was laid on the ground before them, and the senior NCO present proclaimed, "Leap rogue and jump whore, And then you are married for evermore." Thereupon a drummer beat a ruffle, and the couple jumped hand in hand over the sword. This was primarily a British practice, but a similar ceremony took place among American slaves, with a broom instead of a sword.

leather (Antiquity uncertain, but common in World War II) The leather portions of a soldier's uniform and equipment: belts, boots, cap visors, holsters, saddle, harness, etc. Leather had to be kept polished, and the polish had to be of a uniform color. It was work, but it kept the leather in good condition and gave the outfit—especially a mounted one—a swank and swagger that nothing modern quite matches.

leather gun (Spanish-American War) *s.* The penis. Extent of use and origin uncertain.

leave (Modern) Authorized absence from a soldier's place of duty, for the purpose of providing him rest from his working conditions or for specific purposes. At present, leave is earned or accrued at the rate of 2.5 days per month and may be accumulated up to as much as 60 days at a time. All time over 60 days, however, must be used by the end of each fiscal year, or it is automatically forfeited. On separating from the service a soldier may cash in his leave balance. Each day cashed in earns him the equivalent of one day's active-duty pay, but he is permitted to cash in only a total of 60 days during a career. See *furlough.*

Leavenworth long tour (Modern) *s.* Confinement as a prisoner in the US Army Disciplinary Barracks, Fort Leavenworth, Kansas.

Leavenworth short tour (Modern) *s.* Attendance at the Command and General Staff College, Fort Leavenworth, Kansas.

leaves, to get one's (Considerable Antiquity to Modern) *s.* To receive the big promotion from captain and company-grade to major and field-grade status. The insignia of a major is a pair of gold oak leaves—or, at least, they are called oak leaves, although they do not look like any oak leaf that a botanist ever saw.

Lee Cornhole (World War I) *s.* Soldiers' version of Le Corneau, France, where the replacement pool for the Field Artillery was located.

leg leggo lego (Modern) *s.* A soldier or unit that is not airborne, airmobile, or mechanized. "He's a leg." Also used adjectivally, as in *leg unit* and *leg infantry.* See *straight leg.*

legal eagle (Antiquity uncertain to Modern; also Navy) Rhyming slang. The politer name for the Armed Forces' lawyers, now extended to their civilian brethren who intrude increasingly into the military's private business, all in the name of democracy, justice, publicity, and high fees.

Levies (Late 18th century) Temporary regular soldiers, enlisted for six months, for the early Indian campaigns in the old Northwest Territory. Mostly poor material to start with, they were poorly officered, trained, disciplined, and supplied —and they behaved accordingly. Because of the general disorganization of Secretary of War Henry Knox's department, most of them received little or no pay. During the 19th century, such troops were termed *volunteers* and usually were of better quality.

levy (Modern) A personnel requisition to fill vacancies in an understrength unit or command; thus, a designation for overseas duty or special assignment. "You come here on a levy from the airborne?" (Bunting).

liaison (World War I to Modern) Contact between adjacent units or between a unit and its next higher headquarters, to ensure coordinated effort. For example, an artillery battalion will send a liaison officer to the headquarters of the infantry or armored unit it is supporting, to act as an adviser to its commander and transmit his requests for fire support. There are liaison planes to make the task easier and air-ground liaison to try to make certain that the fly-boys hit the enemy and not you.

liberate, to (World War II) *s.* To acquire by various illegitimate or illegal ways—looting, stealing, confiscating, commandeering. Originally applied to property in enemy or occupied areas, but eventually to many other situations. In what is probably the most cynical application, it meant to have sexual intercourse with a native woman.

lick (Modern) *s.* A mistake; anything bad; anything that has gone wrong; hence, particularly in the Vietnam War, a military fiasco. "When something goes wrong, it's a lick on you, see?" (Downs).

lieutenant (Ancient to Modern) Historically, the term *lieutenant* was first applied to an officer who was second in command, without indicating any specific rank. (This usage survives in part in the terms *lieutenant colonel* and *lieutenant general.*) Up into the early 18th century, the lieutenant was the second-in-command of a company and ranked between the captain and an ensign (in the infantry) or a cornet (in the cavalry). The terms *ensign* and *cornet* were gradually replaced by *second lieutenant*, and *lieutenant* by *first lieutenant.* 1. (Army, Air Force, Marines) A commissioned officer of the two lowest grades, second lieutenant and first lieutenant. In the Army and Marines a lieutenant is usually in command of a platoon, but during the absence of a captain, he may temporarily command a company. In the Air Force he may be a pilot, a member of the crew of a large aircraft, or the equivalent of a platoon commander in a support-type unit. Lieutenants may also fill minor staff positions. 2. (Navy) Two commissioned officers—lieutenant, junior grade, and lieutenant. They correspond generally to a first lieutenant and a captain in the other services.

lieutenant colonel (Ancient to Modern) A field-grade officer who ranks just below a colonel and above a major. The modern insignia for a lieutenant colonel is a silver leaf, officially called an oak leaf. The grade was well established during the colonial wars. Nicknames are *bottlecap colonel* and *light colonel.* Abbreviated *Lt. Col.*

lieutenant general (Ancient to Modern) At present a three-star general officer ranking below a (full) general and above a major general. Lieutenant generals usually command corps. Gen. George Washington was the first lieutenant general in the American Army, but after his death the rank existed only intermittently. It was revived for great commanders such as Scott, Grant, and Sherman, or senior major generals such as Nelson A. Miles and Arthur MacArthur, but allowed to lapse at their deaths. After World War I, Hunter Liggett and Robert L. Bullard (who had been temporary lieutenant generals during the war) and Edgar Jadwin were made lieutenant generals on the retired list. The grade of lieutenant general was restored for active-duty commanders in 1939 and is still in use. Abbreviated *Lt. Gen., LTG.*

lifer (Vietnam to Modern; all Services) *s.* A professional, long-service soldier or a soldier who plans to make a career of the Armed Forces. The term is sometimes applied to officers as well as to enlisted personnel, particularly to field-grade officers. It is usually derogatory and implies that the individual in question is a dull, rather stupid person who plods along in his service career because it provides him with a secure living with little effort and (it is to be hoped) at little risk. The term is probably taken from prison slang.

lifer crud (Modern; Air Force) *s.* A noncommissioned officer.

lifer juice (Modern) *s.* Coffee.

lift (Vietnam to Modern) A flight of troop-carrying helicopters. One such helicopter is a *lift ship.*

lift [someone's] stripes, to (World War II) *s.* To bust someone, to reduce someone to the rank of private.

light bob (Late 18th century to early 19th century) *s.* British. A light infantryman.

light colonel (Around 1940 to Modern) *s.* A lieutenant colonel. This term came in, as we recall, when lieutenant colonels began to proliferate in the Army T/Os. Previously they had been rare and awesome beings, rather like regimental sergeant majors.

light company 1. (Colonial to Mexican War) Regimental light infantry companies. See *flank companies.* 2. (About 1821–61) A company of artillery equipped with guns, horses, and vehicles for service as field artillery. (Except for the Civil War, during the period 1783–1901, most of the US Artillery served either as redlegged infantry or at seacoast fortifications.) During the Civil War the term was officially changed to *light battery.* In the Mexican War, the term *field battery* was often used.

light discipline (Modern) In field operations, precautions to conceal light so that soldiers and positions cannot be detected by the enemy. It is equivalent to a civilian blackout. See also *noise discipline.*

light drafts (Civil War; USA) The official name for the tinclad gunboats of the "Mosquito Fleet" of the Mississippi River.

light duty (Antiquity uncertain, but probably very old, to Modern) Temporary excusal from heavy work because of physical disability. Unfortunately, as every GI who has been in a hospital knows, there is no definition of heavy work.

light horse light dragoons light cavalry (Colonial to War of 1812) Lightly equipped cavalrymen, adapted for scouting and skirmishing as well as for shock action. During the French and Indian Wars several of the colonies formed small units of light horse. The light dragoons of the Revolution and War of 1812 were modeled after the British light dragoons, which had been organized to oppose the French hussars. Despite the assertions of various academic historians, they usually fought mounted. The fact that a good many light dragoons served on foot can be attributed to Congress's inability or unwillingness to provide the necessary horses.

light infantry 1. (Colonial through Mexican War) Troops selected for agility, marksmanship, courage, and reliability who were used for advanced guard operations, raids, and skirmishing. In many instances, they were given distinctive uniforms and issued lighter weapons and equipment. 2. (Early 19th century) *s.* Soldiers prone to desertion. "Your family are all light infantry . . . at all times prepared for a march" (*United States Military Magazine*, February 1841, p. 59).

Lightning Bug (Vietnam and later) *s.* A helicopter gunship equipped with searchlights for spotting targets at night. See *Firefly, flare ship*.

light up, to (Modern) *s.* To kill. "Any way you move they can light you up" (Glasser).

line 1. (Colonial into 19th century) Regular troops, as distinct from militia and temporary levies. Thus, our Regular Army during the Revolution was the Continental Line. 2. (European) Regular troops, as distinct from both militia and royal guards. 3. (Early 19th century to 20th century) Combat troops—infantry, artillery, and cavalry—that fought in line, as opposed to staff and specialist personnel, such as quartermasters. Often used as *in the line* or a *line outfit*. The modern term is *combat arms*. 4. A formation in which the elements are side by side or abreast of each other. To achieve precision, the command given is *Line up*, usually with *on*. "All right, you men! Line up on the man on your right!" 5. What the British call a *queue*, an omnipresent aspect of Army life: *pay line, shot line, show line, chow line, issue line*, etc. There is a story, probably apocryphal, of a grizzled sergeant who accosted a young private and growled, "Private, I bet you can't wait until I die so that you can go up and piss on my grave." The private thought this over for a moment and then gravely replied, "No, sergeant, that's not true. You see, I've promised myself that once I get out of the Army, as long as I live, I'll never stand in another line."

line check (Probably at least World War II, to Modern) 1. A routine procedure to determine if communications equipment is working properly and operators are alert to their duty. Often used facetiously, as "Who was that you were talking to?" "Oh, just Jack Anderson [or the Russian Embassy] making a line check." 2. By extension, a call to someone for the purpose of gossiping.

Line 99 (Modern) The space on a manpower authorization listing (the computer printout of authorized manning levels of an organization, by position and name) where personnel excess to the manning table are listed. To be listed here generally means that one is immediately available for reassignment.

I'm feeling fine
On Line 99,
Although treated shitty,
I'm sitting pretty.
If things just move apace,
I'll soon leave this fuckin' place.

line of duty, in (Considerable Antiquity to Modern) An injury or disability incurred while carrying out one's normal duties. If you were hospitalized as a result, the time you lost was "good" and counted as part of your enlistment. If you were permanently disabled, you were entitled to disability pay. Some cases could get very involved. We know of an officer who got VD in line of duty—but that's another story.

line of the Army (At least Old, Old Army through World War II) The combat arms of the Army—now Infantry, Armor, Field Artillery, Air-Defense Artillery, Engineers, and Signal Corps—as distinct from service troops and staffs. We have not heard the term used recently. See *old line*.

Line 1 (Modern) *s.* Dead.

liner (World War II to Modern) The helmet liner. A tough plastic underhelmet that is adjusted to the head by a combination of bands and straps and holds the helmet itself on. Sometimes worn by cadre at training activities and usually adorned with decals of rank and painted variously.

lingerie pins /lon-jer-ˈree *or* lon-jer-ˈray/ (World War I) *s.* Officers' insignia of rank, particularly of company officers. Sometimes spelled more or less phonetically, as *longery*.

linter (Old, Old Army) A lean-to, specifically one built onto the rear of a set of quarters. The quarters for married officers on many early western posts were small. Enterprising officers would create more space by building one or more linters on behind, frequently without permission and from whatever materials were available. The word itself is an early variant of *lean-to*; it seems to have survived longer in military life than civilian.

liquid coffee money (World War I to World War II) A special travel ration —bread, corned beef, canned baked beans, canned tomatoes, jam, coffee, sugar, and evaporated milk—was issued troops traveling "otherwise than by marching, and under conditions where it was impractical to cook." (We remember it as tasting good, even after several days.) When conditions made it impossible to brew coffee, the soldiers were given the cash value of the sugar, evaporated milk, and coffee so that they could purchase "liquid coffee" at stops en route.

liquid cork (Modern) *s.* Medicine for diarrhea; Kaopectate or paregoric.

listen up, to (Modern; all Services) *s.* To pay attention. "Well, listen up, as the sergeants say" (Durden).

Little Buchenwald (Post–World War II) *s.* The stockade of the 82d Airborne Division. Known as an institution ferocious enough to impress even paratroopers with the virtues of self-control in the face of temptation.

Little Chicago (Korea and later) *s.* Tongduch'on-ni, Korea. A town north of Seoul, just behind the US I Corps zone. Principal inhabitants: widows and orphans left by the North Korean attempt to "liberate" South Korea in 1950. Principal occupations: prostitution, begging, souvenir peddling, theft. Principal public institutions: orphanages and relief missions supported by US troops.

Little Friend (World War II; Air Force) *s.* The Mustang P-51 fighter. So called by American and British bomber pilots because it had the range to fly along with them and keep the Luftwaffe off their very vulnerable necks. The term is also applied to fighter escorts in general.

Little Joe 1. (World War II) *s.* The auxiliary motor to the M4 tank. It was a two-cycle, single-cylinder gasoline engine that powered an auxiliary generator to keep the batteries of the tank charged when the main engine and generator were off. We do not know how widely this term was used, but it was current in our division. 2. (Vietnam) *s.* A heavy wrench used for adjusting tank tracks.

Little Men (Vietnam) *s.* The Vietcong or North Vietnamese soldiers.

live ammunition (Colonial to Modern) Service ammunition such as is used in combat, as opposed to blank cartridges or guard ammunition. Exposure to it makes the real soldier. At an earlier date, called *ball cartridge.*

live-fire exercise (Modern) A training exercise where real bullets are fired overhead (or that is what you are told).

liver pad liver patch (1920s to Modern) *s.* The General Staff Identification Badge, worn by officers of the War Department General Staff. So called because it was worn on the uniform blouse above the wearer's liver. There may be a memory here of the liver pads that were sold by medical quacks in the earlier part of the century. They were supposed to keep you from getting an unexpected chill.

Loach (Modern) *s.* The OH-6 (Light Observation Helicopter). Also called *Tadpole* and *white bird.*

lobscouse Primarily a sailor's term, but occasionally used in the Army. See Appendix.

lobster lobsterback (Colonial to Revolutionary) *s.* A contemptuous term for a Redcoat, a British soldier. The term itself was of British origin. In the early 17th century a *lobster* was a heavy cavalryman in armor, but by the mid-17th century, *lobster* and *lobsterback* had come to mean a soldier in a red coat.

lock and load! (Modern) 1. Prepare for firing! A command given to shooters on the rifle range. 2. The act of obeying the command. Also called *rock and roll.*

lock-in (Modern) *s.* A period of time (generally two years) following a promotion, during which a soldier cannot retire without losing his new grade. This rule is occasionally waived in special cases, especially for men retired because of medical disability. "I stayed for twenty-two years, because I got promoted to sergeant major and had a two-year lock-in."

lock into, to (Modern) *s.* To obtain, to consume. "On a good night the soldiers will 'lock into' a few items to make the drive enjoyable" (AT, 18 June 1979). Perhaps the expression grew out of the earlier *latch onto.*

Locks (Mexican War) A mythical culprit among the Tennessee volunteers, responsible for many things that went wrong. A counterpart of *Cogle.*

log bird (Vietnam) *s.* A helicopter that routinely flew resupply missions to a unit's forward elements. The word *log* is short for *logistical.*

logistician (Modern) When a supplyman is promoted to the grade of major, the story goes, he calls himself a *logistician,* in keeping with the dignity of his new rank.

London trade (Revolutionary, at least the winter of 1779–80) *s.* The extensive illegal trade in foodstuffs that American farmers carried on with the British forces in and around New York City. In January 1780, Washington's army had a "starvation week," four days without food and three more with almost none. Men roasted and ate old shoes or gnawed on black birch bark. Washington had only paper money, while the British paid in gold.

longery pins See *lingerie pins.*

longevity (Antiquity uncertain to Modern) 1. A soldier's length of service, particularly with reference to pay. 2. Short for *longevity pay* (which term goes back at least as far as the late 19th century), the rate at which a soldier's base pay increases with length of service, or such increased pay itself. At present longevity increases take place at two, three, and four years of service; after that every two years up to twenty-two; a final increase is given after twenty-six years' service. In the previous system, such increases took place every three years. (See also *fogy.*) In the 19th century the terms *longevity ration* and *fogy ration* were used for such pay.

Long Faces (Revolutionary) *s.* The Continental Line's term for the militia.

Long Gray Line *s.* The Corps of Cadets at the US Military Academy.

long handles long-handled underwear (Possibly pre–World War I and later) *s.* Winter underwear, so called because of long sleeves and legs. Also known as *John L's, long johns.*

long johns Long Johns (Antiquity uncertain, but at least World War II, to Modern) *s.* Probably the commonest slang term for long winter underwear.

long roll (Colonial to about 1885) *s.* The soldier's highly descriptive term for the drum beat for "Assembly" or "Fall in."

long taw (Civil War; USA) *s.* An exchange of artillery fire at long range. Undoubtedly derived from the boyhood use of *taw*, to shoot a marble.

long-time, to (Modern; all Services) 1. *s.* To stay with a woman for the entire night or for several days. As opposed to *short-time*. 2. *s.* To require a long time to ejaculate during sexual intercourse. From Vietnamese pidgin English. "You long time, GI. Beaucoup beer" (Smith).

Long Tom *s.* A name given to several different weapons during various periods of our history. 1. (Revolutionary to War of 1812) Usage here is relatively loose. In general, a long ship's gun—usually a 12-, 18-, or 24-pounder—mounted on a US warship or privateer. 2. (Indian Wars) The trap-door Springfield infantry rifle. 3. (World War I) The 155mm GPF gun. 4. (World War II to Korea) The M2 155mm gun, an improved version of the GPF. It came in both towed and self-propelled mounts, threw a 95-pound projectile over 15 miles, and was extremely accurate. It has been developed further in recent years.

louie looey loot (Pre–World War I to Modern) *s.* Common spoken abbreviations for *lieutenant*, but not usually used with names. One would not say *Looey Jones.*

low crawl, to do the (Modern) *s.* To extricate oneself very quietly from an embarrassing or potentially hazardous social situation. "I did the low crawl right out of there!" In combat, the low crawl is used when concealment is scarce, enemy observation is good, and high speed is not essential. See *high crawl.*

lower than whaleshit (Modern) *s.* A comparative statement indicating where some soldiers rank. "Second lieutenants were 'lower than whaleshit'—which was at the bottom of the ocean" (Groom).

low-order burst (Old Army to Modern) 1. A malfunctioning shell that does not explode properly. 2. By extension, an inefficient person or an event that does not go off as planned.

low quarters (Modern) *s.* The modern plain-toe blucher oxford, chukka boot, or similar commercial-design shoes authorized for wear with the various Army dress and khaki uniforms. The term *quarter* here is a technical term in shoemaking, referring to the portion of the shoe below the ankle bone.

LS Limited Service.

Lt. Lieutenant.

Lt. Col. Lieutenant Colonel.

Lt. Gen. Lieutenant General.

lucifer (World War I) A French match. It could be of the "gopher" variety—going out promptly as soon as lighted, so that you would have to go for another—or the type that fumigated you with sulfur smoke.

lugerhead (World War II and later) *s.* A derogatory term for a German civilian. Derived from the Luger pistol.

Luke the Gook (Korea and later) *s.* Primarily a North Korean soldier, but the term was sometimes applied to his Chinese Communist buddy, who was more commonly called *Old Joe Chink*. Later, a nickname for the Vietcong or North Vietnamese soldier. (See *gook.*) A similar form phonetically was *Luke the Spook*, identified by aircraft factory workers during World War II as a gremlin who ruined work and put "bugs" into aircraft.

lunette 1. (Revolutionary to early 19th century) An officer's telescope. 2. A towing ring, as at the end of the trail of a field gun.

lung warts (1930s and later; all Services) *s.* A woman's breasts.

lurp (Modern) *s.* LRP (Long-Range Patrol) or LRRP (Long-Range Reconnaissance Patrol). After 1969 these units were called *Rangers* and all authorized LRRP units were designated part of the 75th Infantry Regiment.

lurps (Modern) *s.* LRPs (Long-Range Patrol Rations)—precooked, freeze-dried meals in lightweight, flexible packets. You were supposed to add hot water to them to reconstitute them, although cold water would do. You could even chew them dry. They were designed for men traveling fast, light, and far.

LZ (All Services) Landing Zone. A clear area for landing helicopters. These zones may be artificially cleared areas or natural terrain features. They are generally described as hot or cold. Also called *LIMA ZULU*.

☆☆☆☆*M*☆☆☆☆

McClellan cap (Civil War; USA) *s.* A tailor-made French-style kepi such as was fancied by Maj. Gen. George McClellan and many Union officers in place of the issue forage cap. Not common usage.

Mach schnell! (World War II and later; also Air Force) Hurry up! Move it! From German *mach's schnell.* Still occasionally heard.

McNamara's 100,000 McNamara 100,000, the (Modern) A program instituted by Secretary of Defense Robert S. McNamara authorizing acceptance of up to 100,000 men who, because of low mental ability, would otherwise have been excluded from the Army. Many of these men proved to be good soldiers. "McNamara's 100,000—pulled from the compost heaps of America's hopeless" (Durden). Also called *Project 100,000.*

macom /'may-com/ (Modern) Major Army Command.

Maconochie (World War I) Maconochie's Meat and Potato Stew, a British field ration component. Picked up by American troops serving with the British.

made in the shade (Modern) *s.* A catchphrase meaning that a soldier has found the next best thing to heaven on earth—a quiet niche out of the heat of the sun, where officers and NCOs never go. " 'Made in the shade,' he muttered" (Goldman).

mad minute (World War I to Modern) 1. *s.* A lavish display of firepower, when everyone cuts loose with every available weapon, sometimes more as spectacle than for effect. The expression is said to have originated with a British journalist who was describing the British retreat from Mons in World War I. 2. *s.* Climactic moments of firepower demonstrations, especially at the combat arms schools. In the 19th century this used to be called the *grand finale.* One sees the same effect in civilian fireworks displays on the Fourth of July. 3. (Especially Vietnam) *s.* Firing all a unit's weapons simultaneously, either when breaking contact with the enemy or at dawn, in anticipation of an enemy attack. The fire is usually spontaneous, sustained, and at no particular target. "Everyone ready for a mad minute at 0545" (Marshall, 1971).

Mae West *s.* Various items reminiscent of that famous entertainer's mammary equipment. 1. (1940–41) The M2 experimental model light tank. It had two machine-gun turrets just below and on either side of the main turret. 2. (World War II and later) An inflatable life jacket. 3. (World War II to Modern) A parachute malfunction in which one suspension line gets hooked over the top of the inflated canopy, giving it the appearance of a well-filled brassiere. Although it is supposed to be extremely perilous, we would rather ride a Mae West down than risk the extra clutter of getting a reserve parachute mixed up in the thing. If you land hard, so what? Just don't try to slip and you'll be OK.

Maggie's drawers (Old Army to Modern) *s.* A red flag waved from the pits during target practice to indicate that a shot has completely missed the target. Also, the miss itself. We believe that the term was taken from that somewhat improper song "The Little Old Red Flannel Drawers That Maggie Wore." Other terms for the same situation: *artillery bull, lingerie, Aunt Nancy's pants, goose egg*, and *washout*.

magpie (Old Army to post–World War II) *s.* On the rifle range, a shot that hits the number three of the target. It is indicated by a black-and-white disc.

maidless room (Post–World War II) *s.* Old-style officers' quarters usually had a small back bedroom that could be used by a maid or sometimes by an enlisted man and his wife, both of whom helped around the house. (The enlisted man helped in his off-duty time, of course.) The rooms still exist, but maids have gone the way of the Sam Browne belt and the dog robber.

main (Modern) *s.* A paratrooper's main parachute. See also *reserve*.

If my main don't open wide,
I've got another by my side.

main post (At least World War II to Modern) That part of the post where the headquarters and administrative facilities are located. Troop barracks are generally somewhat removed from the main post, thus giving the area an aura of remoteness and inaccessibility in the soldier's mind. The fact that the brass swarm there is all the more reason for the average soldier to stay away.

major (Ancient to Modern) The lowest-ranking field-grade officer. He ranks below a lieutenant colonel and above a captain (who is a company officer). The present insignia of rank is a gold leaf. An officer who holds this grade usually does not command in line units but acts as a chief of staff to the colonel or as a second in command to the lieutenant colonel of the battalion. Abbreviated *Maj.*

major general (Ancient to Modern) At present, a two-star general officer who ranks below a lieutenant general and above a brigadier general. He usually commands a division. Except for a short period in 1798 and again during 1802–12, the rank has existed in the US Army since the Revolution, and for much of the history of the United States the Army has been commanded by major generals. For more detail on this point, see *general officer, General of the Armies, General of the Army, lieutenant general*. Abbreviated *Maj. Gen., MG*.

make 1. (At least 1910 to Old Army; West Point) *s.* A cadet officer or NCO. 2. (Old Army to Modern) To be promoted to rank of a cadet officer or NCO (BN, 1939–79).

make, to (Antiquity uncertain to Modern; also Navy) *s.* To receive the rank of, to be promoted. "Joe just made captain." "I hope to make sergeant in a couple of months." (A possible immediate source for the expression may be the *makes*, an old West Point idiom for the periodically published list of cadets selected for promotion.) We do not recall using the term before World War II. In the British Army and Navy, however, similar expressions date back to the early 19th century.

make company funds, to (At least mid-19th century to Modern) *s.* To build up a large cash balance in the company fund rather than spend it for extras for the mess. Sometimes this was done with a definite end in view, such as the purchase of athletic equipment. But occasionally, in laxly commanded units where the money was left in the care of an NCO, the latter could accumulate money by skimping on meals and by other dodges, and thereafter desert with it (Lowe).

make private, to (1940s and 1950s, but could be considerably older) To be busted back down to private from the grade of NCO. "Charley really had flair. He went from Pfc to topkick in four short years and then made private in one day."

make the scene with eighteen (Vietnam) *s.* A catchphrase often heard on the Armed Forces Radio and Television Service reminding soldiers that no more than eighteen rounds of ammunition should be placed in the standard clip of the M16 rifle.

Malfunction Junction (1940s and 1950s) *s.* The receiving barracks or "frying pan area" of the Parachute School at Fort Benning, Georgia.

malingerer (Colonial to Modern) A soldier who pretends to, fakes, or exaggerates sickness or injury to evade his duty. See *goldbrick, ride the sick book, hospital rat, wagon dogs.*

Man, the (Modern) *s.* The commanding officer. This is really a naval term, comparable to the Army's *Old Man*, but we have heard black soldiers use it. Sometimes as *Big Man.*

management (1950s to Modern; all Services) A pernicious theory that the Armed Forces should be run in a "businesslike" fashion, following the most modern management procedures, rather than being led by forceful example. The theory was welcomed by many persons who happened to be wearing officers' insignia without really being officers in the immemorial sense. Leadership is a demanding and lonely task, whereas anyone can look reasonably impressive behind a desk. Management techniques also spread responsibility for unfortunate goof-offs. Mangement hounds might ponder a German epitaph for the French Army of 1940: "[It] had been administered rather than commanded" (Mellenthin).

manhole inspection manhole (World War II and later) *s.* Physical inspection of WACs to detect VD; equivalent to the short-arm inspection of their male comrades. Some called it *foxhole inspection*, but *manhole* had an appropriate double entendre.

man in the iron stove (Early Civil War; USA) *s.* A soldier wearing one of the "bulletproof" vests peddled to trusting Yankees during the first year of the war. They were heavy and hot, and certainly not bulletproof. The term is probably a play on the famous "Man in the Iron Mask" of Alexandre Dumas *père*'s *Ten Years After.*

Manchu Law (1912 on) *s.* A law limiting line officers' tours of staff duty in Washington to four years out of six. Passed by Congress in 1912, the year in which the Manchu rulers of China were driven out by a revolution, this excellent piece of legislation broke up the comfortable personal empires that the various staff echelons had established and sent their swivel-chair warriors out to the dust and sweat of troop duty to learn how to be soldiers again.

manual of arms, the (Ancient to Modern; all Services) The proper holding of the rifle (or other individual weapon), carrying it through a series of prescribed motions and positions. Training in it is often done initially by the numbers. With the M16A1 rifle the positions used in the manual are: Order Arms, Rest, Port Arms, Present Arms, Inspection Arms, Right and Left Shoulder Arms, and Carry Arms; also Fix and Unfix Bayonets. In the 17th and early 18th centuries this was known as the *manual exercise.*

marching fire See *assault fire.*

marfak (World War II) *s.* Nickname for the "tropical butter" issued to troops in the ETO. It did not melt in hot weather, and there was considerable doubt whether it melted in the human stomach. The term is taken from the trade name of a stiff lubricating grease, or what, a generation earlier, would have been called *axle grease.*

marine, to play someone for a (Civil War; USA) *s.* To fool someone, to make a sucker out of someone. "Say, Dutchy, you rascal, you played me for a marine, didn't you?" (Kelsoe). Based on the common belief that a marine would believe anything. As with *Tell it to the marines*, another instance of the low esteem in which the Army held marine intelligence.

marksman (1879 on) The lowest degree of qualification in arms for which a specific badge is awarded. The higher degrees are *expert* and *sharpshooter*.

mark time, to (Antiquity uncertain, but 1830s in the British Army, to Modern) 1. To march in place, in normal cadence. 2. By extension, also widely used in civilian life, to be in a state of waiting, to be doing nothing, to be stalling.

marmite can (World War I to World War II; also Marines) 1. An insulated container used to carry food forward from the kitchens to the front lines. The term is from French *marmite* 'stew pan' or, in military use, 'camp kettle'. 2. *s.* A large-caliber, high-explosive German shell.

marquee marquis marquise (Colonial to mid-19th century) In common usage, an officer's tent. Originally the *marquise* was an outer shell, pitched over the tent proper, but the term was often used loosely and the exact definition varied over the years.

MASH (Korea and later) Mobile Army Surgical Hospital, with the mission of giving the wounded quick, highly skilled care. (Any resemblance between a real MASH and a certain popular TV show is strictly accidental.) Now, *MUST*—Medical Unit Self-Contained Transportation; see also *bubble*.

massage, to (Modern) 1. *s.* to work over, to develop, to refine a plan or report. "You and George here will have to massage the plan" (Bunting). 2. *s.* Usually as a past participle, *massaged*, killed or wounded.

master blaster (Modern) *s.* A soldier who is authorized to wear the Master Parachutist Badge.

Master of the Sword 1. (Colonial through War of 1812) A select soldier in each troop or company of light dragoons who trained the other troopers in swordsmanship. Like the troop riding master, he was considered an NCO. He was also called the *sword master.* 2. (West Point) A civilian instructor with the "relative rank and . . . pay, allowances and emoluments of a [first lieutenant], mounted" who was at first a teacher of swordsmanship, and later (1901–23) in charge of physical education. The Academy had had a traditional master of the sword since at least 1857, with the official title *Sword Master.* He was officially listed as *Master of the Sword* in 1881. In 1901 "military gymnastics and physical culture" were added to his responsibilities. In 1947 this title was changed to *Director of Physical Education.*

master sergeant (1920 to Modern) At present, a senior noncommissioned officer in pay grade E-8, with, as insignia of rank, a chevron consisting of three bars and three arcs. The title and grade were first created in 1920, and until 1958, when the supergrades were introduced, the master sergeant was the highest enlisted grade in the Army. Master sergeants generally serve in staff and specialist positions that usually do not involve leadership duty. If a master sergeant assumes the duty of a first sergeant, he becomes a first sergeant in rank and adopts the chevron of a first sergeant. At present, although both first sergeant and master sergeant are in pay grade E-8, a first sergeant takes precedence in rank. Before the creation of the supergrades, however, a master sergeant outranked a first sergeant. Abbreviated *M. Sgt., MSG.* A nickname is *three up and three down.*

matross (Colonial to early 19th century) A private of the artillery. The term was adopted from the British artillery during the colonial period. Its ultimate origin is the Dutch *maatgenoot* 'messmate'.

Mattel Messerschmitt (Modern) The TH-Osage helicopter. "The tiny choppers, painted bright orange, look so toylike that students call them 'Mattel Messerschmitts' " (SM 34:11, November 1979). *Mattel* is from the Mattel Toy Manufacturing Company.

Maytag Messerschmitt (World War II) A light American aircraft of the Piper Cub or L-5 type, used for adjusting artillery fire or for courier service. Maytag manufactures household appliances, especially washing machines.

MC Medical Corps.

MCI (Vietnam; also Marines) Meal, Combat, Individual. A replacement for the old C-ration, with more variety and nutritional balance.

Measure the adjusted confusion (World War II and later) *s.* An observation, adapted from artillery fire direction terminology, meaning "Things sure are getting fouled up." Sometimes it squelches a developing flap through its implication that it still can be "measured"—i.e., gotten under control with a little calm thought.

meatball 1. (Old Army to World War II) *s.* The last day of a soldier's enlistment, for which he was paid and fed, although he did no work except to turn in his equipment. When a short-timer was asked how much longer he had to serve, he might reply, "Ten days and a meatball." *Meatball* probably means zero. 2. (World War II) *s.* The circular, red national sun insignia, usually with a white background or edging, painted on Japanese aircraft and tanks. Also the Japanese flag. 3. (World War II and perhaps later) *s.* A stupid person, a strangely acting person. Also *meathead.*

meat can (World War I and later) The official name for the mess kit. Originally made of steel, but soon changed to aluminum, it was an oval pan with a separate cover or lid. A hinged handle clamped the lid in place when the kit was not in use, and could swing out to form a frying pan handle. A knife, fork, and spoon were packed inside it. (They rattled and had to be stowed carefully in combat. Socks were commonly used as soundproofing.) During World War I, the original 1910 model proved too small to hold enough food to satisfy a hungry soldier, and in 1918 both pan and lid were made deeper.

meat wagon (1930s and later) *s.* An ambulance. Also called a *crackerbox.*

mechanical (Modern) *s.* Ambush devices such as flares and mines that are automatically detonated by the enemy as he approaches. "We set up a mechanical before leaving the area."

Medal of Honor (Civil War to Modern; all Services) The highest Army decoration, awarded for acts of extraordinary heroism, above and beyond the call of duty, performed in combat with an enemy. The first Army awards were established for enlisted men in 1862; the legislation was amended in 1863 to include officers and was made retroactive to the beginning of the Civil War. The medal is usually awarded by the President, but any "high official" may make the presentation "in the name of the Congress of the United States." It is thus often called the *Congressional Medal of Honor.* Recipients are entitled to certain benefits: special pensions, free military air transportation within the continental United States, admission of their children (if otherwise qualified) to West Point, and certain pay benefits on retirement from the Army under some circumstances. Contrary to popular opinion, enlisted recipients do not receive a hand salute. The medal is awarded only to American citizens.

medevac (Modern; all Services) *s.* Short for *medical evacuation.* "Critically wounded, already medevacked to Japan" (Smith). "One of them medevac choppers, a dustoff" (Heinemann).

medics medical personnel Terms for enlisted men of the Medical Corps include *bedpan commando, chancre mechanic, clap checker, iodine spiller, ninety-one bedpans* (based on the MOS for a medic), *pecker checker, penis machinist, prick-smith.*

menopause manor (Modern) *s.* An office, staff section, or installation where the average age of personnel is over thirty years.

mess 1. (Ancient to Modern) Originally, in the Army, a group of men who cooked their rations together and ate together or, in the Navy, merely ate together. Hence, *messmate* meant a comrade. Later, the Army applied the term to the building, or portion thereof, in which the food was prepared and the men ate—commonly, the *mess hall.* Similarly, there was an *officers' mess* for unmarried officers. Evening meals there tended to be formal. The term *mess* was naturally much exploited by service humorists:

After eating here for a month or less
I've begun to savvy why they call it
a mess!

Mess has now become something of an official tabu word (see *dining facility or-*

derly), probably because of generations of wisecracks about *mess* as a disorderly jumble. But the word is an ancient term for a meal, which came into Middle English from French, and was probably influenced by a phonetically similar Old English word for a table setting. The modern meaning of *mess* as a disorderly jumble or confusion is 19th century in origin. 2. *s.* A mess sergeant.

mess call A bugle call announcing the beginning of meals. In the Old Army this call was named *Soupy* and sung to the following verses:

Soup—y, soup—y, soup,
  Without a single bean;
Pork—y, pork—y, pork,
  Without a streak of lean;
Coffee, coffee, coffee,
  Without any cream.

As variants, *bacon* was sometimes sung instead of *pork* in the third line, and the final line could be *The weakest ever seen.* Today's less inventive soldiers sometimes sing, "Come and get your chow, come and get it now!'

Mess Dress (20th century; all Services) A special, expensive officer's uniform, modeled after the civilian tuxedo, for wear at formal evening occasions.

mess hall (Ancient to Modern) The place where military personnel eat. The term is still widely used in the Army, but is no longer official. Today, Army "eateries" are called *dining facilities* or *unit dining facilities*. These pretentious, bloodless neologisms were adopted because the word *mess* was felt to have a derogatory connotation.

mess kit messkit (Ancient to Modern) A soldier's personal eating equipment for use in the field. Like the older meat can, it is a shallow metal pan with a separate lid, which may be held in place by a long folding handle. The soldier's knife, fork, and spoon are carried inside the pan. When the handle is extended, the pan may be used for cooking, but modern combat rations have made this use largely unnecessary. Up until the early 20th century, such eating equipment was supplied by the individual soldier or, in some cases, by the unit, but now it is issued. Among soldiers and veterans of World Wars I and II, "I hope to spit [or worse] in your messkit!" was an emphatic expression of agreement.

Mess Kit Repair Company (Modern) *s.* A fictitious organization. Applied facetiously to any unit assigned to trivial, unimportant missions. Also used disparagingly of another person's assignment. "He was sent to the 441st Mess Kit Repair Company at Fort Lost-in-the-Woods," or "to the 131313th Underground Mess Kit Repair Battalion (Unarmored)."

mess sergeant (World War I to Modern) Any NCO who is in charge of a mess hall. In a company unit he works under the mess officer (who is an officer detailed to this duty) and is in complete charge of the eating arrangements for the enlisted men. Under him are first and second cooks, who are usually more or less permanent; perhaps a KP pusher; and KPs. Also called *mess* and (in modern terminology) *mess steward.*

mess tools (Antiquity uncertain) *s.* A soldier's knife, fork, spoon, and mess kit.

messy bucket (World War I) *s.* Soldiers' fractured French for *merci beaucoup* 'thanks very much'. Also *murky bucket.*

metalman (World War II) *s.* The more useless type of retired officer recalled to active duty, with "silver in his hair, gold in his teeth, and lead in his ass." We recall one who (to give him something to do and to get him out from under foot) was told to distribute Purple Hearts to the wounded at a rear-area hospital. He had decorated half the occupants of the VD ward before a medic stopped him.

Mexican promotion (Post–World War II) *s.* The promotion to the next higher grade given all reasonably well-behaved Reserve officers as they were demobilized and returned to inactive status. (If you were recalled to active duty, they took the promotion away from you.) The term is not too widely used.

Mexican rank Mex (Post–Civil War) *s.* Brevet rank. You had it, but you could not exercise it or draw pay for it except under certain rare circumstances. Following the Civil War, the US Army was full of brevet colonels and generals serving as lieutenants and captains. Apparently this reminded soldiers of the Mexican Army, which had almost as many colonels and generals as buck privates.

Mexican standoff (Indian Wars) *s.* A fight from which you escaped with your scalp, shirt, and weapons, but little else. The term, which seems to have been uncommon, was possibly inspired by the Mexican habit of reporting all not too disastrous defeats as glorious victories.

Mex noncom (World War I) *s.* An acting noncommissioned officer. See *jawbone.*

M14 rifle (Modern) The 7.62mm rifle adopted as the standard Army rifle in 1957. It replaced the M1 Garand rifle, which it resembles, and was itself replaced by the M16 in 1967. It also replaced the M1 and M2 carbines, as well as the .45-caliber MA31 submachine gun. Large stocks still exist.

M F W I C (Modern) Motherfucker What's In Charge. Sometimes used in white imitation of black jive talk: "Man I is de M F W I C o' dis M F-in' outfit." Each letter is pronounced distinctly.

MI Military Intelligence.

MIA Missing In Action. Possibly the most tragic of the four casualty classifications—*KIA, WIA, PW,* and *MIA*—especially when the United States fails to ascertain which of the other fates befell its MIAs. This vicious habit began with Korea, at which time the United States apparently decided to quit winning wars.

Mickey Mouse *s.* Various uses, ultimately derived from the animated cartoons about Mickey Mouse created by Walt Disney, although sometimes the connection is not obvious. 1. (World War II) Apparently the original, ironic use: a training film showing the horrors of venereal disease. One of the earlier versions sometimes caused GIs to faint; one of the later versions is said to have stimulated them into trying for themselves. 2. (World War II) A training film of any sort. This meaning survived up into the 1968 edition of *The Airman's Guide.* 3. (Perhaps late 1950s on) Something inane, stupid, chicken shit, trifling. This meaning may have arisen from the simple childishness of the cartoon character, or it may be a reflection on the nature of training films. "There was no saluting here or other Mickey Mouse. . . . This was what the Army was all about. No pressed and starched fatigues, no thrice-daily briefings, no eating in tents with wood floors and electric generators and movies at night and ice cream" (Groom). 4. (Modern) As an adjective, bungled, SNAFU.

Mickey Mouse boots (Korea to Modern) *s.* Insulated cold-weather boots resembling the feet of the cartoon character.

midnight requisition See *moonlight requisition.*

mif-mif (World War I to at least early World War II) *s.* Meteorological information. Temperature and wind direction at the various elevations through which artillery shells would pass in their flight toward the target. Used in computing accurate firing data on a complex pink sheet that also was called, to the best of our memory, a *mif-mif.*

MIG Alley (Korea; mostly Air Force) *s.* A strip of territory along the south bank of the Yalu River, over which Communist MIG-15 jet fighters from safe fields in Manchuria frequently challenged the US Saberjets covering United Nations air operations against North Korea. Thanks to effective radar gunsight and superior flying skills, the Americans shot down eleven MIGs for every F-86 lost.

Mike Force (Vietnam) *s.* A mobile strike force, trained and led by Special Forces. It was composed mostly of Nung (ethnic Chinese) mercenaries, who conducted guerrilla-type operations against the Communists. Also called *China Boy Companies.*

mike-mike (Modern) *s.* Millimeter. From *mike*, the letter *m* in the phonetic alphabet. "Eight-one-mike-mike mortar."

military manner (Antiquity uncertain) A disciplined, responsible, effective attitude revealed through appearance and actions; otherwise, somewhat difficult to define, although readily understood. The expression (which may be old) has been preserved by the second General Order of a Sentinel: "To walk my post in a military manner." It must be added, however, that hundreds of thousands, perhaps millions, of irreverent GIs have finished off the order with the near-rhyme "taking no shit from the company commander."

Military Payment Certificate MPC (1946 on) Scrip issued to US service personnel overseas, intended to reduce black-market speculation in US dollars. In Vietnam and Korea, for instance, MPCs were readily accepted and always brought a much higher rate of exchange than the official one. MPCs were first issued in September 1946 and discontinued in March 1973. Altogether, a total of thirteen different series were issued, with a total of ninety different pieces of currency. MPC is not in use anywhere in the world in 1983.

Military Police Military Police Corps MPs A branch of the service that performs the police functions of the Army. Among the duties of MPs are maintaining order on post, controlling military personnel off post, checking for deserters and AWOLs, controlling traffic, and performing interior guard duty. MPs on duty usually wear a brassard with the letters MP on it and sometimes have distinctive items of uniform, such as white leggings and white helmets. Apart from a short period during World War I, the American Army has not had a separate military police for most of its history; the present corps, under the Provost Marshal General, was established in 1941. MPs are variously regarded by enlisted personnel: as spoilsports, as punching bags, as brutal thugs, and as unfortunates who happen to have landed in a necessary but unpleasant job.

Oh, the MPs, the MPs
With sidearms up and down.
The MPs, the MPs

Who take your pass to town.
The MPs, the MPs
They work and never play.
And I wouldn't be a damn MP
For a million bucks a day.

The letters MP are often expanded as *Miserable Pricks*. See *provost guards*.

milk battalion (Old Army to Korea) *s.* The third battalion of the old-style infantry regiment, which had twelve companies grouped in three battalions. Companies were named alphabetically from A to M (J being omitted to avoid confusion), and the third battalion was composed of companies I, K, L, and M.

milk run (World War II; Air Force) *s.* An easy mission, about as dangerous as delivering milk; also a mission that was flown routinely over the same area.

milk up, to (World War II; Air Force) *s.* Of weather, to turn foggy or very cloudy.

mill 1. (Old Army, and perhaps considerably earlier) *s.* The post guardhouse or stockade. Imprisonment. *To run someone in the mill* was to confine him there:

They ran him in the mill;
They've got him in there still,
His bobtail's coming back by mail. . . .

Probably from prison or general slang, *mill* being a very common Victorian term for a prison. Such prisons often were mills or factories with compulsory labor. 2. (Modern; Air Force) *s.* An aircraft engine.

MILPERCEN (Modern) Military Personnel Center, located in Alexandria, Virginia. From it the worldwide personnel management system of the Army is administered.

MILPO (Modern) Military Personnel Office.

mine (Colonial to World War I) A tunnel system dug under an enemy position for the purpose of blowing it up with high explosives. While this meaning may still be encountered, since the early part of World War II, *mine* generally has meant a relatively small explosive device, such as an antitank mine or antipersonnel mine. See *torpedo*.

minigun (Modern) *s.* A 7.62mm machine gun capable of firing up to 5,400 rounds per minute. It is the main armament of Puff, the Magic Dragon. At night, minigun fire is a dazzling, beautiful pyrotechnic display. "A constant chatter of the mini-guns, spraying red-orange tracers like a cow pissing on a flat rock" (Heinemann).

minnie (World War I) *s.* Short for *Minenwerfer*, the German term for a trench mortar.

minute caller (West Point) A plebe responsible for announcing the minutes (remaining time) until a certain event or formation. He appears in the uniform that is to be worn for the formation or event, and at prescribed intervals announces, "Sir, there are ——— minutes until assembly for ——— formation. The uniform is ———. ——— minutes, Sir!"

missing link (Modern) *s.* A second lieutenant. Perhaps part of the general pattern of denigrating second lieutenants; perhaps the position of the second lieutenant as lowest-grade officer, closest to an enlisted man. (Warrant officers have always been rare mysterious beings occasionally heard of, but seldom seen.)

mission A duty assigned to a soldier or unit by higher headquarters. The order assigning it includes its purpose, thereby clearly indicating the action to be taken and the reason for it. A *small-unit mission* usually is limited and specific—an enemy position to be captured, an area to be reconnoitered. In contrast, the mission given to Gen. Dwight D. Eisenhower in 1943 was, "You will enter the continent of Europe, and, in conjunction with the other Allied Nations, undertake operations aimed at the heart of Germany, and the destruction of her armed forces."

mission-oriented (Modern) Aware, without specific order or instructions, of what to do and how to do it, in order to accomplish a task or mission.

mission-type order (Modern) An order to perform a certain mission that does not specify how it is to be carried out. "The General gives 'mission-type' orders, allowing his staff to take what steps are necessary to fulfill their mission" (Bunting).

Mister (Ancient to Modern; also Navy, Marines) The traditional mode of address to certain low-ranking officers. In the early 19th-century Army, ensigns were officially addressed as *Mister*, as were second lieutenants up to World War II. (The theory apparently was that a second lieutenant really was not an officer yet. It was painful.) Army warrant officers and Marine second lieutenants are still called Mister. When marines serve with Army organizations, they can cause much unhappiness by addressing Army shavetails in the same fashion.

Mr. Charles Mister Charles (Vietnam) *s.* A respectful name for the Vietcong or North Vietnamese soldier. See *Charlie*.

Mr. Ducrot Ducrot Crot (At least the 1930s; and later, West Point) *s.* A plebe, particularly one displeasing to upperclassmen. As a salutation, it was on a par with *Mr. Dumsquat*. Between World Wars I and II the name *General Ducrot* was used by at least one writer in various service journals to denote a mythical general of legendary stupidity. The origin of the name is not known, but it may possibly derive from French *crotte* 'animal dung', 'horse bun', via the AEF. The correct form would be *de la Crotte,* but grammatical niceties did not bother the doughboys.

Mr. No-shoulders (Modern) *s.* A snake. Commonly heard in Vietnam, where snakes abounded. See *Asian two-step*.

MLR (Generally World War II to Korea) Main Line of Resistance. The backbone of a defensive system, where the defending forces plan to stop any enemy attack.

moaks mokes (Civil War to Indian Wars) *s.* Black soldiers. Perhaps derived from *mocha*, not in the sense of a mixture of coffee and cocoa, but as a strong black coffee. Also in civilian use. At the US Naval Academy, a *moak* used to be a black messman who waited on tables.

Molly (Revolutionary) *s* A "woman of the camp," the wife or woman of an enlisted man. Collectively, they were frequently termed Mollies; individually, Molly So-and-so. A formidable lot—sunburned, dirty, and strident—they were wonderful foragers and often thieves. But they cooked, sewed, nursed, and comforted. And there were times when they took a dead husband's place at a gun or hunted cowards back into line with firebrands and screeching imprecations. One of them, an Irish girl named Mary Hays, came to be a minor American heroine under the camp name of Molly Pitcher.

M1 (World War II to Korea) The Garand .30-caliber M1 semiautomatic rifle. It replaced the Springfield '03 in 1940 and was in turn replaced by the M14 in 1957. Less accurate and heavier than the Springfield, it still was excellently designed for a newly raised mass army that did not have time to perfect its marksmanship and had to rely more on volume of fire than individual accuracy.

M1 pencil, to qualify with, the (World War II on) 1. *s.* To qualify in arms by cheating on the score card. 2. *s.* A slighting comment to, or about, desk personnel. "Oh, a company jerk can flub on the range. He qualifies with the M1 pencil."

M1 thumb (World War II on) *s.* A very common injury to the thumb. Closing the bolt to the M1 was a tricky operation. The thumb depressed the clip feed, permitting the bolt to drive forward. The thumb had to be withdrawn instantly, or the bolt, as it drove forward, propelled by a powerful spring, would catch it painfully. Some soldiers are said to have received broken thumbs from this. The least one could expect was a painful and rather discouraging injury.

monkey drill 1. (Old Army to about 1940) *s.* Trick riding practice and exhibitions. Normally a cavalry specialty, but sometimes seen in the field artillery. 2. (Since 1950) *s.* With the passing of mounted units, the term *monkey drill* was transferred to the periods of calisthenics so beloved of physical-fitness experts. It is also applied to nonregulation drill, such as special exhibition performances and trick drills.

monkey meat (World War I) *s.* Canned beef, supposedly purchased in Argentina.

monkey show (Civil War) *s.* A really fouled-up affair, suggestive of the antics of a cageful of apes. The modern equivalent would be *TARFU.*

month and a month (World War I and perhaps later) *s.* A sentence of thirty days in the guardhouse, followed by thirty days restriction to the post or other area. More recently called *thirty and thirty.*

moonlight requisition (Old Army to Modern, probably still in use; also Navy) *s.* A euphemism for theft or misappropriation of government property that is not readily available through official channels or is needed in a hurry. Usually it is taken from a quartermaster dump or an outfit farther to the rear. On occasion, this can be a carefully planned operation. If it is done for the sake of the unit (and not for private gain), it is not considered particularly reprehensible—by those who do it. Also called *midnight requisition.*

moose (Occupation of Japan to Modern; all Services) *s.* A girl, a girl friend, a mistress, a prostitute. From Japanese *musume* 'a young woman'. "Gonna find me a moose, a hooch, and do a shack job."

moose maintenance manual (Modern) *s.* A post or base exchange catalog. From the fact that such a catalog is often needed to keep one's moose in good working order. Also a takeoff on the propensity of the Army to issue maintenance manuals.

more icki tick (Early 1950s; Far Eastern Command) *s.* Very soon, quickly. Origin obscure, but popular barroom Japanese, used by Americans and by Japanese dealing with them. Perhaps a corruption of Japanese *mō jiki ni* 'right away'.

more time in the chow line than you've got in the Army, I've got A statement designed to impress the listener with the speaker's superior knowledge, greater experience, seniority, etc. The line in question can also be the *pay line*, the *shot line*, or any other line.

morning report (At least World War I and later) A daily record submitted to higher headquarters that accounted for all officers and enlisted personnel of every unit in the Army. Prepared on WD AGO Form 1 and later on DA Form 1, this report was a permanent and basic document, and was generally considered the ultimate record from which there was no appeal. Since many commands would tolerate no erasures or other alterations on it, its preparation was often an ordeal for the clerk who prepared it. In some larger units a special clerk was designated to prepare this form, and company commanders and first sergeants took pains to see that nothing was allowed to interfere with him. Now replaced by *SIDPERS*.

MOS (World War II to Modern) Military Occupation Specialty. The assignment you are supposed to be capable of handling; also the code number itself (letters and digits), which is entered on your personal records. You will probably accumulate a number of MOSs during your service, but one of these will be your primary MOS. The system represents a valiant effort to prevent filling round holes with square pegs, even if it is far from perfect in its workings. Also called *MO*.

moskosh morskosh /'moh-skohsh, 'more-skohsh/ (Occupation of Japan and later) *s.* Soon. From Japanese *mō sukoshi* 'a little more' or, in expressions of time, 'a little longer', 'a little later'. Probably contaminated by the English words *more* and *most*. *Moskosh* is the more common form today.

MOS mismatch (Modern) The situation when a soldier who is trained and experienced in a certain MOS is actually put to work in another MOS, often one for which he has little qualification.

Mosquito Fleet 1. (Civil War; USA) *s.* Nickname for the light drafts, the tinclad Mississippi River gunboats. 2. (World War I) *s.* Nickname for a subchaser unit.

mosquito raid (World War II; Air Force) *s.* A raid, usually a strafing run by a single light plane.

mosquito wing (Modern) *s.* The former insignia of rank of a private first class, one chevron.

mothball, to (Mostly Navy) *s.* To place equipment in storage for possible future use. After World War II, surplus ships (mothball fleets) were placed in storage. Many were anchored in fresh water (as in the Hudson River) to inhibit marine growth on their hulls. Their more vulnerable parts were covered or coated with plastic, and dehumidifying equipment was installed. Small caretaker detachments tried to keep the ships in serviceable condition. While mothballing was not completely successful, most of these ships could be restored to service when the Korean War broke out. The Army also mothballed some weapons. Tanks, for example, were rustproofed and stored in sealed containers. They also came in handy.

motherfucker mother fucker (Modern) *s.* Well known in civilian slang, of course, but very widely spread in the Armed Forces. Like many other tabu words of sexual origin, it has lost its literal significance but extends over a broad scale of applications and new meanings. These range from a strong insult and a description of a macho figure on down to uses that are almost drained of specific meaning and are equivalent to *person*. The history of the term is obscure, but the consensus is that although it has been used sporadically since the early 20th century (Gold), it came into wide use from black argot during the late 1940s and early 1950s, probably because of the integration of the Armed Forces during President Harry S. Truman's administration (Norman, 1956; Flexner) or because of the use of black construction battalion workers in the Korean War (Wentworth and Flexner). There are many variants of the expression, ranging from *mother hugger* and *mammy jammer* to *triple clutcher*.

motor pool (World War II to Modern) The area where an organization's motor vehicles are parked, serviced, and—as far as the organization is capable—repaired. Used sometimes in other service arms.

motor stables (Roughly Old Army to World War II) The performance of minor maintenance on a motor vehicle. Probably based on the late-19th-century use of the term *stables*—duty at the stables, caring for the horses and/or mules.

Mount up (Antiquity uncertain to Modern; also Marines) *s.* Informal order from the old horse-soldier days, which passed easily into use with World War II's motorized, mechanized troops. To get your men into their tanks (trucks, choppers, or whatever), ready to move out on order. Often used in ordinary conversation for *Let's get going*.

move on, to (Korea) *s.* To run like hell. See *"Bugout Boogie."*

move out smartly, to (Modern) 1. *s.* To depart quickly, purposefully, and in a military manner. 2. *s.* To scram, to beat it, to disappear. "Move out smartly, Jerry Boy" (Goldman). See *ass in gear*.

mox cocks mox cox (Modern) *s.* A statement of indifference. "It doesn't matter." Sometimes rendered *Mox cocks to me!* or *Mox fucking cocks!* Based on *mox nix*.

mox nix (Occupation of Germany to Modern) *s.* A statement of indifference. From German *es macht nichts*, with the same meaning.

mox nix sticks (Modern) *s.* A signaling device on some European model cars and trucks. It consists of a flashing turn-signal light mounted on an armature that projects from the side of the vehicle when used. The phrase comments more on the Americans' estimation of German driving ability than on the device itself.

MP Military Police.

MPC 1. Military Police Corps. 2. Military Payment Certificate.

MRE (Modern) Meal, Ready-to-Eat. The latest type of combat ration, replacing the C- and E-rations. It provides such precooked meals as Swiss steak, sliced ham, chicken à la king, and beef stew in aluminum foil pouches.

MS Medical Service.

MSC Medical Service Corps.

M16 rifle This became the standard Army rifle in 1967 (as the M16A1 5.56mm rifle), replacing the M14. However, prototypes were used in Vietnam by the Air Force in 1962. Also called *'16*.

M60 machine gun The M60 7.62mm General Purpose Gun began to replace the Browning automatic rifle and the Browning light and heavy .30-caliber machine guns in 1959–60. Its cyclical rate of fire is 5,400 rounds per minute, but the recommended rate of fire under actual combat conditions is only 200 rounds per minute. Even at this rate the barrel heats up enough after only one minute to "cook off" a chambered round in ten seconds.

mud crusher mud thumper *s.* An infantryman. Derisive names undoubtedly invented by the cavalry, some time in the latter part of the 19th century.

mufti (Mid-19th century on; terminal date uncertain) Civilian clothing, as worn by a person who would otherwise be in uniform. Of Indian origin, the term came to the United States through the British army, where it was a common expression. From an Urdu word for *free*, indicating that civilian dress of a fixed pattern was issued free to lower grades of soldiers for walking out or for private use.

muleskinner (Old, Old Army to 1940s) *s.* As in civilian life, the driver of a mule-drawn vehicle, a man noted for his expertise with profane and a long black-snake whip. He also usually chawed tobacco and could spit in a rattlesnake's eye at 20 yards' range. A competent mule-skinner did not skin his mules; instead he kept them moving by voice and the crack of his whip. But, when necessary, he used the whip deftly in a form of North American acupuncture.

mummy sack (Modern) *s.* An OD zippered rubber body bag for holding the dead. "Eighteen mummy sacks lay on the tables in utter stillness" (Smith).

munchkin (Modern; West Point) *s.* A short cadet. The term is taken from L. Frank Baum's *The Wizard of Oz*, possibly from the motion picture version.

murky bucket (World War I) *s.* Soldiers' fractured French for *merci beaucoup* 'thanks very much'.

musette bag (World War I to early World War II) A haversack used by officers to carry immediate necessities when in the field. *Musette* is French for *haversack*; Americans picked it up during World War I and added *bag*, which is somewhat redundant. Maybe it sounded more glamorous than *haversack*. The term continued in use until the early days of World War II, but we have the impression that it has just about died out.

music (Probably Indian Wars, to Old Army) An infantry bugler or cavalry trumpeter. In the Marines *music* is a shortened version of *company musician*—originally drummers, later a bugler. Like their Army counterparts, they sounded the daily calls in peacetime routine or combat.

mustang (Mostly Navy and Marines) *s.* The basic meaning of the term is an officer who has come up from the ranks and is still perhaps a somewhat barbarous character. In the Marines he usually is an ex-gunnery sergeant and notorious smoke bringer. Having hated officers all his life and now finding himself one, he is a most unpleasant person to encounter when one has been late for reveille—especially since he knows all your excuses, having employed them himself in past years. Usually he has a DSC or a couple of Navy Crosses and knows a few things that ordinary second lieutenants do not. He is best avoided in garrison situations, but is quite popular in bush warfare. In the Army, after World War II, *mustang* had the special meaning of an officer who had served in World War II, returned to civilian life, and then came back into service when the cold war began getting hot around the edges. A retread. The history of the term is fragmentary. The first recorded use is in Farmer and Henley (1898), where it is referred back to the Civil War: "An officer entering the U.S. Navy from the merchant service, after serving through the Civil War." But what does a mustang have to do with the sea and how did the term reach the Navy? *Mustang* is derived from Mexican Spanish *mesteño*, 'a wild horse' and, as a slang term, 'a rough uncouth person who enters polite life'. A reasonable guess is that the term was picked up during the Mexican War (like *mustang army*) and that it dropped from Army use, but was revived around the time of the Civil War for the naval situation.

mustang army (Mexican War) *s.* The name the Regulars applied to volunteers and temporary Regulars, from their generally unkempt appearance and unruly behavior.

muster (Ancient to Modern) A periodic head count of every individual in every military unit, to make certain that all men listed as belonging to it were actually present or definitely accounted for. A muster was also customary when militia or National Guard organizations were "mustered in" the federal service. The original purpose of this formation was to keep company and regimental commanders from carrying fictitious names on their rolls and quietly appropriating the pay and rations for these nonexistent soldiers. (The staff system at the time of the Revolution included a number of *commissary generals of musters*, after the British system, for conducting musters.) Later, the muster became merely a handy method of keeping an exact check on the manpower of the Army by ensuring that actual strength of a unit agreed with reported (morning report) strength. From the early days of this custom came a number of old American expressions, such as *to pass muster* and *to muster up*.

mustering-out pay Payment of a set sum of money upon discharge from active duty. This program is now obsolete, but it was followed during the demobilization after World War II.

mystery meat *s.* Meat served in an Army mess. The sneering implication is that the meat is something improper, such as horse meat.

☆☆☆☆*n*☆☆☆☆

name plates and name tapes (Modern) Identification elements worn on the uniform. Name plates are plastic strips, about 1 by 3 inches, worn on the right breast pocket. The soldier's last name is lettered in white against a black background. Name tapes are cloth strips, about 1 by 4.5 inches, sewn above the right breast pocket. The soldier's last name is lettered in black against a background of OG 107 shade. Name plates and name tapes together are called *name tags*.

name, rank, and cigarettes (World War II) *s.* A play on name, rank, and serial number, which was all that a captured soldier was supposed to reveal to his captors. Probably from the fact that during World War II, American POWs were often forced to give their cigarettes to enemy soldiers.

napoo napoo fini (World War 1) *s.* Dead. Done and over with. No more. Soldiers' fractured French for *ne plus* 'no more' and *ne plus, fini* 'no more, finished'. Borrowed from the British.

nappy (World War II) *s.* The company barber.

nasty (Colonial to Revolutionary) Dirty. As in George Washington's description of his New England troops around Boston in late 1775.

National Guard weekend (Modern) *s.* A time of goofing off when an individual or unit is supposed to be working or operational. Based on the tendency of some National Guard (and Army Reserve) units to employ their weekend drill time frivolously. "Another extreme, National Guard weekend" (Herr).

Nazi shatzi Nazi shotzie (Post–World War II to Modern) *s.* A German girl friend, from German *Schatz* 'dearie', 'darling'. The term may already have been familiar from the thousands of dachshunds, Doberman pinschers, and Alsatians that are named Schatzie.

NCO (Also Marines) Noncommissioned officer.

NCO call A formal gathering of the noncommissioned officers of a unit, set up by the commander or sergeant major. Its purpose is exchanging information, resolving problems, and establishing dialogue between brother noncoms. When held as a luncheon, it is sometimes a ready excuse to eat and drink on government time.

NCO club A nonappropriated-fund activity that provides food, drink, and entertainment for enlisted personnel of all grades. Originally, the NCO club was open only to noncommissioned officers.

Near Army (Early World War II) *s.* Anyone not a Regular. We recall a certain camp follower who delighted in asking Reserve officers—usually considerably senior to her husband in age, grade, and service—"Are you Army or Near Army?"

necessaries necessary houses (Colonial to Revolutionary) Latrines. Getting the American soldier to use them has always been something of a task. "[Instead of] repairing to the nessesaries [they still tend to leave their] excrament about the fields Pernishously" (Wade and Lively).

neck out, to have one's (West Point) *s.* To fail to brace properly.

negative negatory (Modern) *s.* Radiotelephone language for *no.*

nervous (18th century to early 19th century) Spirited, active, sinewy, vigorous, strong. A word of praise for man or horse. This now archaic meaning was standard from the 15th century into the 19th century. The more modern meaning, high-strung or fearful, is first recorded in the 1740s. As a result of these two nearly opposite meanings, the word is a booby trap for historical researchers.

nervous in the service (World War II to Modern) *s.* A catchphrase with several related meanings. "Don't get nervous in the service" means "Take things as they come"; "Don't let things get you down"; or "It all counts for twenty." Also, frightened, worried, bewildered, in a state apt to hit the panic button and start a flap. Or it may mean that you just plain do not like the Army, as in a WAC song of World War II, to the tune of "Pretty Baby":

> If you're nervous in the service
> And you crave civilian clothes,
> Have a baby, pretty baby.

netted (World War I to Modern) *s.* A signal communications term indicating that radio sets or stations are in effective communication.

never hachi (Post–World War II to Modern; all Services) *s.* Pidgin Korean for *It will never happen* or *It is impossible.* The origin of the phrase is obscure, and it is often considered derivative from *sucka-hachi* or *shakuhachi,* although such a transformation is difficult to explain. A more reasonable explanation is that *hachi* is from one or another form of the Korean verb *hao* 'to do': *hajianunda* 'they don't do'; *hajianketta* 'they will not do'; or *hajianso* 'they don't do' (polite). Since *-nunda, -nketta,* and *-nso* are common suffixes, it would be easy enough (although ungrammatical) to drop them, leaving just the stem. A related expression is *nevah huckin hachi* 'impossible'. *Huckin* is *fucking,* the combination *fu-* being difficult for a speaker of Korean.

Never happen, said the cap'n (Modern) *s.* A rhyming catchphrase used to express assurance that something will not happen. See *No can do, Madame Nhu.*

Never mind the guard! (Old, Old Army to Modern) The call used by number-one sentry to cancel his previous order, "Turn out the guard!" The dignitary who is approaching does not desire to be so honored. By a natural transition, the expression is used unofficially to halt various activities. Facetiously, a newly made Pfc or a soldier returning from leave might say "Never mind the guard!" when reentering the squadroom.

New Army, the 1. (World War I) The draft Army of 1917–18, contrasted unfavorably with the Regulars. 2. (1945–50) The post–World War II Regular Army, which was designed to conform to the standards of a liberal, permissive society. Discipline was relaxed, sergeants spoke in dulcet tones, and there was great emphasis on travel, education, athletics, and time off. Rough, realistic training was avoided for fear of accidents and the unfavorable publicity that would result. Weapons and equipment were leftovers from World War II. This situation lasted into 1950 and then the backward, semicivilized veterans of the North Korean Army whipped the socks off us, despite our air superiority, for two unhappy months. Later, the Chinese Communists rubbed it in.

newbie newfer (Vietnam and later) *s.* A replacement, a new man in a unit. *Newfer* may have been derived from *new fucker*, reinforced by *FNG*. "To better familiarize those newfers who have just arrived in Vietnam" (AR 7:5, 1 February 1971).

New Guinea salute (World War II; all Services) *s.* The constant waving of a hand over one's mess kit at mealtime in an attempt to keep off the swarms of flies and related insects.

New Regulars 1. (Mexican War) Regular units—one regiment of dragoons, nine of infantry—belatedly authorized by Congress in February 1847 for the duration of the war only. The men were good, but their officers were mostly deserving Democrats, appointed from civilian life, "who might have figured on a race course, or at an election, but evidently had but little acquaintance with barracks or battlefield" (Semmes). So handicapped, these New Regulars had to learn their trade the hard way, but eventually mastered it. See *mustang army, raw levies*. 2. (Civil War; USA) Men who enlisted in the Regular Army after the war began. "The new men were mostly Regulars, or as they were called, the 'New Regulars,' to distinguish them from the Old Regulars, who had been with the Battery before the war" (Buell).

news walkers (Civil War; USA) Soldiers who would go from regiment to regiment after a battle, exchanging news as to what actually had happened. It was reputed to be a point of honor not to give false information.

nickel promotion See *5 percent promotion*.

night fighter 1. (World War I and World War II) Specially equipped fighter aircraft, used to intercept night-raiding bombers. 2. (Mostly World War I, but some use in World War II and perhaps after) *s.* A black soldier. The term originated in World War I, when American black troops allegedly misled trusting mademoiselles by assuring them that they were really white men who had been given a special pill that would darken their skins as camouflage for night fighting. Once the war was over, the story continued, a counteracting pill would restore them as whites.

nightingale (Colonial) *s.* A British Army term for a soldier who "sang" (cried out) while being flogged. In some regiments, grenadiers made it a point of honor not to sing; they chewed on a bullet to bear the pain.

night owl (Air Force) *s.* A night bombing mission.

nine (Modern) *s.* Pay grade E-9, or sergeant major. "I should make the nine list next year" means "I should be selected for promotion to sergeant major next year."

ninety-day loss (Modern) *s.* A soldier who is within ninety days of leaving the service or completing an overseas tour. He will probably be a total loss so far as getting any work out of him goes. See *stack arms.*

ninety-day wonder (World War I and World War II) *s.* A lieutenant commissioned after graduation from a three-month General Officers' Training School. It was not much training, but it was more than the officers newly commissioned from civilian life had had in any of our earlier wars. Also called *three-month wonder.*

95th Article of War "Any officer or cadet who is convicted of conduct unbecoming an officer and a gentleman shall be dismissed from the service." The *Uniform Code of Military Justice* of 1950 changed the last portion to "shall be punished as a court-martial may direct." Old files still mutter about "acceptable degrees of dishonor," and officers' standards of conduct certainly have not improved noticeably. The comparable AW for enlisted men was the 96th.

91 bedpans 91 Band-Aids (Modern) *s.* An Army medical specialist, MOS code 91B.

Nip (World War II) *s.* A Japanese. From *Nippon*, one of the native names for Japan.

nit noy (Modern) 1. *s.* Something trivial, insignificant. "Problems . . . so nit noy they could be overlooked" (Broughton). Broughton claims that this expression is from the Thai for *a little thing.* 2. *s.* Fault-finding, chicken shit. "Let's not be nit noy about this."

No-clap Medal (World War II and later) *s.* A nickname for the enlisted man's Good Conduct Metal, implying that a soldier is assured of getting it if he avoids VD. Also called the *Uninsubordination Medal.*

no doubt in my military mind, There is (Modern) *s.* A mock-serious catchphrase indicating that one is absolutely certain. Poking fun at pomposity and the "military mind."

No guts, no glory (World War II) *s.* A consoling little phrase to be uttered just before you stick your neck out, in the hope that you will believe yourself.

no hair off [one's] ass (World War II; possibly still used) *s.* Whatever is about to happen will cause one neither grief nor loss. "If that goonie wants to get himself killed, it's no hair off my ass." Also, as in civilian slang, *no skin off my ass.*

noise discipline (Modern) A field operating condition in which precautions are taken to deaden or suppress any noise. A blackout of sound.

No Man's Land (World War I) *s.* The space between the two opposing front-line trenches, inhabited only by corpses and occasional patrols.

No Man's Nam (Vietnam and later) *s.* Vietnam. "It's about thirteen thousand miles to No Man's Nam" (Durden).

nomenclature (Antiquity uncertain to Modern; all Services) The detailed naming of each component part of a weapon, vehicle, or other piece of equipment. With a weapon, you disassemble it and then reassemble it, identifying each part as you proceed. This might sound chicken, but you finish knowing each part of the weapon and its function. You are thus not completely helpless if your weapon malfunctions during a night action. Similarly, tankers are expected to know the important parts of their tank. If something about it goes haywire, they can tell their maintenance people what is wrong, instead of babbling about the little gismo behind the whatchamacallit. All this is pretty much the standard meaning of *nomenclature*, but during World War II it was sometimes extended to mean a description, explanation, or process, not necessarily equipment, as in "Hey, sarge, what's the nomenclature on getting a three-day pass next week?" In other words, "How does one go about getting a three-day pass?"

noncom (Ancient to Modern; also Marines, Air Force) An abbreviation of *noncommissioned officer*. In Great Britain this form goes as far back as the mid–18th century. In the US Army, according to Lighter, it dates from at least the 1830s and is probably older.

noncommissioned officer (17th-century British Army to Modern) A person in the chain of command, standing between the commissioned officers, on the one hand, and the privates who make up the bulk of the army, on the other hand. As the title indicates, he is a person in authority, but he does not hold an appointment (commission) signed by the President; he derives his rank and authority from his commanding officer. Since he is an enlisted man, in normal circumstances he serves for limited periods of time (*hitches, enlistments*), which are renewable (all things permitting) until retirement age. His function (depending on his exact position) is leadership, training, and administration. He does not receive the salute or the other recognitions of a commissioned officer and is not addressed as *sir*. At present, the grades of noncommissioned officer, in ascending order, are corporal; sergeant; staff sergeant; sergeant first class or platoon sergeant; master sergeant and first sergeant; sergeant major and command sergeant major; and the position Sergeant Major of the Army. At other times the grades have been different. See the individual grades.

nongraduate (20th century, but possibly somewhat earlier) *s.* An officer who has come into the service, especially the Regular Army, through some other channel than graduation from the US Military Academy. Probably the most illustrious examples have been Winfield Scott and George C. Marshall. Their numbers naturally increase during and immediately after major wars, but dwindle in the lean years between. They probably will be fewer in the future, now that the size of the Academy's Corps of Cadets has been doubled for the sacrosanct purpose of fielding a better football team that can always beat Navy. See *mustang, side-door officer, Tommy-tot*.

nonselect (Modern) *s.* Someone who has been considered, but not selected, for promotion. Like the euphemisms for *kill*, this word, in its sterility, conveys a chilling cynicism that makes its use cruel.

nonseller (Modern) *s.* An action or proposal that won't fly, or won't be approved.

North Joe (Korea) *s.* A North Korean soldier or guerrilla.

North U-Buckle (World War II, but possibly earlier) *s.* A range at the Artillery School, Fort Sill, Oklahoma. It is a tricky bit of terrain. What you think is a small bush in the middle of a flat may be the tip of a tall tree growing at the bottom of a deep-cut gully. Its proper name is the North Arbuckle, but so many students got a *U* (Unsatisfactory) for the problems they fired there that it was unofficially rebaptized.

nothing is too good for the troops (Modern) *s.* A catchphrase: "Nothing is too good for the troops, so that's what they get." Or "Nothing is good enough for the troops, so that's what they get."

Not only *no*, but *hell* no! (Modern) *s.* A famous catchphrase meaning *no*.

novelty troops (World War II) *s.* A nickname for airborne troops that never quite caught on.

nuisance, to commit a (Old, Old Army to World War II) To urinate or defecate elsewhere than at the latrine. Men newly away from home seem to forget the basic decencies of personal cleanliness. Moses had to give the Children of Israel a crash course on camp sanitation (Deut. 23: 9–14), before launching his invasion of Palestine. And, although New Englanders supposedly studied the Bible devoutly, Washington had to instruct them on sanitation after taking command of the Continental Army. The expression itself seems to be peculiarly military.

nukes (1945 on) *s.* Nuclear weapons, whether bombs, artillery shells, torpedoes, demolition charges, or rocket warheads.

number cruncher (Modern) 1. *s.* Any kind of analyst who works with figures. 2. *s.* A computer.

number one (Old Army to Modern) 1. In a post guard, the sentry stationed at the guardhouse. It was his special function to turn out the guard at the approach of the commanding officer, the officer of the day, visiting brass, or "armed parties" other than troops undergoing training. 2. *s.* The first seat (nearest the entrance) in a latrine, reputedly the source of the wildest latrine rumors. "I heard it from number one."

number one . . . number ten (Post–World War II, possibly earlier among troops in the Far East, to Modern) *s.* Number *one* means the best or the most important in American usage, but the concept of numerical classification is much stronger in the cultures of the Far East. *Number-one boy* was the senior servant in the household; *number-one son* (as with Charlie Chan) was the eldest son, and thereby the second most important person in the household. The scale usually goes down to number ten, which is the worst and lowest. "He turned to the girl he'd been with and gave her the finger [made an obscene gesture]. 'So long, pig.' 'You number ten, GI.' 'You number fuckin' ten,' Slagel said" (Smith). GIs often pronounced *number ten* as *numbah ten*, in imitation of Korean or Vietnamese pronunciation. Extension numbers are *number queo* 'number twelve', mimicking Vietnamese pronunciation; *number one thousand* (very bad); and *number ten thousand* or *number ten thou* (very, very bad). In Oriental culture, ten thousand is a more important number than with us.

number-ten can (Modern) A tin can that holds about 2 quarts of liquid; it is a unit size for many kinds of food. When empty, these cans see good service in many ways: holding expended brass on the firing range, serving as butt cans, etc. *Number ten* has nothing to do with the Oriental rank system, as in the previous entry; it is simply a commercial designation of size.

nuoc nam (Vietnam) *s.* Vietnamese name for armpit sauce.

nylon (Modern; Air Force) *s.* A parachute. "He headed for Hanoi via nylon" (Broughton).

☆☆☆☆O☆☆☆☆

oak-leaf cluster A bronze or silver twig of four oak leaves, with three acorns, issued for second or succeeding awards of certain decorations. The silver oak-leaf cluster is worn in lieu of five bronze clusters.

OAO (Late 19th century and later; West Point) *s.* One And Only. Your really important girl.

obstacle course (World War II to Modern) A sadistic training device designed to make you do things—like crossing creeks by swinging Tarzan-fashion from branch to branch—that no sensible person would otherwise attempt. However, even after chipping a toe on a trip wire hidden in tall grass, while wearing a gas mask in heavy smoke, we do not quite buy the story that the first obstacle course was designed by a division surgeon who wanted more practice treating compound fractures. Now called a *confidence course.*

O-club (Modern) *s.* An officers' club, where food, drink, entertainment, and check-cashing are available to commissioned officers, warrant officers, and their dependents.

OCONUS (Modern) Out of the Continental United States.

OCS (World War II to Modern) Officer Candidate School. Such schools were established in July 1941, when Army Chief of Staff George C. Marshall decided that offering draftees a chance to win officers' commissions was necessary to keep up troop morale. Later, as the Army was enlarged, OCSs were an essential source of new shavetails—the modern version of the ninety-day wonder. When first established, OCS consisted of a thirteen-week training program. This was expanded to twenty-three weeks during the Korean War. At the moment, only three schools are still in operation: Infantry, at Fort Benning, Georgia; Artillery, at Fort Sill, Oklahoma; and Engineers, at Fort Belvoir, Virginia.

OCS manual (Modern) *s.* A comic book, from the widespread belief among enlisted personnel that no special intelligence is required to obtain a commission from OCS.

OCS material (Modern) 1. *s.* Facetiously, someone who is definitely not officer material. See *officer material.* 2. *s.* Comic books, pornographic magazines and books, or frivolous reading matter. See *OCS manual.*

OD (Old, Old Army to Modern) Officer of the Day. This is an officer who is detailed daily from a roster of qualified officers, for twenty-four hours of duty in charge of the post guards. After normal duty hours he handles the various affairs and minor emergencies that may crop up. Between midnight and reveille he inspects the guard posts. (There is an ancient Army joke about these night inspections. When challenged by a rookie sentry, the OD identified himself as Officer of the Day. He was again challenged with, "Then what you doin' out this time o' night?")

OD 1. (Old Army to post–World War II) Olive Drab, the official color of Army uniforms and of much of the Army's field equipment, from June 1902 on. Although the color OD was gradually replaced with a dark green, beginning in World War II, the term is still known. Also *od, o.d.* 2. In plural form, *ODs*, the general duty uniform, specifically that version of the uniform issued with the Ike jacket. "ODs rarely showed they were soiled and required only a quick press to look fresh and military" (Doulis).

o-dark-thirty (Modern) *s.* Very early in the morning. Actually, in the military twenty-four-hour clock, 0030, or in civilian use, 12:30 A.M. The first zero may be read as either *zero* or the letter *o.*

officer (Ancient to Modern) A soldier holding a commission or warrant. A commission is a document signed by the President conferring on the recipient the power and authority to carry out a certain task or duty. A warrant is a document signed by the Secretary of the Army certifying and authorizing the holder to perform certain specific tasks or duties.

Officer of Police (Revolutionary) According to Baron von Steuben's *Regulations*, a subaltern who was detailed daily in each battalion to discharge roughly the same duties as the modern Officer of the Day. He saw to the cleanliness and good order of the camp, supervised the distribution of supplies, and organized details to fetch in wood and water. He was assisted by four sergeants and a "drummer of the police."

officer and a gentleman, an (Ancient to Modern) According to the lore of enlisted personnel, an officer is created a gentleman by act of Congress. (Actually, the officer's commission is signed by the President.) This is often a sore point among enlisted men, who also consider themselves gentlemen. They may claim that two different persons are included in this traditional phrase, which goes back to the time when rank tended to coincide with social class. The phrase is often used by EM with uncomplimentary qualifications: "An officer and a gentleman by act of Congress; otherwise he wouldn't have made it." "An officer and a gentleman by act of Congress; everyone else has to earn it."

officer material (Modern) *s.* Not officer material. Ironic.

Officer of the Night (Old, Old Army to at least World War II) *s.* A joking version of *Officer of the Day*, based on the OD's duty to inspect sentries between midnight and reveille.

officers and their ladies, sergeants and their wives (Old Army and later) A thoroughly caste-conscious expression used in invitations to social affairs, such as enlisted men's formal dances. There the commanding officer led the grand march with the sergeant major's wife, followed by the sergeant major with the CO's spouse or, if the CO was a bachelor, the ranking lady on the post. After the first ceremonial dance, the officers and their ladies departed quietly and the fun began.

officers' call (Antiquity uncertain; probably developed during the 1830s) A bugle call summoning officers to report to their regimental or battalion headquarters immediately. It was sounded either for routine meetings or in emergencies. Since it was a peculiarly American call, it was used on occasion during the Indian Wars and Mexican Punitive Expedition as a recognition signal between units trying to establish contact at night. Like most of the other calls, it has faded into disuse. Words associated with it:

Young officers, old officers, field
officers all.
You're ordered to headquarters by
officers' call.

Or

Come to the colonel, the colonel,
the colonel.
Come to the colonel, the colonel,
the colonel.

Officers Call (Modern) An official pamphlet, published at intervals, keeping the Army's officers informed on various current subjects.

Officer's Good Conduct Medal (Generally 1950s to Modern) *s.* Officers are never awarded the *Good Conduct Medal*, which is for enlisted men only. The term, always used in jest (however sardonic) may mean: 1. The Legion of Merit, now awarded to all retiring senior officers who have kept their noses reasonably clean and have not been caught in any display of unusual incompetence. 2. (Among enlisted men) Promotion to first lieutenant. Soldiers consider that this promotion is as easy for a shavetail to achieve as it is for the average soldier to get the Good Conduct Medal.

officer swine (Modern) *s.* Officers. A term used by enlisted swine in reprisal for being called *enlisted swine*. It goes around in a circle.

official terms, on (Old Army to at least World War II) The situation existing when two officers are personally estranged, with no good prospect of reconciliation. They carry out their respective duties as usual without allowing themselves to be influenced by their personal feelings and speak to one another only as is necessary, in "official terms." See *third-person address.*

off limits (20th century) The Army's quaint way of saying "Keep out." It is often overused in rear areas where the Blue Star Rangers of all ranks thus stake out the decent recreational facilities for their own enjoyment. However, it can be used defensively to close off areas and businesses that do not observe proper sanitary procedures or that fleece military customers.

of the Army (Modern) *s.* A soldier who is career-oriented or is serious about his military business. The opposite is *in the Army.*

Oh, Be Joyful (Civil War; USA) *s.* Nickname for hard liquor, especially commissary whiskey, which was noted for its bite-you-back taste. The term sounds as if it might have a biblical reference, perhaps Ecclesiastes 7:14. Other names were *Oil of Gladness, Tanglefoot, How Come You So, Nockum Stiff*, and *Condensed Corn*. The term is somewhat earlier in Great Britain.

OHIO (1941) *s.* Over the Hill In October. A slogan that was written on buildings, vehicles, and anything else that did not run away, in camps where National Guard Divisions were stationed. The National Guard had been called to active duty for one year in late 1940. A good many of its members could see no hostile threat to the United States and had no clear idea why they had been called out. *OHIO* was their threat that if they were not properly demobilized when their year was up, they were going home anyway. However, when Congress extended their service to eighteen months in August, they accepted the extension. Then came Pearl Harbor.

Ohio gas mask (Post–World War II) *s.* An Americanization of Japanese *ohayō gozaimasu* 'good morning'.

-oid (At least 1900 to early World War II; West Point) A slang suffix meaning someone who does things habitually. For example, a *bonoid* (1900) is one who bones, or studies very hard; a *crawloid* (1900) is one who is frequently rebuked; a *hopoid* (1900) is one who is in constant attendance at hops or dances; and a *specoid* (1939) is one who specs, or memorizes verbatim. Now obsolete.

ojo /'o-ho/ (Old Army to World War I) *s.* Eye, from Spanish *ojo.* "Keep an ojo on those greasers."

Old Army (Antiquity uncertain to Modern) The Army not too long ago, before civilians invaded it, when things were tougher but better and soldiers really soldiered. While there is sometimes truth to this, since any institution will have its ups and downs, it is also a state of mind, and the Old Army is invoked by soldiers in a spirit of defiant nostalgia. In 1900, the Old Army was the Army before the Spanish-American War; before World War II, it was the Army before World War I; after World War II, it was the Army in the days before the war; and so on. A good early example of the Old Army is to be found in Croffut's edition of the diaries of Lt. Col. Ethan Allen Hitchcock, Acting Inspector General to Gen. Winfield Scott's army in the Mexican War: "Originally my great hope in joining General Scott's staff was to escape orders of mushroom generals,—political appointments usually—men who know nothing of the science or art of war, and who, in fact, are indebted for all the reputation they ever acquire to the science in the main body of the old regular army, which many of them pretend to despise. Without the discipline, organization, and tactics of the old army, the new army, generals and all, would be but a loose mob." (20 February 1848).

Old Blood and Guts (World War II) *s.* The final, and most common nickname, of Gen. George S. Patton. In a lecture to the officers of his 2d Armored Division at Fort Benning in 1941, he stated that the war would be won by "blood and guts alone"; the phrase was characteristic, and his troops adopted it. Sometimes phrased as "Old Blood and Guts—his guts and our blood!"

old file (Old, Old Army to at least World War I) *s.* A veteran officer of long service, advancing age, and—usually—hardening disposition. Also, he was ahead of you on the promotion list, unless you were a somewhat older file yourself. The term can also be applied to an enlisted man, but with a different meaning. See *file.*

Old Fuss and Feathers (Early 19th century, especially Mexican War) *s.* Maj. Gen. Winfield Scott, possibly the greatest general in the history of the United States and certainly one of the most difficult.

Old Guard (Old, Old Army to Modern) The 3d Infantry Regiment, so baptized by Maj. Gen. Winfield Scott during the

Mexican War. The oldest Regular Infantry regiment in the US Army, the 3d is now the Army's security and ceremonial unit for Washington, D.C.

old ish (Post–World War II to Modern) *s.* Oneself. From German *ich* 'I', in South German pronunciation.

Old Joe Chink (Korea) *s.* Chinese Communist troops.

Old Leatherface (World War II) *s.* Maj. Gen. Claire L. Chennault, an officer of great tactical skill and high-octane ego, commander of the Flying Tigers and later the US 14th Air Force in the CBI.

Old Line Another, not too common way of saying *Old Army*, but emphasizing the combat elements. To us, it is the Regular Infantry, Cavalry, Field Artillery, and Engineers of 1900–40—the men who taught us their trade. From them we learned that a soldier should "go proudly, for he is not as other men."

Old Man 1. (At least Old Army to Modern; also Navy) *s.* The commanding officer. Back before World War II, in the days of fifty-year-old captains and first lieutenants with graying beards, the term made literal sense. But in 1946, C Battery, 24th Field Artillery Battalion (Philippine Scouts) was commanded by an eighteen-year-old shavetail, fresh out of OCS and allegedly too young to be allowed in the bar of the officers' mess without adult escort. His first sergeant was old enough to be his grandfather, but the lieutenant was the Old Man of Charlie Battery. He did age visibly the first few months, but his Scouts liked him and it was a first-rate outfit. As for the term itself, although it may be fairly recent in the Army, it was common usage in the American merchant marine (for the captain of a ship) in the early 19th century. 2. (World War II) *s.* Lower-cased, *old man* was the standard German Army meat ration, so called because it was reputedly made from dead old men.

Old Regulars (Civil War; USA) Men who enlisted in the Regular Army before the war. See *New Regulars*.

Old Rough and Ready (Mexican War) *s.* Maj. Gen. Zachary Taylor. A really rough, brave fighting man, he was as vain as Winfield Scott, but his opposite in almost everything else.

old soldier A term that has the same ambivalence as *GI* or *to soldier*. 1. (Mexican War) *s.* A disciplined, reliable soldier, possibly lacking verve and imagination, never in trouble, but not too popular with his less-steady comrades. 2. (World War II on) *s.* A solid, steady, reliable man who has a sound knowledge of how things are done and is helpful to his juniors. Or his opposite—a sly sneak who manages to escape work and many of the unpleasantnesses of the Army, yet carefully avoids punishment. He is good at goldbricking and brown-nosing, is utterly selfish, and a little crooked. He usually doesn't understand (if he is that perceptive) why his comrades despise him.

Old Soldier's Home (Old, Old Army to World War I) *s.* The latrine, a favorite place of refuge for goldbricks. It is also a handy place to get rid of worn-out articles or incriminating evidence. For that reason, military archaeologists consider a long-abandoned latrine a treasure trove.

on command (Colonial to Revolutionary) Descriptive of soldiers detailed for special duty, such as teamsters, armorers, officers' servants, artificers, butchers, and bakers; or those on detached military service. In 1780, General Washington ordered the first category carried as *on extra service*.

one a-shootin', ten a-lootin' (World War II) *s.* A contemptuous description of units up to division level that appeared lacking in aggressiveness. The implication, of course, was that they could not be got to fight, preferring to rummage through houses behind their front line.

one each (Modern) *s.* One. From the ubiquitous practice of listing individual items on requisition forms as *one each.*

one-eyed zipper snake (Modern) *s.* The penis.

one for one (Old, Old Army to Modern) *s.* A system of loan-sharking that would have made Shylock blush. An improvident soldier would borrow a dollar on the understanding that he would pay it back the next payday with another dollar as interest. This was also termed *1 percent* or *soldier's 1 percent.* In hard times, the going rate might be five for three.

one hundred mission crush (World War II; Air Force) *s.* An Air Force officer's jaunty way of wearing the peaked cap. The grommet that held the crown rigid was removed, allowing the crown to collapse. This style was supposedly restricted by custom to officers who had completed a hundred missions against the enemy, but stateside it was often affected by youngsters on their first leave from flying school and by chairborne types who never flew anything more dangerous than a swivel chair.

one in the hanger, to have (Modern; Air Force) To be pregnant.

one man, one bunk (Old Army into World War II) A basic law of service etiquette. A soldier's bunk was his castle. Another soldier did not touch it. To sit on it without being invited was to risk violent reprisal and public condemnation. The executioner might consider the matter.

One-Oh-Worst *s.* The 101st Airborne Division; also called the *Puking Buzzards.*

one-pounder (World War I) The stubby little French 37mm cannon, used either as the main weapon of the Renault tank or as an infantry support weapon to knock out enemy machine-gun positions and strong points. In later years, it was used for sub-caliber artillery practice.

One-seventy, the (World War II) A drink—half champagne, half cognac—developed in General Patton's 3d Army headquarters in 1944. It was useful in lubricating less aggressive people like Bradley and Eisenhower into a cooperative mood. Although we have seen no explanation for its name, we suspect that it came from the powerful, long-range German 170mm gun.

one-star (Modern) *s.* Brigadier general.

on the deck (Modern; all Services) *s.* To be flying just above the ground itself.

on the line On the firing line.

On your horse, amigo? (Korea and later) *s.* How are you? An American way of saying the Korean greeting variously transcribed as *annyong hasipnika* or *annyøng hasipnigga* 'How are you?'

O pay grades (Modern) The present classification of officers by base pay: O-1, second lieutenant; O-2, first lieutenant; O-3, captain; O-4, major; O-5, lieutenant colonel; O-6, colonel; O-7, brigadier general; O-8, major general; O-9, lieutenant general; O-10, general and General of the Army.

ORB (Modern) Officer Record Brief. A thumbnail record of how you have been doing. Periodically, unit and post bulletins show the notice "Officers may review their ORBs," which somehow sounds hilarious to reprobate old sweats like us.

orderly 1. (Colonial to Modern; all Services) An enlisted person detailed for special duty, usually as a messenger. It was customary for a member of the guard to be selected each day as headquarters orderly on the basis of his personal appearance and alertness. The assignment was much coveted, since it involved little work and fair comfort. It was the source of much competition among soldiers and companies. In other situations, mounted officers were usually accompanied by mounted orderlies who looked after the officers' horses when they dismounted. Dining-room orderlies work in the unit mess hall, and medical orderlies look after hospital wards and assist medical officers. 2. Sometimes called *personal orderly*. A striker or dog robber. In the case of a general officer, the orderly might be an NCO and his duties might be enlarged to those of an enlisted aide-de-camp. Today, in keeping with the New Army's tendency to find nice official names for everyone and everything, an orderly is called an *enlisted aide*.

orderly room (Old, Old Army to Modern) The "office" of a company, battery, or troop commander; the place where company administration is handled by the first sergeant and the company clerk. For historical reasons, it is still called the *orderly room*, and not *company headquarters*.

orderly sergeant (Colonial to Civil War) A duty assignment, not a specific grade of sergeant. Two different usages are apparent. 1. A sergeant detailed as an orderly to a general officer or to other officers (probably senior members of the staff) "entitled to have" a sergeant as orderly. 2. More commonly, a responsible sergeant (usually detailed by roster) in each company, whose duties included reporting to regimental headquarters at prescribed times, or on call, to take down in his company "orderly book" the orders dictated by the adjutant or sergeant major. This done, he immediately brought them to his company commander's attention. (It was strictly prescribed that he wear his sergeant's sash when on such duty.) His responsibilities have passed on to the first sergeant.

order of march The arrangement of troops or units for a march. This necessarily varies according to several factors: the type of troops, day or night, peacetime or wartime, presence or absence of the enemy, and type of road and terrain.

Order of the Concrete Cross the Concrete Cross (World War I and World War II) *s.* A fictitious award. To say that a man had received this decoration meant that he had been killed or possibly just gotten thoroughly in trouble. There were several such fictitious awards, such as the Order of the Barbed Wire Garter for simple nuisances, but most of them were local affairs. The Germans had a widely used one, the "Far behind the Lines Medal, with Knife and Fork."

Order of the Shovel, to get the (World War I) *s.* To be killed (and buried).

Order of the Winged Boot (World War II; Air Force) Formed in 1943, a loose association of Allied airmen who were shot down over German-held territory but managed to avoid capture and to walk back to their own forces. Their insignia was a winged flight boot embroidered in silver bullion (or, for units based in Italy, of cast silver), worn on the upper left pocket flap of the uniform coat, just below decorations and campaign ribbons. These men were also called *Late Arrivals*.

ordnance 1. (Colonial to Modern; all Services) Basically, weapons and ammunition of all kinds. This meaning was common in Shakespeare's time. Stage directions for the ghost scene of *Hamlet* include "a flourish of trumpets, and ordnance shot off, within." 2. (Early 19th century on) All supplies issued by the Army's Ordnance Department, not just weapons and ammunition but, at various times, cartridge boxes or belts, haversacks, saddles, artillery harness, and motor vehicles. There were occasional rows when items of Ordnance issue did not fit together with Quartermaster items—for example, the straps of the Quartermaster infantry knapsack and the Ordnance issue waist belt, during the Civil War. 3. *s.* The individual soldier often refers to his personal weapons as his *ordnance* and—at least before and during World War II—might apply the same term to his knife, fork, and spoon. See also *deliver ordnance.*

ordnance job (World War II and later) *s.* Originally this referred to a damaged vehicle or weapon that could not be repaired by the individual soldier or by battalion or regimental mechanics. It would be turned over to an Ordnance Corps unit for proper work. Later, the term was often applied to any thing, plan, or situation that was going to require extensive alteration by real experts. "That's an ordnance job" just means "That's beyond your ability."

ordnance men men of ordnance (19th century) For some reason, these terms were used officially for enlisted men of the Ordnance Department. They were never called *privates.* We have been unable to determine just when this unusual practice ended.

organic (Modern) Equipment, weapons, or personnel assigned to, and forming an essential part of, a unit. "After all . . . your transport is organic" (Bunting).

organizational shoulder sleeve insignia (Modern) What earlier soldiers, in their naiveté, called simply a *shoulder patch.*

organized grab-ass (Modern) *s.* Physical training, calisthenics.

orgasm in place (Relatively Modern) *s.* An outburst, usually highly vocal, of anger/bad temper. The GI equivalent of what an Englishman means when he says "threw a proper fit." "When I asked for another three-day pass, the topkick really had an orgasm in place."

orioles (Post–World War I) *s.* The plebes taken into the more-than-somewhat disorganized US Military Academy in November 1918 were issued OD enlisted men's uniforms with an orange hatband as a distinctive insignia. Thereafter, they were known throughout their service as the *orioles.*

Orphan Brigade (Civil War; CSA) *s.* A brigade formed early in the war of regiments raised in Kentucky for the Confederate service. Since Union forces soon established control over Kentucky, these troops became "orphans" with no home state to support them. Nevertheless, they maintained a good combat record.

oscar charlie (Modern) *s.* Old Crow bourbon whiskey. From the letters of the phonetic alphabet for *o* and *c.* "Take you some Oscar Charlie there . . ." (Smith).

ossifer (At least World War II to Modern) *s.* A play on *officer.* Perhaps with some indebtedness to the early comic strip "Krazy Kat," with *Ossifer Pup.*

OTC (World War I) Officers' Training Camps. Later renamed *Officers' Training Schools* (OTS). These produced 80,568 ninety-day wonders during the war.

outfit (Post–Civil War to Modern) *s.* In common talk, a soldier refers to the military organization to which he belongs as his *outfit*, a very handy word. A stranger will be asked what outfit he belongs to, rather than what battalion or division.

outgoing (At least World War II to Modern; also Marines) Describing weapons fire, particularly artillery, directed at the enemy. The opposite of *incoming*.

outgoing mail (World War II) Your artillery shelling the enemy. The opposite of *incoming mail*.

outrank, to out rank, to (At least 1840s to Modern) To be another person's superior in rank or senior in grade because of date of rank. See *rank*.

outside (About 1900 to Modern; extensive use 1942 on) *s.* Civilian life; the world outside the post, camp, or fort where a soldier is stationed. "What did you do on the outside?" is a question frequently asked of new soldiers, meaning "What did you do in civilian life?" But to the men of the self-contained Old Army *outside* could be a strange, hostile jungle where their money was welcome, but they frequently were not. To modern soldiers, however, the outside is the place where they want to be. This was almost universally true of the draftee, which led to some very unfavorable comparisons between Army and civilian life. One suggestion is that this term may have been borrowed from prison slang, where similar expressions date from at least as early as the 1880s, reflecting the notion that the Army is an institutional thing. To a professional, however, it simply means outside one's tight-knit little world, as in Kipling's lines:

> There is a world outside the one
> you know
> To which for curiousness 'Ell can't
> compare—

outside man (At least World War II to Modern) 1. A KP detailed to perform certain duties on the outside of the mess hall. It is considered an excellent job, because the outside man is generally out of the mess sergeant's sight. 2. *s.* By extension, anyone who enjoys a cushy job or sinecure. "I missed getting in on the Last Supper because I was outside man that day."

over age in grade (World War II) Age limits were established for commissioned officers, and officers who were older than the limit were termed *over age in grade*. This classification, which probably affected company officers more than higher grades, limited the posts to which an officer could be assigned and his chances of promotion and retention in the service.

overage MOS (Modern) An MOS (Military Occupation Specialty) in which there are more soldiers serving (in terms of the total Army) than are needed. The opposite is *shortage MOS*.

over and under (Modern; also Marines) *s.* An M16 rifle mounted with a grenade-launching tube.

overhead (Modern) 1. The personnel in a unit who provide indirect support (clerical, etc.) for those who perform the direct mission (combat, construction, communications, etc.). The company misfits are often placed with the overhead personnel. 2. The place where the overhead personnel live. 3. (Navy) The ceiling.

overs (Antiquity uncertain to Modern) *s.* Artillery rounds that land over or beyond the target. See *shorts and overs*.

overseas cap (World War I to Modern) Another name for the modern field cap, a cloth cap designed so that it could be folded and carried in the pocket while the soldier was wearing his steel helmet. During World War I, it was authorized for wear only overseas.

overseas service bar overseas service stripe (1946 to Modern) A cloth gold bar worn by officers and EM to denote service in specified overseas combat theaters. Each bar represents six months' service. At present, overseas bars are worn just above the lower outside edge of the right sleeve, but from 1946 to April 1953 they were worn on the left sleeve. The overseas service bar took the place of the earlier service-in-war chevron, which, however, was not phased out immediately for soldiers who had earned such chevrons in World War I. Also called *Hershey bar.*

Oversexed Weekly (Modern) *s.* The *Overseas Weekly*, a private newspaper published for, and distributed among, soldiers in Europe and the Pacific. It publishes such matters as Army scandal and pictures of scantily dressed young ladies, but its publishers deserve credit for being among the first to take the side of the enlisted soldiers and to remind commanders that it is better to admit mistakes than to try to cover them up.

overslaugh, to /over-slah/ (Colonial to early 19th century) Early version of to pass over. To give a promotion to someone junior to the officer entitled to it by seniority. The latter officer was thereby *overslaughed.*

over the fence, to go (World War II) *s.* To sneak out of camp temporarily, perhaps for an evening in town, with the firm intention of returning before bed-check or reveille. Sometimes this was literally over the fence, but in one post, Fort Sheridan, it was around the fence, where it jutted out into Lake Michigan, and in another post, it was crawling under the fence. The soldiers concerned (no matter what the CO might have thought) did not consider this being AWOL.

over the hill, to go (Old, Old Army to Modern) *s.* To desert. The origin of the phrase is not known. Wentworth and Flexner consider it prison slang taken over by the Army. Others have suggested that it arose during the years of frontier service, where a desertion would literally be over the hill. On the other hand, "Over the hills and far away" was a common enough 19th century expression, the refrain of popular songs. It may not be coincidence that in George Farquhar's play *The Recruiting Officer* (1706), in a song describing the life of a soldier, the refrain is "over the hills and far away."

over the hump 1. (Old Army to World War II) *s.* Halfway through your enlistment. You now have the world by the tail with a downhill pull. 2. (World War II) *s.* In the CBI, the aerial supply route from India over the 15,000-foot eastern Himalayas, into China, was called the Hump. It could be far rougher than any Happy Valley raid. So many planes flying it crashed that one bad section became known as the *Aluminum Trail.*

over the shoulder missions (Modern; Air Force) *s.* Indoctrination missions, on which new aircrews on actual combat missions are accompanied by seasoned pilots and navigators.

over-two (Modern) *s.* Two-thirds (two years) through a regular enlistment. "As of tomorrow I'm over-two."

Owls (Civil War; CSA) *s.* Desertion. When men slipped away under cover of darkness, it was said that "the Owls caught them."

☆☆☆☆*P*☆☆☆☆

P 1. (West Point) *s.* Cadet slang for an instructor. Apparently quite old, from the days when the permanent professors handled a large share of the instruction. "Monsieur Micaud is my Frog P." 2. (Old Army to Modern) Prisoner. The letter *p* was stenciled in white or red paint on the fatigues worn by prisoner work details to indicate their status:

He'll soon be down in Comp'ny Q
A-sleeping in a cell.
A big red *p* stamped on his back,
O'Reilly's gone to hell!

3. (Vietnam) *s.* The Vietnamese piaster. In the official rate of exchange, the piaster fluctuated between 73.5 in 1962 to 118 to the dollar during the closing years of the war, but the black-market rate was several times that of the official rate. "Two thousand P buys a lot of short-time, my man" (Heinemann). Also *pee.* 4. (Modern) *s.* Short for *MP* or *AP*.

pack (Modern; Air Force) *s.* An area targeted for bombing; short for *route package*. The packs are usually assigned to specific commands of the US Air Force, or US Navy.

pack battery (20th century) A battery of mountain guns (actually light howitzers) transported by pack mules. Its men had to be taller and stronger than the average artilleryman to get loads onto the big, ornery American mules. Usually the pack batteries could outmarch infantry on the roads or across country.

Oh, I'd rather be a soldier
With a mule and a mountain gun
Than a knight of old
With spurs of gold,
Or a Roman, Greek, or Hun
For when there's something doing,
They always send for me . . .

packer (Old, Old Army to World War II) A soldier or civilian employee who knew how to load and manage pack mules. It was a hard and demanding discipline, and its experts were a proud and touchy lot, frequently as cantankerous as their charges. During the Philippine Insurrection (1898–1901) it was claimed that Moros on the prod would rather take on a troop of cavalry than a Quartermaster pack train. (Our sainted uncle, who served with both, told us this.) Packers were inclined to shoot on first suspicion, without waiting for open demonstrations of hostility.

We are the boys who build the
packs
And throw the diamond hitch.
If anyone says he's better than us,
He's a lying son-of-a-bitch!

Their skills were considered antique and unnecessary by the motorized, mechanized Army that went into World War II. Almost immediately, the jungled hills of Burma and Italy's perpendicular landscape proved packers as essential as ever, and there was a panic flap to find men with the requisite knowledge.

padlock, to (Modern; Air Force) *s.* To make a visual sighting of enemy aircraft; to "lock onto" by sight. Looking away breaks contact.

padre (Old Army to Modern) A chaplain of any Christian denomination. Since the title is respectful, it may be employed as a form of address. The Army first used it for native priests during the Mexican War, but its transfer to American chaplains was limited by their relative scarcity. The term was first commonly used during the occupation of the Philippines.

palace guard (Modern) *s.* A security element formed to provide perimeter security for a fire base or headquarters. Traditionally, a palace guard was a group of elite troops of unswerving loyalty whose duty it was to guard the sovereign or the palace.

paleface (Civil War; USA) *s.* A new recruit. Perhaps from the Indian use of the word. The troops were avid readers of Beadle dime novels.

panda See *bully soup.*

panic button (World War II to Modern) *s.* An imaginary button, usually in the G-3 staff section, that is said to be punched when the situation becomes critical enough for the following verse to apply:

When in danger, when in doubt,
Run in circles, scream and shout!

panic rack (Modern; Air Force) *s.* An airplane ejection seat. When activated in an emergency, it blows clear of the plane, carrying its occupant with it.

papasan stick (Korea and later) *s.* Any of various sorts of walking stick used by elderly men in Korea and Vietnam. The term itself is composed of English *papa* and Japanese *-san*, a suffix added to names, corresponding roughly, at times, to *Mr.*

papa sierra (Modern; also Marines) *s.* A platoon sergeant, from the phonetic alphabet for the initials of his title.

paper asshole (World War II, possibly later) *s.* A term of derision for someone stupid or generally objectionable. Usually expressed as "You talk like a man with a paper asshole." We do not see any direct connection between this use and the following verse, which is a parody of the contemporary popular song "Paper Doll" as sung in the 95th Infantry Division:

I'm going to buy a paper asshole
I can call my own.
An asshole other people cannot
ream.

paper pusher (Antiquity uncertain to Modern; all Services) *s.* Anyone involved in paperwork, from the company clerk to the adjutant general. It was applied to differentiate such people from the "real Army"—"them as shoots and gets shot at." Much like a civilian *pencil pusher,* which term was also used in the Army.

parabundle (World War II and later; Air Force) A package of supplies with an attached parachute, to be dropped from a plane. See *daisy chain*.

Parachute Blondie (World War II on) *s.* A lady who reportedly hung out at Beechie Howard's Bar in Phenix City, Alabama, and personally initiated graduates of the Fort Benning Parachute School. In return for this, she pinned their new paratrooper insignia on her dress. If testimony of surviving paratroopers is to be believed, she could not have pinned all those wings on a circus tent. We believe she was thirty or forty different girls.

Parachutist Badge (World War II on) A badge awarded to soldiers who have completed the prescribed proficiency tests, specified number and types of parachute jumps, instruction at jumpmaster school, and the requisite number of months on jump status in an airborne unit. The badge is awarded in three classes: Parachutist, Senior Parachutist, and Master Parachutist. Also called *airborne wings*. See *ice cream cone with wings, master blaster*.

Parade rest! (Modern) A command in drill. The left foot is placed 10 inches to the left of the right foot. Legs are straight and weight is equally balanced on the heels and balls of the feet. Hands are centered on the belt, at the small of the back, fingers extended and joined, thumbs interlocked, and right palm turned outward. The head is held still, eyes forward. No talking or movement is permitted. The command is given only from the position of attention. Before 1939 this position was called Stand at ease!

parafrags (World War II and later) *s.* Parachute fragmentation bombs that float down gently and then burst in the air just above you.

parasite drag (World War II; Air Force) *s.* The kind of girl who drags her date into a jewelry store instead of an ice cream parlor.

parent unit (Modern) The unit to which a soldier belongs. "All men report to Major Tatum regardless of parent unit" (Doulis).

Parleyvoo (World War I, but also Colonial and Revolutionary) *s.* A Frenchman or Frenchwoman. From French *Parlez-vous français?* 'Do you speak French?'

> Yes, Parlyvoo is true to me—
> 'Cause she is true to the whole
> army!
> Hinky, Dinky, Parley voo!

parole (Ancient to Modern) From the French *parole*, 'a word'. 1. A pledge, in the sense of "my word of honor," given by a prisoner of war that he will fulfill certain conditions: not try to escape, not serve against his captors if released, etc. A prisoner of war who is released on such conditions is *paroled*. A captured officer who broke his parole was subject to execution if recaptured; this punishment was inflicted on at least two Mexican officers during antiguerrilla operations in 1847. While parole was an important feature of premodern war, it is no longer accepted; indeed, is forbidden to the US Army. The practice still existed on a large scale in the Civil War, and parole camps existed on both sides. 2. A secret password. Sometimes called *parole word*.

partisan (Colonial to early 19th century) A soldier—especially an officer—engaged in irregular operations. Brig. Gen. Francis Marion, the "Swamp Fox" of the American Revolution, was an outstanding example.

part pay (Modern) Partial pay issued to a soldier on a special occasion, as just before Christmas. It is deducted from money paid during the next regular pay period or periods.

party (Ancient to Modern; all Services) 1. Not a festivity, but a detail, usually one not involving much joy. A *haying party* would cut, rake, and stack hay. A *GI party* would GI the barracks. 2. A small body of troops detached from the main unit for a particular mission, such as reconnoitering or foraging. 3. (Navy) A boarding party, a portion of the crew of a warship told off to storm aboard an enemy ship and capture it by hand-to-hand fighting.

pasear (Old, Old Army to World War I) *s.* A walk or stroll. From the Spanish verb *pasear* 'to walk'. "Take a little pasear down the road and see if you can spot the rolling kitchen."

pass, to be on To be absent from one's unit for a short time, as time off. Much the commonest form is the three-day pass, which is ordinarily the maximum, although a special pass may be granted for up to ninety-six hours. The term is taken from the pass (a written permission signed by the company commander) that the soldier carries to show that he is legally absent from his unit.

passover (Modern) *s.* A soldier who has been considered for promotion as fully qualified, but not selected. Also, the situation involved. Once used exclusively of officers, but since the centralization of senior enlisted promotions, used also of enlisted personnel. "Someone told me that you'd been through more passovers than a rabbi" (Pratt and Blair).

Pass whiskey (Mexican War) *s.* Liquor of high proof and potency, brewed at El Paso, Texas. It is usually identified as an aguardiente or brandy.

paster (Old Army to Modern) A soldier detailed to patch up the holes in targets on a firing range.

Pathfinder Badge (Modern) A badge awarded by the Commandant of the US Army Infantry School at Fort Benning, Georgia, to soldiers who have completed the Pathfinder course conducted there. Pathfinders are trained in techniques of land navigation.

payday activities (Uncertain antiquity) 1. Time off on payday for settling personal financial affairs, including paying debts, going to the bank, buying PX supplies for the coming month, or goofing off at the snack bar or in the club. Payday activities were once "traditional" in the Army. Today, however, with a fully automated, centralized pay system that spits out checks to individuals on a twice-a-month option, whether or not payday activities are permitted is very much the whim of individual commanders. 2. *s.* To goof off; see *twenty-nine-day soldier.*

pay line Troops lined up to receive pay. Payday was once a very formal occasion. The soldier reported formally to the pay officer, "Private Jones reporting for pay, sir!" delivered with a snappy salute. Pay was disbursed in cash. Collections were made for various charities and company loan sharks hovered in the vicinity (but not too conspicuously) to collect their due. Today, paychecks are disbursed automatically from the finance center to the soldier's bank account or to his regular mailing address.

pay, pack, and follow (Old, Old Army) One of the unwritten responsibilities of a legal camp follower, when a PCS sent her lord and master off to some new assignment ahead of her. She paid the outstanding bills, cleared her quarters and the post, got her household treasures packed, and set off in pursuit. The expression is no longer heard, but the situation still exists.

PC (West Point) *s.* Privileged Character. A cadet who is, or considers himself, above the crowd.

PCOD (Modern) *s.* Pussy-Cut-Off-Date. The date on which a soldier on an overseas tour must cease having sexual intercourse with the native women. After this date there will not be sufficient time to identify and cure a venereal disease. Generally, two months. "Men ask me what is their pussy cut-off-date. I would allow a good four-five weeks anyway" (Bunting).

PCS (Antiquity unknown, but at least 1950s to Modern) Permanent Change of Station. You are ordered somewhere else and probably will never be back again, so clear your quarters and the post. Recently an Air Force staff chaplain pontificated that such a move could be almost as stressful as a death in the immediate family. Our senior author's wife, a "pay, pack, and follow" veteran, remembers eleven PCSs (plus almost as many temporary shifts) in thirty years of following the drum. During the second-to-last one, she quietly and simultaneously married off a best-friend's daughter in full formal style and took care of an ancient, but energetic, aunt from Kansas. She thinks that chaplain needs to see another chaplain—one with a bit more service.

PDA (West Point) Public Display of Affection. An infraction of rules unique to West Point. "PDA—public display of affection. PDA effectively speaking made it illegal . . . to touch a girl in public" (Truscott). Rules or not, we have frequently noticed it going on in public during the last few relaxed years.

pearl diver (World War II and later) *s.* A KP detailed to wash dishes. Also called a *bubble dancer* or *China clipper.*

peas upon a trencher (18th century through early 19th century) *s.* The drumbeat for breakfast. See also *roast beef.*

pebble pusher *s.* An infantryman.

pecker checker **peckerchecker** (World War II and later) *s.* A Medical Corps enlisted man. Like *penis machinist*, the term comes from the Army's periodic short-arm inspections.

pee halt (Old Army to Modern) *s.* A comfort halt.

peep (World War II) *s.* The short-lived original nickname for the quarter-ton truck, better known as *jeep.*

peloncillo /pee-lone-'see-yo/ **peloncí** (Mexican War) Mexican brown sugar issued in place of the unavailable American sugar ration. Quartermasters thought it was an acceptable substitute, but suggested boiling it with the coffee instead of adding it later. From Mexican Spanish *piloncillo* 'a dark, unrefined sugar usually sold in slabs or cones'.

pelican (1930s through World War II) *s.* A glutton. Anyone who has seen a pelican feed will know why.

penis machinist (World War II) *s.* A Medical Corps enlisted man.

Pentagon East (Vietnam) *s.* Headquarters of the US Military Assistance Command, Vietnam (MACV), located on Tan Son Nhut Air Base, on the outskirts of Saigon. This was the headquarters from which the Vietnam War was directed—the military aspects of it, anyway.

Pentagonese (World War II to Modern; all Services) *s.* A peculiar artificial language developed by the aborigines of the

Puzzle Palace for the express purpose of confusing the troops. It is extremely difficult to translate into English.

Pentagoose Noose (Modern) *s.* Nickname for the *Pentagram News*, published weekly and distributed free to Department of Defense civilian and military personnel working at the Pentagon.

peon (Korea) *s.* 1. An airborne term for nearly everyone *not* airborne—but especially for ordinary infantry. 2. An airborne term for their own privates or Pfcs.

Peripatetic Coffin (Civil War; CSA) *s.* The Confederate experimental submarine *H.L. Hunley*, so called because she managed to drown six crews. The last crew went down with her when she sank a Union sloop of war.

permanent party (Modern) Troops assigned to duty at a training center to train or support other troops.

permanent pass (Late World War II to Modern) A small wallet-sized form prepared for every soldier in a unit. It was once mandatory to have such a pass in one's possession at all times when outside the post, particularly overseas.

Pershing cap (Late 1920s to 1930s) *s.* A new style of garrison cap with a larger crown and visor than previously, modeled after one that General Pershing chose to wear during World War I. (Generals can design their own uniforms.) Like other items of our post-1918 uniforms, its style was borrowed from the British. It was far more comfortable and practical than the little 1902 cap, with its tiny visor. You wore it, instead of balancing it on the top of your head.

Persian handicap (World War II; mostly Army) *s.* A game popular (for lack of other amusements) among the exiles of the Persian Gulf Command. Each contestant rolled up a sleeve, crooked an elbow, and let the sweat drip into an empty C-ration can. The first man to fill his can won. A stopwatch was used to time really close games.

personnel (20th century) Pentagonese for *people*, usually male. DACs are *civilian personnel*. A weapon designed to kill soldiers is an *antipersonnel weapon*. A mine designed to check advancing infantry is an *antipersonnel mine*, as opposed to an antitank mine. When many soldiers are being transferred, discharged, and detached, you have *personnel turbulence*, and so on.

peter cheater (Old Army) *s.* A sanitary napkin. The term is blamed, for some reason, on the Cavalry. (One version of the song "She Wore a Yellow Ribbon" features the line "Between her thighs she wore a peter cheater.")

Peter Pilot (Modern) *s.* The pilot of any aircraft.

peter stains (Post–World War II on) *s.* So long. See you again. A naughty play on German *auf Wiedersehen*.

Pfc PFC pfc 1. Private First Class. 2. *s.* Poor Fucking Civilian. To be promoted to Pfc is to be discharged from the Army. 3. *s.* Pretty Fucking Cheap. Many a Pfc's appraisal of his grade.

PGC (World War II; mostly Army) Persian Gulf Command, the logistical command that somehow rushed amazing amounts of lend-lease equipment to the Soviet Union across Iran. (Iran had not wanted any part of the war, but had been clubbed into submission to provide a safe supply line to the Soviets.) US troops in Iran had another reading for the initials: *People Going Crazy*. See *FBI*.

phonetic alphabet A system of easily pronounced, readily understandable words, each representing a letter of the alphabet. It is used to guarantee clarity and dispatch in radio voice and telephone communications. The present system, adopted in 1955, is *Alfa, Bravo, Charlie, Delta, Echo, Foxtrot, Golf, Hotel, India, Juliette, Kilo, Lima, Mike, November, Oscar, Papa, Quebec, Romeo, Sierra, Tango, Uniform, Victor, Whiskey, X-ray, Yankee, Zulu.* In the system used before 1955, the letters were *Able, Baker, Charlie, Dog, Easy, Fox, George, How, Item, Jig, King, Love, Mike, Now, Oboe, Peter, Queen, Roger, Sugar, Tare, Uncle, Victor, William, X-ray, Yoke, Zebra.*

Piccadilly commando (World War II) *s.* A London prostitute, especially the voracious type hunting by night in Piccadilly Circus, where—as one awed correspondent reported—they dragged their prey into any handy doorway and devoured it. See *wall job.*

picket 1. (Ancient to Modern) A guard posted to give warning of the approach of the enemy. Sometimes traditionally called an *outlying picket.* 2. (Colonial and Revolutionary) A punishment in which a soldier was compelled to stand with one bare foot resting on a sharply pointed stake for a given length of time. One account from the Revolution tells of a captured Tory's being punished by "spicketing," but in this case he was "turned round . . . until the pin run through his foot. Then he was turned loose" (Dann).

picket fence, to have a (Modern) *s.* To have a high degree of physical fitness in all the elements of the Physical Profile Serial Code. The systems recorded are *P*, physical capacity, stamina; *U*, upper extremities; *L*, lower extremities; *H*, hearing; *E*, eyes; *S*, neuropsychiatric. The numerical ratings are: 1, high degree of physical fitness; 2, meets standards for military service; 3, assignment restrictions due to physical disability; 4, unfit for military service. The picket fence consists of all ones:

P U L H E S
1 1 1 1 1 1

picket line 1. (Colonial to World War II) A long section of heavy rope to which horses or mules were tethered while in camp. "Water all your horses, and police the picket line." 2. (Colonial to early 20th century) A line of pickets (outposts) guarding the approaches to a position.

pickle button (Modern; Air Force) *s.* The bomb-release button mounted on the control stick of a fighter-bomber. "He centered the target in his sight and pushed the 'pickle button' on the top of the control stick" (TB, p. 39).

pickled mule (Civil War; USA) *s.* Salt meat. " 'I can't give you a very nice breakfast,' she added, as they entered, 'for I haven't got it.' 'Just so it isn't hardtack and pickled mule' " (Kelsey).

pick up [one's] brass, to (Modern) *s.* To leave, to depart. Extended from the rifle range, where, before leaving, soldiers are required to pick up their brass.

picture (Old Army; also Marines) *s.* A little embroidered symbol worn on the sleeve of a specialist, directly under his chevrons if he was an NCO. Examples were a leather-knife for a saddler, a horse's head for a stable sergeant, a bugle for a trumpeter, and a red cross for a hospital steward.

piece 1. (Colonial to Modern) A cannon. Artillerymen are trained in the "service of the piece"; an army or fortification may be described as having a certain number of "pieces of artillery." 2. (Colonial to Modern) A rifle. 3. (At least Old Army to Modern) *s.* The penis. 4. (At least Old Army to Modern) *s.* A woman considered sexually, or sexual intercourse. As in civilian life, *a piece of ass, a piece of tail.*

pie eater (Civil War; USA) *s.* In the 5th New York Volunteer Infantry Regiment, a name given to "country men" (farmers and the like) by the regiment's "city boys." During the first months of service, there was considerable friction between the "country" and "city" companies.

pie pan helmet (World War I and early World War II) *s.* The shallow steel helmet.

pig (Modern) *s.* A gun; any firearm that can be operated by one man. Often applied to the M60 machine gun.

pigeon-shot (Civil War; CSA) "A large cylindrical shot, with iron flanges on each side, known among the rebels as the pigeon-shot, struck the casemates on the port side" (Browne). This must have been the Confederate 3.5-inch "winged shot," an ingenious design intended to get the accuracy of a rifled gun from a smoothbore. When it cleared the muzzle of the gun, springs popped out a pair of triangular "wings," which were supposed to give the projectile greater stability.

pigsticker pig-sticker (At least World War I to Modern) *s.* A bayonet or, much less commonly, a sword.

pill 1. (Modern) *s.* An enlisted man of the Medical Corps. Also called *pills.* 2. (Modern) *s.* As *the pill.* The antimalarial chloroquine-primaquine tablet, taken once a week in most areas of Vietnam. Also called the *elephant pill*, for its size; the *orange pill*, for its color; the *shit pill*, for its tendency to produce cramps and diarrhea.

pill, to (Modern) *s.* To purify water by dropping purification tablets into it.

pill pusher pill roller (At least World War I to World War II, occasionally later) *s.* Enlisted men of the Medical Corps. These are also civilian slang terms for pharmacist or doctor, and probably go back to the days when they made up their own pills instead of purchasing them ready-made.

pills (19th century) *s.* A medical officer, especially the regimental surgeon. A short medical officer might be called *Little Pills.*

pilot killer (World War II; Air Force) *s.* A low-level photographic reconnaissance mission. See *dice.*

pimple on a buck private's ass, to make a (Old Army) *s.* One of the old-time classic put-downs, usually phrased "He wouldn't make a pimple on a buck private's ass." In our fading memory it was used especially in the evaluation of pretentious senior officers and civilians of the political and do-gooder persuasions.

pineapple 1. (World War I to Modern) *s.* A fragmentation grenade. Its tesselated surface looks much like a pineapple's. 2. (At least World War II to Modern) *s.* Things having to do with Hawaii: a *Pineapple*, a native of Hawaii; the *Pineapple Division*, the 25th Infantry Division, activated in Hawaii in 1941 (it preferred *Tropic Lightning*, but *Pineapple* came more naturally); the *Pineapple Navy*, naval units and personnel permanently stationed in the Hawaiian Islands. (It was not exactly a hardship tour of duty.)

pine-top whiskey (Civil War; CSA) *s.* Any potent hard liquor of dubious origin and questionable content. Also known as *corn wine, bust-head,* and *rifle knock-knee.* Sometimes "mellowed" by leaving raw meat in it for several weeks.

ping, to 1. (Modern) *s.* To criticize someone, usually constantly and in small ways. Perhaps from radar and sonar devices, which identify targets by a noise called a *ping.* In World War II naval use, a radar operator might be called a *ping jockey.* 2. (West Point) *s.* To be in a state of agitation.

pinhead distribution (Modern) *s.* A play on *pinpoint distribution,* a system of distributing DA publications, which does not always work the way it is supposed to.

pink bars (Modern) *s.* A second lieutenant's gold bars.

pinks (World War I to 1950s) *s.* Officers' trousers of pinkish-beige wool, worn with a forest-green blouse as the winter dress uniform. Their unique color made it easy to recognize an officer from a distance and thus take any necessary evasion action. If properly tailored, this uniform was smart, but after World War II some of the more sensitive draftees complained that pinks were another offensive aspect of the Army caste system, so pinks were phased out in the mid-1950s. Their passing was not altogether a loss; they were hard to keep properly spotless.

pipe clay (Colonial to mid-19th century) A fine, soft white clay formerly much used for making tobacco pipes. Soldiers used it for whitening their leather belts and for concealing stains on white items of uniform. Pipe clay was therefore associated with the fuss and formality of garrison service. A *pipe-clay parade* was a full-dress affair. In the British Army an *old pipe-clay* was an officer who vigorously observed and enforced every small detail of regulation dress and conduct.

pipeline (World War II to Modern; also Air Force) *s.* The personnel replacement or supply system, on the analogy, probably, of an oil pipeline. People or things go in at one end (usually the continental United States) and come out at the other (usually somewhere overseas). The term may have originated in the Air Force. "The personnel pipeline just couldn't hack the course" (Broughton).

piping (About 1830 to Modern) A narrow band of material used to trim the seams and edges of uniforms, both for ornament and to prevent fraying. Except for Dress Blue uniforms, its use was practically discontinued after 1902. Today (as in World War II) it is worn along the folded-up edge of the garrison cap. Officers have gold piping. During World War II enlisted men wore piping in the color or colors of their branch of the service, but at present piping matches the color of the cap.

pipper (Modern; Air Force) *s.* A tiny dot (2 mils in diameter) in the center of the optical sight reticle (gunsight) of a fighter-bomber. "I pulled the pipper up to the MIG and fired one AIM-7" (AAV, p. 91).

piss call 1. (At least early 20th century to post–World War II; all Services) *s.* Originally a nautical expression arising from the need to close the ship's head (toilet) occasionally for maintenance or repairs. On such occasions it would be a kindly act to awaken the sleeping off-duty watch with, "Wake up and piss. They're moving the head." In this way, the watch would not be confronted with a "closed" sign when they arose at their normal hour with full bowels and bladders. Gradually, this practice became simply *piss call* and—service humor being thoroughly earthy—a good joke to play on a sound sleeper. This passed into Army use during World War II, it being Army custom to close the carefully burnished latrines just before inspections. (One end of a urinal trough and one toilet bowl were usually roped off for emergency use, but this was hardly enough for a company in a hurry.) The sport of awaking sleepers for piss call was not without hazard, for it could result in fat lips and broken noses. Sailors and marines at least might make it less perilous by organizing it as a group activity in which a half-dozen men roused one or two shipmates. In the Army, a recruit of less than two years' service who annoyed his betters in this manner would find life increasingly unpleasant and might expect a chat with the executioner. 2. (World War II and later) *s.* Usage degenerated to meaning "I've got to go to the latrine." 3. (At least World War II) *s.* In disciplinary barracks, where hardened cases were "rehabilitated," piss call was often used as a harassment technique. All the prisoners might be awakened and marched to the latrine.

piss call, to have a *s.* To relieve oneself.

pissed off (Antiquity uncertain to Modern, especially World War II; all Services) *s.* Extremely angry and disgruntled. Like *browned off* or *brassed off*, but decidedly more emphatic.

piss tube (Modern; all Services) *s.* A urinal constructed in the field from any handy kind of tubular metal. The tube is placed in the ground at a 45° angle, sometimes fitted with a funnel and a wire-mesh filter at the receiving end.

pitch tent, to (World War II) *s.* To awaken with an erection. "Betty's not taking care of Sullivan enough. He's pitching tent every morning."

pits (At least 1880s to Modern; all Services) A sheltered area at the target end of the rifle range, where the *sand rats* (also called *pit detail* or *butts detail*) raise and lower targets, score, and paste paper over the holes that have been shot in the target. It is hard work. In some ranges, especially the older types, the pits are actually pits or broad trenches. The more modern pits are usually an open space between the butts and a hillside that forms a backstop for the range.

plain clothes soldier (Shortly after World War I; AEF) *s.* A DCI member who worked in civilian clothing.

plat-daddy (Modern) *s.* A platoon sergeant. If he does his job well, he becomes a surrogate father to his men; if poorly, he sometimes becomes an Oedipal figure.

platoon (Colonial to Modern) A subdivision of a company, consisting of a number of squads; an infantry company is traditionally divided into two platoons. A platoon is commanded by a lieutenant, and its senior noncom at present is a platoon sergeant. The word *platoon* comes from French *peloton* 'a group of things, a knot of things', which in Renaissance warfare had the specialized meaning of a group of soldiers in a prescribed formation.

platoon sergeant (1958 on) A senior noncommissioned officer, serving in pay grade E-7. His insignia of rank is three chevrons above two arcs. He ranks above a staff sergeant (E-6) and below a master sergeant or first sergeant. He is addressed as *sergeant*. His primary function is as senior noncom in a platoon, having command duty in the absence of the commissioned platoon leader. See also *sergeant* *first class*, the counterpart to platoon sergeant on staff and specialized duty assignments. Soldiers are promoted to sergeant first class and appointed as platoon sergeants. Abbreviated *PSG, P. Sgt.*

play it cool in the motor pool (Modern) *s.* A catchphrase meaning that the user does not intend to overexercise himself or bring unnecessary attention on himself. See *It all counts for twenty, nervous in the service*, and *What the fuck, over?*

play switch, to (Post–World War II) *s.* A nasty description of a state of total confusion and indecision. The player has one thumb in his mouth and the other up his anal orifice—and constantly switches them back and forth.

play the white man, to (Civil War; USA) *s.* To be improperly uppity; a phrase used by the first black troops raised, to describe the attitude of their black NCOs.

plebe /pleeb/ (Service academies) The common name for a member of the fourth-year class, equivalent to a college freshman. At West Point, the term was in use at least as early as the 1830s. It is from French *plèbe* 'a member of the lower orders', ultimately from Latin *plebs.*

plebe bible (At least 1939 on; West Point) *s.* A slang term for *Bugle Notes*, the handbook of the Corps of Cadets.

plebe knowledge In part, basic customs and traditions, background information about the Army and military matters, but also, traditionally, verbatim memorization for disciplinary reasons of a considerable amount of nonsense or near nonsense. Upon demand by an upperclassman, stock answers to stock questions have been spouted off by generations of cadets enduring the two months of beast barracks. Examples that are quoted in this volume are *How are they all? How is the cow? What is the definition of leather? What do plebes rank? What time is it?*

plebe pappy plebe pop (Post–World War II; West Point) *s.* An officer of the Military Academy staff and faculty who "sponsored" a plebe. This largely took the form of inviting him to dinner or a picnic, giving him a chance to talk and relax, and to see Army family life. Such hospitality might also be extended to the plebe's parents or girl friends. The program was voluntary on both sides. Someone decided, however, that this experience was too heady for mere plebes, and in 1969 its benefits were switched to yearlings.

plebe skins plebeskins 1. (Late 19th century; West Point) *s.* Civilian clothing. 2. (1920s on; West Point) *s.* The first issue of gray flannel trousers or gym trousers.

ploy, to (Ancient to late 19th century) To shift troops from a line (broad front formation) into a column (narrow front), either for a massed attack or to resume a march. Now archaic. The opposite of *deploy.*

Plunkett's Army (World War I) *s.* Not really an army. The US Navy's heavy railroad batteries in France, commanded by Rear Adm. Charles Peshall Plunkett.

PO Personnel Officer.

POC (Modern) Point of Contact. The name and office telephone number of a staff action officer. This goes on a staff paper so that other action officers will know who the fool is who wrote it.

pocket leave (Modern) *s.* Taking leave but remaining on the post. So called probably because the soldier's papers remain in his pocket. Also called *desktop leave, flagpole leave.*

pod formation (Modern; Air Force) A formation of aircraft in which electronic countermeasures (ECM), self-protective devices mounted in external pods, offer maximum mutual protection.

PO'd (At least World War II to Modern) *s.* Very unhappy, disgruntled. It is usually taken as an abbreviation of *pissed off*, but *pooped out* is also possible.

pogee pogie pogey /'po-'gee/ (Korea and later; all Services, but principally Army) *s.* The female genitals. From Korean slang. Our sergeant major recalls referring to "Georgie Porgie" in the hearing of an elderly Korean lady. She thereupon asked his wife why her husband used such execrably foul language in his conversation. Quick-thinking wife, realizing that the Korean lady had heard *porgie* as *pogee*, replied, "Oh, Porgie is a common American surname." "My goodness," said elderly Korean lady. "Those Americans certainly do have strange names."

pogey (poggie, pogie, pogy) bait (Post–World War II to Modern; all Services) *s.* Originally candy, but around the time of the Korean War, inducements for sexual favors. The term comes from the Navy and Marines, who used it at least as early as World War I. The ultimate origin, however, is not clear. The most reasonable explanation is that *pogey* is related to Irish *pog* 'a kiss', which entered English slang around the end of the 19th century:

> I axed for a pogue,
> The black-eyed saucy rogue.

(*Century Magazine*, 39:892, as quoted in CD)

This in turn may be related to general English-American slang *poke* as sexual intercourse. Another explanation is that *pogey bait* could have been prison slang, parallel to *jail bait* 'a girl below the legal age for sexual intercourse, statutory rape', since *poky* is also a slang term for prison. In such a reading, *pogey bait* would be the candy that a pervert would use to tempt a young girl. Related Marine words are *pogue*, a male homosexual who plays the female role, and its extension, in modern usage, a marine who does rear-line duty in a combat zone.

pogey-bait run (1960s) *s.* Unauthorized breaking of restrictions (such as those imposed in OCS) to visit a wife or girl friend.

Point, the (Antiquity uncertain to Modern) *s.* The US Military Academy at West Point, New York.

Pointer (Antiquity uncertain to Modern) *s.* A graduate of the US Military Academy at West Point.

point man (Old Army to Modern; also Marines) 1. The lead man on a patrol or a small advance guard. It is a lonesome spot. 2. By extension, anyone in a vulnerable position.

Point Purgatory (Revolutionary) West Point. Constantly working to build and strengthen its fortifications on short rations and less rum, soldiers did not have occasion or incentive to enjoy its scenery.

Poison Ivy Division (Modern) *s.* The 4th Infantry Division, because of the ivy design incorporated as part of the division's shoulder sleeve insignia. Also known as *Funky Fourth*.

pole, up the (Old Army) *s.* *To go up the pole* was to refrain from intoxicating beverages. *To fall down the pole* was to go back to drinking, as in the case of Sergeant O'Reilly:

> O'Reilly hit the bottle
> After six years up the pole.
> He blew himself at Casey's place,

And then went in the hole.
He drank with all the rookies,
And shoved his face as well . . .
The whole outfit is on the bum,
O'Reilly's gone to Hell.

In one version of that sad old song, O'Reilly "said the pole was bamboo, and he stopped at every joint." The origin of the expression *up the pole* is not known, but in British usage it means exactly the opposite: getting drunk.

police, to police up, to 1. (Colonial to Modern) To clean, to clean up. A basic Army word. One *polices* the barracks area, and at the end of a day at the rifle range, the troops *police up* the brass. A soldier may say that he is going to *police up*, meaning that he will get himself cleaned up. Originally, the term was somewhat more extensive and included camp sanitation and the general control of the living conditions of the troops. Competent officers had an empirical understanding of the importance of such factors. Brig. Gen. Winfield Scott stressed them in his "camp of instruction" at Buffalo, New York, in early 1814. One of his surgeons was amazed that "even the demon diarrhea appeared to have been exorcised by the mystical power of strict discipline and rigid police!" (Elliott). 2. (Antiquity uncertain) As *to be policed*, in a mounted unit, to be thrown from your horse. 3. (About 1900; West Point) As *to police*, to throw something away. 4. (About 1940; West Point) To fall behind in one's studies and thus be transferred to a lower section in one or more of one's subjects.

police call (Antiquity uncertain) A formation called specifically to pick up trash and litter. "Police call, walking in a straight line picking up cigarette butts and such" (Haldeman).

Polish target pistol (Modern) *s.* A pistol constructed so that the barrel points to the rear (and the person firing it). Such pistols are often illustrated in little "For Sale" posters seen on various unit bulletin boards, always with the legend "Good as new. Used only once." In civilian life called a *Polish dueling pistol.*

polka-dot flare, Send up a (Modern) *s.* A catchphrase used in response to such questions as "What do I do now?" The implication is, "Don't ask me! You're on your own!" (There *is* no such flare!)

POM (World War II to Modern) Preparation for Overseas Movement. It is an intensification of all those tests and inspections you have had previously.

pom-pom 1. (Late 19th century to early 20th century) A general term for various types of quick-firing light cannon, probably derived from the sound they make. During World War II the name was revived for a rapid-fire 2-pounder antiaircraft gun, usually mounted in sets of four, used by the Royal Navy. 2. (Post–World War II; all Services) *s.* Pidgin Japanese for sexual intercourse. A *pom-pom girl* was a prostitute. Perhaps from Japanese *pon-pon* /'pom-'pong/ 'bang, bang!'

pongo honcho (Korea and later) *s.* A person who suffers from excessive flatulence and passes gas frequently and noisily. From Korean *pongu* 'flatus' and *honcho*. See *honcho.*

pony (Civil War; USA) *s.* A boy soldier, underage and undersized. They often were first-class fighting men.

poontang poon tang boontang (World War II and later) *s.* Sexual intercourse, or a woman as a sexual object. Ancient as a term in civilian life, but most common in military in World War II. According to Wentworth and Flexner, *poontang* specifically meant sexual intercourse with a black woman or mulatto, but in our experience the term had no racial restrictions whatever. Probably from French *putain* 'whore', although similar words are found over much of Europe.

poop *s.* Various meanings around study and information, ultimately based on the Victorian architecture of the US Military Academy. On the cadet headquarters building and the tower of the mess hall are two small balconies, which the cadets have called *poop decks* because of their resemblance to the aftermost deck of an 18th-century sailing ship. From the headquarters poop deck the officer in charge observes and supervises formations, and from the mess-hall poop deck the brigade adjutant issues orders to the cadets at mealtimes. Various uses of the word *poop* have emerged from this situation. 1. (At least as early as 1910; West Point) Material to be memorized. 2. (From before 1939; West Point; later Army generally) Information, particularly official or inside information. During World War II this meaning of *poop* spread through the Army and then outside. 3. See *poop, to, 3, 4.*

poop, to 1. (Antiquity uncertain; Artillery) *s.* To fire on a target. "Poop off a couple of rounds at that brush patch." 2. (World War II and later; all Services) *s.* To exhaust, wear out. "That hike sure pooped the rookies." Probably of civilian origin. 3. (West Point) *s.* To memorize verbatim. See *poop.* 4. (West Point) *s.* As in *to poop up*, to inform. "Poop me up on how you do these papers" (Truscott). See *poop.*

poop sheet (Pre-1939 on) *s.* A paper containing information.

poor bundle (Modern) *s.* The A-5 container, used for parachute delivery of equipment.

Poor Lo (Indian Wars) *s.* A fancy name for the American Indian, whether friendly or hostile. Undoubtedly it came from *An Essay on Man* by Alexander Pope (1688–1744), who never saw one:

> Lo, the poor Indian; Whose untutored mind
> Sees God in clouds, or hears him in the wind.

Popcorn Man (World War II) *s.* German light bombers that came over the Anzio beachhead every night, with insulting disrespect for Allied air supremacy, and showered the place with butterfly bombs and other such murderous cargo.

pop off, to (West Point) *s.* To sound off.

pop smoke, to (Modern; also Marines) *s.* To use a smoke grenade, usually to identify a location. "The man who had popped smoke stood facing the direction the chopper would come from" (Downs). Also *to pop one.*

porch climber (Old Army) *s.* A term of opprobrium, much used by older Regular officers when we were new-hatched shavetails. As we remember it, a porch climber was akin to a second-story man, with the possible difference that the porch climber was a brown noser while the second-story man was that and an intriguer to boot. We consulted several older retired officers, but got only one clear-cut definition. "They weren't," said this old file, "very nice people."

porpoise, to do a (Modern; Air Force) *s.* To have an aircraft go into a vertical oscillating dive, out of the pilot's control. Also called *J.C. maneuver.*

portable water (Vietnam and later; all Services) *s.* Potable water, from the ubiquitous signs designating potable or nonpotable water placed near water sources in Vietnam. Sometimes *portable* was a wordplay, but some soldiers really thought that drinkable water was called *portable.*

port call (Modern; also Air Force) Instructions when and where to report for transportation overseas.

portee /por-'tee/ (World War I to early World War II) An early form of motorization, from French *portée* 'carried'. In a portee 75mm battery in the Artillery, the guns were carried on trucks and muscled on and off every time the battery changed position. The system was fast enough on a good road, but trouble off it. The Cavalry, in the early stages of World War II, experimented with portee units, carrying horses in semitrailer trucks, but these proved impractical on backcountry roads.

position of a soldier (Old Army to Modern) 1. Officially, standing correctly at attention. 2. In common usage, stretched out asleep.

possible, a (At least Old Army to Modern) *s.* A perfect score on the rifle range. By extension, a perfect accomplishment of anything difficult.

post Various meanings, some very ancient, involving placement. 1. A permanent military installation, as opposed to a camp, which is temporary. Colloquially, however, either a permanent or temporary installation, as in "I want to get off the post tonight, but the top is sitting on my pass." 2. A soldier's assigned place of duty. 3. The place for an officer or NCO to stand in a prescribed formation. Also the command to take one's place in formation. 4. (West Point) *s.* Generally used by upperclassmen toward plebes, meaning scram, get out, beat it. Probably derived from meaning 3. Also spreading into the Army in general.

post, to To place soldiers on duty or set up information about duty. "I want guards posted around that wing-job [plane] until they get it up again." "That son-of-a-bitch's got me posted for KP again!"

post exchange PX (Old, Old Army to Modern) It has become very much a department store, carrying both necessities and many luxury goods and operating filling/service stations. Sales are restricted to active and retired military personnel and to certain civilians resident at Armed Forces installations. Profits are deliberately limited, and are divided between the upkeep and improvement of exchanges and support of Armed Forces recreational programs. Before the institution of the post exchange, the soldier (especially at isolated stations) had been forced to buy his nonissue necessities and small luxuries from the post trader, who charged fancy prices for inferior goods. Accordingly, in 1880 the officers of the 21st Infantry Regiment at Vancouver Barracks, Washington Territory, opened a *canteen* (cooperative store) modeled on those operated by the British Army. Other organizations soon did likewise. The name was officially changed to *post exchange* in 1892, but the older title survived in *canteen checks.* Soldiers almost always call it the *PX.*

post flag The national flag (10 by 19 feet) usually flown on Army installations. See *garrison flag, storm flag.*

post police (At least Old Army to Modern) 1. Keeping the post neat and tidy. 2. The detail told off to police up the post.

potato masher potato masher grenade (World War I to Modern) *s.* A German hand grenade resembling the old-fashioned wooden potato masher, handle and all.

pot hat (Modern) *s.* The "hat, Army Green" formerly generally issued to female personnel. When inverted, it somewhat resembles a pot. It is still issued for special units, such as the Military Police, but otherwise its use is optional. It is being replaced by the black beret.

pot helmet (World War I and World War II) *s.* The German World War I helmet and the American World War II helmet.

pots and pans (At least World War II to Modern) 1. *s.* The task of cleaning encrusted and burnt food from cooking pots and otherwise keeping them ready for the cooks. A dirty, onerous job, but see *pot walloper* for the positive side. 2. *s.* The KP who does pots and pans.

pot walloper (Old Army, but may still be in use) *s.* The KP charged with the chore of massaging used cooking pots into a state of pristine cleanliness. It took a certain degree of conscience and some skill, and was important enough that a good pot walloper could just about set his own terms with the cooks, who were dependent on a steady supply of clean pots. He might condescend to help scrub the kitchen floor, but dining room help and peeling vegetables were too menial. A really expert pot walloper, like our marine, might even get time off in mid-afternoon.

pound brass, to (Approximately Civil War through World War I; all Services) *s.* To operate a manual telegraph key. This term, like *brass pounder* for a telegraph operator, is taken from civilian life.

pound the bush, to (Modern) *s.* To patrol, or to perform any type of infantry operation.

POV (Modern) Privately Owned Vehicle. "I used my POV all day" (Truscott). Automobiles owned by officers and enlisted personnel, often in conjunction with a finance company. When we first entered the service, they were rare indeed; only master sergeants and first lieutenants on up could begin to afford them. Today, almost every post looks like a mammoth used-car lot, and parking space is an increasingly serious problem. An even more serious problem is what to do with all those vehicles when orders come for a sudden change of station or movement overseas.

POW (World War II and later) Prisoner of War.

powdered (Modern; Air Force) *s.* Destroyed, disintegrated; said of aircraft.

powder house (Modern) *s.* The WAC detachment, WAC barracks.

power band (Vietnam and perhaps later) *s.* A bracelet made of braided bootlaces. It symbolized the Black Power spirit among black soldiers. Some sympathetic white soldiers also wore it.

prairie belt prairie cartridge belt (Indian Wars) *s.* A leather waist belt with canvas loops for carbine cartridges. The Ordnance Department finally got around to issuing it after the troops in the field had been improvising their own for some ten years.

prairie feathers (Pre–Civil War) *s.* Prairie hay, used for stuffing bed sacks in western posts. Straw, which later was the official filling, seldom was available on the frontier.

precedence 1. In communications, the relative order in which messages or telephone calls should be handled. Precedences are, in ascending order, routine, priority, operational immediate, and flash. Flash is used to report initial enemy contact or operational combat messages of extreme urgency. In voice communications there is also flash override. 2. The order in which awards and decorations are worn. The highest decoration is on the wearer's right, followed by US service medals in the order earned and then foreign decorations and medals.

pregnant brass (Modern) *s.* Nonissue convex collar insignia. Whereas issue brass was flat, made in one piece, and burnished gold in color, pregnant brass was convex, made in two separable pieces (thereby easy to clean), and silver plated. It was considered highly desirable. Pregnant brass was never officially authorized and was used at the soldier's peril. (Issue brass today is still burnished gold in color, but is now constructed in two separable pieces.)

pregnant octopus (Post–World War II on) *s.* The insignia adopted for Armor after World War II. It showed a medium tank, represented head-on with turret gun elevated, superimposed on the traditional crossed sabers insignia of the Cavalry.

prep, to (Modern) *s.* To prepare a target for ground assault, by blasting it with artillery or airborne ordnance. To "soften up." "'Prepped' by air strikes and artillery fire" (Downs).

Presbyterian (20th century) A drink affected by virtuous officers who still wanted to be a little sociable. Half ginger ale, half soda water, with a few drops of Scotch as camouflage.

presentos (Post–World War II; Far East mostly) *s.* Small gifts or bribes to win favor. Norman notes this word in Japanese pidgin English in the 1950s, and Algeo observes that it had spread to Korean pidgin by 1960 at the latest. Possibly a Japanese pronunciation of English *present*, although there are also Spanish *presente* and *presentillo*.

prick (Modern) *s.* The AN/PRC-9 or AN/PRC-25 portable radio. The term is an expansion of the letters *PRC*. "There was a little radio . . . a PRC-25 (which everybody called a 'prick-25')" (Haldeman).

pricksmith (Modern) *s.* An enlisted man of the Medical Corps. The term is more associated with treatment of venereal diseases and short-arm inspection than with needle-sticking.

primary zone (Modern) A list of soldiers who meet all the criteria for selection for promotion. Most soldiers selected for promotion come from it. See *secondary zone*.

prisoner chaser (At least World War I to Modern) *s.* A soldier guarding a work detail of garrison prisoners. See *chase a prisoner, tail gunner*.

private (Ancient to Modern) Since July 1961, the lowest enlisted grades in the Army: *private E-1* and *private E-2*, both of whom are addressed as private. A private E-1 wears no sleeve insignia of rank; a private E-2 wears a single bar. Between July 1948 and July 1961, the grades now known as *private* were *recruit* (comparable to E-1) and *private* (comparable to E-2). Before 1948, there was only one grade of private. Abbreviated *PV1, PV2*, and, for older grades, *Pvt.*

private first class (At least 1880s to Modern) At present, an enlisted soldier serving in pay grade E-3. His insignia of grade is a chevron above an arc, and he is addressed as *private*. He is not a noncommissioned officer. He ranks below a corporal and above a private E-2. Between 1920 and 1965 his insignia was a single chevron (bar). Historically, the grade of private first class has often been connected with that of lance corporal. Abbreviated *PFC, Pfc, pfc*.

Private Slipinshits (Modern) *s.* The military equivalent of John Doe, but derogatory; used only of lower-ranking enlisted personnel.

Profane (Mostly World War I) An archaic and primitive language consisting largely of adjectives and expletives. A typical sentence might begin: "*You* goddam, half-assed, pee- [not 'pea'] brained son-of-a-bitch of a yellow-bellied bastard and a Peruvian whorehouse." After such a warm-up, the speaker would expand and reaffirm, often with great originality, always with increasing emphasis. It was spoken by veteran sergeants, petty officers, company commanders, and mule skinners, but not a few senior officers were past masters in its employment. We remember the late Ben Lear, then a colonel of cavalry, speaking to us ROTC cadets in 1931 on the evils of profanity. It was an eight-minute exhortation, the last seven-and-a-half being pure old-vintage Profane; punctuated by whacks on a field desk with a sort of leather-covered ball bat that he used for a riding crop. He didn't repeat himself once and left us convinced that our amateur noises were indeed "low and degrading." But even that example was as a single firecracker unto the thunders of the Almighty when compared to the great George S. Patton in full vocal array. Employed by such experts, Profane could propel infantry through uncut barbed wire or reduce hardened QMs to tears of repentance. Animals also comprehended it. Sulky, tired mules would put their weight into their collars; ancient, sinful troop horses would allow scared recruits to saddle them.

professional privates (Pre–World War II) *s.* Regular Army enlisted men who refused promotion to corporal (or sometimes, even to Pfc). Their motto was "I've got no responsibilities and they can't bust me." World War II changed all that.

prog (Colonial to Revolutionary) *s.* Provisions. Maj. John André's mock ballad "The Cow Chace," written in 1780, mentions Anthony Wayne's

Horse that carried all his prog,
His military speeches
The cornstalk whiskey for his grog
Blue stockings and brown britches.

prog, to (Colonial to Revolutionary) To forage.

Project Transition (Modern) A program (terminated on 31 May 1974) that prepared soldiers for their return to civilian life by providing training in various marketable skills, ranging from motor mechanics to motel management. The instruction was on government time and at government expense, and could begin as much as six months before scheduled date of discharge. It could be either full-time or part-time.

projo (Probably since early World War II) *s.* An artillery projectile. Also called *prodge, jo, joe.*

prolonge (19th century) A heavy rope carried on the trail of a field gun. Its most important use was during rear-guard actions when continuous artillery fire was required. One end of the prolonge was fastened to the limber, the other to the lunette at the tip of the trail of the gun. The limbers then moved off at a walking pace, dragging the guns. The cannoneers could load the guns as they moved. When the guns were ready, the teams were halted just long enough for the cannon to be aimed and fired. The withdrawal was then resumed.

promotion hump (Post–World War I) *s.* No promotions, the incubus of the officers' corps during the 1920s and early 1930s. Cutbacks in the strength of the Regular Army and restrictions on promotion left it with a large proportion of captains and majors who would have to retire before lieutenants could hope for promotion. Those were the days of forty-year old captains who hoped to make major before they retired. Adolf Hitler came to their rescue. Also called *the Hump.*

prone position (Modern) *s.* Sexual intercourse. From the prone position used in firing the rifle.

prop (20th century) *s.* In aviation outfits, the habitual name for a propeller.

prop wash (About World War II and later; Air Force) 1. *s.* The breeze stirred up by a rotating propeller—a lot of air going nowhere and serving no useful purpose. 2. *s.* By extension, gossip, idle talk, bragging, general oral nonsense. About the same as *windjamming, working your bolt, slipping your clutch, scuttlebutt, slushing oil.*

prosign (Modern) 1. Officially, any symbol (usually a number) used as a code to express a standard message. 2. *s.* Unofficially, a series of highly colorful statements, expressing attitudes about Army life, fellow soldiers, hopes and fears, etc. These expressions are usually preceded by a number, which is then shouted or written down instead of the whole statement. For example, someone shouting "124" might mean "Pardon me, sir, you obviously mistook me for someone who really gives a shit." The numbers are arbitrary and only locally understood; one verbal expression might have several different prosign numbers in different outfits. Examples of such prosign statements: "Answer your fucking phone!" "Be nice!" "Fuck you. A strong letter follows." "Fuck you very much." "Go pound sand in your ass." "Happiness is a warm pussy." "Oh joy, oh fucking rapture." "Show us your tits." "You eat shit, chase rabbits, and bark at the moon." "You just stepped on your dick." "You've got to be shitting me." See *proword.*

pro station (World War I to Modern) *s.* Short for *prophylaxis station,* a medical station where men who have had sexual intercourse are given prophylactic treatment. Its distinguishing sign was a blue light. Such stations antedate our entry into World War I, for treatment of this sort was compulsory under General Pershing in Mexico in 1916 and may have been used earlier.

protargol (Old Army to 1950s) Albuminate of silver, a prophylaxis against venereal disease, administered by syringe at a pro station. If used within an hour after exposure to disease, it was effective.

provost courts /'pro-voast *or* 'pro-vo/ Military courts set up in occupied countries to try civilians for offenses against our forces.

provost guards (Revolutionary to Civil War) Troop units or individual soldiers put under the authority of the provost marshal to check desertion and straggling, prevent pillaging, and generally maintain law and order. Except for temporary units activated in the AEF in 1918, the US Army had no regular Military Police from 1783 to 1941.

provost marshal (Colonial to Modern) A staff officer who functions as the chief of police (in the civilian sense of *police*) of a command. Since 1941 he has been an officer of the Military Police Corps. The US Army has a *Provost Marshal General*. The same title is used for the provost marshals of armies and major commands.

provost sergeant (Ancient to Old Army) In peacetime, a sergeant who assigned work to garrison prisoners on work details and looked after the tools used in keeping the post clean and trim. Now obsolete.

proword A word used to express a standard message. The most common are *Roger, Over, Wilco, Affirmative.*

PSP (Modern) Pierced Steel Plate. PSP or steel or aluminum matting (sometimes called planking) is used on airfields and other constructions to provide a smooth, sturdy surface capable of supporting heavy traffic. It is molded with holes to make it lighter and easier to handle.

psywar (World War II to Modern) *s.* Psychological warfare.

PT (About World War I to Modern) 1. Physical Training. All those organized calisthenics and such, designed to give you health, strength, and grace. 2. *s.* Loafing, goofing off. Where organized grabass is not practical, soldiers are given time off to conduct their own PT. This may mean a chairborne warrior's taking a sunny afternoon off from urgent business to improve his physical condition by riding a motorized cart around a golf course.

P-38 1. (World War II) The German Walther 9mm automatic pistol, developed as a replacement for the Luger. It was an outstanding weapon, highly desired as a souvenir. 2. (World War II to Modern) A small hinged can opener issued with combat rations. It has been described as the most perfectly designed tool in history and has been standard issue since as early as 1943. "Slightly smaller than a razor blade. Weighs one-fifth of an ounce, can be carried on a key ring" (*Yank* 1:51, 11 June 1943).

ptomaine domain ptomaine palace (At least World War II to Modern) *s.* The mess hall.

public animal (Old, Old Army to Modern) A horse, mule, ox, carabao, camel, dog, or other animal belonging to the Army—or, technically, to John Q. Public. (Officers usually purchased their own horses.) Public animals were to be given the best treatment possible. If a mule kicked you, you could be court-martialed for kicking him back. Kicking was a mule's prerogative, and anyway, you should have been more careful.

pucker factor (Modern) *s.* The degree to which any exacting or hazardous set of circumstances causes a tightening of the anal muscle. "Pucker-assed frightened" means something like "too frightened to shit"—*really* scared.

puddle jumper (World War II and later) *s.* A light aircraft, a Grasshopper.

Puff, the Magic Dragon (Vietnam and later) *s.* A C-47 aircraft armed with 7.62mm machine guns, each firing 5,400 rounds per minute. It provided ground troops with devastating firepower support. The ability of the aircraft to stay aloft for long periods of time, place accurate fire on targets, and provide flare illumination made it one of the most successful counterinsurgency weapons. The name was probably inspired by Peter Yarrow's song "Puff, the Magic Dragon." "Puff the Magic Dragon, with three rapid-fire 7.62mm guns" (Marshall, 1969). Also called *dragon ship, spooky*.

PUFO (Modern; Canadian origin) Pull Up [your tent pegs] and Fuck Off. To move out. Obviously the Canadian interpretation of *fuck off* differs from American, which is to loaf, to shirk, to waste time.

puke pills (World War II) *s.* Motion-sickness pills issued to airborne troops to prevent air sickness. They were potent and so relaxing that they made many men quite sleepy, even in combat.

Puking Buzzards (Modern) *s.* The 101st Airborne Division, because of the eagle on their shoulder patch; also called the *One-Oh-Worst*.

pull, to (At least pre–World War II to Modern) *s.* To perform a duty. You *pull a detail* or *pull guard*. "I pulled KP again yesterday." The origin of this use is not clear, and it is not to be found in any of the various reference works on slang, even though it is an extremely common Army term. It might be related to prison slang, *to pull ten years*.

pull a Hank Snow, to (Korean) *s.* To run for your life, to bug out. The reference is to *"Bugout Boogie."*

pull and paste, to (Modern) To operate the targets on a rifle range. In some Army posts the targets were mounted on wooden frames, which slid up and down on metal tracks and were counterweighted. After a soldier had finished firing, the pit detail would pull the target down and apply little paper patches over the bullet holes so that the next shooter would have a clear target.

pull a profile, to (Modern) *s.* To avoid duty by capitalizing on a physical disability. The profile concerned is the Physical Profile or Temporary Profile. (See *picket fence.*) The expression does not refer to the soldier who is legitimately disabled and does his best, but to the malingerer who looks forward to invoking his profile on every occasion, extending it indefinitely, and applying it to every conceivable circumstance.

pull [one's] stripes, to See *pull rank*.

pull rank, to (Considerable Antiquity to Modern; all Services) *s.* To make use of one's seniority to impose one's wishes on juniors, especially when off duty. The expression seems to have been used originally for officers, but in World War II at least it was used for enlisted men as well. Similar conduct by a noncommissioned officer (as, for example, when off duty, in a beer hall) is called *pulling his stripes*, a usage that seems to have become common only in the early 1940s. It is sometimes expressed as *pushing one's stripes*.

pull [someone's] belt, to (At least World War I to World War II) *s.* To remove a soldier from guard duty with the intention of trying him or punishing him for an offense. It amounted to disarming the soldier, for a soldier under arms wore either a cartridge belt or a pistol belt, depending on the weapon he carried. In the Old Army, if an inspecting officer found a guard derelict in his duty, he might order the sergeant of the guard to pull the soldier's belt. A soldier thus singled out was disarmed and went from being on guard duty to being under guard. He would receive due attention from his company commander. The expression was also occasionally used loosely for arrest for any reason.

pull the pin, to (Vietnam) *s.* To leave, to depart, to go. Presumably from pulling a hand-grenade pin.

pumpkin (Colonial) *s.* British soldiers' term for a New Englander.

pumpkin rinds (Civil War; USA) *s.* Second lieutenants, so called because of their plain cloth shoulder straps. Second lieutenants had no distinctive insignia of grade until the present "single gold bar" was introduced during World War I.

pumpkin rollers (Civil War; USA) *s.* Belgian-manufactured smoothbore muskets that were issued to some Union infantry units during the first year of the war, because of the shortage of modern weapons. They were heavy-caliber weapons with a brutal recoil. (It was claimed that you could tell how many had gone off by counting the number of men who had been kicked flat.) Their bayonets were made of soft iron "apparently designed to coil around the enemy," and their locks had a tendency to bend once the gun was heated from firing. A French officer with the Army of the Potomac termed them "the refuse of Europe."

punch box (West Point) *s.* A calculator.

punch out, to (Post–World War II; Air Force) *s.* To bail out.

punishment tour (West Point) A punishment consisting of walking a prescribed number of hours under arms in the area. It is usually given in conjunction with a certain number of demerits. See *area bird, century man, tour*.

punji pongi (Vietnam) A razor-sharp bamboo stake, part of a mantrap consisting of a number of such stakes, often smeared with human excrement or other infectious material in order to produce a festering, incapacitating wound. Punjis were also used in defensive works to impede attackers.

punk 1. (Old, Old Army to World War I) *s.* Bread. The *punk sergeant* was the dining-room orderly whose duty was to keep the mess tables supplied with sliced bread. Also called *bread sergeant*. The origin of the term is probably from *punk* as soft, dry, decayed wood, ultimately an American Indian word. 2. (Also Marines) *s.* A derisive term for the company clerk.

pup tent (Civil War to Modern) *s.* Popular term for the soldiers' small tent erected out of two shelter halves. Each soldier is issued half of the tent and the accoutrements needed to set it up. The halves, made of heavy canvas, are buttoned together along the ridge seam and the end flaps. "Such as had no tents Drew those Little Pup or Dog tents as the Boys call them" (Ayers, diary entry of 16 October 1864).

Purple Hard-on (World War II and perhaps later) *s.* A cynical nickname for the Purple Heart. See also *Purple Shaft*.

Purple Heart **Purple Heart Medal** (1932 on) A decoration awarded to a member of the Armed Forces (and in some circumstances to a civilian) who has been wounded or killed, or has died as the result of a wound. The present version bears the profile of George Washington and, on the reverse, the words *For Military Merit*. The award is connected symbolically with the original Badge of Military Merit established by George Washington in 1782. This earlier decoration, although it was not concerned with wounds, was heart-shaped and made of purple cloth edged in narrow lace or binding. It lapsed after the Revolutionary War. Recognition for wounds received in war was first given in 1918 with the award of wound chevrons. The present award was established in 1932.

Purple Heart boxes (World War II; North Africa) *s.* A half-track, especially one used as a tank destroyer. Its light armor and open top gave its crew next to no protection against enemy fire. See *Seek, Strike, Destroy.*

Purple Shaft (Modern, perhaps earlier) *s.* Grossly unfair treatment, a royal screwing. A play on the *Purple Heart.* Expressions like the "order of the purple shaft, with barbed wire cluster" (Algeo) were common during the Korean War. Implicit is the understanding that the shaft is rammed up one's anus. "Overhead got the Purple Shaft with horseshit cluster" (Smith). The *Military Order of the Purple Elbow* (a naval expression) is apparently a "lower order" of the Purple Shaft.

purple-suiter (Modern) *s.* An officer assigned to duty on a staff where no particular service predominates. This may be a joint staff, where all services cooperate, or a combined staff, where two or more allied nations participate. He is called *purple* because he loses the identity (and color) of his particular service, and the color purple is not used by any of the services. The official colors are green for Army, blue for Air Force, and white for Navy. See *regreening process.*

pushing daisies **pushing up daisies** (World War I) *s.* Dead and buried.

> Casey Jones tried to stop a flying
> Whizbang
> And now he's pushing daisies out in
> No Man's Land!

pussy cut-off date See *PCOD*

put on the roots, to be (Civil War; CSA) *s.* To be assigned extra tours of guard duty as punishment for minor military offenses.

Puzzle Palace (Modern) 1. Headquarters. The things that go on are mysterious, even to the staff. 2. Especially the Pentagon, which is also known as the *Cave of the Winds*, referring to the undercut beneath Niagara Falls. An Army joke of the 1950s and 1960s told of a Russian spy who had been dispatched on a suicide mission. During a crisis in the cold war his superiors gave him a miniaturized nuclear bomb and ordered him to penetrate into the innermost sanctum of the Pentagon and detonate the bomb. He had no trouble in entering the Pentagon but, naturally, promptly got lost. A week later he staggered out and reported that his intimate view of the Pentagon in action had convinced him that its undisturbed existence was essential to the safety of the Soviet Union.

PX See *post exchange.*

☆☆☆☆ *q* ☆☆☆☆

Q Quarters.

Quad .50 (World War II to Modern) Originally a half-track vehicle (later a full-track) armed with four .50-caliber machine guns mounted so that they could be aimed and fired together. Intended as a defense against low-flying enemy aircraft, it was also a potent antipersonnel weapon, capable of chopping a stone house in half or turning an attacking Chicom horde into next year's manure.

Quaker gun (Colonial to Civil War) An imitation cannon made of wood, so called because of the pacifistic beliefs of the Quakers. Quaker guns were employed both on shipboard and in fortifications. In late 1861 and early 1862 Confederate Gen. Joseph E. Johnston used them to buffalo Maj. Gen. George B. McClellan.

qualify, to (At least Old Army to Modern) To achieve a prescribed degree of proficiency with a weapon. This was formalized, and in the Old Army (up into World War II for a short time) it was recognized (in some circumstances) with awards and extra pay. A soldier could qualify with several weapons, including the bayonet, although the rifle was the most important. See *marksman*.

Qualitative Management Program (Modern) A program (still operative as of 1983) that reviews the records of enlisted personnel periodically to eliminate marginally effective soldiers from the service. Soldiers selected for elimination are notified by letter and are allowed to remain on duty until the expiration of their current enlistment, after which they are denied further enlistment. Unlike officers eliminated in an RIF, these soldiers receive no extra compensation on discharge or options to continue in a lower grade. Appeals are seldom granted.

quarantined in camp (Civil War; USA) *s.* Restricted to camp for disciplinary reasons. "Unless something was done to keep our boys [a Regular battery] from disturbing the infantry camps, fighting, etc., their liberty would be suspended—in other words, that the Battery would be 'quarantined in camp' as we used to say" (Buell).

quarter (Colonial to Modern, though some uses are now obsolete) Mercy. *To give quarter* was to spare a defeated enemy's life and accept him as a prisoner. *No quarter* meant that no prisoners would be taken. *To cry quarter* was to plead for mercy. An offer of *good quarter* or *fair quarter* to besieged enemy troops meant a promise of mercy and good subsequent treatment. The origin of the term is uncertain. The accepted theory is that *quarter* originally referred to a specific area or quarter where such prisoners might be held. It has also been claimed however, that the term arose from the practice of demanding one quarter of a soldier's yearly pay or of his possessions for ransom. See *Tarleton's quarter*.

quarter, to (Colonial and Revolutionary to Modern) To house troops in private residences, "quartered on the inhabitants." A sore point in pre–Revolutionary War days, this practice has been most uncommon since. It is forbidden in peacetime in the United States (except with consent) by the Third Amendment to the Constitution. During World War I the word *billet* officially replaced *quarter*.

quartermaster (Ancient to Modern) A staff officer responsible for the procurement and delivery of equipment, fuel, and supplies. Food was added in 1912, when the Quartermaster Department became the Quartermaster Corps and took over the responsibilities of the old Subsistence Department.

Quartermaster Corps QMC Founded in 1912 by the consolidation of the Quartermaster, Subsistence, and Pay departments. The Old Army considered it a repository for "fat men and slow mules"; responsibility for the Army pay was rescued from it in 1918. Unlike the former Quartermaster Department, it had its own troops, including motor transport, salvage, graves registration, laundry, refrigeration, bakery, and fumigation and bath units. By 1953, the problems involved in procuring and distributing the increasing variety of supplies had become too complex for any one branch of the service, and so, they were divided among several new staff offices. For example, truck, sea, and rail transport was passed to the Transportation Corps, and the Supply and Maintenance Command was created to receive, store, and distribute weapons and equipment. However, the Quartermaster Corps still provides the trained personnel to handle many of the tasks involved. The easier and safer life of Quartermaster organizations naturally drew acrid comments from combat troops, such as this anonymous verse:

The Devil's displacing to the rear,
Because, so he confessed,
The infantry took most of hell
And the QM stole the rest.

Actually, it usually delivered—sometimes under the most real difficulties. Still, come to think of it, we never saw a hungry quartermaster. Usually referred to as simply *QM*.

Quartermaster Department Private contractors having proven energetic and capable only in enriching themselves and swindling the Army, and war with England clearly being at hand, Congress authorized a Quartermaster Department in March 1812. This department consisted of a few officers supported by an elaborate hierarchy of civilian storekeepers, wagon masters, clerks, and other employees hired as required. Army officers and enlisted men might be detailed to duty with the department in emergencies. During the Civil War, the department had its own navy, armed vessels to escort its chartered transports and supply ships. The Civil War was its great period, its performances during the War of 1812, Mexican War, and Spanish-American War being an affront to the service. Reputedly it was a Quartermaster Department officer who protested in 1898 that he had just gotten his office running smoothly—and then somebody had to go and start a war with Spain.

quartermaster gait *s.* A leisurely walking pace.

Quartermaster General (Revolutionary to World War I) The staff officer who, as head of the Quartermaster General's Department (Quartermaster Department, Quartermaster Corps), was responsible for providing the Army with quarters, clothing, fuel, and transportation, plus (after 1912) food. After World War I, the Quartermaster General was downgraded to a member of the Army's Special Staff, responsible to the Deputy Chief of Staff for Logistics. His responsibilities, since approximately 1958, have been assigned to the Chief of Support Services.

Quartermaster General's Department Established on 16 June 1775 by the Continental Congress, to handle the supply of clothing and equipment to the troops and of forage for their animals. Except for the period when it was headed by Maj. Gen. Nathanael Greene (1778–80), it had a hand-to-mouth existence at best and was frequently reorganized but not improved. Its responsibilities included transportation of supplies; in 1780 it had some 3,000 employees organized in quasi-military units of teamsters, bateaux men, and artificers, controlled by wagon masters, forage masters, harbor masters, conductors, and overseers of boats. In 1785, Congress abolished the department, turning supply over to the pinch-penny Treasury and civilian contractors.

quartermaster hunting (Civil War; USA) *s.* Artillery fire that passed over the battle line and landed well behind it, where the only people it might accidentally hurt were quartermaster personnel and coffee boilers. Gen. Robert E. Lee's artillery preparation before Pickett's charge on the third day of Gettysburg was a classic example.

quartermaster property (World War II to Modern) *s.* Dead. Since the Graves Registration Service is part of the Quartermaster Corps, a soldier theoretically becomes its property when he dies.

quartermaster, regimental (Colonial to World War I) An officer of the regimental staff, usually a lieutenant, charged with procurement, issue, and maintenance of camp equipage, arms, equipment, provisions, fuel, and forage. He also was responsible for laying out campsites and seeing to their cleanliness. (Because of the shortage of available officers through the 19th century, he often also functioned as a company officer.) Appointed regimental quartermaster of the 4th Infantry Regiment in 1846, Lt. Ulysses S. Grant ran the regimental pack train with its Mexican mules and muleteers and took care of the regimental fund. When the 4th Infantry was sent from New York to California in 1852, Grant's chores included getting the regiment and its legal camp followers across the Isthmus of Panama by train, boat, and mule, with cholera ravaging them. Note that these regimental quartermasters belonged to their respective branches of the service—Infantry, Cavalry, Artillery, or Engineers—and not to the Quartermaster Corps. On occasion

—as when Grant rode with dispatches under heavy fire at Monterey, or Lt. James M. Bell brought up the ammunition wagons at the Washita—they were combat officers. Their present equivalent is the battalion S-4. Regimental quartermaster sergeants (three chevrons and a tie of three bars) existed in the Army from 1902 to 1917. The term *regimental supply sergeant* replaced that of *regimental quartermaster sergeant* (*Special Regulations* 42, 15 August 1917) and persisted in the Army until the Reorganization Act of 1920, which redesignated them as simply *master sergeants, first grade*.

quartermaster sergeant 1. (Revolutionary to 1917) An enlisted assistant to the regimental quartermaster; with the sergeant major and the senior musician, he was part of the regimental noncommissioned staff and an individual of pomp, pride, and circumstance. 2. A company noncommissioned officer charged with the issue and care of clothing and equipment. He makes a momentary appearance in the Infantry in 1814 (Ganoe) and then reappears in the Army at large from 1832 onward. His title was changed to *supply sergeant* in 1917; possibly he had some of the responsibilities of the modern mess sergeant.

quarters (Colonial to Modern) Housing for troops. In modern usage, it means buildings on a military post, such as *officers' quarters* and *NCOs' quarters*. The noncommissioned officer in charge of a barracks is a *CQ* or *Charge of Quarters*, and soldiers may be *restricted to quarters* as a punishment. See *quarter*.

quarters and rations **Q & R** (At least Old Army to Modern) "Room and board" furnished to soldiers temporarily assigned to a unit. The abbreviation *Q & R* is frequently met. Sometimes called *rations and quarters*. "With us for quarters and rations while doing their liaison work" (Marshall, 1979).

Queen Anne **Queen Anne's musket** **Queen's Arm** (Colonial and Revolutionary) A very loose classification of muskets, generally any such weapon sent to the colonies during the reign of Queen Anne (1702–14) or bearing her cypher. Most of them were heavy, rather crudely made flintlocks of approximately .75 to .81 caliber, manufactured for the armies of her predecessor, King William III. Many of them had the old-fashioned *dog lock*. Since better muskets (the first models of the famous Brown Bess) were being provided for British troops, Queen Anne's muskets were used to arm troops raised in America. Although they were practically obsolete by the American Revolution, during the first years a good many were used for lack of anything better. It is rumored that some turned up in the hands of Confederate militia during the Civil War.

queer degen (Colonial) *s.* An ordinary sword, with a brass or iron hilt, of the type issued to British infantry enlisted men. They soon proved to be a nuisance in North America and were turned in. The term itself is British cant of the late 17th century, *queer* meaning inferior or of bad quality, while *degen* (related to German *Degen*) means a sword.

queer toast (At least World War II; 1930s in the Marines) *s.* French toast. *Queer bread* was French bread. The term is based on the half-serious belief that the French had sexual "customs quaint and rare." See *cocksucker bread*.

querida (Mexican War to at least 1925) *s.* A girl friend, a mistress. From Spanish *querida* 'loved one', 'sweetheart', 'mistress'.

quibbling (West Point) A broadly defined violation of cadet honor codes.

quickstep 1. (19th century) *Quick time.* 2. (Early 19th century on) A military march performed at the tempo of quickstep, which was then slower than modern quick time, being about 107 beats to the minute. 3. Derived from 2, in civilian use, a very popular sort of marchlike dance music, often fancifully titled. 4. (Civil War) *s.* Diarrhea, dysentery, or similar bowel disorders, usually lumped together by doctors as the *flux.* Union soldiers (parodying civilian quickstep names) often added the name of the state in which the affliction struck them, as, for example, the *Virginia quickstep.* The Rebels often spoke of the *Confederate quickstep.* For a modern parallel, see *Saigon quickstep.*

quick time (At least early 19th century to Modern) The normal rate of march or cadence; at present 120 counts or steps to the minute. In premodern times, the rate was slower.

quill (Early 20th century on; West Point) *s.* A report of delinquency. The origin of the term is unclear, perhaps from writing down with a (quill) pen, perhaps from being stuck with a porcupine's quill. Other forms are *quill sheet* and *quill book.*

quill, to *s.* To record delinquency. "Before I pull out my two-dash-ones [2–1, Disciplinary Report Form] and quill you" (Truscott).

quitter (Post–World War II; Airborne) *s.* A subtle, special use: one who chickens out from parachute duty before the end of his enlistment. A soldier who reenlists for other duty at the end of his enlistment is not considered a quitter.

quoin (Colonial to Civil War) A wedge-shaped piece of hardwood, with a short handle, to be placed under the breech of a gun to adjust its elevation. Each gun had a set of quoins of different thicknesses.

☆☆☆☆r☆☆☆☆

RA (At least World War II to Modern) Regular Army, in various aspects. 1. Regular Army, as distinguished from draftees, the Army Reserve, and the Army National Guard. Before the use of Social Security numbers, when serial numbers were still used, Regular Army serial numbers were sometimes prefixed with the letters *RA*. Such men were known as *RAs*. They received a tiny bit of preferential treatment as enlisted men in being placed first in the pay lines. It used to cause wisecracks when the RA private (and fuck-up) got paid before the draftee sergeants. The RA often looked down his nose at the other components of the Army, and the others reciprocated in kind. 2. *s.* Regular Asshole. From definition 1. In use at least as early as 1956 (Norman). 3. Continuing the insult, *RA* is any soldier who takes to the Army with enthusiasm, regardless of his official classification.

rack **rack time** (West Point) *s.* A newer version of *sack* (sleep).

Rackensackers (Mexican War) *s.* The Regular's name for the Arkansas volunteer cavalry, which was usually more of a nuisance than the Mexican Army. The term is probably a typical soldier's satirical rendering of *Arkansas.*

'rad **rad** (Post–World War II) *s.* A German male. As *the 'Rads*, Germans in general. Probably from the habit many German males had of calling all Americans *Kamerad* 'comrade'. *Kamerad* was also the common surrender cry of German troops in the last days of World War I.

RA5 (Modern) *s.* A draftee who enlisted in the Regular Army. He kept his original serial number, which began with 5. The draftee prefix *US* was dropped, and the letters *RA* substituted. A knowledgeable person, on looking at a number like RA55123456, could see immediately that it was an ex-draftee's number.

ragbags (Modern) *s.* Sloppy, ill-disciplined troops. "When they get here they're ragbags (the paratrooper's favorite word for anyone whose style is less than airborne)" (*Washington Star*, 29 August 1979).

rag carrier (Colonial to early 19th century) *s.* An ensign or color-bearer. From British usage.

rag fair (Colonial to early 19th century) *s.* An inspection of enlisted men's clothing and equipment, comparable to modern showdown inspection.

Rag Tag Circus (World War II) *s.* The 83d Infantry Division, so called in 1945 because of the number of German combat vehicles and trucks that it picked up, repainted, and used. An aggressive, fast-moving division, it much preferred its original nickname —*Thunderbolt*— and occasionally used *83d Armored Division.*

Raiders (Civil War; USA) A criminal gang, reportedly mostly Irish toughs and thugs from the stews of New York, who terrorized the other prisoners at Andersonville, assaulting and robbing the "fresh fish" as they arrived. The Raiders were charged with currying favor with the Confederates, acting as informers, and being a major source of Galvanized Yankees. Similar groups seem to have existed in other prison camps.

rail (Antiquity uncertain to Modern) *s.* A first lieutenant, whose insignia of grade is a single silver bar.

railhead (Civil War to Modern) A point to which supplies and troops are delivered by railroad, thence to be moved forward by other means of transportation. The term differs from civilian use in not necessarily designating the end of the line.

railroad tracks (Old Army, still occasionally heard) *s.* A captain's insignia of grade; two silver bars, connected by thin silver strips. Somewhat resembling crossties and rails.

rainbows (Modern) s. Recruits, so called because when they initially arrive at Army reception stations they are wearing a mixed bag of civilian clothing. "The young men and women are called 'rainbows.' Their bright clothing distinguishes them as civilians."

rainmakers (World War I) *s.* Heavy artillery, from the superstition that massed bombardments caused the heavy rains so characteristic of "sunny France." Reputable authority says that this term lasted into World War II, but we have never heard it.

rain room (Old Army to World War II; mostly Army) *s.* The bathhouse, where large numbers of men could shower together.

> Then they took me to the wash room—
> Place like I'd never seen before!
> Water runs in through a hole in the
> ceiling—
> Runs right out through a hole in the
> floor!

raise five, to (Modern) *s.* To salute.

Raise the flagpole, sergeant! (Antiquity uncertain to Modern) *s.* A catchphrase meaning that officers should not bother NCOs, but should let them do what they are supposed to do. The expression comes from a pre–World War II anecdote illustrating a teaching method said to be used at an OCS (or West Point) class: An eager class of students (or cadets) has been given the problem of erecting a flagpole in the shortest, most efficient way. A sergeant and several other enlisted men are present to do the actual work. Many minutes pass while the candidates (or cadets) argue about the best way to approach the job. They make several false starts, all ending in confusion. At last the tac takes charge. "Gentlemen," he says. "Observe how it is done." He turns to the sergeant and says, "Sergeant, raise the flagpole." Within a few minutes the flagpole is in place.

RAMF (Modern) *s.* Rear-Area Mother Fucker. See *REMF.*

ramp tramp (Vietnam and later; Air Force) *s.* The officer responsible for coordinating all flight-line activities at an air base. Such duty required him to be all over the place, usually in a jeep.

ramrod, to (Probably Modern) *s.* To provide leadership, backbone, or inspiration to an outfit, particularly to an outfit that is slack. "He's being sent in to ramrod that outfit." Surprisingly enough, despite the soldier's obsession with reaming, *ramrod* does not usually have an unfavorable connotation.

ramrod bread (Civil War; CSA) *s.* A field expedient for hardtack. Corn meal mixed with water was plastered over a rifle ramrod and cooked over the campfire. After it was more or less cooked, another layer was added. The final result was successive layers of soot between successive layers of scorched corn meal. Some Confederates called it *Jeff Davis bread.*

R & R (Korea to Modern) Officially, Rest and Recuperation leave; unofficially, Rape and Restitution or Rape and Ruin, in which instances it was identified with I & I. Usually a five-day leave period for combat soldiers (to Japan for soldiers in the Korean War). Frequently the soldier returned twice as tired as before he left, but without his previous thousand-yard stare. It was during the initial phase of this activity that serious consideration was given to issuing a special Close Combat Badge to all MPs serving in Japan. However, things soon more or less quieted down. It was only after the fighting in Korea had dwindled, and the men on leave were not so weary that R & R really became I & I. R & R is not chargeable against the soldier's leave time and is also given to personnel on hardship overseas tours. It was sometimes called *the little R*, to distinguish it from *the big R*, for *rotation* (Algeo).

range guard (Antiquity uncertain to Modern) A guard detail posted around the firing range to keep hunters, berry pickers, nature enthusiasts, lovers, drunks, and second lieutenants with compasses and maps from wandering into the impact area. It is amazing what shows up at times.

ranger (Colonial to Modern) A soldier specially trained for irregular warfare, raids, and long-range reconnaissance. The term originated in England, where it was applied to keepers of the royal forests, who waged constant guerrilla warfare against poachers. During the colonial period, many colonies raised small ranger units for border patrol, to apprehend escaped slaves, intercept Indian war parties, or escort surveyors and other officials. During the French and Indian Wars, British commanders enlisted ranger companies, chiefly for duty in Nova Scotia and New York. Service was for one year; rangers received high pay (plus bounties for scalps), but provided their own weapons and equipment. An infinite amount of nonsense has been written about these units, useful though they were. Needing cavalry in the West, Congress authorized a battalion of Mounted Rangers in 1832, the men to provide their own horses and weapons, but the unit proved ineffectual and was replaced by the 1st Dragoons. The Texas Rangers, however, were a mounted state police. The same title was given to Texas volunteer cavalry units during the Mexican and Civil wars. In World War II the United States organized six

Ranger Battalions for commando-type operations. They were useful troops, but were disbanded at the end of the war. During 1951–52, separate ranger companies were formed for service in Korea. Today, the tendency is to give all combat troops ranger training.

ranger killer (Korea; also Marines) *s.* The Russian 14.5mm antitank rifle. Allegedly nothing lighter could hurt a ranger.

ranger tab (Modern) A tab bearing the word *Ranger* worn on the left shoulder a half inch below the seam, by a soldier who has completed a Ranger course conducted at the Army Infantry School at Fort Benning, Georgia.

rank (1500s to Modern) 1. A line of soldiers abreast; also applied to horses, vehicles, teams, etc. In this sense of width, *rank* is opposed to *file*, which involves depth. 2. By extension, *the ranks* means those soldiers who would stand in mass formation, or corporals and privates as a group. (Sergeants would stand outside the formation.) 3. (Ancient to Modern) A soldier's relative position in the military hierarchy. Your rank is your relative position of superiority or inferiority in the Army as a whole and within your grade. A colonel (grade 0–6) *ranks* (is superior to) all officers in grades below 0–6, all warrant officers, and all enlisted personnel. Within his grade, he ranks all other colonels who were promoted to that grade after he was. He *is ranked by* (is subordinate to) all general officers and all colonels who received that promotion before he did. As an example, if the brigadier general commanding a brigade is killed or disabled, the ranking colonel assumes command. If no colonel is available, the ranking lieutenant colonel takes over. A goodly number of American regiments have come out of action under the ranking surviving lieutenant. See *grade, seniority, rank out, RHIP.*

rank, to 1. (Mid-19th century on) To outrank, to be superior or senior in rank. "Yes, sir. Times have changed since I was in the Army. In my day, a master sergeant ranked a first sergeant, but now it's the other way around." Or, "Jones may be ranking corporal because he was made before me, but he still doesn't know his ass from a hole in the ground." 2. (World War I) To pull rank: "He comes ranking in" (Nason, 1926).

rank and file (Colonial to late 19th century) Men carrying muskets (later, rifles) and standing in the ranks. In other words, corporals and privates, the effective strength of an army. Nowadays, unofficially, *rank and file* has come to mean the average soldier.

ranker (Colonial to Modern) *s.* A British term meaning a soldier serving in the ranks, particularly such a man when later commissioned as an officer. (Kipling's "gentlemen rankers" were men of good family whom circumstances forced to enlist and serve as privates.) Not used much by Americans, except by convinced anglophiles.

rank out, to (Ancient to approximately World War II) *s.* To force someone out of his quarters by right of seniority. A particularly vicious application of RHIP. You and your wife would spend considerable time and money fixing up a battered set of officers' quarters. Then an officer senior to you would be assigned to your post and could, if he wished, rank you out of them. If he did, unless you possessed more than normal human virtue, you did the same to the next junior officer, and so on down until the lowest-ranking married officer was forced to hunt up any available shed. By 1918 some common sense had been applied. Most post commanders forbade the practice. After that, to everyone's relief, it vanished. See *falling bricks*.

rate a drag, to (World War I) *s.* To have influence, to know someone with influence. Today we say *to have a drag*.

rater (Modern) The officer or NCO who is responsible for first filling out an *ER*.

ration (Ancient to Modern; also Marines) The amount of food allowed for one person (or one animal) for one day. It is a point of professional pride to bitch about your rations while putting them away as rapidly as possible.

ration breakdown (20th century) A place or point where the rations issued for a large organization (say a battalion) are divided up for issue to its component companies or batteries. Also, the act of dividing up the rations. Your company or battery representative there had better have a knack for basic arithmetic, a no-nonsense disposition, and eyes in the back of his head.

ration drawer (Modern) *s.* A soldier who takes his food, pay, and benefits with alacrity, but does little to earn them.

ration of shit (Modern) *s.* A hard time. "Don't hand me a ration of shit, George" (Bunting).

ration savings See *garrison rations*.

rattlesnake (Mid-19th century) *s.* The salt pork served to troops on board chartered transports.

rattlesnake colonel (Colonial) *s.* A dignitary of the outer frontier, usually an Indian trader or land speculator with a self-bestowed military title. Someone with Braddock used the term to describe "Colonel" Thomas Cresap, a noted frontier capitalist, who was then busy trying to sell badly spoiled meat to the British Army.

raven (Modern; Air Force) *s.* An intelligence or electronic-warfare technician flying as a nonrated member of an aircrew. Folk etymology attributes the origin of the term to the "black bird" aircraft, which were once used for electronic-warfare missions.

raw levies (Mexican War) *s.* A term used by the Old Regulars for the New Regulars, who were raised for the duration of the war only and were officered by deserving Democrats. See *mustang army*.

read, to (World War I to Modern) 1. *s.* To tell another radio operator how clearly you are receiving his message. "I read you five-by-five" ("I understand you perfectly"). 2. *s.* To understand, to comprehend. "I don't read you." 3. *s.* To give a pilot a heading, navigational data concerning his aircraft's exact location. See also *wet read*.

reading your shirt (World War I) *s.* Picking body lice out of the seams of one's shirt.

ready finders (Civil War; USA) *s.* Civilians who followed marching Union troops to pick up anything they discarded.

Ready on the firing line! (Modern) *s.* Ready for action. Taken from the command usual at the rifle range, where it is preceded by "Ready on the right" and "Ready on the left."

ready rack (World War II to Modern; also Marines) A rack handy to the breech of a tank's gun, holding an assortment of rounds—HE, AP, or others—that might be required at once. Hence, a handy place to keep anything that might be needed on short notice.

real army, the That part of the Army (possibly somewhat idealized in the minds of soldiers exiled to school or staff duty) that has weapons and trains at using them, because combat arms duty "is what the Army is all about." Some people can feel useful doing almost anything, like pushing papers for an Equal Opportunity Officer, whose function is to heckle busy commanders to make sure all minority members in their organizations are happy, especially if working conditions are comfortable. The real soldier, however, gets nervous in the service in an outfit that seems to have lost interest in the basic purpose of his profession.

real estate transfer (World War II) The meteorological condition prevailing at Camp Roberts, California. In the morning the wind hurled vast clouds of dust in one steady direction. (We do not remember which.) In late afternoon, an opposite wind blew it all back. An old-timer or two claimed the term came into use at Pershing's camps around Dublán, during the Mexican Punitive Expedition in 1916 —"the windiest place in the world" Lt. George S. Patton, Jr., called it.

real world (Modern) *s.* A TAD (Temporary Active Duty) reservist's name for civilian life, from which he recently departed and to which he will shortly return. See *outside.*

rear-rank Rudy (World War II, perhaps earlier) *s.* A low-quality soldier. His sergeant has put him in the rear rank so that he will not be too obvious during drill and inspections.

recall (Old, Old Army to World War II) A bugle call, originally a signal for troops in action to retire. Later, it was used to indicate the end of a period of drill or fatigue.

recognize, to (At least 1920 and later; West Point) 1. *s.* To admit a plebe formally to upper-class status. After the graduation parade, in a formal ceremony, each plebe shakes hands with each upperclassman in his company and is thereby "recognized" or accepted. 2. (For upperclassmen) *s.* To treat a plebe as an equal.

records manglement (Modern) *s.* A play on records management. See *career manglement.*

Recreational Services (Modern) An organization within the Department of the Army responsible for administering arts and crafts, youth activities, sports, libraries, music and theater, and outdoor recreation programs. Until 1974 this organization was called *Special Services.*

recruit (Ancient to Modern) 1. While in the Renaissance a recruit was primarily a body of auxiliary troops or reinforcements, since the 18th century the term has meant a new soldier, particularly a young and inexperienced enlisted man. He may have enlisted without persuasion, been recruited by a recruiting officer or NCO, or been drafted. Also called a *rookie* or a *john.* 2. (August 1948 to July 1961) Officially, the lowest grade in the Army, used for new soldiers and soon outgrown. Abbreviated *Rct.* In July 1961 the title of the grade was changed to *Private E-1.*

recruiter (Modern) A soldier, operating outside, whose mission is to persuade others to join the Army or, if they are eligible and need no persuasion, to facilitate their enlistment. The modern descendant of the old recruiting sergeant or recruiting officer. At present recruiters are carefully selected, highly motivated young men and women in pay grades E-5 through E-7, whose assignments are controlled by the US Army Recruiting Command (USAREC, also known as *Useless Wreck*). For the most part, their work is very hard and is complicated by the fact that each recruiter must cope with a quota system. This quota system has been a major contributing factor to the scandals that have rocked the Recruiting Command periodically. The need for high-pressure salesmanship makes the recruiting service unpopular with many professional NCOs.

recruiting NCO (Modern) An NCO whose mission is to counsel active-duty soldiers about reenlistment opportunities and actually to reenlist them. He is assigned to a unit or post and performs his duty among the soldiers at his installation. Previously called a *career counselor*. Not to be confused with a *recruiter*, who operates among civilians.

recycled, to be (Modern) *s.* To be put back in a training course because of incompetence or sickness.

recycle platoon (Modern) *s.* A platoon in a training unit into which are put soldiers who have been recycled—slow learners or physically unfit individuals who cannot keep up with their comrades. The Army, always ready to soften today's watered-down form of basic training, has banned the expression. See *awkward squad, bolo, goon platoon.*

red ass, to have the (World War II) *s.* To be angry. "Pete sure has the red ass since he got his Dear John." Later, the expression was often simplified to *to have the ass*, but by around 1955 it had expanded into *to have the .30-caliber ass,* meaning extremely irritated. The anger involved seems to have been of a more enduring type than that involved in an *orgasm in place*, which was just a blowup.

Red Ball Express (World War II on) *s.* Various high-priority transportation systems. During and after World War II the term referred to Army supply trucks, in carefully planned one-way route systems, that supplied the troops. During the Vietnam War, the Red Ball Express was a special delivery system for transporting repair parts rapidly, in order to remove equipment from deadline status. From railroad name for a fast freight train.

Red Diamond (Modern) The 5th Infantry Division, so called because of its insignia.

redirects (Modern) Mail that is returned from a unit for forwarding to a new address.

red disturbance (Old, Old Army) *s.* Whiskey or any available substitute. We *think* that the term *red ruin* may also have been used.

First I drunk red liquor,
Then I drunk brown.
Now I'm a deadbeat
In San Antone town!

redeploy (World War I to Modern; all Services) To move organizations (or supplies or individuals) from one theater of operations to another.

red eye redeye (World War II) *s.* Ketchup. A common civilian nickname, brought into the service by new recruits. Ketchup was also occasionally called *blood.*

red leg 1. (Post–Civil War to Modern) *s.* An artilleryman. Artillerymen formerly wore a red stripe down the outside seam of their trousers. The term persisted on up through the days of OD uniforms. The fact that horse artillerymen wore (at a later date) high-laced leather boots that were highly polished, usually with a reddish tinge, may have helped the term survive. 2. (Civil War) *s.* A Union militiaman or home guard in the Kansas area, so nicknamed because he wore leggings made of red sheepskin. The Red Legs gave occasional good service, but were generally given to horse-stealing and to robbing any citizens against whom a suspicion of southern sympathy could be invented. Also called *Red-Legged Scouts, Jayhawkers.*

red-legged infantry 1. (Mexican War, possibly earlier) *s.* Artillerymen serving as infantry. During the early days of our republic, only one or two companies in each artillery regiment were equipped and armed as field artillery. The other soldiers were employed as garrisons for coastal fortifications or as infantry in the field. In the latter service, only the red stripes along the seams of an NCO's trousers distinguished him at a distance from an ordinary doughboy. 2. (Civil War; USA) *s.* Zouave and other regiments fancying red trousers were frequently referred to as *red-legged.*

red phone (Modern; all Services) A special telephone, to be used only in the direst emergencies. It is colored bright red so that you will not use it by mistake —another reason for not having colorblind soldiers. The hookups vary in different headquarters, but normally, taking the handset off the hook rings other special phones in the offices or quarters of everyone who needs to know that the balloon is about to go up—or has already gone. Really complex command systems may have phones of many colors, permitting a high degree of flexibility in who gets scared to death (and later registers his feelings forcibly) when the cleaning detail accidentally knocks a handset off the hook while dusting the phone next to it.

regiment (Ancient to Modern) An administrative and tactical unit below a division or brigade and above a battalion. It is normally commanded by a colonel. While the composition of a regiment has varied from time to time and from branch of service to branch of service, it typically is composed of three battalions, each consisting of four companies (or troops or batteries), headquarters, supply, and miscellaneous personnel.

regimental monkey (World War II and probably earlier) *s.* The regimental bandmaster.

regreening process (Modern) *s.* Reorientation; a periodic briefing given to officers who have been serving on non-Army joint staffs or at the Office of the Secretary of Defense to inform them of developments in the Army at large. See *purple-suiter.*

regroup, to (At least World War II to Modern) To rally or reorganize; to move activities from one spot to another.

regular (Modern) *s.* A member of the Regular Army, a professional soldier. "The two sergeants, both regulars" (Marshall, 1971). See also *RA.*

Regular Army regular army (As a general term, since early 18th century in Great Britain, and from early 19th century to 1920 in the United States; as an official component of the US Army, 1920 on) The permanent standing army of the United States, recruited on a volunteer basis. For much of the history of the United States, it has been the only active component of the Army. After the ending of hostilities in the Revolutionary War, Congress declared almost complete demobilization, but a permanent armed force soon became necessary, both for internal use and against Indian attacks on the frontiers. This body of men developed into the Regular Army. For most of the 19th century it was a very small organization (approximately 6,500 officers and men at the outbreak of the Mexican War, about 15,800 at the beginning of the Civil War), but it served as the skeleton for the enormous expansions of the Civil War, the Spanish-American War, and the wars of the 20th century. See *RA, Old Army.*

Regulators (Civil War; USA) *s.* A vigilante group formed by responsible prisoners within Andersonville. They crushed the Raiders gang, executing some of its leaders.

relook (Modern) *s.* A board of officers convened to reconsider those officers who have been passed over for promotion.

REMF (Modern) *s.* Rear-Echelon Mother Fuckers. Support and noncombat troops.

Remington Raiders Remington Rangers (Modern) *s.* Army clerk typists and office workers in general. *Remington* here means the typewriter.

remount (About 1800 to World War II) A new horse or mule acquired by the Army. The term was applied indifferently to saddle, draft, and pack animals.

remount station 1. Officially, a place where newly purchased horses or mules were trained for military use. Also called a *remount depot.* 2. (Mexican Punitive Expedition, 1916–17) *s.* The official red-light district at General Pershing's base camp at Dublán, Chihuahua, Mexico. Like all of Black Jack's doings, it was strictly regulated. A soldier had to have a medical certificate and $2 to go in, and could stay thirty minutes. The women (all Mexicans, to avoid racial disputes) were regularly inspected. Professionally virtuous Americans were shocked, but the VD rate of the troops hit a record low, and public order and decency were much encouraged.

re-orgy week (West Point) *s.* Reorganization Week in August, at which time cadet organizations are reorganized for the beginning of classes in fall.

Repertorial Corps (Civil War; USA) *s.* In the Army of the Cumberland, a name given to the war correspondents—"that lying body of men"—accompanying it. The nickname obviously was adapted from *repertorial company,* a group of ham actors who regularly repeat a limited sequence of dramas. See *Bohemian Brigade.*

repple depple (World War II to Modern) *s.* A replacement depot, where they kept the human spare parts until needed.

reserve 1. (Ancient to Modern) A body of troops held back for later use. Often in plural form, *reserves.* 2. (Modern) By analogy, a parachutist's second parachute, on which he relies, should his main fail. The reserve is much smaller than the main.

Reserve/Reserves (Properly Organized Reserves) For the Army, these are the Army National Guard and the Army Reserve. In general service talk, however—such as "Reserve officer"—*Reserve* applies only to the latter. Established in 1916 and several times reorganized, the Army Reserve is a federal force, unlike the National Guard, which functions as state military organizations when not in federal service. It provides trained units and additional qualified individual soldiers in times of national emergency. The Navy, Marines, and Air Force have similar Reserve components; the Air Force has Air National Guard units.

reserve ration (World War I) A ration consisting of a pound of canned meat, a pound of hard bread, coffee, sugar, and salt. Each soldier was issued two of them, which were supposed to be saved for use in case the supposedly automatic supply of field rations failed. Somehow, they tended to evaporate.

respects (Old, Old Army to World War II) The customary mode of address of a junior officer to his senior: "Lieutenant Bender's respects, sir, and may he report that the colonel's tent is on fire." (The lieutenant is speaking in the third person to the colonel himself!)

Rest! A command in drill, permitting troops to move (although the right foot must remain in place), talk, smoke, or drink from their canteens. It is given from "At ease!"

restriction Short for *restriction to quarters.*

retread (World War II to Modern) *s.* A soldier who has been discharged or retired, and then is called back to active duty. The term is based on the practice of retreading automobile tires that have been worn smooth, and reusing them. As applied to people, the term has no unfavorable connotation. Also *tread.*

retreat (Ancient to Modern) 1. As defined by Garber and Bond, "An involuntary retrograde movement forced on a command as a result of an unsuccessful operation or combat." Since at least World War I, a traditional and somewhat hypocritical use of words. If the enemy is defeated, he retreats; but if we are defeated, we retire—which sounds much more dignified. 2. An evening formation, held on all Army posts, just before the firing of the evening (or sunset) gun and the lowering of the flag. Also, the drumbeat or bugle call used to signal this formation. In earlier days, all troops not then on duty were to go to their quarters. (Tradition has it that this was a means of getting them inside the fort before dark.) Even in the early 1940s it was customary to go indoors when retreat was sounded.

return, to (Colonial to World War II) To place on the records officially, in some instances amounting to *to classify*; to report. "There were five or six others who 'showed blood,' but not enough to be returned as wounded" (Buell).

re-up, to (At least early 20th century to Modern) *s.* To reenlist. There are several theories for the origin of the term. When a soldier enlists, he raises his right hand when taking the oath; reenlisting would be re-upping his hand. A soldier also *signs up*, by affixing his signature to the necessary papers. Thirdly, if one up and enlisted in the first place, perhaps one re-ups for the second hitch. Moe (AS 37:3, October 1962) quotes a 1913 usage:

I hated to leave those Isles [the
 Philippines]
Of prickly heat and itch
But I had to go or else re-up
For seven long years hitch.

Dr. Lighter traces the term to a 1906 Army source.

re-up bonus (Modern) *s.* A specified amount of money paid to a soldier when he reenlists. The amount varies, but in recent years soldiers qualified in special skills have received thousands of dollars for reenlisting.

reveille (Ancient to Modern) The second bugle call of the soldier's day. From the mid-17th century to shortly after the Civil War, it was a drumbeat to "advertise the army that it is day-light, and that the sentinels are to forbear challenging" (James). At present it is a ceremony that accompanies the raising of the flag, involving a special formation, when practical, and a roll call. Reveille is not used to awaken the troops; that should have been done a quarter-hour earlier by first call. But in popular usage, reinforced over the years by thousands of sergeants who have delighted in snapping on the lights and running through the barracks shouting, "Reveille, reveille! Hit the deck! Everybody up! Drop your cocks and grab your socks!" and similar invitations, it has come to mean a call to awaken and get up. The words most commonly associated with the call are:

I can't get 'em up, I can't get 'em up,
I can't get 'em up in the morning;
I can't get 'em up, I can't get 'em up,
I can't get 'em up at all.
The corporal's worse than the
privates;
The sergeant's worse than the
corporals;
The lieutenant's worse than the
sergeants;
And the captain's the worst of all.

But there are many other versions, which have little in common except the refrain, "I can't get 'em up." Some of them were not intended for publication. We recall one that began:

Get up you sons-a-bitches
Pull on your lousy britches
Oh, I can't get 'em up. . . .

One officer from each company is expected to *stand* or *take reveille* (meaning to be present at this formation). As the Old Army captain told a newly assigned shavetail, "I believe in sharing the work equally. I've stood reveille for the past sixteen years. You do it for the next sixteen."

review (Ancient to Modern) 1. A formal inspection of an organization. 2. A ceremony to honor a dignitary or to present decorations to military personnel. During a review, the person honored may troop the line (pass slowly before the front rank of the troops drawn up) or the colors may be trooped.

reviewer (Modern) The individual responsible for examining the comments of the rater and indorser on ERs. If the reviewer considers that there is a discrepancy between the comments of the rater and the indorser, he can add his own comments or may initiate action to obtain further information. Now called the *senior rater* on OERs.

RFA (Modern) Reserve Forces Act. A soldier brought to active duty by the act of 1957, which prescribed that members of the Army Reserve and Army National Guard (recruited after a certain date) should serve six months' active duty before beginning their seven-year obligation in the Reserve or Guard. The RAs and draftees often despised the RFA as a shirker who took the easy way out; the RFA looked down his nose at the others as being too stupid or shortsighted to avoid longer active service.

RHIP Rank Has Its Privileges. A basic fact of life in any profession. Today, it means just the little things that make a senior officer's life less harassed, like a reserved parking lot, but in the Old Army (see *rank out*) it could be rough as a cob:

The Captain told the Looie
To sweep the mess hall floor.
The Looie told the Sergeant,
And gosh but he was sore.
The Sergeant yelled at the Corporal
As mad as mad could be,

And I've just talked with the
Corporal
—So I guess it's up to me.

rhubarb 1. (Antiquity uncertain to Modern, but from late 19th century in civilian use) *s.* Any sort of minor engagement, from a barroom brawl to a spat between two staff sections. Probably from stage use, where players muttered or shouted the word *rhubarb* to create the impression of crowd noises or turmoil; perhaps ultimately from *hubbub*. 2. (World War II) *s.* A small-scale, low-level harassing mission by fighters, fighter-bombers, or light bombers against targets of opportunity. Probably adopted from the British.

rice-belly (Modern) *s.* A derogatory term for any Oriental, especially one with an enlarged abdomen.

rice-paddy daddy (Modern) *s.* A soldier who lives with a native woman who is not his wife, especially if he fathers children by her. A common expression in the Far East.

ride the sick book, to (At least Old Army to Modern) *s.* To go on sick call constantly, usually as a trick to avoid work, discomfort, or danger. Separating such goldbricks and malingerers from the genuinely sick is always a rough job for medical personnel.

RIF riff (20th century) *s.* Reduction In Force. A controversial (because it sometimes seems grossly unfair) way of reducing the Army's officer strength for economic reasons. In theory, the least effective officers are riffed, but in practice favoritism has been alleged. When an officer is selected for RIF, he is notified by official letter that his services are no longer required. He may become a Reserve officer or he may be permitted to remain on active duty as an enlisted man in order to qualify for retirement benefits. When an officer is released from duty, he is given a cash settlement, but if he remains on active duty as an enlisted man, he must eventually pay the money back. "Now he'll come under the Reduction in Force the Army's putting through and be riffed" (Doulis).

rifles (Modern) *s.* Infantrymen. "How many rifles wounded?" (Smith).

Right of the Line The 14th Infantry Regiment. The right of the line was traditionally the post of honor, reserved for picked troops. At the final review of the Army of the Potomac, in 1865, the V Corps, of which the 14th Infantry was a part, was told to take this post.

right-shoulder patch (Modern) A patch worn on the right shoulder of the uniform coat with the insignia of the unit in which a soldier has served during wartime. To have the patch of a line unit is considered best, but a support or headquarters-type unit patch is better than nothing. The right-shoulder patch is the mark of a real veteran who has seen wartime service, and soldiers who are not authorized to wear such patches are often looked down upon as tyros.

ring knocker (Old Army to Modern; also Navy) *s.* A disagreeable type of graduate of the US Military (or Naval) Academy. He is overwhelmingly proud of his achievement and looks upon nongraduates as inferior species. His class ring is his patent of nobility. If you do not notice it and genuflect immediately, he will irritably bang it against the table or bar to call you to your senses. Fortunately, the breed is somewhat rare. Of the three we met in thirty-nine years of service, two had come close to being the goats of their respective classes.

Rinkydink (Modern; principally Air Force) *s.* Incirlik Air Force Base, Adana, Turkey. The word itself is a civilian slang term for rubbish or the third-rate.

rip cords (Modern) *s.* The small bits of thread or string that fringe or unravel from chevrons, shoulder patches, uniform fabric, etc. Also called *Irish pennants.*

Rise and shine! (Antiquity uncertain) *s.* A traditional exhortation used by NCOs while getting soldiers awake and moving in the chill, gray dawn. It may alternate with strictly professional urgings. Reportedly borrowed from the British.

roach coach (Modern) *s.* A mobile snack-bar vehicle operated by the PX service. So called because the food offered is often unappetizing and stale, and is widely believed to be the staple of roaches and other insects.

roadguards (At least World War II to Modern) Men detailed to run ahead of a marching formation to stop oncoming traffic at intersections. The commands for placing them and returning them are "Roadguards left [or right], post!" and "Recover!" The term *roadguard* also appears in the catchphrase *Since Caesar was a roadguard*, meaning that something has not happened for a long, long time.

roadrunners (Vietnam) Members of reconnaissance teams serving with Green Beret long-range reconnaissance detachments. They were selected from the Civilian Irregular Defense Group, an organization of Vietnamese (mostly from ethnic minorities) recruited for service with the Special Forces. They operated in four-man teams, wearing native clothing and carrying captured weapons and equipment. Inserted by helicopter deep within enemy-held areas, they moved openly by designated roads and trails to prearranged pickup points, collecting intelligence en route.

roast beef (Possibly Revolutionary to at least early 19th century) *s.* The drumbeat for noon and (sometimes) evening meals. It was obviously borrowed from the British, who used *roast beef of Old England* to summon officers to dinner. The beat may have been used during the Revolution, although it is not on Steuben's listing of official calls. See *peas upon a trencher.*

rock and roll, to rock 'n' roll, to (Modern) 1. *s.* To lock and load a weapon. 2. *s.* To place a weapon on full automatic. This would produce (with a rifle, such as the M16) a burst of fire that would last as long as you squeezed the trigger—or until the magazine emptied.

rockers (World War II to Modern) *s.* The arcs at the bottom of sleeve insignia of grade of senior NCOs and, at present, certain other grades. When a sergeant wins promotion to staff sergeant, he is said to *get his first rocker*. This means that an arc has been added below the three chevrons that he already has.

Rock of Chickamauga 1. Maj. Gen. George H. Thomas. Old Pop Thomas, a Virginian who remained loyal to the United States in 1861 and never lost a fight. Also known as *Old Slow Trot* and *Old Pap*. 2. The US 19th Infantry Regiment, for its part in Thomas's grim rear-guard battle at Chickamauga in September 1863. Its men were called *Chicks*, at least during the 1950s.

Rock of the Marne (World War I to Modern) The 38th Infantry Regiment, thus honored for its outstanding valor and efficiency during the Second Battle of the Marne, in which it saved the left flank of the French 9th Army. This title is carried also by the 3d Infantry Division, to which the 38th then belonged, since its other regiments also did well that day.

Rocky Mountain canary (Indian Wars) *s.* A rule or burro, so called for its plaintive hee-haw.

rodeo (World War II; Air Force) *s.* A fighter sweep over enemy territory. It differed from a *circus* in that no bombers were included to stir up enemy fighters.

"Rogue's March, The" (Old, Old Army to Old Army) The traditional tune played when a soldier was drummed out of the service for dishonorable conduct.

ROK Rock (Korea and later) *s.* A soldier of the Republic of Korea (South Korea).

rolling kitchen (World War I) A large iron range mounted on two wheels. Its chimney was hinged so that it could be folded down into a horizontal position for traveling, giving it the appearance of a heavy gun. Also called a *chow gun, chow cannon, slum cannon, slum gun, slum burner, soup cannon.*

roll out, to (Ancient to Modern) *s.* To get up, to get out of bed.

First thing in the morning,
Guy with a horn makes an awful
noise.
Then along comes the First
Sergeant,
Says "Wake up and roll out, boys."

roll over (Old Army to World War II) *s.* The last day of a soldier's enlistment. He does no duty. If he has reenlisted, he gets the afternoon and night off. The term probably comes from rolling over and going back to sleep, instead of getting up. In World War II the custom was sometimes followed for soldiers who were being transferred.

roll up one's flaps, to (Some antiquity, sporadic popularity) *s.* To stop, especially to stop talking. "Roll up your flaps" means "Shut up." Also, a soldier might say, "Guess I'll roll up my flaps" when he was dropping out of a crap game. We would guess that the flaps mentioned are tent flaps, which would be rolled up for better ventilation when the soldier turned in.

Ronson (World War II) *s.* The M4 Sherman tank. Since it was gasoline-propelled, it had the tendency to burst into flames when hit. From the advertising slogan for Ronson cigarette lighters: "They light up every time." Probably of British or German origin.

rookie (Old, Old Army to Modern) 1. A new recruit, particularly one that is inept, green, and naive. In years past, at least, frequently shortened to *rook.* Recorded in England from the 1890s. Sometimes taken to be a distortion of the word *recruit*, sometimes referred to as *rook*, a cant word for a sucker. 2. Something new. A "rookie regiment" or "rookie outfit," meaning one newly organized.

Roosevelt's Butchers (World War II) A title claimed by the 30th Infantry Division because some German supposedly called it that. The official nickname is *Old Hickory.*

ropey (World War II; Air Force) *s.* Defective, displeasing, not up to accepted standards. Adopted from the RAF.

roster duty roster (At least Old Army to Modern; all Services) A list of the men in a company, used in assigning them to various duties and details, such as guard, KP, CQ, and the like. Sometimes there was a separate KP roster and guard roster. Whatever the system, it was remarkable how often your name would turn up, particularly in short-handed outfits. There are also rosters of officers for various jobs, usually that of duty officer. In higher headquarters, pulling duty officer entitles you to try to sleep in an inner sanctum with a red phone next to your ear.

rotary-wing (Modern) A helicopter, because the "wings," or rotors, rotate. The opposite of *fixed-wing*.

rotation rotation date (World War II to Modern) The day on which a soldier leaves for the United States from an overseas tour.

ROTC (1920 to Modern) Reserve Officer Training Corps, established during the reorganization of the Army in 1920. It is a training program established at civilian educational institutions to provide training and to qualify selected students for appointment in the Army as second lieutenants. Graduates must serve two years on active duty.

rough rider 1. (Mid-18th century to perhaps late 19th century in Great Britain) A reliable cavalry soldier who assisted the regimental riding master in training remounts and teaching recruits horsemanship. There was usually one rough rider to each troop. He had de facto status as an NCO and received extra pay. The practice was followed in early American cavalry units, but the term *riding master* seems to have been preferred during the Revolution and War of 1812. 2. (Late 19th century) Various secondary meanings, such as irregular cavalry and cowboys. "When finally the Generals of Division and Brigade began to write in formal communications about our regiment as the 'Rough Riders,' we adopted the term ourselves" (Theodore Roosevelt, quoted by *OED*). 3. (Spanish-American War) A soldier of the 1st Regiment of US Volunteer Cavalry, alias Roosevelt's Rough Riders. (Three regiments were authorized, but the 2d and 3d never left training camps.) The 1st had that consummate politician and military amateur, Theodore Roosevelt, for a lieutenant colonel. It was very much pampered in matters of equipment, weapons, and assignments, and the newspapers trumpeted its uprisings and down-sittings with great fervor. Its men were excellent. Roosevelt saw to a publicity-inspiring mix of rugged westerners and eastern college boys. But the war really could have been won without them. Also known as *Teddy's Terrors, Rocky Mountain Rustlers*, and —in Cuba—*Wood's Weary Walkers*, after their own Col. Leonard Wood, another expert conniver.

round 1. (Ancient to Modern) An inspection tour of the guards, sentries, and/or outposts by an officer or NCO to see that they are properly alert. 2. (Mid-18th century to Modern) A cartridge, shell, or other form of ammunition for a single shot. "The clip of the American M1 rifle held eight rounds." "The German MG42 light machine gun could fire 1,200 rounds a minute." *Round*, in this sense, grew out of the older meaning of a single shot fired by every soldier in a unit—that is, *all around*.

round brown (Modern) *s.* Another name for the Smokey the Bear hat, which is round and brown. "Smokey the Bear hats, known as 'round browns' " (Rogan).

roundeye round-eye (Occupation of Japan and later) *s.* An Occidental, especially a female of the sort. As opposed to *slanteye*. "Five thousand men without a round-eye white female in sight" (Broughton).

route order /rout *to rhyme with* about/ (Ancient to Modern) A relaxed manner of marching in which soldiers are permitted to talk, smoke, carry their weapons in the most comfortable and convenient manner, and march out of step. It is used on long marches and on crossing bridges (to avoid the serious vibrations set up by troops marching in cadence).

route-step 1. Marching in route order, hence out of step and relaxed. 2. (At least 1930s on) *s.* Sloppy, untrained, undisciplined, indifferent; used of either a person or a unit. "You know—Bravo Company—the one that's been doing the fucking fighting while you route-step bastards sit on the water so's we all die of thirst" (Groom).

RSOP (Old Army to Modern) Reconnaissance, Selection, and Occupation of a Position. The art of picking out a good position and getting into it without attracting undesirable attention.

rubber bitch rubber lady (Modern; also Marines) *s.* An inflatable rubber air mattress issued to troops in the field.

ruffles and flourishes (Ancient to Modern) A form of military honors rendered to visiting dignitaries. A ruffle is a low vibrating drumbeat; a flourish, a short run of notes from a bugle or trumpet. The number varies according to the status of the visitor.

Ruff-puff (Vietnam; all Services) *s.* The RF/PF (Vietnamese Regional/Popular Forces). Paramilitary troops used to supplement the regular forces by performing static defense and regional security missions. Lightly armed and not very well trained, these troops were often poorly led and motivated. Their effectiveness, according to even their American advisers, was considered equivalent to a rough puff of wind.

rug rats (Post–World War II) *s.* Legal dependent children.

run a Mick, to shove a Mick, to (Civil War; CSA) *s.* Junius H. Browne, one of the Bohemian Brigade, war correspondent of the *New York Tribune*, was captured by the Confederates and imprisoned for a time at Castle Thunder, Richmond. On one occasion he was confined with a group of Confederate military criminals, who told him of their exploits. " 'Running a Mick' was to get an Irishman drunk, induce him to enlist for two or three hundred dollars, obtain five times that sum from some citizen desirous of procuring a substitute, and after sending the Hibernian to Camp Lee in the forenoon, to go out for him towards evening, bring him in again, and sell him to some other individual requiring a representative in the field" (Browne).

run a sandy, to (World War I and perhaps later) *s.* To fool someone, to pull the wool over someone's eyes. "Don't try to run a sandy on me. I didn't get these stripes yesterday." Also civilian slang.

runners (Early 20th century to World War II; also Marines) Volunteers picked for intelligence, agility, and reliability who served as messengers for front-line units. They were the most effective means of communication available when shell fire cut the field telephone line.

runt company (Antiquity uncertain; West Point) *s.* A company of soldiers shorter than average. Until recent years cadets were assigned to company by height, in order to present a more uniform appearance on parade. The company with the shortest men was the *runt company.* Since it was at considerable disadvantage in intercompany athletics, the custom was finally abandoned.

run the guard, to (Considerable Antiquity, at least 1848) *s.* Evading the guard around a camp, usually by literally running through the guard lines. The practice was especially prevalent among Civil War volunteers, who, as freeborn American citizens, frequently felt that they had a perfect right to duck out to have a drink, steal chickens, see a wench, or simply wander around the countryside.

run the mail, to (Early 19th century) *s.* To smuggle intoxicating liquor into camp. Smugglers were known as *mail runners*; and the liquor, made from the cheapest possible ingredients, sold for exorbitant prices, and requiring "a copper-lined throat and a stomach of gutta percha," was the *mail* (Prucha).

runt with a runt's complex (World War II and later) *s.* A shorter-than-average soldier who tries to compensate for his lack of inches by being extra tough. Such men are not uncommon. Sawed-off officers and sergeants may be regarded with considerable suspicion when they join a new unit.

ruptured duck 1. (World War II and immediately after) *s.* The awkward-eagle lapel pin given to all personnel mustered out of the Armed Forces at the end of the war, and generally mislaid as quickly as possible. 2. (Modern) *s.* An honorable discharge certificate. The coat of arms of the United States (a "flattened" eagle) appears on it. 3. (Modern) *s.* The basic insignia of grade for an Army specialist. A *ruptured duck with an umbrella* is a specialist of the fifth class; the arc over the eagle device resembles the curve of an opened umbrella. Also called *chicken coop with a roof*. 4. (Vietnam) *s.* The badge of the signal corps, Army of the Republic of Vietnam; so termed by American advisers.

☆☆☆☆S☆☆☆☆

sabot (Civil War) A wooden disk turned to fit the bore of a muzzle-loading, smoothbore field gun. In a complete round of ammunition, the cannon ball (whether solid shot or explosive shell) was fastened to the front of the sabot by thin metal strips; the woolen powder bag, containing the propelling charge, was fastened to the rear face of the sabot. Sabots were usually made of poplar wood. Their function, besides holding the complete round together, was to make it easy to center the round in the bore of the gun.

sack (Antiquity uncertain; all Services) *s.* A bed or any sort of place to sleep. A *sack artist* is a soldier who sleeps at every possible opportunity. To go to bed or go to sleep is variously *to hit the sack, to sack in*, or *to sack out*. *Sack time* is sleep. While the term would seem to point at least to a memory of the time when a bed was likely to be a sack of straw, the earliest recorded use, cited by Partridge (1970) is for the British Navy of the early 19th century, where a *sack* was a hammock.

sacred cow (World War II to Modern; originally Air Force, but now general) *s.* The private airplane of some VIP.

SAD S & D (Modern; also Marines) Search And Destroy. Clearing an area of enemy troops and of anything that serves to feed or shelter them. A tactic widely employed during the Vietnam War.

Sad Sack (World War II and later) The hero of a comic strip in *Yank* (and, after the war, commercially syndicated), drawn by Sgt. George Baker. The Sad Sack did his best, but he was not very bright, always had bad luck, and was often victimized. From the expression a *sad sack of shit*.

Safety-First 7th (Spanish-American War and later) *s.* The famous, socially elite 7th Regiment of the New York National Guard. During the Spanish-American War, it refused to accept active duty for fear its pristine elegance might be contaminated by contact with West Pointers and "Tom, Dick, and Harry."

SAFU /'saf-foo/ (World War II; rare) *s.* Self-Adjusting Fuck-Up. Used for situations like the confused and scattered drops of US paratroops during the invasion of Sicily. The troops involved somehow sorted themselves out and saved the day.

Saigon commando Saigon warrior (Vietnam; all Services) *s.* A soldier who spent his time in a rear-echelon environment, especially Saigon. Sometimes applied to persons who were not in fighting units, regardless of where they were assigned in the war zone.

Saigon quickstep (Vietnam; all Services) *s.* Diarrhea. "The salad is guaranteed to induce a malady known as the Saigon 'Quick Step' " (Mulligan). See also *quickstep.*

Saigon tea (Vietnam; all Services) *s.* A small glass of real tea or colored water hustled by Saigon bargirls. Each girl made a small percentage from every glass of tea bought for her by patrons. The expression was familiar throughout Vietnam, wherever American soldiers congregated. Our sergeant major claims to have first heard it in a Saigon bar in 1962.

Saint Agony (World War I) *s.* Soldiers' version of *Saint Aignon*, France, where the replacement pool for the Infantry was located.

salt horse (Civil War; also Navy) *s.* Corned beef, usually containing as much salt as beef, and therefore difficult to cook in the field. Also called *old bull.* From earlier sailors' slang.

salt junk (Civil War) *s.* Salt pork. From earlier sailors' slang. *Junk* is a technical term for a piece of old rope, to which the toughness and stringiness of the meat are compared. In nautical and civilian slang, *salt junk* can also be salt beef.

salvage (World War I to Modern) 1. Basically, material gathered from the battlefield or from an abandoned installation for sorting, repair, and reuse. In World War II, salvage was also a system whereby a GI could turn in worn or misfit clothing (and sometimes other defective equipment) in exchange for new items. This, at least, was the theory. The articles were taken to the local QM, sorted out, and often reissued back, worn and misfit. This was done on *salvage day*, the first of the month in some outfits. 2. *s.* A euphemism for theft, whether from a dump or another outfit.

Sam Browne (Brown) belt (World War I to early World War II) A sword belt invented by Gen. Samuel James Browne of the British India Army during the late 19th century. According to report, an old wound made it difficult for him to carry and draw a saber with the regulation belt. The belt he devised consisted of a waist belt supported by a narrower belt worn diagonally over the right shoulder. Officers of the AEF adopted it from the British. They did not wear sabers, but the belt was dramatic-looking, and it soon became official US gear. It was abolished about halfway through World War II. During the period of its use, it was the symbol of becoming an officer, much like stripes for an enlisted man. *He got his Sam Browne* meant that a man had become an officer. "Hell of a note goin' home without a Sam Brown [*sic*]" (Dos Passos).

same-same samo-samo samey-samey (Post–World War II; Far East; all Services) *s.* Just like, the same as, in Pidgin English. Norman reports *samey-samey* and *samo-samo* in Japan prior to 1955, and Algeo reports *samee-samee* in Korea in 1960. These expressions also were widely used in Vietnamese pidgin and are still used in Korean pidgin. Our sergeant major confesses to using *same-same* frequently in his everyday conversation, out of force of habit, to the utter perplexity of most of his listeners. *Samey-samey* goes back at least to the early 20th century in civilian pidgin in China.

SAMI /'sam-my/ (West Point) *s.* Saturday Morning Inspection.

Sammie (World War I) An unsuccessful nickname for the American soldier, favored only by civilians, and that, briefly. It was probably inspired by *Uncle Sam.* According to some sources, the British started it. The average Yank or doughboy regarded it as a professional insult. See *doughboy.*

samshu (1930s; Asiatic Fleet of the US Navy, but occasional Army use after World War II) In the earlier use, a beverage peddled by bumboat men to EPDs and men restricted to the ships. It was brewed from concentrated garbage and hoof parings swept from the floor of a farrier's shop and then distilled in a modified brass radiator from a 1915 Model-T Ford. It sold for about 3 cents a quart and was not worth it. From Cantonese *sam shao* 'triple distilled'. (According to the reference books, it should be distilled from millet.)

-san (Post–World War II; Far East especially) *s.* As used by Americans, a suffix applied to names or persons, with various meanings: the one in charge, Mr., an expletive without much meaning, etc. Thus, *papasan* 'an old man'; *mamasan* 'lady of the house', 'madame of a whorehouse'; *heitaisan* 'soldier boy', etc. The Americans, who had the notion that all Orientals understood the term, took it to Vietnam, where it came to be used extensively in Pidgin English. Our sergeant major recalls being told by very serious Vietnamese that *-san* was an English word-ending. "Single girls were baby-san, married ones mama-san" (Flood). From Japanese *-san (sama)* originally meaning lord, but roughly equivalent to *Mr., Mrs., Miss, Ms.*

sand (Considerable antiquity to at least World War II) *s.* Sugar. Possibly an echo of the old times when patriotic contractors did adulterate the flour and sugar furnished to the troops—but more likely just routine bitching over rations. Our editor has heard *sand* used in the United States, during World War II, as meaning salt.

sandbagging (1950s) *s.* Goofing off on the job.

sand-lappers (Civil War; CSA) *s.* Troops from South Carolina. One serious explanation is that in the early history of the state poor whites and blacks sometimes ate clay during famine times. There are other versions, some of them printable.

sandpaper (Modern) *s.* Issue toilet paper. We have seen it with splinters in its texture.

sand rat (Old Army) *s.* A soldier detailed for duty in the pits or at the butts during target practice.

sand socks (Modern) Knee-length, gray stockings worn with the now-discontinued Bermuda shorts issued to soldiers prior to 1960. Most soldiers did not wear their sand socks, except as padding around their knees and elbows when crawling through the infiltration course.

sandwich (Modern; Air Force) *s.* A situation where one aircraft is caught between two enemy fighters.

San Miguel San Mic (Late 19th century to Modern; all Services) *s.* A superior beer brewed in the vicinity of Manila, Philippine Islands. Cynics attribute its unusual flavor to the fact that the Pasig River, from which it gets its water, is too thick to drink, but not quite thick enough to walk on. But even cynics drink it. It is available throughout the Far East, and our sergeant major fondly remembers that it was served in American clubs in Vietnam in the early 1960s.

sao [to] sow [to] (Vietnam; all Services) *s.* To lie, to be a liar. Commonly heard among Vietnamese bargirls as *You sao, GI!* meaning, *You are lying!* This expression has often been misunderstood. Wentworth and Flexner define it as "a repulsive, disagreeable, dishonest, or stupid person," and Groom uses it as meaning "bad." The expression is from Vietnamese *xao* 'cleverness', 'cunning', and the mistranslation has probably been caused by the similarity in sound between *xao* and *sow* (a female pig).

sapper (Early 19th century) An enlisted man in the Engineers. From French *sapeur*, via British Army use. In 1846 a "Company of Sappers, Miners, and Pontoniers" was added to the Army, but after the Mexican War this title was changed to "Engineers."

sarge (Antiquity unknown) *s.* An abbreviated form of *sergeant*, used as a form of address, without the sergeant's name.

saucer cap (Modern) *s.* The modern service cap. Also called a *flying saucer cap*.

"Saul Was a Jew" (Old Army) Soldiers' name for the "General's March," which was played when a general officer appeared at a military ceremony. Nason (1926), in a story set in World War I, refers to it as "Sam Was a Jew."

save, to (Modern; Air Force) *s.* To refuel an aircraft that has insufficient fuel to return home.

sawbones (At least Civil War to 1930s) *s.* A surgeon. While the term was of common civilian use in Great Britain during the early 19th century, it was particularly applicable to a military surgeon because of the number of amputations he was called upon to perform. It was generally safer to cut off a badly wounded arm or leg than to risk the chance of gangrene's setting in and killing the patient. Medical officers also have been called *pills, quinine*, or *butcher*.

Sawney (Revolutionary) *s.* A Scot, particularly a Scots soldier in the British Army. The term itself was a common English term, much resented by the Scots, since it referred to the wicked deeds of Sawney (Alexander) Bean, a semilegendary criminal. Sawney and his family were highway robbers, murderers, and cannibals.

sayonara (Occupation of Japan and later) So long, goodbye, farewell. It is a melodic word, and quite a few Americans even learned how to pronounce it correctly. From Japanese *sayonara*, literally 'if it must be so'.

scandal sheet (World War II) *s.* The company payroll, also sometimes termed the *swindle sheet*.

scarecrow (Mexican War) *s.* A false alarm. Gen. William J. Worth, a brave and able combat officer but one given to nervous imaginings between battles, started so many of them that *Worth's scarecrows* became a byword.

scarf up, to (Modern) *s.* To eat, to gobble up; also to seize, to take, to steal. Perhaps from Scottish dialect *scaff*, meaning food or to eat. The word has otherwise never been common in the United States (except in black slang), but it seems to have been popular in the British colonies around the turn of the century. "Well, she sent me them Christmas cookies that you scarfed up" (Herr).

scatter gun (Some antiquity; mostly Army) *s.* The "riot gun" carried by tail gunners, prisoner chasers, and other guard details.

schnell-like (Post–World War II to Modern; also Air Force) *s.* Fast, quickly, right away. From German *schnell*, of the same meaning. The *-like* would seem to put this expression into Hippie days. "Report to the motor pool, schnell-like."

schnitzel schnitz (Post–World War II to Modern; all Services) *s.* As in *To get the schnitzel*, to be treated shabbily, to be undone, to get a fucking. From various possible German originals: *Schnitz* 'a slice'; *schnitzeln* 'to carve', *Wienerschnitzel*, etc. Originally picked up during the occupation of Germany, but now spread into general American slang. "Looks like the Imperial City's had the schnitz" (Herr).

school of the soldier (Early 19th century to Modern) A period of instruction (or the instruction itself) in basic drill and behavior for the individual soldier; the first training given to a new recruit. The term is no longer official, but it continues in use by veteran officers and NCOs. In the Old Army, it was followed by the schools of the squad, platoon, and company. The word *school* here is used in a sense that is archaic in civilian life. See also *garrison school*.

school solution (Probably early 20th century to Modern) Service schools do much of their teaching by requiring their students to solve problems—a tactical problem in the field, a strategic problem on a set of maps, or a practical matter like getting the engine out of a disabled tank with no crane handy. Each problem has a solution favored by the school faculty, the school solution. Usually it is sound and practical, if sometimes lacking in inspiration. Being American soldiers, however, the students tend to regard it with skepticism. The following verse was popular at the Armored School at Fort Knox, Kentucky, and probably many other places:

Here lie the bones of Lieutenant Jones,
A product of this institution.
In his very first fight,
He went out like a light,
Using the School Solution!

scoop out, to (World War II; Air Force) *s.* To send out a force of fighter planes to extricate a bomber formation from enemy air attack. Used mostly by fighter pilots.

scope head (Modern; Air Force) *s.* A radarman. "One of his scope heads had plotted a launch" (Broughton).

scout 1. (Ancient to Modern) An individual sent out to obtain information. 2. (Colonial through Mexican Punitive Expedition) A civilian expert who served as a combination of information gatherer, guide, interpreter, and adviser. A competent scout knew the country, spoke the languages of its inhabitants, and could find food, water, and the enemy. 3. A member of certain military units, such as the Indian Scouts and the Philippine Scouts. See *Kit Carson scouts*.

scouting belt See *prairie belt*.

scrambled eggs (Post–World War II; all Services) *s.* The gold embroidery on the visors of the caps of field-grade and general officers. Also on those of their naval counterparts.

screamer (Modern) *s.* A staff action paper of such importance that evertyhing else must cease until it is processed. From civilian newspaper slang.

screaming meemies (World War II) *s.* The German six-barreled 150mm rocket launcher, the Nebelwerfer 41 (and a five-barreled 210mm later model). Its rockets had a gut-curdling sound like "a thousand gates on rusty hinges being opened." British soldiers called them *moaning minnies.* As civilian slang, from a somewhat earlier period, the *screaming meemies* were the DTs.

screenhouse *s.* The stockade (prison).

screwed, stewed, and tattooed, to get screwed, blewed, and tattooed, to get (Antiquity uncertain, but at least as old as the 1930s, to Modern) 1. *s.* To paint the town red, to have a wild time. The expression sounds as if it is naval in origin, referring to a sailor's wild orgy on liberty in port after a long cruise. He went to a prostitute or made a pickup, got very drunk, and ended by getting himself tattooed at some waterfront dive. (On the other hand, it must be admitted that many Old Army men did have tattoos.) In modern usage *blewed* is taken to mean *got a blow job* (fellatio), but in the original expression, *blewed* or *blued* was common slang for drunk, like *stewed.* 2. World War II at least) *s.* As *screwed, blewed, and tattooed,* to be shamefully mistreated, to get a raw deal, to get a royal fucking. "As usual, I get screwed, blewed, and tattooed. They picked that asshole Johnson for OCS and not me!" Here, it would seem that the notion of mistreatment in the word *screwed* was so strong that it destroyed the original literal meaning of the phrase.

scrub, to (World War II and later) *s.* To cancel. "Our mission's been scrubbed. The field's all socked in." Apparently the expression goes back before World War I in the British services. See *abort.*

SD Special Duty.

sea gull (World War I and later) 1. *s.* Chicken, as served in Army mess halls. 2. *s.* A prostitute who catered to sailors and marines and often followed the fleet from port to port.

seam squirrel (World War I) *s.* A body louse, cootie. Lice apparently laid their eggs and concentrated in the seams of clothing.

Sears Roebuck officer (Philippine Insurrection to World War II) *s.* A newly commissioned officer who was not up to the standard you expected. (In the Philippine Insurrection he was probably from one of the volunteer regiments, and in World War II, from the ROTC or OCS.) He was insistent on his privileges as an officer, not much concerned with his responsibilities, and inclined to pull rank—even when he was a mere shavetail. (In the early days, Sears, Roebuck was solely a mail-order business, and the implication was that he got his commission through the mail by sending for it.)

secesh (Civil War; USA) *s.* Short for *secessionist.* This term was applied to Confederate soldiers and civilians alike. A southern girl might be described as a *pretty secesh.* See *Johnny Reb.*

secondary zone (Modern) A list of soldiers eligible for promotion, but either too junior in grade or in length of service to be put into the primary zone. Soldiers selected from this zone must be outstanding in all ways. At any given time, usually only 5–10 percent of the personnel in this zone are picked for promotion. Also called *below-the-zone, 5 percent promotion, nickel promotion.*

second balloon (Modern) *s.* A second lieutenant.

second eight (Modern) *s.* The advanced individual training (usually eight weeks in length) that follows basic training.

Second-Horse Punch (Revolutionary) A tipple attributed to Maj. Benjamin Tallmadge of the 2d Regiment of Continental Light Dragoons, the senior regiment of US Cavalry. It consisted of a pint each of light-bodied rum, peach brandy, and lemon juice; 10 tablespoons of bitters and 8 tablespoons of brown sugar, all mixed in a bowl containing a rusty stirrup and, if available, ice. Whether this punch had anything to do with the fact that the 2d Light Dragoons were generally more effective than all three of the other Continental cavalry regiments together cannot now be established. But even when it is diluted, according to modern taste, with equal amounts of club soda, two snorts would leave a trooper willing to take a Russian T-62 heavy tank apart with a dull saber.

second john See *second lieutenant.*

second lieutenant (1839 to Modern) The lowest-ranking commissioned officer, in pay grade O-1. His insignia of rank is a single gold bar. As junior man in the officer ranks, the second lieutenant has traditionally caught much abuse and is the subject of many catchphrases and slurring remarks about his inexperience, stupidity, and general uselessness. Among his nicknames are *butter bar, brown bar, shavetail, second john, missing link, twink.* Abbreviated *2Lt., 2d Lt.* See *lieutenant.*

seconds (Considerable Antiquity to Modern) *s.* Second helpings of chow. A qualified chow hound was going through the mess line for seconds before you had figured out whether the stuff in your canteen cup was coffee, tea, soup, or dishwater.

second-story man (Old Army to 1930s) *s.* Officer slang for another officer who was neither on the level nor honest. In civilian slang of the period, a *second-story man* was a burglar.

Section 8 (Old Army to World War II) A discharge for mental or emotional problems, which covered a multitude of sins. Also a soldier who had such a discharge, was up for such a discharge, or should get such a discharge. Or just a common insult. "Come on, look where you're going, section 8!"

Seek, Strike, Destroy (World War II) The original motto of US Tank Destroyer units, which sent them out looking for trouble in the form of German tanks with thicker armor and better guns. See *Purple Heart box, Hide and Hope.*

seep (World War II) *s.* An amphibious version of the jeep. It was not especially successful. The only two we ever saw in use apparently wanted to be bathtubs.

See the chaplain! Tell it to the chaplain! (World War II and Korea; also Marines) *s.* Shut up, go tell your troubles to someone else, tough shit. (Answer: "But I don't want to listen to his troubles.")

see the elephant, to (Mexican War to Civil War) *s.* To be in combat. "The Twenty-Fourth Ohio Volunteer Infantry had seen the elephant several times, and did not care about seeing him again unless necessary" (Wiley). The original expression in full—*I've heard the owl and have seen the elephant*—meant approximately *I've* *been around*. It seems to have been common on the western frontier before the Mexican War.

Seminole-Negroes (Indian Wars) Descendants of Seminole Indians who had been expelled from Florida and had taken refuge in Mexico. In both Florida and Mexico many of them had interbred with escaped slaves. After years of vengeful border raiding, they reentered the United States and provided the Army with a small but expert contingent of scouts.

sencero /sen-'sehr-o/ (Mexican War to Indian Wars) The bell mare of a pack train. From Spanish *cencerro* 'the bell worn by a lead animal'. The Army's first packers were Mexican arrieros, and traces of their professional language remained long after they had been replaced by North Americans. The bell mare, traditionally white or gray for better visibility, carried nothing but the bell hung around her neck; the pack mules were trained to follow her on the trail and graze in her vicinity during the night.

senior enlisted swine (Modern) *s.* Senior noncommissioned officers. See also *enlisted swine, officer swine.*

seniority (Ancient to Modern) Another way of saying *rank*. From corporal to general, your rank within your grade depends on the date on which you were promoted into it. Even one day makes the difference in who takes command or gets a particular job. Although *grade, rank*, and *seniority* are loosely used, *ranking officer* should mean officer highest in grade, and *senior officer*, the one with the greatest length of service in his particular grade. In assigning duties to a number of officers of the same grade, it is customary to determine first who is senior. However, it was an Old Army principle that seniority among second lieutenants was comparable to virtue among whores. The same principle applied to privates first class and specialists fourth class. See *senior service.*

senior NCOs 1. (1958 to Modern) Sergeant first class and platoon sergeant, master sergeant and first sergeant, sergeant major and command sergeant major. 2. (World War II) T/3, staff sergeant, technical sergeant, first sergeant, and master sergeant.

senior service The oldest of a nation's armed forces, which, other things being equal, is superior in rank to the others. In Great Britain, the senior service is the Royal Navy; in the United States, the Army is the senior service, a state of affairs that the Navy and Air Force find barely tolerable. Actually, it is a matter of little practical application except in the unlikely situation where officers of equal seniority and grade may find themselves on the same interservice committee or board. In that case, the representative of the Army is automatically the honcho.

separation allowance (Modern) Money paid on a monthly basis to officers and enlisted men in pay grades E-4 through E-9 when they are separated from their families for more than thirty days while on an unaccompanied or hardship tour.

sergeant (Ancient to Modern) As a general designation, any noncommissioned officer above the grade of corporal. At present, this includes sergeant (E-5), staff sergeant (E-6), sergeant first class and platoon sergeant (both E-7), master sergeant and first sergeant (both E-8), sergeant major and command sergeant major (both E-9), and Sergeant Major of the Army. The unifying concept for these grades is that they are expert soldiers, highly practiced and skilled in Army administration or drill and discipline. (Only grades E-5 through E-7 are addressed as *sergeant.*) The title of *sergeant* is very old, appearing in European armies from the Middle Ages on. It is ultimately derived from Latin *servientem,* which came to mean a servant, although without necessarily any connotation of low status or servitude. Many high officials carried the title *sergeant* in combination with various other titles. *Sergeant,* in the modern military sense, as the senior noncommissioned officer, is found at least as early as Elizabethan times in England. It was carried over into Colonial America.

sergeant [As a specific grade] 1. (Revolutionary to 1920) A noncommissioned officer ranking above corporal and below sergeant major. During the first half of the 19th century, sergeants were distinguished by a red sash, sword, epaulettes, a broad stripe of their branch color on their trouser legs, and varying types of chevrons. The traditional three-stripe chevron seems to have become official in 1832; originally, it might be worn with its points either up or down. The latter became regulation in 1851, and remained so until 1902. 2. (1920–48) A junior noncommissioned officer, ranking above a corporal and below a staff sergeant. He was officially classified as fourth grade. (In the old system grades began at the top, so that a master sergeant was first grade.) His nicknames were *buck sergeant, three-striper.* 3. (1948–58) In the somewhat complex reorganization of grades in 1948, the seven enlisted grades were reduced to six, and the rank of sergeant was established as third grade, pay grade E-5. His insignia was a chevron of three bars above an arc, the former insignia of the staff sergeant, the title and grade of *staff sergeant* being dropped. 4. (1958 to Modern) With the reorganization of 1958, the grade of sergeant was reestablished as above corporal and below staff sergeant. The present-day sergeant once again has three stripes. Abbreviated *Sgt.*

sergeant first class 1. (At least 1891 to 1920) Various noncommissioned officers concerned with technical matters in different branches of the service: the Signal Corps, the Hospital Corps, the Coast Artillery Corps, and the Quartermaster Corps. Their insignia of rank generally consisted of three stripes, usually with a bottom arc (or bar for the Quartermaster Corps), enclosing various corps devices. These grades were all swept away in the reorganization of 1920 and have no connection with the modern grade. 2. (1958 to Modern) A senior noncommissioned officer in pay grade E-7, whose insignia consists of three stripes above two arcs. Soldiers are *promoted* to the rank of sergeant first class. They may then be *appointed* to platoon sergeant, which is also in pay grade E-7. Platoon sergeants, because they exercise actual functions of enlisted command, take precedence over sergeants first class, who are usually concerned with administrative or technical work. Abbreviated *SFC, Sgt. 1st Cl.*

sergeant major 1. As a generic term in the present Army, a soldier in pay grade E-9. This includes sergeant major, command sergeant major, and Sergeant Major of the Army. These men are all addressed as *sergeant major.* 2. As a premodern position or grade, *sergeant major* has a long and complex history. At times the term *sergeant major* has designated a job or position without distinctive grade, and at other times it has designated a specific grade. (The term itself goes back to the Renaissance, when the sergeant major general and sergeant major were, respectively, the third-ranking officer in an army and the second-in-command of a regiment. These terms were eventually shortened to *major general* and *major.*) By the early 18th century the sergeant major, as an enlisted man, had become the principal noncommissioned officer of the British Army. This role was carried over into the Continental Army during the Revolutionary War, and from this time until 1920 the sergeant major constituted a rank, usually the highest noncommissioned grade. His work was primarily administrative. From 1917 to 1920 there were two grades of sergeant major, battalion and regimental. In the reorganization of 1920 the grades of sergeant major were abolished, although the position of sergeant major as administrative NCO of a large unit, from battalion to post, remained, usually filled by a master sergeant. 3. (1958 to Modern) In 1958 the supergrades were created and sergeant major was reestablished as a grade. He is a senior noncommissioned officer in pay grade E-9, ranking above a first sergeant (and master sergeant) and in precedence below a command sergeant major. For a short time (April 1968 to November 1969) he was titled *staff sergeant major*, which term describes his work well, since he is usually concerned with staff and support-type work of a technical or supervisory nature. His insignia of rank is three chevrons above three arcs, enclosing a five-pointed star. He is addressed as *sergeant major*. His nicknames (if one dares to use them) are *smadge* and *top*. Abbreviated *SGM, Sgt. Maj.*

Sergeant Major of the Army (1966 to Modern) The highest enlisted office in the US Army. He is the senior enlisted assistant and adviser to the Chief of Staff and reports directly to him in all matters. He is appointed by the Chief of Staff from the ranks of the command sergeant majors, and his term of office is normally that of the Chief of Staff. The insignia of grade has varied, but at present it consists of three chevrons above three arcs, enclosing two five-pointed stars. Abbreviated are *SMA, Sgt. Maj. of the Army.*

sergeant of the floor (Civil War; USA) In the large warehouse-type Confederate prisons, a noncommissioned officer elected by the prisoners. He drew rations and enforced what little discipline was observed.

serial number (1918–69) A distinctive number given to each individual in the US Armed Forces in order to avoid confusion between individuals with identical or similar names. For enlisted men this practice began in February 1918; officers were assigned serial numbers (beginning with O) shortly after World War I. On 1 July 1969 the Army, to avoid confusing Uncle Sam's computers, switched to the use of Social Security numbers for identification. In the older system the number proper was at times prefixed by letter codes giving information about status of service—Regular Army, draftee, Reserve, etc. The current number is known as *Social Security Account Number (SSAN).*

servant (Colonial to Revolutionary) A private detached from his company to act as an officer's personal orderly. (*Servant* and *waiter* seem to have been used interchangeably.) The practice was a severe drain on combat strength. The mercenary

German regiments therefore had extra officers' valets attached for such duties. Higher-ranking or wealthy officers might also hire one or more civilian servants.

service cap (Modern) A flat-crowned felt hat of Army Green, with a black leather visor and chinstrap. On the front is worn a metal insignia. Officers wear a representation of the Great Seal of the United States; warrant officers, an eagle with wings open, standing upon arrows, with a wreath superimposed; and enlisted men, the Great Seal, but on a plain disk. The visors of field and general officers display oak leaves. The hat is very similar to what was termed a *garrison cap* just before and during World War II. Nicknames are *flying saucer cap, saucer cap*. It is called a *barracks cap* by the Marines and a *flathat* by the Navy.

service club (World War II and later; principally Army) An institution introduced in World War II with the intention of offering troops in training camps wholesome entertainment and conveniences, thereby keeping them out of beer joints. Sometimes within the post limits, sometimes just outside the post, a service club might furnish library service, space for reading and writing, pinball machines, snack bars and food services, various entertainment programs, Ping-Pong tables, radios and record players, and the like. For the GI, service club detail used to be one of the best. After a perfunctory sweep-up, he could doze in comfortable chairs, read, listen to music, or chitchat with nubile young civilian librarians. Service clubs sometimes had guesthouse facilities for visiting parents and girl friends. It was noted that the same young lady might appear frequently as the guest of various soldiers from the same outfit, but as long as public decencies were observed, there was nothing in the regulations to forbid such carryings-on. Service clubs still exist under that phase of the Recreational Services program known as the *Outdoor Recreational Program*, but the scope of services is somewhat less than it was in earlier years.

Service of the Rear (World War I) The second designation for the logistic organization of the AEF. (The first was *Line of Communication.*) It was an unfortunate choice of words, giving rise to all sorts of vulgar jokes. Another change made the organization *Services of Supply*.

Service Medal A circular bronze disk indicating honorable performance of military duty in specified geographical areas within specified dates. It is a one-time award, conferred automatically.

service ribbons Ribbons representing decorations or service medals. Mounted on small bars with clasps like safety pins, they are identical in pattern and color to the suspension ribbon of the medal they stand for. Decorations take precedence over service medals and are worn with the highest displayed above, and to the right of, others. Service medals are worn in the order in which they were earned. All are worn singly or in rows of three or four above the left breast pocket. Also called *fruit salad*.

service school service stripe (Modern) *s.* A V-shaped patch of darker-colored cloth resulting when the seat of khaki trousers is let out to accommodate an expanding rear end. Used derogatorily of soldiers who have been gaining weight, on the assumption that long periods of physical inactivity in Army service schools permit the accumulation of fat (but nothing else).

service star A bronze or silver five-pointed star worn on a service ribbon to indicate participation in a campaign. A silver star is worn in lieu of five bronze stars. Also called *campaign stars, battle stars.*

service stripes See *hash marks.*

serving detail (Modern) Soldiers picked to serve food in the mess hall. They are generally selected from among the soldiers waiting to enter the mess hall. Some mess sergeants pick the first men in line, on the principle that if they have nothing better to do than stand in line waiting to eat, they should be given something useful to do. Others pick the last men on the grounds that they are slothful and badly organized and need a little pepping up. Others just pick at random.

seven (Modern) *s.* Short for *pay grade E-7,* sergeant first class or platoon sergeant. "I should make seven on the next list."

seven and seven (Vietnam, from 1971 on) *s.* One week of R & R with one week of leave.

Seven Steps to Hell (Modern) The US 7th Army, so called because of seven steps in the design of the pyramid on its shoulder patch. Possibly reinforced by the fact that the 7th Army spends much of its time on NATO field maneuvers.

seventy-niner (Modern) *s.* The M79 grenade launcher. Also called *blooker, chunker, thump gun, '79.*

sewer trout (Modern) *s.* Fish, particularly white fish, served in the mess hall.

shack boots (Late 1940s; Japan) *s.* Parachute boots with zippers cleverly installed on the inside of the legs. This was a dead giveaway that the wearer was spending a lot of time inside a certain native house and did not want to lose time untying bootlaces once he got there. Of course, it is possible that some wearers were learning how to play the koto, but we doubt it. See *tatami burn.*

shack man (Early 20th century on; occasionally other Services) 1. *s.* In the earlier period, a more or less married soldier living off the post where his unit was stationed. A shack was usually all he could afford in the way of housing. 2. *s.* Later, a soldier who kept a mistress in some sort of off-post housing—anything from a room in a house of ill-repute to a cosily domestic temporary home. The process was called, as in civilian life, *shacking up.* A soldier who was expert in finding females willing to cohabit with him was a *shack artist*, although more strait-laced types might dismiss him as a *shack rat.* The woman might be called a *shack rat* or a *shack job.* There are many other combinations.

shade 44 shade 385 (Modern) *s.* A black. From the color of shade 44 (Army Green, which is very dark) and 385 (the color of the black raincoat or overcoat).

shadow soup (Civil War; USA) *s.* Weak chicken soup served to men in the hospital. To make it, one veteran claimed, the hospital cooks put a large kettle of water on to boil, hung a chicken so that its shadow fell on the water, and boiled the shadow for a half-hour. They then added salt and pepper and served it.

shaft, to get the (World War II to Modern) *s.* To be given the works suddenly, painfully, and with no regard whatever for Emily Post or your finer sensibilities. The implication, of course, when you use the word to describe your own misfortunes is that the act was grossly unfair and completely undeserved. Also, *to get shafted, to be shafted,* and *to give someone the shaft.*

shag ass, to (World War II to Modern) 1. *s.* To run away, to depart quickly. "We were talking to Murphy when he was on guard, and just then we saw the looey coming. Did we shag ass out!" 2. *s.* To hurry, to stop stalling, to get moving. Usually as a command, as in "Come on, you! Shag your asses down to the QM depot and get that coffee. The CO's waiting."

shakedown (Post–World War II to Modern) 1. *s.* A search or unannounced inspection for stolen property, narcotics, and the like. Probably from civilian police slang, via detective stories. Also *shakedown inspection.* 2. *s.* A charity drive or related form of extortion. The major charity organizations (and the US Treasury with its savings bonds) have found the Armed Forces a vulnerable and lucrative target. Frequently given the official blessing of the White House, their campaigns for generous donations progress down the chain of command. Various COs, smitten by the hope of making useful brownie points with their superiors, twist their subordinates' arms a little harder in an effort to set a record for joyful giving. It is hard on morale, family budgets, and Christian charity.

Shape up or ship out! (Korea to Modern) *s.* Start behaving like a proper soldier or you get transferred! (presumably to the 99th Submarine Paratroopers, currently stationed in Antarctica).

sharp point (Modern) The advance guard or any unit in energetic contact with the enemy. A graphic Canadian term picked up by US units on joint exercises.

sharpshooter 1. (About 1800 to Modern) A soldier who is a good shot, especially one who is acting as a sniper. The term was first recorded in Great Britain and America around the time of the Napoleonic Wars, and may be a translation of German *Scharfschütze* 'expert marksman'. The theory that the term originated during the Civil War from the use of the Sharps rifle by the 1st and 2d Regiments of US Sharpshooters is false. 2. (Late 19th century to Modern) The second highest grade of rifle marksmanship. See *shooting pay.* 3. (World War II to Modern) *s.* A person who harasses the instructor of a military class by asking questions intended to confuse or confound him. Some draftees with college degrees were prone to try it with ungrammatical senior NCOs, only to discover that an NCO's syntax is no reliable indication of his savvy. At the US Military Academy and other service schools, this practice may be termed *sniping.*

shavetail 1. (1870 and probably earlier, as a term, to pre–World War II) An unbroken mule. The tails of newly purchased mules were trimmed, so that they could be distinguished from those properly trained. The practice goes back to before the Mexican War. 2. (Indian Wars to Modern) *s.* A second lieutenant. The term is based on the first definition. "My stomach's emptier than a shavetail's head" (Nason, 1928).

She ain't got no yo-yo (Occupation of Japan to Modern) *s.* A catchphrase, sometimes sung, meaning *She hasn't any boyfriend* or *She isn't getting any sexual intercourse.* It is a parody of the popular song "Shina no yoru" ("Chinese Nights"), theme song from the Japanese motion picture of the same name. *Yo-yo* can signify either the male organ or bouncing up and down. The expression is still very popular among Korean War veterans, but is dying out in the Army at large.

sheep racks (Civil War; USA) *s.* *Chevaux de frise*, a type of obstacle used before the introduction of barbed wire.

sheepskin fiddler (Early 19th century; British) *s.* A drummer.

shellrep (World War II and later) *s.* A report detailing what the enemy artillery and mortars have been doing to you—how many rounds of what calibers and types have landed on your position within a certain period.

shelter half (Civil War to Modern) One half of a two-man tent as issued to the individual soldier. Each soldier is also issued a tent pole, five tent pins, and a guy rope. The tent halves are put together by buttoning them along the top and (if needed) the end flaps.

sheriff (Modern) 1. *s.* The duty officer on a post or installation, command, etc. See *CQ*. 2. Sergeant of guard.

shield of shame (Modern) *s.* The insignia of the Adjutant General's Corps, so called because of the rear echelon, noncombat nature of the AGC.

Twinkle, twinkle, little shield,
Keep me off the battlefield.

shined with a chocolate bar (Modern) *s.* Unshined, messy-looking. Essentially an expression from the brown-shoe Army, but still very common even in these days of black footgear. "Nothing they did was right. Their shoes looked like somebody had shined them with a chocolate bar" (Truscott).

ship out, to (At least World War II to Modern) To be transferred out. "They cut my orders, and Friday I ship out."

shirtman (Colonial to mid-19th century) *s.* A frontiersman, especially a frontier rifleman; so called from the hunting shirts customarily worn. See *Dirty Shirts.*

SHIT (Post–World War II to Modern) *s.* South Hudson Institute of Technology, a name given to the US Military Academy by embittered nongraduate officers. Unlike *West Point Protective Association*, this term is used rarely, but never in jest.

shit-burning detail (Vietnam) *s.* Burning out cesspools with fuel oil to sanitize them. To make sure that the odious contents of the cesspool were thoroughly burned, the cesspool had to be stirred constantly with a long pole. A dirty and disgusting task. After a soldier finished the detail, his clothing was permeated with the odor of excrement. Often men were selected for this chore as punishment for minor infractions of local rules and regulations. Also called *shithouse detail*. It is not to be confused with *shit detail* per se, but it was one.

shit detail (Probably fairly old, to Modern) *s.* An onerous, dirty, disgusting, difficult job, sometimes given out as punishment. "He's going to give me every shit detail in the book" (Groom).

Shithook (Modern) *s.* The CH-47 Chinook helicopter. Possibly a play on *Chinook*, combined with *shithook*, a common slang term for the hand, from the resemblance between the CH-47 and the hand. Also called *go-go* and the *Hook.*

shit in your mess kit, I hope to (World War I to Modern) *s.* A catchphrase (jokingly or for emphasis) threatening someone with dire consequences. (Lighter records a World War I AEF euphemism, *spit in your mess kit.*) Also *I will shit in your mess kit.* "You don't believe me? I hope to shit in your mess kit if it isn't true."

shit-on-a-shingle SOS (20th century; also Navy) *s.* Creamed beef on toast, a frequent breakfast dish. Actually, two or three different dishes were involved under the slang term *SOS*. One was creamed ground beef, and another was creamed chipped beef. Creamed chipped beef, if the slivers of meat were large enough, was often called *creamed foreskins* or *foreskins*. Actually, despite its bad reputation, SOS was usually quite tasty and within the capabilities of the average service cook.

shot rolls downhill, the (Antiquity uncertain) *s.* An expression that has been around, in varying forms, as long as there have been armies. It is the enlisted man's version of *RHIP* (*rank has its privileges*) and *The buck is passed, downwards.* Since the EM has little rank and less privilege, he is always on the receiving end—in combat from the enemy and, between episodes of combat, from his own army. It is his assertion, somewhat obliquely, that he can take it, come what may.

shit-shower-shave-shine (At least World War II to Modern) *s.* A catchphrase for the sequence of events when a soldier prepares himself for the duty day, a heavy date, or a night on the town. There are many variants: *shit-shine-shower-shave, shit-shave-and-shower, shit-shower-shampoo, shine-shit-shower-shave,* etc. Mardis refers to *the three s's,* a West Point cadet expression for *shat-showered-and-shaved.* In the contexts above, *shine* can refer either to one's shoes or one's brass.

shoat brands shoat bars (Civil War; USA) *s.* An NCO's chevrons.

shock action (Ancient to Modern) The effect of charging cavalry, massed infantry, or armored vehicles to ride down, knock over, or smash opposing troops or obstacles. Some academic historian has recently "discovered" that there never has been any such thing. Obviously, Alexander the Great, Napoleon, and Jeb Stuart suffered from delusions—they thought there was, and employed it successfully.

shoddy (Civil War; USA) A type of material usually put together out of scraps and ravelings "pounded, rolled, glued, and smoothed to the external form and gloss of cloth" made into uniforms by some patriotic manufacturers at the beginning of the war. A little wear or rain quickly reduced it to its component parts. The word arose in the mills of Great Britain in the early 19th century, but it came to world prominence with the American Civil War experience.

shook (World War II) *s.* Shaken, nervous, apprehensive, and far from being your normal heroic self.

shoo-shoo sho-sho (World War I) *s.* Phonetic approximation of *Chauchat*, the French automatic rifle issued in large numbers to American troops. It was cumbersome, unreliable, and unpopular. Replaced by the BAR.

shooting pay (Late 19th century to Modern; also Marines) Extra pay for demonstrated expertise with weapons. (Through the 1930s, shooting pay was limited to the rifle.) A man who qualified as a sharpshooter before World War II drew $3 extra per month; an expert rifleman drew $5. These were princely sums on top of a buck private's pay. Between the World Wars, Marines got to fire for qualification every year, but the impoverished Army held full qualification tests only at three-year intervals. Dear as this extra pay was, we remember one infantry company (afflicted with a capricious and arbitrary captain) that deliberately and unitedly shot bolo scores when up for qualification. The captain's career was badly blighted.

short 1. (All Services) *s.* Near the end of one's overseas tour or enlistment. Often heard today in catchphrases: *I'm so short I could walk under the door. I'm so short I can't carry on a long conversation. I'm so short I've given up smoking king-size cigarettes.* 2. (Army) *s.* A discharge taken before one's normal enlistment is up, in order to reenlist for some option. "I took a short and reenlisted for Germany." Also called *short discharge*. 3. (Antiquity uncertain to Modern) *s.* An artillery projectile that falls short of its target.

shortage MOS (Modern) A Military Occupational Specialty in which there are fewer soldiers serving throughout the Army than are authorized. The opposite of *overage MOS*.

short arm 1. (Perhaps pre–World War I to Modern) *s.* The penis. There may be a pun buried here. An *arm* is a rifle, and a pistol (*piss tool*, long a slang term for a penis) may be considered a short arm. 2. (Perhaps pre–World War I to Modern) *s.* In its most common usage, the abbreviated form of *short-arm inspection*—the medical inspection of male soldiers' "primary sex organs" to determine whether they have contracted venereal disease. In the rough days of old, *short-arm* could be a unit formation. 3. (Modern) *s.* Also, although not a common usage, rifle inspection.

short-arm practice (Old Army) *s.* Copulation.

short-fuze (Modern) *s.* A very short deadline or suspense date; applied to any kind of action or requirement. "This staff paper has a very short fuze."

short-legged (Reasonably Modern; primarily Air Force, but occasionally applied to vehicles) *s.* Able to travel only a short distance without refueling. Officially, having a "short radius of action."

short round 1. (Antiquity uncertain to Modern) An artillery round that falls short of its target. The same as *short*. 2. (Modern) *s.* A short person.

shorts and overs (20th century) 1. *s.* In artillery, rounds that do not hit the target, some falling short and some falling over. 2. *s.* Trouble of any sort that hits an innocent bystander. A bystander who suffers damage during anything from a barroom brawl to a high-level interservice dispute over allocation of funds "gets [hit by] all the shorts and overs."

short sheet (As a term, antiquity uncertain, but at least Old Army to Modern) A barracks prank in which the top sheet is folded in two so that it looks like two sheets, top and bottom. When the victim tries to get into his bed, his legs are stopped short by the fold. Soldiers consider this hilarious when the victim is a little drunk and cannot understand what is happening. Grose (1788) calls this an "apple-pye-bed . . . a common trick played by frolicsome country lasses on their sweethearts, male relations or visitors." At times short-sheeting has been practiced to deceive inspecting officers, giving the appearance of two sheets when in fact only one was in use.

short time (Perhaps Occupation of Japan to Modern) 1. *s.* "Anyone who has served in the Far East knows that a 'short-time' is a brief visit to a brothel" (Pratt and Blair). 2. *s.* Any quickly dispensed sex, whether it is paid for or not. 3. (Perhaps before World War II to Modern) *s.* The condition in which the individual is close to the end of his enlistment or overseas tour. "Come on, get off your asses! Just because you're on short time doesn't mean you can fuck off on detail!"

short-timer (Perhaps Occupation of Japan to Modern) 1. *s.* See *short time* 1. A prostitute who sells instant sex, often in doorways and alleys. 2. *s.* Her customer, especially one who prefers this sort of encounter. 3. (Perhaps pre–World War I to Modern) *s.* See *short* 1. A soldier who is approaching the end of an overseas tour or enlistment. The term has been known in the Army since at least 1921, and Dr. Lighter has traced it to 1906 in a Navy source.

short-timer's attitude short-timer's fever (Modern; all Services) *s.* See *short-timer* 3. Indifference, irresponsibility, FIGMO. *Short-timer's fever* is stronger and more obvious than *short-timer's attitude*.

short-timer's calendar (Modern; all Services) *s.* A special calendar used to count the days remaining on an overseas tour or enlistment. Such calendars are often intricate works of art, and the process of checking off each passing day can be a serious and complicated ritual.

short-timer's party (Modern) *s.* A party held to celebrate a soldier's imminent departure from an overseas station for home or his impending discharge from the service. "Besides, he hadn't had a shower in a week, since before Fisher's short-timer's party" (Smith).

short-timer's stick (Modern) *s.* A baton or stick, usually ornately decorated, conspicuously displayed or carried by soldiers on short time. Sometimes the happy short-timer will give his stick to the next shortest soldier in his outfit.

short-timer's wheel (Modern) *s.* A homemade device, popular among soldiers in Germany around 1968–74, consisting of a metal washer, the rubber seal from a fliptop bottle of German beer, etc., worn somewhere on the uniform to indicate that the wearer was nearing the end of his tour. Our sergeant major reports that some evil-minded NCOs objected to the wearing of these "wheels" because they were not authorized by the uniform regulations.

short tour (Modern) An overseas tour of eighteen months or less.

shot (Early Colonial) A man equipped with firearms, as opposed to a pikeman. In 1611, Governor Sir Thomas Dale of Virginia ordered that "every shot shall either be furnished with a quilted coat of canvas, a headpeece, and a sword, or else with a light Armor" (*Military Collector*, Winter 1955). The term went out of use during the first half of the 17th century as the colonists discovered that pikes were useless against the Indians. All citizens were required to have firearms.

shot at and missed and shit at and hit (Modern) *s.* A catchphrase indicating that one has come safely through vast troubles and hardships only to be brought down, finally and foully, by official shit.

shot group (Modern) *s.* The accuracy and depth of a person's understanding of a problem or situation. Taken from the official term *shot group*, the pattern in which rounds hit a target. (The dispersal pattern of the shot group shows the shooter how to adjust his sights.)

shotgun envelope (Modern) *s.* The standard-design commercial perforated envelope used to transmit papers in interoffice communications. It is called *shotgun* because the holes suggest holes made by shotgun pellets. Also called *stop-go* or *holey joe*.

shots (World War I to Modern) 1. Medical inoculations and injections of all sorts against various diseases. For some reason, the little runts take them and grin; the big fullback types turn white, roll up their eyes, and faint. *To receive shots* sometimes is *to get shot*. "Oh, Christ. We get shot today. I hope it isn't yellow fever." 2. (Post–World War II on) *s.* A German girl friend or mistress. From German *Schatz* 'dearie', 'darling'. Also *shotsie, schotzie, schatz*. See *Nazi shatzie*.

shoulder cord (Post–World War II to Modern) A cord worn around the right shoulder, under the shoulder loop, by Infantry officers and EM who have been awarded the Combat or Expert Infantryman badges or have otherwise been deemed qualified. It is of Infantry blue and is formed of a series of interlocking square knots around a center cord.

shoulder knots Ornamental devices worn on the Blue and White Mess and Evening Dress uniforms. They are gold-colored and are attached with snaps. Regimental officers wore them with their Dress Blue uniforms from 1872 until World War I.

shoulder patch (Perhaps World War I to Modern) A cloth insignia worn on the outer sleeve, half an inch below the shoulder seam. At present, the shoulder patch worn on the left shoulder is obligatory and designates the soldier's unit; that on the right side is optional and indicates the soldier's former combat unit. Shoulder patches were first (but irregularly) used in World War I and were formalized in the early 1920s. The present system went into effect in October 1945.

shoulder straps (Civil War; USA) *s.* Officers in general. With the plain field service uniform of the Civil War, an officer was distinguished chiefly by his transverse shoulder straps and crimson sash—and many officers discarded their sashes as nuisances. *To get shoulder straps* meant to receive a commission; *to have shoulder straps* meant to be an officer.

shove, to shove up, to (Old Army) 1. *s.* To dispose of government property illegally:

O'Reilly swiped a blanket
And shoved it up, I hear;
He shoved it for a dollar
And invested that in beer.

2. *s.* As in *to shove your face*, to demand credit without offering any security other than your honest appearance. Probably from civilian slang *to shove* meaning to hock or to pawn.

show 1. (World War II on; especially Air Force) *s.* A performance, operation, or deed. A *bad show* is a defeat or sorry mess; a *good show*, the opposite. A *wizard show* is something really outstanding. Thus, the exclamation *Good show!* means applause, while *Bad show!* means emphatic disapproval. Of British origin. Partridge (1970) records it from the 1920s, and it may go back to World War I in Great Britain. 2. (Antiquity uncertain to Modern) *s.* In *Let's get this show on the road*, let's get started. From old circus or theatrical jargon.

show-and-tell (Modern) *s.* A briefing that uses various visual aids.

show blood, to (Civil War) 1. (USA) *s.* To be slightly wounded, but not seriously enough to be reported as wounded or to be sent to the rear. 2. (CSA) *s.* According to one account, a challenge used by Confederate provost guards to men attempting to go to the rear during combat was *Show blood* (in other words, *Prove that you are wounded*).

showdown inspection showdown (Uncertain antiquity as a term, but at least World War I to Modern) A strict inspection in which all of a soldier's clothing, equipment, and weapons are laid out for examination. (Unlike a shakedown inspection, a showdown is not primarily concerned with stolen or illegal articles.) Since some inspecting officers are known to suffer exceedingly if every man does not have the same size and brand of toothpaste, veteran soldiers often have an extra set of toilet articles for inspections only. Inspections of this sort go back to colonial times (see *rag fair*) but the term *showdown*, which is derived from poker, is probably from the 20th century.

show-horse outfit show-horse (At least Old Army, possibly still in use) *s.* An outfit noted for its snap, spit, and polish. When show-horse outfits are good fighting units, they are usually very good, but when they are not, they come unglued rapidly. A show horse is great on style and appearance, and wins ribbons at horse shows, but it may or may not be capable of hard service.

shrapnel 1. (Spanish-American War to World War I) An artillery projectile designed to explode in the air, releasing a shower of small spherical missiles. (An earlier type used in the Civil War was called *spherical case shot.*) Shrapnel fire was comparatively difficult to adjust. If the shell burst too high, the missiles lost momentum as they fell; if it burst too low, most of the missiles went harmlessly into the ground. Also, it was ineffective against dug-in troops. The use of shrapnel had been discontinued by World War II, and stocks of shrapnel remaining on hand were used for gunnery training. 2. (World War II and Modern) A popular term for fragments of exploding bombs or shells, often misapplied by war correspondents.

Siberia (Origin hazy, but probably pre–World War I; probably still in use) *s.* An isolated post, camp, or station, usually in the northern states, assignment to which lively souls considered exile. The 4th Infantry was apt to apply the term to Fort Missoula, Montana, when we were there in the 1930s. Its next duty station was in Alaska.

sick book (Antiquity uncertain to Modern) A form prepared in the orderly room that listed the soldiers who were going on sick call. Since old-time topkicks were very suspicious, knowing that many soldiers would use any excuse to get out of training or details, the sick book was very frequently a source for KP assignments. See *ride the sick book*.

sick call (At least early 19th century to Modern) Originally, a bugle call informing soldiers that it was time to report for medical care. In later days, reporting to the orderly room, being entered on the sick book, being marched by a noncom over to the dispensary, and being treated. (See *CC pill, APC pill, iodine.*) Nowadays, an established time at a medical facility when outpatients are seen.

sick in quarters Sick enough to be excused from turning out for duty in the rain, but not sick enough to go to the hospital. The earlier term was *sick, present*. The medic lets you take it easy in your squadroom, tent, dugout, or wherever you are quartered, for a day or so. You either get well or get sick enough to go to the hospital—or else it will be decided that you are riding the sick list (sick book) and need a little therapeutic fatigue detail.

sickness (1800–50) Drunkenness.

sick slip (Modern) A form signed by the first sergeant or company commander authorizing a soldier to go on sick call.

side arms 1. (Colonial to Modern) Officially, weapons that are usually worn at the side. In the old days, *side arms* would have included swords, bayonets, knives, as well as firearms, but nowadays the term indicates primarily pistols or revolvers. 2. (Perhaps 1920s on) *s.* Colloquially, salt and pepper in the mess hall. In the Navy and Marines, sugar and cream; probably sometimes also in the Army.

side-door officer (Old Army to 1930s) *s.* Officers who entered the Regular Army otherwise than by graduation from the US Military Academy—in other words, through a side door. The term apparently was used for the most part by West Pointers, but seldom, if ever, by enlisted men.

side knife (Civil War) A large fighting and utility knife carried by enlisted men, especially among the Confederates. These knives were locally procured by the men themselves and varied from 6 to over 18 inches in length, with hilts of many patterns. Often called *Bowies* or *Arkansas toothpicks*.

side walls sidewalls See *whitewalls*.

SIDPERS (Modern) Standardized Installation/Division Personnel System. A personnel management system covering personnel actions, centralized at the Military Personnel Center. Input to the system is provided by data cards prepared at unit level. Before the creation of SIDPERS, personnel management and accounting were decentralized and the basic source of information was the morning report. SIDPERS is also read as *Stupid Individuals Desperately Pretending Everything Is Running Smoothly.*

sierra (West Point) *s.* Summer uniforms, from *Sierra*, the letter *s* in the phonetic alphabet.

sight picture (Modern) *s.* Understanding of a situation or a task. The term is taken from the rifle range, where a *sight picture*, in aiming a weapon, is the proper alignment of the rear sight, front sight blade, and the target. "He doesn't have the proper sight picture on this problem."

silence (West Point) A traditional form of punishment whereby a cadet guilty of a serious (but not illegal) moral trespass is shunned by his fellows. All members of the Corps of Cadets are on their honor not to speak to the victim, under threat of expulsion. Silence is invoked by the cadets, under the provisions of their honor code. It cannot be suggested or ordered by the command or faculty.

silk (World War I and later) *s.* A parachute. *To hit the silk* was to jump from a crippled airplane and trust that your parachute would function properly.

silo (Modern) An underground installation mounting a ballistic missile ready for firing.

silo sitters (Modern) *s.* Air Force personnel assigned to intercontinental ballistic missile launching sites. The Wild Blue Yonder boys of the 1950s are the Silent Silo Sitters of the 1970s and 1980s.

Silver Fox (1950s; Far East; possibly other Services) A Japanese imitation whiskey, selling for approximately 15 cents a pint and tasting like an inferior cedar oil polish. Impoverished dipsomaniacs occasionally could bring themselves to drink small quantities of it, usually in those parched two days just before the eagle screamed. One version of it bore a label (obviously prepared by some improper American for an uninformed Japanese distiller): "Genuine Scotch Whiskey. Distilled in the basement of Buckingham Palace by King George VI in person."

Silver Star (1932 on) The third-highest award for heroism, ranking below the Distinguished Service Medal and above the Legion of Merit. It was authorized as such in 1932, superseding citation stars (authorized in 1918). Despite its title, it is a gilt bronze star 1.25 inches across, on the obverse of which is a tiny silver star.

Simonize your watches (Modern) *s.* A play on *Synchronize your watches*, a favorite line in grade-B war movies.

since Caesar was a roadguard since Christ was a corporal since George Washington was a lance jack (Antiquity uncertain to Modern) *s.* Catchphrases indicating, in a jocular way, that it is a long time since something has happened, or perhaps that it has never happened. The general pattern seems to be of British origin, although Americans have altered names and positions suitably. Lighter has recorded the comment about Washington for the AEF in World War I. One of the best of these expressions, recorded by Partridge (1970) for the British RAF, is *since Pontius was a pilot.*

sin hound (Generally World War II) *s.* A chaplain. Also called *GI Jesus, sky pilot.*

sink (Colonial to Civil War) A latrine pit. Also, occasionally, a garbage pit. According to Baron von Steuben's *Regulations*, sinks were to be 300 feet from the camp. They were to be "filled up, and new ones dug every four days, and oftener in warm weather." The term is an old English word that died out (in this sense) about a hundred years earlier in civilian life.

sinkers (Mexican War) A variant of *sink*. Not to be confused with the modern edible variety.

sin loy (Vietnam) *s.* Sorry. From the Vietnamese interjection *xin lôi*, 'beg pardon', 'excuse me'. Commonly used by American soldiers.

Sir Charles (Vietnam) *s.* The Viet Cong soldier. Although most Americans who served in Vietnam regarded the Vietnamese people with feelings only slightly higher than contempt, they had high respect for the Communist soldier.

SI shoes (West Point) *s.* Special Inspection or Saturday Inspection shoes, maintained only for display on these occasions.

SITREP (Modern) *s.* Situation Report. A report on the conditions and circumstances affecting a unit or command at any given time. "The reading of the sitreps (situation reports) had confirmed his skepticism" (Marshall, 1968).

SIW (World War I to Modern) Self-Inflicted Wound. Also, a person who has intentionally wounded himself. An age-old method of evading combat duty, it was probably practiced in the armies of ancient Babylon and Egypt. All armies take a dim view of this practice, but some SIWs are hard to convict—for example, when a soldier manages to drop a case of ammunition on his foot while loading a vehicle. Such an injury hurts more and does more permanent damage than a self-inflicted flesh wound. It will not get him a Purple Heart, but is is hard to prove that he did it on purpose.

six (Modern) *s.* Short for *pay grade E-6* or *specialist six.*

six-by (Modern) 1. *s.* Short for *six-by-four*, or a vehicle of six wheels, of which four are driving wheels. Usually written *6 x 4*. 2. *s.* Short for *six-by-six*, or a vehicle that has six driving wheels. Usually written *6 x 6*.

six-pack of asskick, bring a (Modern) *s.* A catchphrase used to put down any boasting, obstreperous person: "Screw around with me, Jones, and you'll need to bring your whole platoon and a six-pack of asskick with you." *Six-pack* refers, of course, to the packaging of beer.

six Ps (At least 1940s to Modern) *s.* Abbreviation of a catchphrase used in various service schools—"Gentlemen, always remember the six *P*s: 'Prior planning prevents piss-poor performance'."

six-striper 1. (West Point) *s.* A cadet brigade and regimental commander, brigade deputy commander, and executive officer. 2. (General Army) A master sergeant.

skag (Perhaps 1920s on) *s.* A cigarette. *Skag me* meant "Give me a cigarette."

skillygalee (Civil War; USA) Hardtack soaked in cold water until soft and then fried in salt pork or bacon grease. The term itself comes from British sailors' slang of the Napoleonic period, but the earlier recipe seems to have been very different.

skin (1888 on; West Point) *s.* A delinquency report, or the making of such a report. Now synonymous with *gig*.

skin, to *s.* To punish in some fashion, often by the application of that deadly weapon, the human tongue. Inspecting officers and camp followers are usually superefficient at it in their different ways. One theory holds that the term is derived from the West Point use of *skin* and, like *poop*, was taken into the expanding Army in 1940–42. We doubt this, having childhood memories of parental warnings to behave "or I'll skin you alive," and suspect that the term came from frontier civilian life.

skinhead skin job 1. (Modern) *s.* A haircut where the cut is so close to the scalp that skin is visible all over the head. (Although military haircuts are still much shorter than those found in civilian life, the skin job is no longer very popular.) To a soldier the term may have phallic meanings, for *skin it* or *skin it back* are the usual instructions at short-arm inspection. 2. *s.* A person with such a haircut or a bald man. 3. (Modern; Marines) *s.* A boot, because of the boot's short haircut. See *boot* in Appendix.

skinner 1. (Revolutionary) An irregular, especially in New York, who professed allegiance to the United States, but frequently was a mere bandit. 2. (Civil War; USA) *s.* A sutler, obviously from his typical business practices.

skivvies (Antiquity uncertain to Modern; early 20th century in the Marines) *s.* Underwear, particularly summer underwear.

skivvy skivvie (Post–World War II, perhaps earlier, to Modern; especially Vietnam and still used in Okinawan and Korean Pidgin English) *s.* A prostitute. A *skivvy honcho* is an oversexed man; a *skivvy-girl* is a prostitute; a *skivvy-house* is a brothel. The origin is almost certainly Japanese *sukebei* /skay-bay/ 'lechery', 'lecher', 'bum', etc.

skoshi skoshee skosh /sko-shee/ (Post–World War II to Modern; especially in the Pidgin English of Korea and Okinawa; all Services) *s.* A little. Often used as *skoshi bit, just a skosh,* and *skoshi-timer* (short-timer). From Japanese *sukoshi* /sko-shee/ 'a little'. Many Japanese loanwords are found in Korean

Pidgin English, either imported by the Americans from Japan during and after the Korean War or picked up by the Koreans themselves during the lengthy Japanese occupation of their country. Succeeding generations of GIs have perpetuated expressions like *sukoshi*, thus proving groundless the fear expressed by Norman (1955) that the Bamboo English of the occupation of Japan would eventually die out.

skrag, to (Post–World War II to Modern) *s.* To murder, from gangster talk. The word entered Army use around 1946, but soon acquired new meanings. If your sergeant skragged you, you had a bad time, but if you skragged your date, you seduced her.

skull (Approximately World War II) *s.* A person who is exceedingly stupid, inept, and prone to inappropriate action—in other words, solid bone above the Adam's apple. Rarely heard now.

sky pilot (Antiquity uncertain, but especially World War II to Modern) *s.* A chaplain. The term goes back at least to the early 19th century in British naval slang (Ware) and apparently had consistent naval and civilian use up to World War II. It acquired new vitality when *pilot* came to include *airplane pilot* as well as *ship's pilot*. Colby, in his excellent *Army Talk* (1942), mentions it as a new term from "civilian slang of long standing, but used primarily in the Air Corps." We first heard it in the popular "Praise the Lord and Pass the Ammunition," which was written just after Pearl Harbor. Also called a *sky scout*.

sky up, to (Modern) *s.* To take a trip, usually in an airplane or helicopter ("Welcome Edition," AR, p. 24). The expression seems to have originated fairly late in the Vietnam War.

slack man (Modern) The backup man for the point man of a column of troops. He provides security for the point man and also keeps him on the proper route.

slanteye slant-eye (World War II to Modern) *s.* An Asiatic, especially a Japanese girl or woman. From general American slang, but probably more common in the Army than outside. Unlike most of the ethnic terms for peoples of the Far East, *slanteye* was descriptive and not necessarily derogatory, for Japanese women were usually very highly regarded by American soldiers. Besides being more available than roundeyes, they had the art of deftly building up their escort's self-esteem. Many Americans, especially nice mother's boys, found them essential to their morale, and the US Armed Forces' legal camp followers now include a respectable slanteye contingent. The term *slant* was supposedly used for male Asiatics in a more contemptuous way, but we have never heard it.

sleeping dictionary (At least pre–Spanish-American War to Modern) *s.* A mistress taken in a foreign country. Otherwise respectable soldiers have maintained that this was the best and quickest way of learning the local language, but it is doubtful that their motivations were primarily intellectual or that the first words they learned were of any use in handling native allies under fire. There is the further problem that in some cultures there is a special woman's language, and it does not do for a tough NCO to go around talking like a dress designer at a fashion show.

slick (Modern) *s.* A troop-carrying or supply-carrying UH-1 Huey helicopter.

"It was called a slick because it didn't have any weapons fastened on the outside of the fuselage" (Downs). Slicks have door gunners, who are armed with M60 machine guns. See *gunship*.

slickie boy (Korea to Modern; also Air Force) *s.* A particular type of clever, nimble-fingered thief. The term is widely used in Korean Pidgin English today, as is the verb *slickie*, to steal. Korean slickie boys are so deft that they can slip an unwary American's wristwatch off his arm and be away before he knows it is gone. This same sort of criminal legerdemain was also widely practiced by young Vietnamese. Our sergeant major recalls the story of a friend whose wristwatch was stolen while he was riding down a Saigon street in a cyclo. He also lost his lunch, which he left in the cyclo when he leaped out to chase the thief, and his shoes, which fell off as he ran down the street.

slick-sleeve (Modern) *s.* A soldier with no rank, a private E-1, whose sleeves are bare of insignia.

sliders (Revolutionary to early 19th century) *s.* An early form of overalls, probably established in America by 1750. They were worn by troops (particularly, it would seem, by cavalrymen) while they were mounted as fatigue dress or as a protection for their boots and britches. Boots were difficult to obtain during the Revolution. American horsemen therefore sometimes had to make do with long overalls and ordinary shoes.

slipping your clutch (World War II) *s.* Talking too much on subjects where your ignorance is apparent. Also called *slushing oil, working your bolt*.

slope slopehead 1. (Vietnam on) *s.* A Vietnamese. Perhaps the worst of the many derogatory ethnic terms. It was based on the popular American misconception that the Indochinese were so stupid that their heads were pointed. This misconception was possibly reinforced by the fact that some Indochinese are extremely brachycephalic. 2. *s.* An Oriental. Less commonly used than more specific terms like *Nip* and *gook*.

slope, to (Civil War; USA) *s.* To desert. According to a contemporary parody of "Just Before the Battle, Mother" by George Frederick Root,

> Softly falls the twilight, mother.
> Gently slopes the battle plain.
> But still more gently, mother,
> Am I sloping home again.

sloper (Civil War; USA) *s.* A deserter.

slop over, to (Civil War) *s.* To wax unnecessarily enthusiastic, laudatory, and/or sentimental, whether about the charms of some female or some regiment's behavior in action.

slow deer (Civil War; USA) *s.* A Confederate farmer's pig, frequently considered legal game.

slow Joe (World War II) s. A soldier slow above and/or below the eyebrows. Apparently little used.

SLUF (Post–World War II; Air Force) *s.* Short Little Ugly Fellow. The A-7 attack aircraft.

slug (West Point) 1. *s.* Punishment for infraction of the rules. Usually in demerits and punishment tours. 2. *s.* Any disagreeable duty.

slug, to (West Point) *s.* To impose punishment.

slum slumgullion (Antiquity uncertain, but probably very old; possibly still used) Stew, usually beef stew, but it can be made with whatever is handy around the mess. According to one authority, "You don't make it. It just accumulates." The term goes at least as far back as the early 19th century on shipboard. Mencken (1945) lists it as in current use during World War I and "of very respectable antiquity" at that time. It is recorded for West Point (as *slum*) in 1900.

slum burner (World War I and somewhat later) *s.* A rolling kitchen, a sort of large kitchen range on wheels. Also called a *slum cannon, slum gun.* Cooks were sometimes called *slum burners.*

slum diver (World War I and somewhat later) *s.* A soldier who is fed slum excessively.

slushing oil (Modern) 1. A light oil used for a quick preliminary cleaning of a gun bore after firing. 2. *s.* By extension, anything superficial or of little value, especially talk.

smack smackhead (West Point) *s.* A plebe. Female plebes are called *sugar smacks*, probably with reference to the popular breakfast cereal.

smadge (Modern) *s.* Term of address to a sergeant major. From the now obsolete abbreviation *SMaj. Smadge* itself is still in wide use. " 'Smadge,' he said, using the contraction for Sergeant Major" (Flood).

small arms (Colonial to Modern) All arms, including automatic weapons, up to and including .50-caliber weapons and shotguns. In other words, all firearms smaller than a cannon.

small bowl (West Point) *s.* A dessert bowl used in the cadet mess hall.

small rations (Mid-19th century) Hardtack, coffee, salt, and sugar. These, properly packaged, could stand rough handling and were comparatively light. On long marches into hostile territory, such as Sherman's across Georgia in late 1864, a command could carry several weeks' small rations with it, and forage for meat, vegetables, and whatever else was available from the countryside as it advanced.

small-unit coward (Modern) *s.* A fictitious MOS title applied jokingly to oneself or derisively to someone whose courage is questionable.

smart bomb (Vietnam to Modern; Air Force) *s.* A bomb that can be guided to its target by a laser beam or television camera, giving amazing accuracy. See *dumb bomb.*

smoke bringer (World War II and later) *s.* A person or piece of equipment that has great potentialities for causing acute discomfort. "That new colonel's a real smoke bringer." The thought may also be expressed as "That new colonel will bring smoke on you." Also *pee-bringer.*

Smoke if you got 'em! (Modern) *s.* A catchphrase meaning *Relax!* or *Take it easy!* From a situation on a march or in formation: troops are often put at rest and told they can "smoke if you got 'em."

smoke jumper (Late 1940s; Airborne) *s.* One who crossed the color line sexually.

smoker (World War II and later; all Services) *s.* An enemy aircraft that goes down out of a dogfight trailing smoke. He is probably hurt, but possibly faking. Unless he is seen to crash, he does not count as a kill.

Smokey Bear (Vietnam and later) *s.* A UH-1 Huey helicopter with a smoke-screening device. Smokey Bears were used to lay protective screens of smoke during assault or recovery operations. They could lay smoke in a path 4,000 meters (about 4,372 yards) long.

Smokey the Bear hat (Modern; also Marines) *s.* The campaign hat worn by Army drill sergeants. So called after the hat worn by forest rangers and the Smokey the Bear figure used by the National

Council on the Prevention of Forest Fires. Also called *cowboy hat*.

smoking lamp (Modern; all Services) A lamp at formal officers' mess dinners and NCO dining-ins that indicates, when it is lit, that smoking is permitted. A naval custom originally.

SNAFU snafu (World War II) *s.* Situation Normal, All Fucked (or, in polite conversation, Fouled) Up. This handy definition of the basic facts of life soon begot a breed of equally terse acronyms, beginning with *TARFU* and *FUBAR*. The original *SNAFU*, however, has had the most vitality.

snake 1. (Modern) *s.* The AH-1G Cobra helicopter. 2. (West Point) *s.* Based on similar civilian uses of *snake* as a ladies' man, a cadet who cuts in at dances or hops. Since at least as early as 1939, a *parlor snake* has been a cadet who volunteered to escort female visitors around the post.

snake, to (West Point) *s.* To cut in at a dance. To make off with another cadet's date.

snake-bite medicine (Old, Old Army, but still occasionally heard) *s.* Hard liquor, especially whiskey. A term in common American use, it reflects the popular belief that the venom of a poisonous snake could be neutralized by drinking whiskey. The cure probably killed as many people as the snakes did.

snaked, to be (1950s to 1960s; West Point) *s.* To be the victim of underhanded treachery, as when a friend steals your date while you are off getting her a hot dog.

snapper (18th century to early 19th century) 1. (British) A flintlock pistol. 2. A piece of wood or horn used during drill to take the place temporarily of the expensive flint. With the snapper in place, the musket could be snapped without injury to the lock. Also called a *driver*.

snapsack (Colonial) An early spelling of *knapsack*.

snap shit, to (World War II and later) 1. *s.* To be really on the ball, to turn out or perform with exceptional smartness. "Those honor guard guys really have to snap shit." 2. *s.* As a command, "Hurry up!" "Get on with it!" "Do it better!"—or any similar exhortation to speed and efficiency. "Come on, snap shit! We don't have all day!"

sneak and peek (World War II) *s.* Reconnaissance patrol operations specializing in the collection of information by stealthy scouting, avoiding combat if possible.

Sneaky Pete 1. (1920s to 1930s) *s.* Canned heat (Sterno), used as a beverage by the more thrifty members of the Army during Prohibition days. In civilian life *Sneaky Pete* was rotgut liquor of any kind. 2. (Modern) *s.* The Special Forces.

sniper 1. (Antiquity uncertain, but late 18th century in British Army, to Modern) A soldier, usually an expert shot operating from concealment, who picks off individual enemy soldiers. 2. (West Point) *s.* A cadet who tries to harass, confuse, or embarrass an instructor with questions. Called a *sharpshooter* elsewhere in the Army. 3. (Post–World War II; especially paratroopers) *s.* An enlisted man suffering from compelling thirst and financial embarrassment. While nursing a small beer, he sneaks other customers' change off the bar. A long-winded civilian drunk makes an ideal victim, particularly if the sniper has comrades to distract the victim's attention. The more professional Regular Army types disdained this as a crude form of graft, considering a sponsor safer and more profitable.

snowbird 1. (Early Indian Wars to early 20th century) *s.* A soldier who enlisted in the autumn to get food and shelter during the winter and then deserted in the spring. 2. (Modern) *s.* A soldier who receives a temporary assignment while awaiting orders. Also called a *blackbird.*

snow drop (World War II) *s.* A very rear-echelon MP standing guard in London, Paris, and other safe spots. So called because of gleaming white helmet liners such MPs wore. The suggestion is also that he might melt, if in a place where things got hot.

snow-excluder (Indian Wars) The Army's first (1874) issue overshoe, a primitive, low-cut affair, but a lot better than nothing. A related model was called a *bucket gaiter.* Both models were replaced by the higher and better arctic shoes, commonly called *arctics.*

snow job (World War II to Modern) *s.* Deliberately confusing and flattering speech designed to make the listener believe something he knows is not so, or to go along with a proposed course of action he knows he should oppose. It should be said that a snow-job expert can be a handy adjunct to a headquarters when it becomes necessary to obfuscate visiting congressmen, minions of the mass media, higher headquarters, and other nuisances. *I snow you not* is a pledge of sincerity, and sometimes the biggest snow job of all.

snuffy (Modern) *s.* A basic trainee or a soldier detailed to perform a menial, unimportant task; hence, any low-ranking, unimportant person. In the Marines, however, *snuffy* can indicate any low-ranking marine, up to lance corporal. Possibly from the comic strip "Barney Google" or its successors.

Soap Suds Row (Old, Old Army to World War I) *s.* The quarters assigned to married enlisted men. Their wives and daughters customarily eked out the soldiers' scant pay by taking in washing from officers and unmarried enlisted men. See *Hungry Hill.*

socked in (World War II and later; Air Force) *s.* Unable to fly because of the weather. The soup is right down on the runway and the birds are walking.

soft duty (Civil War; USA) *s.* Duty well behind the front, especially clerical work. A Regular artilleryman returning to duty with his battery recorded that "the old fellows hazed me a little to make up for my six months of soft duty! The specifications were 'Six months' absence on soft duty' " (Buell).

soft money (World War II) *s.* Paper money.

soft-stripe (Modern) *s.* A specialist rating; a soldier with a specialist rating. His rank does not entitle him to troop leadership duties or the privileges of a noncommissioned officer. See *hard-stripe.*

soft-tack (19th century to Civil War) Ordinary baker's bread, as contrasted to the issue *hardtack.*

SOI (Modern) Signal Operating Instructions. The rules and bylaws for using your outfit's different types of signal communications.

SOL (World War I to Modern) *s.* Shit Out of Luck.

soldier of the month (Modern) A soldier selected by competitive examination as the sharpest individual in his unit or the competing units. The individual appears before a board of officers and noncommissioned officers, who grill him on a variety of topics, from job knowledge to general military subjects. His appearance and bearing are noted. The award is fairly substantial and may be an official certificate to go in his records, excusal from extra duties for a time, a special pass, or even money in the form of a US Savings Bond. Similar competitions may be held on weekly, quarterly, and yearly bases.

Soldier's Medal (1926 to Modern) The fifth highest award for heroism, ranking just below the Distinguished Flying Cross. It is awarded to US and foreign military personnel in recognition of heroism not involving actual combat with an enemy. The action for which it is awarded must involve personal hazard and voluntary risk of life. EM who have received this award and retire with more than twenty years of service may receive a 10 percent increase in base pay.

Soldiers of the Sea (Approximately World War I) A fanciful title the Marines occasionally give themselves. (The original British term was *Sea Soldiers.*) There is a fleeting record, however, of its use by the AEF, referring to Marines doing duty as MPs, in a song (Nason, 1928) with the chorus:

> So yell to hell with Kaiser Bill
> And the Soldiers of the Sea

soldier's wife (At least Civil War to Modern) *s.* A sewing kit with needles, thread, buttons, etc. with which a soldier can perform minor tailoring jobs. They are usually available in the PX. Also called a *housewife.*

someone else's war (Modern; also Marines) *s.* Any action not involving the speaker, even if it is happening only a short distance away. "Someone Else's War a mile away" (Webb).

somewhere between shit and syphilis (Modern) 1. *s.* Serious and compromising circumstances, equivalent to the standard slang *between a rock and a hard place.* 2. *s.* A catchphrase used to reply to any silly question.

son-of-a-bitch (Old Army) *s.* Water, bacon fat, and hardtack boiled together. Something soldiers liked as a bedtime snack.

Sop (World War I) *s.* Any of the various models of the British Sopwith aircraft, flown to a limited extent by US pilots.

> Mother, hang out your service flag!
> Your son's going up in a Sop.
> The engine's a-stutter, the wings
> are a-droop
> It'll fall to bits if he loops the loop.

SOP (World War II and later; all Services) Standard Operating Procedure—the way we do things around here. This is especially useful in major joint headquarters, which have a multiplicity of problems involving several services. For example, you are an Army officer on red phone duty in the Far East at midnight. An Air Force radar station reports that a US Navy aircraft appears to be buzzing the Vladivostok naval base. (Parenthetically, it develops that the pilot, besides being stupid, is in complete despair because his wife is arriving and his josan refuses to move out.) What *do* you do, first, second, and finally? Believe it or not, a good SOP can tell you.

sorry A word that, if used in official conversation by a Marine of the 1920s and 1930s, would have gotten him about four hours of pack drill. The idea behind that was that you were either right or wrong. If you were right, regrets were indicative of unbecoming weakness of character. If you were wrong, such idle chatter merely further irritated an already irked superior. The Old Army had much the same attitude, especially among its officers. Traces survive even into these lax times. If you get chewed out, do not waste energy and your superior's time apologizing; just do it right the next time.

Sorry about that (Modern) The exact meaning of this phrase is somewhat hard to define, except that it ranges roughly from *C'est la guerre* to *tough shit.* "The expression 'Sorry about that' was repeated at least six thousand times between Reveille and Taps" (Groom).

SOS 1. (World War I) Services of Supply. The communications and supply organization that supported the combat units of the AEF.

Oh, mother, take in your service
flag.
Your son's in the SOS.
He isn't helping to win the war,
But he's getting a wonderful rest.

2. See *shit-on-a-shingle.* 3. (Fairly modern) *s. Same Old Shit.* It means that there has been no improvement recently in whatever subject is under discussion. "I wanted leave, but they gave me that SOS about how they couldn't spare me right now."

"Sound Off" (Modern) *s.* The name of a cadence marching or Jody song that uses the refrain *sound off.*

sound off, to Several related expressions ultimately going back to the command *Sound off!* given by the adjutant during a formal parade or guard mount, as the signal for the band to march the length of the line and back, playing loudly. 1. (Old, Old Army to Modern) *s.* To talk loudly and long on some subject, monopolizing the conversation. 2. (Probably Old, Old Army to Modern) As *Sound off!* A command to speak more loudly, as during a roll call, cadence counting, etc. 3. (Modern) *s.* A preparatory comment before breaking wind.

Sound off like you've got a pair! (Modern) *s.* A catchphrase for *Speak up, Make yourself known,* etc. The implication is that one who does not sound off must lack one or both testicles and so not be a complete man.

Airborne sergeant went to heaven,
Never cussed and had no lovin'.
When he didn't see God anywhere,
He said: "Sound off, Lord, like
you've got a pair!"

soup (World War I to Modern; Air Force) *s.* Fog, low clouds, rain, or snow that means instrument flying or no flying at all.

Soupy See *mess call.*

sour krauts (Civil War; USA) *s.* German-American volunteers, usually much derided by native Americans and blamed for anything that went wrong.

sow (West Point) *s.* A nickname used by cadets for a second-class (equivalent of college junior) woman cadet. It conveys the proper gender and rhymes with *cow,* but we doubt very much that it will meet with official approval.

sow belly (Civil War to early 20th century) *s.* Salt pork, usually fat. It had an acceptable, if strong, flavor and could be prepared in various ways or even eaten raw. In later years, sometimes bacon.

SP (World War I, but especially World War II, to Modern) Self-Propelled. An *SP gun* is mounted on a truck, half-track, or full-track chassis, which usually is armored. Such a gun has better cross-country mobility and can get into action faster than towed guns.

Space A (Modern) *s.* Short for *space available.* Space on military aircraft that is left open after official-duty travelers are seated. Space A seating is available on a first-come, first-served basis, according to category of potential riders.

space cadet (Vietnam and later; Air Force) *s.* A pilot, usually young, sometimes skillful, but always a show-off. Also *hot dog, hot rock.*

Spad 1. (World War I) A single-seater biplane. 2. (Vietnam) *s.* Affectionate nickname for the A-1E Skyraider single-engine fighter plane, which despite its age was widely used during the Vietnam War. "We called them Spads, because the A1E's age and performance approached that of the WWI machine" (Broughton).

Spam Ribbon (World War II and later) *s.* The European–African–Middle Eastern Campaign Medal awarded for service in those areas. The name was coined by troops in North Africa who got an overdose of Spam in 1943. By the time we got there, Spam was a luxury item.

Spanish dinner Spanish meal (Mexican War and later) *s.* Southwest frontier slang for tightening your belt another notch; in plain fact, going hungry. Also called *Mexican dinner.*

spaz (West Point) *s.* A plebe; a sort of human malfunction. A handy new cadet expression.

spaz around, to (West Point) *s.* To waste time and to foul things up.

speak sergeant, to talk sergeant, to (Considerable Antiquity) To use especially profane, objectionable, and/or blasphemous speech. The implication is that such was a sergeant's native language. These days, they are supposed to speak gently and sweetly.

spec (West Point) *s.* Since at least as early as 1900, verbatim memorization of information.

spec /spek/ (Modern) *s.* Short for *specialist.* "A Spec/4; not quite a sergeant" (Haldeman).

special feces (Modern) *s.* A play on *Special Forces.*

Special Forces (Modern) The Green Berets. Airborne soldiers who are cross-trained in a variety of military, linguistic, medical, and survival skills. They are organized into small detachments and have the mission to train, organize, supply, direct, and control guerrilla forces and to conduct unconventional warfare. They were first organized at Fort Bragg, North Carolina, in 1952 as the 10th Special Forces Group. Also *Green Beanies, Snake Eaters, Sneaky Petes.*

Special Forces Prayer (Modern) A parody of Psalm 23:4. It exists in many variants. The Special Forces may not have originated it, but it represents the devil-may-care bravado of men who live under desperate circumstances. Herr notes that it was very popular among marines along the DMZ in Vietnam.

> Yea, though I walk through the
> valley
> Of the shadow of death, I will fear
> No evil: For I am the meanest
> Motherfucker in the valley.

Also *Airborne Prayer, Infantryman's Prayer, Marine's Prayer.*

specialist grades The concept of the military specialist is probably as old as organized warfare, and the history of organizational development is in very large part a proliferation of specialists. The men who specialized in ordnance, supplies, music, veterinary care, motor maintenance, and radio repairs all did work that could not be expected of combat troops and had to be recognized. But a problem has always existed: their relation to the fighting men. It is a problem that the Army has historically treated in seesaw fashion. From colonial times until 1920, specialists were not recognized as a separate class, but there were de facto specialists who did technical work of various sorts in what amounted to an exuberant welter of special positions and grades: farrier, stable sergeant, saddler, electrician, etc. In 1920 the Army faced up to the problem and created the first specialist category per se. 1. (1920–42) Men who performed technical duties were rated in rank as privates or privates first class, but were further graded as specialists, ranging from specialist sixth class to specialist first class, first being the top. These ratings were eventually awarded to 227 specialties that amounted to forerunners of the MOS system. Although the specialists did not receive rank, they did receive pay increments, so that a first-first (private first class specialist first class) might under some circumstances receive almost as much pay as a master sergeant. In 1942, however, these specialist ratings and their extra pay were canceled, and soldiers who held the ratings were converted to the new technician grades, or remained privates and privates first class. 2. (1955 to Modern, in stages) In 1948 the technician grades were abolished and holders of the grades were converted to the corresponding command grades. This change proved unsatisfactory, and in 1955 the specialist grades were revived as specialist first class, specialist second class, specialist third class, and master specialist. These all ranked below a corporal. After several fairly complex changes, the present system was arrived at in 1958, with some small changes in 1977. At present, the specialist grades consist of specialist four (E-4), specialist five (E-5), and specialist six (E-6). (Specialist seven was abolished in 1977. Specialists eight and nine, while announced, were never created, and the grades were abandoned.) Specialists are not noncommissioned officers, and in each specialist grade, the specialist is immediately inferior in rank to the comparable command grade. Thus, a specialist five ranks below a sergeant (who is E-5) and above a corporal (who is E-4). The general insignia for the specialist grades is an eagle. A specialist four wears just the eagle; a specialist five, the eagle with an arc above it; and a specialist six, the eagle with two arcs above it. General nicknames for the specialist grades are *speedy* and *spec*. A specialist four is called a *bird corporal*; a specialist five, *chicken coop with a roof*. A specialist is addressed as *specialist*.

Special Processing Company SPC (Modern) A facility located at battalion or separate-company level where soldiers are confined for short periods as a form of "correctional custody," under the orders of their immediate commanders, for such minor infractions as are punishable under Article 15 of the *Uniform Code of Military Justice* with short-term deprivation of liberty. (Personnel in pay grade E-4 and above may not be confined to an SPC unless their punishment also includes an unsuspended reduction to grade E-3 or below.) SPC confinement is light, the offender being allowed out to work during the day. He also may take passes and have visitors. Time spent in the SPC is not considered "lost time" or "bad time." The SPC is the lowest rung on the ladder of the military penal system. Next is the stockade, where confinement and discipline are much stricter and sentences are served for longer periods than in the SPC. Soldiers who commit court-martial offenses are placed in a stockade. Most military installations have one. The next step is the US Army Retraining Brigade, located at Camp Funston, Fort Riley, Kansas, where confinement is for a maximum period of six months under conditions designed to remotivate the offender, with the object of eventually restoring him to full military duty. The final stop for the military miscreant is the US Disciplinary Barracks, Fort Leavenworth, Kansas, where sentences range from a mere thirty days for being AWOL to life for murder.

speckalist (Modern) *s.* A specialist.

speedy (Modern) *s.* A specialist, as in *speedy four, speedy five, speedy six.*

Spick Spic (West Point) *s.* The Spanish language as taught at West Point.

spiderholes (Modern) *s.* Small concealed firing positions from which snipers emerge to shoot at patrolling troops. Probably from the ingenious lair of the trapdoor spider, which darts from its hole to snatch unwary prey.

spin, in a tail spin, in a (World War I to Modern) *s.* Confused, dizzy, distracted. Originally an aviator's technical term, but soon in general use.

spit and polish (Antiquity uncertain to Modern; all Services) *s.* A term with a double meaning. At worst, excessive attention to outward appearance; at best, equal devotion to efficiency, with effort expended to maintain uniform and equipment in a high state of cleanliness and readiness. The origin of the term would seem to be one of the basic methods of polishing something—spit on it and then rub hard. The term is recorded for the 1890s in the British Army and was even then considered an old term (Partridge, 1970). The American Army adopted it some time before World War II.

Spitfire Battery (World War II) *s.* An anti-aircraft unit attached to the US 5th Armored Division. It had a bag of four planes—all British Spitfires. We were present when it got the fourth and must say it was an impressive feat. How its gunners ever managed to pick that lonesome little Spitfire out of a sky full of German planes really baffled everyone—especially the Spitfire pilot.

spit-shine, to (Modern; all Services) *s.* To shine shoes with polish, water or saliva, and a wet rag, resulting in a surface finish glossier than patent leather. The technique involves building a thick and even coat of polish on the leather before buffing it. Some soldiers advocate washing the dye completely out of the leather and then working a commercial shoe polish (Kiwi is recommended) into the leather until it is completely recovered and redyed. The recommended buffing material is a baby diaper wrapped tightly around the hand. The rag should be damp, but not wet. A quick circular motion is used to apply new polish and small amounts of water and saliva. While spit-shining produces a high gloss that is fairly easy to maintain, it dries out the leather and reduces the life of the shoe. Deep scratches cannot be covered. Some soldiers keep one pair of shoes or boots with a spit-shine for display and inspection only.

spittoon (Antiquity uncertain, probably recurrent) *s.* Soldiers' way of saying *platoon.*

splash (Modern; Air Force) *s.* Visual or radar verification of the destruction of a target. "Splash! I got him! Splash!" (AAV, p. 22).

splinter blind (Ancient to at least World War I) A wall of sandbags or gabions partially closing off a section of a trench. Troops were supposed to duck behind the splinter blind when an enemy mortar shell or grenade landed in the trench, to avoid being hit by metal "splinters."

Spock's Army See *Dr. Spock's Army*.

sponsor 1. (1940s to 1950s) *s.* Someone, usually a well-heeled drunk, who treats a soldier at a bar. The soldier acquires a sponsor when suffering pecuniary embarrassment. The soldier's modus operandi is to nurse a beer for a long time, until he spots a loquacious customer anxious to talk about his war experiences. In order to retain the attention of his audience, the talker keeps setting up drinks. One paratrooper we know was so skilled at this that he saved up a tidy fortune and got the DTs. 2. (Modern) An enlisted man or officer appointed to "host" a newly assigned officer or enlisted person during the first days of assignment to a new post. The sponsor attends to such things as arranging for temporary billeting for the soldier and his family, meeting him when he arrives in the local area, and escorting him about as he does his processing. The sponsor is usually of the same rank as the person he is detailed to assist and, when possible, the person who is being replaced by the new arrival.

spoof, to (World War II) *s.* To try to trick the enemy in electronic operations. Spoofing includes setting up temporary radio nets to simulate the presence of nonexistent units (sometimes the enemy tries to jam them, a useless expenditure of energy); transmitting radio messages containing false information; continuing to transmit on a frequency the enemy has jammed, so that the enemy will think he has not been successful; and other plots and ploys.

spooks (Modern) *s.* Counterintelligence Corps personnel, perhaps because of the covert nature of much of their work. Spooks are not to be confused with CID agents.

Spooky (Vietnam and later) *s.* Another name for Puff, the Magic Dragon. The nickname is appropriate, because Spooky, which operated at night, could seldom be seen or heard by ground troops until it opened fire. Its miniguns produced a weird grinding, groaning noise and the tracers fired from them seemed to pour out of the night sky like sparks from a welder's torch. All this usually happened unexpectedly to most observers on the ground and the overall effect was awe-inspiring.

spoon, to (Civil War; USA) *s.* To sleep very close together, spoon fashion. In such crowded conditions, *Right spoon!* or *Left spoon!* was a command to shift positions. "The room . . . was barely large enough for all of us to lie down at once. It required pretty close 'spooning' together—so close, in fact that all sleeping on one side would have to turn at once. . . . All for instance would be lying on their right sides. They would begin to get tired, and one of the wearied ones would sing out to the sergeant in command of the row, 'Sergeant, let's spoon the other way.' . . . 'Attention! Left SPOON!' and the whole line would at once flop over on their left sides" (McElroy).

spoons (Modern) *s.* Cooks and mess personnel in general.

spoon up, to (West Point; 1920s and later) *s.* To clean up, to put in proper order. Now obsolete.

spoony (West Point; early 20th century to about 1950s) *s.* "Showy, brilliant, clear, beautiful, pretty stylish" (*Howitzer*, 1900). In modern usage, by 1942, neat in personal appearance. Perhaps now obsolete.

spoony button (West Point) *s.* "A Full Dress button a cadet used to give his girlfriend" (*Bugle Notes*, 1979, p. 272).

spread-eagle (Early 19th century to late 19th century as a civilian term) *s.* Exaggeratedly patriotic. Thus, Samuel E. Chamberlain in his *Recollections of a Rogue* tells of his campaign to be elected an officer of Illinois volunteers in 1846: "I made a spread eagle speech, with plenty of the 'Halls of Montezuma' and 'Golden Jesus's of Mexico.' " (He lost to an opponent who promised whiskey immediately.)

spread eagle *s.* (Colonial) A soldier who had been tied to the halberds for flogging. "His attitude bearing some likeness to that figure, as painted on signs."

spread-eagled, to be (Early 19th century to Civil War) A form of field punishment, often inflicted for cowardice. The offender was lashed to a wheel or pegged out on the ground with his arms and legs spread as widely as possible, and left to contemplate the state of his conscience. If he was noisy, he was gagged. On at least one occasion, a coward was spread-eagled between two trees in full view and easy range of the Confederates.

sprechen, to (Post–World War II to Modern) *s.* To talk. From German *sprechen* 'to talk, to speak'. Usually heard as in "Let's you and I sprechen about this."

Springfield '03 (1903 on) The US Magazine Rifle caliber .30 Model 1903, first manufactured at the Springfield (Massachusetts) Arsenal. It replaced the Krag-Jorgensen in 1904. A Mauser-type bolt-action weapon, it is probably the most accurate military rifle ever produced. During the Mexican Punitive Expedition, Capt. Aubrey Lippincott of the 13th Cavalry shot a Mexican officer out of his saddle at 800 yards. And in 1928, Gunnery Sergeant Satterfield, USMC, is reported to have hit one of Sandino's "Patriots" in Nicaragua at 1,200 yards. Although replaced by the Garand semiautomatic rifle at the beginning of World War II, the Springfield is still used as a sniper's weapon.

spruce beer (Colonial to Revolutionary) A drink made by boiling the end shoots of the black spruce for three hours, straining the resulting liquid into casks, adding molasses, and permitting the mixture to ferment. This is a basic recipe, but recipes varied, some including ginger, hops, and yeast, which seldom were available on the frontier. It was a useful antiscorbutic, of great benefit to troops campaigning on salt rations. Although the military no longer indulges in spruce beer, civilians still occasionally make it.

sprung (Revolutionary) *s.* Drunk. Sgt. Benjamin Gilbert of the 5th Massachusetts Regiment noted in his journal on 5 March 1778 that he "stopt and Drinkt Sling until we all got well Sprung." (A sling was not exactly the modern cocktail of the same name, but a drink composed of hard liquor, lemon juice, and bitters—or any reasonable equivalent—served either hot or cold.)

spy company (Late 18th century on, but somewhat uncommon by the Civil War) A unit of scouts and guides that performed the general duties of a modern reconnaissance company. The Mexican Spy Company (actually three companies), recruited by Gen. Winfield Scott from underemployed bandits during the Mexican War, proved efficient and loyal.

squad (Ancient to Modern) 1. The smallest tactical unit in the Army. Although *squad* was a common military term even before the American Revolution, it denoted only an informal grouping. To each sergeant was assigned a number of men whom he supervised in matters of appearance, care of equipment, and conduct. Usually these men messed together and shared the same tent or hut. The squad as a combat unit appeared in the 1904 revision of the *Infantry Drill Regulations.* Until just before World War II, the standard squad consisted of a corporal and seven men. At present, under optimal conditions, an infantry squad consists of one staff sergeant, two sergeants, and seven men. 2. A group of men temporarily associated for a certain activity. As in *bolo squad* or *awkward squad.*

squad bay An area in the barracks or troop billets large enough to accommodate a squad of soldiers. It is usually open to the general area of the billets and affords minimum privacy.

squadron (Colonial to Modern) 1. A squadron of horse cavalry normally consisted of four troops or companies. The typical modern Armored Cavalry squadron has a headquarters troop, three ground reconnaissance troops, a tank company, and a self-propelled howitzer battery. 2. (Air Force) A basic administrative and tactical unit, smaller than a group, and consisting of two or more flights.

squad room (Old, Old Army to Modern) The sleeping quarters in the older-style barracks.

squads east and west (Old Army and later) *s.* Close-order drill. The *Infantry Drill Regulations* of 1904 established the eight-man squad as the smallest division of a company, and most drill movements thereafter were by squads—squads right, right by squads, and so forth. It was a sharp, effective system, but one that required considerable practice. Possibly for this reason it was replaced by simpler drill just before World War II, but old-timers called any drill by the old name for many years thereafter.

> It's "Squads East" and "Squads West"
> And "Squads right into line."
> And then the dirty gentlemen
> They give you "Double time."

square division (World War I to early World War II) An infantry division containing two brigades, each consisting of two infantry regiments. It was big and a trifle unwieldy, but just right for long slugging matches like the Meuse-Argonne. (One factor that French and British historians of World War I always overlook is that one of our divisions equaled at least two of theirs.)

squared away (Antiquity uncertain to Modern) *s.* In order, ready for action, prepared. Early 19th-century British nautical jargon, but fairly common in the US Army.

squat (Modern) *s.* Nothing; something that is absolutely useless. " 'Squat,' said the third. 'They don't worry about squat' " (Groom). Probably from a contemptuous phrase we recall from boyhood: "He doesn't amount to diddly squat!"

squaw A native woman. Army usage is broader than civilian usage here. Originally a North American Indian woman, but later, a Chinese, Filipino, or Latin American woman. A white man who wed or lived with such a woman in a jawbone marriage was a *squaw man.*

squelch, box of (Modern) *s.* An imaginary commodity that evil-minded persons sometimes send naive recruits to fetch.

squints (Modern) *s.* Personnel trained to read aerial reconnaissance photos and interpret intelligence data gained from them; image interpreters MOS 96D.

squirrel rancher (1920s to 1930s) *s.* A small-scale, barely-scrape-by rancher-farmer whose barren holdings produced little except children, ground squirrels, mortgages, and debts. The term was widely used in the Rocky Mountain area when the Army was busy with the Civilian Conservation Corps. We suspect that it was a borrowed civilian term like *ridge runner* and *briar jumper*, which were local descriptions of back-country citizens around Fort Knox, Kentucky.

stabilized tour (Modern) A tour of duty of a specified length of time, during which a soldier cannot be levied for assignment elsewhere. Usually a tour of from two to three years.

stack (Air Force) 1. *s.* Short for *exhaust stack.* 2. Planes in a holding pattern over an airfield.

stack, to (Air Force) 1. To arrange aircraft at various altitudes, usually over an airfield awaiting landing instructions. The situation above the airport is a *stack up.* 2. *s. To crash.*

stack arms, to (Ancient to Modern) 1. As *Stack arms!* Officially, an order for soldiers to put their rifles into tripod arrangements, so that they would not fall over, yet could be easily retrieved when needed. In certain weapons, like the Springfield and the M1, this was done with the *stacking swivel.* After a march or battle, the command for stack arms would be given, indicating that it was time to rest or to pitch camp and eat. 2. *s.* By extension, to retire from active duty. 3 *s.* To loaf on the job, especially just before retirement or after having attained that last possible promotion.

stacking swivel (20th century; also Marines) A small metal part near the muzzle of certain rifles that permitted the rifles to be hooked together and form a standing group. The expression *to grab [someone or something] by the stacking swivel* could range in meaning from grabbing someone by the throat to getting a problem or job firmly in hand.

stack pencils, to (Modern) *s.* To loaf on the job just before retirement, discharge, or transfer. Used primarily by support and staff personnel, in parody of *stack arms.*

staff 1. See *general staff.* 2. (1920s to Modern) Short for *staff sergeant.*

staff sergeant 1. (1818–30; West Point) *s.* A cadet noncommissioned officer ranking just below sergeant major. He was appointed from the class just below that of the sergeant major and generally succeeded to that office on the sergeant major's graduation. Abolished in 1830. 2. (1920–48; 1958 to Modern) At present, a junior noncommissioned officer serving in pay grade E-6. He ranks just above sergeant and just below platoon sergeant and sergeant first class. The grade was created in 1920 as staff sergeant (third grade), ranking above a sergeant and below a technical sergeant. The title and grade were abolished in 1948, but revived in 1958. In both periods, the insignia of a staff sergeant has been three stripes, with a connecting arc below. A staff sergeant is addressed as *sergeant.* His nicknames are *rocker* and *staff.* Abbreviated *SSG, S. Sgt.*

stake out, to (Colonial to Indian Wars) A rough form of field punishment, often applied for drunkenness. The prisoner was spread out on the ground with his limbs extended in an X-shape, and both wrists and ankles were lashed to stakes or tent pegs. If he were impolitely noisy about it, a fifth tent peg was fastened across his mouth. See *spread-eagled.*

stand, to (Antiquity uncertain to Modern) To perform certain duties or to be present at certain occasions: *to stand formation, to stand guard, to stand sentry, to stand reveille,* etc. While the age of these expressions is uncertain in the US Army, *stand sentry* extends back to the Renaissance in Great Britain.

standby alert (Modern) An exercise in which a unit's strength is mustered, but not deployed.

stand down from, to (Modern) As in *to stand down from* an alert, to assume a lower level of combat readiness.

standing order (Antiquity uncertain to Modern) An order announced at a unit formation or posted on its bulletin board.

standing tall (Modern; all Services) 1. *s.* At attention. 2. *s.* Ready for any contingency. 3. *s.* On the carpet for disciplinary action. "Have PFC Clarke standing tall in my office" (Doulis).

stand of arms (Colonial to late 19th century) A musket, complete with ramrod, sling, and bayonet.

stand to, to (World War I) *s.* To be in position, ready and waiting. Undoubtedly a shortening of the very old "cautionary" orders *Stand to your arms* and *Stand to your guns,* used to alert troops for action. Because of the natural tendency of both sides to raid the enemy's trenches in the early morning, both sides would stand to. "We stood-to at dawn in white mists which peeled slowly away and kept us waiting" (Chapman).

star man (West Point) *s.* An academically distinguished cadet.

Stars and Gripes (Modern) *s.* A play on the newspaper *Stars and Stripes.*

stars and stripes (Old Army to World War II) *s.* Baked beans. A very common dish. *Stripes* referred to the strips of bacon included.

Stars and Stripes (1918–19; 1942 to Modern) An unofficial newspaper for military personnel overseas, operated under the sponsorship of the Army. It was first published for the AEF from February 1918 to June 1919, with a total of seventy-one weekly issues. Among its contributors were Alexander Woollcott, Franklin P. Adams, Harold Ross, and John T. Winterich. It was revived as a weekly newspaper in April 1942, and became a daily by November 1942. Among its contributors were Irwin Shaw and Ernie Pyle. In October 1945 a Pacific edition appeared, and at present both European and Pacific editions are in existence.

state connection (Modern) *s.* The airplane that takes soldiers home from an overseas assignment. The term is very commonly used in Germany. Also called *freedom bird.*

stateside (Old Army to Modern) *s.* The continental United States. "I'm shipping out stateside next week."

static line (World War II to Modern; Airborne) *s.* 1. A snow job to a woman. 2. Connects troop parachute to anchor line cable in an aircraft.

stealee-boys (Post–World War II; all Services) *s.* The professional criminal class on the island of Okinawa. They were reputed to be the most skillful thieves in the

Orient, capable of extracting the gold from your teeth while carrying on a conversation with you. One of their exploits was cutting several hundred feet of wire out of a live, high-voltage electric power line, just outside the provost marshal's office one night.

steam and cream, to get a (Vietnam to Modern; all Services) *s.* To visit a massage parlor where one is treated to a steam bath (of sorts), a massage (often only perfunctory), and then sexual intercourse and/or fellatio (not necessarily in that order). The reference to *cream* is in association with ejaculation. There were many of these establishments in Vietnam and the expression probably gained popularity among the Armed Forces through Vietnam service during the period from 1962 to 1973. These establishments still exist in Korea. Also called *steam job* and *blow bath.*

steel pot (World War II to Modern) *s.* The steel helmet.

step (Antiquity uncertain to Modern) The distance covered in completing a single movement of the foot in drill. *Normal step* is 30 inches; *double time* is 36 inches; *half step* is 15 inches; *side step* is 10 inches.

Stetson (Old Army to World War II; also Marines) An expensive, commercially produced brand of campaign hat, favored by officers and senior NCOs. You could park it in a seabag, water your horse out of it, and otherwise subject it to the exigencies of the service, yet it still kept its shape.

stewburner (Antiquity uncertain to Modern) *s.* An Army cook.

We sent that cook to CBS
And all he learned to do
Was boil water and burn the stew.

CBS was Cooks and Bakers School. Later generations of soldiers may have substituted OCS as a more familiar abbreviation.

stick (Modern) All the parachutists who jump from one door of an aircraft during one run over a drop zone.

stockade 1. (Colonial to mid-19th century) A fortification, usually consisting of a rectangular palisade with blockhouses at its corners. Barracks, officers' quarters, storerooms, and stables were built against the inside of the walls. Hollywood melodrama aside, such forts were seldom built west of the Mississippi. The Plains Indians were not dangerous enough to warrant such constructions. On the few occasions when the Indians did pluck up courage to attack an Army post, the troops were able to stand off greatly superior numbers of tribesmen from behind defenses improvised from woodpiles or wagon boxes. 2. (Old Army and a little earlier) As during the Mexican Punitive Expedition, at Dublán, Chihuahua, Mexico, a fenced and guarded area where prostitutes were quartered to exercise their profession under medical supervision. 3. (Old Army to Modern) A military prison. At present, the place where military prisoners are confined under somewhat stricter discipline than that imposed in the Special Processing Company, for crimes that do not warrant a sentence in the retraining brigade or federal prison. Colloquially, variously known as *Box Three, Box Thirteen, Crossbar Hotel, Crowbar Hotel, screenhouse, Wire City, the mill,* etc.

stockade, to (Modern) *s.* To fold mattresses and bed linen in a prescribed manner on the day that old linen is exchanged for fresh. The mattress is folded into an

S-shape, and the pillow, linen, and blankets placed on top of the mattress.

stockade population (Modern) Pentagonese for that portion of the Army that is under confinement at any one time. The pressure to keep it low and lower—no matter how—can get pretty heavy.

stockade shuffle (Modern) 1. *s.* A peculiar bouncing, shuffling, half-marching, half-dancing step supposedly used by military prisoners. 2. *s.* As in *to do a stockade shuffle,* to be confined in the stockade as a prisoner.

stonk (Antiquity uncertain, perhaps World War I, and later) *s.* A salvo or heavy barrage of artillery or mortar shells. Of Australian origin (Baker, 1945). Now rarely heard. "A stonk of about eight mortar rounds dropped on both tents and finished them" (Marshall, 1968).

stonkered (World War I to World War II) *s.* Put out of action, struck by a shell, killed. Australian origin (Baker, 1945). Not commonly heard.

stooge company stooge (1930s into World War II) *s.* Another impolite name for the company clerk.

storm flag (At least World War I to Modern) A small national flag (5 by 9.5 feet) flown by military installations during bad weather. By a natural transition, *the storm flag's flying* can mean that the old man is on the prowl with blood in his eye and that it could be your blood.

stout (18th century into 19th century) Physically strong and well built; brave, bold, and determined. Like *nervous,* it was a complimentary term for much of our history, without the present-day meaning of corpulent.

stovepipe (World War I) *s.* The British "Stokes" trench mortar, used to some extent by the AEF. It killed Germans, but very seldom the ones its crew was trying to hit.

STRAC /strak/ (Modern) 1. Strategic Army Corps. Formerly a command consisting of various units in a high state of combat readiness, capable of being deployed to any part of the world on very short notice. 2. *s.* By extension, of an individual, sharp, prepared, on the ball. *He is STRAC* is still a common expression, although the Strategic Army Corps as such has long been phased out. 3. *s.* Shit, The Russians Are Coming.

straddle trench (Antiquity uncertain to Modern) A field latrine consisting of a trench 1 foot wide, 2.5 feet deep, and 4 feet long. The dirt from its excavation is left alongside it to cover up feces as they are deposited. Also called a *slit trench.*

strafe, to (World War I to Modern) Originally, an attack on ground troops by low-flying airplanes using machine guns and light bombs. Later, any sort of sudden and violent attack, including a verbal one by a superior. From German *strafen* 'to punish'. The word became widely known through the German motto of World War I, *Gotto strafe England* 'May God punish England'.

straight dope (1930s to World War II, but still heard occasionally) *s.* The Absolute Truth—which turns out to be a straight-faced lie half the time and an unsubstantiated rumor the other half.

straight leg leg (World War II and later) 1. *s.* An airborne soldier's term for the rest of the Army, which did not share his exalted status. And, by compensation, a term of pride when used by nonairborne soldiers to describe themselves. A straight leg is thus a foot soldier. The origin of the term lies in the fact that paratroopers land with bent legs. 2. *s.* As in *straight-leg in-*

fantry or *straight-leg outfit*, reliable, workmanlike, non-elite, without frills.

straitjacket (1930s to World War II) *s.* The World War I Army issue blouse, which fitted snugly and had a tight, stand-up collar. Since World War I ended earlier than our planners foresaw, there was a large surplus of these jackets on hand when the looser, roll-collar blouse was introduced in 1926. These older jackets were issued to recruits and men in newly activated units for temporary wear until new-style blouses could be procured. (We are still of two minds concerning that old-style blouse. It was comfortable enough when properly fitted and certainly gave better protection around the chest and throat in cold weather. Also, you did not have to mess with that most unmilitary of all items of clothing—the necktie.)

straphanger (Modern) *s.* A useless person, one who goes along for the ride only. "A strap of the type one encounters standing up in the New York subway, to indicate that [he] was a nonproductive 'strap-hanger' " (Tregaskis).

strawfoot straw-foot (Civil War; USA) *s.* A recruit, especially a stupid or confused one, right off the farm. Presumably, such recruits did not know their left feet from their right. Sergeants would tie bits of hay to their left feet and straw to the right feet, and then drill them to the chant of "Hay foot! Straw foot! Belly full of bean soup!" With elaborations and modifications, this verse endured into our early years. The earliest example of the teaching system that we have found is from the colonial period in New York. Lacking haversacks, militiamen carried their bread and cheese rations in their coat pockets, bread on one side, cheese on the other. Their sergeants chanted, "Bread foot! Cheese foot!" During the Spanish-American War, a variation consisted of giving the recruit a small stone to carry in his left hand.

streamer 1. (Ancient to Modern) A long, narrow pendant strip of cloth affixed to an organizational color or distinguishing flag to commemorate each award of a unit decoration, campaign participation credit, or war service. Streamers are attached to the pike or lance of the flag staff and are a component part of colors, flags, and/or guidons. 2. (World War II to Modern) The complete failure of a parachute canopy to deploy. Although fairly common among equipment chutes, streamers are rare in personnel chutes. In fourteen years of parachute duty, one of our authors has seen exactly seven personnel chutes become streamers. When the T-7 chute was used, a streamer was usually caused by a poor exit—the jumper spun and twisted the suspension lines during deployment, so that the skirts of the canopy could not deploy. With the "improved" T-10, it did not matter what sort of exit you made. A streamer was purely a matter of luck. It also became very easy to break a static line. Such is the price of progress.

> If my main don't open wide
> I've got another by my side
> If that should fail me too
> Look out below, I'm comin' through.

strewn platoon (Modern) *s.* A sloppy drill or troop formation.

strike, to (Modern) *s.* To go bar-hopping, to hit the local bars.

striker (Civil War to World War II; also occasionally Marines) An enlisted man who voluntarily looked after an officer's leather, quarters, and (in mounted units) horse in off-duty time for a fee. The officer paid him out of his own pocket. Enlisted men often termed him a *dog robber*. The origin of the term *striker* is unknown, although it appeared earlier in civilian life as a man who did odd jobs, and it may ultimately refer to a blacksmith's assistant, the man who does the hammering while the smith holds the iron. When first encountered in the Army, the striker was much like the earlier British servant. He cooked, washed dishes, and helped around the house in addition to looking after the officer's equipment. In return, he received $5 a month and his meals, and was excused from guard duty, fatigue details, roll calls, and sometimes drills. If the officer's quarters were large enough, the striker might have a backstairs room. Married enlisted men often found this very desirable. The custom of the striker as a general personal servant definitely weakened the small companies of the frontier Army, and in 1881, Army regulations forbade it. Thereafter, the striker became an officer's personal orderly: he would shine the officer's boots, but not his kitchen floor. A reliable striker was a useful man. He kept a busy officer looking smart and could be an unofficial spokesman for the enlisted men. He had to be careful, however, not to be considered a tale-bearer. The term *striker*, as well as the institution, rather faded away during World War II. An officer's driver might handle a few essentials like his sleeping bag and perhaps a Jerry can of water for washing up, but that was about all. The postwar Philippine Scouts were a little more traditional, and the older custom seems to have lingered in some regiments through the Korean War. See *dog robber*, *enlisted aide*, *waiter*.

Strip (Modern) *s.* The main road leading up to an Army base. The Strip is usually lined with civilian business establishments catering to the physical and other needs of the troops. See *gate ghetto*, *Ville*.

stripe (Considerable Antiquity to Modern) 1. A small, straight piece of cloth, usually of a different color from the rest of the uniform, sewn on the sleeve to indicate enlistments or, in earlier times, wounds received. Called *service stripes* or *hashmarks*, and *wound stripes*. 2. A chevron indicating grade among enlisted men. In this meaning, the word *stripe* enters into many combinations and idioms: *one-striper*, (formerly) private first class; *two-striper*, corporal; *three-striper*, sergeant, etc.; *to get a stripe*, to be promoted; *to lose one's stripes*, to be demoted; *to be stripe heavy*, to have many stripes, to be a senior NCO; *to get one's stripes*, to be promoted to noncommissioned officer, etc.

striped-ass ape stripe assed ape (World War II) *s.* An imaginary creature capable of moving with great speed. "We took off like a batch of striped-assed apes." Perhaps based on the cavortings of sexually excited mandrills in a zoo.

Stud Book (Antiquity uncertain to Modern) *s.* *The Army Register*. So called because it gives the "pedigree" of every officer in the Army.

stump jumper *s.* An infantryman.

stupor juice (World War II) *s.* A generic term for high-proof brave-makers improvised by US troops in the Normandy hedgerows. It was generally Calvados, more or less diluted with wine or cider.

subaltern (Colonial to Revolutionary) Any officer below the grade of captain. A British term (still in use in Great

Britain) that lingered on in the Army through the Revolution.

subcaliber (20th century) 1. Officially, as in *subcaliber practice*, an economical way of gaining practice in firing a large gun by actually using a smaller gun. A common example of subcaliber practice involved using a World War I model of the 37mm gun in training 75mm-gun crews. The 37mm was mounted on the tube of the larger gun and their bores aligned. The gun crew used the sights of the 75mm, but fired the 37mm. 2. *s.* Colloquially, something less than completely satisfactory.

Submarine Messkit Repair Company (Modern) *s.* An imaginary unit assigned even more ridiculous and frivolous missions than the imaginary Messkit Repair Company.

Subsistence Department (1818 to World War I) A staff section, headed by a commissary general of subsistence, who was responsible for the procurement and issue of the Army's food. Formed in 1818, it was put into the Quartermaster Corps in 1912.

substitute 1. (Colonial through Civil War) A soldier serving in place of the man originally designated. This was a common circumstance in American militia service as early as King Philip's War (1675–76). A man of some means called up for active duty usually was able to hire a poorer or more adventuresome neighbor to go in his stead. This was not considered dishonorable. There is one story of a man who successfully sued his hired substitute for failing to report for duty. On another occasion, a substitute became bored with frontier duty and so hired a substitute to take *his* place. The system continued through the Revolution, in which a gun-shy white might offer up his black bondsman as a substitute sacrifice to freedom. During the Civil War, a drafted man again could avoid service by furnishing a substitute, but the resulting abuses (see *bounty jumper*) and the obvious unfairness of the practice caused its termination. 2. A soldier who took over a work detail for another. In some circumstances an enlisted man could pay another man to pull a detail like KP or CQ for him. The first sergeant or commanding officer had to give permission for the exchange of work, but no official cognizance was taken of it. The detail was accredited to the man who paid, not the man who did it. This practice was not officially authorized, but it was considered a custom of the service and was usually honored by the orderly room.

suckahachi (Post–World War II to Modern; all Services) *s.* Fellatio, both literally and figuratively. In the figurative use, *suckahachi* is an expression of defiance, equivalent to *Suck my dick!* or, in politer terms, *Go to hell!* From Japanese *shakuhachi*, the traditional 18-inch bamboo flute.

Suckahachi, GI watchee (Post–World War II to Modern) *s.* An offer by a Japanese or Korean prostitute to commit fellatio for the price of a cheap wristwatch or the wristwatch itself.

suckers (Civil War especially) *s.* Troops from Illinois.

Sudstown (Old, Old Army) *s.* Another version of *Soap Suds Row*.

sugar (Air Force) A code word formerly used in filing a flight plan when there was a VIP going along who wanted no special treatment during the trip. It means "accord no honors, provide servicing only"—about the same as the Old Army's *Never mind the guard.*

sugar report (World War II and later) *s.* A letter from the (or a) girl friend.

suicide squad (World War I into World War II) *s.* A machine-gun unit. Because of their deadly fire, machine guns are priority targets for enemy artillery and tanks. At least one history of World War I machine-gun battalions calls them *suicide battalions.* See *three-minute man.*

suitcase drill (Modern) *s.* Packing up to leave.

summer soldier (About World War II) *s.* A member of the National Guard, which normally has its annual active-duty training during the summer months. Consequently, most Regulars see them only when they come in for that "summer camp."

Sunny France (World War I and World War II) *s.* A mythical nation with an ideal climate, not to be confused with the actual France, where

> There's mud in the jam, the bread,
> and the stew!
> You open an egg—and there's mud
> in it too!

Sunny France was spoken with a carefully controlled shudder so that the rain or snow accumulated on your helmet would not spill down the back of your neck.

Sunsetters (World War II; Air Force) The 7th Fighter Command, which served with credit in the Pacific. Some of its personnel having been caught on the ground at Pearl Harbor, it tended to regard the war as a grudge fight dedicated to the soonest possible setting of Japan's "rising sun."

sunshiner (Old Army, possibly still surviving) *s.* A soldier who has served too long in the tropics and has begun to act as if the hot sun has crisped his brain around the edges. Another variety of sunshiner is the returned veteran of the tropics, who may still be all right in the head, but has gotten so thin-blooded that a summer day in Washington, D.C., seems uncomfortably chilly to him.

suntans (1930s to 1950s; also Marines) A cotton summer uniform, light golden brown in color, introduced during the 1930s. It replaced the post–World War I summer uniform, which had consisted of an OD wool shirt and OD cotton breeches. Oldtimers still called them *khakis.* (The Marines adopted the pants, but not the shirt; they preferred a thinner, lighter-colored shirt.) See also *chino khaki.*

supe (Considerable Antiquity to Modern; West Point and other Service academies) *s.* The superintendent.

supergrades (1958 to Modern) Senior noncommissioned officers in pay grades E-8 and E-9: master sergeant, first sergeant, sergeant major, command sergeant major. During 1956 and 1957, large numbers of noncommissioned officers left the Army to take more remunerative employment in the civilian job market. A committee appointed by the secretary of defense pinpointed the problem: "Too many enlisted men . . . reach the top rung of their ladder at a young age with little opportunity for further advancement" (Cordiner). As a result of this report, the grade structure of the Army was reorganized in 1958, and pay grades E-8 and E-9 were added. See also *sergeant, specialist.*

supernumerary A soldier detailed to stand by for guard duty in case someone detailed is not available.

supernumerary payday (Old Army) See *jawbone.*

suspension ribbon The ribbon that holds the actual medal of an award; it is fastened at the top to a metal bar with a clasp. The suspension ribbon is significant in displaying the official colors of the award and in being the place where devices representing later awards of the same decoration are affixed.

sutler (Colonial to late 19th century) A civilian who followed an army and sold food, toilet articles, tobacco, and items of clothing to the soldiers. Until the early 19th century he also sold liquor; thereafter, he could have been a bootlegger on the side. He was frequently the object of the regimental surgeon's wrath because of the poor quality of the foodstuffs he offered. The whole system was a source of corruption, but until the establishment of the PX system, the sutler was usually the soldier's only source of small necessities and comforts.

swabby (World War II) *s.* A member of the US Navy, of any rank whatever. From naval slang *swab*, for a common seaman, because swabbing decks was one of his major occupations.

swabs (Early 19th century; possibly of naval origin) Epaulettes. "I hope to get both swabs next year"—i.e., to be promoted from captain (one epaulette, worn on the right shoulder) to major (two epaulettes).

swaddy (Probably post–Civil War to perhaps late 19th century) *s.* A soldier. The term was occasionally applied in the western United States after the Civil War. Undoubtedly from British *swad*, *swadkin*, *swaddy* (late 18th and early 19th century), which meant a soldier, sometimes a discharged soldier.

swag (Revolutionary) A peddler of small objects, sometimes trashy, or such objects themselves. (The word was still used in this sense in Mayhew's 19th-century London.) Benjamin Gilbert and a comrade, returning home to Massachusetts after being discharged from the 5th Massachusetts Regiment, "rode as old swags" (Symmes).

swagger stick (Antiquity uncertain) A stick or small cane carried for show. Once these objects were very common in the US Army, and on some installations it was mandatory that officers and noncoms carry them. In this instance, they were the descendants of the various batons that were carried as badges of rank and the clubs and staves with which early noncommissioned officers corrected sloppy drill and bad habits. As a term, *swagger stick* is recorded for the British Army in the 1880s and still continues in use. In the US Army, happily, the swagger stick has gone the way of the third person form of address and other demeaning military customs. Grose (1783) tells the sergeant major, "When telling off the divisions . . . be sure to lay your rattan pretty smartly upon those you name . . . which will impress it to their memory; as well as upon their shoulders."

sweat (World War II to Modern) *s.* Waiting and worrying, especially the latter. *No sweat* means that something is easy or no trouble at all. But you *sweat out* the delay in getting an expected sugar report or orders. *No sweat, GI. MPs no come* was a come-on Korean women would give a soldier to let him know that it would be safe—in one respect—for him to dally with her.

swinging dick (1940s to Modern) *s.* A male soldier. The penis of a good soldier supposedly swings in time to the cadence count during drill. The sergeant's yell *Every swinging dick!* is equivalent to the naval *All hands,* meaning everyone. In the modern integrated Army, the expression is not so appropriate, but our proper sergeant major reports himself having been shocked and surprised when a woman buck sergeant referred casually to *swinging Richards.* There does not seem to be a generally accepted comparable term for female soldiers, although *double-slotted kitchen mechanics, dovetails,* and *crack troops* commonly exist.

swing team (Early 19th century to World War II) The middle team of horses for a field gun or caisson. In weight and size, they were intermediate between leaders and wheelers.

SWNCC SWINK /swink/ (World War II and later) State-War-Navy Coordinating Committee. A hardworking bunch of staff officers charged with developing policies mutually acceptable to their respective departments.

tab (Modern) An embroidered strip of cloth, worn on the shoulder, that indicates that the wearer has completed special training or has demonstrated proficiency in arms.

table commandant (West Point) The senior cadet at each table in the mess. "The upperclassman in charge of his ten-man mess hall table" (Truscott).

tac (At least as early as 1900 to Modern; West Point) *s.* Short for *tactical officer,* an instructor in military tactics. With the introduction of women into the national academies, West Point naturally acquired female tacs. Cadets promptly christened one of them the *Iron Dumpling.*

tac air (Modern) *s.* Short for *tactical air support,* provided to ground troops by the Air Force, Navy, and Marine fliers.

TAD Temporary Active Duty.

tadpole 1. (World War I) *s.* A French child, as the young of a *Frog.* Perhaps synthetic. 2. (Modern) *s.* When capitalized, the nickname for the OH-6 helicopter. See *Loach.*

tail 1. (Civil War; USA) The staff officers, orderlies, and escort accompanying a senior officer. "General Blunderbuss came galloping up, his tail strung out along the road behind him." A long-established informal derisive British term for a retinue, especially such as might follow a Highland "bonnet-laird" or a minor Arab chieftain, it seems to have had limited American use. 2. (World War II and later) That part of any air force or airborne organization that does not move by air. This is usually the service units and heavy equipment. It may be a *land tail* if it moves over land or a *sea tail* if it follows by ship.

tail-end Charlie (World War II; Air Force) *s.* A single fighter stationed above and behind a fighter formation to keep the other planes from being bounced. Since this position usually resulted in tail-end Charlie's getting bounced, new formations that gave all-around visibility were adopted.

tail gunner (World War II to Modern) *s.* A guard over prisoners on work details; his normal position was behind his charges.

tailormade (Old Army) *s.* A commercial cigarette, as opposed to a hand-rolled butt.

Highly desirable in the Old Army, which could seldom afford such luxuries. See *bull.*

take a blanket, to (Old, Old Army) *s.* To enlist. The Marines' term is *to draw a bucket.*

take fire, to (Modern) To be shot at, to receive fire from the enemy. "This is where they took fire earlier today" (Smith).

take it in the ear, to (World War II; possibly other Services) *s.* An unusual form of sexual perversion, attributed to a person one dislikes. *You take it in the ear!* was an insult direct. The proper non-physical retort was "I do—every time I listen to you."

take off, to take on, to (World War II) *s.* To reprimand someone. Not as common as *to chew* or *to chew out*, and apparently not as strong.

take on, to (Old, Old Army) *s.* To enlist.

Take six for the benefits! (Modern) *s.* A recruiting slogan used to encourage soldiers to reenlist (six years) for the benefits of an Army career. Generally employed facetiously, as in "Don't get pissed, reenlist! Take six for the benefits."

Take ten! (World War II; mostly Army) *s.* Take a ten-minute break. From the old practice of a ten-minute halt in every hour of marching. Our sergeant major remembers *Take ten! Smoke if you got 'em.* Still in use under all circumstances to announce a break from work.

takusan See *toksan.*

talk button (Modern) *s.* A radio, when it is used to transmit simple messages in the clear (as, for example, the size of an enemy force) by repeatedly depressing the talk button. "The 'talk button,' a pet name for the radio telephone when it is used for signaling. They would 'break squelch' on the instrument according to the count of the enemy force they saw" (Marshall, 1969).

Tallyho! (Modern; Air Force) *s.* Sighted! Seen! Meaning that visual contact has been maintained or established with one's flightmates or the target. An old fox-hunting cry used to excite the hounds when the fox was in view. Undoubtedly from the RAF.

tango boats (Vietnam and later) *s.* Mechanized landing craft (LCM), modified to carry troops on riverine operations. *Tango* is from the phonetic alphabet, *t* for *troop.*

tanker (World War II and later) A soldier in a tank unit. Less specifically, any soldier assigned to Armor.

I'm a tanker!
I'm a tanker!
Glory be to God on high!

tape and turn (Modern) *s.* Fastening two small-arms magazines together with tape in such a way that when one is empty, the other can be inserted by removing them and reversing them in one swift, fluid motion. Taping and turning thus doubled the magazine capacity of a weapon. It can be done with any sort of magazine, provided the feed is external to the weapon. See also *banana clip.*

taps The last bugle call of the military day. It is also traditionally played at all military funerals. The present music for taps was written in 1862 by Brig. Gen. Daniel Butterfield (USA), during the Peninsular Campaign. Before this, the American Army had used the French call *l'extinction des feux* ("lights out") for the last bugle call. The association of taps with funerals is also said to date from the Civil War. The derivation of the term *taps* is uncertain. It has been derived from *tap,* as a drumbeat, and from Dutch *taptoe* 'close the taps', with reference to curfew for a tavern. See also *tattoo*.

tap the black rock, to (Mid-19th century) *s.* To obtain whiskey surreptitiously or illegally. The expression is said to refer to a large black rock formation, a favorite recreation spot for off-duty soldiers, near Fort Defiance, Arizona. The first payday at Fort Defiance was to be celebrated with a reasonably orderly fandango. This unexpectedly developed into a monumental drunk, involving even the guard. When the musician in charge was summoned to explain where he got the extra whiskey, he said, "Why, sir, I tapped the Black Rock."

tar bucket 1. (About 1825–32) *s.* A heavy, bell-crowned shako made of jacked black leather, worn by company-grade officers and enlisted men. 2. (West Point) *s.* Nickname for the shako worn with full-dress uniform since 1899.

TARFU (World War II and later; all Services) *s.* Things Are Really Fucked Up. The next higher degree to SNAFU.

Tarleton's quarter (Revolutionary) No quarter, no mercy. Lt. Col. Banastre Tarleton, commanding the British Legion (made up of American Loyalists), was a brave and dashing partisan officer, but a hard man who seldom bothered to take prisoners.

Tar River Tar Riverman (Mexican War) *s.* A soldier from North Carolina. Pine tar was an important state product. By the time of the Civil War, the term had changed to *tarheel*, a name the North Carolinians reinforced by their stubborn fighting qualities.

task, to (Modern; all Services) *s.* To tell someone to do something. An affected bit of verbiage lately used in service talk. "You are now tasked to dig a new latrine pit."

tatami burn (Post–World War II) A friction-type burn on the toes and top of the foot. An unexpected medical problem that appeared following the occupation of Japan. Research soon determined that it resulted from energetic contact with tatami, the thick mats of woven straw that covered the floors of most Japanese homes and places of entertainment. The average American was too long for the traditional Japanese bed-on-the-floor, and his feet protruded from the lower end.

tattoo (Renaissance to Modern) A bugle call directing that lights should be extinguished within fifteen minutes. As late as 1813, it was called *tapto* in the US Army and was a signal for all soldiers to return to their areas for evening roll call. The term came from the British (or possibly Dutch) service: drummers beat the tattoo (Dutch, *taptoe*) through the camp or garrison town as a signal for everyone to return to his quarters. Tavern keepers and sutlers were to turn the taps of their liquor barrels "to"—meaning close them—and stop business for the night.

taught to follow, too tired to lead (Modern) *s.* A catchphrase expressing reluctance to take the responsibility of leadership.

TC 1. Tank Commander. 2. Track Commander.

TDY Temporary Duty.

TDY cap (Modern) *s.* The garrison cap. Officers assigned to certain duty stations are authorized to wear this cap only when they are traveling in the status of temporary duty. At most other times they must wear the cumbersome service cap.

tea party (Old Army) *s.* A real big roaring drunk, whether one man or most of the company.

tear off a strip, to (World War II and perhaps later) 1. *s.* To reprimand severely, to chew out, to bring smoke on. There are many variants, most of them with references to the human fundament. "Tear a strip off both sides of your ass." 2. *s.* To have sexual intercourse. Equivalent to *to knock off a chunk*. Both definitions seem to be of British origin.

technical sergeant (1920–48) A senior noncommissioned officer in the second grade, ranking below a master sergeant and above a staff sergeant. His insignia was a chevron of three stripes above and two arcs below. His nicknames were *teck* and *T-sergeant*, and he was addressed as *sergeant*. In 1948 the grade of technical sergeant was changed to sergeant first class, and this in turn, in 1958, became platoon sergeant and sergeant first class. Abbreviated *T/Sgt., Tech. Sgt.*

technician grades (1942–48, as grades) A now obsolete system of enlisted grades roughly equivalent to the present-day specialist grades. In 1942, during the reorganization of the Army, the earlier specialist ratings were abolished, and in their places were established the technician grades. These consisted of technician fifth grade (T/5), who drew the pay of a corporal; technician fourth grade (T/4), who drew the pay of a sergeant; and technician third grade (T/3), who drew the pay of a staff sergeant. In each case, the insignia was that of the comparable combat grade, but with a *T* centered under the stripes. Thus, a T/3 had three upper stripes and a bottom arc, like a staff sergeant, but enclosing a *T*. The duties of the T-grades were often technical or administrative, but commanding officers sometimes used the technician ratings as probationary grades before giving line ratings. Thus, a newly appointed company clerk might first be made a T/5, even though the T/O permitted a corporal for the position. If the soldier did not work out, it was easier, through a technicality, to reduce him to the ranks than if he had a line rating. The T-rating also provided an incentive for advancement. The technicians, unlike the present-day specialists, were noncommissioned officers, who ranked "among themselves (according to date of rank), below staff sergeants, sergeants, and corporals, respectively" (DA Circular 204, 24 June 1942), with comparable pay and allowances. There was, however, some confusion about their status because of memories of the earlier specialist ratings. In 1948 the technician grades were abolished and their holders were transferred to the comparable line ratings. Abbreviated *T5*, *T/5*, *T-5* or *Tech-5*, etc.

ted (West Point) *s.* A new name for the sort of cadet who is a confirmed bookworm, carries a calculator attached to his waist belt, and wears a coat and necktie on summer leave.

tee-tee ti-ti (Vietnam; all Services) *s.* A little bit, very little. From a reduplication of Vietnamese *ti* 'a little'. "Got me a tee-tee Heart tonight" (Webb).

teeth-to-tail ratio (Modern) *s.* Combat power as compared to combat support base; the number of men shooting as compared to the number engaged in the supply, service, and administrative jobs believed necessary to keep the others shooting.

telegraph dispatch (Mid-19th century; West Point) A warning that an officer was inspecting the cadet barracks. Cadets in the first-floor rooms would tap lightly on the gas pipes with a pencil or knife. The sound would not be noticed by the officer, but could be heard in every room from the first to the fourth floor.

Tell it to the Marines (Antiquity uncertain to Modern) *s.* A widely used expression of disbelief, probably derived from the Royal Navy. Marines were landsmen and, as such, more gullible about sea matters than sailors. The earliest quotation located (Partridge, 1970) is from 1806, but it is often said to go back to the times of Charles II and Samuel Pepys. In the earlier forms it was sometimes *You may tell that to the marines, for the sailors won't believe it* and *That will do for the marines, but the sailors won't believe it.*

temporary duty **TDY** Duty up to 180 days performed away from home station; upon completion of temporary duty, the soldier is to return to his original unit or station.

temporary profile (Modern) A temporary change in a soldier's physical profile to reflect a physical disability. The change can be made on the authority of one doctor. It is usually effective for thirty days and authorizes light duty for its duration. Also, the physical disability itself.

tender meat list (Antiquity unknown; West Point and probably many other posts, camps, and stations) A legendary secret list—supposedly including the superintendent, dean, commandant of cadets, and professors—who get the pick of the meats in the post commissary. It seems to be largely legend, or at most, an instance of RHIP.

ten forty-nine (Modern) A now obsolete form (DA Form 1049, "Request for Personnel Action") designed specifically for submitting individual requests for personnel actions, such as requests for transfer, reclassification of MOS, schooling, etc. Older soldiers still occasionally refer to personnel actions as *ten forty-nines.* "Morgan typed the 1049 forms requesting service in Vietnam" (Smith).

ten miles beyond the flagpole (Old, Old Army through World War I) *s.* A catchphrase embodying the unwritten law for heavy-duty philanderers and libertines among the officers: Keep your messy affairs well away from the post and out of sight.

tent city (Modern) *s.* Popular name for any cantonment using tents for troop housing. The most famous recent tent cities were Tent City A and Tent City B on Tan Son Nhut Air Base, just outside Saigon.

10/10 cloud (World War II; Air Force) A completely overcast sky. 1/10 would mean that only one-tenth of the sky was obscured by clouds.

tenth (Before 1900; West Point) The smallest unit of marking.

"Ten Thousand Dollars for the Folks Back Home" (World War I) *s.* Soldiers' title for the "Dead March" from Handel's *Saul,* frequently played at Army funerals. *Ten thousand dollars* refers to the customary value of a soldier's government life insurance.

tent pegs (Modern) *s.* Stupid or ineffective troops.

tent wrench (Old Army and later, possibly still current) *s.* An imaginary piece of equipment that eager rookies could be sent to fetch from the company supply sergeant. Some supply sergeants would explode forthwith; others, of a meaner stripe, would send the poor devil on to higher echelons or to the next company. Similar articles were the *stove jack,* the *bed jack* or *bunk jack*, (if one were in garrison), *squelch oil*, and *five yards of skirmish line*.

terminal flap (Modern) *s.* The ultimate stage of flap or confusion and panic; total disaster. "In a state of terminal flap, *spastic* you were so scared" (Truscott).

T/5 T-5 Technician fifth grade. See *technician grades* and *fucking up like a T/5 going to an NCO meeting.*

T/4 T-4 Technician fourth grade. See *technician grades.*

theater (All Services) A geographical area. In the sense of a locality where action takes place, the term goes back to Jacobean English. 1. (Considerable antiquity) As *theater of war*. All the land, sea, and air areas that are or may become involved directly in the conduct of the war. A theater of war is normally divided into several theaters of operations. Also *area of war*. 2. (World War II and later, although occasionally earlier) As *theater of operations*. A portion of the theater of war, operations in which are directed at achieving one particular mission and are under one command. A typical example is the World War II *ETO (European Theater of Operations)*, comprising Western Europe, under General Eisenhower. The term *area* was used for similar commands in the Pacific, such as the *Southwest Pacific Area*, under General MacArthur. Also *area of operations*.

There it is! (Modern) *s.* You're right! That's the way it is, and there's nothing that you can do about it. A common expression in Vietnam. Perhaps developed from the older *There you go* meaning *You're right* or *Now you're talking* (Norman).

there was I there I was (World War II and later) *s.* A war story, so called from the expression usually sprinkled through a typical version. (It is a good example of universal military verbiage. For centuries the French "old moustache" has salted his war stories with *ainsi moi qui vous parle* 'I who speak to you [did thus and so]'.) On occasion, after the speaker would say, "There was I," the yarn would be interrupted by a chorus of "but I kept a stiff upper lip because I am British."

thermonuke (Post–World War II; Air Force) *s.* A thermonuclear weapon, specifically a thermonuclear bomb.

Third Herd (Modern; also Marines) *s.* Any unit designated as the 3d. The nickname for such diverse units as the 3d Armored Division and 3d Infantry Division. It also goes down to smaller units. "The Third Herd [third platoon] had a new Papa Sierra" (Webb).

third lieutenant 1. (West Point, perhaps elsewhere) An unofficial term for a cadet who is undergoing a thirty-day active orientation by assuming the duties of a company-grade officer with an active Army unit. 2. (Early 19th century) A grade established in January 1813, each company in the Regular Army being authorized one third lieutenant. (In the Cavalry, at least after March 1814, he was titled a *cornet*; in the Infantry, the term *ensign* was adopted.) This grade was abolished in the Infantry in 1815, and in the Artillery three years later. (The Cavalry had been abolished at the end of the War of 1812.)

third-person address (Ancient to at least 1930s, and sporadically thereafter) A formal style of official address, designed for complete impersonality. An enlisted man, for example, after obtaining the top kick's permission to see the company commander, would say, "Sir, Private

Jones has the first sergeant's permission to speak to the captain." Or, as an NCO speaking to the company commander, "Sir, would the captain like to see the paper?" It is hard to believe in this modern, liberated age that soldiers once actually addressed their superiors in this manner, but they did. Our sergeant major remembers an old sergeant at Fort Sam Houston, Texas, in 1958, who habitually talked to his officers in the third person. Today, the third person is almost unknown as a standard mode of address, but it is occasionally used facetiously or as a subtle form of protest, since it immediately conveys to the person addressed the fact that, were it not for military discipline, the speaker would disagree strongly and forcefully. It can be a deadly weapon when employed by a veteran to bring a Sears, Roebuck shavetail or a ring-knocker lieutenant colonel back down to earth. See also *compliments, respects.*

third wiper (Air Force) *s.* A beginner in an aircraft crew. Presumably from *wiper*, a person who does menial or cleanup work around a stationary engine and in other engineering situations.

Thirsty First /*traditionally*, thoisty foist/ The 31st Infantry Regiment, which may have acquired its famous thirst from long service in the Philippines.

> We's lower dan de scum of de eart'.
> We's always after booze!
> Ho! We is de boys of de Thoisty-Foist!
> Who in de hell is youse?

thirty-year man (Old Army to Vietnam) A career soldier who intended to serve the full thirty years allowed. In the draftee Army of World War II, sometimes an insult. During Vietnam the term *lifer* became more common.

thousand-yard stare (World War I to Modern) *s.* A gaze characteristic of combat troops, especially infantrymen, who have been in action for prolonged periods. They always seem to be looking over your shoulder, watching for the first sign of the enemy, while you are talking with them.

three and two-thirds *s.* A short way of referring to a common court-martial sentence. "To be confined at hard labor . . . for three months, and to forfeit two-thirds of your pay per month for a like period."

three answers (West Point) Plebes are taught by upperclassmen that there are only three proper answers to any question put to them: "Yes, sir"; "No, sir"; "No excuse, sir." Sometimes a fourth answer is permitted: "I don't understand, sir."

three-day pass (Antiquity uncertain, but at least World War II to Modern) An authorized absence for a period not exceeding three days; also, the paperwork authorizing such absence. It is not chargeable to leave. A *three-day pass* now may extend up to ninety-six hours.

three drunks (Revolutionary) *s.* A Continental's term for his month's pay (if he got it) in depreciating Continental currency.

three-hundred-dollar man (Civil War; USA) *s.* A derisive term for soldiers who volunteered later in the war, after increasing bounties were authorized. By 1863 the Union was offering $300 for new three-year volunteers and $400 for veterans who reenlisted. Subsidiary bounties offered by states and communities sometimes raised the total to over $1,000. Many of these men were bounty-jumpers, but many served faithfully and well.

I'm a new recruit, with a bran' new suit.
Nine hundred dollars bounty
And I've come down from Derbytown
To fight for Oxford County.

three-minute man (1920s, apparently derived from World War I) *s.* A machine gunner, the three minutes representing his supposed life expectancy in action. To be perfectly truthful, we have heard the term used only in the 163d Infantry Regiment, Montana National Guard. But see *suicide squad.*

3.2 /three-point-two/ 1. The first modern field gun adopted by the Army after the Civil War, used from 1885 to 1905. It existed in two models, 1885 and 1897, which were very similar to each other. Designed by an American officer on the model of the best foreign guns of the 1870s and 1880s, it had no recoil system and was soon obsolete. It performed poorly in Cuba in 1898, because of its black-powder ammunition, but some 3.2s gave good service in the Philippines and the Boxer Rebellion. 2. (World War II) Beer. The maximum percentage of alcohol permissible in beer sold at the PXs was 3.2, but 3.2 multiplied by ten or twelve bottles can mount up. Also called *Army brew.*

three-star (Modern) *s.* A lieutenant general.

three-striper (Antiquity uncertain, still heard occasionally) *s.* A sergeant, so called because of his chevrons with three stripes. Similarly, *two-striper* for a corporal and *six-striper* for a master sergeant.

three up and three down (Modern) *s.* A master sergeant. His chevrons have three stripes on top and three arcs below. Similarly, *three up and two down* is a sergeant first class or platoon sergeant. His chevrons have three stripes on top and two arcs below.

throttle jockey (Modern; Air Force) *s.* A fighter pilot. "The wing weenies have worked it over long before our throttle jockey walks out to his Thud" (Broughton).

Thud (Vietnam; Air Force) *s.* The F-105 Thunderchief fighter-bomber; replaced by the Phantom F-4s by 1972. Originally the nickname was applied disparagingly, but during the height of the war, Thud pilots had come to use the name affectionately. Other nicknames for the plane were *lead sled, ultra-hot*, and *squash bomber*.

Thud Ridge (Vietnam; Air Force) *s.* A hill mass near Hanoi, where a number of Thuds augered in.

thumbing the vent (Colonial to Civil War) Temporarily blocking the vent (touchhole) of a cannon to prevent premature discharge. When a muzzle-loading cannon became hot from firing, air coming in through its touchhole might cause it to discharge while being loaded. One of the crew, normally the gunner, kept his thumb firmly over the vent until the charge was rammed home. (By 1861, gunners were using their second left fingers instead of their thumbs.) Since a heated gun could sear flesh to the bone in seconds, the gunner wore a thumbstall (a protective sheath of heavy leather) while thumbing the vent. Later, this became a fingerstall.

thump gun (Modern; also Marines) *s.* The M79 grenade launcher. Probably so called because of the thumping noise the weapon makes when it is fired. Also called *blooker, chunker, '79.*

TI & E (World War II to Modern) Troop Information and Education. An Army-wide program to keep troops informed about current events and official Army policy on a wide variety of subjects. TI & E was at one time a full-time job for the noncom assigned to this duty in a unit. He was responsible for preparing and often delivering lectures, performing demonstrations, and showing films. The program was not very successful, since those responsible for it often took the easy way out by simply showing training films by the dozens and since soldiers resented the fact that TI & E usually took place on Saturday mornings. It was entirely possible for a soldier on a two- or three-year tour of duty to see the same films dozens of times. This program has been superseded by one called *Training*, which, if not superior in quality, is at least scheduled mostly during duty hours.

ticket-punching (Post–World War II to Modern) *s.* The process of making certain that you get all the service assignments and attend all the schools necessary to keep you a bright prospect for promotion and prestigious jobs. An advanced degree from a civilian college—on the Army's time if possible, on your own if necessary—also helps. Most officers ticket-punch out of reasonably honest ambition, but really aggressive wheeler-dealers, who are interested only in advancing their careers, can be destructive. They merely want, for example, their ticket punched as having commanded a battalion and do not care what happens to the battalion in the process.

Tiger beer (Vietnam) Bière La Rue, a brand of beer brewed in Saigon by the French-owned Brasseries et Glacières de l'Indochina (BGI). The label showed the silhouette of a tiger. Tiger beer was milder than ba-me-ba and came in much larger bottles.

tiger suit tiger stripes (Modern) *s.* The camouflaged jungle or tropical uniform, so called because the stripes of color look somewhat like a tiger's stripes. "Looking tall, lean, and blond in his camouflaged tiger suit" (Tregaskis). "You don't wear tiger stripes in Japan" (Glasser).

time-tick (World War II; Air Force) *s.* Synchronizing watches before a mission.

tinclad 1. (Civil War; USA) *s.* A light-draft sternwheel river steamer converted into a gunboat for service on the Mississippi and its tributaries, so called because of the thinness of its improvised armor. The iron plating of the tinclads was only .5–.75 of an inch thick (although sometimes reinforced over the boilers) and their guns were light, but they could operate in 2 feet of water, "anywhere the ground was a little damp." 2. (World War II) *s.* A general term, occasionally used, for lightly armored vehicles like armored cars and half-tracks.

tin hat (World War I on; also Marines) *s.* The old soup-dish–shaped steel helmet of World War I. It was replaced in 1941 by the steel pot.

tinhorn (Also Marines) *s.* An adjective applied to National Guard units, never kindly and sometimes undeserved.

tin school (Old Army, but still occasionally heard) *s.* A private military school, ranging from institutions like the Virginia Military Institute on down.

tiswin talk (Indian Wars) *s.* Any wild, exaggerated rumor or story. Tiswin was a crude beer brewed by the Apache from partially fermented corn. A few drinks of it made them completely irresponsible. *Tiswin juice* apparently has the same meaning as *tiswin talk*. The word is from Spanish *tejuino*, ultimately from Nahuatl.

tit cap See *garrison cap*.

titless WAC (World War II on) *s.* A male clerk or office worker. A rather devastating commentary on the masculinity of noncombat soldiers. See *ball-bearing WAC.*

T/O Table of Organization. It shows how many men are in a particular organization and the grade and assignment of each of them.

toadsticker (Old Army, but still heard) *s.* The bayonet. Also called a *pigsticker.*

T/O & E Table of Organization and Equipment. The T/O, plus lists of vehicles, weapons, and equipment assigned to an organization.

tobogganing (Modern; Air Force) *s.* A temporary loss of altitude of two planes during midair refueling. This occurs when a fighter-bomber reduces speed to match that of a tanker. If the fighter-bomber reduces speed too much, it can lose lift, fall off the refueling boom, and sink downward. If the tanker pilot drops his nose and follows, both aircraft "are falling down hill together, or tobogganing" (Broughton).

toe popper (Modern) *s.* A small antipersonnel mine detonated by foot pressure.

toggle, to (Modern; Air Force) To jettison a fighter-bomber's bombs short of the target.

TOG rule (Vietnam and later) *s.* They're Only Gooks. A "rule" stating that one need not worry about killing or injuring the Vietnamese, because they are not quite human to begin with.

toilet seat (Modern) *s.* The original Meritorious Unit Emblem, first awarded in 1944. This was a gold laurel wreath, 1⅝ inches in diameter, worn on the lower part of the right sleeve of the uniform dress coat. In 1966 this was changed to a scarlet ribbon encased in a gold frame, authorized to be worn above the right breast pocket of the appropriate uniform coat or shirt.

toksan taksan takosan (Post–World War II to Modern; all Services) *s.* A large amount, plenty. The term is widely used in Korea and Okinawa today and has spread throughout the Army and Air Force. From Japanese *takusan* /tahk-sahn/ 'a lot', 'a large quantity'. "They got takosan (lots) of cover" (Mulligan).

Tommy (World War I to World War II) *s.* A British soldier, from the British slang term for a private soldier. From Thomas Atkins, originally a fictitious legal name (like John Doe or Richard Roe); applied to soldiers from the 1880s on. See Rudyard Kipling's poetry and prose.

Tommy cookers (World War II) *s.* English tanks, especially the lend-lease US M4 Sherman, which caught fire regularly. The term is of German origin.

Tommy gun (World War II) *s.* The US Thompson .45-caliber submachine gun. It was a good weapon, but too intricate for field service. Also, it tended to "climb" unless fired in very short bursts.

Tommy-tot (1930s) *s.* A Reserve officer on active duty with the Regular Army under the provisions of the Thomas Act. This farsighted act provided that a thousand Reserve officers would be ordered to a year of active duty annually. The fifty outstanding officers each year would be selected for permanent commissions.

too close to payday, It's (Modern) To be near the end of the month and out of funds. Traditionally, payday for soldiers has been at the end of the month.

Toot Sweet Express (World War II) *s.* A special train that made an express run from Cherbourg, via Paris, to Namur and Verdun in thirty-six hours, carrying small quantities of urgently needed supplies, the lack of which might affect Allied operations. Its run was later extended to Liège and Bad Kreuznach. From *toot sweet*, the GI version of French *tout de suite* 'at once'.

top top sergeant (Modern) 1. *s.* A sergeant major. 2. *s.* A first sergeant.

top junior (Modern) *s.* The company clerk. Traditionally, the company clerk has run his outfit in the absence of the first sergeant.

top kick top top man topper tops top sergeant (Old, Old Army to Modern) *s.* The first sergeant of a company, battery, or troop, the captain's right hand and alter ego. We can remember the time when his word was law and his fist the physical embodiment of the *Articles of War*. The green earth cracked and smouldered where he spat. A competent top kick was a master psychologist and a red hand in battle. As the Old, Old Army captain said to the new shavetail,

All I want you to do
Is turn out for reveille,
And after that, remember
The Top Kick runs the company

Of these equivalent terms, *top* and *top sergeant* seem the oldest, *top* being recorded as early as 1898 (Lighter, *American Speech*). *Top kick* is less definite, and its origin is not clear. It might be a parallel to civilian *sidekick*, which seems to have come into use in the period of World War I and the 1920s. *Topper* may be fairly modern. Note that while a modern sergeant major and a modern first sergeant may both be called *top* or *top sergeant*, only a first sergeant is a *top kick*. See also *first sergeant, sergeant major*.

topos (Mid-19th century) *s.* The Corps of Topographical Engineers, formed in 1813 as part of the Corps of Engineers and given independent status from 1838 to 1863. They were the Army's mapmakers, surveyors, and explorers.

torpedo (Civil War on) Originally, an explosive device buried in the ground or placed on, or just under, the surface of the water. The latter was what Adm. David Farragut meant when he said, "Damn the torpedoes, full speed ahead!" at Mobile Bay in 1864. Torpedoes could be detonated by a variety of devices, ranging from the primitive slow match to electricity. Their use in land warfare was considered unsporting. Confronted by them, irked Union commanders would send Confederate prisoners to the head of their column to locate and remove them. From around 1900 the word *torpedo* began to be used in its present sense, a self-propelled explosive device launched from a submarine or light surface warship. The former torpedoes took on the names of *land mines* and *naval mines*. See *mine, pink lady* (in Appendix).

TOT (Modern) Time On Target. A method of firing so that several battalions' shells reach the target at the same time. "The TOT zapped this formation dead on" (Marshall, 1971).

to the color A bugle call played immediately after retreat. As the call is played, the flag is lowered and military personnel face the direction of the flag and render an appropriate salute. On many posts the sunset gun is fired between the sounding of retreat and to the color. To the color is also played as a salute to the President, the Vice-President, ex-presidents, and heads of foreign states.

Tough shit! (Before World War II to Modern) *s.* That's too bad! Usually indicating utter lack of sympathy, interest, or desire to help, or a hard-boiled recognition that that's the way things are. More commonly encountered as the initials *TS.*

Tough titty! (World War II on) 1. *s.* Too bad! The equivalent of *Tough shit!* but by no means as commonly met. 2. *s.* Something difficult, unpleasant. We recall a soldier muttering, as he looked at the next ridgeline, "*That's* gonna be tough titty to chew!"

tour 1. (Ancient to Modern) An assignment of duty or a period of duty. This may be either short, like guard duty, or it may be a prolonged assignment, like overseas duty. Also called *tour of duty.* 2. (At least 1920 on; West Point) Punishment assigned to a cadet for infraction of rules. It consists of walking for a specified period of time under arms in the area. See *area, punishment tour.*

towed target infantry (World War II) *s.* The glider infantry regiments of the US Airborne Forces. The nickname stresses the resemblance between a towed glider and the sleeve target towed behind an airplane and used for antiaircraft artillery target practice. Glider troops were country cousins of the Airborne Force, treated with disdain by lordly paratroopers. They had a dangerous job, but did not draw extra pay until July 1944. They were not issued jump boots or other special equipment. Also *glider riders.*

tracer (20th century) Ammunition containing a chemical composition that burns in flight and shows the path of the projectile.

tracks 1. (Probably World War II on) *s.* The insignia of a captain, two silver bars. 2. (World War II to Modern) Vericles with caterpillar treads, such as tanks and half-tracks, as opposed to wheeled vehicles(*wheels*).

train (Colonial to Modern) Service elements, such as vehicles and operating personnel, providing supply, evacuation, and maintenance services. Duane (1810) described a train "as all the necessary apparatus, implements of war, such as cannons, &c. that are required at a siege or in the field."

trained killer (World War II to Modern) A term cynically and facetiously applied by soldiers to themselves. Used seriously (by civilians), it is only a little less detestable than *cannon fodder.*

trainee (Antiquity uncertain, but mid-19th century in civilian life) A soldier who is undergoing basic combat, advanced, or initial skill training. Innocuous as this word may sound when compared with *gomer, burrhead,* and *Private Slipinshits* (all favorite terms for trainees), it has been banned. " 'Trainee' . . . seeming to strip the recruit of dignity [has been proscribed. The proper form] in speaking to recruits [is] 'soldier,' 'private,' or the soldier's surname" (*Army*, November 1979, p. 11).

trap-door Springfield (Indian Wars on) *s.* The US caliber .45-70 Springfield rifle and carbine. This was the Civil War Springfield muzzle-loading rifle converted to a breechloader according to a system developed by Master Armorer Erskine S. Allin. (It is also called the *Allin conversion.*) It was a single-shot weapon, but was powerful and accurate, especially in the infantry Long Tom version. The Regular Army used it during the Indian Wars; volunteers carried it in the Spanish-American War (where the smoke from its black-powder cartridges was a handicap); and a few were still in state arsenals at the beginning of World War I.

traps (Civil War; USA) *s.* Equipment in general. From contemporary civilian slang.

tray man (Modern) *s.* A KP assigned to clean and wash the metal or plastic compartmented trays used in Army mess halls. To be tray man is not so bad as pots and pans, but harder work than DRO. See *pots and pans.*

triage (Antiquity uncertain, but World War I in British Army, to Modern) Deciding which of the wounded should be treated. A cheerful term used by Armed Forces medics. In emergencies, when the number of wounded or injured persons exceeds the medical facilities available to care for them, they are sorted into three categories: those too severely hurt to survive with reasonable care (give them morphine, put them in a corner, and let them die quietly); those too lightly injured to require expenditure of time and skill (apply Band-Aids and send them back to duty); and those who need care and, with the facilities that are available, have a reasonable expectation of survival (concentrate on them). The term itself is an old French agricultural term, going back to Roman times in one form or another, and originally meant hulling grain and, later, sorting out produce. Despite the *tri-* and the threefold classification, it has nothing to do with three.

trimmings (Pre–Modern West Point) *s.* A cadet's cross belts, cartridge box, and the like.

troll, to (Modern; Air Force) *s.* To fly a random pattern in order to detect enemy electronic emissions. Probably taken from fishing vocabulary.

trombone (World War I; also Marines) *s.* A grenade-launching attachment for the muzzle of the Springfield '03 and the Enfield. (There was a similiar rig for the English infantry musket in the early 18th century.) It kicked too hard to be fired from the shoulder, was apt to malfunction, and was never very popular with the doughboys.

troop 1. (Ancient to Modern) Up to World War II, a mounted unit comparable to an infantry company or an artillery battery. At present such a unit in armored cavalry. 2. (Ancient to Modern) In combinations like *troop train, troop bay, troop training,* soldiers in general. 3. (Modern) *s.* An individual soldier, on the misapprehension that troop is the singular form of troops (or perhaps as humor). When used as in "Now get this, troop!" talking down to the soldier. Also *troopie,* which is very informal and usually applied jokingly.

troop bay (Modern) An open area below decks on a troop ship. A wing in a barracks reserved for troop occupancy. Such accommodations are Spartan.

trooper 1. (Ancient to Modern) Originally a mounted soldier; at present, a member of an armored cavalry unit. Since World War II, *trooper* has been colloquially applied to airborne and paratroopers, and sometimes to marines, although the last use is officially frowned on. 2. A cavalry horse or troop horse.

trooper ladder (Modern) *s.* A series of qualification bars (Rifle, Pistol, Machine Gun, etc.) suspended from the Marksmanship Qualification Badge. From the rope ladders used to exit from helicopters during air assault operations.

truck (Ancient to Modern) A small wooden disk at the top of a flag staff; it usually has holes in it for reeving the halyards. Originally a naval term. This word is almost never used outside Army promotion or soldier-of-the-month boards, where a nervous candidate will suddenly be asked, "How many trucks are there at Fort So-and-so?" Only the canniest soldier can avoid falling into a state of blank astonishment when first asked this ridiculous and possibly unethical question.

try another touch, to (Revolutionary) *s.* To reenlist.

TS (World War II, sporadically later) *s.* Tough Shit or, bowdlerized, Tough Stuff. A very common expression indicating disgust, commiseration, or lack of commiseration. See *TS card.*

TS box (World War II) *s.* An imaginary box, usually located in the chaplain's office (but sometimes in the orderly room), into which a soldier could put written complaints. We have never met anyone stupid enough to believe that it existed, but it was occasionally referred to.

TS card (World War II to present) *s.* Tough Shit card, also sometimes read as Theological Service or Trouble-Shooting card. At first a joke like the TS box, but after a time real cards were printed. These were usually wallet-sized cards, sometimes with blank boxes for the chaplain to punch as an indication that he had heard your complaint, and sometimes with various options indicated in the boxes around the margin. Typical options would be *See the chaplain, Get screwed, Kill a bottle,* or *Shoot the bugler.* The idea here, too, was that the card would be punched. It is rumored that TS cards were first devised by the chaplains themselves during the early years of World War II, but that the cards caught on so rapidly (with unforeseen variations) that the chaplains soon came to regret their little joke. In some commands, TS cards were banned. TS cards were very popular in World War II and were also present during the Korean and Vietnam wars.

TS slip (World War II) *s.* Tough Shit slip. An imaginary slip that one could obtain from the chaplain (or the orderly room), fill out, and deposit in the TS box.

T/3 T-3 A technician third grade. See *technician grades.*

tuba (Old Army to World War II) A native Philippine beverage, palm wine. Originally it was made from the sap of certain palm trees, later from coconuts, but the stuff sold to American soldiers as tuba—especially during the bull market of World War II—too often was made from God knows what. Anyone who overindulged in it supposedly could be identified by his habit of falling out of banyan trees, where he was trying to hang by his tail with the other monkeys. (During the Japanese occupation of the Philippines, guerrilla units ran the motor generators of their radio stations on a high-proof alcohol distilled from tuba.) Its worst feature was that it induced a nasty hangover. In derivation, no connection with the musical instrument, but from Malay and Tagalog *tuba,* the name of a plant.

tube Technically, the barrel of a cannon; loosely, the whole gun.

tube steak (Modern) *s.* Mess-hall frankfurters. Perhaps in association with the penis; probably simply from their shape.

TUIFU (Modern) *s.* The Ultimate In Fuck-Ups.

tunic (Modern) The plain, tight-fitting, long-sleeved jacket that is worn as part of the women's Army Green Pantsuit uniform. It is a pullover garment with a turtleneck collar and a zipper in the back.

Strictly speaking, a military tunic is any close-fitting garment. Tunics have not been worn by male soldiers since the World War I–style garment was abolished.

tunnel rats (Vietnam) *s.* A hardy breed of volunteers whose mission it was to explore and assist in the destruction of the enemy's labyrinthine tunnel complexes. They had to be smaller than average so that they could pass through tight places underground, and were equipped with knee pads and gloves. They carried aerosol sprays against insects, and smoke bombs as signals to comrades on the surface that they were about to emerge, so that they would not be shot by mistake. They were armed with .22-caliber pistols because it was found that the standard-issue .45-caliber automatic would deafen the shooter in the confined spaces underground.

turkey shoot (World War II; Navy, Air Force) *s.* A one-sided battle in which the enemy suffers disproportionately heavy loss. In the great Marianas turkey shoot of 19 June 1944, the Japanese Combined Fleet lost two aircraft carriers and 346 airplanes in eight hours; American casualties were 26 planes.

turnaround time (Modern) *s.* The amount of time between overseas tours for soldiers in any given MOS. This varies for each grade within each specialty. During peacetime it can be as long as five years or as short as only eighteen months.

turnback (At least 1900 on; West Point) *s.* A cadet who, because of academic deficiency, is forced to repeat a year or who is dismissed and later readmitted to a lower class. This seems to have little effect on his subsequent career. Gen. George S. Patton, Jr., who had trouble with mathematics, was such a turnback.

turret-head (Modern) *s.* An argumentative person. Perhaps from the turret of a tank, and shooting off.

turtle (Modern; all Services) *s.* One's replacement, probably because he always seems so slow in coming.

twelfth general order (Antiquity uncertain) *s.* Before August 1967, when there were only eleven official general orders for sentries, an imaginary twelfth was variously repeated as *Remember the other eleven; To walk my post from flank to flank and take no shit from any rank*, or *To walk my post in a military manner and take no shit from the company commander.*

twenty-nine-day soldier (Antiquity uncertain) *s.* A man who would be a model soldier up until payday, which traditionally fell at the end of the month. When he received his pay, he would go on a bender, often winding up in the guardhouse, drunk and disorderly.

twenty-thirty man (Modern) *s.* A professional soldier who says he is going to stay in the Army twenty years and thirty minutes, or absolutely no longer than is required to be eligible for retirement.

twink (World War II to Modern) *s.* A second lieutenant. In World War II there was a little verse,

Twinkle, twinkle, little bars,
How I wish that you were stars.

two-dash-one (West Point) A Disciplinary Report Form. See *quill.*

two-digit fidget, to have a (Modern) *s.* The nervous state that often overcomes a soldier on an overseas tour when he has from ninety-nine to ten days left before going home. Also *two-digit midget* and *double-digit midget.*

two grains of rice with two sticks (Vietnam) Part of a disparaging statement about the Vietnamese people: *It took these people a thousand years to figure out how to eat two grains of rice with two sticks and another thousand to learn how to carry two buckets of shit with one stick.* Or *It took these people a thousand years to figure out how to carry two buckets of shit with one stick and another thousand to figure out how to eat it with two.* A similar line had been applied earlier to Koreans.

two hots and a Charlie (Modern) *s.* Two hot meals and one meal of C-rations per day, the common fare of soldiers in the field. "Two hots and a Charlie, that's what awaits us" (Mulligan).

two months' walk (Revolutionary) *s.* A Continental's sardonic name for the militia's short term of service in emergencies. This service always was counted from the date on which militiamen left their firesides, and it was an unfortunate fact of American military life that militia usually marched very slowly toward the enemy. Also, it would leave the Army in plenty of time to get home by the day its enlistments expired.

201 file /two-oh-one file/ (Early World War II to Modern) The military personnel file for the individual soldier. It contains the soldier's Form 20 or its successor documents, copies of orders, citations, personnel actions, etc.

two-star (Antiquity uncertain to Modern) *s.* A major general.

two-striper (Antiquity uncertain to Modern) *s.* A corporal.

two up, one back, and feed 'em a hot meal (Pre–World War II; possibly still used) *s.* A catchphrase purporting to be the universal solution to any tactical problem presented in the classroom of a service school; hence, the solution to any problem, whether tactical or not. The phrase is based on a combat situation in the days when an infantry regiment consisted of three battalions. Two battalions would engage the enemy, and one would be held in reserve. The hot meal would be the morale-boosting factor.

tying-up (19th century) An unofficial punishment used through the Mexican War and into the Indian Wars. The usual form of punishment was to tie the culprit's thumbs to a branch or pole so that he could take his weight off them only by standing on tiptoe. A milder form was simply tying the offender to a tree or post so that he could not move.

typewriter (World War I and later) *s.* A British nickname for a machine gun; borrowed by the AEF. Its use seems to have died out during World War II. Another term was *devil's piano.*

☆☆☆☆U☆☆☆☆

ultimate weapon (Modern) *s.* The infantryman. But all bets are off if the next war is fought with atomic missiles. In that case, he will be the ultimate weapon of World War IV.

unaccompanied (Modern; all Services) Without dependents. Said of a married serviceman who moves to a new duty station without his wife and children, or other dependents.

unass, to (Modern) 1. *s.* Basically, to get off one's ass, to get up from a comfortable position. 2. *s.* To leave, to depart. "The VC'll unass their main positions" (Bunting). 3. *s.* To get to work.

uncle (Antiquity uncertain; probably intermittently used) *s.* Uncle Sam. The US government.

Uncle Benji's Resthome (Modern) *s.* Fort Benjamin Harrison, Indiana. This post, the home of the US Army Finance and Personnel Records Center, is an extremely good duty station. Its proximity to Indianapolis, a very hospitable town, adds to the fact that Uncle Benji's is a rather nice place to be.

Uncle Sam's bad bargains (19th century; West Point) *s.* Cadets who had been found deficient and were dismissed from the Military Academy.

uncover, to 1. (Ancient to Modern) To remove a cap or hat. 2. (Late 18th century in British usage, to Modern) When a regiment in column deployed into line, each company in turn moved off to the right or left, as ordered, thus "uncovering" the company behind it.

under arms (Ancient to Modern) Basically, a soldier who is actually carrying his weapons, but in peacetime, a soldier wearing his web equipment is considered to be under arms. In matters of military courtesy, a soldier under arms remains covered indoors when reporting to a superior.

underload, to (Modern; West Point) *s.* To carry fewer elective courses than you could manage if you really wanted to.

Underwear! Underwear! (World War I; also Marines) The AEF's version of the refrain—"Over there! Over there!"—a popular contemporary song titled, oddly enough, "Over There."

Unfortunate Soldiers Sadly Sold (Civil War; USA) Unofficial reading of *USSS* (United States Sharpshooters), used by soldiers of the two sharpshooter regiments.

unicorn (Apparently intermittently from Civil War to Modern) *s.* A wordplay on *uniform.* "I've got my unicorn ready for tomorrow." Dr. Lighter (letter to Cragg, 19 July 1980) writes that the term was current in the Civil War.

Uniformed Services (Modern) An official designation, encountered in various regulations and official papers, for the Army, the Navy, the Air Force, the Marine Corps, the Coast Guard, the Commissioned Corps of the Public Health Service, and the Commissioned Corps of the National Oceanic and Atmospheric Administration.

unit award (Modern) Recognition given to a unit for certain acts, services, or skills. Awards include the Presidential Unit Citation, the Valorous Unit Award, and the Meritorious Unit Commendation. Each consists of a streamer, emblem, and certificate.

unit crest (Modern) Popular name for Distinctive Unit Insignia, which is an unhandy mouthful and so was replaced—in defiance of strict heraldic rules—by *crest.* An enameled metal insignia worn on the uniform by personnel assigned to a unit that has been authorized a coat of arms or historic patch. Crests are worn on the shoulder loops of the khaki and Army Green uniforms and on the garrison cap.

United States Terms for the continental United States include *America, Big PX, Big Rice, Cuntsville, Land of the Big PX, Land of the Round Doorknob, Land of the Twenty-four-hour Generator, stateside, the world.*

universal scout (Civil War; USA) *s.* A double agent. "Possibly Graham was a universal scout and . . . divided his services impartially between Meade and Lee" (Buell).

up from the ranks (Antiquity uncertain to Modern) Risen from the status of an enlisted man to that of an officer. While the age of this exact phrase is not known, comparable expressions, *risen from the ranks* and *from the ranks,* are recorded for mid-19th-century Great Britain but are probably considerably older. See also *ranker.*

uphill (Modern) *s.* The first half of an overseas tour or enlistment. The opposite of *downhill.*

upperclassmen (Early 19th century to Modern; West Point and other Service academies) Second- and first-year cadets, equivalent to college juniors and seniors, respectively.

up Shit Creek (Pre–World War II to Modern; all Services) *s.* Either you have been semimortally shafted or else the blind workings of fate have put you into a predicament that would wring tears of sympathy from a Levantine loan shark. It is not quite hopeless, but it is worse than damned unpleasant. In extreme cases, one customarily adds *without a paddle.*

Up your ass with bugs and gas (Modern) The unofficial motto of the Nuclear, Biological, and Chemical Warfare experts. Formerly Chemical, Biological, and Radiological.

US (Post–World War II to 1 July 1969) A draftee, from the fact that the letters *US,* standing for *Army of the United States,* were prefixed to his serial number. There was a fair amount of intraservice rivalry between the US and the other components of the Army, the RA and the RFA. The US looked down on the RA as too stupid to have avoided military service and not courageous enough to have remained a civilian until "they came and got him." The US spoke of the RFA in terms unprintable, because the RFA was committed to only six months of active duty, while the US had two years. But this was mostly in good humor. The draftee, during the more than thirty years that this country had the draft, proved himself an excellent soldier. There are those in the Regular Army today who miss him.

USASMA /yew-'sass-ma/ United States Army Sergeants Major Academy, the most sophisticated of the various charm schools for noncoms. It trains selected master sergeants and sergeants major for top enlisted staff and troop leadership roles.

use a light coat of oil, to (Modern) *s.* A catchphrase meaning to do everything necessary to get ready for an inspection, a special event, or any kind of military operation. It probably originates from the practice of placing a light coat of oil on weapons just before an inspection or before returning them to the arms room.

Useless Dick (Modern) *s.* The US Army Criminal Investigation Command (USACIDC). See *CID* for an explanation of the superfluous *D*.

Useless Wreck (Modern) *s.* The US Army Recruiting Command (USAREC).

use up, to (Modern; all Services) *s.* To kill. "Zap that slope. Waste that gook. Use them up" (Bunting).

US is always right, The (At least 1958 to Modern) Not jingoism, not sarcasm, but a mnemonic device for the position of the collar brass insignia. The *US* piece is always affixed to the right lapel of the uniform coat.

USMA United States Military Academy at West Point, New York.

USMC (Modern) *s.* U Suck My Cock, a left-handed salute at the US Marine Corps.

USO (World War II to Modern) United Service Organizations, which operates centers where servicemen can relax in pleasant surroundings or enjoy a Saturday-night dance. Also, more commonly, the center itself.

USO card (World War II) *s.* By and large an imaginary card that was said to entitle the holder to sexual privileges from the hostesses. A few such cards were printed as jokes, sometimes with obscene pictures of very ugly women, but they were by no means as common as TS cards.

USO commando (World War II) *s.* A stateside hero who specialized in thrilling pretty hostesses with tales of derring-do. He was frequently equipped with decorations and insignia he had not earned.

U-T (Vietnam) U-Tapao, Thailand, where the 307th Strategic Wing (B-52) was stationed.

☆☆☆☆V☆☆☆☆

valise (Colonial to 1855) A cloth and/or leather container, usually tubular, attached to the cantle (rear) of a saddle. It was used to carry spare clothing and toilet articles.

VC 1. (Vietnam) Viet Cong. 2. Veterinary Corps.

VC National Forest (Vietnam) *s.* An area in Vietnam controlled by the Vietcong or their North Vietnamese counterparts. See *Indian country*.

VD Venereal Disease. At present, VD is handled like any other disease: treat the soldier and return him to duty, no matter how many times he contracts it. In the past, however, a soldier lost pay and enlistment time while he had the disease, and could well be reduced in rank (see *bad time*). There are also legends of brutal treatment for gonorrhea. According to one account, during treatment in the Old Army, an instrument was inserted in the urethra without anesthetic. The handle of the instrument was turned, and tiny blades emerged from the shaft. The instrument was then yanked out, as the patient fainted. Another story involved using a rubber mallet to break abscesses. Behind these horror stories, whether true or not, and the disciplinary actions was the official position that the soldier was blamable. Pro stations were available. If they were not used and VD resulted, it was the soldier's fault for not obeying orders. If the soldier had used the pro station, he was held blameless.

V-device (Modern) A bronze block letter *V* worn on service and suspension ribbons to denote an award for valor. At present Vs are authorized for the Bronze Star Medal, the Air Medal, the Army Commendation Medal, and the Joint Service Commendation Medal.

VD movie (World War I to Modern) A motion picture showing the nature of the diseases and methods of avoiding them—and then scaring the bejasus out of the audience by illustrating what VD can do. Sometimes they are called *horror movies*. They are a major part of VD control efforts, but their effectiveness is hard to gauge. In 1947 some paper-pushing idiot insisted on showing such a movie to the 13th Infantry Division (Philippine Scouts), which had practically no VD troubles. A couple of weeks after the movie, it did!

It seems that the Scouts got so excited over the cute blond prostitutes exhibited in full color that they did not pay attention to the subsequent clinical details. See *Mickey Mouse.*

vedette videt 1. (18th and 19th centuries) A cavalryman on sentry duty. The line of vedettes was the most advanced part of an army's outpost system. They were supported by a second line of small detachments or pickets, approximately a quarter of a mile to their rear. 2. (Old Navy) A small, fast launch used for scouting.

veep (World War II and later) *s.* A jeep equipped with a VHF radio for contact with tactical aircraft supporting the ground forces.

Venus fixers (World War II) *s.* Personnel of the Allied Subcommission for Monuments, Fine Arts and Archives, assigned to rescue and preserve Italian art treasures.

Verey light Very light (World War I, British usage) An illuminating flare projected from a special pistol. The AEF tended to apply the term *Verey light* to a variety of pyrotechnic signals. See *Verey pistol.*

Verey pistol Very pistol (World War I to Modern) A pistol (and signaling system) devised by Lt. Edward W. Very of the US Navy in 1877. Originally the Very pistol shot balls of fire, but in more recent years it has fired colored signal flares.

veteranize, to (Civil War; USA) *s.* In 1864 the US government was confronted by the unpleasant fact that the three-year enlistments of troops recruited in 1861 were about to expire. Since loss of these seasoned soldiers would have taken the backbone out of the Union armies, Congress passed the Veteran Volunteer Act, providing all veterans who reenlisted with a thirty-day furlough, a $400 bonus (which states and communities usually increased), and the status and distinctive chevron of a "veteran volunteer." If three-fourths of a regiment reenlisted, it could retain its regimental organization and colors, and the men could take their furloughs at the same time. In a proud response, approximately half of these men did veteranize and reenlist. See *first-call men.*

V-girls Victory girls (World War II) *s.* Women—usually teenagers—who were khaki-whacky and hung around military installations and bus and railroad stations to offer their favors to any interested military personnel. This patriotic activity was deeply resented by commanding officers and hospital personnel, because it raised the VD rate—and also by regular practitioners of the Oldest Profession, many of whom were forced to take jobs in shipyards or munitions plants because of this amateur competition.

Victor Charlie (Vietnam; all Services) *s.* The Vietcong soldier, from *Victor* and *Charlie*, the letters *v* and *c* in the phonetic alphabet.

Viet-speak (Vietnam) *s.* A mixture of standard English, slang, patois, and miscellaneous terms from various Oriental languages that was widely used by Americans in Vietnam. It was not far enough removed from English to be called a pidgin. A fragment from the story of Little Red Riding Hood in Viet-speak (*Army Reporter*, 1, February 1971, p. 5) reads thus:

> Little Red Riding Hood is leaving her hootch with a basket of chop-chop to take to her sick grandma-san. . . . As she places the basket next to the

bed, she makes a double-take and exclaims, "Choi-oi! What big eyeballs you have!"

"There it is," says the wolf. "All the better to see you with."

"And your ears are maxed to the onions," comments the hood.

"Check it out. All the better to hear you with."

Ville vill (Modern) *s.* Short for *village.* Used most often at present in Korea and earlier in Vietnam, where most US military camps and installations were situated near small native villages, which provided various physical and material services. Dr. Lighter notes that *ville* was used by soldiers of the AEF in 1919 (when it was probably taken from French *ville* 'town'), but it is doubtful that the World War I term survived to the present. Tregaskis notes that Saigon, in the early years of the war, was called *the Ville.*

vinegar blanc (World War I) *s.* An AEF twist to French *vin blanc* 'white wine'. Possibly the term reflects on the quality of wine sold to Americans.

Vinegar Joe (World War II and earlier) Lt. Gen. (later Gen.) Joseph W. Stilwell, American commander in the CBI. He seems to have acquired the nickname much earlier in his career, but the CBI fully justified it.

violin case (World War II; Paratroopers) *s.* The Griswold (or G) bag, a specially padded canvas gun case for carrying a knocked-down M1 rifle during airborne operations. Obviously the name came from the alleged use of real violin cases by American gangsters to carry submachine guns.

VIP (World War II to Modern; all Services and general civilian use) Very Important Person. VIPs are supposed to be treated with care and respect. Armed Forces air terminals sometimes have special VIP lounges, usually quieter, with more comfortable chairs than the others. VIPs may be military or civilian, and the qualifications to be considered a VIP vary from time to time. Mere Army or Air Force colonels and Navy captains may be so classified when the supply is short. Another manifestation of the ancient human truth that RHIP.

visibility (Modern) The fact of being visible, a state that is highly undesirable on the modern battlefield. Uniforms and the paint patterns of vehicles and heavy weapons are selected to provide low visibility. You also may want to maintain low visibility when the Old Man is on the prowl with blood in his eye or with some extra duty to hand out. Of recent years, a soldier whose ERs and general service are so outstanding that he is certain to be noticed for promotion or a choice assignment is said to *have visibility.*

vivandière (Civil War) An authorized female camp follower after the style of the French Army, where vivandières had been a regular institution since the 18th century. The vivandière wore a feminized adaptation of her regiment's uniform and marched at the head of its column. Her particular equipment consisted of a small keg, appropriately painted, from which she dispensed hard liquor to those in need. Some American volunteer regiments—especially zouaves or those containing many foreigners—copied the idea, usually without a clear notion of what a vivandière should do, other than be decorative. Most of the girls soon went, or were sent, home. A handful, mostly thoroughly respectable and courageous young ladies, stayed on as combination cooks and surgeons' assistants.

V-mail (World War II; all Services) A special type of letter for overseas troops, introduced in May 1942. The letter form was furnished to the troops without charge. When the letters were written (and censored), they were placed on microfilm, which was flown to the United States, where the letters were reproduced in reduced size and delivered. The *V* stood for *victory*.

VOCO /*usually* 'vo-co *but sometimes pronounced as initials*/ Verbal Order of the Commanding Officer. Usually applied to short leaves for officers, granted orally rather than in official orders. "The Old Man gave me a weekend VOCO."

VOLAR /'vo-lar/ (Modern) Volunteer Army, the new, all-volunteer service.

VPL (Modern) Visible (Verified, Verifiable) Panty Line. The outline of a woman's panties, which can be seen when she wears tight-fitting shorts or trousers, especially when she is well endowed in the derrière. This expression was once common in Vietnam, where the women wore silk pantaloons under their exotic *áo dài*, the traditional woman's costume.

VT fuze (World War II to Modern) The "proximity" fuze for artillery projectiles. It contains a miniature radio receiving and transmitting oscillator, which sends out a continuous signal while the projectile is in flight. When this signal is reflected by a solid object (such as an enemy aircraft or the ground), the fuze detonates the projectile within optimal killing distance. A British invention perfected and mass-produced in the US, it greatly improved the speed and accuracy of antiaircraft fire and allowed the use of shell air-bursts over enemy troops. A popular translation of *VT* is *very touchy*.

☆☆☆☆W☆☆☆☆

WAAC /wak/ (Early World War II) 1. Women's Army Auxiliary Corps. Established 14 May 1942 and redesignated the Women's Army Corps on 1 July 1943. 2. Often as *Waac* or *waac*, a member of the WAAC.

WAC /wak/ (World War II to 1978 as an organization; as a term, gradually dying out) 1. Women's Army Corps (see *WAAC*). First established as the WAAC in 1942, the WAC was officially disestablished on 28 April 1978 and its personnel integrated with the male portion of the Army. Women have been totally integrated into almost all phases of Army life. In many places men and women share the same billets (separate rooms within the same building—"coed barracks") and are administered by fully integrated detachments. As of 1 September 1982, however, integrated basic training was discontinued. 2. Often as *Wac* or *wac,* a member of the WAC.

WAC detachment (World War II to 1978) The WAC quarters on a post or the WAC complement in toto. The WAC detachment was commanded by a female officer and the cadre and overhead were also all women. Nicknames for the WAC quarters were *Bay of Pigs, convent, chicken house, crackshack, henhouse, hen pen, heifer barn, powder house, wackery, wackshack, wacs' works.* See also *latrine orderly in the WAC barracks.*

waccoon (World War II) *s.* Derogatory nickname for a black WAC.

wackie whacky (World War II) *s.* A WAC.

wads (World War II) *s.* Cookies. Usually in the plural form. Apparently of British-Indian origin.

wagon dogs (Civil War; CSA) *s.* Soldiers who pretended to be hurt or sick so that they could remain with the supply trains where life was more comfortable and the chances for profitable thievery greater.

wagon gun (Indian Wars) *s.* An Indian name for a field gun. It was a gun, but it had wheels like a wagon. Up through the 1860s, it was usually the smoothbore 1840–41 12-pounder mountain howitzer. Later, it was the rifled 2-pounder Hotchkiss mountain gun.

wagon soldier (Indian Wars to 1940s) *s.* An artilleryman. The term continued in use, as in some versions of the "Caisson Song," into World War II. Oddly enough, most of the soldiers who manned the wagon guns during the Indian Wars were "instant artillerymen"—infantrymen or cavalrymen detailed to such duty, often with very little training.

waiter 1. (Colonial to post–War of 1812) An enlisted man serving as an officer's personal orderly. See *dog robber, striker.* 2. (By 1814 and after) A civilian servant hired by the officer himself. Officers received extra pay for the hire of such servants. A major general was allowed wages for four men; the four officers of a company, as a group, were allowed wages for three men. A soldier could no longer be taken from the ranks to work as a waiter. Shortly after, the term disappeared.

wait one (Modern) *s.* Just a second, wait a minute, hold on. Usually in phone conversations.

wake-up (Modern) *s.* The day the soldier leaves for the United States if he is overseas or the day of his discharge from the service. The time before the event and the event itself may be described as *three days and a wake-up* or *three days and a greasy egg* (referring to breakfast).

walk-a-heap (Indian Wars) *s.* An Indian name for *infantryman.* To the "Horse Indians" of the Far West, walking to war was an inexplicable thing. Only the Blackfeet customarily did this, and even they tried to steal horses to ride home. Obviously, therefore, walk-a-heaps were crazy and should be approached with caution—an idea soon converted into a conviction by the range and accuracy of the infantry's .45–70 trap-door Springfields.

walking wounded (All Services) 1. Those able to walk despite wounds. 2. *s.* Persons not too badly traumatized as the result of any sort of confrontation.

wall job (World War II; ETO) *s.* A peculiar method of sexual congress, utilizing a wall as a backstop. It was particularly favored by the female guerrillas who haunted Piccadilly Circus after dark, dragging their prey into doorways. Even GIs from New York City were amazed at what they could do, fully clothed, and standing up.

wandering Jew (World War I and somewhat later) *s.* A soldier who seems to have no permanent post, but is transferred many times.

war hat (Indian Wars) *s.* The stiff, black felt hat adopted in 1855 for the two newly organized cavalry regiments. It was issued to the remainder of the Army in 1858 as its full-dress headgear. It was also known as the *Jeff Davis hat* or *Hardee hat*, after, respectively, Secretary of War Jefferson Davis and Maj. William Hardee, who were blamed for inflicting it on the Army; the *Kossuth hat* after a similar headgear sported by that Hungarian insurgent; and the *Fra Diavolo hat*, after a similar one worn by the Italian brigand in Auber's comic opera.

war hotel (Civil War; CSA) *s.* A place of confinement for prisoners of war. "[I can] give you free transportation to Richmond, and a letter of introduction to a first-class 'War Hotel.' The gentleman in charge of it will be pleased to entertain you, free of cost" (Kelsey).

warm body (Modern) *s.* The individual soldier, particularly the subnormal variety.

warrant officer (1918 to Modern; the office also exists in the Navy, the Marine Corps, and the Air Force) In the Army, officers appointed by warrants signed by the

Secretary of the Army (as opposed to officers' commissions, which are signed by the President). Warrant officers for the most part serve as administrative or technical specialists in positions too specialized for commissioned officers. They generally have the same privileges as commissioned officers and rank below second lieutenants and above enlisted men and cadets. Historically, the rank of warrant officer evolved (ultimately) from civilian employees of the Army who handled finances and (immediately) from field clerks in the Quartermaster Corps in World War I. The rank was created in a small way in 1918 for the Mine Planter Service of the Coast Artillery Corps (for the command of vessels) and was greatly expanded in the reorganization of 1920. While details of rank and insignia have varied over the years, since 1954 there have been four grades: warrant officer 1 (WO, WO-1) (the lowest); chief warrant officer 2 (W-2, CWO-2); chief warrant officer 3 (W-3, CWO-3); and chief warrant officer 4 (CWO, W-4, CWO-4). Their insignia is a silver bar with black squares, ranging from one for warrant officer to four for chief warrant officer 4. Warrant officers are addressed as *Mister* and enlisted men salute them as if they were commissioned officers.

war story *s.* A military tall tale. It has been the immemorial prerogative of a fighting man to remember publicly "with advantages what feats he did that day," and such veterans usually have a degree of tolerance for one another's stories, if only because they, too, have hair-raising yarns of their own to tell. But sometimes such stories strain all willing belief, or the teller's credentials seem dubious. In such cases, military listeners may quietly get up and put on their steel helmets as a polite protest. The more uncouth may remark, "That stuff's sure getting deep in here. Where's my hip boots?" Generally, *war story* equals *damned lie.*

warwhoop (Indian Wars) *s.* An Indian warrior, particularly a hostile. See *Poor Lo.*

washed-out (World War II, perhaps earlier) *s.* Disqualified, failed. The term was originally used by aviators, but soon became widely accepted. The airplane used to check the flying proficiency of pilot trainees was called a *washing machine.*

washout (World War II on) *s.* Complete failure to hit the target on the rifle range.

WASP (World War II) Women Airforce Service Pilots. A ladies' auxiliary organization that ferried aircraft, towed aerial targets, and was otherwise useful and sometimes ornamental. Also, as *WASP, Wasp, wasp*, a member of the organization.

waste, to (Vietnam to Modern) *s.* To kill. Gold notes that the term was popular among jazzmen from at least as early as 1955. See *use up* and *zap.*

watash watashi /wah-'tahsh, wah-'tahshee/ (Post–World War II to Modern; all Services) *s.* I, me, oneself. From Japanese *watakushi*, colloquially spoken as *watashi*, 'I'. Sometimes used as *old watash.*

watch and watch (Ancient, but still occasionally encountered) A nautical term denoting a system of watches stood alternately by two groups of men. Occasionally it "came ashore." During the Civil War, a Regular artilleryman noted that "the whole of the Ninth and Fifth Corps stood watch and watch, twenty-four hours on and twenty-four hours off, half of each corps being on duty at a time" (Buell). A *watch*, in naval usage, is a division (roughly half) of a ship's crew that takes turns on duty.

water cure (Philippine Insurrection) A form of interrogation favored by the Spaniards and Filipinos, and adopted by Americans once they had experienced the uncertainties of guerrilla warfare. (Our senior author's sainted uncle's outfit used it in the Philippines after they found one of their missing men buried up to his chin in an ant hill.) When a prisoner refused to talk, a tube was thrust down his throat and water poured into him. He could either swallow or drown. Eventually he indicated his willingness to talk and was drained.

water walker (Modern) *s.* Anyone who receives a maximum rating on his efficiency report from both his rater and his endorser.

wax, to (Modern) *s.* To kill.

web feet web-footed boys (World War II) Navy personnel in general. A favorite expression of Gen. Curtis LeMay when describing his Navy associates and superiors in the Pacific.

web gear (Antiquity uncertain to Modern) Individual field equipment made of sturdy webbing (now nylon, earlier cotton): pistol belt, canteen cover, ammunition pouches, first-aid packet, entrenching tool carrier, combat field pack, sleeping-bag carrier, etc. The term *web* was used for this sort of material in World War I by the British Army.

wedge (West Point) *s.* Cadets normally apply nicknames to their officer instructors and tactical officers, who (if they are wise) show no curiosity whatever about the practice. One unwise tactical officer did learn that cadets called him *the Wedge*. He was quite proud, until he also learned the cadet definition of *wedge*: the simplest tool known to God or man.

weekend warrior (Modern) *s.* A Reservist or National Guardsman.

weenie (Vietnam; Air Force) *s.* Someone from higher headquarters. Obviously derogatory, with phallic suggestions.

wee-wee (World War I) *s.* A Frenchman. Undoubtedly from *oui, oui*.

West Pointer (Early 19th century to Modern) An officer who is a graduate of the US Military Academy at West Point.

West Point Protective Association WPPA (20th century) *s.* A not quite imaginary organization that still is considerably overworked by Reserve, National Guard, OCS, and other nongraduate officers in explaining why they did not get certain choice assignments, promotions, and/or decorations. But there is a camaraderie among West Pointers, a sense of shared experience and doctrine, and a strong tendency to look after one another, even in unofficial matters. And occasionally this does stick in the craw of equally competent nongraduates. See *ring knocker, SHIT*.

wet read (Modern) *s.* An initial interpretation of an aerial reconnaissance photo while it is still wet.

WETSU /wet-soo/ (Modern) *s.* We Eat This Shit Up. Used derisively with reference to gung-ho units, generally by the soldiers assigned to such units.

wetting them down wetting [one's] stripes wetting [one's] stripes down (Probably Ancient to Modern) *s.* A custom whereby an NCO who has been newly promoted stands his cronies and comrades to free beer or liquor in celebration of the event. Sometimes the newly promoted serviceman is expected to place his new chevrons at the bottom of a huge glass, fill it with beer, and then drink it dry without stopping. But as one gets older and rises in rank, these shenanigans become less and less attractive. Our sergeant major claims not to have celebrated his promotion to that rank and feeling very good about it the morning after. While this custom may provide the only occasion on which a sergeant buys beer for a private, such parties sometimes got out of hand and the new sergeant got an opportunity to start all over again from the bottom. The earliest recorded instance of the term is 1910 for the British Army (Partridge, 1970), but the custom undoubtedly goes back to the armies of the pharaoh. Comparable terms for officer promotions are *wetting one's bars, wetting one's oak leaves, wetting one's eagles*, etc.

What do plebes rank? (West Point) A stock question asked plebes by upperclassmen, part of plebe knowledge. The stock answer is "Sir, the Superintendent's dog, the Commandant's cat, the waiters in the Mess Hall, the Hell cats, and all the Admirals in the Whole blamed Navy."

What is the definition of leather? (West Point) A question of plebe knowledge. The stock answer is "If the fresh skin of an animal, cleaned and divested of all hair, fat, and other extraneous matter be immersed in a dilute solution of tannic acid, a chemical combination ensues; the gelatinous tissue of the skin is converted into a non-putrescible substance, imperviout to and insoluble in water; this, sir, is leather."

What the fuck, over? (Modern) *s.* A catchphrase meaning *What does it matter?* or *Who cares?* "The typical radio transmission among the helicopter pilots is: 'What the ———! Over' " (Tregaskis).

What time is it? (West Point) An element of plebe knowledge. The plebe replies to this question (according to the 1939 *Bugle Notes*), "Sir, I am deeply embarrassed and greatly humiliated that due to unforeseen circumstances over which I have no control, the inner workings and hidden mechanisms of my chronometer are in such inaccord [*sic*] with the great sidereal movement by which time is commonly reckoned, that I cannot with any degree of accuracy state the exact time, sir; but without fear of being very far off, I will state, that it is so many minutes, so many seconds, and so many ticks after the Xth hour." Alas, this ritual seems no longer performed at West Point.

What's los? (Post–World War II to Modern) *s.* What's up? What's the matter? From German *Was ist los?* with the same meaning. " 'Orville!' Morgan yelled, jumping to his feet. 'What the fuck is *los*?' " (Smith).

wheelers wheel team (Early 19th century to World War II) The rear team of horses pulling a gun or caisson in a Field Artillery battery. Each gun and caisson was normally pulled by three teams. The rear team, that directly harnessed to the limber, was known as the wheelers. They were bigger, more powerful animals than those in the swing and lead teams. As a 114-pound ROTC cadet, our senior officer had a stint as wheel driver. One of his team weighed 1,500 pounds, the other 1,550, and both stood over sixteen hands. Fortunately, they were docile, well-trained creatures.

When in doubt, whip it out (Modern) *s.* A catchphrase meaning that if a soldier is not sure whether he should salute a superior, he should play it safe and salute.

when the balloon goes up (Antiquity uncertain, but probably 19th century, to Modern) *s.* A catchphrase meaning when the show really starts, when things get rough. Although many explanations have been given for this expression, we believe that it originated in the last half of the 19th century, when a balloon ascension was the big point of a country fair. *When the shit hits the fan* is a modern equivalent, but *when the balloon goes up* remains in general use.

whip, to (World War II) *s.* To steal, especially to steal with great deftness. A term borrowed from the British by the Americans in Italy and apparently not used in other theaters. "A Neapolitan can whip the gold out of your eyeteeth while you're yawning."

whirlybird (Korea and later) *s.* A helicopter.

white arm (19th century to 20th century) The cavalry sword or saber. The term is derived from French *arme blanche*, meaning any cold-steel weapon—saber, lance, or bayonet. There was a constant dispute, waged with apostolic zeal from approximately the Civil War on, as to whether American cavalry should carry sabers or should rely solely upon firearms. The sabers eventually vanished. The cavalry followed shortly thereafter.

Whitebird (Modern) *s.* The OH-6 helicopter. See *Loach* and *tadpole.*

white-glove inspection (Old Army to Modern) A particularly rigorous inspection, especially of barracks, mess halls, and personal equipment. In plain fact, some inspecting officers did wear white gloves, and the slightest spot to appear on them as the officer checked kitchen gear, locker tops, and odd corners meant collective and selective woe for the outfit and individual responsible. Cleanliness was not only next to godliness, it was essential for the health and self-respect of the service.

white mice (Vietnam) *s.* The Vietnamese National Police, so called for their white uniforms and apparent lack of backbone when faced with danger.

white-oak chips (Civil War; USA) *s.* Hardtack. White-oak wood is noted for its toughness.

whites (Antiquity uncertain; all Services) *s.* White uniforms or articles of uniform. Modern examples of whites are the white working uniforms of mess and medical personnel, the Navy Undress Summer Uniform, and the Army officers' Summer White Dress Uniform. We have been unable to ascertain whether the term *whites* was applied to the Army summer fatigue uniform worn in southern states from about 1802 to sometime in the 1840s, but the term seems to have been in use by the last years of the 19th century.

white sergeant (Early 19th century) *s.* An officer's wife, particularly one who, taking advantage of her husband's uxoriousness, neglected her household concerns to meddle in the command of his outfit. We recall one modern example who insisted on a division symphony orchestra. If your driver or radio operator could tootle a flute, you saw him only at paydays, some meals, and concerts.

whitewall (Modern; also Marines) *s.* A haircut in which the sides of the head are so closely trimmed that no hair is visible when a hat or cap is worn. The hair on the top of the head (under the cap) is usually flat-topped.

whizbang (World War I) *s.* A German field gun (and its shells) employed for direct fire against troops and tanks. The exact caliber and model of this weapon are much disputed; probably several different guns were used. The whiz of the passing shell and the bang of its explosion hit your ears at practically the same time. The term was of British origin, usually spelled *whizzbang*.

whores de combat (World War I and later) *s.* Prostitutes. A play on the French *hors de combat,* 'disabled', 'out of action', a state to which they can reduce the careless soldier.

WIA (20th century) Wounded In Action. A soldier so wounded. "Send the crackerbox. We've got six WIAs."

wife (Service academies) *s.* A roommate.

wigwag (Late 19th century to 1930s) The two-flag semaphore system of signaling that replaced the one-flag system used during the Civil War. It was employed as an alternate means of communication into the 1930s.

wild blue yonder (World War II) The domain of the Army Air Corps. A *wild blue yonder boy* was an aviator (fly-boy). The phrase came from an Air Corps song beginning "Up we go, into the wild blue yonder." When it was sung, lowly ground-troop types were apt to interrupt it with disrespectful amendments, such as bellowing "Crash!" just as the fly-boys caroled "yonder."

willie peter **willy peter** (World War II to Vietnam) *s.* White phosphorus ammunition, wonderful stuff so long as the other fellow does not use it on you. From the old phonetic alphabet terms for *w* and *p*. "Brilliant white smoke from phosphorus ('willy peter/make you a buh-liever')" (Herr).

Willow Run (World War II) *s.* The Consolidated Officers' Mess, set up in the Great Ball Room of the Grosvenor Hotel, Park Lane, London. It fed decent meals to hosts of officers, local or transient. Named after the big new Ford aircraft plant near Detroit, it was operated considerably more efficiently.

windjammer (Old Army) *s.* A bugler or trumpeter.

windsucker (Old, Old Army to 1940s). *s.* A horse that swallows air, to the detriment of its digestion.

wings (18th century to early 19th century) 1. Crescent-shaped pieces of cloth sewn on the shoulder seams of grenadiers', light infantrymen's, and musicians' coats during the 18th and early 19th centuries. 2. An elaborate type of shoulder strap used by US dragoon officers (1812–15) and later by the whole Army (1820–30) in place of epaulettes.

wings (Probably before World War II to Modern) *s.* The traditional insignia—a spread pair of bird wings—awarded to qualified aviation personnel.

> I wanted wings, till I got the ——— things!
> But now I do not want them anymore.

wings, to get one's 1. (Probably pre–World War II to Modern) *s.* To qualify as a pilot. 2. (Probably World War II to Modern) *s.* To qualify as a paratrooper. The parachutist's badge is a parachute flanked by a pair of wings.

wing weenie (Modern; Air Force) *s.* An officer of an Air Force wing who serves as one of the commander's principal staff assistants. "Lumped together, these people become wing weenies to the fighter pilots" (Broughton). See *weenie*.

Wipe it off! (Considerable Antiquity to Modern; also Marines) *s.* A command to "take that idiotic grin off your face, quit goofing off, and get back to work."

Wire City *s.* The stockade.

wire hangers (Vietnam) *s.* Rear-echelon troops who could take their clothes off and hang them up at night rather than sleeping in them, like combat troops.

wire happy (World War II; all Services) *s.* Intense despondency, which afflicted some Allied prisoners of war and occasionally ended in suicide. See *happy*.

wizard (World War II) 1. *s.* Much used by the British to indicate something of superlative quality, like a *wizard show*. Its origin is not clear, but it may derive ultimately from British schoolboy slang. Partridge (1970) cites it from 1924, but the term may have been reinforced by *The Wizard*, a popular British boys' serial magazine of the 1930s and by the motion picture *The Wizard of Oz*. 2. US Army Air Corps) *s.* A very special girl friend.

wobbly one (Modern) *s.* A warrant officer W-1, possibly because he is so junior and so new to the warrant officer ranks that he is unsure of himself.

Wolfhounds (Korea) The US 27th Infantry Regiment. In Korea, at night on the front lines, they would howl loudly to let the North Joes know who was there. Also called *Russian Wolfhounds*.

wolf patrol (World War II; all Services) *s.* Clean-cut, red-blooded young Americans on pass, looking for wine, women, and song—in whatever sequence available.

wood butcher (Probably pre–World War I to Old Army) *s.* A carpenter, usually a post civilian employee. Or, as recorded for World War I, the company artificer. As a civilian term, recorded from the 1880s.

wooden horse, to ride the (Colonial to Revolutionary) *s.* To suffer a particularly harsh form of military punishment. The "horse" consisted of two wide planks perhaps 8 feet long, fixed together to form a sharp angle along the "back." This was supported by four posts, for legs, A rough neck, head, and tail might be added for show. Offenders were seated astride the sharp back, with their hands tied behind them. Sometimes weights were attached to their feet. The results could be crippling.

wooling (Early 19th century) *s.* A quick form of company punishment, especially designed for those of limited understanding. The offender was taken by the ear and shaken vigorously. The term refers to pulling wool.

Woo Poo (West Point) *s.* West Point, site of the US Military Academy. "Brought him up here to Woo Poo" (Truscott).

wopper (West Point) *s.* WOPR (Written Oral Partial Review).

word one (Modern) *s.* One word. "I never got to say word one." Possibly from the Army supply system, where items are listed by basic nomenclature and unit of issue.

wordsmithing (Modern) *s.* Rewriting a staff paper to smooth out wording without changing substance.

working (Modern) A signal word used to let the telephone switchboard operator know that a line is open, is in use, and should not be cut off. All too often it is spoken into lines that are already dead.

working your bolt (Old, Old Army to World War II) *s.* Idle chatter, a lot of activity with no visible results. The term comes from the bolt-action rifles that were used before the adoption of the semiautomatic M1 rifle. The soldier raised his bolt handle to unlock the firing chamber, pulled the bolt back to extract the fired cartridge case, shoved it forward to seat a fresh cartridge and cock the rifle, and pushed it down to lock the firing chamber. Before target practice with live ammunition, recruits were given bolt manipulation training to accustom them to carrying out the sequence rapidly and correctly. This was called, in soldier talk, *working the bolt*. The expression has apparently died away except among old-timers.

world, the (Vietnam) *s.* The United States. Vietnam was somewhere, but to most of the Americans fighting there, not of *this* world.

World War II barracks These were temporary wooden buildings constructed principally to provide billets for troops at training centers. They were two-story buildings, consisting mostly of open floor space. Latrine facilities were located at one end of the building and small rooms for cadre personnel (or noncoms) were usually provided at the other. In between was the troop living space, which could accommodate approximately one platoon per floor, or sixty men or more to a building. Soldiers slept in double bunks, as a rule. Each man had a footlocker, and most barracks had open-shelf storage and clothing racks mounted on the walls for hanging uniforms. These buildings sometimes had tiny porches, upper and lower, connected by wooden stairs or ladders. Such barracks are now becoming rare sights, since new construction is replacing them. They were Spartan places to live, but because they forced men to live together intimately, they fostered a sense of belonging that is missing in today's Army, with its much more comfortable and private three-man rooms in brick buildings.

worm wormer (Colonial to Civil War) A corkscrew-shaped device used to draw an unfired load (or pieces of half-burned wadding) from the bore of a muzzle-loading weapon.

woxof (Modern; Air Force) *s.* Completely socked in. Formed by combining the weather report code letters for ceiling zero.

wrapped around the flagpole, to be (Modern) *s.* To be overcome by an issue, to concentrate too much attention on petty matters to the detriment of more important things. "Don't wrap yourself around the flagpole over some minor uniform regulations."

wrist breaker (Civil War; USA) *s.* The issue cavalry saber.

writ (West Point) *s.* A recitation or examination.

☆☆☆☆ X/Y ☆☆☆☆

XO (Modern) Executive Officer.

---

yaki-waki (World War II) *s.* Phonetic approximation of a drink invented by US Army nurses in the skimpy Anzio beachhead, where, as Bill Mauldin remembered it, "wounded men got oak leaf clusters on their Purple Hearts when shell fragments riddled them as they lay on hospital beds." Yaki-waki was made of medicinal alcohol flavored with the synthetic powdered lemonade from C-rations. None of us having been there, we can only express amazement that the hospitals continued to function.

yaller dogs (Civil War; CSA) *s.* The Confederate infantryman's term for staff officers and couriers, who "were regarded as noncombatants and a nuisance, and the average private never let one pass without whistling and calling dogs" (Watkins).

Yard (Vietnam) *s.* Abbreviation of *montagnard*, a general term for several different tribal groups living in the central highlands of South Vietnam. They are subsistence farmers and hunters, organized along tribal lines. Their assistance was sought after by both sides during the war. The US Army Special Forces had much success training and organizing these primitive people, but there has long existed a warm and mutual hatred between them and the Vietnamese. Their fate since the United States "crawled out standing up" from Vietnam apparently has been thoroughly unpleasant.

yardbird (World War II) *s.* A term with varied meanings, rather hard to pin down. In general, a substandard soldier who might, if carefully supervised, be capable of policing up the area. In 1941, however, when privates with less than four months' service received only $21 a month (as compared to the standard rate of $30), a yardbird could be such a rookie or recruit. The term itself is apparently taken from the "Barney Google" and "Snuffy Smith" cartoon strips. The Navy, however, considers a *yardbird* to be personnel stationed at a Navy yard or, in a somewhat contemptuous sense, the civilian employees of a Navy yard.

yearling (West Point) *s.* A cadet third classman, the equivalent of a college sophomore. Also *youngster, yuk.*

yellowhammer yaller-hammer (Civil War; CSA) *s.* A soldier from Alabama. When an Alabama regiment behaved poorly in action, other Confederates would jeer "Yallerhammer, Alabama, flicker, flicker, flicker!" Apart from the rhyme with *Alabama*, a play on words was involved, since *yellowhammer* is a local term for a variety of flicker, and the verb *flicker* was hardly complimentary.

yellow leg (Old, Old Army) *s.* A cavalryman, yellow being the Cavalry branch color. Specifically, cavalry officers and NCOs had yellow stripes down the outside seams of their trousers.

Y-man (World War I) *s.* A YMCA man who performed small services for the doughboys in France. The Y-men seem to have been cordially hated and detested, being considered mealymouthed slackers and hypocrites.

The YMCA went over the top
To pick up the pennies the
Doughboys drop!
Hinky Dinky Parley Vous.

yobo (Modern) *s.* A lover. From Korean. The word can be applied to either men or women, although it is generally used to mean a girl friend.

yodel in the canyon, to (Modern) *s.* To perform cunnilingus.

youngster (West Point) *s.* A cadet third classman (sophomore). A yearling.

You're not paid to think! (Antiquity uncertain to Modern) *s.* A cynical rejoinder to statements beginning with *I think . . .* or *Do you know what I think?*

Your last four? (Modern; all Services) A request for the last four digits of one's Social Security number. The numbers are largely used in hospitals and personnel and finance offices to help locate individual record folders and to identify the soldier with the correct record.

You sao! See *sao.*

yuk (West Point) *s.* A cadet third classman (sophomore). A yearling.

☆☆☆☆ Z ☆☆☆☆

zap, to (World War II to Modern) *s.* To kill. A very common expression during the Vietnam War. Perhaps adopted from underworld jargon, perhaps from comic books (notably *Captain Marvel*). "They threw three grenades into your old location and zapped two men" (Downs).

zebra (Early World War II) *s.* A short-lived term for a noncommissioned officer, based on his stripes.

zep (World War I) *s.* A Zeppelin.

zero defects program (Mid-1960s) One of those stunts dreamed up by underemployed inmates of the Puzzle Palace, in defiance of human nature, common sense, and the laws of probability. Everyone was to sign a pledge to do absolutely perfect work—*zero defects* in Pentagonese. We remember a nice general who made the required exhortation to his assembled headquarters and then announced that he would then and there publicly sign his pledge. He reached for his pen—and found that he had left it on his desk.

zero hour (World War I) British for *H-hour*, picked up by Americans serving with the British Expeditionary Force in northern France.

zero-zero (World War II; Air Force) *s.* The same as *socked in*: clouds down to ground level, visibility nil, birds walking, our fly-boys sleeping late, and the supposedly nonexistent Luftwaffe somehow on the prowl overhead.

ZI (20th century) Zone of the Interior. That part of a territory involved in a war in which no active operations are taking place. Between long-range missiles and aircraft, and guerrilla warfare, the ZI tends to get smaller and smaller.

zig zig zigzig (World War II) *s.* Sexual intercourse of the casual kind. A common approach was *Vooleyvoo fair zigzig?*

zip (Modern) *s.* An Oriental. Possibly an acronym of *Zero Intelligence Potential.*

zippo (Vietnam) 1. *s.* Any of various Armored Cavalry Assault Vehicles equipped with M10-8 flamethrowers. 2. *s.* Any flame-throwing device. "Yet another carried a tank of liquid napalm and was used as a flamethrower. With a fine sense of nonchalance men called it a 'Zippo'" (Bunting). From the commercial cigarette lighter Zippo.

zippo squad (Vietnam) *s.* The last element of a tactical unit to go through an enemy village; it put the torch to the place as it passed through.

zoomie 1. (West Point) *s.* A cadet at the US Air Force Academy. 2. (World War II) *s.* An aviator. Also used by submariners, especially for US Navy planes. Until the last year of the war, zoomies were a major hazard to US subs.

zoo-zoo zoo-zoo-zoo (Civil War) *s.* A zouave.

zouave (Civil War) A soldier of a volunteer regiment that copied (more or less) the showy North African dress and sometimes the special light-infantry drill of the French Zouaves. Contrary to popular belief, a good many zouave regiments, most of them first-rate combat units, served in the Union forces throughout the war. One 1862 northern definition of a zouave was "an Irishman and six yards of red flannel." Confederate zouaves soon wore out their colorful uniforms and became plain graybacks and butternuts.

Appendix of Naval ☆☆☆☆ and Marine Terms

AB (Old Sailing Navy) Able-bodied seaman, one grade above an ordinary seaman. Today, used only in the merchant marine.

acey-deucy A board game derived from backgammon. Understood only by the Old Navy, which had time enough to master its complexities.

acorn (World War II and later) A special unit with the personnel and equipment necessary to establish an advanced air base capable of servicing, rearming, and performing routine maintenance and minor repairs on the aircraft of one carrier group or one patrol plane squadron.

actual (Modern; Marines) *s.* A unit commander. A call sign used to distinguish the commander from his radio operator. "Getting a new actual today" (Webb). If, for example, the call sign is *Fox-6*, the officer is *Fox-6 Actual.*

adrift (Considerable antiquity; Navy, Marines) Out of its proper place, mislaid, or lost. "My cigarette lighter's gone adrift." Anything found adrift aboard ship goes into the lucky bag.

airedale (World War II; Navy) *s.* An enlisted man in the air department of an aircraft carrier. They moved, armed, fueled, and guided planes between flights. Also called *sheepdogs.*

all hands (Ancient to Modern; Navy) The entire crew of the ship, from captain to cabin boy, or a call on the boatswain's pipe, to turn them out in the morning or for some other purpose. In the Old Sailing Navy the call might be to shorten sail in a sudden storm or to man the sweeps.

Amgrunt (Modern; Marines) *s.* A member of a Marine amphibious unit. Probably from *amtrack*, an amphibious tracked vehicle, and *grunt*, an infantryman (Lighter, 1980).

AO (Navy) Auxiliary Oiler. Oil tanker.

AR (Navy) Auxiliary Repair Ship.

A72 (Navy, Marines) A seventy-two-hour liberty, the equivalent of the Army three-day pass.

ball cap (Modern; Navy) Short for *baseball cap.* "Current regulations permit wearing of command (organizational) ball caps" (*All Hands*, March 1977).

BAM (World War II; Marines) *s.* Broad-Assed Marine, the Corps's unofficial title for a member of its female contingent.

Banana Fleet (Early 20th century) The Caribbean Special Service Squadron, made up of converted destroyers used as assault transports for Marine detachments. In those days it was neither fashionable nor safe for Latin American countries to kidnap American citizens or nationalize their property. That is why *US Marine* is still a cussword in those parts.

barge (Colonial to Modern; Navy) Originally a large (typically 28–34 feet long; 6-foot beam; 2.5-foot depth) ship's boat that could either be rowed or carry light sail and was used for boarding or landing operations. Some boats of this type did good service as small gunboats, chasing picaroons in the shallow waters of the Caribbean after 1815. Traditionally, however, admirals at sea used barges, suitably appointed and decorated, when they wanted to go ashore or visit other ships of their fleet. Later, the admiral's barge became a motor launch of the same general type as a captain's gig, if somewhat more embellished. As the Navy's "Destroyer Song," which dates from some time around World War I, puts it,

> The captain rides in a gig,
> The Admiral rides in his barge.
> It ain't cause it goes any faster
> It just makes the bastard feel large.

bargeman (Old Sailing Navy and later) *s.* A weevil maggot inhabiting ship's biscuit. They, or their relatives, also got into the Army's hardtack.

battlewagon (20th century; Navy) *s.* A battleship.

BB (Navy) Battleship.

beat, to (Old Sailing Navy) To tack to windward by sailing close-hauled. "Only a master seaman could beat up the channel in such weather."

beat 'em, to (1930s through World War II; Marines) *s.* To complain. shortened from *beat [one's] gums.*

beat to quarters (Old Sailing Navy) The drum signal for general quarters.

before mast (Navy, Marines) Called before the commanding officer to explain one's misdoings. The nautical equivalent of the Army's *on the carpet.* Also *up for mast.*

belay (Old Sailing Navy to 20th century) Disregard that last order. Old salts still use it.

bells (Colonial to Modern; Navy, Marines) A seagoing way of telling time. At 8:30 A.M. or P.M., a bell is sounded once and then one bell is added on every half hour until eight bells, when the cycle starts over. Each such four-hour cycle constitutes a *watch.*

bend, to (Ancient to Modern; Navy, Marines) To attach or to fasten. For example, the first Marines to reach the top of Mount Suribachi during the conquest of Iwo Jima in 1945 bent an American flag to the piece of Japanese water pipe they used for an improvised flagstaff. The term itself is probably a variant of *bind.*

Bent-Wing Widow Maker (World War II; Marines, Navy) *s.* The Chance-Vought Corsair F4U fighter plane. It was a swift, agile, deadly aircraft, first developed for land-based Marine air units, later employed aboard aircraft carriers. It was still highly effective in Korea, where one of them shot down a MIG-15 jet fighter.

big chow (World War II; Navy, Marines) *s.* The meal served before a "big day" (major carrier aircraft strike). Usually big steaks, fried eggs and potatoes, buttered toast, and coffee.

Big Portsmouth (Navy, Marines) *s.* The Joint, the Naval Prison at Portsmouth, New Hampshire.

bilge rat (Navy) *s.* A boiler technician or machinist's mate.

binnacle list (Ancient to Modern; Navy) The ship's sick list. In the Old Sailing Navy, the sick list was hung on the binnacle in front of the steering wheel. There the officer of the deck could check it against the men on duty. The term seems to be dying out.

bird farm (Navy) *s.* An aircraft carrier.

black gang (Coal-burning Navy) *s.* The engine-room stokers and coal-passers.

Black Pit (World War II; Navy) The so-called Greenland Gap, an area in the mid-Atlantic, south of Greenland and out of range of land-based aircraft from either North America or the United Kingdom. It was a happy hunting ground for German U-boats until about April 1943, when hunter-killer groups moved in.

blank file (Early 20th century; Marines) *s.* Someone who wears a uniform but otherwise is not exactly with you. He has to be watched, since he is prone to create accidents. Sometimes useful as a horrible example.

blood tub (Old Steam Navy, possibly earlier) A ship under brutal, often erratic discipline.

Blue Coffin (World War II; Navy) *s.* The amphibian Catalina PBY, a big, steady aircraft excellent for long-range overwater patrols. In the Aleutians, however, they were pressed into service as bombers, torpedo planes, and even dive-bombers—roles for which their size, low speed, and matronly maneuvering qualities did not exactly qualify them.

blue shirts (Modern; Navy) *s.* A species of airedale. Aircraft handlers aboard an aircraft carrier. They wear blue jerseys to identify themselves. Blue shirts work for the yellow shirts.

boat (Ancient to Modern; Navy, Marines) A small craft that can be hoisted aboard a larger vessel, which is properly called a ship. (The motor torpedo boat is the one exception to this definition, but even MTBs are carried as cargo aboard large ships for long-distance movements.) No matter how small a warship may be, do not tell its skipper than he has a "nice little boat."

boatswain /'bo-sun/ (Ancient to Modern; Navy) A warrant officer in charge of rigging, anchors, cables, boats, and the like. His pipe (usually blown by a bosun's mate) sounds the ship's calls.

bolshevik (Post–World War I; Navy, Marines) *s.* Undisciplined, disorderly, disobedient, or bearing the outward aspect of incipient mutiny. A *bolshevik ship* is poorly run, with a surly, disobedient (or would-be-if-they-dared) crew. The traditional result was the court-martial pennant run to the masthead of the flagship. After a half-dozen stiff sentences—and usually a new captain—the bolshevik became the smartest one in the squadron. We are not entirely certain as to what happens today.

boomers (Modern; Navy) *s.* Officers and men of the new nuclear-powered elements of the US Navy. They have their own language, which we hope to learn.

boot (Marines) *s.* A new recruit. He gets his initial training in a boot camp, where his muscles are toughened (including some he did not know he had), his civilian priorities ruthlessly rearranged, and his psyche carefully inoculated with the importance of being a marine. Also called *boots.*

boot brown-bar (Modern; Marines) *s.* A new second lieutenant. "I was alliteratively known as the 'boot brown-bar,' slang for a raw second lieutenant" (Caputo).

bottle baby (Marines) *s.* An alcoholic or rummy—raised on a bottle and never weaned.

Boxhead (1920–30; Navy) *s.* A Swede or Norwegian.

break out, to (Old Sailing Navy to Modern) To display a hoist of signal flags that have been so attached to a signal halyard that they unfurl simultaneously as they are raised.

brig (Navy, Marines) The jail of a warship. Also, a jail on a naval base.

brightwork (Colonial to Modern; Navy, Marines) Ornamental brass fittings in a barracks or aboard ship. Shined every day. Masters-at-arms often lose their minds because of the tendency of marine detachments to paint over brightwork when they are not closely watched. (In wartime, it *is* painted over.)

brig rat (World War II; Navy, Marines) *s.* A prisoner serving time in the brig.

bubbly wubblies (World War II; Marines) *s.* Projectiles from Japanese rocket mortars, so named from their noise in flight.

bulkhead (Navy) A partition between two compartments of a ship. Sailors use the term for what the rest of us call a *wall*.

bumboat (Colonial to Modern) A small craft used for peddling various items—frequently illegal—to ships anchored off a port.

bursting fart (Marines) *s.* A marine gunner's insignia.

By your lee, sir (Old Navy) An expression used by sailors to request permission to pass an officer in a congested area or as an apology when overtaking him from the rear. Reputed to have originated in the days of sail when sailors passed officers only on the downwind (lee) side. Going out of use. *By your leave, sir*, is the modern form, which both officers and enlisted sailors use when passing a person senior in rank. It, too, is reported to be going out of style.

CAM ship (World War II; Navy) Catapult Aircraft Merchant. The Royal Navy term for a merchant ship modified to launch a fighter plane from a catapult. One such ship was frequently attached to a Murmansk-bound convoy in the hope that the plane could knock down the German long-range reconnaissance planes that haunted such convoys. The returning pilot had to ditch his plane in the sea near the ship and wait to be picked up.

can (World War I to Modern; Navy) *s.* A destroyer. Short for tin can.

candy assholes (Korea; Marines) *s.* Lifesavers.

captain of the head (Navy) A sarcastic title for the sailor responsible for keeping the ship's head clean and functioning.

captain of the yard (Navy) The officer in command of a naval shore installation. Despite the title, he may be a rear admiral.

cat fever (Navy, Marines) A very informal medical term covering everything from a mild cold to double pneumonia. Catarrhal fever. A marine witness of unimpeachable probity assures us that a fever of more than 3° got you medical attention; one of less than 3° got you forty hours of EPD for malingering.

Channel fever (Old Navy) Homesickness. Probably from the British Navy.

Charlie Noble (Old Navy to Modern) The smokestack of a ship's galley. Many a tearful, pregnant miss has come to a naval base inquiring for Seaman First Class Charlie Noble, often of the "USS *Tuscarora*," who got her that way. According to Partridge (1970) the term originated in the British Navy, from a Commander Noble "who insisted that the cowl of the galley funnel be kept bright."

cheat shoes (Modern; Navy) *s.* Shoes made of a shiny plastic, for off-duty wear. They do not require polishing.

Chinese rot (Old Navy) *s.* A severe case of one of the several fungus infections that could be picked up east of Suez and west of Guam. During World War II the term shifted to *jungle rot*.

chips (Navy) A ship's carpenter's mate.

Cinderella liberty (Navy, Marines) *s.* A period of liberty (or pass) ending at midnight.

clothes stops (Navy) Pieces of line used for tying laundry to a clothesline. See *tie-tie*.

Coffin Corner (World War II) *s.* The rear starboard (right) corner of a Murmansk-bound convoy. Being closest to the Norwegian coast and having little supporting antiaircraft fire from other ships in the convoy, it was a favorite target for German dive-bombers.

common shell (Early 20th century to World War II; Navy, Marines) A special shell used for target practice. It was loaded with sand rather than with high explosives.

com orderly (1920s to World War II; Navy, Marines) *s.* Communications orderly. A marine orderly detailed to carry messages from the bridge to other places aboard ship.

comosellama (Navy) *s.* A whatchamacallit. Derived, according to a salty submarine commander, from Panamanian nightclub Spanish.

coxswain /cock-s-n/ (Old Sailing Navy to Modern) 1. A seaman or petty officer in charge of a boat or light landing craft. The *captain's coxswain*, for example, is in charge of the captain's gig as a full-time duty when not at battle stations. The *spud coxswain* is less aristocratic and on occasion may even be a marine. 2. Formerly, a petty officer, the lowest-ranking of the boatswain's mates. The rating, as such, no longer exists, but it is used as a temporary designation.

Crabtown (Antiquity uncertain; US Naval Academy) Neighboring Annapolis, possibly because of the famed seafood of the area, but *crab* was once midshipman slang for a "femme of the local order" (*Lucky Bag*).

Crotch (Marines) *s.* The US Marine Corps. "Gonna get married, as soon as I get out of the Crotch" (Roth). "I couldn't make lance corporal if I stayed in the Crotch for thirty years" (Caputo).

crow (Modern, but probably of some antiquity; Navy) *s.* The spread eagle on a petty officer's sleeve insignia. *To get your crow* is to be promoted to petty officer.

cruise (Old Sailing Navy to Modern; also Marines) An enlistment. In early days sailors and marines were recruited for a cruise instead of for a definite period of time.

crumb (Marines) *s.* A marine with unclean personal habits. If he did not mend his ways, he could end up getting a special sand and canvas bath. Old-time marines were very unsympathetic people who never studied Freud, but their treatment for such asocial behavior was 100 percent successful.

cub (World War II and later; Navy) An advanced supply base with the necessary wharfs, warehouses, tank farm, and equipment for storing and handling all types of materials needed by the fleet. It has its own service and harbor defense units.

CV (Navy) Aircraft carrier.

CVE (World War II; Navy) Escort carrier. Also known as *jeep carriers* and *baby flattops*, these were small ships (approximately 10,000 tons) capable of carrying some thirty aircraft. The crews read *CVE* as *Combustible, Vulnerable, Expendable.*

DD Destroyer.

dead horse (Old Navy) 1. Indebtedness for items used or consumed. *Working off dead horse* was trying to pay up, frequently while attempting to make additional purchases on credit. 2. Drawing up to three months' pay in advance, to meet expenses incidental to a change of station, is *drawing dead horse.* An old custom, sanctioned by law.

deck (Navy) What a sailor says when he means *floor.* See *hit the deck.*

deck apes (Navy) *s.* Enlisted seamen assigned to deck or gunnery duties. Cooks, yeomen, electricians, and the engine-room gang are not entitled to this distinction. Sailors also apply the term to the boatswain's mates.

deep six (Navy, Marines) Davy Jones's locker at the bottom of the sea, taken from the last mark on the lead line (see *heave the lead*). Burial at sea may be referred to as *the deep six. To give something the deep six* is to get the article or problem concerned permanently out of sight and mind.

destroyer (Navy) 1. (20th century) A light warship, next below a light cruiser, much used for escort and hunter-killer missions. Also called *can, tin can.* 2. *s.* (1930s and 1940s) A very attractive woman.

Devil Dogs (World War I and later) A name pinned on the US Marine Corps, supposedly by awed German prisoners after the Battle of Belleau Wood. It is more likely that the nickname originated with a war correspondent or with Secretary of the Navy Josephus Daniels, a gentleman given to orotund oratory and glowing press releases. The Navy remembers him as the nice-Nelly who prohibited the "use or introduction for drinking purposes of alcoholic liquors" on board any vessel. Do not use the term *Devil Dogs* when addressing marines. They are trying to forget.

Dilbert dunker (Modern; Navy) A device used in the training of Navy air pilots. It simulated an aircraft ditching at sea (*All Hands*, April 1977).

dirty dog and no sailor (Old Sailing Navy) A sailor's supreme expression of contempt for a shipmate. As ordinarily used, this expression probably would contain several additional adjectives.

doggie (Marines) *s.* An Army infantryman.

dog's body dogsbody (Navy) Dried peas boiled in a cloth. The only use we have seen was during the Civil War, but we believe that it is far older.

dolphins (Modern; Navy) *s.* The submariner's badge. Also called *silver fish.*

double irons (Ancient to post–Civil War) Punishment for serious misconduct aboard ship, with fetters (irons) on both wrists and ankles.

down the throat (World War II; Navy) *s.* A submarine crewman's term for a torpedo fired at the bow of an enemy ship from a position straight ahead of it.

draw a bucket, to (1920s to 1940s; Marines) *s.* To arrive at the recruit depot after enlistment. There each recruit was issued a galvanized iron bucket, which he was supposed to retain for his entire service. It was charged against his pay.

eagle boat (World War I) A destroyer substitute for antisubmarine work. It displaced 500 tons, mounted two 4-inch and one 3-inch guns, and made 18 knots. The Ford Motor Company built them on an assembly line, but slowly. Only eight of an authorized sixty were completed in time. Most were gradually disposed of before World War II.

Eat the apple and fuck the Corps (Modern; Marines) A catchphrase indicating a certain degree of dissatisfaction with the US Marine Corps. See *Semper fi.*

ensign (Navy) The lowest commissioned grade in the Navy. The title was adopted in 1862 to replace *passed midshipman.*

EPD (Navy, Marines) Extra Police Duty. Awarded as a punishment. It can be worked out only aboard ship. Some captains seem to have restricted such working hours to time the ship spent in a liberty port (one where your well-behaved comrades are allowed ashore). Also called *extra duty*, which may be a more modern form. Also, person who does EPD.

fast cruise (Navy) *s.* A rather paradoxical description of a simulated cruise at pierside—the ship is *fast* to its moorings.

Fideli certa merces (From at least 1837; Marines) The Latin motto found on Marine honorable discharge certificates. The accepted translation is *To the faithful one there is certain reward.* Others include *Certainly a faithful mercenary* (Navy) and *Let's go get a beer* (a marine gunnery sergeant).

field day (Modern; Navy) A day, or part thereof, devoted to cleaning up a ship or base. It usually is Friday morning, before the Friday afternoon inspection.

field scarf (Marines) A necktie. The Marine Corps picked the term because it sounds tougher (and is harder to say).

first luff (Old Sailing Navy) *s.* The first lieutenant/executive officer of a warship.

fish (Modern; Navy) 1. *s.* Torpedoes. 2. *s.* Torpedo-shaped side-scanning sonar devices towed by surface ships.

flag officer 1. (Roughly Old Sailing Navy to 19th century) The senior officer, regardless of actual grade, in command of a number of ships. 2. An admiral or a commodore. Like an Army general, he is entitled to display a flag indicating his rank.

flake down, to (Navy, Marines) 1. To lay out lines on deck in a long, rectangular pattern. 2. Another way of saying *to sack out* or *to be in the sack*, except that it usually means that the sleeper is not in his usual berth or hammock. "Joe's flaked down on deck near the after stack."

flank flank speed (Navy, Marines) A ship's top speed. By extension, applied to individuals. "When the Gunny yells, you'd better hit flank speed your first jump!"

flatfoot (1930s) *s.* A marine's term for a sailor. It probably refers to the deck apes' habit of going barefoot on steel decks.

flathat, to (Navy) *s.* To buzz, as when a Navy aviator dives low in peacetime over a base or a civilian community just to give everyone a thrill. When the first Japanese plane hit Pearl Harbor on 7 December 1941, the story goes, the Navy operations officer thought it was a US pilot flathatting and started to make out a report of violation of flight rules. A bomb explosion interrupted him.

fleet, to (Ancient, probably now obsolete; Navy) To move or change position.

fleet up, to (Of some antiquity but still used; Navy) To be advanced in position or grade, usually in the same ship or organization. It is similar to the Army *frocking*, except that an officer who is fleeted up also gets the increase (if any) in pay that goes with his new job, as well as the right to wear the appropriate insignia. Probably derived from *fleet*.

floating staff (Navy) A seaborne staff, like that of an admiral assigned to command a carrier task force.

flopdoodle (1930s; Marines) *s.* A game popular in Chinese seaport cabarets, especially in Shanghai, where the sport seems to have originated. The first marine to expose a mammary appendage of a hostess got free drinks from the others. The Russian "refugee princesses" in the more expensive places took the game in good spirits if the players were big spenders. (If the players were not, they needed their steel helmets.) Chinese hostesses were more difficult. The game was revived in Japan in the 1950s, but war and rotation had removed too many of the skilled players for it really to catch on.

foo-foo water (About 1930–41; Marines) *s.* After-shave lotion, hair lotion, or other cosmetic liquid. Most old-timers used more of it internally than externally. The onetime post motor sergeant at the Navy Mine Depot noted that bay rum drunk straight out of the bottle with a milk chaser had a pleasant spicy flavor, rather like cloves, but if you burped, it tasted like a barbershop.

fore-and-aft cap (Navy, Marines) The soft garrison cap. Also called the *piss-cutter cap*.

fourpiper (World War I to World War II; Navy, Marines) *s.* A World War I type of US destroyer, built with four "stacks."

four-point-oh attitude (Navy, Marines) *s.* The highest rating an enlisted sailor or marine can achieve on a fitness report is 4.0; thus, the attitude that would earn such a rating. " 'I like liberty' would be considered less than the reflection of a 4.0 attitude" (*All Hands*, July 1979).

four-striper (Navy) *s.* A captain; from the four stripes on his sleeve. He is the equivalent of an Army colonel, although from a junior service.

Freshwater Navy (Modern; Navy) The US Coast Guard, because part of its mission is to patrol and guard inland (freshwater as opposed to saltwater) waterways. See *Brown-water Navy*.

furry thing (Old Sailing Navy) A rabbit, which was supposed to produce incredible misfortune if brought aboard ship. Even mentioning the word *rabbit* was bad luck, whence the circumlocution. Only clergymen and coffins were considered comparable hoodoos.

galley (Ancient to Modern; Navy, Marines) A ship's kitchen. Out of force of habit, the Marine Brigade of the AEF referred to its rolling kitchens as its *galleys*.

galley yarn (Ancient to Modern; Navy, Marines) A rumor aboard ship. Much the same as *scuttlebutt* or the Army's *latrine rumor*. In the Old Sailing Navy, the cook and his helpers often were the source of gossip based on what they thought they had overheard officers say.

gammerhootching (1930s; Marines) *s.* A high old time with female company, with seduction as a distinct possibility. Here the use seems to be different from civilian use, in which *gammerhootchee*, in various spellings, usually means fellatio or cunnilingus.

gangway (Old Sailing Navy to Modern) 1. A portable bridgelike structure used by people boarding or leaving a ship at a pier. Also called *gangplank* and *gangway ladders*. 2. A cry uttered loudly to clear a passage for an officer or an awkward or dangerous load through a crowd of enlisted seamen or a work party. 3. An opening or entry post in the side or rail of a ship by which one enters or leaves the vessel.

gate guards (Modern; Marines) A derogatory term for troops performing static security missions. "This is a grunt battalion, not a buncha gate guards" (Caputo).

geedunk (Navy, Marines) *s.* Ice cream, candy bars, chewing gum, and such.

general quarters (Ancient to Modern) The most urgent call aboard a naval vessel, ordering all hands to their battle stations.

gig (Navy) Originally a light boat rowed by four to eight long oars, particularly for transporting officers between ships or from ship to shore (the "captain's gig"). This title is still applied to a roomy, comfortable motorboat carried aboard warships for the captain's use. See *barge*.

Gitmo (20th century; Navy, Marines) *s.* The US Naval Base at Guantánamo Bay, Cuba. For a wonder, we still have it.

glory hole (Navy) *s.* The chief petty officer's quarters aboard ship.

gob (World War I to 1930s) *s.* An enlisted man in the US Navy below the rank of chief petty officer.

goof hat (1930s; Marines) *s.* A cotton khaki overseas cap, with *RD* (Recruit Depot) stenciled in black on both sides. It was worn by boots for the first day or two, until they were issued their uniforms.

gooner (Marines) *s.* A gook.

green shirt (Modern; Navy) *s.* Another type of airedale. A member of the catapult, arresting gear, and maintenance crews aboard an aircraft carrier. He wears a green jersey as identification.

grinder (Marines) *s.* A parade ground. "Where do you think you are—on some grinder back at boot camp?" (West).

grog (18th and 19th centuries in original meaning) Rum mixed with water. Adm. Edward Vernon reputedly introduced it to the Royal Navy around 1740, in order to keep his sailors from getting drunk on their allowance of straight rum. (It is called *grog* because his nickname was *Old Grogram*, for a grogram cloak that he wore.) Later, a mixture of any strong liquor and water. Today, intoxicating drinks in general.

grog 'em and flog 'em (Old Sailing Navy) Supposedly the principle followed by the tougher captains to keep their ships both happy and taut. Extra grog for good performance of duty; flogging for derelictions.

Gtwotmo (Navy, Marines) *s.* Guantánamo Bay, Cuba.

guarro (Navy) A very cheap Central American drink of unknown and probably variable composition and violent effectiveness. Properly *guara*.

gummer's mate (Navy) *s.* A dental technician.

gun deck (Generally World War II; Navy and Marines) *s.* The equivalent of the Army's *snow job*, a convincing explanation that has very little relationship to what actually happened.

gunner's daughter (18th century to early 19th century) A limber cane, usually of rattan but sometimes made from the dried backbone of a shark, carried by the master gunner of a warship. Unruly ship's boys might get to *kiss the gunner's daughter* by being laid across a gun and flogged with it.

gunny (Marines) *s.* A gunnery sergeant; in actual practice, the field first sergeant and NCO in charge of training for a company and battery. A good person to stay well clear of, because he is not noted for his good disposition. The assistant warden of the post brig is usually a gunnery sergeant.

guns 1. (Old Sailing Navy) *s.* A gunner's mate. 2. (Modern Navy) A ship's gunnery officer or an ordnance warrant officer.

gun striker (Marines) A member of a gun crew on sea duty charged with the permanent care of the gun. As a special privilege, he is the only man aboard who is permitted to set up his shaving gear on the breech of the gun. This was a great advantage on the crowded gundeck of a pre–World War II battleship.

handsomely (Ancient to Modern; Navy) To do something (for example, lowering a lifeboat) very carefully, keeping it under full control.

happy ship (Navy, Marines) *s.* A ship with a contented crew. It also may be a taut ship if its captain is an expert leader of men, but often it is somewhat sloppy and inefficient.

harness cask (Old Sailing Navy) A barrel of salt horse (corned beef).

hawsehole hawsepipe (Navy, Marines) A hole in the stern or bow of a vessel through which an anchor cable passes. *To come through the hawsehole* meant to come up through the various grades in the Navy from common seaman to commissioned officer, a comparatively rare and very difficult feat. This expression was well established in the merchant marine at the beginning of the 19th century and is probably much older. *Hawsepipe* is a modern version of hawsehole.

head The Navy's term for latrine (toilet), derived from its traditional location in the beak-head of a sailing ship.

headman head orderly The sailor responsible for the cleanliness of the head. Sometimes he is mock-grandiloquently styled *captain of the head.*

head yellow shirt (Modern; Navy) *s.* The officer who is in charge of aircraft aboard a carrier, because of the yellow jersey he wears as identification. See *yellow shirt.*

heave the lead, to (Navy) An old, old term with two very different meanings. 1. To heave a sounding lead to determine the depth of water under the ship's bow. Also, on occasion, to check the composition of the sea bottom, samples of which stick to a soaped or pitched lead. This is a hard, demanding job. 2. *s.* To goof off, to ghost. A possible source of this meaning is that the leadsman would be a picked seaman or petty officer who seldom got the really dirty jobs aboard. Also, since one would only heave the lead in shallow water, for most of a cruise there would be no occasion to do it.

heavy sugar (1930s to 1940s; Marines) *s.* A steady girl friend, for whom one felt more than a casual affinity. In the highly professional Corps prior to 1940, this was considered a disaster, since if one ranked below platoon sergeant, nothing much could come of it.

hell below zero (World War II; Navy) The Murmansk run, over which lend-lease supplies were brought to the Soviet

Union by sea around the northern tip of Norway.

hell-bird (World War II; Navy) *s.* A Japanese kamikaze plane.

hell's bells (World War II; Navy) *s.* A warning device (technically, a frequency-modulated sonar) used on submerged submarines to detect the presence of a minefield. It made an unholy uproar when activated.

hit the deck, to (Old Navy, Marines; later borrowed by the Army) To get up in the morning; generally, to stop resting or loafing, and get moving. During World War I and subsequent unpleasantries, marines might instinctively use it for *hit the dirt.*

hog waller (1930s; Marines) *s.* A dance hall, usually with country and western music, square dancing, and fistfighting as its primary attractions.

hoist (Navy) One or more flags run up together on a warship's signal halyards as a message to adjacent ships.

Horn, the (Navy) Cape Horn, either the mainland or the adjacent islands, where the seas are notoriously rough and passage is among the most difficult in the world. To have been around the Horn was considerable proof that you were a foul-weather sailor.

Horse Marines (World War I to World War II) The US Marine Corps's mounted detachment at Peking, China. The term was undoubtedly borrowed from the British.

Hot stuff! (Navy) Look out! Out of the way! The yell of a messman to clear the way when he is carrying a rack of hot food to the mess deck.

hunter-killer group (World War II and later; Navy) A small naval force usually consisting of one escort carrier and four destroyer-type warships. This combination was especially effective during 1943–45 in hunting down German submarines in the mid-Atlantic.

huss, to give a (Modern; Marines) *s.* To give a helping hand. From the UH-34 helicopter (originally designated the HUS). When calling for medical evacuation helicopters in Vietnam, marines asked for the huss (*Leatherneck*, March 1976, p. 3).

inaptitude (Through World War II; Marines) The equivalent of the Army Section 8, discharge for mental incompetence. It was neither honorable nor dishonorable.

Indian drawers (1930s; Marines) *s.* A type of issue underwear that would "creep up on you and cut you."

in his boat with his colors flying (Colonial to Modern) An archaic English expression still used to indicate that the officer referred to is going about his official duties and not just taking a recreational joyride in his gig or launch.

in ordinary (Sailing Navy) A term of great antiquity, probably borrowed from the British, and used into the later part of the 19th century. A ship was in ordinary when decommissioned and laid up—the equivalent of modern *mothballing.* Ships were anchored in shallow harbor areas; their yards and spars were sent down, and all running gear was removed. Usually they were roofed over to protect them from the weather. The crews would be discharged, except for a few men to guard and maintain the ships.

jack 1. (Old Sailing Navy to World War I) A sailor, especially an ordinary seaman. *Jack*, as a generic name for the common man, dates from the Middle Ages. *Jacks, Jackies,* or *Jackys* frequently were daubed with tar from the rigging of their ships, and so came to be *Jack Tars.* (A politer term, *blue jacket*, seems to have been more literary than nautical.) See *gob, Jack Nastyface.* 2. (Navy) A small flag flown at the bow of a warship. The US jack is a blue flag with fifty white stars in rows—the union portion of the national ensign. The name probably comes from the old use of *jack* for an unimportant person. It is flown from a *jack staff* and is not saluted or given any of the honors accorded the national ensign.

jackass officer (World War I and later) *s.* A Navy officer who had come up through the hawsehole by promotion from enlisted ranks. He would be snubbed by Naval Academy graduates and given the most undesirable assignments. Gradually, this term has been replaced by the slightly kinder *mustang.* See *mustang* in Army definitions.

Jack Nastyface (18th century; British) A common sailor.

jack-o'-the-dust (Ancient to Modern; Navy) An enlisted sailor in the ship's supply department. His regular work includes keeping the storerooms clean—hence, his title.

jeep carrier (World War II; Navy) *s.* An escort carrier.

Jimmy Legs (Old Sailing Navy) A warship's master-at-arms. May still be heard occasionally.

Joe (Navy, Marines) *s.* Coffee. "Pass the Joe, please, with sidearms."

khaki sacker (Post–World War II; Marines) *s.* A man who carries his lunch in a brown paper bag. Equivalent to *brown-bagger.*

kid 1. (Ancient to Civil War) A small wooden tub used to carry the cooked food of a mess (six to eight men) of sailors from the ship's galley to their usual eating place on deck. Originally, messmates ate directly out of it, but gradually individual plates or bowls came into use and *kid* became a serving dish. 2. (Old Sailing Navy) A sailor's individual eating bowl, usually made of pewter or enameled metal.

kiwi (Modern; Marines) *s.* A goof-off. Named after the kiwi bird. See Army entry.

knot (Ancient to Modern; Navy, Marines) A unit of speed: 1 nautical mile (6076.115 feet) per hour. The origin of the word is from actual knots tied in the log line, which, with an hourglass, was used anciently to reckon a ship's speed. Thus, when a sailor is *making knots*, he is moving rapidly, perhaps as a member of a liberty party heading for the nearest bar.

ladder (Ancient to Modern) A sailor's term for a stairway. A naval officer begins this usage when he arrives at the Naval Academy at Annapolis; an old salt uses the term to describe any staircase ashore, no matter how grandly designed.

lance lance corporal (Marines) An old British term for a probationary corporal; recently adopted by the US Marines to distinguish a somewhat similar enlisted grade between private and corporal. See Army entry.

landsmen landmen (Old Sailing Navy) Members of a ship's crew who were not seamen. During the Revolution and the War of 1812, privateers might enlist landsmen for service as marines. The term might also mean would-be sailors on their first cruise.

lash-up (Marines) A potent term of disapproval, applicable to almost anything. "What kind of damn lash-up is this outfit?" However, Marine officers have told us that during the 1940s *lash-up* meant merely a group of anything, without a derogatory implication. An ancient naval term, *Lash up!* was originally the command for newly awakened sailors to tie their hammocks and bedding into snug, cylindrical bundles, which would then be stored in the rope nettings along the spar deck's bulwarks. Failure to make a neat, tight lash-up was reprehensible—and probably unhealthy.

lay, to (Ancient to Modern; Navy) To go. *To lay aloft* was to get up into the rigging; *to lay out*, to man the yards; *to lay below*, to come down from the rigging (or, if on deck, to go below); *to lay aft*, to go toward the ship's stern; etc. 2. To aim a gun, whether in the artillery ashore or on a warship.

letter of marque (Colonial to War of 1812; Navy) Properly *Letter of Marque and Reprisal*. A commission granted by a government in time of war authorizing a privately owned vessel to engage in hostilities against the enemy. Such a ship might be termed a *letter of marque*, but the common American name was *privateer*.

liberty (Ancient to Modern; Navy, Marines) Permission to spend time ashore, or the time so spent; the equivalent of the soldier's *pass*. Officially termed *shore leave*. It is a really happy event after being at sea for a long time and a time of profit for bars, curio shops, and sea gulls. A liberty party is a group going ashore to enjoy liberty; *liberty blues* are the Dress Blue uniforms marines wear on liberty in cold weather. Not all ports are *liberty ports*; some are closed for reasons of health or international politics.

line (Navy) Naval officers are divided, similarly to Army officers, into line and staff. Only line officers exercise command of ships and major shore installations.

Link the Chink (Vietnam; Marines) *s.* A Vietnamese. See *Luke the Gook* in military definitions.

lion (World War II and later; Navy) The largest type of advanced naval base. It has facilities for docking and repairing the largest warships, ordnance shops, tank farms, hospitals, and necessary defensive installations. See *acorn, cub*.

Little Portsmouth (Navy) *s.* The Naval Detention Prison at Portsmouth, Virginia. It is a combination of station disciplinary barracks and accommodation for transient prisoners en route to Big Portsmouth.

loblolly (Old Sailing Navy) A thick gruel fed to sick or wounded sailors. It later "came ashore" to mean a mudhole or any mess in general.

loblolly boy (Old Sailing Navy) A ship's boy, assigned to its sick bay. This term was standard in the Royal Navy in the early 18th century; as late as 1881 it was used in America for a sick-bay man or nurse.

lobscouse (Old Sailing Navy) The nautical version of Army *slum*—salt beef, broken biscuit, and onions stewed together and "well peppered." Some accounts describe it as a hash of crushed biscuit and any odds and ends available.

lucky bag (Navy) A ship's lost-and-found department, kept by the M/A to store articles left lying around. To recover an article from it, you have to put in an appropriate number of hours of police duty, just to remind you to be neat and tidy in the future. Unclaimed articles are sold at auction for benefit of the ship's fund. In the Old Sailing Navy, it really was a bag.

M/A (Navy) Master-at-Arms, the ship's chief janitor and custodian of its minor criminals. His actual rating is usually chief boatswain's mate or chief gunner's mate. He reports directly to the ship's executive officer and is not noted for responding to reasonable arguments, no matter how intelligently presented. He sees that the EPDs do not get too fat and lazy.

Madame Kiss-Kiss (1920s and 1940s) A somewhat legendary madame in Shanghai who reputedly ran her house on a street known as the Street of a Thousand Delights, or some such picturesque Chinese name. (Marines called it the *Street of a Thousand Ass Holes.*) During actual interviews in the field from 1937 to 1941, we never could find anyone who had met Madame Kiss-Kiss. However, all old China hands insisted that she was real. All of them had buddies who knew a guy who had met her, even if no two of them agreed as to her age, size, hair color, and original nationality. Otherwise, we would swear that she was as mythical as the unicorn. May she rest in peace.

maggot (World War II; Marines) Form of address used to a prisoner undergoing sentence. Originated at The Joint, the Naval Prison at Portsmouth, New Hampshire.

make a hat, to (Modern; Marines) *s.* To escape, to run away. "I can hear them splashing through the paddies, sir. They're making a hat" (West).

make a swoop, to (Modern; Marines) *s.* To make a long trip in a short period of time, like traveling home on weekend liberty.

making colors (Antiquity uncertain; Navy) The ceremony of raising the national colors in the morning and lowering them at sunset. The ceremony is similar to the Army's *retreat.* The band, if available, and the guard are present. If warships of other nations are near by, their national anthems are also played after ours at morning colors.

man-eater (Marines) An attractive nymphomaniac. It has always been a marine's fondest dream to be captured by a man-eater and held in captivity for an indeterminate period.

Man, the (Generally World War II and later; Navy) The commanding officer; equivalent to the Army's the *Old Man.*

marine officer (Old Sailing Navy; primarily British) An empty bottle, "marine officers being held useless by the seamen."

mate (Old Sailing Navy to Modern) Originally, an assistant to a warrant officer. Today, an enlisted petty officer, equivalent of an Army or Marine NCO. The titles of mates—*boatswain's mate, gunner's mate,* and the like—often are unchanged from the days of the sailing navy, but now there are also *pharmacist's mates, electrician's mates,* and similar new handles. Usually they are still known by an abbreviation of their function. Thus, a *gunner's mate* is *guns*; the *boatswain's mate, boats.*

mership (World War II) A handy contraction of *merchant ship.*

middie mid (Colonial to Modern; Navy) Midshipman. Originally a boy or young man serving aboard a warship as an officer candidate, ranking between the warrant officers and the petty officers. In 1845, Secretary of the Navy George Bancroft assembled them at the new US Naval Academy, and the title since then has meant a student of that school. A midshipman ranks below an ensign.

midnight small stores (Navy) *s.* Theft or misappropriation of government property that is not readily available through normal supply channels. The equivalent of Army *moonlight requisition, midnight requisition.*

midrats (Modern; Navy) *s.* Leftovers. Food such as soup, crackers, sandwiches served to sailors before and after mid-watch (*All Hands*, July 1979).

Mister (Navy, Marines) The traditional form of address to warrant officers, ensigns, and Marine second lieutenants. When marines are serving with Army organizations, they cause much unhappiness by addressing Army shavetails as *Mister.* (The Army also followed the custom before World War II, apparently on the theory that a second lieutenant really was not an officer yet. It was painful.)

monitor fever (Civil War; Navy) A form of ship's fever, resulting from a combination of malaria, typhoid, combat fatigue, and the general strains of life aboard the cramped, poorly ventilated, stiflingly hot armored warships on blockade duty off southern ports.

monkey dicks (Generally World War II; Marines) *s.* Vienna sausage.

monkey fist (Navy) A length of halyard line woven around a hunk of lead and attached to a heaving line. It is used in docking a ship. As the marines describe its use, a coxswain throws the monkey fist at the marine sentry on the dock. If he misses, the marine takes the line, heaves a hawser to the dock, and drops the eye over a bollard. If, on the other hand, the monkey fist kills the marine, the ship's company take up a collection to buy beer for the coxswain, the marine is replaced, and the game starts all over again.

mosquito fleet 1. (Civil War; USA) *s.* The Light Drafts, the tinclad Mississippi River gunboats. 2. (World War I) *s.* A subchaser unit.

move the head, to (Old Navy to Modern) Every warship of any size has more than one head for enlisted personnel. Ships large enough to carry a marine detachment have a separate head for the marines. Periodically, one head would have to be closed for repairs, and the men normally using it would have to go to another one. See *piss call* in military terms.

nails (Old Sailing Navy) A ship's carpenter's mate.

nigger steak (1940s–1950s; Marines) *s.* Fried liver.

no-moon night (Modern; Marines) A night on which there is no moon is a good night for an ambush or sneak attack. "Beware the no-moon night" (Webb).

North China Marines (Pre–World War II) The Marine guards stationed at the American legations at Peking and Tientsin. They were trapped when the Japanese suddenly entered World War II, and had to fight the war in a Japanese prison camp.

office hours (Marines) *s.* Up before the company commander for disciplinary action. The same as the Army's *on the carpet.* "Okay, Donovan. It's office hours for you."

officer of the deck (Navy) The naval version of the Army's *OD.* He is a line officer, responsible for the operation of the ship during his watch. All persons aboard her, except the captain and the executive officer, are subject to his orders. His station is on the bridge when the ship is under way and on the quarterdeck when she is at anchor.

officers' country (Navy) That portion of the ship where the officers' cabins and wardroom (dining room and lounge) are located. It is out of bounds to enlisted men, except those on duty there.

old Joe (1930s; Navy, Marines) *s.* Syphilis.

one-way (1930s; Marines) *s.* Selfish, mean. "He's a real one-way bastard."

our chickens (World War II) *s.* Term given by submarine crewmen to US fighter aircraft detailed to escort submarines engaged in rescuing downed pilots. It was a major relief to have US Navy aircraft on their side for a change.

overhead (Ancient to Modern; Navy, Marines) The ceiling.

over the side (Marines) Disembarking from a warship or transport at sea, usually by means of a cargo net hung over the side, into small boats or landing craft.

Panamanian love call (Navy) *s.* Pssssst! The traditional signal of a prostitute that she is open for business.

petty officer (Ancient to Modern; Navy) The equivalent of an Army or Marine NCO.

picture window (Navy) *s.* The faceplate in the helmet of the Mark 12 mixed-gas diving outfit; so called because the plate is so large.

pigboat (Old Navy) *s.* A submarine. Living conditions in the early submarines were rough. The British developed this expressive term before World War II; we borrowed it from them.

Pineapple Navy (World War II; Navy) *s.* Naval units and personnel permanently stationed in the Hawaiian Islands.

pink lady 1. (1930s; Navy) A drink based on torpedo juice, the alcohol fuel that drove the American steam-propelled torpedo of the period. Jolly tars of the Asiatic Squadron's destroyers would bleed it off for festive occasions. Thereafter, the torpedoes ran crooked—and so did those sailors. 2. (World War II to Modern) A drink used for social occasions by Navy medical personnel. Medicinal alcohol with either pink coloring matter or phenolphthalein added.

pipe (Ancient to Modern) A whistle carried on a fancy lanyard by a boatswain's mate. He tootles it on official and ceremonial occasions. But do not call it a *whistle.* He will be outraged enough at such an insult to Navy tradition to hurl you down the slop chute. Also sometimes known as *boatswain's call.*

pipe, to To sound a call on the pipe. With marines, even when serving ashore, mess call is *pipe for chow.* See *pipe down.*

pipe down (Ancient to Modern; Navy) Properly, a call on the boatswain's pipe, signaling the completion of an all-hands evolution. The watch on deck can resume duties; the off-duty watch can go below and try to get some sleep. From this, it also has become an order to keep quiet and, as such, has passed into general use.

piss and punk (Navy) *s.* Bread and water, a diet formerly fed inmates of the brig.

piss-cutter hat (Marines) *s.* The soft garrison cap.

plane-pushers (World War II and later; Navy) *s.* Plane-handlers, the airedales detailed to hanhandle carrier aircraft into position preparatory to launching or after landing.

plank owner (Considerable Antiquity; Navy) A member of the original crew aboard a newly commissioned warship. By tradition, each man owned one plank in the vessel.

pogue poge (Considerable Antiquity; Navy, Marines) 1. *s.* A male sex pervert who plays the female role, the opposite of a Turk. 2. By extension, a rear-echelon, noncombat marine. "The rear pogues wore them curled up" (Webb).

pogey bait (Navy, Marines) *s.* Candy. See Army entry.

poop (Old Sailing Navy) A superstructure at the stern of a ship. It was officers' country, and the captain's command post in battle.

port (Navy) Left. The port side of a ship is to your left when you are on board ship and are facing the bow (front). It is a comparatively new word, as US nautical terms go, having replaced the older *larboard* within the history of the United States. In a howling gale, *larboard* and *starboard* sounded too much alike.

powder monkey (Old Sailing Navy) A ship's boy who carried the powder cartridges from the magazine to a gun in action.

Private's Delight (1930s; Marines) *s.* A small bottle of bay rum, purchased at the ship's store for 18 cents, a beverage within the means of a private paid 70 cents a day.

PT boat (World War II; Navy) Patrol Torpedo boat, typically a 35-ton boat, 81 feet long, armed with torpedo tubes, two 20mm or 25mm guns, and depth charges. Capable of 45 knots.

puffing (Late 1930s; Marines) *s.* Getting drunk.

purple shirt (Modern; Navy) *s.* Another species of airedale. A member of the fueling crew aboard an aircraft carrier. He wears a purple jersey as identification.

Q-boat (World War I; Navy) A merchant ship armed with concealed guns and depth charges; used in areas where enemy submarines were operating, in the hope that the Germans would take such a ship for a helpless tramp steamer and surface to sink her by gunfire.

quarterdeck (Navy) In ships of normal construction, on which the officers' country is aft, the quarterdeck is that portion of the main deck from the main mast to the stern. Most of the ship's ceremonial functions are performed there. In those ships where the officers' quarters are not in the stern, the captain defines the location of the quarterdeck. By old custom, Navy personnel never smoke on the quarterdeck, never appear on it unless they are properly uniformed, and never walk on the starboard side of the quarterdeck. That area is reserved for the captain.

quartergunner (Ancient) A master gunner's assistant. A member of the master gunner's department, ranking below the gunner's mate(s). Normally, there was one quarter gunner to each "division" (a variable number) of the ship's guns. This rating existed in the US Navy from 1797 to 1893; some American privateers and pirates also had quarter gunners.

quartermaster 1. (Old Navy) The man at the wheel of a Navy ship, regardless of his actual rating. Today, he is called a *helmsman.* (The term *wheelman* is for freshwater sailors only; it makes bluewater sailors wince.) 2. (Navy) A petty officer whose duties are related to navigational equipment. Over the years his functions have changed considerably. They once included signal equipment, now handled by signalmen.

queer toast (1930s; Marines) *s.* French toast. Also called *queer bread.* See Army entry.

railroad trousers (Considerable Antiquity) The Navy officer's name for his gold-striped full-dress trousers.

range ponies (Modern; Marines) *s.* Ragamuffin kids in general, especially Armed Forces offspring.

red lead (Navy, Marines) *s.* Tomato ketchup.

red-lead fleet (Post–World War II) *s.* Decommissioned ships, mothballed and kept for future emergencies.

red shirt (Modern; Navy) *s.* A crash, salvage, and fire-fighting airedale on the flight deck of an aircraft carrier. He wears a red jersey as identification.

Reveille Special (Marines) *s.* The 0300 train from Washington, D.C., to Quantico, Virginia.

Rocks and Shoals (Pre–1960; Navy) *s.* The Navy's equivalent of the Army's *Devil's Article*. Both vanished in 1950 when the civilian-minded *Uniform Code of Military Justice* was imposed on the Armed Forces.

ro-ro (Modern; Navy) *s.* A roll-on/roll-off type of vessel, designed to take aboard or discharge a cargo of fully loaded vehicles in a hurry.

run up, to (Probably as early as World War I; Marines) *s.* To put an offender on charges (or on the crime sheet) for misconduct.

saltwater call (Pre-1940; Navy, Marines) A bugle call either used only aboard ship or having a different meaning when afloat than when on shore. For examples of the first type: (*a*) "Motor launch number ———." Two bars, followed by a series of toots corresponding to the number of the launch, and (*b*) Liberty Call, the same. As an example of the second type, the saltwater call "Torpedo defense" was the same as the on-shore "To arms."

salty salt (Navy, Marines) Seasoned to sea duty; veteran. Often used as a sarcasm when the individual is not salty and insists on talking as if he were. "That ain't salt! That's dandruff! Now shut your mouth!" Other nautical put-downs for such an occasion include "I've spent more time on a life raft than you've got in the Navy" and "My seabag's been past more lighthouses than yours has telephone poles."

sand and canvas (1930s; Navy, Marines) *s.* An unofficial beauty treatment (an enforced bath, with canvas for washrags and sand for soap) used to cure a crumb. If forcibly administered, it could hospitalize the recipient. Usually just the threat that a vigilance committee of tough enlisted types would administer it was enough to make the most confirmed crumb become exceptionally fastidious. (The Old Army had an equivalent ceremony, employing issue scrub brushes and GI soap, but we regret to report we cannot recall its name.)

scuttlebutt (Ancient to Modern; Navy, Marines) Originally, an open cask of drinking water placed on deck. The crew could help themselves from it unless water was in short supply and being rationed. It traditionally served like the water cooler or Coke machine in a modern office: sailors gathered there for a few minutes of loafing and gossip. It thus became the ship's major source of rumors and misinformation, collectively termed *scuttlebutt*, the nautical equivalent of the Army's *latrine rumors*. Today, the name may also be applied to the drinking fountain of a ship.

seabag (Ancient to Modern) A sort of canvas sack used by sailors and marines as a steamer trunk. It was designed to prove that all matter can be compressed to the point of infinity. Theoretically, an old-time marine could pack a locomotive and a string of boxcars into his seabag and still have room for a Shanghai cabaret and twelve White Russian princesses.

Sea Bees (World War II to Modern; Navy) From *CB*, short for *Construction Bat-*

talion. CB is translated by the Sea Bees themselves as *Confused Bastards.*

sea daddy (Old Navy) *s.* An experienced seaman who teaches a new sailor his trade. In the old days, he literally helped him to learn the ropes.

seagoing bellhop (World War I and later; Navy) *s.* A marine.

sea gull (Navy, Marines) *s.* A prostitute who specializes in sailors and marines. She often follows the fleet from port to port. Frequently a purveyor of old Joe.

sea lawyer (Navy, Marines) *s.* Someone who is a self-appointed expert on how to beat all the rules, a soul brother to the Army's guardhouse lawyer. He usually winds up with a tail gunner.

secure, to (Ancient to Modern; Navy, Marines) To stop doing something and/or put it away. *Secure the butts* means put away the targets on the firing range, and get ready to march back to the cantonment area.

Semper fi (Modern, and perhaps somewhat earlier; Marines) From the motto of the Marines, *Semper fidelis* 'always faithful'. 1. A brief way of stating "I've got mine. How are you doing?" If your buddy drinks your whole pitcher of beer while you are in the head, and you complain about it, all your fellow marines present will yell, "Semper fi," and wave their index fingers in a mysterious voodoo sign. This shows that they are highly sympathetic to your misfortune and that, if you will buy another pitcher of beer, they guarantee it will not vanish the next time you turn your back. For some reason, no one has ever tested them in that way. 2. Go to hell, screw you, fuck you. When pronounced with the appropriate degree of cynicism and gestures or facial expressions indicating the speaker's dissatisfaction or contempt. "We're in the Corps, P. J. The Crotch. Semper fi and fuck your buddy" (Caputo). 3. Take your choice of the two above, or try to combine them for a true picture.

shakedown cruise (Antiquity uncertain; Navy) The first cruise by a Navy vessel after being commissioned or after a major overhaul. Its purpose is to check out the vessel and its equipment, and to familiarize the crew with the vessel's characteristics, in short, to shake everything down into place.

Shake out a reef (Old Sailing Navy, and later) Hurry up! A reef was a portion of a sail rolled up and tied down in order to reduce the area exposed to the wind. When reefs were loosened—shaken out—the vessel would sail faster.

shellback (Old Sailing Navy to Modern) One who has been initiated into the ceremonies of sailing across the equator—hence, a veteran seaman.

She sails! (Old Sailing Navy) She (a woman) is easily conquered; she is an easy lay.

ship over, to (Ancient to Modern; Navy, Marines) To reenlist.

ship's corporal (Navy) An assistant to the master-at-arms. The term was well established by the Civil War. Its origin can apparently be traced to the assignment of a Marine NCO to this duty.

ship's service The Navy equivalent of the *PX*. It may be in the middle of the Mohave Desert, but it still is the *Ship's Service Store.*

shivering Liz (20th century; Navy) *s.* Jello.

shooting pads (1930s; Marines) *s.* Pancakes. Like the thick elbow and shoulder pads on a shooting jacket, which were supposedly equally edible.

shot at your feet (Navy) Burial at sea. The dead man was sewn into his hammock with a cannonball at the bottom to take him down to Davy Jones's locker feet first.

shove off, to (Old Sailing Navy to Modern) Originally, to push a boat away from the beach, but the expression has spread through the Armed Forces as a synonym for *to leave*. "Let's shove off." In the imperative mood, it is an or-else invitation to do so.

sick bay (Navy) A ship's dispensary.

sidearms (1930s; Marines) Sugar and cream, to go with coffee. "Pass the Joe and the sidearms, please."

sight in, to (1930s; Marines) *s.* To take a good look at something, probably with future action in mind. If a comrade is sighting in on your girl friend or the bottle hidden in your laundry bag, you had best be vigilant.

Silence! (Antiquity uncertain; Navy) A command given by an officer or any member of a gun crew when it is necessary to stop firing the gun, usually because of a malfunction of some sort. When the command is uttered, all members of the gun crew immediately stand still and await instructions.

silver fish See *dolphins*.

simple servant (Modern; Navy) *s.* A play on *civil servant*. Any derogatory implication is undoubtedly intentional.

skinhead (Prior to 1960; Marines) *s.* A *boot,* because of his new, close haircut.

skids (Modern; Navy) *s.* Sailors' bunks aboard a submarine.

skimmer (Modern; Navy, submarines) *s.* A surface vessel.

skipper (Ancient to Modern) The commanding officer, especially the captain of a ship.

skivvies (Early 20th century to present; Marines) Summer underwear, a *skivvy shirt and shorts.* Not to be confused with the English *skivvy*, a chambermaid, also sometimes found next to a marine's skin. See Army entry.

skunk (Modern; Navy, submarine) *s.* An unidentified surface-ship contact.

sky out, to (Modern; Marines) *s.* To run away or to leave precipitously. "Looks like you'll be skying out on us, huh?" (Webb).

slop chest (Old Sailing Navy) A ship's store, controlled by the purser. It sold articles of clothing to the seamen. Before naval uniforms were officially adopted, a captain could get his crew into standardized clothing by stocking his ship's slop chest with it.

slop chute (Navy, Marines) 1. The ship's garbage chute. 2. *s.* An enlisted man's "wet canteen," one where beer is sold.

slops (Old Sailing Navy) Clothing and bedding used by seamen.

slush (Old Sailing Navy) Fat and grease from the galley, used to lubricate and waterproof masts and spars.

slush fund (Modern; Navy) A fund originally based on proceeds from selling excess slush to commercial firms; the fund was used for the benefit of the enlisted men.

slushing oil (Navy) A mixture of fish oil and Copenhagen tar used as a rust preventive on steel decks.

small stores (Navy) A wholesale clothing store operated by the Navy, where sailors may purchase uniforms and accessories.

smoking lamp (Apparently Ancient to Modern; Navy) A now-legendary lamp that used to be kept lighted during the hours when smoking was permitted in certain parts of the ship. Such lamps were actually used into the first years of the 20th century, but it is doubtful if any sailor now alive ever saw one. Nevertheless, aboard ship today, the announcement that "the smoking lamp is out throughout the ship" is the signal to put out your butt or knock out your pipe. See Army usage.

snapping in (1930s; Marines) *s.* Practice of any sort. The term originated from dry firing (going through the motions without using ammunition) at rifle practice.

snipe (Navy) *s.* A seaman assigned to the ship's engineering branch. See *deck ape.*

snooper (World War II and later; Navy) *s.* A reconnaissance plane, which first locates and then maintains contact with enemy forces.

snotty The old, old Royal Navy nickname for a midshipman, undoubtedly coined during the early years when many midshipmen were in their earliest teens, living under rather miserable conditions, and thus frequently apt to have running noses. The term is well known in the US Navy, but apparently has never been applied to American mids. *A snotty's nurse* was the officer, usually a lieutenant, in charge of a warship's midshipmen.

son of a bitch from out of town (World War II; Navy) *s.* A visiting expert—someone from higher authority who thinks he can solve all your problems without ever having experienced them.

soldier soger sojer (Old Sailing Navy) A lazy sailor, a shirker.

sorry See Army entry.

SP (Antiquity unknown; Navy) Shore Patrol, the Navy's version of Military Police. They patrol areas where the natural exuberance of sailors on liberty ashore might become annoying to the taxpayers.

SPAR (World War II to Modern) The women's reserve of the US Coast Guard. Individual members are called *Spars.* From the Coast Guard motto, *Semper paratus* 'always ready'.

spick itch (20th century; Navy, Marines) *s.* Athlete's foot.

spit kid spit kit 1. The Navy equivalent of a spittoon, usually a square wooden box filled with sand. Spit kids are now more often found in barracks ashore than on ships afloat. 2. An old nautical term for a small vessel. During World Wars I and II, the Navy applied it to a variety of little warships "larger than a PT boat and smaller than a destroyer," like subchasers, minesweepers, and oceangoing tugs.

Splice the main brace! (Ancient to Modern; Navy) A ship captain's traditional command for the issue of a ration of intoxicating liquor (usually in the diluted form of grog) to all hands. Also known as *top off the boom!* or *Sweat up the halyards!* Virtuous souls in and out of the Navy, especially Adm. Andrew H. Foote of Mississippi River gunboat fame, finally ended the official practice of this honorable custom on 30 September 1862. The words, however, have survived, and certain antiquarians still use them before personal libations.

splinter fleet See *subchaser.* In World War II, *splinter fleet* was sometimes used to designate a force of Navy minesweepers or any wooden vessels.

spud 1. (Relatively Modern; Navy, Marines) *s.* Vodka, or a person who overindulges in vodka, normally identified by his jaundiced complexion. 2. A potato. Potatoes are stored in *spud lockers.*

spud coxswain (Navy) *s.* A KP. He peels potatoes (today, he runs the machine that peels them) and prepares green vegetables. Generally considered a good detail to pull.

squilgee (Navy) 1. Originally a small swab. Later, by the time of the Civil War, the equivalent of the modern squeegee. 2. A contemptuous term for a lazy, worthless sailor.

SS Submarine. Slang name is *pigboat.*

stamps (Modern; Navy) *s.* The mail orderly.

starboard (Ancient to Modern; Navy) Right. When you face the bow (front) of a vessel aboard ship, the starboard rail is to your right.

start, to (Old Sailing Navy) 1. To encourage a seaman to move quickly and smartly about his duties by the application of a rope's end or other handy stimulator. This was a special responsibility of the bosun and his mates. 2. To discharge the ship's water supply. This was sometimes done to lighten a ship so that it could get off a shoal or sail faster when pursued by a superior enemy.

starter (Old Sailing Navy) A length of rope, usually carried coiled inside the hat of a bosun's mate. Used for starting laggard seamen.

Street of a Thousand Ass Holes (1930s; Marines) A famous street, just off Bubbling Well Road in Shanghai, the site of flourishing businesses that specialized in soothing fevered brows of foreign servicemen and relieving them of their money. Madame Kiss-Kiss supposedly began there as a hatcheck girl or something of the sort. Another such street is reported to have flourished in Tsingtao.

striker (Navy) A sailor who is training for promotion to a specific rating. See also *gun striker.*

stripes (Navy) Commissioned officers' insignia of grade, worn on the cuffs of their coats.

subchaser (World War I; Navy) A 100-foot wooden antisubmarine vessel employed in coastal waters. Called collectively *Cinderellas*, *mosquitoes*, and the *splinter fleet.*

sundowner (Old Sailing Navy, still occasionally heard) A martinet who runs a supertaut ship. Originally, the term was applied to captains who gave their crews liberty ashore only until sundown.

swab (Old Navy to Modern) A common seaman, so called because swabbing decks and guns was one of his major occupations. Also *swab jockey.*

For he ain't like some of the swabs
I've seen
As would go and lie to a poor marine.

swabs (Late 18th century on) The epaulettes formerly worn with Navy officers' full-dress uniforms.

sweeps (Old Sailing Navy) Very long, heavy oars used in emergencies to move the smaller warships, such as sloops, cutters, or brigs. For some reason, the same implement aboard a galley was called an *oar.*

sweet mama (1930s; Marines) *s.* A marine's paramour, usually older than he is and possessed of either a wealthy husband or a good job. Provides food and drinks as well as bedroom gymnastics. The ideal sweet mama owns a flourishing bar two blocks from the gates of the navy yard. Some sweet mamas have a touch of nymphomania and a half-dozen young sailors and marines in attendance.

swipes (Colonial; Navy) Small (weak) beer, usually of low quality, issued aboard ships of the Royal Navy. Since the ship's purser issued it, frequently termed *purser's swipes.*

tadpole (Modern; Navy) *s.* A sailor who is engaged in basic underwater demolition or SEAL (Sea-Air-Land; usually used as *Sea-Air-Land team*) training, possibly because he has not yet become a fully qualified frogman.

tail-end Charlie (Modern; Marines) *s.* The rear element in a unit on the move.

tarpaulin (Old Sailing Navy) *s.* A sailor. A tarpaulin hat was a characteristic sailor's headgear, typically a stiff straw hat covered with canvas and lacquered black to make it waterproof. When worn for full dress, it usually had ribbons with the ship's name on them. Also called a *glazed hat.*

taut ship A ship with a well-trained, highly disciplined crew, always ready for anything, but possibly not a happy ship. An officer may be described as *running a taut ship.*

TBS (World War II to Modern; Navy) Talk Between Ships. A short-range voice radio.

That's high (Ancient to Modern; Navy) Cease hoisting! An order.

three-way woman (Navy, Marines) *s.* A woman who practices all the more exotic heterosexual acts.

tie-tie (Late 19th century to 1940s; Navy, Marines) A short piece of ⅛-inch line with a brass ring at each end to prevent raveling. It was used as a clothespin at sea, where the stiff breezes would be too much for conventional wooden pins. Similar to *clothes stops.*

timberclad (Civil War; USA) A wooden warship protected by a heavy extra sheathing of timbers, preferably oak. Most timberclads were river gunboats, hastily improvised early in the war when there was a shortage of armor plate.

tin can (World War I and later; Navy) *s.* A destroyer, particularly appropriate for the small four stackers.

tin fish (20th century; Navy) *s.* A torpedo.

top (Colonial to early 20th century) A platform built about the head (or top) of the lower portion of a ship's mast. It furnished a working area and a support for the rigging of the mast's higher sections. In combat in the Old Sailing Navy, it was a handy post for marine sharpshooters. Later, it became a fire-control station. Today, it has been replaced by radar installations.

top cutter (Early 20th century; Marines) *s.* The company first sergeant.

topmen (Old Sailing Navy) The elite of the enlisted seamen. Their primary duties were aloft in the rigging.

topside ratings (Navy) Nonspecialist ratings.

Turk (20th century; Navy, Marines) *s.* A homosexual who likes to play the masculine role in the act. He used to face a dishonorable discharge and twenty years' confinement.

Turk's head (Old Sailing Navy to Modern) A bit of rope or string fancy work, woven or knotted onto an object such as the head of a swagger stick or the junction of a lanyard. When you see an object covered with tassels and Turk's heads, you will know that someone had very little to do during duty hours or chose not to expend his off-duty time in riotous living.

twins *s.* A term used by an old-time marine drill instructor when particularly irritated. "You—stupid! Yes, you—da guy wit da two left feet! You must be twins! One guy couldn't be so damn stupid!" After this, the culprit is usually called *Twins* by the drill instructor. His fellow boots also adopt that salutation, at least until he punches the heads of a few of them.

under the gun (Marines) *s.* Under guard. That is how you find yourself after attending your company commander's office hours where you unsuccessfully tried to convince him that the Reveille Special did not run yesterday.

under way (Ancient to Modern; Navy) Moving through the water. The ship has weighed (raised) anchor and is now in motion. *Way* is another of those peculiarly naval terms. *To have way on* is to be moving in the direction you want to go; *to be in way of* means to be beside, or adjacent to, something.

USS Tuscarora (1930s) An imaginary warship, usually mentioned in spinning an outrageous yarn or in a sarcastic vein. "Oh, yeah. Well, *my* daddy was a warrant cook with Dewey at Manila Bay on the old *Tuscarora.*"

up the kilt (World War II; Navy) *s.* A submarine crewman's term for a torpedo fired from dead astern of an enemy ship.

vedette (Old Navy) A small Navy launch used for scouting. Sometimes *vedette boat.*

vulture's row (Vietnam; Navy) *s.* The "island" side of an aircraft carrier's flight deck, where the mechanics, armorers, plane-pushers, and other airedale specialists wait, ready to swarm over incoming planes. If a plane landed on the wrong carrier by error, they might decorate it with impolite graffiti.

waisters (Old Sailing Navy) The lowest caste aboard a warship, usualy made up of landsmen, ship's boys, and apprentice seamen. Their principal duties were hauling on braces and downhauls amidships—in other words, in the ship's waist.

walk to the wire, to (Modern; Marines) *s.* To put out observation or listening posts beyond the lines of a defensive perimeter. "He'll walk us to the wire every night" (Webb).

warrant (Up to 1941; Marines) A certificate stating whether a promotion was permanent, temporary, Regular, or Reserve. This was effective for all enlisted grades, including PFC. The holder of a permanent warrant, Regular Marine Corps, took precedence of all others of the same grade in the pay line, and was senior to all others of the same grade who did not hold Regular permanent warrants. He could be reduced only for cause, whereas others could be reduced by a reduction in force.

warrant officers' champagne (Civil War; Navy) Grog mixed with ginger ale. On larger warships, the warrant officers—engineers, gunner, boatswain, carpenter, and sailmaker—had a separate mess and were able to add such extra touches to their meals. If there was a marine detachment aboard, its sergeant would be accepted as a member.

wash (1920s and 1930s, perhaps earlier and later; Marines) *s.* Excuses, meaningless explanations, insincere professions of esteem or affection. Perhaps an abbreviation of *eyewash* or *hogwash.* As Capt. John W. Thomason, Jr., has a marine captain say, in "Luck," to the girl who has just turned him down, "Anyway, you didn't give me any wash about wantin' to be a sister to me."

watch (Colonial to Modern; Navy, Marines) The division—roughly half—of a ship's crew that is on duty. The *watch* *on deck* is on duty even if part of its members are actually working in the engine room and elsewhere below decks. The *watch below* is off duty, but available on call for emergencies. See *bells, all hands*.

WAVES (World War II) Women Accepted for Voluntary Emergency Service, the Navy's equivalent of the WAC. There is the story of a preacher in a seaport town who unintentionally reduced a service congregation to helpless laughter by declaiming, "And what might have happened to Saint Paul, tossed on the bosoms of the angry waves, had he not clung tightly all night to a spar?" See *SPAR*.

Way enough! (Ancient to Modern; Navy) The order given when an oar-propelled boat is sufficiently under way. The rowers finish their stroke, then toss and boat their oars. The command can also be used to signal the termination of a scuttlebutt session or other activity.

weep list (World War II; Navy) *s.* A list of needed repairs and replacements turned in by a ship's captain at the completion of a cruise.

WET (Modern; Navy) Week-End Training. Common among US Naval Reserve personnel.

whifflesnifter (1930s; Marines) *s.* A potently derogatory term, supposedly the name for a rare type of pervert who got his kicks by breaking wind while in the bathtub and then biting the resulting bubbles.

White Ace (Marines) An excellent white shoe polish used for whitening the fuzzy-surfaced suede belts issued for wear with dress blues. (The belts were made smooth with steel wool and sandpaper, and then coated with White Ace.) In 1940 the suede belt was replaced with a white canvas dress belt.

white-blue-white (20th century; Marines) The official code for the Marine Corps summer dress uniform worn afloat, at Pearl Harbor and Washington, D.C., and at embassies abroad: white cap, blue tunic, white belt and trousers.

white rat (1930s; Navy, Marines) *s.* One who courts favor with higher authority. Resembles the Old Army handshaker, but is more sinister, willing to do any sort of dirty work to get ahead.

Willie Fudd (World War II and later; Navy) *s.* A large airplane modified to serve as an airborne control center for a large carrier strike force. It has a conspicuous mushroom-shaped projection on the top of its fuselage, suggestive of the bald head of the character Elmer Fudd in "Bugs Bunny" cartoons.

windjamming (Navy, Marines) *s.* Gossiping, making idle talk. Was used through and after World War I, but is now seldom heard. A modern substitute is *beating [one's] gums*.

wing wiper (Modern; Marines) *s.* A pilot. Any marine who serves with an aviation unit.

worker bees (Modern; Navy) *s.* See *blue shirts*.

writer (Antiquity uncertain, but probably considerable; Navy) The yeoman who serves as secretary to the captain of a ship; sometimes *the captain's writer*. Another example of the nautical habit of naming a man for his duties.

yellow shirt (Modern; Navy) *s.* Yet another breed of airedale. An aircraft spotter on the hangar and flight decks and catapults aboard a carrier. He wears a yellow jersey as identification. See *head yellow shirt*.

yeoman (Navy) A petty officer with clerical duties.

Y-gun (World War I and later) A Y-shaped depth-charge launcher designed to throw two depth charges simultaneously, one to each side of the stern of a destroyer. The charges are thrown a considerable distance.

your head?, Where is (Navy) A question put only to an officer of the watch or the quartermaster. If the captain asks, "Quartermaster, where is your head?" You do *not* reply, "Right under my hat, sir." Instead, you give him the compass heading on which you are now holding a course.

☆☆☆☆ Bibliography

Aces and Aerial Victories. See U.S. Department of the Air Force.

Airman. See U.S. Department of the Air Force.

Airman's Guide, The. Harrisburg, Pa.: Military Service Publishing Co., 1955; Stackpole Books, 1968.

Algeo, John T. "Korean Bamboo English." *American Speech*, 25:2 (May 1960).

All Hands. See U.S. Department of the Navy.

American Speech. See Algeo, John T.; Lighter, Jonathan; Neubauer, Philip; Norman, Arthur M. Z.

Army. Arlington, Va.: Association of the U.S. Army. Published monthly. Successor to the *Infantry Journal* (last issue July 1950) and the *Army Combat Forces Journal*, which became *Army* in February 1956.

Army and Navy Journal. Washington, D.C.: Army & Navy Journal, Inc. 6 March 1937–25 February 1950. Published weekly.

Army Digest. See U.S. Department of the Army, *Soldiers*.

Army Information Digest. See U.S. Department of the Army, *Soldiers*.

Army Reporter, The. See U.S. Department of the Army.

Army Times. Washington, D.C.: Army Times Publishing Co. Published weekly.

Ayers, James T. *The Diary of James T. Ayers, Civil War Recruiter*. Springfield: Illinois State Historical Society, 1947.

Baker, LaFayette C. *The United States Secret Service in the Late War*. Chicago: Thompson and Thomas, 1902. First published in 1868 as *History of the United States Secret Service*.

Baker, Sidney J. *The Australian Language*. Sydney: Angus and Robertson, 1945.

Barrère, Albert, and Leland, Charles G. *A Dictionary of Slang, Jargon and Cant*. 2 vols. London: 1889, 1890; reprint, Detroit: Gale Research, 1967.

Bibliography

Bellard, Alfred. *Gone for a Soldier*, edited by David H. Donald. Boston: Little, Brown, 1975.

Boatner, Mark M. *Military Customs and Traditions.* New York: David McKay, 1956.

Bourke, John G. *Mackenzie's Last Fight with the Cheyennes.* Reprint, New York: Argonaut Press, 1966.

Brosig, Elly. "American Army Slang in Germany. Sociolinguistic Aspects of Slang." Read before Hauptseminar, *Aspects of American English*—ss 1981. Stuttgart: University of Stuttgart.

Broughton, Jack. *Thud Ridge.* Philadelphia and New York: Lippincott, 1969.

Browne, Junius H. *Four Years in Secessia: Adventures within and beyond the Union Lines.* Reprint, Washington, D.C.: National Tribune, 1900.

Brunn, Michael. "Military Dress. 1902 Service Dress Chevrons." *The Military Collector and Historian,* 30:2 (Summer 1978).

———. "U.S. Army Service Dress Rank Chevrons—1905–1926." *The Military Collector and Historian,* 31:2 (Summer 1979).

Buell, Augustus. *The Cannoneer. Recollections of Service in the Army of the Potomac.* Washington, D.C.: National Tribune, 1897.

Bugle Notes. West Point, N.Y. Issues of 1939–42, 1979.

Bunting, Josiah. *The Lionheads.* New York: George Braziller, 1972.

Caputo, Philip. *A Rumor of War.* New York: Holt, Rinehart and Winston, 1977.

Carman, William Y. *A Dictionary of Military Uniform.* New York: Scribners, 1977.

Catton, Bruce. *Mr. Lincoln's Army.* Garden City, N.Y.: Doubleday, 1951.

Cavalry Journal. Fort Leavenworth, Kan.: U.S. Cavalry Association. March 1888–January 1920. Published quarterly.

Century Dictionary, The. See Whitney, William D., ed.

Chamberlain, Samuel E. *My Confession.* New York: Harper, 1956. Also published as *Recollections of a Rogue.* London: Museum Press, 1957.

Chapman, Guy. *A Passionate Prodigality.* Greenwich, Conn.: Fawcett, 1967.

Claerbaut, David. *Black Jargon in White America.* Grand Rapids, Mich.: W. B. Eerdmans Publishing Co., 1972.

Clendenen, Clarence C. *Blood on the Border.* New York: Macmillan, 1969.

Colby, Elbridge. *Army Talk.* Princeton, N.J.: Princeton University Press, 1942.

"Cordiner Report, The." See U.S. Department of Defense, *Report of the Defense Advisory Committee.*

Craigie, Sir William A., and Hulbert, James R., eds. *A Dictionary of American English on Historical Principles.* 4 vols. Chicago: University of Chicago Press, 1938–44.

Croffut, W. A., ed. *Fifty Years in Camp and Field: Diary of Major-General Ethan Allen Hitchcock, USA.* New York: Putnam, 1909.

Dann, John C., ed. *The Revolution Remembered.* Chicago: University of Chicago Press, 1980.

Dauzat, Albert. *L'Argot de la guerre d'après une enquête auprès des officiers et soldats.* Paris: Librarie Armand Colin, 1919.

Detzer, Karl W. *True Tales of the D.C.I. Division of Criminal Investigation.* Indianapolis: Bobbs-Merrill, 1925.

Dolph, Edward A. *"Sound Off!" Soldier Songs from Yankee Doodle to Parley Voo.* New York: Cosmopolitan, 1929.

Dos Passos, John. *Three Soldiers.* New York: George Doran, 1921.

Doulis, Thomas. *Path for Our Valor.* New York: Simon and Schuster, 1963.

Downs, Frederick. *The Killing Zone: My Life in the Vietnam War.* New York: Norton, 1978.

Duane, William. *A Military Dictionary.* Philadelphia: William Duane, 1810.

Durden, Charles. *No Bugles, No Drums.* New York: Charter Books, 1976.

Dyer, Frederick C. *The Petty Officer's Guide.* 6th ed. Harrisburg, Pa.: Stackpole Books, 1966.

Eaton, Brig. Gen. R. P. *Recollections of World War I by a First Aid Man.* [Privately printed. Place and date of publication not indicated.]

Elliott, Charles W. *Winfield Scott, the Soldier and the Man.* New York: Macmillan, 1937.

English Language Institute of America. *A Dictionary of Contemporary and Colloquial Usage.* Chicago: 1972.

Farmer, John S., and Henley, W. F. *Slang and Its Analogues.* 7 vols. London and Edinburgh: Thomas Poulter and Sons, Harrison and Sons, Neill and Co., 1890–1904.

Finke, Detmar H. "Insignia of Rank in the Continental Army, 1775–1783." *Military Collector and Historian,* 7:4 (Fall 1956).

Flexner, Stuart Berg. *I Hear America Talking.* New York: Van Nostrand Reinhold Co., 1977.

Flood, Charles B. *The War of the Innocents.* New York: McGraw-Hill, 1970.

Fraser, Edward, and Gibbons, John. *Soldier and Sailor Words and Phrases.* 1925; reprint, Detroit: Gale Research, 1968.

Freeman, Douglas S. *Lee's Lieutenants.* New York: Scribners, 1942.

Ganoe, William A. *The History of the U. S. Army.* Rev. ed. New York: Appleton-Century, 1943.

Garber, Max B., and Bond, P. S. *A Modern Military Dictionary.* 1942; reprint, Detroit: Gale Research, 1975.

Gaynor, Frank. *The New Military and Naval Dictionary.* New York: Philosophical Library, 1951.

George, Victoria, and Dundes, Alan. "The Gomer, a Figure of American Hospital Folk Speech." *Journal of American Folklore,* 91:359 (January–March 1978).

Giles, Herbert A. *A Chinese-English Dictionary*, 2d ed. Shanghai, 1912; reprint, Taipei: Ch'eng Wen, 1972.

Glasser, Ronald J. *365 Days*. New York: George Braziller, 1971.

Gold, Robert S. *Jazz Talk*. Indianapolis: Bobbs-Merrill, 1975.

Goldin, Hyman E., ed. *Dictionary of American Underworld Lingo*. New York: Twayne, 1950.

Goldman, William. *Soldier in the Rain*. New York: Bantam Books, 1970.

Gove, Philip M., et al., eds. *Third New International Dictionary of the English Language*, Springfield, Mass.: G. and C. Merriam Co., 1965.

Groom, Winston. *Better Times than These*. New York: Berkley Books, 1978.

Grose, Francis. *Advice to the Officers of the British Army with the Addition of Some Hints to the Drummer and the Private Soldier*. London: 1783; reprint, New York: Agathynian Club, 1867.

———. *A Classical Dictionary of the Vulgar Tongue*. London: 1788; reprint, New York: Barnes and Noble, 1963.

Haldeman, Joe. *War Year*. New York: Pocket Books, 1978.

[Haliburton, Thomas C.] *The Clockmaker: or, The Sayings and Doings of Samuel Slick, of Slicksville*. Philadelphia: Carey, Lea, and Blanchard, 1837.

Hazelton, Joseph P. *Scouts, Spies, and Detectives of the Great Civil War*. Washington, D.C.: National Tribune, 1899. First published in 1866 as *The Camp, the Battlefield, and the Hospital*.

Heinemann, Larry. *Close Quarters*. New York: Farrar, Straus and Giroux, 1977.

Heinl, Col. Robert D. *The Marine Officer's Guide*. Annapolis, Md.: Naval Institute Press, 1977.

Herr, Michael. *Dispatches*. New York: Knopf, 1977.

Hill, Jim D., ed. *The Civil War Sketchbook of Charles Ellery Stedman, Surgeon, United States Navy*. San Rafael, Calif.: Presidio Press, 1977.

Hitchcock, Ethan Allen. *See* Croffut, W. A.

[Hotten, J. C.] *The Slang Dictionary*. London: Chatto and Windus, 1905.

Howitzer: The Yearbook of the Graduating Class of the United States Military Academy. West Point, N.Y.: 1900, 1910, 1920.

James, Charles. *An Universal Military Dictionary, in English and French*. London: T. Egerton, 1816.

Jones, James. *From Here to Eternity*. New York: Scribners, 1951.

Journal of American Folklore. See George, Victoria.

Journal of the Military Service Institute of the United States. Governor's Island, N.Y.: Military Service Institute. 1879–1917. Published quarterly.

Kelsey, D. M. *Deeds of Daring by Both Blue and Gray*. Philadelphia: Scammell, 1884.

Kendall, Park, and Viney, Johnny. *A Dictionary of Army and Navy Slang*. New York: M. S. Mill Co., 1941.

Kerbey, Joseph O. *A Boy Scout in Dixie, Service under the Shadow of the Scaffold*. Washington, D.C.: National Tribune, 1897.

Kong, Le Ba. *English-Vietnamese Pronouncing Dictionary*. Saigon: Zien-Hong, 1966.

———. *Vietnamese-English Pronouncing Dictionary*. Saigon: Zien-Hong, 1967.

Landy, Dr. Eugene E. *The Underground Dictionary*. New York: Simon and Schuster, 1971.

Leatherneck. Quantico, Va.: Marine Corps Association. Published monthly.

Lee, Chang Hei. *A First Course in the Korean Language*. Seattle: University of Washington Press, 1965.

Lighter, Jonathan. "A Historical Dictionary of American Slang." Vol. I, A Ph.D. diss., University of Tennessee, 1980.

———. "The Slang of the American Expeditionary Forces in Europe, 1917–1919: An Historical Glossary." *American Speech,* 147:1, 2 (Spring–Summer 1972).

Linebacker. See U.S. Department of the Air Force.

Lowe, Percival. *Five Years a Dragoon*. Reprint, Norman: University of Oklahoma Press, 1965.

Lucky Bag. The Annual of the Regiment of Midshipmen. Annapolis, Md.: 1920.

Maledicta. The International Journal of Verbal Aggression. Waukesha, Wis.: Maledicta Press. Issued semiannually, 1972–80; annually, 1981–82.

Manchester, William. *American Caesar*. Boston: Little, Brown, 1978.

Mardis, Jaime. *Memos of a West Point Cadet*. New York: David McKay, 1976.

Marshall, Samuel L. A. *The River and the Gauntlet*. New York: William Morrow, 1953.

———. *Pork Chop Hill*. New York: William Morrow, 1956.

———. *West to Cambodia*. New York: Cowles, 1968.

———. *Ambush*. New York: Cowles, 1969.

———. *The Fields of Bamboo*. New York: Dial Press, 1971.

———. *Bringing up the Rear*. San Rafael, Calif.: Presidio Press, 1979.

Mauldin, William Henry. *Up Front*. New York: World Publishing Co., 1945.

Mayhew, Henry. *London Labour and the London Poor*. 4 vols. London: Griffin, Bohn and Co., 1861–62.

McElroy, John. *Andersonville: A Story of Rebel Prisons*. 2 vols. Reprint, Washington, D.C.: National Tribune, 1899.

———. *Si Klegg, His Transformation from a Raw Recruit to a Veteran*. Reprint, Washington, D.C.: National Tribune, 1910.

Meek, Capt. S.P. *The Monkeys Have No Tails in Zamboanga*. New York: William Morrow, 1935.

Mellenthin, F.W. von. *German Generals of World War II as I Saw Them.* Norman: University of Oklahoma Press, 1977.

Mencken, H.L. *The American Language.* 4th ed. New York: Knopf, 1979.

———. *The American Language. Supplement One.* New York: Knopf, 1945.

———. *The American Language: Supplement Two.* New York: Knopf, 1948.

Military Collector and Historian: Journal of the Company of Military Historians, The. Washington, D.C.: Company of Military Historians. Published quarterly.

Military Service Publishing Company. *The NONCOM's Guide.* Harrisburg, Pa.: 1948–62. Published annually.

Moe, Albert F. "Gung Ho." *American Speech*, 42:1 (February 1967).

———. "Gyrene—A Lexicographical Stumbling Block." *American Speech*, 37:3 (October 1962).

Morris, William, ed. *The American Heritage Dictionary of the English Language.* New York: American Heritage, 1969.

Morris, William, and Morris, Mary. *Dictionary of Word and Phrase Origins.* New York: Harper and Row, 1962.

Moss, James A. *Officers' Manual.* 5th ed. Menasha, Wis.: George Banta, 1917.

Mulligan, Hugh A. *No Place to Die.* New York: William Morrow, 1967.

Murray, Sir James, et al. *The Compact Edition of the Oxford English Dictionary* (OED). 2 vols. New York: Oxford University Press, 1971.

Nason, Leonard. *Chevrons.* New York: George H. Doran, 1926.

———. *Sergeant Eadie.* Garden City, N.Y.: Doubleday Doran, 1928.

———. *A Corporal Once.* Garden City, N.Y.: Doubleday Doran, 1930.

Neubauer, Philip, and Norman, Arthur M. Z. "German and the GI." *American Speech,* 31:2 (May 1956).

Neilson, William A., et al., eds. *Webster's New International Dictionary of the English Language.* 2nd ed. Springfield, Mass.: G. and C. Merriam Co., 1943.

Norman, Arthur M. Z. "Army Speech and the Future of American English." *American Speech*, 31:2 (May 1956).

———. "Bamboo English, The Japanese Influence upon American Speech in Japan." *American Speech*, 30:1 (February 1955).

———. "Linguistic Aspects of the Mores of U.S. Occupation and Security Forces in Japan." *American Speech*, 24:4 (December 1954).

O'Brien, Tim. *Going after Cacciato.* New York: Dell, 1978.

Oxford English Dictionary, The. See Murray, Sir James.

Partridge, Eric. *A Dictionary of R.A.F. Slang.* London: Michael Joseph, 1948.

———. *A Dictionary of Forces' Slang.* London: Secker and Warburg, 1948.

———. *Slang To-day and Yesterday.* 3rd ed. New York: Macmillan, 1950.

———. *A Dictionary of Slang and Unconventional English.* 4th ed. New York: Macmillan, 1970.

———. *A Dictionary of Catch Phrases.* New York: Stein and Day, 1978.

Pentagram News. Alexandria Va.: Alexandria Gazette Corp. Published weekly.

Peterson, Mendel L. "American Epaulettes, 1775–1820." *The Military Collector and Historian,* 2:2 (June 1950).

———. "American Army Epaulettes, 1814–1872." *The Military Collector and Historian,* 3:1 (March 1951).

[Post, J. B.] *The Dark Other.* Verdun, France: Nasty Nearprints, 1963.

Pratt, Don, and Blair, Lee. *Salmagundi Vietnam.* Tokyo: E. Tuttle, 1970.

Prucha, Francis P. *Broadax and Bayonet.* Madison: State Historical Society of Wisconsin, 1953.

Read, Allen W. *Classic American Graffiti.* Waukesha, Wis.: Maledicta Press, 1977.

Reifer, Mary. *Dictionary of New Words.* New York: Philosophical Library, 1955.

Rogan, Helen. *Mixed Company.* New York: Putnam, 1981.

Roth, Robert. *Sand in the Wind.* Boston: Little, Brown, 1973.

Ruffner, Fred G., and Thomas, R. C. *Code Names Dictionary.* Detroit: Gale Research, 1963.

Safire, William. *Safire's Political Dictionary.* New York: Random House, 1978.

Sanders, Clinton A., and Blackwell, Joseph W., Jr. "Words of the Fighting Forces: A Dictionary of Military Slang and Terminology." Richmond, Va. (Unpublished manuscript, September 1942.)

Santamaria, Francisco J. *Diccionario general de Americanismos.* 3 vols. Mexico City: Editorial Pedro Robredo, 1942.

Semmes, Raphael. *The Campaign of General Scott, in the Valley of Mexico.* Cincinnati: Moore and Anderson, 1852.

Smith, Steven P. *American Boys.* New York: Putnam, 1975.

Soldiers. See U.S. Department of the Army.

Stanton, Shelby L. *Vietnam Order of Battle.* Washington, D.C.: U.S. New Books, 1981.

Stars and Stripes. New York: National Tribune, 1926 (8 February 1918–13 June 1919).

Stephenson, Edward A. "GI-ese and Instant Replay." *American Speech,* 48:3, 4 (Fall–Winter 1973).

[Steuben, Baron Friedrich von.] *Regulations for the Order and Discipline of the Troops of the United States.* Boston: I. Thomas and E. T. Andrews, 1794. (Author cited as Baron de Steuben.)

Suddick, Tom. *A Few Good Men.* New York: Avon Books, 1978.

Sunoo, Hag-Won. *A Korean Grammar.* Prague: Statni Pedagogicke Nakladatelstvi, 1952.

Symmes, Rebecca D., ed. *A Citizen Soldier in the American Revolution.* Cooperstown: New York State Historical Association, 1980.

Tale of Two Bridges, The. See U.S. Department of the Air Force.

Taylor, A. Marjorie. *The Language of World War II.* 2nd ed. New York: H. W. Wilson, 1948.

Thomason, John W., Jr. *Red Pants and Other Stories.* New York: Scribners, 1927.

The Times Magazine. Washington, D.C.: Army Times Publishing Co. Published monthly.

Tregaskis, Richard. *Vietnam Diary.* New York: Holt, Rinehart and Winston, 1963.

Truscott, Lucian K., IV. *Dress Gray.* Garden City, N.Y.: Doubleday, 1979.

U.S. Department of Defense. *Joint Chiefs of Staff Publication 1, Dictionary of Military and Associated Terms.* Washington, D.C.: Joint Chiefs of Staff, 1974.

———. *Report of the Defense Advisory Committee on Professional and Technical Compensation.* Vol. 1: *Military Personnel.* Washington, D.C.: 1957. (Also known as "the Cordiner Report.")

U.S. Department of Health, Education and Welfare. *A Comparative Study of Urban Black Argot.* San Francisco: HEW, 1972.

U.S. Department of the Air Force. *Aces and Aerial Victories.* Washington, D.C.: Office of the Air Force Historian, 1976.

———. *Airman.* Kelly Air Force Base, Tex.: Air Force Service Information and News Center. Published monthly.

———. *Linebacker II: The View from the Rock.* Maxwell Air Force Base, Ala.: Airpower Research Institute, 1979.

———. *The Tale of Two Bridges and the Battle for the Skies over North Vietnam.* Washington, D.C.: U.S. Government Printing Office, 1976.

U.S. Department of the Army. *Army Regulations 310-25, Dictionary of U.S. Army Terms.* Washington, D.C.: Headquarters, Department of the Army, 1977.

———. *Army Regulations 670-1, Wear and Appearance of Army Uniforms and Insignia.* Washington, D.C.: Headquarters, Department of the Army, 1981.

———. *Army Regulations 672-5-1, Military Awards.* Washington, D.C.: Headquarters, Department of the Army, 1981.

———. *The Army Reporter.* U.S. Army, Vietnam. 4 January 1971–20 December 1971. Published weekly.

U.S. Department of the Navy. *All Hands.* Washington, D.C.: U.S. Navy Department of Information. Published monthly.

———. *Small Unit Action in Vietnam.* Washington, D.C.: Headquarters, U.S. Marine Corps, 1977.

———. *Soldiers.* Washington, D.C.: Army Chief of Public Affairs, published monthly. (This is the successor to the *Army Information Digest* [May 1946–Dec. 1965] and *Army Digest* [June 1966 to May 1971].)

U.S. Military Magazine. Philadelphia: William M. Huddy and Peter S. Duval, April 1839–June 1842. Published monthly.

Wade, Herbert T., and Lively, Robert A., eds. *This Glorious Cause.* Princeton, N.J.: Princeton University Press, 1958.

Wainwright, Charles S. *A Diary of Battles.* New York: Harcourt Brace and World, 1962.

Ware, J. Redding. *Passing English of the Victorian Era.* London: Routledge, 1909.

Watkins, Samuel R. *Co. Aytch.* New York: Collier, 1962. First published in 1882 as *1861 vs. 1882.*

Webb, James H. *Fields of Fire.* New York: Bantam Books, 1979.

Wentworth, Harold, and Flexner, Stuart B. *Dictionary of American Slang.* 2nd supp. ed. New York: Thomas Y. Crowell, 1975.

Whitney, William D., ed. *The Century Dictionary: An Encyclopedic Lexicon of the English Language.* New York: Century Co., 1889–1900.

Wiener, Col. Frederick B. "Three Stars and Up." *Infantry Journal,* 56:6–57:5 (June–November 1945).

Wiley, Bell I. *The Life of Billy Yank.* Indianapolis: Bobbs-Merrill, 1952.

———. *The Life of Johnny Reb.* Indianapolis: Bobbs-Merrill, 1943.

Willcox, Cornelis de Witt. *A French-English Military Technical Dictionary.* Washington, D.C.: Government Printing Office, 1917.

Williams, Dion. *Army and Navy Uniforms and Insignia.* New York: Frederick A. Stokes, 1918.

Yank. New York: U.S. War Department, 1:46–4:27 (7 May 1943–21 December 1945). Reprint, Arno Press, 1967.

Yoshitaro, Takenobu, ed. *Kenkyusha's New Japanese-English Dictionary.* Tokyo: Kenkyusha, [n.d.]